1987

Medical and Health Annual

Encyclopædia Britannica, Inc.

CHICAGO

AUCKLAND • GENEVA • LONDON • MANILA • PARIS • ROME • SEOUL • SYDNEY • TOKYO • TORONTO

1987 Medical and Health Annual

Editor	Ellen Bernstein
Senior Editor	Linda Tomchuck
Contributing Editor	Charles Cegielski
Editorial Assistant	Lavonne Nannenga
Medical Editor	Drummond Rennie, M.D.
	Chairman of Medicine,
	West Suburban Hospital Medical Center, Oak Park, Ill.;
	Professor of Medicine,
	Rush Medical College, Chicago;
	Senior Contributing Editor, *The Journal of the American Medical Association*
Art Director	Cynthia Peterson
Senior Picture Editor	Holly Harrington
Picture Editors	Rita Conway, Kathryn Creech
Layout Artist	Dale Horn
Illustrators	Anne H. Becker, John L. Draves, William T. Soltis
Art Production	Richard A. Roiniotis
Art Staff	Daniel M. Delgado, Patricia A. Henle, Raul Rios, Lillian Simcox
Director, Yearbook Production and Control	J. Thomas Beatty
Manager, Copy Department	Anita Wolff
Senior Copy Editor	Barbara Whitney
Copy Staff	Ellen Finkelstein, Anthony L. Green, Patrick Joyce, Elizabeth Laskey, Gerilee Martens-Hundt, Steven Maxey, Julian Ronning
Manager, Production Control	Mary C. Srodon
Production Control Staff	Marilyn L. Barton, Mayme R. Cussen, Timothy A. Phillips
Manager, Composition and Page Makeup	Melvin Stagner
Composition Staff	Duangnetra Debhavalya, Morna Freund, Van Jones, John Krom, Jr., Thomas Mulligan, Gwen Rosenberg, Tammy Tsou
Page Makeup Staff	Marsha Check, *supervisor* Michael Born, Jr., Griselda Cháidez, Arnell Reed, Philip Rehmer, Danette Wetterer
Director, Editorial Computer Services	Michael J. Brandhorst
Manager, Editorial Systems and Programming	I. Dean Washington
Computer Services Staff	Steven Bosco, Clark Elliott, Rick Frye, Daniel Johnsen, Vincent Star
Manager, Index Department	Frances E. Latham
Assistant Manager	Rosa E. Casas
Senior Index Editor	Carmen Hetrea
Index Staff	Edward Paul Moragne, Lisa Strubin
Librarian	Terry Miller
Associate Librarian	Shantha Uddin
Assistant Librarian	David W. Foster
Secretarial Staff	Dorothy Hagen, Kay Johnson

Editorial Administration

Philip W. Goetz, Editor in Chief
Michael Reed, Managing Editor
Karen M. Barch, Executive Director of Editorial Production
Nathan Taylor, Executive Director of Planning and Technology
Carl Holzman, Director of Budgets and Controller

Encyclopædia Britannica, Inc.
Robert P. Gwinn, Chairman of the Board
Peter B. Norton, President

Foreword

The 1986 *Medical and Health Annual* featured an article entitled "Too Busy to Despair" by Jacob K. Javits. For six years Javits suffered the progressive, debilitating effects of the neuromuscular disease amyotrophic lateral sclerosis (Lou Gehrig's disease). The former senator from New York died on March 7, 1986. Mr. Javits's article for Britannica was one of the last things he wrote. He was a meticulous worker to the last and put a lot into the writing. When he completed his manuscript, he commented, "There is nothing that concentrates the mind like the need for putting down one's experiences and feelings."

Despite his physical incapacitation he lived his last years to the fullest, continuing to be active in politics—he was one of the most respected and influential political figures in the United States—and acting as an advocate for the sick and the dying. He waged a vigorous battle against his terminal illness; it was that battle that he wrote about eloquently for the *Medical and Health Annual*.

Among those who eulogized Javits at his funeral were New York Gov. Mario Cuomo, Sen. Edward M. Kennedy of Massachusetts, Sen. Daniel P. Moynihan of New York, Sen. Charles McC. Mathias, Jr., of Maryland, and Sen. Alan K. Simpson of Wyoming. The illness that crippled Javits, said Simpson, "could have imprisoned a lesser man," but in the former senator "the spirit soared." Simpson compared Javits to Winston Churchill; both shared a personal philosophy: "Never give up, never give up."

The 1987 *Medical and Health Annual* is a bigger book than previous issues—96 pages longer. In this volume we introduce a new section—an *Encyclopædia Britannica* Medical Update—consisting of major revisions of medical articles from the 1986 printing of the *Macropædia*. Additionally, other sections of the *Annual* have been expanded.

A topic that is covered extensively in the 1987 *Medical and Health Annual* is heart disease. Coronary heart disease (CHD) is a modern epidemic that is most prevalent in industrialized countries of North America and Europe. Each year in the United States it claims over 500,000 lives; some 800,000 patients are admitted to hospitals with heart attacks; an estimated six million are diagnosed as having coronary artery disease; and an inestimable number of middle-aged adults are developing the disease but have not yet experienced symptoms.

The feature article "Rethinking the Good Life: 40 Years at Framingham" (page 24) focuses on findings of the most comprehensive epidemiological study of a population and its life-styles. Framingham has delineated a portrait of the prime candidate for heart attack by establishing the major personal risk factors leading to CHD.

A Special Report in this volume (page 356) considers what has been learned about so-called Type A behavior and why *it* is a risk factor for CHD. The report raises an important question: Can people who are overaggressive, impatient, and hostile change their ways and improve their health?

David E. Rogers is a physician and president of the Robert Wood Johnson Foundation, Princeton, New Jersey; he has been treating patients with heart disease for well over 30 years. Last year he learned "from the inside" what it is to have the most feared form of CHD. In "On Having a Heart Attack" (page 231), he describes "the quality of the pain" during his myocardial infarction, and he recalls his overwhelming presentiment that he was going to die. He did not die; he was saved by the best of modern treatments. Not surprisingly, his insights as a doctor and a patient into the number one killer of American men are highly illuminating.

The article "Heart and Blood Vessels" (page 361) examines one of the most far-reaching advances in cardiology in recent years—the use of clot-dissolving drugs that are given during acute myocardial infarction to arrest the process that causes heart muscle damage. The variations of this promising new strategy have the potential to reduce mortality significantly and prevent vast numbers of cardiac cripples.

A very common treatment for those who have suffered the damage of CHD is coronary bypass surgery. In the United States coronary operations number over 180,000 per year and cost approximately $25,000 per case. The Health Information Update article "Coronary Bypass" (page 451) describes the procedure in which clogged areas of the coronary arteries are "bypassed" to restore normal blood flow. The article provides instructive and practical information about what the patient undergoing this major form of surgery can expect in the short term and in the long run.

Two articles (pages 254 and 433) examine yet another facet of heart disease treatment: transplantation. There have been significant advances in transplanting human donor hearts. The viability of artificial heart implantation, however, has been called into question owing to the results of mechanical heart implantations in five patients, the first of which occurred in December 1982. On Aug. 6, 1986, the last surviving implant recipient, William Schroeder, died after having lived 620 days with his Jarvik-7 heart.

The participation of growing children in competitive sports is the subject of a series of three articles (pages 148–183), which we call "The Sporting Life." A special contribution is by world champion middle-distance runner Sebastian Coe and his father and coach, Peter Coe. Together they look back on nearly two decades of Sebastian's training, from athletic obscurity at age 12 to Olympic fame in 1980 and 1984.

All three "Sporting Life" articles stress that athletics are among the healthiest sources of fun, fitness, and learning for children. However, youngsters are not "little adults" and, therefore, their special physical and mental vulnerabilities must always be considered. And a further caveat: children should *never* be pushed into competition by overeager parents.

Ellen Bernstein —Editor

Contents

Features

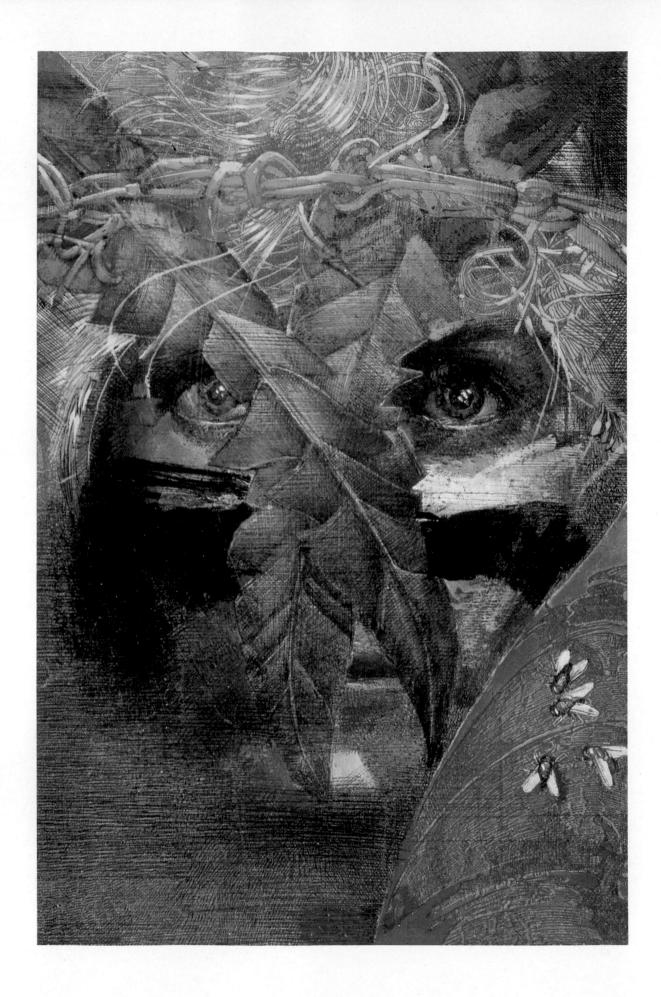

The Nature of Nightmares

by Ernest L. Hartmann, M.D.

When you're alone in the middle of the night and you wake in a sweat and a hell
  of a fright
When you're alone in the middle of the bed and you wake like someone hit
  you in the head
You've had a cream of a nightmare dream and you've got the
  hoo-ha's coming to you.
>   —T. S. Eliot, "Fragment of an Agon"

The word nightmare suggests a night horse. And horses have indeed figured in tales of nightmares and in works of art, such as the well-known painting "The Nightmare" by the 18th-century Swiss artist Henry Fuseli. However, most scholars agree that the "mare" in "nightmare" derives not from the root *myre,* meaning "female of the equine animal," but from the Old English and old German root *mara,* "an incubus or succubus" (a kind of demon). The *Oxford English Dictionary* defines "nightmare" as "a kind of goblin supposed to produce nightmares by sitting on the chest of the sleeper." Over the centuries "nightmare" has been used in a loose, general sense to mean anything that wakes one up in fright, the supposed creature or demon that produces the terror, the frightening dream itself, or the actual awakening.

A third of human life is spent sleeping. Yet only in recent years has a considerable amount of research focused on the formerly elusive process of sleep. As a result, many sleep disorders are now not only much better understood but treatable. The process of dreaming, too, has been taken out of the realm of the impenetrable and has become the subject of serious scientific inquiry. As a result of work conducted in sleep laboratories, beginning in the 1950s, it is now possible—through electrical monitoring of brain activity, eye movements, and muscle tonus—to know precisely when a sleeper is dreaming.

While in-depth study of sleep and dreaming has amassed a wealth of information, only a small segment of the research has focused on nightmares per se. Thus, what is known about them is still quite limited. Nonetheless, very recent work is beginning to shed new light on these intense, emotional, and highly disquieting dreams. Most notably, it has been discovered that there are two important and very different phenomena that can wake us in fright in the night. One of them we now call "night terror"; the other, "nightmare."

Ernest L. Hartmann, M.D., is Professor of Psychiatry at Tufts University School of Medicine, Director of the Sleep Research Laboratory at West-Ros-Park Mental Health Center, Boston, and Director of the Sleep Disorders Center at Newton-Wellesley Hospital, Newton, Massachusetts.

(Opposite) Cover illustration for Lord of the Flies, *by 1983 Nobel laureate William Golding. The novel tells a nightmarish tale of a group of English schoolboys, stranded on a tropical island during an atomic war and reduced to wanton savagery in their attempt to survive. Illustration, Barron Storey, reproduced by permission of the Putnam Publishing Group*

The Swiss artist Henry Fuseli believed dreams were "one of the most unexplored regions of art," and in many of his paintings he personified his own acutely experienced dream sequences—the best known example being "The Nightmare."

The etching below was executed at a time when the Spanish artist Francisco Goya was left physically wasted and totally deaf by a paralytic stroke. The work reveals Goya's theme that when man allows reason to sleep, hobgoblins and demons— the nightmarish creatures of the irrational world—control his life.

"The Sleep of Reason Produces Nightmares" by Francisco Goya; photograph, Jean-Loup Charmet, Paris

Dreaming elucidated

To understand the differences between these two events, we must first briefly examine what happens in the brain and body during a typical night of sleep. When we fall asleep, we pass through several distinct stages before we wake up in the morning. Drowsiness, or relaxed wakefulness, characterized in brain-wave recordings by alpha waves (about ten waves per second), gradually gives way to what is known as stage 1 of sleep, the lightest stage, with reduction of alpha activity. Then we enter stage 2 of sleep, characterized by fairly regular brain-wave activity in which there are 13 to 15 tightly packed waves per second (called sleep spindles) as well as some jagged electrical spikes (K-complexes). Next comes deeper and deeper sleep, characterized by slow delta waves (stages 3 and 4).

In a normal night the sleeper progresses through more than one of these cycles—generally four or five. At the "top" of each cycle, there is a period in which the brain waves resemble the light sleep of stage 1. These four or five periods during a night's sleep are characterized by electroencephalogram (EEG) readings that resemble drowsy wakefulness and by distinct physiological changes. There is profound muscle relaxation; pulse and respiration become faster and more irregular; and there are bursts of rapid, darting eye movements. Someone awakened during these periods will usually report a dream. These four or five periods are called rapid eye movement (REM) sleep or sometimes dreaming sleep (D sleep). The first REM period is the shortest, and each succeeding one is longer, so that the last may continue for up to 45 minutes. Such periods occur not only in human sleep but in the sleep of almost all mammals.

Probably the most dramatic and unexpected finding of recent years of sleep research is that dreaming does not occur in a split second as one wakes up, as had previously been thought. Rather it happens during regu-

"The King wanted the Jury to settle whether the Knave of Hearts was guilty or not guilty—that means that they were to settle whether he had stolen the Tarts, or if somebody else had taken them. But the wicked Queen wanted to have his punishment settled, first of all. That wasn't at all fair, was it?. . .

"So Alice said 'Stuff and nonsense!'

"So the Queen said 'Off with her head!'. . .

"So Alice said 'Who cares for you? You're nothing but a pack of cards!'

"So they were all very angry, and flew up into the air, and came tumbling down again, all over Alice, just like a shower of rain.

. . ."The next thing was, Alice woke up out of her curious dream. And she found that the cards were only some leaves off the tree, that the wind had blown down upon her face."

—from chapter XIV, "The Shower of Cards"

Tenniel's illustration from The Nursery "Alice," an adaptation of Lewis Carroll, Alice's Adventures in Wonderland (London: Macmillan and Co., 1890)

lar, fairly long REM periods, each lasting 10 to 25 minutes or more. Also, all of us, whether we remember dreams or not, have three to five such periods of dreaming every night.

With this background we can now examine what happens when a person who suffers from nightmares or other frightening episodes during the night is studied in the laboratory. (Such investigations have been done in several laboratories. Roger Broughton at the University of Ottawa and Charles Fisher at Mount Sinai School of Medicine, New York City, performed some of the earliest lab studies specifically on nightmares and night terrors in the 1960s.)

Night terrors versus nightmares

It has been learned that the frightening event now called the night terror involves an awakening early in the night—usually within an hour or two after the onset of sleep. This abrupt awakening usually occurs from deep,

Christopher Springmann

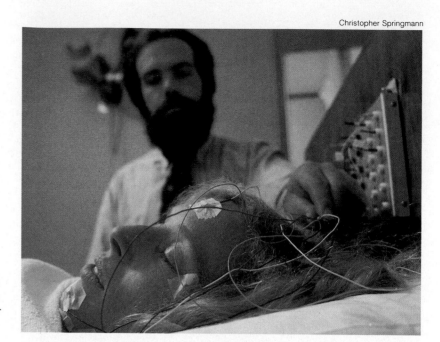

Monitoring brainwaves (right) in sleep laboratories has produced a wealth of information about the processes of sleeping and dreaming.

slow-wave, stage 4 sleep. A person will sleep normally for an hour or so, then show some body activity or movement, then suddenly scream uncontrollably or cry out (something like "Help! Help!") and awaken in terror. The night terror is sometimes accompanied by intense physical movement. Children, especially, may thrash about, hit out, sit up in bed, or sometimes even get up and move around. A night terror may even continue into a sleepwalking episode. Recordings of pulse and respiration taken in the sleep laboratory during night terrors have demonstrated that rates may double during the 30 seconds or so involved in these awakenings.

By studying the cat's brain, researchers are gaining knowledge that may explain many of the mysterious aspects of human dreaming. Both brains consist of two large globes of nervous tissue (the cerebral cortex and cerebellum) and an enlargement of the spinal cord (the brain stem). Both cat and human appear to depend on the brain stem in particular to regulate the mind's activity during dreaming.

From "Dreamstage," a multimedia exhibition, supported by Hoffmann-LaRoche Inc.; photographs, Ted Spagna

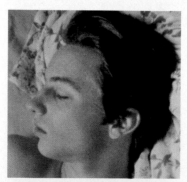

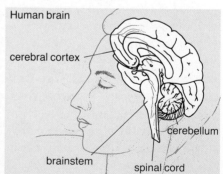

Human brain

cerebral cortex

cerebellum

brainstem

spinal cord

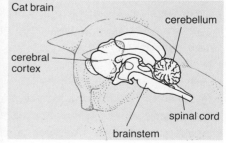

Cat brain

cerebellum

cerebral cortex

spinal cord

brainstem

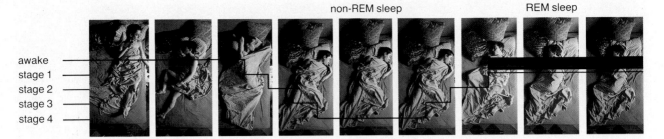

awake
stage 1
stage 2
stage 3
stage 4

When someone asks what has happened, the sleeper either remembers nothing at all—sometimes even returning to sleep without a full awakening—or may say, "I don't know what it was. Something awful. My heart's pounding." Occasionally the person will remember a single image—"Something was crushing me and I couldn't breathe," or "It felt like the ceiling fell on me"—but the terrifying episode is generally not described as a dream.

The other kind of experience—the nightmare—sometimes called REM-nightmare or dream anxiety attack—is quite different. A nightmare usually occurs late during the night—during the last three hours of the sleep period. Recordings in the laboratory show that it occurs during REM sleep—usually from a long REM period that has continued for 20 to 30 minutes. Pulse and blood pressure may show some increase but not as much as in a night terror, and there is no sitting up in bed or sleepwalking.

The experience also *feels* different to the one who has it. The person waking with a nightmare usually remembers very distinctly a long, vivid dream, ending with a frightening sequence; *e.g.,* "Someone was chasing me," or "A man attacked me with a knife." The sleeper usually can recall a long dream leading up to the frightening ending: "I was at a party with a bunch of people. Suddenly, the door blew open; the wind came howling in; I saw these strange, threatening characters who seemed to be coming in. Then it turns out my friend was one of the bad guys. He started after me as if to attack me, and I tried to run away. . . ."

In contrast to night terrors, in which there is either no dream content or, sometimes, a single image, the nightmare is a long dream, and it is almost always vivid, colorful, and lifelike. The nightmare often includes sensations other than vision; *e.g.,* "It was a wartime scene. I could *hear* awful noises: bombs bursting around me, screams. Something hit me in the shoulder; I could *feel* the pain and the blood flowing down my arm."

Although it may require a number of nights of recording and observing in a sleep laboratory, the two different events—nightmares and night terrors—can be quite clearly distinguished. Luckily, though, a sleep laboratory is seldom necessary for establishing whether a person who is plagued by terrifying sleep events is experiencing nightmares or terrors. When a patient reports having frightening sleep interruptions, usually the answer to one simple question—"Are these experiences dreams?"—will indicate the nature of the experience. Those who have nightmares say, "Yes, of course they are dreams." To them it is perfectly obvious that their nightmares are long, frightening dreams. Those who have night terrors also find the answer obvious: "Definitely not." They sometimes remember dreams like anyone

During a typical night the sleeper passes through several sleep cycles (above) that include four or sometimes five distinct stages—each characterized by particular brain-wave patterns and body movements. Researchers have used time-lapse photographs taken at various intervals during the night to link body positions to brain-wave activity and other physiological indicators. During dreaming there is profound muscle relaxation and the body is quite still, but pulse and respiration quicken and become irregular; especially notable is the phase with bursts of eye movements—known as rapid eye movement, or REM sleep—in which dreaming occurs (below). A quite unexpected finding of sleep research is that all *people,* whether they remember dreams or not, *go through several periods of dreaming (REM stages) each night. Sleep investigators have speculated that the sporadic eye bursts may be connected with the curious changes in a dream's sequences of action.*

Time-lapse photographs, Ted Spagna

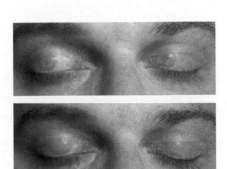

11

Andrew Shachat

else, and they know perfectly well that the night terror experience, which they may call a nightmare, is not a dream. They may not know what it is, but it is obviously something different from a dream.

In the study of nightmares and night terrors, it has been determined that they are different experiences psychologically, they differ physiologically, and they usually occur in different individuals. Rarely does one experience both phenomena.

Almost all "nightmare" events can be classified as night terrors or nightmares. However, there are a few that are not easily classified. An occasional person suffers from what we call hypnagogic nightmares—a terrifying nightmarelike fantasy upon just falling asleep. Also, there are people who have a condition called nocturnal myoclonus—many jerking muscle movements during the night—and occasionally these people will report a nightmarelike phenomenon as they are awakened by muscle jerks. Finally, there are people who have chronic posttraumatic stress disorder,

Very recent dream research has distinguished a phenomenon called "night terror" from the "nightmare." Night terrors occur in the early hours of a night's sleep—often within an hour of falling asleep—i.e., during very deep sleep. Nightmares, on the other hand, occur toward morning during long periods of REM sleep.

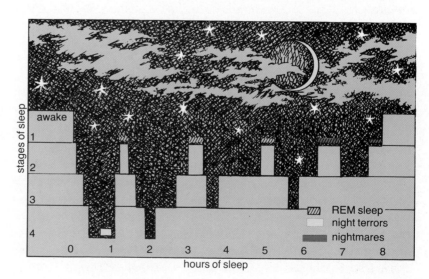

(Left) Jean-Loup Charmet, Paris; (right) "Nightmare" by Rockwell Kent, 1941; collection, Philadelphia Museum of Art, Print Club Permanent Collection

who have repetitive nightmares depicting the traumatic experience long after the event. These are in some ways nightmares, but they have some characteristics of night terrors as well, and they can occur in various stages of sleep. Combat veterans figure high in this group. Recently studies have been conducted of the many Vietnam veterans who suffer from profound sleep disturbances, among other posttraumatic stress symptoms.

Nightmare incidence

Nightmares are by far the more common of the two distinct occurrences that have been delineated; therefore, what follows will focus mainly on the nightmare. Most people, and possibly all people, have had at least an occasional nightmare. For many these may have occurred in childhood and been forgotten or half-forgotten. Some people with especially frequent or especially vivid nightmares, however, remember them clearly throughout their lives.

From many studies of nightmares, sleep specialists estimate that approximately 50% of adults have no nightmares at all, though they may have had them as children. Most others remember at least an occasional nightmare but in most cases experience only a few per year. Only a small percentage, then, have nightmares that are frequent enough or severe enough to be overwhelmingly disturbing to their lives. (The subgroup of people who report very frequent nightmares—at least once a week—has recently been studied in depth and will be discussed further below.) One recent study showed that 4% of a sample of 1,000 city dwellers in the U.S. had reported nightmares to their physicians, though nightmares were seldom the principal reason for seeing the physician. Other studies have shown that between 5 and 10% of the population reported having a nightmare once a month or more, although the nightmares were not necessarily considered a problem. The average is perhaps one or two nightmares per year.

The artistic conceptions (opposite page and above) are suggestive of night terrors. A person experiencing a night terror will progress from peaceful sleep to a quite agitated state, often with thrashing about in bed, then will usually scream or cry for help and abruptly awaken. The night terror is experienced not as a dream but as a single, overwhelmingly terrifying fantasy, most often accompanied by a specific image—for example, falling off a cliff. In some cases a night terror will continue into an episode of sleepwalking.

Photographs, Jean-Loup Charmet, Paris

Nightmares, especially those involving terrifying encounters with horrible creatures, demons, goblins, and monsters, are quite common at ages three through five. Such dreams often cease after childhood but can persist throughout life.

Elderly persons—in their sixties and seventies—usually continue to have nightmares if they previously had them. But overall, the incidence of nightmares decreases with age and is relatively low in older healthy adults.

Is there a sex difference? It has been difficult to determine if, in fact, one sex is more prone to nightmares. Women mention nightmares to their doctors somewhat more frequently than men do. When sleep specialists at Tufts University, Boston, sought study subjects with nightmares, more women than men responded. But in interviews with adolescents and adults with nightmares, investigators also found that men tend to be much more reluctant to talk about their nightmares than women. It may be that having nightmares is not considered manly. So the conclusion seems to be that there is probably not much difference—men are likely to have nightmares as much or almost as much as women, but they may be more hesitant to mention them.

Childhood nightmares

The results of various studies on childhood incidence of nightmares are not completely consistent, but they give a rough indication of a general pattern. Nightmares are definitely more frequent in occurrence in children than in adults. They are especially common at ages three through five. From the accumulated studies and clinical work by sleep specialists, it is evident that nightmares are probably present before that age as well, probably as early

14

"Oh, to dream once more the untroubled dreams of childhood!"

as age one, but children are unable to communicate the presence of these preverbal nightmares. Only later are they able to distinguish dreams and nightmares from waking experience and describe them to adults. Nightmares become less frequent after the age of 6 to about 12 or 13. The incidence may increase again in adolescence, at ages 13 to 18. In childhood there is no apparent gender difference; thus, five-year-old boys indicate they suffer from nightmares just as frequently as do five-year-old girls.

The causes of nightmares: demons? pizza? stress?

We no longer believe that demons, goblins, fiends, furies, monsters, or other evil spirits descend upon the sleeper to produce nightmares. But are there perhaps some simple factors, such as spicy foods, that cause nightmares? There is a rather widespread belief that eating certain foods can trigger nightmares; this has led to what is sometimes called the "pepperoni pizza theory." Many people remember once having eaten something that

15

The cause of nightmares continues to elude researchers. Many potential triggers have been suggested, but most seem unlikely. The 1853 caricature (above) "Memoires of a Stomach," depicting an overstuffed man dozing and dreaming rather unpleasant things, is suggestive of one such possibility. What has in modern times been dubbed the "pepperoni pizza theory" holds that indulging in spicy foods produces nightmares. But recent surveys of what people have eaten prior to their nightmares provide no evidence that any specific foods are consistently linked to the occurrence of their most terrifying dreams.

disagreed with them (*e.g.,* pepperoni pizza) and then having had a nightmare or nightmarelike experience. However, there is no solid evidence for this association. Most of us have nightmares so rarely that it would be hard for us to say what might be associated with them. In a recent study of 100 people who reported having nightmares at least once per week, 99 saw no association between foods and their nightmares. Only one woman thought she had more nightmares when she had eaten something that disagreed with her, but she could be no more specific than that.

Another prevalent view is that lack of oxygen or lack of air to the lungs can produce nightmares. The fact that a night-terror awakening is sometimes associated with a feeling of being crushed or choked perhaps lends some credence to this view. Moreover, it seems quite plausible that being deprived of air could be a frightening, nightmarelike experience that would result in a nightmare. However, recent evidence seems to be against this.

There are some people who suffer from a sleep disorder known as obstructive sleep apnea—a condition in which air simply does not get through the throat to the lungs, usually because of some obstruction such as excessive fatty tissue or poor muscle function in the pharynx, at the back of the throat. People who have this condition literally can be said to be choking, and this happens 100 or more times per night. In sleep apnea the chest and abdomen heave and the patient tries hard to get air, but the air does not get through. After 10 to 20 seconds there is a brief awakening, and the sleeper can then breathe normally again. It has been shown that the blood oxygen levels of these patients drop during periods when they are deprived of air. If choking and deprivation of air or oxygen were to produce nightmares, as has been theorized, one would expect that sleep apnea sufferers would experience frequent nightmares. In fact, this is an extremely rare occurrence. Apneic patients either go right back to sleep and do not even remember the awakenings or occasionally complain that their sleep has been restless. Sometimes they even mention that they woke up choking or gasping. But they do not report nightmares.

There is some evidence that various physical conditions produce nightmares. Children often have them during febrile illness. Adults, too, appear to have more nightmares than usual during high fever or around the time of an operation. Certain neurological conditions have sometimes been associated with nightmares—notably epilepsy and postencephalitic parkinsonism.

Guilt, also, seems to have a penchant for triggering nightmares. At least in literature, there is rich evidence of nightmares visiting murderers. Clarence, in Shakespeare's *Richard III,* relates the following dream:

O! then began the tempest to my soul.
I pass'd, methought, the melancholy flood,
With that grim ferryman which poets write of,
Unto the kingdom of perpetual night. . . .
A shadow like an angel, with bright hair
Dabbled in blood; and he shriek'd out aloud,
"Clarence is come—false, fleeting, perjur'd Clarence. . . .
I trembled wak'd, and, for a season after,
Could not believe but that I was in hell,
Such terrible impression made my dream.

16

Aside from these specific and rare causes, is there anything then that can be said to produce unexplained, frequent, and troublesome nightmares? Thus far the only factor investigators have been able to identify is what they broadly call "stressful events." When people who report having nightmares off and on throughout their lives are asked under what circumstances they have had more frequent or more disturbing nightmares than usual, they almost always recount a period involving stress. Many different kinds of stress can have this effect. In some a specific event such as being attacked in the street produced an increase in nightmares lasting days or weeks. In some the loss of an important relationship was associated with an increase in nightmares, often for months. And sometimes a long period such as a turbulent adolescence was associated with more nightmares for several years.

Revelations of recent studies

What is known about the personalities of those who have nightmares? That question could not be attacked properly until recent years, when we were able to distinguish nightmares from night terrors. Associates at Tufts University and the Sleep Research Laboratory at West-Ros-Park Mental Health Center in Boston have completed several in-depth studies to examine this question more closely. For two similar studies in the late 1970s, the researchers placed ads in newspapers to recruit subjects who had frequent nightmares as a long-term condition. The first study looked at 38 adults with nightmares. The second study compared 12 nightmare sufferers with 12 people who reported that they had vivid dreams but no nightmares and 12 others who reported neither nightmares nor vivid dreams. Study subjects were interviewed and given psychological tests, including Rorschach inkblot tests and personality and fear surveys. Some were also monitored in the sleep laboratory.

The vampire, who drinks the blood of his victims only in the darkest dreaming hours, is indeed the stuff of nightmares.

Anecdotal and literary associations between nightmares and profound emotional states abound. But about the only factor scientific investigations have uncovered as a potential trigger of nightmares is what can be broadly termed "stress." Overwhelming fears can be extremely potent "stressors"; such fears are vast and varied—e.g., fears of insects or sharks, of taking examinations, of speaking in public, of having a baby, of failing, and even of succeeding. Whether these are powerful enough to translate into a nightmare depends upon the individual and the situation. Fear of pain is represented at left as nightmarish anticipation of a visit to the dentist.

"Spirit of the Dead Watching" by Paul Gauguin, 1892, oil on burlap mounted on canvas, 28½ x 36⅜ inches; collection, Albert-Knox Art Gallery, Buffalo, New York, A. Conger Goodyear Collection, 1965

Among the distinctions that appear to set nightmare sufferers apart is that they tend to experience uncertain states of identity and consciousness. They may, for example, be confused about their sexual identity or their status as adults or children or, at times, they may not be sure if they are awake, asleep, or dreaming. The paintings of Paul Gauguin (right) and Ferdinand Hodler (opposite page) are suggestive of such "thin boundaries." Both works were executed at the end of the 19th century—a time when Sigmund Freud was writing his Interpretation of Dreams *and the mysterious realm of the unconscious was beginning to be explored in art.*

Investigators found, among many things, that there were no clear-cut physical differences; *e.g.,* people who had frequent nightmares were not taller or shorter or fatter or thinner than others. Nor were they more or less intelligent. The thing that immediately stood out was that those individuals in the nightmare groups often had jobs or life-styles related to art or creativity; included were painters, poets, musicians, and craftspersons as well as some teachers and therapists. There were no traditional blue-collar jobholders in the nightmare groups, nor were there white-collar executives or other office workers who had frequent nightmares; however, there were many blue-collar and white-collar workers in the ordinary-dream and vivid-dream groups.

Next, it was clear from interviews that the artistic or creative interests of nightmare subjects were not something that these adults had acquired recently. Rather, they described themselves as having been in some way "unusual" as children. Generally they used words such as "unusually sensitive"—"sensitive" being a commonly used self-description. It referred sometimes to being especially reactive to stimuli, *e.g.,* bright lights or loud sounds; more often to being easily hurt ("Everything gets to me"); and sometimes to possessing the quality of empathy—*i.e.,* being sensitive to the feelings of others. Thus, the nightmare sufferers saw themselves as "different" throughout their lives. However, insofar as investigators could tell, their childhoods were not marked by extreme trauma.

People with nightmares almost always described their adolescence as stormy, difficult, often characterized by periods of depression and thoughts of suicide. They tended to go through a rebellious stage involving drugs, alcohol, fights with parents, running away from home, and so forth. While adolescent upheaval is not unusual, it was much more common in those with nightmares than in those without them.

Further, as adolescents and adults the nightmare sufferers appeared to be extremely open and trusting people. They seemed to be, in fact, too trusting for their own good. They often became involved quickly in difficult, entangling friendships and love relationships from which they found it hard to escape.

Finally, the nightmare groups appeared to be neither especially anxious, especially angry, nor especially depressed people, as might have been expected. Rather, they appeared very open and trusting and at the same time somehow defenseless or vulnerable. In fact, there was evidence that some were vulnerable to mental illness; a strikingly high proportion of nightmare sufferers had been in psychotherapy (76% in one study group; 67% in the second study group), and several had been admitted to mental hospitals at some former time (11% in one study and 17% in the other). Psychological tests confirmed a certain vulnerability to mental illness. As a group, however, at the time of interviews, they were functioning quite well in life.

Using these findings, investigators attempted to characterize those with nightmares. Having "thin boundaries" was the term researchers found best described the creative, sensitive, and vulnerable nightmare groups. This meant that they had thin interpersonal boundaries—*i.e.,* they tended to get involved with others very quickly; thin ego boundaries—they were very aware of their inner wishes and fears; and thin sexual boundaries—they easily imagined themselves to be someone of the opposite sex, and many had fantasized about or engaged in bisexual activity. Further, they had thin group boundaries in that they did not see themselves firmly as members of a single community, a particular ethnic group, etc. Another distinction noted was that they had thin sleep-wake boundaries—*i.e.,* they often had in-between states in which they were not sure whether they were awake or asleep or dreaming. Their responses on Rorschach inkblot tests confirmed this "thin boundary" description; the individuals who had nightmares on a regular basis gave frequent responses involving seeing imprecise boundaries—blending of one figure into another—and noting a general amorphous quality in the inkblot pictures they viewed. Such responses were common only in the nightmare groups.

19

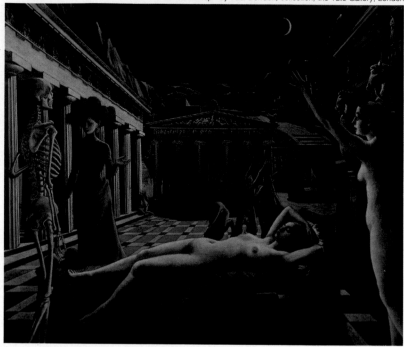

"Venus Asleep" by Paul Delvaux; collection, the Tate Gallery, London

The Belgian painter Paul Delvaux created disquieting, contrasting, and mysterious dream worlds peopled with phantoms and nude sleepwalkers.

People suffering from frequent night terrors have also been studied recently. They are quite different from those with nightmares and do not have the above personality characteristics, but currently there is no single personality description that fits the night-terror group.

Interpreting nightmares

Nightmares, like other dreams, come from the mind of the dreamer and thus have meaning; they are likely to refer in some way to the dreamer's memories, wishes, or fears or to events in recent or past life. One can interpret a dream—*i.e.,* understand the subtle or obscure connections—only when one knows the dreamer very well, and even then it is not always possible.

Though every dreamer's dreams are highly personal and unique, studies of nightmare sufferers indicate that at least one generalization seems to hold: their nightmares almost always involve feelings of helplessness and most often helplessness dating from childhood. Thus, nightmare sufferers often have adult adjustment problems and difficulties with certain ego functions. Situations involving being attacked, chased, thrown off a cliff, or in some way at the mercy of others were among the most frequent situations in their dreams. Almost invariably it was the dreamer himself who was in danger and utterly powerless—not someone else. (The only exceptions were nightmares reported by two mothers of young children, in which it was the child who was in danger.)

One theory that specialists have formed to explain the occurrence of adult nightmares is that certain stressful periods in adulthood may produce feelings of helplessness that remind them of childhood feelings. Helplessness is, of course, normal in childhood. Humans, unlike most animals, are

20

almost completely dependent (*i.e.,* helpless) for many years. It has been noted in both research subjects and patients that among those adults who have nightmares, it is not uncommon for them to be plagued by nightmares only for a certain period in their adult lives. Then over the course of years (with or without psychotherapy), the number of nightmares decreases, and in some cases they cease to occur entirely. What causes the change? Usually it occurs as people feel more confident, more mature, and thus less close to their childhood helpless feelings. They develop better coping styles to meet the stresses in their lives.

Are nightmares treatable?

Usually nightmares in themselves do not require treatment. At ages three through six, when nightmares are most common, the most important thing is for the parents to be aware that the occurrence is not abnormal. Night terrors are also common in young children. Parents may want to talk to their children and give them a chance to express fearful feelings, which all children have. Parents should also examine the family or school situation to check for sources of fears that might not be obvious. Usually nothing more drastic is required.

Neither do adults, in most cases, require treatment for nightmares per se. In interviews with researchers, most adults who had very frequent nightmares reported that they had never sought treatment or really desired treatment for their nightmares. They almost always said that they felt their nightmares were part of them. Some claimed they had learned to live with their terrifying dreams and even made use of the nightmares in their creative endeavors. However, these same people *had* sought treatment for other conditions—such as stress or depression—that may have contributed to or exacerbated their nightmares. The nightmare, then, is sometimes an

Jean-Loup Charmet, Paris

The image we have of hell is typically a place inhabited by helpless creatures in the face of powerful, punishing forces (devils). Likewise, nightmares are "hellish" in that they almost always involve the dreamer in a position of utter helplessness and vulnerability.

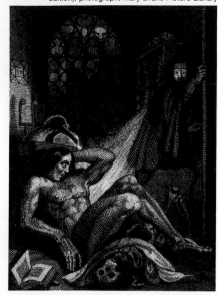

Mary Shelley's classic novel of terror, Frankenstein, *was directly inspired by a nightmare.*

indication that there is a condition requiring treatment, but it is not the nightmare that is treated.

A sudden onset of nightmares is sometimes a sign of an impending mental illness. Nightmares have been found to occur frequently at the onset of schizophrenia. They can also precede or accompany the development of depression or other serious illness.

More commonly, stressful conditions are associated with an increase in nightmares. It is obvious that recognizing potential sources of stress and trying to make some change—internal or external—may be helpful. Overwhelming feelings of helplessness, emptiness, or deprivation and prolonged depressions can require examination and sometimes medical or psychological treatment. Adults who have never overcome their childhood sense of helplessness may need help in restructuring their lives, finding hidden strengths, and discovering the reasons that they continue to feel helpless.

When a traumatic event is followed by nightmares, short-term psychotherapy is often extremely beneficial. Typically, a person who has been through an experience such as a fire or has been the victim of some kind of violence has nightmares for several weeks. This is a time when counseling or therapy can give people a chance to talk about the lingering fears and thus render their memories of the traumatic event less haunting.

Research directions

In very recent studies of the biology of the nightmare, it has been found that certain medications may produce nightmares. These include reserpine, a widely used antihypertensive; beta-adrenergic blockers such as propranolol, which block substances in the body that affect the central nervous

Robert Louis Stevenson based his famous Strange Case of Dr. Jekyll and Mr. Hyde *(1886) on a nightmare in which he saw a dapper upper-class English gentleman change into a hideous monster.*

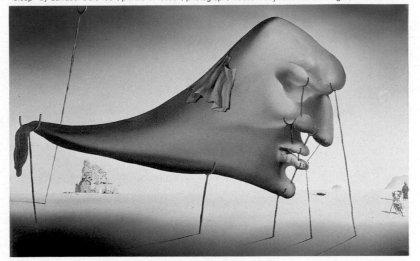

"Sleep" by Salvador Dali, 1937; private collection; photograph, Museum Boymans-van Beuningen, Rotterdam

A great many of the works of Spanish artist Salvador Dali create nightmarish worlds. Even though nightmares are now the subject of scientific inquiry, much about these uniquely terrifying dreams remains beyond the grasp of investigators. Indeed, it is unlikely that science will ever unravel the ultimate mysteries behind these haunting dreams. And for perhaps that we should be thankful, because it is clear that nightmares have inspired and will continue to inspire works of art.

system and are used to treat cardiac and other conditions; L-DOPA, an antiparkinsonism drug; and anticholinesterase drugs, which are sometimes used in the treatment of the neuromuscular disorder myasthenia gravis. The precise mechanisms of action of each drug are complex and by no means fully understood.

Less information is available about drugs that may decrease or prevent nightmares. Antipsychotics appear to have this effect, but there may be others. In any case, such drug studies are fertile ground for further investigation and are one way of better defining the nightmare as a distinct psychological and biologic phenomenon.

The creative solution

Some well-known people have let nightmares shape their creative endeavors. For instance, Mary Shelley reported using her nightmares as a basis for *Frankenstein.* Robert Louis Stevenson used his nightmares to create Dr. Jeckyll and Mr. Hyde. Many painters have painted scenes from their nightmares.

The list of artists and other creative individuals who have had frequent nightmares is indeed a long one, though in most cases little is actually known of the exact link between their dreams and their creativity. Bram Stoker, who wrote *Dracula,* is reported to have had frequent nightmares. Samuel Taylor Coleridge had nightmares (though these may have been opium induced). Others who were allegedly haunted by their dreams include André Gide, both Richard Wagner and his wife Cosima, René Descartes, Fyodor Dostoyevsky, and August Strindberg.

If we cannot beat our nightmares, perhaps we can join them. It may well be that for many of us the healthiest approach is to allow nightmares to be self-enriching rather than incapacitating—using them either in getting to know ourselves better or in artistic creation.

Rethinking the Good Life:

Forty Years at Framingham

by William B. Kannel, M.D., M.P.H.

The town of Framingham, Massachusetts, has served as a model community for the longest-running and most comprehensive project of its kind, which has generated information that has been used to save millions of lives around the world. The now famous enterprise, known as the Framingham Study, has become a classic of preventive medicine—evolving methods, concepts, and substantive findings that are now part of the curriculum of virtually all medical schools in the United States and in many other countries as well. There is hardly a prevention-minded physician anywhere in the world who has not heard of the study and its major findings.

The study has delineated a portrait of the prime candidate for a heart attack or stroke by identifying those persons who are vulnerable and modifiable predisposing ("risk") factors (and, therefore, is sometimes called the Framingham Heart Study). The risk factors identified have been confirmed in many parts of the world. The Framingham Study has dispelled the fatalistic notion that cardiovascular disease is an inevitable consequence of aging and genetic makeup. It has demonstrated that this disease is largely a product of how people live and that avoidance of heart attacks is in the hands of the potential victims, who, with guidance, must take a measure of responsibility for their own health.

Many physicians, as a result of the study findings, are now unwilling to accept prevalent physical activity and dietary practices, usual cholesterol and blood-pressure levels, or average body weights as optimal standards for their patients' health. The day is now approaching when a heart attack or stroke in a patient under health maintenance programs will be considered a medical failure.

The impact of the ongoing, world-renowned Framingham Study now extends well beyond the science of epidemiology. The periodically published results have begun to influence the way people live. In the United States the findings are stimulating a change in the notoriously atherogenic (cardiovascular-disease-promoting) American life-style.

(Opposite page) "The Endangered Heart" by Lucia Kellner; photograph, Bayer AG (Bayer–Berichte, 53/1985)

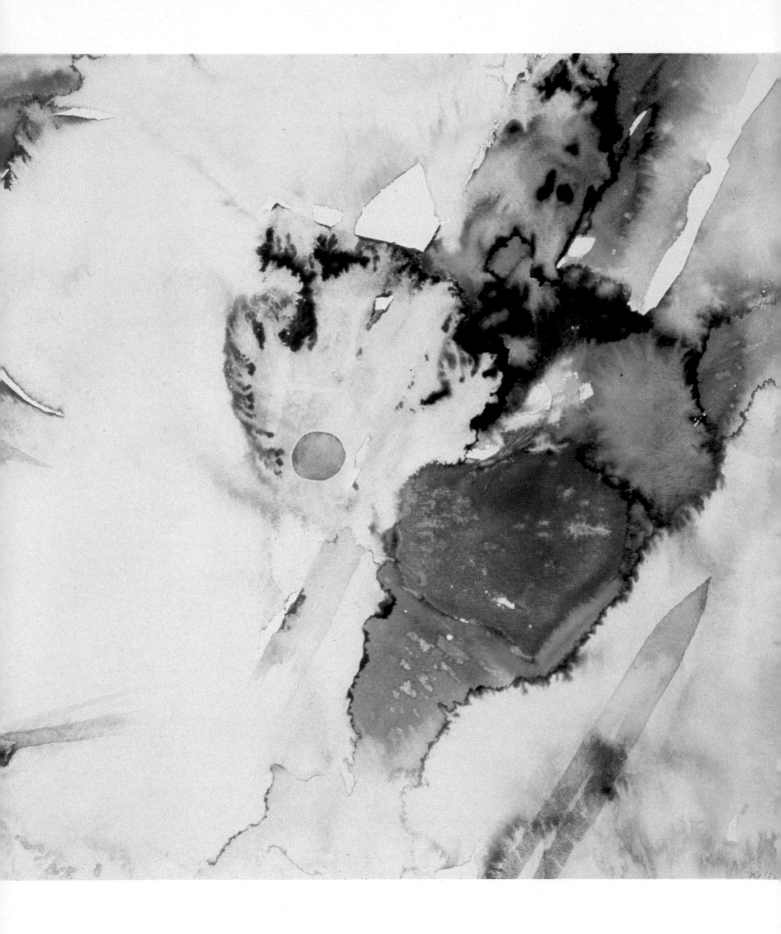

William B. Kannel, M.D., M.P.H., is Professor of Medicine and Public Health at Boston University School of Medicine and former director of the Framingham Study.

The participants

The success of the Framingham Study is to a large extent owed to the steadfast cooperation and long-term commitment of the good townspeople of Framingham. When the study began nearly four decades ago, the participants from this typical New England town had the same atherogenic life-styles as most urban or suburban Americans—*i.e.*, characterized by too much of a too rich diet, cigarette smoking, too little exercise, unrestrained weight gain, and, as a result, elevated blood pressures, high blood cholesterol and blood sugar, and, often, electrocardiographic abnormalities. Despite this, they were without symptoms—thus completely unaware of impending heart attacks and strokes. In fact, as most Americans, these prime candidates for early death from coronary attacks were living what they believed was the "good life."

The long-term commitment of the study's participants has meant being reexamined every two years, and in over 30 years only 2% have completely deserted the cause. They have submitted to a complete cardiovascular examination including a medical history, physical examination, electrocardiogram (ECG), echocardiograms, drawing of blood samples, exercise treadmill tests, X-ray examinations, and long questionnaires on their dietary practices, their exercise, smoking, and drinking habits, and their behavior patterns. Although these examinations, carried out in a locally established clinic, were free of charge, the subjects often had to take a morning off from work; sometimes they have had to save urine for 24 hours or keep a diary of food intake.

This is indeed remarkable dedication, since no medical care is offered; the medical personnel only report any abnormalities discovered to the participants' own physicians. Nor has there been any materialistic inducement. In fact, there has been no tangible reward for those participating other than the knowledge that they are contributing to medical illumination.

Motivation for and organization of the Framingham Study

In the decades of the 1930s through the '50s, there was an ever mounting epidemic of coronary heart disease (CHD) in the U.S. and many Western countries, so that it became the leading cause of untimely mortality. By 1950 one out of every three American men would develop cardiovascular disease before age 60. This rise came about with the improvements in sanitation, nutrition, and overall standard of living. Thus, the former leading lethal forces—the infectious and enteric diseases—had come under control only to be replaced by atherosclerotic cardiovascular disease. Although life expectancy from birth had increased steadily in the 1950s and '60s, there had been no increase in expected length of life beyond age 45, chiefly owing to unabated mortality beyond that age from cardiovascular disease.

In one of every six coronary attacks, sudden death was the first, last, and only symptom. Moreover, half of all CHD deaths occurred outside the hospital and out of reach of immediate medical care. In 1950 there was no known treatment capable of prolonging life even in those who were fortunate enough to survive the critical first hour of a heart attack. Thus, it was concluded by the U.S. surgeon general that only a preventive approach

(Opposite) The site of the now famous Framingham Heart Study is the small, self-contained community of Framingham, Massachusetts, within commuting distance of Boston. Every two years participants in the longest-running epidemiological undertaking of its kind visit the modest white frame house (center left) to undergo extensive medical evaluation. The residents of Framingham, a "typical" New England town, have "typical" American life-styles. Their diets are too high in fats, salt, and calories; they exercise too little; and they smoke too much—in other words, they are prime candidates for heart attacks.

26

could make substantial inroads against this number one killer.

In 1948 a division of chronic disease had been established within the U.S. Public Health Service, and programs were under development to determine whether cardiovascular disorders, so highly prevalent, might be prevented and what remedial measures might be undertaken. Studies of the epidemiology and possible prevention were then begun. Two of these were located in Massachusetts, in Boston suburbs, with Framingham to undertake epidemiological investigations while preventive programs were implemented in Newton.

Largely because of the recommendation of the late public health expert David D. Rutstein of the Harvard Medical School, Framingham—as a small, self-contained community of, at that time, about 28,000 inhabitants, and 29 kilometers (18 miles) west of Boston and thus in close proximity to that city's major medical research community—was chosen as an ideal locale. The residents were of all walks of life and largely employed in well-established business and manufacturing enterprises. The Framingham population is composed largely of Irish- and Italian-Americans. The major blue-collar employers are a General Motors plant, Hodgman Rubber Co., and Dennison Manufacturing Co., a paperworks company. There are also farms, small businesses, and an upper-middle-income group of professionals who work in Boston. The town is served by a medical community comprising a well-trained cadre of local physicians and two hospitals. These physicians and other town leaders agreed to cooperate with the proposed plans and to assist in recruiting townspeople to participate in the study.

The plan was to select a stable sample of adults (the "cohort") who would vary in the factors thought to be related to development of heart disease. An initial examination of these participants was carried out to detect the presence of already existing disease and to identify those free of disease who would be followed for 20 years in order to determine who would and who would not develop initial cardiovascular disease. Each subject was to be characterized biennially so that changes in suspected predisposing personal attributes, living habits, and other factors could be tracked.

Gilcin F. Meadors, a young public health officer, was first charged with organizing the Framingham Study by enlisting volunteers. When the National Heart Institute (NHI) was established in 1948, its head, Cassius J. Van Slyke, who was committed to an epidemiological approach, transferred the incipient study to the auspices of NHI. The new institute reconsidered the initial selection of the cohort, or population at risk. In order to ensure that the findings of the study would be applicable to other areas of the country, it was determined that approximately 5,000 to 6,000 adult men and women would be required in the cohort so that over 20 years a sufficient number of cardiovascular events would emerge to permit an examination of the relation of suspected predisposing factors to development of disease.

With the transfer to the NHI, Thomas Royle Dawber accepted responsibility for the study and became its chief architect. He guided it for the next 16 years. Under his direction, a set of hypotheses to be tested was conceived; these hypotheses were largely based on clinical experience of noted Boston cardiologists.

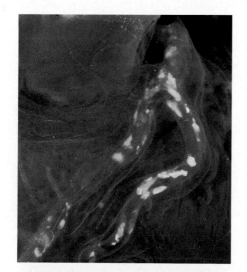

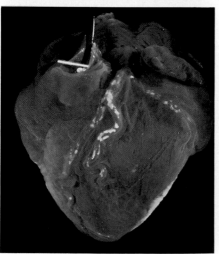

Photographs, Lou Lainey/Discover Magazine ©
1984 Time, Inc.

28

The study established headquarters in a modest three-story white frame house in downtown Framingham, with a staff of some 20, including doctors, nurses, technicians, and researchers, to perform the medical examinations of volunteers. As the study progressed and the population sample was brought back for reexamination at two-year intervals, increasing numbers of participants developed atherosclerotic cardiovascular disease. Not until seven years after the start of the study did a sufficient number of events accumulate to permit even a preliminary report.

New questions posed and a new generation to study

The seven-year report suggested that some of the hypotheses under investigation would be substantiated. With each successive reevaluation after a substantial number of cardiovascular events had accumulated, a more in-depth analysis of the factors under investigation was possible. This generated questions not originally anticipated, which required further follow-up.

Even before a major 20-year follow-up was completed, extramural committees had been appointed to consider the wisdom of continuing the program. By 1970, after 20 years of operation, a review committee had advised that clinical examinations be discontinued, since the major hypotheses had been sufficiently tested. This decision was widely disputed. The Boston University Medical Center then sponsored a campaign to finance an additional five-year period of follow-up with the help of a number of foundations, industrial enterprises, insurance companies, and private individuals. Upon completion of this phase of the study in 1975, during which 48 scientific publications were generated, support of further clinical follow-up under a contract to Boston University was reinstituted by the National Heart and Lung Institute. (The NHI became the National Heart and Lung Institute from 1969 to 1976, and in 1976 the name was changed to the National Heart, Lung, and Blood Institute [NHLBI].)

A Framingham Offspring Study (sometimes called "Son of Framingham") was initiated in 1971 to assess familial and hereditary factors as determinants of CHD. Among the 5,209 original participants were 1,644 families in which both husband and wife were enrolled. Some 2,656 children from 1,202 of these families have been examined. Hence, the study is engaged in determining to what extent factors known to increase susceptibility to atherosclerosis and coronary heart disease tend to cluster in families.

The children were examined at about the same ages as their parents had been two decades previously, making meaningful comparisons possible. The offspring examinations, like those of the parents, included a medical history, an examination of the cardiovascular system, an ECG, lung function tests, blood analyses for cholesterol, lipoproteins, sugar, sodium, and uric acid, and various other tests. Future examinations will permit study of changes in the major risk factors. As new technologies have evolved, better methods of testing have been introduced into the offspring study. A determination of the risks is now accomplished with sophisticated ultrasound devices that detect abnormalities, exercise stress tests, noninvasive blood flow studies, and special studies of blood lipid makeup and of blood clotting factors, among others.

As a result of the findings of the Framingham Study and other epidemiological investigations, many physicians are now unwilling to accept usual cholesterol levels in their patients. It is now well established that cholesterol in the blood leads to an accumulation of excess fat particles that become plaque deposits inside arteries, obstructing the flow of blood to the heart muscle and causing heart disease. Photographs (opposite page) dramatically show the fatty, yellowish plaque material that clogs coronary arteries. Only recently has it become clear that reducing cholesterol in the diet reduces risk of heart attacks.

29

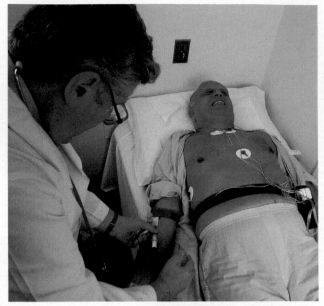

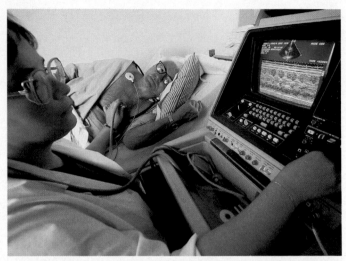

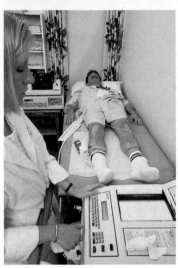

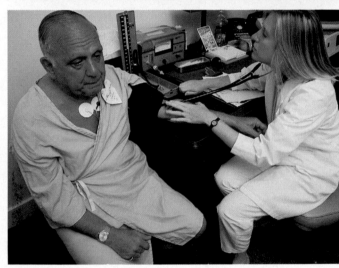

The epidemiological approach

At the inception of the Framingham Study, the application of an epidemiological approach to unraveling the causes of chronic cardiovascular disease was novel. The science of epidemiology has since undergone a metamorphosis. The epidemiologist now explores the way disease processes arise, evolve, and terminate fatally in relation to possible factors that may affect them. Epidemiologists are concerned chiefly with the circumstances surrounding the development of disease in general population samples rather than in individuals, but findings are relevant to an understanding of disease occurrence in individuals. Epidemiological investigations constitute not only statistical studies but a study of people in their total environment. An especially valuable outcome of epidemiological research is the revelation of unexpected information about health and disease.

To date, as a prospective epidemiological investigation, the Framingham

30

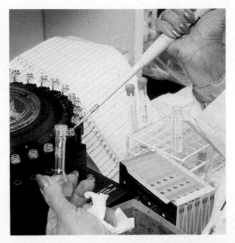

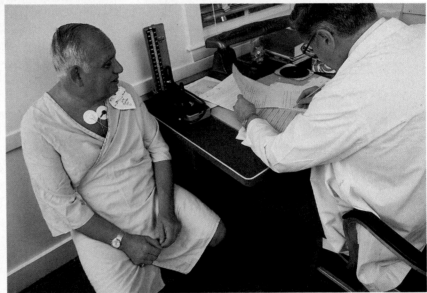

Study has uncovered an undistorted clinical spectrum of CHD in those who have it, has provided a perspective on the importance of CHD as a force of disease and death, and has established the chain of events leading to CHD occurrence. Numerous clues to pathogenesis also have been discovered. While the focus of study has been the most pervasive medical problem—cardiovascular disease—much has been learned about other maladies as well.

Major findings

The Framingham Study has successfully identified major contributors to cardiovascular disease, which include atherogenic personal habits typified by a diet excessive in calories, fat, and salt; a sedentary rather than active life-style; unrestrained weight gain; and cigarette smoking—factors elaborated upon below. Alcohol, if used in moderation, may be beneficial since it

(Top left) Lung capacity is checked as a volunteer exhales into a device called a spirometer. (Top right) Sophisticated new laboratory techniques enable precise detailing of blood lipid makeup from regularly collected blood samples (bottom left). (Bottom right) A medical history and a long questionnaire on life-style practices are an important part of the thorough medical exam that Framingham participants submit to.

Photographs, Dan McCoy—Rainbow

31

was found to be associated with a reduced risk of CHD. Postmenopausal estrogenic hormones were found to aggravate the atherogenic traits that predispose to CHD, and when used by women for long periods, beyond age 50, and in conjunction with cigarettes, they were associated with increased risk of heart attacks and strokes. Type A behavior, characterized by excessive time-urgency, drive, and competitiveness, was common in individuals of both sexes prone to develop coronary heart disease. Men married to more highly educated women were found to be at increased risk of CHD if their wives worked outside the home, particularly in white-collar jobs.

In the Framingham Study many heart attacks were found to go unnoticed. About 28% of men and 35% of women who sustained a myocardial infarction were not aware that such an event had taken place. These "silent" heart attacks were detected only by means of routine biennial ECGs. The clinical signs of a compromised coronary circulation determined by ECG were found to be highly predictive of future, overt clinical events. Despite the apparent benign manifestation of these attacks, their outlook was found to be just as serious as those in persons who had obvious symptoms. In fact, after ten years 45% of those with unrecognized infarctions were dead, compared with a 39% death rate in those with symptomatic attacks. Later-onset strokes and heart failure also occurred in the silent group at the same rates as they did in symptomatic heart attack patients.

Another major finding was that of innate susceptibility when family history included premature cardiovascular disease—*e.g.*, those with a brother who developed CHD had more than twice the risk (which was not accounted for by other cardiovascular risk factors).

Cholesterol. Physicians are now realizing that what is *usual* may be far from *ideal*. It has been shown that within the so-called normal range of blood cholesterol reported by most laboratories (*i.e.*, 180–310 milligrams

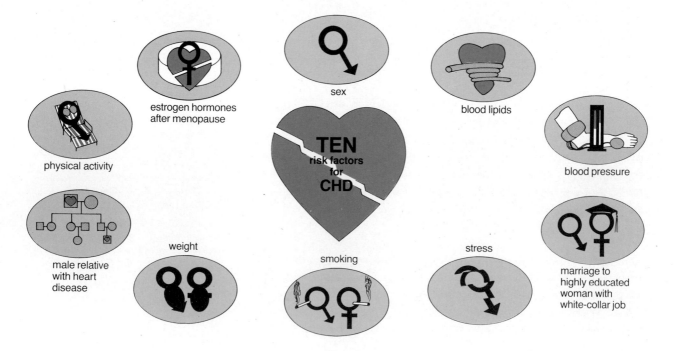

physical activity

estrogen hormones after menopause

sex

blood lipids

blood pressure

TEN risk factors for CHD

male relative with heart disease

weight

smoking

stress

marriage to highly educated woman with white-collar job

Source: Framingham Heart Study

**Risk of developing CHD in four years
by HDL and LDL cholesterol** (men ages 50–70)

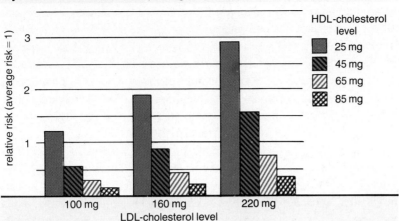

*Framingham investigations helped to
determine that serum total cholesterol
involves a "two-way traffic" of low-density
lipoproteins (LDL) in the blood carrying
cholesterol into arteries, where it
accumulates as plaque, while high-density
lipoproteins (HDL) serve a protective
function, flushing cholesterol out of
arteries. Risk of coronary artery disease
is directly proportional to the level of
LDL cholesterol, inversely related to
HDL-cholesterol levels.*

per deciliter), risk of a coronary attack varies with the level. Ideal cholesterol
values are now thought to be somewhere between 150 and 180 milligrams
per deciliter, values associated with low CHD rates and a low overall
mortality rate. In the Framingham cohort the average cholesterol level was
about 225. In Framingham subjects who succumbed to CHD, levels were
almost invariably over 200.

Early in its investigations the study measured the lipoproteins to which
cholesterol is joined in the blood. It came to be recognized that the serum
total cholesterol reflected a "two-way traffic" of cholesterol; low-density-
lipoprotein (LDL)-linked cholesterol was atherogenic, carrying cholesterol
into the lining of the arteries. This component then was responsible for the
serum total cholesterol-coronary disease relationship. Another component,
the high-density-lipoprotein (HDL)-linked cholesterol, was found to be protective since it is involved in transport of cholesterol out of the tissues.
Framingham, in collaboration with other epidemiological studies, has convincingly demonstrated that risk of coronary disease is directly proportional
to the LDL cholesterol and inversely related to the HDL cholesterol.

Because the final link in the chain of evidence connecting cholesterol
and its lipoproteins to atherosclerosis and its clinical manifestations has
now been forged, many physicians and health officials are taking action
to modify the typical, atherogenic American diet. There is now indisputable
evidence that what people eat is related to their serum cholesterol and
to their subsequent CHD mortality rate. A Chicago-Western Electric Study
after 20 years of follow-up showed that the saturated fat and cholesterol
content of the diet is related to mortality. A Boston-Ireland collaborative
study showed the same and, in addition, that the fiber and vegetable
content of the diet is protective. A long-term study in Zutphen, The Netherlands, showed that fish consumption is protective. Two intervention studies
have further convincingly shown that lowering elevated cholesterol by diet
or drugs reduces the risk of CHD. This cumulative evidence should dispel
much of the resistance some cardiologists have had to supporting public
health action—*i.e.,* recommending wide-scale changes in the national diet.

33

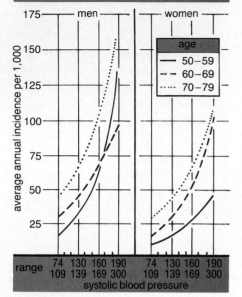

Source: Framingham Heart Study

Risk of CHD according to systolic blood pressure in persons with diastolic blood pressure under 95 (20-year follow-up, men and women ages 50–79)

Prior to Framingham findings, medical thinking held that high blood pressure (hypertension) was unhealthy only if the diastolic pressure (the bottom figure in a blood pressure reading) was elevated. But it was found that elevation of the systolic component (the top measure) is equally or more dangerous to cardiovascular health.

Further, it was learned that although hypertension increases risk of mortality from various vascular diseases, the risk for coronary heart disease is by far the greatest.

Hypertension. At the time of the initiation of the Framingham Study, the clinical dogma held that the negative cardiovascular consequences of hypertension (high blood pressure) derived from the diastolic component of the blood pressure. It is now widely recognized by physicians, largely from Framingham data, that the systolic component is as potent, or more so. In persons in the Framingham cohort who had never had any elevation of their diastolic pressure (the residual arterial pressure between heartbeats when the heart is "filling" with blood), CHD risk was distinctly related to their associated systolic pressure (the peak pressure when the heart muscle contracts and squeezes blood out into the arteries).

There was also a belief in a threshold critical "hypertensive" blood pressure value that designated where normal left off and abnormal began. This widely held concept has evaporated as data from Framingham have shown that risk of cardiovascular sequelae is simply proportional to the blood pressure level, from the lowest to the highest pressures, and even within the so-called normotensive range. It is blood *pressure* that kills, and even mild or "borderline" elevations double the risk. Also mild elevations beget severe elevations, and so it is not safe to await the appearance of "true hypertension" before treatment is instituted.

When the Framingham Study began, many physicians believed that older people required higher pressures to compensate for more rigid, sclerotic (*i.e.,* narrowed) blood vessels—in order to adequately perfuse their tissues with blood. It was held by some that it might actually be dangerous to lower elevated pressures in such elderly persons. The study has shown that, comparing normotensive with hypertensive persons within each sex by age, the risk of cardiovascular disease associated with any degree of hypertension is at least as great in the elderly as in the young and that the absolute risk is substantially greater in the elderly.

Hypertension is now recognized as a threat to life, despite its silent nature, at any age in either sex. Despite a common belief to the contrary, women were found not to tolerate hypertension any better than men do.

A further widely believed concept at the inception of the study was that

Risk of cardiovascular disease according to hypertensive status
(26-year follow-up, men and women ages 35–84)

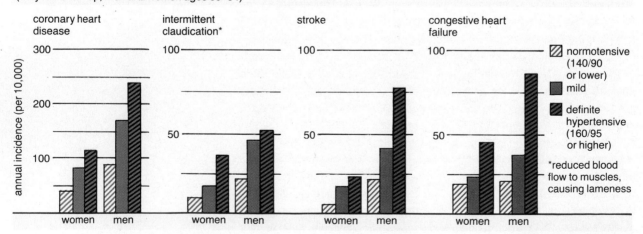

Source: Framingham Heart Study

because blood pressure was naturally variable, it was necessary to obtain a measure of basal (*i.e.,* resting) pressure in a sedated patient in order to determine whether "true hypertension" was present. That blood pressures taken routinely in a doctor's office would not correctly characterize the blood pressure status has, however, been disproved by the epidemiological investigations, which had to rely on such determinations. These casually obtained pressures were found to be good predictors of the cardiovascular sequelae of hypertension. The belief in the need for elaborate medical evaluation to seek out specific causes in all hypertensive persons has largely been dispelled, except where there is some clinical clue to suggest a specific correctable cause.

Controlled clinical trials were undertaken that demonstrated the efficacy of treating high blood pressure while still asymptomatic. Such treatment with a variety of antihypertensive drugs has been shown not only to effectively lower the blood pressure but also to prolong life and to reduce certain cardiovascular sequelae such as stroke, cardiac failure, and kidney insufficiency. Since these benefits have been achieved with few and, in most instances, tolerable side effects, physicians have been stimulated to detect elevated blood pressure in their patients early and to treat it vigorously.

Cigarette smoking. When the Framingham Study was initiated, there was no reliable evidence that the use of tobacco was detrimental to the cardiovascular system (other than possible occlusive peripheral arterial disease affecting the circulation to the legs). Framingham investigations provided the first clear knowledge that cigarette smoking was indeed a major contributor to the development of coronary heart disease (in addition to lung disease), which was sustained by the first Surgeon General's Report in 1964 on the hazards of cigarette smoking. Further epidemiological studies at Framingham and elsewhere extended these findings so that cigarette smoking is now known to be a powerful independent contributor to heart attacks, sudden coronary death, peripheral arterial disease, and premature strokes.

The impact of this information on the smoking habits of physicians themselves has been truly profound. The general public has also responded to the adverse findings. Middle-aged men have responded most dramatically but, unfortunately, the persuasive evidence has not prevented young women from taking up the habit in ever increasing numbers.

Physicians now do not condone cigarette smoking in any of their patients, and especially in their high-coronary-risk patients. Although doctors have been as effective as any group in inducing smokers to quit, overall accomplishments have been modest. The search for a safer cigarette has proved fruitless, and filter cigarettes carry as great a risk as unfiltered cigarettes. Better methods of helping people overcome or never to begin smoking are clearly needed.

Obesity. Aside from some life insurance statistics, there was little to incriminate obesity as a factor in the development of cardiovascular disease until Framingham and other epidemiological population studies demonstrated the link. It has been shown that excessive weight is accompanied by increased blood pressure, blood sugar, and atherogenic blood lipids. Largely as a consequence of the worsening of these atherogenic traits,

"Three Smokers" (detail) by Roy Carruthers, 1977; photograph, ACA Galleries, New York

In the early 1950s, the initial years of the Framingham Study, there was no reliable evidence that smoking was involved in heart disease. In fact, many of the now well-known dangers of cigarette use were not detailed until the U.S. Surgeon General's Report on Smoking and Health in 1964.

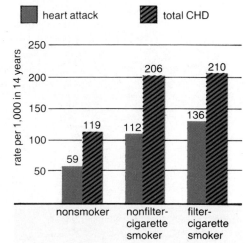

Heart disease and smoking
(men under age 55)

Source: Framingham Heart Study

Source: Framingham Heart Study

Changes in blood cholesterol level with changes in relative weight

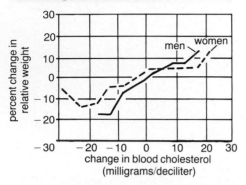

Changes in systolic blood pressure with changes in relative weight

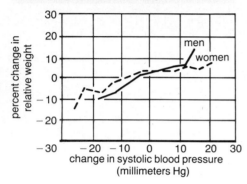

obesity is associated with a high rate of heart attacks. This evidence induced most physicians to advise their heavy patients to lose weight. Unfortunately, however, effective means for preventing and treating long-standing obesity are unavailable. Massive obesity has proved to be virtually an intractable condition, a fact that indicates the urgency for modestly overweight individuals to correct the problem before it gets out of hand.

Physical activity. Physicians formerly counseled against physical exertion in patients with coronary disease, and some believed that vigorous physical exertion contributed to cardiovascular disease. These concepts have been radically altered by epidemiological data that have indicated that, if anything, *lack* of physical activity is associated with occurrence of coronary attacks. Hence, many physicians now recommend vigorous endurance exercise for the purpose of avoiding coronary disease. Exercise is also now used to help reduce blood pressure, raise HDL-cholesterol, improve glucose tolerance, and control obesity. And physical exercise programs are now standard for recovering heart attack victims.

Justification for and obstacles to public health action

Indeed, the Framingham Study has helped to identify, with reasonable certainty, major precursors of cardiovascular disease that are modifiable and the life-style that tends to promote them. Despite some lingering uncertainties and the fact that knowledge is incomplete, there now is enough information for action. Reducing the huge annual toll of cardiovascular mortality is now possible.

In a disease like coronary disease, which characteristically strikes with little warning, in which the first symptom may be the last, in which more than half the mortality occurs outside the hospital in a matter of minutes, and which can be silent in its most dangerous form, a preventive approach

Obesity is a risk factor for heart disease because it is associated with other major risk factors—increased blood pressure, high blood sugar, and elevated cholesterol. But the battle to reduce and maintain a weight loss permanently is not easily won by most who try. Moreover, motivating people to alter their eating patterns has proved to be one of the most difficult challenges to modern medicine. Indeed, in a society of plenty, it is no easy task for most people to be prudent when the temptations of overabundance and the offerings of the "good life" are so ever present.

"Thanksgiving Still Life" by David Bates; collection, Mr. and Mrs. George M. Young, Fort Worth, Texas; photograph, Charles Cowles Gallery, New York

is the best means of achieving a substantial reduction in mortality—especially in light of the fact that some 80% of U.S. males have one or more major risk factors, from which 90% of all coronary events evolve.

Unfortunately, there are a number of impediments to implementation of preventive programs. A successful preventive program would have to be integrated into the medical care delivery system without competing for scarce resources and endangering the system's ability to deliver quality care to those already ill. But the medical care system as it currently stands in the United States is overburdened with those already ill and is oriented toward crisis and therapeutics—not to helping people alter life-styles.

Despite the great health rewards to be gained, motivating people to give up practices they enjoy for some future benefit remains an exceedingly difficult enterprise. Futher, there is no secure basis for precisely estimating the reduction in coronary and stroke events that will ultimately be achieved by applying current knowledge about risk factors to the task of prevention.

Cardiovascular mortality declines

After decades of increasing incidence of coronary heart disease, reaching epidemic proportions in the 1950s, rates peaked in the late 1960s and then began a dramatic downturn, which has continued to the present. The proportion of all deaths due to cardiovascular causes decreased from 54 to 49% between 1968 and 1982, and the proportion of deaths ascribed to CHD decreased from 35 to 28%. Overall, deaths from CHD dropped 37% between 1963 and 1982, and stroke mortality declined by a remarkable 45%. As a result, the gap in mortality between coronary disease and cancer is now closing rapidly. Life expectancy has increased 2.5 years in whites and 4 years in blacks, and for the first time a substantial increase in life expectancy beyond age 45 is being experienced. These improvements in cardiovascular mortality have occurred for both sexes, in all races, and in all geographic areas in the U.S. They have been greatest in the better educated, in young adults, and in blacks. The decline in the U.S. exceeds that in other countries, and it has not occurred in some European countries with equally sophisticated medical care. Those countries most active in risk-factor control, including Canada, New Zealand, and Australia, have had the greatest declines.

This dramatic decline in the leading cause of death has been substantial, universal, sustained, and real. It is continuing and is clearly not due either to changes in death certification practices or to other artifacts. The improvements have coincided with improvements in the levels of predisposing risk factors in the general population and are also due, in part, to better access to more sophisticated medical services. Blood-cholesterol values and blood pressures are lower; cigarette smoking has declined from 43 to 32% (1966 to 1983); and middle-aged Americans are exercising more. Dietary changes toward a less saturated fat, lower cholesterol intake, more fiber, and less salt are taking place. It has been estimated that changes in disease-promoting life-styles have accounted for more than half the decline and medical interventions for about 40%.

How have the people of Framingham fared in correcting their athero-

Source: Framingham Heart Study

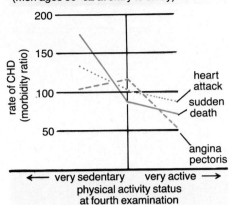

Risk of developing CHD in 12 years according to physical activity
(men ages 30–62 at entry to study)

Doctors once believed that vigorous physical exertion was dangerous to the heart. Now it is clear that regular exercise, in addition to providing many other substantial health benefits, substantially lowers the risk of developing most forms of heart disease.

37

*"This weekend, I thought I'd pop over to
Vegas and grab a smoke."*

genic ways? Although they are perhaps the most sensitized Americans to the dangers of cardiovascular life habits, they have *not* become shining examples of healthful living. Their role as participants in the now famous study has been for observation and tracking as representative "typical" Americans. They may be more conscious of risks, but that has not kept them from taking the risks. Nonetheless, there have been some changes. For example, half of the male participants have quit smoking, and their coronary attack rates have been halved, compared with those of counterparts within the cohort who elected to continue to smoke. However, more of the Framingham women are now smoking than did formerly.

Mission for the future

The Framingham Study has always attempted to stay at the frontier of epidemiological research by adapting new technology and by testing new hypotheses as they emerged. Hence, the study is now engaged in a variety of new research initiatives.

With the advent of noninvasive ultrasound techniques, it is now possible to examine the thickness of the heart muscle, the way it contracts, and the amount of blood it pumps with each beat (echocardiograph). The prognostic significance of these sorts of abnormalities is being determined. It has also become possible to better assess underlying processes that are related to the well-established risk factors. The atherosclerotic plaques that clog the arteries now can be visualized and the degree of clogging measured by ultrasound techniques, which pick up the velocity of blood flow through arteries.

New laboratory techniques have enabled the study to refine further the examination of the blood lipid-CHD connection by investigating subfractions of the atherogenic LDL cholesterol and of the protective HDL cholesterol.

Nearly four decades of studying heart disease in Framingham are paying off—and not just in the United States. Many Western nations are now witnessing a real and sustained decline in deaths from cardiovascular disease. A major accomplishment of the kind of health information that has emerged from Framingham is that people the world over are changing their habits. Notably in the U.S., smoking rates (at least among men) have declined. Moreover, smokers are fast becoming an unpopular minority. At least 39 states now have laws banning smoking in certain public areas, and increasingly restaurants, hotels, public transport, businesses, and workplaces are prohibiting smokers from exercising their habit where it might affect others.

Declining cardiovascular mortality, U.S.

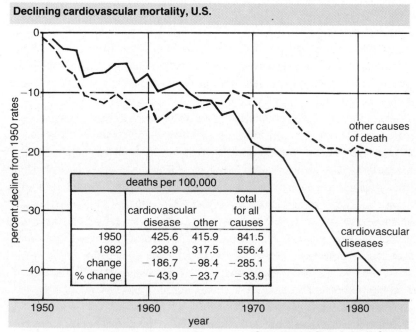

deaths per 100,000			
	cardiovascular disease	other	total for all causes
1950	425.6	415.9	841.5
1982	238.9	317.5	556.4
change	−186.7	−98.4	−285.1
% change	−43.9	−23.7	−33.9

Source: National Center for Health Statistics

Photographs, Dan McCoy—Rainbow

Additional insights are being sought through examination of the precise makeup of these lipoproteins that transport cholesterol in and out of the arterial wall.

Ambulatory monitoring is allowing a long-term look at blood pressure and the ECG characteristics of persons while they go about their daily lives. It has been found that ischemic ECG changes, signifying a compromised coronary circulation, occur many times during the day without provoking symptoms. This ECG monitoring will also allow an examination of the significance of transient, asymptomatic cardiac rhythm disturbances that have been linked to sudden-death heart attacks.

Detailed work histories of Framingham participants are being examined to determine whether working conditions and unemployment predispose them to heart attacks and strokes. Likewise, sociodemographic and a variety of psychosocial factors are being explored to extents that they have not been previously.

As the population sample has reached advanced age, many geriatric problems have become prevalent. Accordingly, the health problems that bedevil the elderly and can take the joy out of reaching a venerable stage in life will constitute a major portion of future Framingham investigations. In addition to the specific influence of cardiovascular risk factors as they affect this age group, hearing, eye disease, senile dementia (Alzheimer's disease), arthritis, osteoporosis, and emphysema are also being studied.

These and other activities will occupy investigators in the Framingham Study for some time to come. Currently the NHLBI is negotiating new contracts to extend the study mandate until 1992. Also, the National Cancer Institute and the Institute for Neurologic Disease are now providing support through grants and contracts for the investigation of cancer and Alzheimer's disease, respectively.

As the Framingham Study enters its 38th year, perhaps the biggest question is: Will the investigators survive the devoted volunteers who originally "enlisted" in this longest continuously running epidemiological study and who have been so central to the making of medical history?

(Above) Ronald and Linda Isaacson are current participants in the Framingham Offspring Study, which was initiated in 1971 in order to assess coronary heart disease and life-style habits in second-generation Framingham residents. The offspring of original participants undergo the same kind of evaluation as their parents did, at similar intervals, making it possible to study hereditary and familial patterns. The Isaacsons are notable in their adoption of a healthful life-style. Both stay trim and active. Linda (center) plays tennis regularly, while Ronald (right) has a vigorous thrice-weekly workout on the squash court. The people of Framingham may be the most acutely aware of all Americans of just how their habits affect their health. Nonetheless, not everyone in this Massachusetts community has altered his or her ways. Even though they have taken part in the world-renowned study that has delineated a portrait of prime candidates for early death from heart disease— a study that has so conclusively defined unhealthful life-styles that people can modify—a great many still opt to take the risks.

Comfort Me with Apples

by Bonnie Spring, Ph.D.

At least three times daily, most of us choose and eat the foods we wish. Food supplies the calories needed for energy and the nutrients needed to preserve life and health. Moreover, eating is pleasurable—so pleasurable, in fact, that 25 million–50 million people in the U.S. alone are overweight. The effects of foods on energy, health, and weight are accepted and reasonably well understood. But another kind of dietary influence has only recently captured the attention of scientists and the public—the possibility that foods affect such behaviors as mood, sleep, and performance at work or school or elsewhere in society.

The thought that foods might affect the body in ways that influence behavior, although new to science, has long commanded a place in folk wisdom. The poet of the biblical Song of Solomon wrote, "Stay me with flagons, comfort me with apples: for I am sick of love." Both the Egyptian Ebers papyrus, a compilation of medical texts dating from 1550 BC, and ancient Chinese writings contain the advice that eating liver can improve vision, a perceptual skill underlying behavior. Chinese folklore also recommended ginseng root as a prescription to stimulate libido, while modern folk wisdom holds that eating oysters accomplishes the same goal. Other beliefs about the way foods affect behavior have been incorporated into popular lore as well; e.g., the claims that warm milk helps one relax before bedtime, sugar makes one peppy and alert, and fish provides "brain food" (i.e., sharpens one's mental processes).

Recently some folk beliefs based on anecdotal stories have attracted extensive public interest and occasionally have even been presented as established fact. A prime example occurred during the 1979 trial of Dan White, who was charged with murdering San Francisco Mayor George Moscone and Supervisor Harvey Milk. White's attorney noted that his client had been undergoing a financial crisis and had gorged himself on packaged snack cakes and other "junk" foods before committing the crime. A prominent psychiatrist giving testimony for the defense argued that the client's diet resulted in an aberrant mental condition, causing diminished capacity to discriminate right from wrong. The "Twinkie defense" was apparently one factor that led jurors to render the more lenient judgment of voluntary manslaughter rather than murder.

Bonnie Spring, Ph.D., is *Professor of Psychology at Texas Tech University, Lubbock.*

(Opposite page) "Adam and Eve" by Titian, c. 1570; collection, Museo del Prado, Madrid; photograph, Giraudon/Art Resource

41

The idea that foods might affect behavior, although new to science, holds a well-established place in folk wisdom. Over the centuries various cultures have attributed aphrodisiacal powers to a host of spices, vegetables, and seafoods, including oysters.

From anecdote to observation to explanation

It may be that anecdotes about foods and behavior have deterred as much research as they have stimulated, since many claims have been so overstated that they seem implausible. While collecting stories is indeed a first step in establishing that foods affect behavior, it is only the first.

A good example of the way that anecdote has led to meaningful controlled investigations is found in the work of Joseph Goldberger, a founding figure in the field of psychiatric epidemiology and perhaps the first major researcher of diet–behavior relationships. During the early 20th century, Goldberger, a physician with the U.S. Public Health Service, unraveled the cause and cure for pellagra, a condition characterized by skin lesions, gastrointestinal disturbances, and a psychosis that can include depression, confusion, delusions, and hallucinations. Pellagra was prevalent among poor sharecroppers in the southern U.S., and anecdotes suggested that it often struck members of the same family and patients who were institutionalized at certain hospitals. Because the condition affected persons in close proximity to one another, it first seemed that the illness might be infectious. Nevertheless, it was noted that some hospital staff slept in the same rooms as their patients, and yet staff members did not develop the syndrome.

Observing that pellagra was most common among the poorest farmers who ate little meat and that some hospital diets were also poor in meat, Goldberger speculated that people who ate such impoverished meals over an extended period might develop a nutritional deficiency that manifested itself as pellagra. Staff members were presumably protected from the deficiency because they ate many meals at home. Goldberger also noticed a similarity between the inflamed tongue of the pellagra victim and the brownish eroded mouth surfaces of dogs with a fatal condition called blacktongue. Since dogs developed this illness when they were restricted to a diet consisting only of vegetables, Goldberger reasoned that blacktongue might represent an animal model for pellagra. After producing blacktongue in dogs by feeding them vegetable diets, Goldberger attempted to prevent the condition by adding specific foods to the animals' intakes. By the time of his death, he had established that liver and yeast contained a heat-stable, water- and alcohol-soluble factor that prevented both blacktongue and pellagra, and he had reduced deaths from pellagra by 75% by orally administering extracts of yeast and liver. Not long after Goldberger's death, other investigators discovered that niacin is the pellagra-preventing factor and were able to cure pellagra by administering injections of B vitamins.

An interesting aside is that Goldberger was offered financial support to pursue similar studies leading toward a cure for schizophrenia. Schizophrenia is a serious mental disorder that others have since sought, unsuccessfully, to treat with injections of large amounts of vitamins. Goldberger declined the award, expressing disbelief that he could accomplish the task.

As befits an era of relative plenty, today's questions about foods and behavior extend beyond exclusive concern with the consequences of dietary deficiencies. Attention is now being devoted to learning the effects of foods and food constituents that are already present in the diet. In the industrialized countries people consume higher levels of food additives, preservatives, environmental toxins, highly processed and refined foods, salt, caffeine, and sugar than many believe to be desirable for long-term health. But what about the short-term consequences for behavior of eating those foods and food constituents naturally present in the diet, about which the most is known? What are the behavioral consequences of eating carbohydrates or protein, eating large meals or skipping meals, or consuming food constituents like tryptophan, tyrosine, choline, or lecithin that are readily available at health food stores? Enough progress has been made to separate out three kinds of links between diet and behavior: those that are established, those that are suspected, and those that are merely purported by anecdotes.

Foods and hyperactivity in children

Hyperactivity is a behavior disorder typically first diagnosed in children of elementary school age, with boys more likely to be affected than girls. The restlessness and high levels of activity that mark the disorder are only part of the difficulty; problems in concentration are equally troublesome. Stimulant-type drugs such as Ritalin, which, paradoxically, calm the hyperactive child, have been the primary treatment.

Many parents firmly believe that food substances play a role in triggering hyperactive behavior. In 1975, prompted by the anecdotes of parents and pediatricians, Benjamin Feingold, a California allergist, published a diet alleged to produce dramatic improvement in hyperactive children. The Feingold diet restricts a child's intake of putatively troublesome synthetic food dyes and flavorings, as well as salicylates. One type of salicylate is the active ingredient in aspirin; some salicylates also occur naturally in fruits. After years of numerous controlled studies, the effectiveness of the Feingold approach remains controversial. Certainly the diet has not produced the dramatic benefits originally claimed. When, unbeknownst to the children being studied or their parents, researchers have reintroduced food additives into the diet, only a very small number of children have shown behavioral disturbances. These few children, for unknown reasons, may be sensitive

An impoverished black farmer (below) awaits death from pellagra in early 20th-century Georgia. Prevalent among poor sharecroppers, pellagra remained a baffling illness for years until Joseph Goldberger's investigations showed it to be the result of a dietary deficiency. Alabama sharecropper's cottage (below left) captures the plight of its residents, whose livelihood depended on a luxurious cotton crop that left little land for edible plants or livestock.

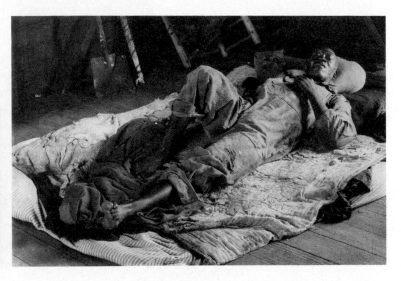

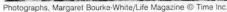

Photographs, Margaret Bourke-White/Life Magazine © Time Inc.

"Fidgety Phil" (above), a fictional denizen of a 19th-century collection of moral tales for children, epitomizes the restless behavior of the hyperactive child. Although the German physician who wrote the tales labeled the behavior simply as "naughty," many modern parents have laid the blame on food substances and additives. Allergist Benjamin Feingold (below) displays foods whose elimination from the diet, he believed, would dramatically improve hyperactive behavior. Feingold's diet, published in 1975, has not produced the broad, striking benefits first claimed for it and, after more than a decade of controlled studies, its effectiveness remains controversial.

to food additives and be helped by the elimination diet. Most, however, do not benefit substantially when additives are removed. The cost of helping the few who do respond positively must be weighed against the great effort required to maintain the diet. An enormous number of foods must be eliminated from the household, and restaurant dining becomes virtually taboo.

Since food additives failed to prove troublesome to many children, another culprit was proposed—sugar. Consumption of sugar has increased dramatically over the past several centuries. Three hundred years ago 1.8 kilograms (four pounds) of sugar satisfied the average English citizen for an entire year; current tastes call for 1.8 kilograms every two weeks. At one time sugar was a luxury item eaten primarily by the rich in elaborate ceremonial cakes and even edible sculptures. As Sidney W. Mintz points out in the book *Sweetness and Power,* working-class families during the 17th and 18th centuries consumed sweet meals as a way of imitating the rich. At one time a special treat, sugar is now staple fare for both adults and children.

James D. Wilson/Newsweek

As a side effect of its intended restrictions, the Feingold diet reduces carbohydrates, including as much as 86% of products high in sucrose (table sugar). Because parents frequently nominate sugar as a trigger for their children's unmanageable behavior, some people speculated that the elimination of sugar caused some of the sporadic successes of the Feingold diet. Many careful studies have since been undertaken to test the claim that sugar exacerbates hyperactivity. In one study conducted at the U.S. National Institute of Mental Health, Rockville, Maryland, David Behar, Judith Rapoport, and their colleagues advertised in the newspaper for parents who believed that sugar caused their children's disruptive behavior. These children were taken to the laboratory on three different days and given drinks containing the artificial sweetener saccharin or one of two natural sugars, sucrose or glucose. The children did not know which substance they had received, nor did the investigators who measured each child's behavior for five hours after the drink. Over the course of the study, neither natural sugar produced an increase in activity. Surprisingly, in fact, the sugars slightly decreased movements. Comparable results amassed from many similar studies fail to support the popular belief that sugar increases hyperactive behavior.

If sugar does not worsen hyperactivity, why do so many parents remain convinced that it does? The answer might be that a high level of sugar intake and a high degree of activity and aggression occur together in hyperactive children even though the first element does not cause the second. That is, children who are the most active and restless do indeed eat more sugar than their peers. Observing this relationship, parents may infer that sugar causes the hyperactivity. Laboratory findings, however, suggest that this conclusion is erroneous.

The correlation between high sugar intake and high activity levels may exist for at least two reasons. First, children who are highly active, for reasons that remain unknown at present, may burn up many calories

Sugar consumption has risen more than 20-fold in the past three centuries and has entrenched itself in the diet of both children and adults. Although parents of hyperactive children frequently have condemned sugar for their children's problems, many careful laboratory studies fail to support this idea. It is possible that hyperactive children unconsciously seek out a great deal of sugar to meet their increased energy demands or even to control their high levels of activity.

Joe McNally—Wheeler Pictures

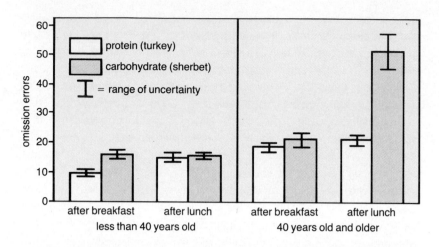

(Above) From Bonnie Spring *et al.*, "Effects of Protein and Carbohydrate Meals on Mood and Performance: Interactions with Sex and Age," *Journal of Psychiatric Research*, vol. 17 (1982–83), pp. 155–167; (opposite page, top) from C. Keith Conners *et al.*, "Experimental Studies of Sugar and Aspartame on Autonomic, Cortical, and Behavioral Responses of Children," *Diet and Behavior: An Interface Among Psychology, Medicine, and Nutrition*, ed. B. Spring, J. Chiodo, and J. Elias (Lubbock: Texas Tech University Press, in press)

The common wisdom that a high-carbohydrate meal supplies extra energy and improves concentration has not been supported in laboratory studies. The graphs above summarize results of a listening test used to measure concentration in adults who had consumed either carbohydrates or protein for breakfast or lunch. Those subjects who had eaten the carbohydrate meal generally made more errors than those who had eaten protein; the most striking difference was seen in adults age 40 and older after lunch. School-age children also have been found less attentive after eating carbohydrates (opposite page). As the graph indicates, children given a carbohydrate breakfast and then administered either an attention test or a test of response speed performed more poorly than children who had fasted or had eaten a protein breakfast.

and turn to sugar as a way of replenishing their energy supplies. The high intake of sugar in hyperactive youngsters might reflect an increased metabolic rate, since such children are able to eat a great deal without becoming overweight. Second, since sugar has a mild calming influence on behavior, highly active youngsters might even select sugary foods, albeit unconsciously, in an effort to control their own high activity levels.

Both of these explanations for the association between sugar and hyperactivity are speculative, but they indicate what may be a fruitful way of thinking about relationships between foods and behavior. Ordinarily, foods are something that we voluntarily select and administer to ourselves. Although we may not be able to articulate the reasons for our choice of foods, these selections, when examined objectively, might contain important information about the way diet affects us, not only in terms of long-term health but also in terms of short-term behavioral effects that we wish to induce. Ultimately they may fill out a picture that begins with an understanding of how we are what we eat and concludes with an understanding about how we eat what we are.

Food, mood, and mental performance

Adults who work at desk jobs and children who attend school depend on appropriate moods and levels of mental alertness to function effectively. Maintaining these states can be made easier or more difficult by the food choices that are made for meals or snacks. When feeling sluggish or lacking the time for a full lunch, people commonly dash to the vending machine for a candy bar. This practice is usually rationalized, though perhaps not entirely without guilt, with the folk wisdom that sugar provides the extra energy needed to perform demanding work. The lore that carbohydrates supply extra pep may hold true for those who face feats of physical endurance, although even this case remains untested. Anecdotally, marathon runners claim that eating large quantities of carbohydrates before a race increases their stamina. For those who face primarily mental marathons, however, carbohydrates appear to be a poor prescription.

Several studies conducted by Bonnie Spring and co-workers at Harvard University and later at Texas Tech University, Lubbock, compared what happens to mood and performance after adults eat meals that consist chiefly of carbohydrates or chiefly of protein. The carbohydrate test meals comprised sugary lunch bars, pita bread, or a nondairy fruit sherbet. Turkey breast served as the protein meal. Both test meals contained equal amounts of fat and supplied fewer than 1,000 calories. The investigators found no evidence to support the common wisdom that a high-energy mood follows a sugary meal. Instead, two hours after eating a high-carbohydrate meal lacking in protein, test subjects experienced fatigue, sleepiness, and lapses in concentration.

In one study Spring and her colleagues used a dichotic listening test to measure the concentration of subjects who had eaten either sherbet or turkey for breakfast or for lunch. While hearing distracting sounds through one earpiece of a set of stereo earphones, the subjects listened to long tape-recorded strings of words through the other earpiece and were required to repeat each word aloud as soon as it occurred. The investigators kept track of how many of the tape-recorded syllables the subjects omitted. The most striking results were seen in older subjects, who after eating the carbohydrate lunch left out many syllables, indicating that they were having trouble concentrating. This finding suggests that older people may be especially sensitive to the loss in performance efficiency that follows a midday meal that is carbohydrate rich but protein deficient. Even though younger people are apparently not as adversely affected, other studies have shown that college-age adults also do more poorly after a carbohydrate lunch than after a protein one. Moreover, it is not only simple sugars that reduce mental alertness; meals high in starch, a complex carbohydrate, produce the same result.

Sedentary adults are not the only ones who become less attentive after eating carbohydrates, for children were found to respond similarly. C. Keith Conners of Children's Hospital, National Medical Center, Washington, D.C., recently studied three groups of children: one group skipped breakfast; a second group was served a high-carbohydrate toast meal; and the third was fed a protein-rich breakfast of eggs. After eating, those children who ate the carbohydrate-rich breakfast performed slowly on measures of response speed. They also scored more poorly on tests of attentiveness than children who had fasted or eaten protein.

The advice that sugar provides energy could be correct when the task ahead is physically demanding work. Eaten alone, however, carbohydrates are not the best energy source for mental activity. Still, it would be a mistake to conclude that a high-protein, low-carbohydrate meal will improve mood and enhance mental alertness; the study results described above contain no implied support for following such a diet. Moreover, much evidence suggests that fad diets prescribing unbalanced meals lacking either carbohydrates or protein are detrimental to health. At present, the tried-and-true balanced meal remains the best diet for mood, work, and health.

Foods and behavior: looking for a causal connection

Until recently most scientists dismissed any connection between foods and behavior as the product of an overactive imagination, or at best a placebo

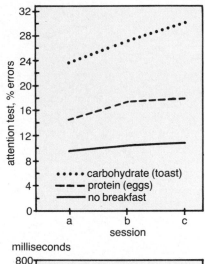

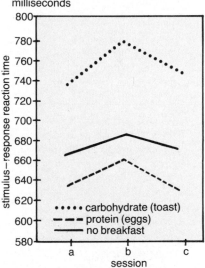

Burt Glinn—Magnum

47

(Left) Laboratory of Behavioral Medicine, Children's Hospital, National Medical Center, Washington, D.C.; (right) Department of Psychology, Texas Tech University; photograph, Cindy Mather

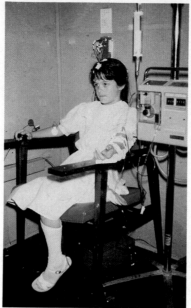 

Schoolgirl in full "hookup" (left) participates in a performance evaluation task in a sound-deadened booth at the Children's Hospital in Washington, D.C. Electrodes placed on the scalp monitor brain-wave changes during the task, while arm and leg electrodes follow cardiac patterns and body movements. An intravenous line draws blood samples for hormonal analysis. The child gives her responses to the presented task by pressing a button in her right hand. (Right) Woman wearing earphones receives instructions for dichotic listening test from Texas Tech investigator Bonnie Spring. A tape recorder connected to the microphone records the subject's attempts to repeat syllables heard through the earphones while enduring distracting noise. Such experimental designs are providing new insights into the relations between food, mental performance, and the body processes that affect behavior.

effect. A placebo is an inert substance that brings about an effect simply because it is expected to do so. Beliefs or expectations can create self-fulfilling prophecies. Two factors, however, cast doubt on the argument that all diet–behavior relationships can be attributed to placebo effects. First, there is no prevailing folklore suggesting that carbohydrates should make people sleepy. Indeed, one piece of folk wisdom suggests that sugar should be activating; another suggests that it triggers feelings of depression. Consequently, people swayed by these beliefs might be expected to become active or depressed after eating carbohydrates. Yet, as discussed above, these moods have not been seen in controlled laboratory studies. Second, it has proved difficult to induce placebo effects in studies of food and behavior. Neither an individual's preexisting expectations nor those created by an experimenter have been able to trigger food-induced symptoms in laboratory experiments. Typically, subjects say that they expect foods to affect other people but that they personally feel immune to such effects.

It is known, however, that placebo effects work most powerfully in a formal therapeutic program involving a relationship between client and therapist. Both persons share strong beliefs about how the treatment should work and hold enthusiastic expectations for a cure. In such cases beliefs alone can become a powerful curative force. Many professionals believe that the occasional successes produced by the Feingold diet or by other elimination diets are, in fact, placebo effects. This question remains an important one for future research.

What mechanism, other than placebo effects, could cause the behavioral changes brought about by foods? A leading theory is that foods affect behavior by altering the biochemistry of the brain. John Fernstrom, Richard Wurtman, and their colleagues at the Massachusetts Institute of Technology (MIT) proposed this theory after making the interesting observation that the level of the brain's neurotransmitters, chemical messengers that the brain

48

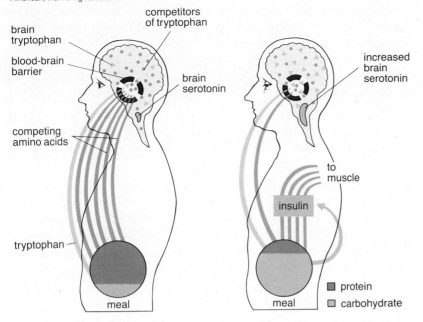

uses to send a specific signal from one nerve cell to another, fluctuates during the day. Neurotransmitter elevations occur after mealtimes, raising the question of whether food intake affects the brain. At the time of the initial MIT work, most scientists believed this to be an unlikely possibility. A long-standing assumption had been that the brain is relatively impervious to what the body eats. The brain was thought to be highly protected, having its energy needs met before those of other bodily organs and rendered immune from transient changes in bloodborne nutrients by the blood-brain barrier. This barrier is a lining of specialized cells within the brain's capillaries that blocks many kinds of molecules from passing from the bloodstream to the brain. But certain food constituents are the precursors—the raw materials—from which the brain manufactures its neurotransmitters. The human body cannot synthesize some precursor substances, a fact that suggests that the brain must be able to extract them from the diet.

One such food constituent is the essential amino acid tryptophan, the precursor for the brain neurotransmitter serotonin. Since tryptophan is found in protein, it might seem that a protein-rich meal would elevate brain tryptophan and cause more serotonin to be manufactured. But, in fact, a high-protein meal, even though it contains some tryptophan, causes brain tryptophan and serotonin to decrease. The reason is that protein contains proportionally much more of other similar amino acids such as tyrosine, leucine, and valine. These amino acids and others compete with tryptophan for access to the same limited transport system to get across the blood-brain barrier. Since a protein meal introduces more of tryptophan's competitors to the bloodstream than it does tryptophan, tryptophan's uptake into the brain declines, as does the manufacture of serotonin.

Paradoxically, even though a carbohydrate meal lacks tryptophan, it causes the brain's influx of tryptophan and its production of serotonin to increase. The reason is that carbohydrate foods cause the body to secrete

Some scientists believe that foods influence behavior by affecting the concentration of the brain's neurotransmitters. One neurotransmitter, serotonin, is made in the brain from the food constituent tryptophan, an essential amino acid. Since tryptophan is found in protein, a high-protein meal might seem likely to elevate brain tryptophan and promote serotonin manufacture. In fact, a high-protein meal lowers brain tryptophan and serotonin because other amino acids in the meal compete with tryptophan for access through the blood-brain barrier to the brain (left). Paradoxically, a high-carbohydrate, low-protein meal, while comparatively low in tryptophan, raises levels of brain tryptophan and serotonin (right). Carbohydrate foods stimulate the body to make insulin, which diverts many amino-acid competitors of tryptophan from the bloodstream into muscle. Consequently, tryptophan enters the brain in increased amounts. Since serotonin is believed to play a role in triggering sleep, the above explanation can account for the drowsiness that follows a carbohydrate meal.

49

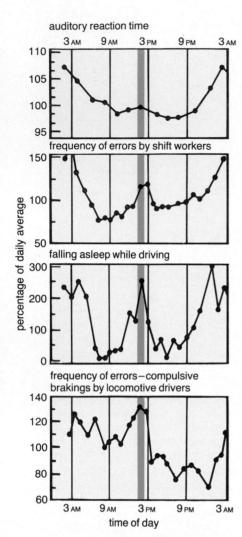

auditory reaction time

frequency of errors by shift workers

falling asleep while driving

frequency of errors—compulsive brakings by locomotive drivers

Investigations of food-behavior relationships from a practical perspective have been prompted by statistics culled from different occupational groups. In the graphs above, which summarize the results of four separate studies, a drop in performance efficiency—signaled by rises in reaction time and in error and sleep frequency—appears around 2 PM. Subsequent laboratory studies have shown that the dip does not reflect a natural biologic rhythm but appears only when subjects eat lunch.

(Above and opposite page) From A. Craig, "Acute Effects of Meals on Perceptual and Cognitive Efficiency," *Diet and Behavior: A Multidisciplinary Evaluation,* Nutrition Reviews/Supplement, vol. 44 (1986), pp. 163–171

insulin. Insulin prompts amino acids to leave the bloodstream and be taken up into muscle. Tryptophan, however, is an exception to this rule; it remains in the bloodstream after its competition for the blood-brain transport system has been removed. Consequently, tryptophan enters the brain in increased amounts after a carbohydrate meal or snack, triggering more manufacture of brain serotonin.

What is the likely behavioral consequence of increasing brain serotonin? In a healthy person sleepiness is a probable outcome. Much of the brain's serotonin is found in structures that play a role in triggering sleep to begin. One theory is that raising tryptophan and serotonin in the brain by eating carbohydrates may simulate a state of readiness to fall asleep, thus accounting for the drowsiness. Although not yet proved correct, this explanation can account for the fact that a balanced meal containing both protein and carbohydrates produces less drowsiness than a meal supplying the same number of calories from carbohydrates alone. The protein in a balanced meal contributes enough competing amino acids to prevent tryptophan from having such easy entry into the brain.

Whether and how much to eat

Applied psychologists investigate relationships between eating and behavior from a largely practical perspective. What, if anything, they have asked, should we eat for breakfast and lunch in order to optimize performance at work and school? Research done in England by Angus Craig of the University of Sussex was prompted by some distressing statistics. Averages culled from many occupational groups show a drop in performance efficiency around 2 in the afternoon. Around that time, shift workers are prone to make errors, locomotive engineers make braking mistakes, and automobile drivers fall asleep at the wheel.

Are these occurrences due to chance, or do they reflect a meaningful phenomenon? Craig studied the 2 PM efficiency drop in the laboratory and found that it did not reflect a natural biologic rhythm. The midafternoon dip did not appear unless subjects ate lunch. When they consumed a balanced three-course meal of 1,000 calories, the postlunch dip in performance efficiency was approximately 10%. At first glance a 10% loss in efficiency seems small, the difference perhaps between peak and excellent performance. But 10% is the same degree of impairment that occurs after an entire night of sleep deprivation. Craig's findings suggest that people should be no more cavalier in trusting themselves with demanding work after a three-course lunch than they would be after a sleepless night.

The British results initially seemed to carry the unsettling suggestion that from the standpoint of performance efficiency, it might be best to eat nothing before attempting to work. Other results, however, contradict this notion. Studies of classroom performance suggest that deficits show up later in the day when children skip meals entirely. Very recent work from Craig's laboratory indicates that a low-calorie lunch containing both protein and carbohydrates (for example, a 300-calorie sandwich) does not impair work efficiency. It has also proved important to take eating habits into account. The person who usually eats a light lunch is the most adversely

50

affected by a large midday meal. On the other hand, the gourmand who regularly enjoys a noontime banquet tolerates a large meal far better.

Food substances as treatments

A new and growing field of study involves the use of food substances to treat disorders of the body and mind. As potential treatments, foods represent a tremendously appealing alternative to synthetic drugs, holding out the promise of altering body chemistry in a natural way while inducing relatively few side effects. Thus far some of the research results in this area have been negative, while others have been mixed or encouragingly positive. The most extensive efforts have gone toward testing whether food components can reverse or slow the development of disorientation, memory deterioration, and thinking difficulties seen in people with Alzheimer's disease. The brain neurotransmitter acetylcholine, which plays an important role in learning and memory, is known to be in abnormally short supply in the brains of Alzheimer victims. Findings from animal research initially suggested that eating either choline, the precursor of acetylcholine, or lecithin, the major dietary source of choline, could reverse the decline in learning ability associated with the disorder. Unfortunately, after many trials it appears that acetylcholine-precursor therapy does not alleviate memory disturbance in Alzheimer's disease, possibly because simply making more precursor available to the brain does not encourage it to synthesize more acetylcholine. The need for alternative treatments for memory disorder remains a pressing clinical problem, especially since available drugs have limited effectiveness and many undesirable side effects.

Tryptophan has also been tried as a treatment for several clinical problems, including depression, for which it has produced mixed results. One complication is that there appear to be various kinds of depression, not all of which are accompanied by alterations in brain serotonin. This work should be especially promising if valid techniques can be developed to discriminate among the different biologic subtypes of depression. Tryptophan

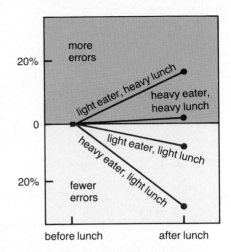

Researchers who have studied the effects of meals on performance efficiency have had to take into account not only the type and amount of food consumed but also personal eating habits. The graph above depicts the prelunch and postlunch performances of people given the task of crossing out certain letters from a passage of prose; the percentage of target letters they omitted is plotted for various combinations of the subjects' usual lunch habits and the size of the test meal. People who ordinarily eat lightly at lunch were shown to have the most difficulty performing well after a large midday meal. The regular noontime gourmand (below) tolerates a heavy lunch far better.

Jean-Loup Charmet, Paris

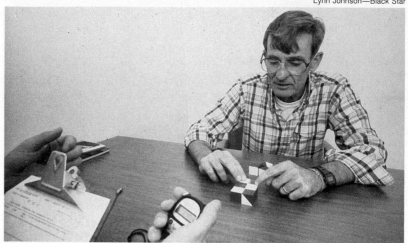

A victim of Alzheimer's disease fails a simple color-matching test. The brains of Alzheimer victims are known to be deficient in the neurotransmitter acetylcholine, and extensive efforts have gone toward determining whether acetylcholine-precursor substances found in food could reverse or slow the decline in thinking and memory abilities associated with the disorder. After encouraging findings from animal research, investigators have found acetylcholine-precursor therapy disappointing. Nevertheless, the need for effective treatments for Alzheimer's disease remains pressing, and food substances that would alter body chemistry in a natural way still represent an appealing alternative to synthetic drugs.

has proved more consistently helpful in treating two other troublesome conditions, insomnia and pain. In dosages of one to five grams, tryptophan is a safe and effective sleep aid for treating mild to moderate insomnia. It reduces the time taken to fall asleep without disrupting the natural stages of sleep. Tryptophan taken alone, or especially in combination with carbohydrate foods, also reduces pain sensitivity. Because it enhances pain tolerance, tryptophan holds considerable promise in the treatment of chronic pain stemming from such afflictions as neuralgia, arthritis, and temporomandibular joint problems.

For a field that originated only recently, exciting progress has already been made in translating knowledge about the behavioral effects of foods into useful treatments. But many people are eager for diet therapies to do a great deal more. For example, can large doses of vitamins provide hope of a cure for schizophrenia? Can criminal behavior arise from treatable sensitivities to milk or sugar? Can people with the potential for unprovoked violence be identified by analyzing their hair for deficits of essential trace elements? If the scientific community has been slow to accept findings linking foods to behavior, others have leapt at preliminary results, eager to convert them into therapies. What scientists regard as an overzealous translation of tentative findings into treatments is understandable in light of the socially pressing and personally distressing problems at issue.

Whereas scientists advocate caution and debate the meaning of research findings, some members of the public clamor that there are fires to be put out now. If there is even the slightest hope of a cure or improvement through dietary intervention, they argue, then it is worth trying; such experiments surely cannot hurt. Scientists answer, though, that such adventures into treatment sometimes do hurt. The financial costs of subsidizing ineffective and possibly even harmful treatments can be painful. The costs in dashed hopes and resources unwisely invested are also great. Some families of individuals with schizophrenia spend a substantial fortune on unreliable hair analyses and on megavitamin treatments that may even be dangerous, since certain vitamins and minerals taken in large amounts are toxic. Juvenile justice programs have been known to invest $5,000 per child

52

If foods work like drugs to alter brain chemistry, what can our choice of foods tell us about the brain's needs? The study of food choices, one likely direction for future research, may take us beyond a comprehension of how we are what we eat and into an understanding of how we eat what we are.

in questionably valid tests for food sensitivities. Such resources are lost to work that could lead to the development of truly effective treatments.

Challenges for the future

The practical goal of studying the way foods affect behavior is to provide insight into food choices that work to human advantage. It is hoped that in the relatively near future such wisdom will be applied in the classroom, the workplace, and the clinic, although a viable contribution to the treatment of criminality may have to await a more distant future. Social needs in this last-mentioned domain are pressing, but sound knowledge about the links between diet and criminality has been slow to develop. On the other hand, promising research is under way on the involvement of foods in other psychobiological disorders such as depression, stress-related disturbances, substance addictions, and eating disorders.

Two themes are likely to thread through future discussions of the influence of foods on behavior. One is the nature of individual variation in the response to foods. Many findings point to gender- and age-related differences in responsivity to foods, and other important dimensions of individual variation will no doubt emerge. Such results may help characterize people who show special sensitivity to food substances, rendering them good candidates for diet therapies. For example, cravings for carbohydrates occur among a subgroup of individuals enduring nicotine withdrawal or suffering from obesity, depression, bulimia (a disorder characterized by episodic binge eating), or hyperactivity. What this diverse group has in common and whether they derive benefits from carbohydrate consumption remain important unanswered questions. The second and related theme will probably be that the diet–behavior relationship is a two-way street. If foods act like drugs to affect brain chemistry, what does the choice of foods tell about what the brain needs? Food selections may be guided by a lawfulness considerably deeper than anything that is perceived. The study of food choices might even lead to a science of the way people use diet intuitively to modulate their own brain chemistry and behavior.

A Secret Garden in Chelsea

by Jerry G. Mason

The Chelsea Physic Garden opened its doors to the public without much commotion in April 1983, after 310 years of private patronage. Since then some 40,000 visitors from all over the world have entered its gates off a quiet Chelsea street and experienced the delights of the four most intensively cultivated acres of London. The garden is open to the public from April to October each year. On top of the gates that shut out the din of the modern Royal Hospital Road along the Chelsea Embankment on the garden's south end is the coat of arms of the Worshipful Society of Apothecaries, which founded the garden in 1673. Its function was the study of and research into medicinal plants, all plants being then thought to have medicinal properties, after the tradition of "physic" gardens established in Renaissance Europe. Today the Chelsea Physic Garden is unique in that it is one of the few such gardens still thriving in the world.

Medieval foundations of physic gardens

The culture and preparation of "simples" (medicines from plants) had long been part of the education of medieval ladies. Medicinal plants were grown in the cramped gardens of castles and fortified places of the Middle Ages, where they would be useful in times of siege. In most districts monks cared for people's bodies as well as their souls, dispensing at the monastery gates the remedies produced within their cloistered grounds. At the monastery of St. Gall, Switzerland, there is extant an architect's plan of the ideal monastery drawn up circa 816–820. It shows a physic garden next to the physician's house and infirmary, a *herbularius* divided into 16 beds, each with a named herb.

Seeds and cuttings of medicinal plants were exchanged between monasteries throughout Europe, although surviving correspondence tells us that many of the cuttings arrived dead. Alcuin, the founder of Charlemagne's Palace School, the first real university in northwestern Europe, sent cuttings from France to monasteries in his native Britain. He is also known to have corresponded with and sent plants to Benedict of Aniane, the reputed compiler of Charlemagne's famous list of 73 herbs and 16 fruits and trees that were by decree to be grown on crown lands in every city of the em-

Jerry G. Mason is a free-lance photojournalist specializing in science and technology. He resides in London.

(Opposite page) The coat of arms of the Worshipful Society of Apothecaries atop the gates to the Chelsea Physic Garden; photograph, Jerry Mason

A treatise from the 12th century depicts a medieval herbalist supervising the gathering of medicinal plants.

pire. This list, the *Capitulare de Villis* (published 812), had some surprising omissions. Betony (*Betonica officinalis*) was not included, yet it was highly esteemed from the classical age of Greece onward as a panacea for all ills of the head. Agrimony (*Agrimonia eupatoria*) was also absent from the list, despite its fame as a vulnerary herb (used in the healing of wounds), and for reasons unknown, violet (*Viola odorata*), a useful purgative, was omitted. But the list of 89 plants, with directions for their maintenance, shows that Charlemagne was the patron of physic gardens throughout his vast empire. However, the empire did not long survive its founder, and the fate of hundreds of physic gardens thereby became obscure.

Few references to physic gardens in Europe survive before the flowering, as it were, of the Renaissance. Another helpful list of herbs was published by John de Garlande in 1250. In a garden's shrubbery, for instance, he advised "pimpernel, mouse-ear, self-heal, bugloss, adder's tongue, and other herbs good for men's bodies." Flowers were also to be grown for their use rather than for purely ornamental reasons. The rose was grown because it "despatcheth all corrupt and evil humours in and about the veins of the heart."

In the 13th century the study of medicine flourished at Salerno. In the first years of the 14th century, the Salernitan Matheaus Silvaticus built a physic garden to which he brought seeds from Greece and plants of *Arum colocasia*. Scholars such as Silvaticus were probably aware that Aristotle had kept a botanical garden with the great botanist Theophrastus (371–287 BC) as its curator. Theophrastus devised the first system of botany using Aristotelian methods of classification by genera and species; this sophisticated Greek botanical system has survived to this day. But during the medieval period it was in the world of Islam rather than in Europe proper that progress was made in the comparative study of plants and the systematic introduction of exotic species.

Islamic influence

The botanist and gardener Ibn Wafid, born in 999, founded a physic garden within the palace grounds of the sultan of Toledo. It was a genuinely scientific garden in which experiments were conducted in the cultivation of plants, and the treatises Ibn Wafid wrote on his work were widely studied by later generations of Moorish gardeners. Sadly for Ibn Wafid's own physic garden, Toledo was conquered by Christian crusaders ten years after his death in 1075.

Ibn Wafid's successor, the equally illustrious Ibn Bassal, fled to Seville, there to improve the gardens of Sultan al-Mu'tamid (1069–91). Ibn Bassal's writings built on his mentor's work, and a century later the scientific collection of plants in a physic garden reached its peak in the work of Muhammad ibn 'Ali ibn Farah for the Almohad Sultan Mu'tammad an-Nasir (1199–1214). The mid-13th-century pharmacopoeia of Ibn al-Baitar of Malaga contained 1,400 plants, a remarkable number in the time before the New World was revealed to the Old.

Other botanists wrote local floras, or compendiums of medicinal plants, of Moorish Spain. But by 1482 the whole of Spain had at last been reclaimed by its Christian monarchs, and the scientific traditions of Islamic gardeners were temporarily lost to Europe.

The Islamic tradition of gardens and the cultivation of medicinal plants in part inspired the physic gardens of Renaissance Europe that were to become so famous. A great deal of knowledge reached Europe in translation from Arabic at this time. But the physic gardens of the Italian city-states of the 16th century owed their inspiration above all to the botanical discoveries made by conquistadores and explorers as they circumnavigated the globe. The theme of the gardens was always the gathering together of plants and seeds from all over the world so that they might be named and their nutritive and medicinal properties communicated. In biblical terms the gardens were designed to bring together the scattered pieces of creation into a living encyclopedia that would increase man's power over nature and recover direct knowledge of God lost since Adam and Eve were evicted from Eden.

A depiction of a late medieval herb garden from a Flemish illuminated manuscript, c. 1470.

The great physic gardens of Italy

Physic gardens had been established at both Padua and Pisa by 1545. The Orto Botanico of Padua was founded in 1545 by a decree of the Venetian Republic. Soon thereafter the monastery of St. Giustina in Padua ceded to the republic and the University of Padua an area of about 20,000 square meters (216,000 square feet) for the planting of a physic garden. The Padua garden had long been campaigned for by Francesco Bonafede, who held the "Chair of Simples" at the university's School of Botanical Medicine. He wanted live material rather than the plant illustrations and dried specimens that were as a rule the only aids for the study of plants. The garden specified by Bonafede would also provide the opportunity for the study of the life cycles of plants.

The Padua garden was designed on formal lines by Giovanni Moroni da Bergamo. The central feature was a circular brick wall that enclosed 5,555 square meters (59,793 square feet) of garden, the *Hortus cinctus*. Paths

An Arabic manuscript from Iraq (1199) shows the growing and gleaning of medicinal plants.

(Right) An 18th-century view of the Orto Botanico of Padua—one of Europe's earliest gardens, established as part of the University of Padua to be a living laboratory for scientific research on pharmaceutical plants. Overlooking the garden is the Basilica of Santo Antonio. A botanical institute that housed an herbarium and a library is visible at the garden's northern end. Giovanni Moroni da Bergamo's original design for the garden (below), a perfect circle 84 meters (92 yards) in diameter, had four central mandalas that were intricately subdivided. The plans took several decades to complete and set the pattern for future physic gardens throughout Europe. The planting scheme represented a living textbook—with trees, plants, flowers, and herbs spread out page by page on the ground.

divided the *Hortus cinctus* into quadrants to represent the four corners of the Earth; plants from the East were to occupy the beds of the eastern section, and so on. The quadrants were further subdivided into intricate geometric designs, each containing a fountain and 250 small, mosaiclike beds, with each bed devoted to a single species. The desired effect, as in all physic gardens to this day, was that the plants spread out like flora, the manuals that compiled plants and herbs—*i.e.,* page by page on the ground. The sequence of the plants has changed greatly since the Orto Botanico at Padua was founded, with new methods of classification and advances in botany, yet then as now the physic garden was fashioned as a living laboratory for scientific research.

Outside the enclosed *Hortus cinctus,* the garden at Padua was later landscaped to provide a range of environments suitable for different types

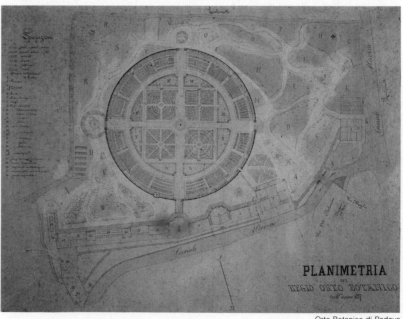

Orto Botanico di Padova

of plant, from alpines to mosses, with ponds for water lilies, sedges, and lotus. There are now seven greenhouses and an arboretum as well.

Moroni's plans took decades to complete, but in 1561 the University of Padua instituted a new chair, *Ostensio Simplicium,* charged with the duty of "reading, showing and speaking in the Medicinal Garden about herbs." In 1564 Melchiorre Wieland of Königsberg took up the new post, and under him the narrow specialization of the garden, in plants related to medical botany, began to expand to include all the plants that could be grown both outdoors and under glass. This was a prelude to modern botany and set the pattern for future physic gardens.

Although aesthetic considerations were secondary in the founding of the physic garden at Padua, Moroni's design, with its four central mandalas, was not without ornament. The large tank for the water garden was held up by four statues representing great figures of medicine—Galen, Hippocrates, the god Asclepius, and at the fourth corner Mithradates, famous for his immunity to poison and perhaps an obvious choice in the Italy of the Borgias. When the inner wall was rebuilt in the 18th century, statues of the famous Italian botanists of the age were added to it. Around this time, in 1786, Goethe visited the garden. He was so inspired by a palm (*Chamaerops humilis*), which had been planted in 1585, that he wrote a long study of its morphology: *Metamorphosis of Plants* (published 1790). The garden recently celebrated the palm's 400th anniversary. Housed in its own greenhouse, the palm has been known as the Goethe Palm for 200 years.

Many plants that were to become common or garden species in Europe were first cultivated at the Paduan Orto Botanico. The potato (*Solanum tuberosum*) reached Padua via England in 1590, and first cultivated there in the same year were sesame (*Sesamum orientale*), *Hyacinthus orientalis, Cyclamen persicum,* and *Jasminum nudiflorum,* with its lovely yellow winter flowers. In 1662 the first *Robinia pseudoacacia* was cultivated; also known as the locust tree, it has since taken its place in the landscape of much of Europe, where its grooved and angular limbs and feathery leaves have transformed many an ordinary street into stately avenues. A number of bamboos, and in 1713 the ice plant (*Mesembryanthemum crystallinum*), were first grown at Padua. The geranium (*Pelargonium cucullatum*) made its appearance in the Orto Botanico in 1801.

The classification of the beds by the Engler system—devised by German botanist Adolf Engler in the late 1800s—gradually gave way to the present Linnaean arrangement. (The Linnaean system of nomenclature, established in the 1750s by Swedish botanist, physician, and explorer Carolus Linnaeus, was an early and important general biologic classification system.) The garden has kept its original layout and maintains its original function as a physic garden. One tree, a chaste tree (*Vitex agnus-castus*), was planted in the same year the garden was founded, and both the tree and garden flourish to this day.

The garden at Pisa was founded in the same year as the Padua Orto Botanico, and it had the advantage of being instigated and directed by the great teacher Lucca Ghini. One of his pupils, the botanist Ulisse Aldrovandi, founded another physic garden, the Orto dei Simplici, at Bologna in 1568.

The potato (Solanum tuberosum)*, at top, and the sesame plant* (Sesamum orientale)*, bottom, were first cultivated in the physic garden at Padua. Both were to become common species throughout Europe.*

59

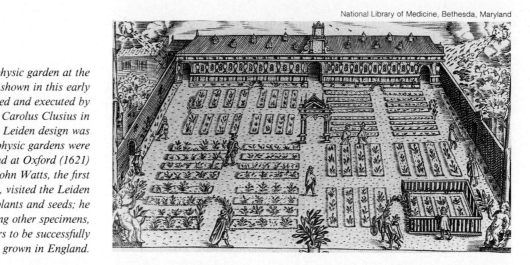

The scheme for the physic garden at the University of Leiden shown in this early engraving was devised and executed by the Dutch botanist Carolus Clusius in the late 1500s. The Leiden design was later adopted when physic gardens were established in England at Oxford (1621) and Chelsea (1673). John Watts, the first curator at Chelsea, visited the Leiden garden to exchange plants and seeds; he returned with, among other specimens, the first Lebanon cedars to be successfully grown in England.

From Ghini there followed a line of outstanding prefects at Pisa. Andrea les Alpino systematized plant taxonomy; Georgio Santi was the first botanist to publish a Tuscan flora; and to Biagio Longo's research into caprification (artificial insemination of fig plants) is owed the proliferation of the edible fig. The horse chestnut (*Aesculus hippocastanum*) reached Pisa from Albania in 1597. The tree of heaven (*Ailanthus glandulosa*) and the evergreen magnolia or bull bay (*Magnolia grandiflora*) were first grown in Europe at Pisa, and in 1720 the unique maidenhair tree or ginkgo (*Ginkgo biloba*) made its appearance there, a tree common in Jurassic times but long since reduced to a single genus with a single species, from China.

Physic gardens extend across Europe

As well as the Orto dei Simplici at Bologna, physic gardens had been established at Florence, Italy; Ferrara, Italy; Leipzig, Germany; Leiden, The Netherlands; and Montpellier, France, by the end of the 16th century. The University of Leiden, which was soon to rival the fame of Montpellier as a medical school, was founded in 1575. The Dutch botanist Carolus Clusius finally agreed to plant the *hortus botannicus* for the university in 1592, five years after the plot of land (39.9 × 30.9 meters [130 × 100 feet]) had been set aside for the purpose. Clusius chose the long, straight, narrow bed, the *pulvillis,* to organize the plants, a design later used in the English physic gardens at Oxford and London. The *pulvillis* design was a far cry from the elaborate geometry of the Paduan garden. The physic garden founded in Paris in 1635 by King Louis XIII's physician, Guy de la Brosse, took up the Paduan design again, but the *pulvillis* has been the more enduring pattern for the scientific garden.

The curator of the Jardin Royal des Plantes Medicinales in Paris was Vespasien Robin, an extremely influential figure in the flourishing community of physic gardens of which 17th-century Europe could boast. Considering Robin's achievements at Paris, it is surprising that the Jardin Royal remained a physic garden only until 1718, when its name was changed to Jardin des Plantes and it became a general, and principally ornamental, botanical garden. Robin was the mentor of Robert Morison, the exile from

Cromwell's Britain who was later to become the University of Oxford's first professor of botany and from 1669 curator of the Oxford Botanical Garden.

The Oxford garden had been founded in 1621 by the earl of Danby, and by 1658 its catalogue listed 2,000 plants, 600 of which were English. The 1.2 hectares (three acres) of the garden were originally divided into four quarters as in Padua and Paris, but the Leiden arrangement was later adopted. Morison is a giant figure in the history of the garden. He had already built a garden for the de Blois family in France, and from 1660 he had been both the king's physician and keeper of the Royal Garden under Charles II.

In 1670 Morison published his opus *Praeludia Botanica*. The book convinced the Scot Robert Sibbald, who had studied at Leiden in the 1650s, that the university of his native Edinburgh needed a physic garden. Sibbald bought a plot of land 12 meters (40 feet) square, and in partnership with the physician Andrew Balfour, he planted 1,000 species of plants to improve the study of medicine. The University of Edinburgh remains an important medical school, and the garden Sibbald planted has grown in both size and fame.

The garden in Chelsea

Its beginnings. Three years after Edinburgh, the Worshipful Society of Apothecaries founded the Physic Garden at Chelsea. John Watts, the first curator, visited Leiden to exchange plants and seeds, returning to Chelsea with four Lebanon cedars (*Cedrus libani*), which were among the first to be successfully grown in England. Two had to be cut down in 1771 because they were taking up too much space, and the last survived increasing atmospheric pollution until 1904.

The manor of Chelsea containing the garden was bought in 1712 by Sir Hans Sloane from William Cheyne. Sir Hans Sloane's statue in white marble, by Michael Rysbrack, still stands at the intersection of the two

A physic garden, the Jardin Royal des Plantes Medicinales (below, left), was founded in Paris in 1635 by King Louis XIII's physician, Guy de la Brosse. Although it was among the most highly cultivated and influential physic gardens of 17th-century Europe, it remained a physic garden only until 1718.

Jean-Loup Charmet, Paris

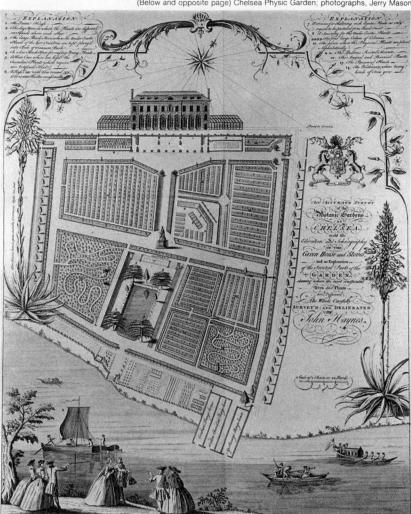

central paths. Sloane had studied at the garden during his early training as a physician, and he had also studied at the University of Montpellier's Jardin de Botanique under Magnol. In 1722 Sloane granted a lease *ad perpetuam* on "3 acres, 1 rood and 35 perches, plus greenhouse, stoves, and barges" to the Worshipful Society of Apothecaries, on the condition that the land remain forever a physic garden. The garden had fallen into some neglect when the new head gardener, Philip Miller, took over.

The greatest botanical horticulturist of his age, Miller stayed at the Chelsea Garden for almost half a century. He immediately set about delivering to the leaseholders the 50 plant specimens, pressed and mounted, that were required annually as part of the lease. Famed for his skill in germinating seeds of new species received from the Americas, Miller continued to honor the requirement. During his time the first cotton seeds were sent to Georgia in exchange for native American seeds. Miller's *Dictionary of Gardening* is recognized as the first modern encyclopedia of horticulture, although his *Dictionary* did not adopt Linnaeus's botanical classification until its seventh edition. The book is still of practical use.

62

An early 19th-century view (left) shows the Chelsea Physic Garden's four lushly cultivated acres, situated along the Thames. (Opposite page) Philip Miller, head gardener at Chelsea in its early years for nearly half a decade, was considered the greatest botanical horticulturist of his day. He was the author of the Dictionary of Gardening *(1731), the first comprehensive compilation of medicinal horticulture. The tree map is from 1751.*

The Chelsea Physic Garden flourished for more than a century. William Curtis (founder of the *Botanical Magazine* and author of the beautiful horticulture treatise *Flora Londinensis*) was demonstrator of plants and *praefector horti* at the garden when Sir Joseph Banks, in the late 1700s, brought back from his travels enough Icelandic tufa for a rock garden. The tufa was added to a huge pile of old building stone taken from the Tower of London. Banks also supplied 500 packets of seeds from his world voyage.

A new greenhouse in the classical orangery style was built in 1732, as well as lean-to houses heated both by stoves and by beds of fermenting tanbark (a bark rich in tannin bruised or cut into small pieces and used in tanning). Until sewer construction led to their demolition in the middle of the 19th century, the buildings provided good conditions for the cultivation of tropical plants. A long-term associate of the garden, Nathaniel Bagshaw Ward, developed in the 1830s a technique of transporting living tropical plants, which vastly increased their number in Europe. The so-called Wardian Case, a miniature portable greenhouse, also allowed 20,000 tea plants to be taken from Shanghai to the foothills of the Indian Himalayas, and in 1876 Brazilian rubber (*Hevea brasiliensis*) traveled from South America to the famous Royal Botanic Gardens at Kew, outside London, and from there to Malaya.

Decline and rebirth. Then, sadly, in 1870 the construction of a road along Chelsea's embankment cut the garden off from the Thames and drastically changed the water table; the third Lebanon cedar was then felled; a greenhouse was sold off and heating was discontinued in others. Pharmacists had long been losing interest in botany, and by the end of the last century the Chelsea Physic Garden had been virtually closed.

The Society of Apothecaries applied to the charity commissioners for a scheme to save the garden, which led eventually to funds being supplied from the public purse and a committee of management set up to ensure that the garden continued to be used for educational purposes. The heir of

Photographs, Jerry Mason

In the Chelsea Physic Garden's northeastern corner—virtually unchanged for 300 years—is the herb garden (top left), comprising a culinary herb collection as well as herbs valued for their medicinal qualities. The white marble statue of Sir Hans Sloane stands at the intersection of the two central paths. It was Sloane who bought the manor of Chelsea, containing the garden, in 1712 and granted a lease on the land to the Worshipful Society of Apothecaries, with the stipulation that the land always remain a physic garden. (Right) Ordered beds of plants run east and west beneath a magnificent Chinese willow pattern tree (Koelreuteria jeaniculata). *The willow is among the unusual specimen trees transplanted from remote areas of the world.*

Sir Hans Sloane was represented on the committee. A new curator, William Hales, was then appointed. Much of the present layout of the garden is the work of Hales (who cared for the garden until 1937), in collaboration with Sir John Bretland Farmer of Imperial College.

The garden today. To the left of Sir Hans Sloane's marble statue, open beds stretch to the wall beyond a magnificent Chinese willow pattern tree (*Koelreuteria jeaniculata*). Down the central path in winter, with ordered beds running east and west, the outlines of dozens of species of unusual trees strike the eye: a couple of ginkgos, a Kermes oak (*Quercus coccifera*), black mulberry (*Morus nigra*), storax (*Styrax officinalis*), an ancient olive tree (*Olea europaea*), and a *Magnolia kobus* with its white blossom. The Chelsea Garden as a whole contains about 5,000 species of plants, of which 126 are specimen trees.

In the northeastern corner is the herb garden, which virtually has not changed in 300 years. Owing to the general deterioration of the garden in recent times, the list of herbs is incomplete, but the accompanying table lists the major medicinal plants from which drugs are made. The table also lists the various applications of the plant-derived drugs as remedies. Many such plants have now been replaced by synthetic drugs or by other plants that are more suitable sources.

64

Photographs, Jerry Mason

Today's Chelsea Garden has a culinary herb collection comprising 56 herbs, ranging from hyssop (*Hyssopus officinalis*) to skirret (*Sium sisarum*), a popular Renaissance root vegetable similar to salsify (*Tragopogon porrifolius, ssp. porrifolius*). There are 57 plants that either are used in modern drug manufacture or have traditional homeopathic associations, as well as 13 plants such as woad (*Isatis tinctoria*), madder (*Rubia tinctorum*), and dyers' greenwood (*Genista tinctoria*) used in the making of dyes before the advent of synthetics. The herb garden continues to be used for teaching, and plants newly threatened by whatever hazards the 20th century creates will be added.

Plants as drugs

All plants were once thought to have medicinal value, even if the use of their active ingredients remained to be discovered. The shared ground of botany and medicine was far greater when both were arts rather than sciences—*i.e.,* when traditional plant lore as well as chemistry accounted for the therapeutic properties of plants. By the time Nicholas Culpeper wrote his famous herbal in the middle of the 17th century, scientific people condemned the book because astrology was an integral part of it. But while the importance of medical botany was steadily declining in the teaching of physicians, the effectiveness of some old remedies could not be denied.

Mandrake (*Mandragora officinarum*), for instance, is now known to yield the alkaloid hyoscine, a powerful analgesic, which under the name scopolamine is a standard preoperative medication. In Roman times Dioscorides used it for surgery and cautery, and it was also the major ingredient of the "death sponge" used to relieve the sufferings of the crucified. The more mysterious powers once attributed to the plant—to drive out demons, for instance—have lapsed, while new uses have been found for the drug in the treatment of travel sickness and of Parkinson's disease.

Opium, from the Greek word *opos* for "juice," is the dried exudate from the unripe seedpods of the opium poppy (*Papaver somniferum*). It contains over 20 alkaloids, 4 of which have medicinal value. These are morphine, codeine, papaverine, and noscapine. The effects of opium, including relief of pain, anxiety, and sleeplessness, were familiar to the Babylonians (4000 BC), and opium was used before 2000 BC in Egypt to pacify children, a practice that persisted in Europe and America until the early 20th century. The Swiss physician Paracelsus gave the name laudanum, in Latin "to praise," to preparations from the plant, although this later came to mean a tincture of opium in alcohol.

Today morphine is obtained from the plant for its analgesic properties, as is codeine, also an analgesic but weaker than morphine. Papaverine is used to treat intestinal colic and vascular spasm. Noscapine is an antitussive drug used in cough mixtures. The Chelsea Physic Garden continues to supply opium poppies to industry for routine pharmacological screening.

Another plant growing in the garden, the autumn crocus (*Colchicum autumnale*), contains colchicine, an effective anti-inflammatory medication used in the treatment of gout. Specimens of deadly nightshade (*Atropa belladona*) are also grown at Chelsea. As its name suggests, the plant

Among the visual delights are the flowers, the Japanese tree peony (Paeonia soffruticosa), *top, and the* Abutilon ochsenii. *Not all the plants in the Chelsea garden today are of a "physic" nature; many are simply ornamental, valued for their beauty or rarity.*

For 1,500 years the ancient Greek botanist Dioscorides reigned as the supreme authority on medicinal substances. His efforts to systematize knowledge of the healing properties of plants were contained in his important treatise, De materia medica. *The picture above of Dioscorides and a student discussing the mandrake* (Mandragora officinarum) *is from an Arabic translation of* De materia medica *(1229). The mandrake, with its forked root resembling the human form, was once thought to have magical applications, such as the ability to drive out demons. Today it is valued for the narcotic and sedative properties of the alkaloid it contains.*

is potentially lethal. It is a source of atropine, an alkaloid with properties similar to the analgesic derived from mandrake, hyoscine. Licorice (*Glycyrrhiza glabra*) is the source of carbenoxolone, used in preparations to heal peptic ulcers.

The purple foxglove (*Digitalis purpurea*) was mentioned in Welsh writings as long ago as 1250, but it was not until 1775 that the physician William Withering identified the leaves as the active ingredient in a mixture of some 20 herbs used by an old woman in Shropshire, England, to cure the dropsy, a condition marked by abnormal accumulation of fluid in the body. It fell into disrepute because of indiscriminate use by later physicians, but interest in the plant was revived early this century when two kinds of foxglove, purple (*D. purpurea*) and woolly (*D. lanata*), were found to contain cardiac glycosides, from which the powerful modern drugs digoxin and digitoxin are made. The effects of the plant extracts have been clinically observed in patients. Glycosides produce a marked inotropic effect on ailing hearts; they augment the force of contraction of the heart, specifically in the condition known as congestive heart failure. Although the pharmacological and toxic properties of semisynthetic derivatives and other natural substances have been examined, no suitable substitute for the foxglove has yet been found.

The search for new drugs

Of the estimated 250,000 to 500,000 higher plants, only between 5 and 10% have been investigated for their medicinal-therapeutic properties—and those usually for one specific activity. The ongoing search for new drugs renders the Chelsea Physic Garden a vital laboratory.

Recent interest has focused on possible new drugs of botanical origin for cancer. In 1756 Philip Miller described a plant introduced from Madagascar via the Paris Jardin des Plantes. Originally called *Vinca rosea* by Linnaeus, the Madagascar periwinkle, now *Catharanthus roseus*, was taken from the garden and spread to the West Indies, where it became naturalized. The plants were first collected because of their folklore reputation as an oral antihypoglycemic for treating diabetes. Apparently by chance, extracts of

the plant were among some 2,500 plant extracts screened in the early 1960s under the auspices of the National Cancer Institute in the United States. The plant was found to have antileukemic activity. In fact, over 60 alkaloids have been isolated, among them vincaleukoblastine (VLB) and leurocristine (VCR). VLB and VCR have been developed into the commercial drugs vinblastine, used as a cure in Hodgkin's disease, and vincristine, used to help induce remissions in children with leukemia.

In a similar way, the mayapple (*Podophyllum peltatum and Podophyllum hexandrium syn. P.Emodii*) has led to the discovery of useful anticancer agents. The roots of the plant yield an extract called podophyllum resin, used for centuries by people in the Himalayas and by North American Indians against worms and constipation. An irritant action on the skin led to its use locally to treat venereal warts (condyloma acuminate and human papilloma virus infections). From its usefulness in genital ailments an antitumor activity was suggested, which was confirmed in 1971 when two semisynthetic drugs (etoposide and teniposide), derived from the mayapple, were developed. These drugs had the advantage of causing less systemic toxicity than many other of the available chemotherapeutic agents.

The Chelsea Physic Garden now is host to a number of research programs in pharmacognosy (the study of natural substances used in medicine), as well as in taxonomy and the effects of pollution on plant growth. Specimens of feverfew (*Tanacetum parthenium*), a member of the compositae family, are supplied to Kings College, London, for chemical and pharmacological studies. The name feverfew is probably a corruption of the word febrifuge, from its traditional use as a tonic and fever-dispelling agent. Work carried out on the wild type of feverfew has suggested that the plant may be efficacious in the prophylaxis of migraine headaches and rheumatoid arthritis. In a study done in 1983, 300 migraine sufferers consumed fresh leaves of the plant daily for a prolonged period; of this sample some 70% said their migraine attacks were fewer and less painful. The active constituents of the feverfew plant that account for the relief experienced by the patients appear to be sesquiterpene lactones, the major one being parthenolide. These compounds exhibit a wide range of biologic effects, including cytotoxicity (antitumor activity), antimicrobial, anthelmintic, analgesic, anti-inflammatory, and antihyperlipidemic activities. Other studies have shown that feverfew extracts act by interfering with the biosynthesis of prostaglandins (a kind of local hormone). Evidence has accumulated that suggests that prostaglandins may be involved in physiological and pathophysiological processes and may therefore have therapeutic applications.

A variety of plants go by the name feverfew, but members of this botanical family are rather variable in chemistry and morphology. The content of parthenolide and other sesquiterpene lactones varies considerably with season and part of plant. The work of Peter Hylands at Kings College has demonstrated that the amount of parthenolide in each leaf could vary by a factor of seven. Since a number of products—herbal remedies sold without prescription for migraine relief—using the feverfew plant are already on the market, detailed chemical investigation is needed to facilitate control of the level of active ingredient.

In the late 1700s the English physician William Withering identified the leaves of the purple foxglove (Digitalis pupurea) *as the active ingredient in a cure for dropsy. The modern drugs digoxin and digitoxin, derived from powerful cardiac glycosides contained in foxglove, are widely used today in the treatment of congestive heart failure. The above drawing of the foxglove is from Withering's 1785 account of his discoveries.*

Four of the 20 alkaloids in the opium poppy (Papaver somniferum) *are recognized for their pharmaceutical effects. The man in Eastern dress depicted in the engraving (opposite page), c. 1674, is shown slashing the poppy bud in order to harvest its highly valued medicinal contents. For centuries—indeed, into the early 20th century—the opium alkaloids morphine and codeine were widely used in patent medicines such as those for soothing the pain suffered by teething babies.*

67

Other research projects

The department of biochemistry at Imperial College, London, has used the plot and greenhouse facilities of the Chelsea Garden for the last 25 years in order to grow rye, wheat, and grasses. These have provided hosts for ergot fungi such as the rye ergot fungus (*Claviceps purpurea*), which yields complex alkaloids useful in migraine relief and in obstetrics (for prevention of postpartum hemorrhage). The sclerotium of *Claviceps purpurea* contains ergotinine and ergometrine. Researchers have been able to study mechanisms that regulate normal synthesis of ergot alkaloids during plant parasitism, and subsequently ways have been found of stimulating these fungi to biosynthesize the alkaloids in laboratory fermentations. Recently a mutant strain of the rye ergot fungus, which does not produce any completed alkaloid, has been shown to operate only the first step of the alkaloid biosynthetic pathway but still has appropriate enzymes for catalyzing some of the later steps. Such a variant strain may have potential for producing novel substances.

Medicinal plants in the Chelsea Physic Garden

plant	common name	medicinal use
Achillea millefolium	yarrow	tonic, carminative, spasmolytic, hemostatic
Aconitum napellus	monkshood	analgesic, febrifuge
Adonis vernalis	false hellebore, pheasant's eye	heart tonic, diuretic
Angelica archangelica	angelica	tonic, antispasmodic
Arctium lappa	burdock	dermatic
Arctostaphylos uva-ursi	bearberry	used in liniments and embrocations, diuretic
Arnica montana	arnica, mountain tobacco	stimulates circulation, used to treat bruising
Artemisia vulgaris	mugwort	used in epilepsy, vermifuge
Asperula odorata	sweet woodruff	antispasmodic
Atropa belladonna	belladonna, deadly nightshade	antispasmodic, sedative, mydriatic, narcotic
Avena sativa	oats	stimulant, treatment of arthritis, rheumatism, liver infections, skin disorders
Bellis perennis	common daisy	treatment of bruises and sprains
Borago officinalis	borage	reduces inflammations, diuretic
Calendula officinalis	marigold	heals wounds and ulcers
Catharanthus rosea	Madagascar periwinkle	used in treatment of cancer
Chenopodium ambrosioides var. *anthelminticum*	worm seed	vermifuge to expel intestinal worms
Clematis recta	clematis	bronchitis, tracheal irritations
Cnicus benedictus	holy thistle	liver disorders, rheumatism, arthritis, emetic and diuretic
Colchicum autumnale	autumn crocus, meadow saffron	anti-inflammatory
Conium maculatum	hemlock	circulation disorders
Convallaria majalis	lily of the valley	heart tonic
Datura stramonium	thornapple	antispasmodic
Digitalis lanata and *lutea*	woolly foxglove and yellow foxglove	heart tonic
Ferula asa-foetida	asafetida	sedative
Fragaria vesca	strawberry	digestive stimulant
Galega officinalis	goat's rue	diuretic, galactogenic
Gentiana lutea	yellow gentian	used as a tonic for the digestive system

The useful aspects of ergot alkaloid pharmacology arose from their toxic properties, which are still a potential agricultural hazard, causing "ergot disease" in cereals like millet and sorghum. Hence, this research has a bearing also on the control of ergot disease, important in semiarid regions of the world. In India millet is being bred to produce new disease-resistant strains.

Rye grasses are also being grown at the Chelsea Garden to facilitate studies on the biosynthesis of lolitrem B, a neurotoxin that arises when the rye grass is infected by an endophytic fungus. Structurally similar neurotoxins produced by several other fungi are known to cause protracted tremor in animals.

Also grown at the garden are the tropical legumes *Erythrina crista-galli* and *E. caffra*. These are currently sources for the study of the potentially therapeutic alkaloids they contain, having once been used as a muscle relaxant in surgery.

The department of pure and applied biology at Imperial College uses the garden's facilities for another program of research. For several years

Medicinal plants in the Chelsea Physic Garden

plant	common name	medicinal use
Glycyrrhiza glabra	licorice	anti-inflammator and antispasmodic
Grindelia robusta	gum plant	antispasmodic, antiasthmatic
Hyoscyamus niger	henbane	sedative, analgesic
Hypericum perforatum	perforate St.-John's-wort	sedative, also used in a lotion with olive oil for treating burns
Inula helenium	elecampane	tonic, diuretic
Iris germanica and *florentina*	orris root	used as a basis for medicinal preparations
Juniperus sabina	savin	contains an oil that has irritant properties; *e.g.,* purgative
Lactuca virosa	wild lettuce	used in laryngitis
Leonurus cardiaca	motherwort	dysentery, menstrual and pelvic disorders
Mandragora officinarum	mandrake	formerly used as a sedative and anesthetic
Mentha x piperita	peppermint	antispasmodic, tonic, carminative
Paeonia officinalis	peony	cures itching and chronic ulcers
Papaver somniferum	opium poppy	sedative and painkiller, source of morphine
Podophyllum hexandrium and *peltatum*	mayapple	anticancer properties, purgative
Pulsatilla vulgaris	pasqueflower	sedative, antispasmodic
Ricinus communis	castor-oil plant	purgative
Ruta graveolens	rue	rheumatism, neuralgia, bone injuries, and strains
Saponaria officinalis	soapwort	detergent, used to treat skin disorders
Scopolia carniolica	scopolia, Japanese belladona	sedative, mydriatic, narcotic
Scrophularia nodosa	figwort	diuretic, also used as a poultice
Scutellaria lateriflora	skullcap	sedative, diuretic, antispasmodic
Solanum dulcamara	woody nightshade	used in nervous disorders and skin conditions
Tanacetum parthenium	feverfew	febrifuge, treatment of migraines
Urtica dioica and *urens*	greater and lesser nettle	eczema, diuretic, tincture used for ulcers and wounds
Veratrum album	white hellebore	reduces blood pressure
Veratrum viride	American hellebore	reduces blood pressure; used for congestion of the lungs

(Top and bottom, left) Photographs, Jerry Mason; (bottom, right) Fred Ward—Black Star

Only a small proportion of all plants have been investigated for medicinal potential. At the Chelsea Physic Garden the search goes on for new plant-derived medicines and new applications of plants that already are part of the therapeutic armamentarium. (Right, top and bottom) The antineoplastic properties of both the Madagascar periwinkle (Catharanthus roseus) and the mayapple (Podophyllum Emodii) are under study. The feverfew plant (Tanacetum Parthenium; far right) is also being studied. Feverfew is known to have many biologic effects, from lowering fats in the blood and pain relief to shrinking tumors. Several drugs containing feverfew are marketed as nonprescription agents, but levels of the active therapeutic alkaloids that these products contain are not known or controlled. More precise understanding of how the plant's powerful alkaloids exert their effects is one of the present goals of pharmaceutical research at Chelsea.

investigators have carried out experiments in and around London to examine the effects of city air on plant growth. The Chelsea Garden is one of the sites used to grow varieties of pea, spinach, barley, and clover. Similar experiments were done in Leeds in the 1950s using lettuce plants. It was found that plants grown 11 kilometers (seven miles) from central Leeds weighed three or four times as much as those grown in an industrial area near the city's center.

For the London investigations 18 sites lying along a transect from central London to a laboratory 40 kilometers (25 miles) away are used to examine the problem in detail. The test plants at each site are grown in bags of

(Far right) A relatively new drug-delivery method uses a pharmaceutical patch that continuously releases the drug scopolamine through the skin to prevent the nausea and vomiting of motion sickness. Scopolamine is the most pharmacologically active alkaloid found in the belladonna plant. Japanese belladonna (Scopolia carniolica), which is grown in the Chelsea garden, is shown at right.

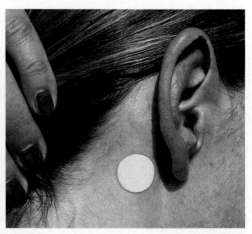

standard soil. The mean concentrations of sulfur dioxide (SO_2), nitrogen dioxide (NO_2), and ozone (O_3) are measured. Ozone is evaluated in the summer using tobacco indicator plants. The leaves of these plants, *Nicotiana tabacum,* are sensitive to increased concentrations of ozone gas and develop spots. Maximum and minimum temperatures are also recorded, as well as rainfall.

In the summers of 1983 and 1984, spinach and four varieties of pea (Banff, Douce Provence, Progeta, and Waverex) were grown for testing. Results showed an increasing yield with increasing distance from London. Closer to the city, the weight of stems and leaves was lower, and plants showed visible leaf damage after periods of high ozone concentration.

In October 1985 clover was sown for analysis in September 1986. In a paper published in the *London Environmental Bulletin* of autumn 1985, researchers Mike Ashmore and Cathy Dalpra had not drawn any definite conclusions from the study so far but speculated that complex reactions between SO_2, NO_2, and high summer concentrations of ozone were to blame for the damage to and deficiencies of the plants grown near the center of the city. The research is funded by the Natural Environment Research Council and money from the EEC environment program.

In the northeastern end of the Chelsea Garden, Mary Gibby of the British Museum's natural history department has about 120 species of wild pelargoniums under cultivation. Here the research is primarily taxonomic, tracing the evolution of the species within the genus pelargonium. There are about 200 species of pelargonium in the wild, most of them from southern Africa, and they are extremely variable in their growth forms, from root to leaf. Gibby studies the chromosomes of individual plants. Samples are taken from the young buds or root tips, and the number (which can vary from 8 to 88), the size, and the morphology of chromosomes are observed. For instance, *Pelargonium elongatum* has 8 chromosomes, while *Pelargonium alch emilloides* can have 16, typically with one particularly small pair, or 18, typically with one particularly large pair, or 34 or 36 chromosomes.

(Left) In greenhouses tropical legumes are being cultivated and investigated for their potential as therapeutic agents. In the past, legume alkaloids were used as muscle relaxants for surgery. (Center) Samples of pearl millet (Pennisetum glaucum) *are the subject of a current Chelsea-based research project sponsored by Imperial College, London. Millet and other grains serve as hosts for ergot fungi; ergot alkaloids are extremely potent agents that are used for migraine relief and other pain-quelling purposes. New ergot analogues are being investigated for multiple medical uses. Not all research at the Chelsea garden focuses on the therapeutic potential of plants. (Right) An investigator from the natural history department of the British Museum is involved in cultivating over 100 species of wild pelargoniums (mostly from Africa) in order to develop a more detailed classification system of the genus.*

Photographs, Jerry Mason

(Left) John Sims—Click/Chicago; (right and opposite page) photographs, Jerry Mason

The department of pure and applied biology at London's Imperial College is currently sponsoring a series of experiments that are attempting to determine the effects of pollution on plant growth. The map below shows a 40-kilometer (25-mile) transect with sites plotted at various distances from central London. Laboratories at these points test various plants for concentrations of ozone, sulfur dioxide, and nitrogen dioxide. Barley and clover samples are shown growing at one of the experiment sites (right).

Another species from the southwestern Cape areas of South Africa has 22 or 44 chromosomes, again with distinctive forms. To establish the relationships between plant types, hybrids are being made. Chromosomes from their young buds are examined at meiosis (when the cell divides to form gametes) to see whether there is pairing. An understanding of the relationships between species within the pelargonium genus will almost certainly result in a revision of the plants' classification.

The future

Despite these significant research programs, the Chelsea Physic Garden is much underfunded. Interest in pharmacognosy has only recently revived, and as yet the greenhouses and laboratories at the garden have not been modernized. Curator Duncan Donald says that an endowment of £1.2 million ($1.8 million) is needed for the upkeep of the garden. To this end the

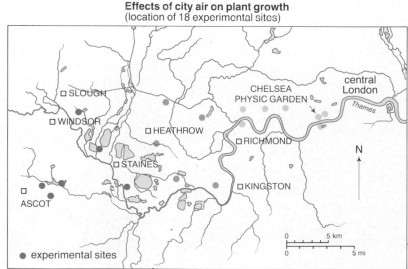

Effects of city air on plant growth
(location of 18 experimental sites)

• experimental sites

Adapted from Mike Ashmore and Cathy Dalpra, "Effects of London's Air on Plant Growth," *London Environmental Bulletin* (Autumn 1985)

Those who visit London's "secret" garden in Chelsea are almost certain to be surprised and delighted by what they discover.

garden is continuing to keep close links with the pharmaceutical industry and has supplied poppies to Glaxo Holdings PLC. Glaxo has made a substantial gift, and the garden has also received some funds from Imperial Chemical Industries' plant protection division. Other funding comes from the Apothecaries Society and the Pharmaceutical Society.

About one-third of the garden is taken up with botanical order beds. To the south, sloping toward the river, these systematic beds contain 100 genera, from *Ranunculaceae* to *Labiatae* on the east and from *Plantaginaceae* to *Grámineae* on the west side. Nearer the river is a pond with flowering rush shaded by a dawn redwood (*Metasequoia glyptostroboides*); next to it is a definitive collection of *Hypericum.*

In the southwestern corner, overlooking the cytologists' fern house, is a mimosa (*Acacia dealbata*), which brightens the winter landscape with its yellow blossom. A winter garden is taking shape nearby containing species that flower between October and April, such as *Galanthus* (snowdrops), *Cyclamen,* and *Helleborus.* There is a striking collection of variegated plants flanking the path to the north of Sir Hans Sloane's statue. Plants from Australasia, South America, California, and southern Africa all have beds to themselves in the densely vegetated 1.6 hectares (four acres) of the garden, which are a pleasure to the senses as well as an aid and a research tool in the study of botany.

Physic gardens were established in other cities after the founding of the Chelsea Physic Garden in 1673. By the end of the 18th century, there were gardens in Urbino, Turin, Cagliari, Pavia, Siena, Palermo, and Milan in Italy and Uppsala in Sweden. This century a physic garden was built in the Maison Nevve Park of Montreal, containing a historical collection of medicinal herbs from medieval monastery gardens, medicinal plants of the American Indians, a modern pharmacopoeia, and poisonous and allergy-provoking plants. Though physic gardens in the world today are a dying breed, those few that blossom are continuous sources of fascination, delight, and scientific possibility.

73

Psychoanalysis on the Couch

by Allan Hobson, M.D.

Psychoanalysis is the brainchild of Sigmund Freud, a turn-of-the-century Austrian physician who became interested in psychology through his association with Jean-Martin Charcot, with whom he studied hysteria and hypnosis in Paris. With his Viennese colleague Josef Breuer, he developed the idea that it was repressed sexuality that was pathogenic in hysteria and that it was the transference of those unconscious sexual feelings to the doctor that provided the basis of symptom relief in a cathartic treatment process called free association.

Freud: his couch and his theory

Freud sat in an armchair behind the head of the couch on which his analytic patients lay supine. The couch and its relaxing posture were carryovers from the hypnosis era from which psychoanalysis emerged. But, in contrast to the hypnotist, the psychoanalyst neither touched the patient nor initiated verbal interchange. By also avoiding the social inhibition of a face-to-face confrontation, the couch thus encouraged the patient to follow the "analytic rule" of saying whatever came to mind, without suggestion or censorship.

This "classic" couch technique is still used by orthodox Freudians, whose patients typically come for 50-minute sessions at the same time three to five days a week for durations of one to five or even ten years. Allowing for the standard August vacation, this comes to between $15,000 and $20,000 per year at the current rate of $80–$100 per session. The annual cost of psychoanalysis is thus three or four times the annual income of poverty-level families in the United States. Even in affluent America psychoanalysis is affordable by few. Many psychoanalytic "patients" are would-be psychoanalysts who may be paying their own psychoanalytic bills by treating "control" cases referred to them by their psychoanalytic institutes.

However rare in numbers of patients treated by psychoanalysis, this exclusive practice is extremely influential as a model since the assumptions on which it is based permeate many of the psychotherapies that now constitute the mental health scene. While most psychotherapy variants are shorter in total duration, are less frequent, take place sitting up, or may even be conducted in hot tubs or in groups, a fundamental assumption is

Allan Hobson, M.D., is Professor of Psychiatry, Harvard Medical School, and Director of the Laboratory of Neurophysiology at the Massachusetts Mental Health Center, Boston.

(Overleaf) "Piazza d'Italia" by Giorgio de Chirico; collection, Bergamini, Milan; photograph, Scala/Art Resource

that loosening of restraint will not only reveal hidden pathology but relieve it by discharging its associated emotional energy. These assumptions carry forward Freud's idea that by saying everything that came to mind, no matter how apparently nonsensical or even outrageous, the patient could, with the help of the analyst, discover the pathogenic idea or memory and so discharge the associated pent-up feelings.

In Freud's first systematic theoretical formulation, *The Interpretation of Dreams,* this central dynamic model was elaborated as a universal process governing not only dreams but clinical psychological phenomena as well. The essence of the idea is that instinctual drives such as sex press constantly for expression in thought and deed; their denial or postponement in conformity with socially imposed restraints leads to their burial via repression in the unconscious, where they fester and sometimes find their way to the surface. In response to the threat they pose to the conscious mind, these repressed drives (or wishes) are neutralized and emerge in compromised form as apparently nonsensical dreams or as slips of the pen or tongue. Freud went on to elaborate a comprehensive theory that accounted for individual human psychological development, family interactions, social structures, politics, art, and even the religious beliefs and practices of normal people as well as for all the neurotic and psychotic disturbances of the mentally ill.

From the outset, psychoanalytic theory was under sporadic attack, but today it is so besieged as to raise the concern of its most loyal defenders. Indeed, scholars from disciplines as disparate as neurobiology, history of science, clinical psychology, and philosophy of science are finding evidence that (1) weakens the ultimate logic of its original clinical claims; (2) suggests more plausible alternative hypotheses regarding the causation of dreams, slips, and neurosis; and (3)—most damaging of all—indicates that the treatment based upon the theory may be ineffectual—or even harmful—as well as inefficient. Psychoanalysis is thus clearly in need of treatment. But can the couch alone help so severely impaired a patient?

Storm of criticism

In the face of such strong attack on every front, the defense of psychoanalysis is surprisingly weak. Why? Perhaps because, like Rome at the height of decadence, psychoanalysis has so greatly overextended its empire that it hardly knows where to take a defensive stand. The psychological theory has been splintered, diluted, and bastardized in its application to such far-flung fields as literature, anthropology, sociology, linguistics, history, aesthetics, and economics.

Furthermore, psychoanalysis has provided vast ranks of unscientifically trained helping professionals (such as social workers, occupational therapists, and teachers) with an easily understood perspective. Using oversimplified psychoanalytic theory, members of this ever widening psychotherapeutic "fringe" are widely promoted as "therapists."

Even the professional cadre—that sitting within the psychoanalytic citadel itself—has split into a multitude of factions. This infinite branching has rendered the identification of a centrally shared theoretical basis impossible.

New York and Paris have at least three psychoanalytic institutes apiece—each with a quite different ideology. Jacques Lacan (the "French Freud") singlehandedly founded two institutes, which are now at swordpoints with each other. The theoretical spectrum of splinter groups has ranged from unreconstructed Freudian orthodoxy on the right (with Jacob Arlow and Charles Brenner among the leaders), through progressive ego psychologists (like Anna Freud and Erik Erikson) in the center, to a radical ("hermeneutic") wing (with Paul Ricoeur and Jurgen Habermas) on the left.

These three main groups are distinguished by their basic differing emphases. In brief, the orthodox view supports the primacy of biologic instinctual drives as determinants of mental life. The ego psychology perspective focuses on the continuously evolving and adaptive nature of defensive conflict reduction and resolution. And the hermeneutic school holds to the importance of multiple and subjective meanings of thoughts, words, and actions, whatever their veracity, mechanism, or function.

In practice today psychoanalysts, in treating their patients, may be witheringly cold—insisting that signs of human kindness on the part of the therapist would rob the patient of independence. Or they may be smotheringly warm—holding that only a positive emotional experience in therapy can really make a difference.

How did such disarray arise? And what can be done about it? Some answers to these questions become clear in the course of examining the history of psychoanalysis. But another, prior, question nags: Why bother? Who cares about psychoanalysis anyway?

To the extent that psychoanalysis is a general theory of human nature, it can be said that everyone has a stake in it. Psychoanalysis is as much point of view as it is a set of formal propositions about the workings of

Freud sat in the armchair behind his famous couch while his patient lay supine. Freud believed that the lack of face-to-face contact with the analyst stimulated the patient to free-associate and to talk uninhibitedly. The picture (above left) was taken in his London Maresfield Gardens home, where he settled at the end of his life after being forced by the Nazis to leave Vienna in 1938. At the stage of his life when the photograph (opposite page) was taken—in 1931, eight years before his death—Freud was in ill health and saw that his time and opportunities for making fresh observations were limited—unlike his earlier years, when he was the only worker in a new field with vast expanses of unexplored territory ahead. Many of his pioneering theories had been challenged; many of his early followers had deserted him; and psychoanalysis itself had become fragmented and factionalized.

77

Practitioners of psychoanalysis, perhaps more than any other group of doctors who apply remedies to diseases, have been viewed as everything from gods to mystics to the most devious of con men. Any number of interpretations are possible for René Magritte's sculpture "The Therapeutist" (above).

The extent to which Freudian psychiatry has penetrated the popular consciousness, especially in the United States, is reflected by the number of widely eclectic therapies that have arisen. There has been little opportunity to study or validate most of these unorthodox approaches, many of which are led by a single charismatic leader or "guru." (Opposite page) In a lesson on "sensory awareness," participants at California's Esalen Institute at Big Sur practice "head tapping" as a form of nonverbal communication (left). In a "Gestalt" therapy session (center), a group member unleashes pent-up anger. One form of group therapy (right) encourages people to touch as a way of knowing themselves and communicating their feelings.

the human mind. And since psychoanalytic interpretations have been widely adapted in explaining human nature, it has become critical to people's self-image, self-knowledge, and self-esteem. Finally, because so many people are potential psychotherapy patients, knowledge about how the various types of therapists, including the psychoanalytically inclined doctors, think about people is needed. While some might assert that as a medical specialty psychiatry would be better off without psychoanalysis, there is no competing comprehensive psychological theory to take its place, and biology—despite its many strengths—is not ready to replace psychology as the entire basis of human behavior.

Evolution of psychoanalysis in America

Nowhere in the world has psychoanalysis so firmly entrenched itself as in the United States. Ask junior high school students today to give dream reports and they will offer instant Freudian interpretations—though they may never have heard of Freud. So deeply embedded are psychoanalytic hypotheses that they are unrecognized as such and have instead become articles of cultural faith. Yet, perhaps ironically, these ideas have never passed the test of science, which is a prerequisite for intellectual longevity in pragmatic America.

The basic psychoanalytic concept of the dynamic determination of personality—together with its corollary assumption of inherent ability to change with treatment—fits perfectly with the so-called American dream. Not only is everyone created equal, but equality can be constantly renewed since environmental disadvantage can be overcome by reeducation. As a doctrine psychoanalysis thus gives liberal impetus to child-rearing reforms, progressive educational programs, and the mental health movement itself.

This, of course, is not at all what Freud had in mind, either for his theory or for America. Although he was sympathetic to the idea of the lay (or nonmedical) analyst, he would have been surprised—and probably horrified—to see today's uncritical acceptance and distortion of his ideas. In 1930 he wrote:

I often hear that psycho-analysis is very popular in the United States. . . . My satisfaction over this is, however, clouded by several circumstances. It seems to me that the popularity of the name of psycho-analysis in America signifies neither a friendly attitude to the thing itself nor any specially wide or deep knowledge of it.

Freud went on to castigate the lack of financial support for American psychoanalytic institutes and the paucity of scientific research before concluding:

Many of the evils which I have mentioned with regret no doubt arise from the fact that there is a general tendency in America to short study and preparation and to proceed as fast as possible to practical application. There is a preference, too, for studying a subject like psycho-analysis not from the original sources but from second-hand and often inferior accounts. Thoroughness is bound to suffer from this.

Nowhere in the world has psychotherapy been given so glorious a chance to fail as in the United States. It is ironic that it may be Americans (who have so casually and widely accepted psychoanalytic ideas) who will now prove that Freud's own late-life pessimism about the value of psychoanalysis as a treatment was justified.

Failure in treating mental illness

Psychoanalytic theory began as an explanation of psychiatric symptoms. For Freud the neurotic and even the psychotic symptom was a failed compromise between a biologic drive (and its psychic correlate, the wish) and a social demand for postponement. Thus, the symptom was an effective negation of the drive (of which the psychic mediator was repression, which banished the wish to the unconscious). So repressed, the drives (and associated wishes) were potentially pathogenic because they constantly exerted pressure for release, and occasionally they escaped—in disguised form— as dreams, slips, and symptoms. This mechanistic model of the mind had an intellectual appeal, even for those physicians who might have questioned some of its details, because it was analogous to the classic and successful infectious disease model, where symptoms—such as fever—signaled a deeper pathogenic process—such as infection.

To proceed with this analogy, to reduce a phobic patient's fear of pigeons—without relieving the repressed drives deep within the unconscious, *e.g.,* infantile sexual feelings toward a parent—was tantamount to supressing a tuberculous patient's night sweats or cough while leaving the tubercule bacillus to continue to feast on the lungs. At the same time, complementing this analogy of pathogenesis was the promise of relief by psychotherapeutic intervention—just as antibiotic therapy destroyed the microorganism, which then relieved the cough and sweats. Interpretation of the symptom in the context of a transference relationship to the therapist (as stand-in for the eroticized parent) relieved not only the symptom (fear of pigeons) but also its deep cause. And only such deep interventions could provide lasting relief, according to Freud and his followers.

Unquestionably, this was a neat idea. But, as contemporary cognitive psychologists are learning, not all slips are Freudian. And today the record actually indicates that the treatment of phobias by behavioral techniques, which directly attack the fear and not its presumed deep cause, is both

"Listen . . . You've got to relax . . . The more you think about changing colors, the less chance you'll succeed . . . Shall we try the green background again?"

Inherent in psychoanalytic theory is the idea that people can change. Thus the joke: How many psychiatrists does it take to change a light bulb? Answer: just one, provided the light bulb wants to change.

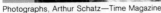
Photographs, Arthur Schatz—Time Magazine

Perhaps the ultimate spoof on Freud and his theories is the publication of Freud's Own Cookbook *(1985). "Eat your way to sanity the Freudian way, with recipes from Sigmund Freud's long-suppressed private cookbook. Here is the definitive work Freud would have given us had he not been distracted by his patients, anxieties, and professional articles." Among the culinary delights are Erogenous Scones, Incredible Oedipal Pie, and Sublimation Sandwiches.*

Illustration, Jeff Fisher; reproduced by permission of Harper & Row

more effective (*i.e.,* the symptoms are more often relieved) and more efficient (the treatment is faster and less expensive) than psychoanalysis. Moreover, and perhaps most important, symptom substitution does not occur following behavior therapy for phobias. In other words, the treatment's effects endure.

Phobias may be behaviorally and socially crippling, but as signs of psychic turmoil they pale beside the hallucinations and delusions of psychotically deranged schizophrenic patients. In the mid-1960s, fully ten years after effective schizophrenic symptom reduction had for the first time been achieved by use of the so-called psychiatric wonder drugs—the phenothiazine tranquilizers—it was asserted in some major American university hospitals that such "chemical restraint" definitively countered the need for treatment by psychoanalytic psychotherapy. The hallucinations and delusions of schizophrenic patients had previously been viewed as deflections of repressed wishes and impulses. But put to the test this notion did not stand up as correct, and even in the hands of highly skilled and respected psychoanalysts, effective and significant symptom reduction in severely impaired schizophrenics could not be achieved. The tranquilizers proved not to be as "miraculous" as first believed, and it is now evident that not all patients respond to such medication. Nevertheless, a great many do. And no psychiatrist today would withhold medication while waiting for psychoanalysis to effect its promised deep cure.

In light of its obvious shortcomings and clear failures, how can the persistence of psychoanalytic ideology be accounted for? The reasons are many and often complex. For one thing, it can be said that the social causes that have been linked to psychoanalytic theory are noble ones. In its complexity and in its argumentation, it is also quite beautiful. Freud was an impressive thinker and a superb writer. The members of the psychoanalytic institutes rightly revere Freud's texts as treasure. To some extent, like the artwork preserved in great cathedrals, these works of genius are not to be defaced even if the anticlerical and antitheological tenets of the revolutionary spirit are fully justified.

Freud's shortcomings come to light

Today's complaints about psychoanalysis are clearly traceable in psychiatric history and are largely founded in Freud's character, his relationships with his colleagues, and his way of handling his theory and the clinical data about his patients.

The intellectual link between Freud's early career as a neurologist and physiologist and his later development of psychoanalysis was set down in 1895 in *Project for a Scientific Psychology,* held to be a virtual Rosetta Stone, and in the *Interpretation of Dreams,* published in 1900, which is still acclaimed as the cornerstone of psychoanalysis. That Freud's ideas about the nervous system—which became his ideas about the mind—were dated is not surprising. One can hardly blame him for being a product of his times. Thus, although Freud recognized the neuron as the cellular unit of the brain, he was ignorant of such important physiological processes as nervous system chemical inhibition, by which neural transmissions may be suppressed

80

and signals effectively canceled, and spontaneous activity, which endows the system with degrees of independence of the environment for both its energy needs and its information.

Coupled with other misconceptions regarding the nature of the workings of the nervous system, these oversights prompted Freud to view the brain (*i.e.,* the mind) as the necessary and permanent slave of "drives" such as sex and hunger—drives that had their origin elsewhere in the body or outside it. According to Freud, once these forces entered the system, they could not escape unless discharged in motoric (behavioral) activity. They generated conflicts that could be resolved only by banishment to the unconscious but that perpetually pressed for discharge. They emerged in disguise as dreams, as slips, and as symptoms.

Freud's dream theory deposed

All of these Freudian assumptions about the nervous system are now known to be either incomplete or downright wrong. For example, Freud thought that dreaming was actually *caused* by the pressure of the unconscious infantile wishes, which threatened to overcome the relaxed guard of the sleeping ego. We now know that the energy for dreaming is intrinsic to the brain since REM (rapid eye movement) sleep, in which most dreaming occurs, is an automatic physiological function, like respiration and temperature control. It is not caused by wishes.

In generating REM sleep, the brain utilizes its own metabolic energy captured from basic chemicals like glucose (sugar) and oxygen, which circulate in the blood. The automatic regulation of REM sleep by the brain relies heavily on modulation of the spontaneous activity of neurons. It is thus nervous system inhibition and not ego repression that declines in sleep and allows the brain to become active and to dream. Some psychoanalytic theorists would say that nervous inhibition and ego repression are the same thing. But most modern neurophysiologists and many practicing psychiatrists now see that this reasoning is flawed.

Since unconscious wishes have been eliminated as causes of dreaming, their possible role in the determination of dream content should be explored. According to Freud, dreams were bizarre and apparently nonsensical precisely because consciousness could not bear to face the unconscious wishes that were their root cause in undisguised form. The ego's censor, therefore, used such defensive processes as condensation, displacement, symbolism, and pictorialization to obscure and detoxify the wishes, thereby allowing sleep to proceed basically undisturbed.

Now that the nature of brain activation in REM sleep has been recognized, the disguise-censorship hypothesis can be confidently replaced by an alternative idea, that of so-called activation-synthesis. Activation-synthesis sees dreams as visual because the visual system is activated as an integral part of REM sleep. More strikingly, condensation, displacement, and symbol formation may be explained quite simply as the activated mind's attempt to create—not disguise—meaning. In the absence of external information, dreams are not surprisingly disoriented and not surprisingly fanciful. It now seems clear that there is no way to save Freud's dream theory.

Keith Bendis

Psychoanalytic theory as conceived by Freud held that repressed drives and the wishes associated with them constantly pressed for release; when they escaped they did so in disguised form—such as in slips of the pen and slips of speech. Freud wrote about these "mistakes" in Psychopathology of Everyday Life; *he believed that behind every such blunder lived a meaning, and often that meaning was hidden. According to Freud, the route to uncovering the repressed drives that emerged as slips, dreams, and symptoms was the psychoanalytic process of digging deep into the unconscious, as the French illustration below suggests. Today few scientists believe all slips are Freudian; rather they allow that some are just amusing mistakes.*

Jean-Loup Charmet, Paris

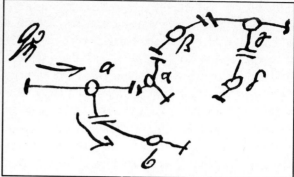

The illustration (above left) depicts a lecture on the brain at the University of Vienna, where Freud was a student from 1873 to 1881. Freud, a trained neurologist, held ideas about the brain and the nervous system that are outmoded today. He and other neurologists of his day lacked important knowledge of physiological processes, such as chemical inhibition of neural transmissions. In the diagram (above right) Freud attempted to show what happened in the brain during dreaming—i.e., that there was a physiological diversion of nervous energy consistent with his psychological concept of repression. Recent studies have delineated a much more precise picture of what really occurs in the brain at every stage of sleep, including the view that dreaming is an automatic physiological function that is not controlled by wishes.

The contemporary outlook on dreaming allows "wishes," whether they be unconscious or conscious, a place in dream creation, but it views the resulting dreams as directly revelatory, not concealing, of them. By also allowing fears, persistent worries, and traumatic memories a direct role in dream content formation, the new theory gets around an important problem that Freudian psychoanalysis could not resolve—the obvious presence of undisguised or directly threatening feelings in dreams.

In addition to alleging that psychoanalytic dream theory is based on outmoded neurology, modern scholars have also shown that Freud was inconsistent, illogical, and unscientific in interpreting dreams. The philosopher of science Adolf Grünbaum points to Freud's inconsistency in interpreting his own famous "Irma" dream. This dream of July 23–24, 1895, was considered by Freud to have been a turning point in his life. From his exhaustive analysis of the Irma dream, he established that "dreams really do possess a meaning." Yet, as Grünbaum has shown, Freud did not use his own dictum—i.e., he did not attribute the dream's meaning to unconscious infantile wishes at all but based his analysis entirely upon a recent event. In Freud's own words: "It is at once obvious to what events of the preceding day it relates." Now it is a commonplace belief that recent events are represented in dreams.

Is psychoanalysis scientific?

Grünbaum's critique of psychoanalysis is much more broadly based. Whereas many are now questioning whether psychoanalysis is indeed a scientific theory—i.e., one that can be "tested"—Grünbaum holds that psychoanalysis is testable. A key test, advanced by Freud himself, is related to the outcome of treatment. If an analyzed subject feels that the insights gained tally with his or her own experience and feelings, then the psychoanalytic theory upon which therapy is based is vindicated. Although

82

he agrees in principle with the "tally argument," Grünbaum shows that the evidence in favor of it is hopelessly flawed. The essential flaw is in the failure of psychoanalysts to account for the effects of suggestion that are inherent in the treatment setting. In giving psychoanalysis a chance to become a science, Grünbaum specifies that as-yet-untested predictions—for instance, that dreaming should change in amount, bizarreness, and defensive content during treatment—are testable. But here, too, control for suggestion would be essential.

Most psychoanalysts today scoff at attempts to test the theory experimentally. In fact, there has been a historical tendency of psychoanalysts to rely on Freud's beliefs and assertions as truth without attempts to verify or provide other proof. Freud argued that the clinical evidence was too strong to admit contradiction from experimental science. The British psychologist Hans Eysenck has made the important point that those few scientific studies that have been interpreted as favorable to psychoanalytic theory are either methodologically flawed or allow equally plausible alternative explanations. Indeed, the serious consideration of competing hypotheses has been absent from the psychoanalytic literature since Freud swept all previous theories off the table in chapter one of *The Interpretation of Dreams*. In this sense, at least, those who allege that psychoanalysis is nonscientific are correct.

While Freud disclaimed—and even ignored—the obvious influence of his early neurobiological education, he was quite clear in his ultimate commitment to physical science, especially biology. He confidently predicted that the physical basis of psychology would someday be established through the growth of physiology and chemistry.

At the same time, he was loathe to admit for theoretical consideration evidence from extrapsychoanalytic sources. This narrow attitude, which is not only unscientific but antiscientific, has become institutionalized to the point of completely depriving psychoanalysis of the benefits of self-correction.

Now that brain activation in sleep is understood, the disguise-censorship hypothesis proposed by Freud (left) can be replaced by the activation-synthesis model (right). The latter sees dreams as visual because the visual system is normally activated during the physiological stage of sleep known as rapid eye movement (REM) sleep. The brainstem contains a clock-trigger mechanism that turns the dreaming state on and off. Condensation, displacement, and symbol formation, which Freud saw as the "scrambler's" action of disguising meaning, actually are the activated mind's attempt to create meaning. The present view allows wishes, worries, and traumatic memories, whether conscious or unconscious, a place in dreams; thus, this model is a psychophysiological model. With present understanding, it now seems clear that there is no way to save Freud's dream theory.

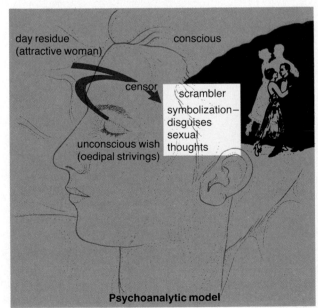

Psychoanalytic model

day residue (attractive woman)

conscious

censor

scrambler symbolization—disguises sexual thoughts

unconscious wish (oedipal strivings)

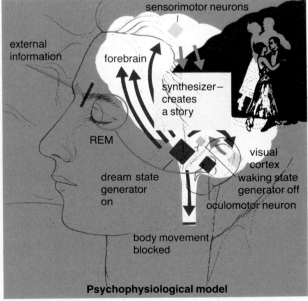

Psychophysiological model

sensorimotor neurons

external information

forebrain

synthesizer—creates a story

REM

visual cortex

dream state generator on

waking state generator off

oculomotor neuron

body movement blocked

Drawings adapted from *Dream Theory and Neurobiology* by J. Allan Hobson, M.D.; © 1979 J. Allan Hobson, M.D., and Roche Products, Inc.

A small select committee of psychoanalysts was founded in 1912 as a reaction against the crises and quarrels surrounding various defections among Freud's early followers. Certain members of the committee advocated making a film on psychoanalysis, though Freud was opposed: "My chief objection is still that I do not believe that satisfactory plastic representation of our abstractions is at all possible." Nonetheless, the film was made. The poster for the film (above) translates as "Psychoanalysis: Puzzle of the Unconscious."

Further, the narrowness of psychoanalytic thinking deprives the discipline of the vigor that would result from communication with mainstream science (by incorporating the relevant findings of modern neurobiology and scientific psychology into the theory).

One point to consider, for example, is the failure of psychoanalysis to study scientifically the process of free association, which is so central to its methodology. Today, after some 90 years of psychoanalysis, no one is any wiser regarding such crucial questions as: Can people ever speak of associations as free? Given the well-established powers of suggestion, of expectation, and of context, is there any experimental evidence that any starting point in thought is different from any other in determining where a given subject's train of associations will ultimately lead? Are dreams any different from fantasies or even daytime ruminations in terms of the kind of associations that they trigger and the course that they run? What systematic evidence now exists—after what must be at least a million hours of psychoanalytic "work"—for the claim that dreams are the royal road to the unconscious? There is none.

Carl Jung, who was expelled from Freud's inner circle for his mystical backsliding, was in many respects more scientifically critical than Freud himself. His early experiments on the associative process, his skepticism regarding the sexual etiology of the neuroses, and his recognition of the creative nature of dreaming all make his rejection by Freud the more disappointing and the more telling. The famous Freud-Jung letters show clearly that their falling out was the end of a personal power struggle that had little or nothing to do with science. The same is true of Freud's clashes with psychiatric colleagues Otto Rank, Alfred Adler, and—most tragically—

The unscientific nature of psychoanalysis is the theme of this German caricature, "Der Psychiater" ("The Psychiatrist").

Ralph Steadman

The drawing at left caricatures the brewing upheavals that were occurring in the psychoanalytic ranks when the third congress of the International Psycho-Analytical Association met at Weimar in 1911. At the time, Carl Jung and Freud were still good friends but Alfred Adler had already clashed with Freud, and in 1912, owing to irreconcilable scientific disagreements, Adler was obliged to resign from Freud's inner circle.

Victor Tausk (whose touching story has been told by Paul Roazen in his book *Brother Animal*).

This pattern of rejection from the movement of anyone strong enough to challenge Freud's ideas is clearly at the heart of the current problems in the field. The failure to change, to integrate new ideas and new facts, has led to the rigidity and backbiting that today characterize the psychoanalytic in-group. At the same time, the resulting exclusions and expulsions of dissenters have led to the wild proliferation of offshoot sects, each with its own gratuitous claims and its own impassioned guru.

Second- and third-generation analysts

Freud's alliance to his own family and to his lifelong friends led to the group of second-generation analysts that became interested in what they called ego psychology. Anna, Freud's daughter, worked with Dorothy Burlingame

Freud is shown in the early 1890s with Wilhelm Fliess (at right in the picture). Fliess was a Berlin otolaryngologist who from 1887 to 1901 was closely linked with Freud as a scientist and friend. In an extensive correspondence they shared their discoveries. Fliess was thus the sole witness of the birth of psychoanalysis, and he was indispensable to Freud during a period that included the most important years of the latter's self-analysis. Many of Freud's ideas about infantile sexuality were of Fliessian origin, but Freud later took steps to suppress that fact and even to repudiate his relationship with Fliess.

The assaults on Freud today are rampant. One contemporary defector from the inner Freudian ranks is Jeffrey Masson (top), who had been an ardent disciple. But in 1984 Masson published a vehement exposé, The Assault on Truth: Freud's Suppression of the Seduction Theory, *in which he charges that the way Freud abandoned his early ideas about childhood sexual traumas was an act of ethical cowardice. It was Freud's daughter Anna (above) who allowed Masson special access to her father's private papers.*

to foster the direct observation of children, a tradition that has been carried on in London and in the U.S., especially at Yale University. Ego psychology, while accepting much of psychoanalytic orthodoxy, has been genuinely progressive.

Ego psychologist Erikson extended the so-called developmental schema of Freud, holding that personality is a continually evolving process, to the full human life-span, which he described as a continuous sequence of tasks. His work inspired the burgeoning school of psychobiography, which has "analyzed"—in absentia—the lives of such great men as Mahatma Gandhi, Martin Luther, and T. E. Lawrence.

There are a few, such as the English analyst John Bowlby, who have made attempts to establish the relevance of post-Darwinian ethological science to human psychobiology. But the attempts to pursue this link have not been systematic and thus represent an important missed opportunity.

The hermeneutic "left wing" of the contemporary psychoanalytic squadron, which is interested in meanings, not causality, alleges that "truth" is relative and thus so heavily context-bound as to defy the usual canons of science. Alarmed by this posture, critic Grünbaum, for one, has attacked Ricouer, Habermas, and other hermeneutic theorists as condemning psychoanalysis to an essentially literary exercise.

Misunderstood genius?

Freud conceived of himself as an ostracized hero whose message was too ultimately painful to be believed by his more timid fellow humans. He actively promoted an image of himself as single-handedly exploring the forbidden ground of the human unconscious. However, the historian of science Frank Sulloway has presented extensive evidence that, contrary to Freud's claims of ostracism, his ideas were, in the main, respectfully and even flatteringly received. Sulloway shows that Freud was in intense, sympathetic, and frequent communication with his friend the otolaryngologist Wilhelm Fliess and that he extensively borrowed from him intellectually. Indeed, it has come to light that the emphasis upon sexuality was of unacknowledged Fliessian origin. When Freud's ardent dependence upon Fliess became personally strained, Freud took active steps to obliterate evidence of the relationship. This suppression of historical evidence, not surprisingly, has outraged many in the field.

Suppression of the truth

The active concealment of historical data has continued to characterize psychoanalysis to this day. Claiming discretion and protection of patient anonymity, Anna Freud and Kurt Eissler have conspired to keep secret many documents in the Freud archives that are crucial to a clear picture of the origins of psychoanalysis. This policy of censorship has inspired some sleuthlike students of psychoanalysis. The psychoanalytic "double-agent" Jeffery Masson had to hoodwink both Anna Freud and Eissler to gain access to documents showing how Freud abandoned his seminal seduction theory—*i.e.,* real sexual traumas in childhood accounting for neuroses in later life—for the idea that people are ruled by events that were only

imagined as young children and that they remain unconscious of imagining. Hence, it was fantasy, not reality, that really counted for the psyche. This important shift in emphasis—from objectivity to subjectivity—probably was hidden by Freud for complex personal reasons and because he saw how damaging it was to his theories and his treatments. Although Masson himself, according to many, comes across as an unsavory character with a sackful of exaggerated claims, his exposé has shown that the psychoanalytic establishment actively violated its own central rule: to say everything.

Two analytic "victims" of Freud

Why should analysts have gone to such lengths to suppress the truth? Recently the world has been treated to a rash of new and startling truths—one by German journalist Karin Obholzer and another by the independent historian Peter Swales. Both have unearthed painfully embarrassing details about the true course and outcome of some of Freud's major cases involving two of the best known psychoanalytic patients.

Obholzer has provided a penetrating account of her conversations with Freud's famous patient the Wolf Man (Freud's pseudonym for the Russian nobleman he treated for an obsessional neurosis). Obholzer learned that there was really no clinical evidence that the white wolf, dreamed of by the patient at age four, was a symbol disguising the Wolf Man's vision of "the primal scene" (his parents' intercourse). Freud simply told his dependent, credulous patient that it was so, and he believed it. And there was no evidence that the Wolf Man's lack of confidence and his romantic failures with women who were his social equals—or his penchant for prostitutes— were either correctly analyzed or relieved by his work with Freud. The Wolf Man continued in treatment in Vienna for some 60 years after Freud left off. In fact, it appears that the Wolf Man's successor analysts went to great lengths to keep him quiet about Freud's failings.

Obholzer's account strongly suggests that the Wolf Man was a victim of Freud's exaggerated claims. Not only did he not get well in six months—as promised by Freud—but, when his treatment dragged on for several years, he stayed in Vienna and thereby lost his property in Russia and most of his fortune. In fact, he never really got well at all. When he finally died in a public hospital in Vienna in 1979, he was still under the spell of analysis.

That Freud was not forthcoming about important details regarding his clinical results is echoed—and amplified—by the follow-up case study of hysterical patient Frau Cecilie M., who has been identified by Peter Swales as Anna Lieben (née von Tedesco), one of the wealthiest women in Europe. Though she was described as cured by Freud in his *Studies in Hysteria* (1895), it now seems clear that Cecilie M. was neither hysterical nor really cured. This case is doubly important because Freud claimed that it was this patient who helped him discover that free association could be as effective as hypnosis in effecting the cathartic release of repressed wishes and symptomatic improvement. Thus began the "talking cure." As Swales determined in Frau Cecilie's case, her treatment did not effect a cure, nor was it exclusively founded upon talk.

Among Freud's most famous cases was that of the Wolf Man, a Russian nobleman treated by Freud from 1910 to 1914 for an obsessional neurosis. But recent investigation has brought to light the fact that Freud failed totally to get to the root of the Wolf Man's problems. In fact, after his analysis with Freud, the Wolf Man continued in therapy for some 60 years until his death in 1979. The man known as the Wolf Man is shown at right on a street in Vienna during the Nazi occupation. The picture (far right) of wolves in a walnut tree was the patient's own depiction of a vivid dream at age four. Freud based much of his treatment of the Wolf Man on his extensive analysis and interpretation of the wolf dream.

According to Swales, Freud saw the patient twice a day for three years, even during their vacations, which took place at the same time and in the same fashionable Austrian watering place. The evidence is strong that besides talk, an unacknowledged ingredient in the treatment was morphine, to which Frau Cecilie was addicted. No wonder Freud's frequent visits were required. And no wonder the patient's agitated state was calmed during Freud's visits. It is now known that it is dangerous to attribute any change in any patient who is addicted to narcotics to anything but the addiction. And to say nothing—in a case report—about the use of a potent drug or the presence of an addiction is at best disingenuous. Not surprisingly, when Freud left the case after three years of "talk," the patient had made no substantial improvement.

Psychoanalysis tomorrow: a prescription

As a prospective science, psychoanalysis is living on borrowed time. As such it has everything to gain and nothing to lose by getting back to the basic principles that constituted its origins. If the field is to become the scientific discipline that Freud dreamed of, these are some of the principles that must be followed: (1) acknowledgement of the origin and continuing rootedness of psychoanalysis in the mind-brain problem; from this it follows that psychoanalysis—as a patient on the couch—would profit from attention to the exponentially growing data base from the fields of modern neurobiology, of ethology, and of cognitive psychology to refresh, refurbish, and reconstruct all of its fundamental assumptions; (2) adherence to the psychoanalytic rule; *i.e.,* being honest about its history and acknowledging the baseness of many of its own deep motives; and (3) use of the resulting insights to grow up; *i.e.,* abandoning the infantile narcissism that has led to parochialism, divisiveness, and isolation from the mainstream of scientific progress.

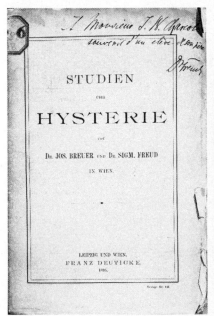 

Frau Cecilie M. was treated by Freud for hysteria. In his Studies in Hysteria *(1895), he claimed to have cured her, but according to contemporary historian Peter Swales, who has looked into the case, Frau Cecilie was neither hysterical nor cured. Moreover, Swales found that Freud had treated the patient with morphine (to which she became addicted), but he never acknowledged the use of the drug or the addiction in his report of the analysis. Cecilie M. (whose real name was Anna Lieben) is pictured at left in the early 1880s with one of her children.*

(Left) Jean-Loup Charmet, Paris; (right) Collection, Peter J. Swales

Some last words

The storm of controversy is not likely to let up soon; the analyses of Father Freud no doubt will continue. To this scientifically inspired critique of psychoanalysis may be added some caveats offered by modern literary humanists.

Alarmed by the influence of Freudian psychoanalytic theory on modern introspective literature—"this business of analysis and pondering one's complexes"—contemporary Jewish writer Isaac Bashevis Singer inveighs against writing in the first person:

I'm against the stream of consciousness because it means always babbling about oneself. The writer who writes about himself all the time must become a bore, just like the man who talks all the time about himself. When the writer becomes the center of his attention, he becomes a *nudnik.* And a *nudnik* who believes he's profound is even worse than just a plain *nudnik.*

In Thomas Mann's great novel *The Magic Mountain,* two tuberculosis inmates are discussing the merits of Dr. Krokowski's theory that all organic

Freud psychoanalyzing Freud is the theme of the drawing at right. Much of Freud's theory, upon which the discipline of psychoanalysis was based, came from his own extensive self-analysis. But it would appear that he did not go far enough, especially in light of the current barrage of criticism that is calling into question the ultimate logic of Freudian theories and, indeed, the effectiveness of psychoanalytic therapy.

Drawing by Charles B. Slackman; courtesy, American Heritage Publishing Company; photograph, Bildarchiv Preussischer Kulturbesitz, Berlin

Psychoanalysis is living on borrowed time. If it is to become the scientific discipline that Freud dreamed of, it must begin to heal itself now. Otherwise, scholars and scientists from widely diverse fields will continue to find evidence of its weak foundations and wrongly conceived concepts, evidence that ultimately will lead to its demise.

disease including tuberculosis is a secondary phenomenon. Hans Castorp asks Herr Settembrini:

"You are down on analysis?"
"Not always—I am for it and against it, both by turns."
"How am I to understand that?"
"Analysis as an instrument of enlightenment and civilization is good, in so far as it shatters absurd convictions, acts as a solvent upon natural prejudices, and undermines authority; good, in other words, in that it sets free, refines, humanizes, makes slaves ripe for freedom. But it is bad, very bad, in so far as it stands in the way of action, cannot shape the vital forces, maims life at its roots. Analysis can be a very unappetizing affair, as much so as death, with which it may well belong—allied to the grave and its unsavory anatomy."

FOR ADDITIONAL READING:

Eysenck, Hans J. *Decline and Fall of the Freudian Empire.* New York: Viking, 1985.

Grünbaum, Adolf. *The Foundations of Psychoanalysis: A Philosophical Critique.* Berkeley: University of California Press, 1984.

Malcolm, Janet. *Psychoanalysis, the Impossible Profession.* New York: Alfred A. Knopf, Inc., 1981.

Malcolm, Janet. *In the Freud Archives.* New York: Knopf, 1984.

Obholzer, Karin. *The Wolf-Man: Sixty Years Later.* New York: Continuum, 1982.

Reiser, Morton F. *Mind, Brain, Body.* New York: Basic Books, 1984.

Roazen, Paul. *Brother Animal: The Story of Freud and Tausk.* New York: Knopf, 1969.

Sulloway, Frank J. *Freud, Biologist of the Mind: Beyond the Psychoanalytic Legend.* New York: Basic Books, 1983.

The Family in China:

Happy, Healthy, and Small

by Elizabeth B. Connell, M.D., and
Howard J. Tatum, M.D., Ph.D.

A Western visitor to this vast country is initially overwhelmed by the crush of people. The sight of thousands of workers thronging the streets on their bicycles on their way home at night is never to be forgotten. The Chinese are healthy, energetic, and extremely friendly, and the children are utterly delightful. People who spent many years in China before the revolution and only recently returned are constantly amazed everywhere they go. One member of a visiting U.S. medical delegation, a woman born and raised in China, could hardly believe the changed appearance of both the country and the people. She kept exclaiming everywhere she went, "China doesn't smell anymore!"

Report from the People's Republic—1986

In the past year the authors of this report were privileged to be leaders of a medical delegation to the People's Republic of China, invited by the Chinese Medical Association. We and our colleagues were able to observe firsthand the impact of the numerous changes in the medical care system, particularly in the area of family planning. It was a visit full of new vistas, excitement, and ideas, unlike anything the members of the group had ever experienced before. We returned home full of admiration for what the Chinese people had been able to accomplish, leaving behind many new and valued friendships to be continued in the future.

Nowhere in the world have such dramatic changes in health and health care taken place in such a short period as in China. In the years since 1949, the time of the revolution, a health care system has been built up, medical education has undergone tremendous changes, and new types of health care workers have been trained. Many infectious diseases have been virtually eliminated. In view of the vast problems China faced because of its rapidly growing population, the development of a national family-planning program was a major economic, political, and social priority. The success of this program is only one of many testaments to the determination and adaptability of the Chinese people.

Life before the revolution

Prior to the revolution the majority of the Chinese people, particularly those living in the rural areas, suffered from both acute and chronic malnutrition.

Elizabeth B. Connell, M.D., and Howard J. Tatum, M.D., Ph.D., are Professors in the Department of Gynecology and Obstetrics, Emory University School of Medicine, Atlanta, Georgia.

(Opposite page) Leshan (Le-shan), Sichuan (Szechwan) Province, China—billboard promoting population control; photograph, Charles Kennard—Stock, Boston

Disease and starvation were ubiquitous in prerevolutionary China. The drawing at far right by a Chinese artist of the late 19th century shows parents selling children into prostitution, a not uncommon practice during times of starvation. Another drawing from the same series, right, is entitled "Mother and Child Dead from Hunger." Syphilis, smallpox, diphtheria, tuberculosis, and other infectious diseases ravaged the Chinese population until well into the 20th century. The last case of smallpox in China was recorded in 1952. (Below) An 18th-century illustration of a girl with smallpox.

Their lives, wretched by today's standards, were made more miserable by periodic crop failures, natural disasters, war, and disease. Living in poverty, without decent housing and sanitation, and lacking even the most primitive forms of modern health care, the Chinese were unable to cope with the recurring epidemics that ravaged the population. The little medical care that was available was dispensed by poorly trained local practitioners, using traditional herbs and ancient techniques, with no knowledge of the advances of Western medicine.

Infants died of tetanus and congenital syphilis, and children died of mumps and measles. Contaminated water supplies and the use of raw human feces as fertilizer led to the spread of hookworm, schistosomiasis, typhoid, cholera, and dysentery. Diseases carried by insects were also common, including kala-azar (a parasitic infection transmitted by sand flies), malaria, typhus, and plague. Thousands of people were either killed or rendered chronically ill by smallpox, diphtheria, influenza, and tuberculosis.

The inferior status of women in traditional Chinese society contributed to their poor health and often to that of their female offspring as well. Under the pressures of extreme poverty and lack of food, parents sold children into prostitution, a practice that increased the extent and seriousness of sexually transmitted diseases. Syphilis at one time infected almost one-quarter of the urban population. Preventive health care was unknown.

After the revolution

In 1950 the First National Health Conference was convened to assess the state of China's health and to make recommendations for improvements. After a careful review of the entire problem, the conference targeted smallpox and syphilis for eradication and selected public sanitation and the training of midwives as top priorities. At about the same time, an important decision was made that was to have a major impact not only on health

In the engraving "The Manchurian Plague" at left, bubonic plague—the Black Death—is personified as a grotesque hag from whose tattered skirts a horde of rats emerges. The deadly plague that spread across Europe during the Middle Ages is believed to have originated in the Eurasian steppe, where the infection was carried by burrowing rodents native to the region. For centuries the population of northern China and the adjacent areas was repeatedly decimated by plague.

care but also on all aspects of life in China—the apportionment of the entire population into communes. These collective units circumscribed all aspects of the individual's life—home, school, and place of employment— and provided the context of day-to-day events. As a self-contained unit, the commune facilitated the provision of education and health care. Moreover, communal life ensured that policy decisions made by the government were universally enforced.

A second critical decision made in the 1950s—inasmuch as there were very few professionally trained doctors and nurses in China—was to use amateurs to provide basic health care. Training consisted of short, intensive courses focusing on how to detect and treat various diseases. The first program employing these new health workers was a campaign to eliminate syphilis. The medical workers carried out a highly effective screening program; houses of prostitution were closed; and tremendous social pressures were brought to bear against sexual promiscuity. These combined efforts were remarkably, and quite quickly, successful.

Two important lessons were learned from this experience. The first was that the infectious diseases that had plagued China for centuries could be eliminated within a relatively short time by a combination of health education

95

and medical care. The second was that this result could be obtained by using dedicated health care workers with only minimal training. The latter conclusion was particularly important, as China at that time was in no position to pattern its health care system along Western lines.

Remarkable results

On the basis of this success, the medical objectives were expanded to include other health problems and a program of public education in proper sanitation and nutrition. The Chinese cooperative medical system has, in just three decades, produced truly remarkable results. There are many notable examples. The last case of smallpox in China was seen in 1952. Not only syphilis but also most of the other major sexually transmitted diseases have been virtually eliminated. The incidence of tuberculosis has decreased sharply. All babies are vaccinated against tuberculosis at birth and, if necessary, revaccinated when they enter school at the age of seven. DPT vaccine—a combined vaccine against diphtheria, tetanus, and pertussis, or whooping cough—is also given at birth, and there has been a major decline in infant and childhood deaths from these diseases. Between 1949 and 1981 infant mortality dropped from about 250 deaths per 1,000 live births to 40 per 1,000. (The U.S. rate in 1983 was 11.2.) During the same time interval, the prevalence of malaria went from 5.5 to 0.3% of the population. Finally, with the institution of Pap smear screening programs in the female population, the rate of cancer of the cervix has decreased by 97%.

Much of the improvement in the general health of the Chinese people stems from improved waste-disposal techniques·and sanitary treatment of drinking water, both of which have had a direct effect on the incidence of infectious and communicable diseases. Another key factor has been the greatly improved food supply. The Chinese today are, in general, very well nourished. And better nutrition has undoubtedly contributed to the increased life expectancy, which rose from 35 in 1949 to 68 in 1981. The average Chinese derives only 20% or less of his caloric intake from fat, compared

Unlike their forebears, the Chinese people of today are extremely well nourished, a factor that contributes to their general good health. Fruits and vegetables, sold in colorful outdoor markets, are in plentiful supply.

(Left) Ed Grazda—Magnum; (right) William Campbell—Sygma

Foreign visitors frequently notice that all of the Chinese people—men, women, the young, and the old—seem to be in better physical condition than their Western counterparts, a fact undoubtedly influenced by a life-style that includes a great deal of exercise. Private cars are virtually unknown, and bicycles are a primary mode of transportation. Typically at rush hours in Chinese cities, streets are thronged by cyclists (left) commuting to work. Organized calisthenics are regularly practiced by schoolchildren (below).

with about 40% in the typical American diet. In addition, traditional Chinese foods are high in bulk and fiber, dietary factors that probably contribute to the population's low rates of diverticular disease and cancer of the colon.

The Chinese people get a great deal of exercise. Their primary means of transportation is the bicycle; private cars are virtually unknown. Children up to the age of two are carried by their parents; older children ride as passengers on their parents' bicycles. Visitors to China frequently comment that both men and women are in excellent physical condition. There is very little obesity and, in general, the older people appear to be healthier than their counterparts in the U.S. In fact, contemporary life in the Chinese countryside is very much like rural life was in the United States at the turn of the century, when 80% of the people lived on the land, walked, rode bicycles, drove wagons, and did much of their work by hand.

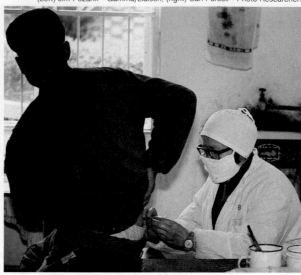

The health care system

Some level of medical care is available to all Chinese. Most accessible are the "barefoot doctors" (above left), who provide primary care. The next level of care can be found at the commune or district hospital; (above right) a patient gets a shot at the Shanghai Commune Hospital. The highest level of expertise exists at teaching hospitals like the Beijing (Peking) Children's Hospital (below right). With medical education decentralized, students in remote locations such as Kashgar (K'a-shih) have a chance to become doctors (below right).

Health care in China is available at four different levels. Primary care is provided by "barefoot doctors." China currently has approximately 1.2 million of these workers, serving in both rural and urban areas. They are usually graduates of primary schools and have approximately six to nine months of formal training in public health and basic primary care. They also receive periodic refresher courses. Barefoot doctors treat minor illnesses and complaints and identify those individuals who should be referred to the second level of medical care, commune or district health centers with 10–30 beds and outpatient clinics, each serving 10,000 to 30,000 people. These facilities are run by more highly trained individuals, assistant doctors, junior high school graduates who have two years of medical training. They can perform minor surgery and prescribe antibiotics.

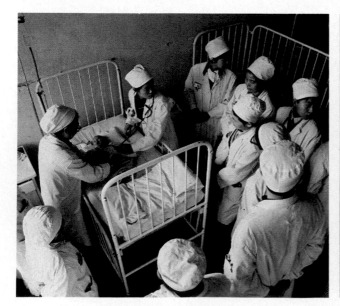

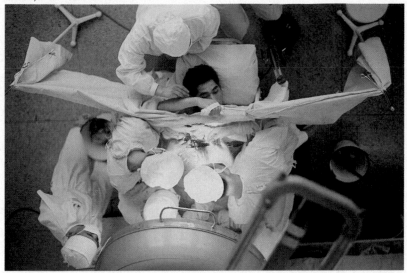

The third level is the county hospital, one to each county, serving 200,000 to 600,000 people. Patients in these institutions are cared for by senior doctors, high-school graduates who have completed a five-year medical school program. They practice both traditional Chinese and Western-style medicine. At the fourth and highest level is the teaching hospital, of which there are approximately 30 to 40 in China.

Medical education in China has also undergone an evolutionary development. There have been three major stages: the ancient period (before 1840), the modern period (1840–1949), and the contemporary period (1949 to the present). In the ancient period medical education was conducted primarily by the apprenticeship method, first within the family structure and later in more traditional settings, under private physicians and ultimately medical schools. The modern period saw an influx of foreigners into China,

Although modern medicine is practiced throughout China, traditional ways have not been forgotten. Sometimes the two are complementary; (left) a woman giving birth by cesarean section receives acupuncture anesthesia. Some practitioners still specialize in traditional techniques (below). Acupressure (left) is an ancient form of pain-relieving massage in which the fingers are used to apply pressure to specific points on the body. In moxibustion (center) warmth is used to relieve pain. A small packet of medicinal herbs is lit and held near designated areas, usually the same points used in acupuncture. Some treatments use acupuncture and moxibustion in combination. Cupping (right) is a variation on moxibustion in which the applied heat is concentrated under a cuplike device.

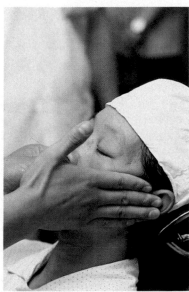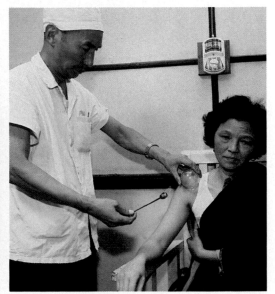

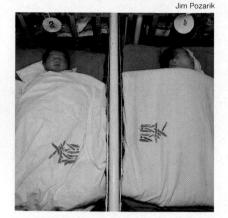

The Chinese population increased by 25% between the fall of the last feudal dynasty in 1911 and the revolution in 1949. During this time the birthrate rose and, with better medical care, infant mortality declined.

looking for new colonies and new markets for foreign goods. Ahead of the colonial settlers came missionaries and medical doctors, who sought to gain the confidence of the Chinese people by becoming involved in medical education and health care.

A number of major changes occurred in the contemporary period with the founding of the People's Republic. The government seized control of the medical schools, all of which were located in the major cities, and relocated some of them in smaller towns. New schools were established in the more remote areas. The training in the various medical schools and the curriculum content were standardized. One of the major changes in medical education was the inclusion of Western medicine in the curriculum. It now accounts for about 90% of the study time, the remainder being devoted to traditional Chinese medicine. There are 116 medical schools in China; more than 415,000 doctors have been trained since the founding of the republic. In addition, there are 556 secondary medical schools, which have trained more than 940,000 practitioners. Finally, there are 25 schools that focus almost entirely on traditional medicine.

Birth control: top priority

China's population has grown dramatically in the last half century. In the years between the collapse of the last feudal dynasty in 1911 and the revolution in 1949, the population increased by 25% to 500 million. However, between 1949 and 1982 the Chinese population doubled, reaching one billion—or 22.6% of the world's total population. As in many less developed countries, this change came about because the old pattern of high birthrates and high death rates was replaced by a new one with high birthrates and low death rates. In feudal times the large number of deaths caused by political upheavals, natural disasters, and multiple diseases had tended to counteract the effect of a high birthrate, so that the natural population increase was slowed or even decreased in some areas.

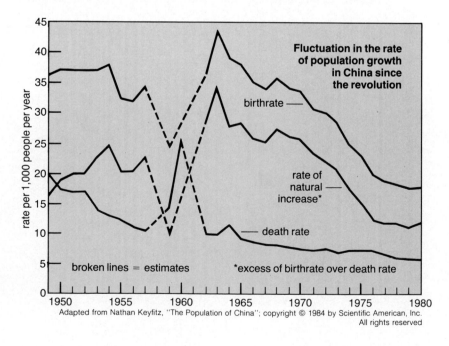

Fluctuation in the rate of population growth in China since the revolution

birthrate ———

rate of natural — increase*

— death rate

broken lines = estimates   *excess of birthrate over death rate

rate per 1,000 people per year

Adapted from Nathan Keyfitz, "The Population of China"; copyright © 1984 by Scientific American, Inc.

With the many cultural and health improvements instituted by the new government, there was rapid growth in the economy; life expectancy increased and the birthrate also increased. In the early years of the republic, it was still considered desirable to have many children, particularly many sons. As health care improved, fewer babies died in infancy. By 1953 the annual birthrate was between 30 and 40 per 1,000 population. This translated into an increase of 100 million people within the six years from 1953 to 1959. In the mid-1950s, realizing the implications of such vast growth, the Chinese government began a major family-planning program.

There has been considerable argument over the years as to which is more important in attempting to control population, the promotion of fertility-regulation (*i.e.,* family-planning) programs or reliance on the pressures generated by economic development. It is now generally recognized that both play a significant part. Among the many socioeconomic factors known to promote a decline in the birthrate are decreased infant mortality, increased urbanization, longer life expectancy, improved level of literacy, and expanded opportunities for employment, especially for women. The effectiveness of family-planning programs has also been documented. Data from a number of countries including China have been used to dispel the argument that family planning is not effective in checking the birthrate, that population growth can be controlled only by social change. Obviously, as the Chinese experience demonstrates, an active program to promote birth control can have a tremendous impact.

Four major birth-planning campaigns have been carried out in China. The first began in 1956 but came to an abrupt end in 1958 when Chairman Mao Zedong (Mao Tse-tung) instituted the movement known as the Great Leap Forward. During this attempt to improve the economy of China by decentralizing industry and collectivizing agriculture, widespread economic problems developed. There was a drop in the birthrate—not because of contraception but because of economic decline, crop failures, and widespread famine.

At the end of this disastrous experiment, in 1962, a second birth-planning campaign was undertaken. This effort was just beginning to show results when the Cultural Revolution, Chairman Mao's ill-fated attempt to reawaken revolutionary zeal, was promulgated. This program, which lasted from 1966 to 1968, disrupted the production and distribution of contraceptives and interfered with family-planning services, resulting in a marked increase in the birthrate.

The third campaign to control fertility lasted from 1971 to 1979. During these years population growth was a major concern of the government, and a number of laws were passed to deal with the problem. As a consequence of this campaign, China reduced its birthrate from 34 per 1,000 in 1970 to 18 per 1,000 in 1979, an achievement unequaled by any other major nonindustrial country.

The one-child limit

At the outset of the third birth-planning campaign, great emphasis was placed on the two-child family. However, it soon became clear that, because of the previously high birthrates, particularly during the Cultural Revolution,

By the mid-1950s, with birthrates rising and death rates falling, the Chinese government realized that birth planning would have to be made a national priority. Today the one-child family (above) is the model of socially conscious Chinese couples.

Having established population control as a top social priority, the government uses every possible means of publicizing the necessity for family planning. In rural areas loudspeakers are particularly effective in reaching people. In Zhengzhou (Cheng-chou) a loudspeaker truck (right) decorated with slogans emphasizes the importance of the one-child-family policy. The poster pictured below shows how Chinese agricultural produce and imported foodstuffs are distributed among the population, stressing that reducing population growth increases the standard of living for everyone.

even limiting families to two children would not make a major impact on the population problem. Therefore, in 1979 the fourth campaign was undertaken with the one-child family as its goal.

Many social incentives and disincentives have been instituted in order to achieve this goal, reinforced by a complex system of financial rewards and penalties. First, it has been made abundantly clear to all of the Chinese people that population growth is regarded as a major problem by the government. Propaganda is constantly being dispensed throughout the country via a massive educational program. All types of communications media are used, including radio, television, films, filmstrips, pamphlets, newspapers, lectures, public exhibits, songs, slogans, billboards, and posters. These media efforts are conducted in the residential areas and also at the workplace. It has been estimated that there are more than 100 million loudspeakers in the rural areas of China, capable of reaching 70% of the population. Adult study and discussion groups focus on the population issue, and married couples are frequently visited at home by medical corpsmen and party officials, whose messages reinforce the goal of the one-child family. Communities also have "health technicians"—local women who are responsible for keeping track of the contraceptive practices and the menstrual cycles of the married women in the neighborhood.

Family-planning activities in the various factories are intense. For example, in Shanghai there are 80,000 women employed in the local textile factories. Nurses in the factories keep menstrual calendars and family registration cards for all female employees. They collect data on the child, or children, in the family, the contraceptives that are being used, and the dates of future planned pregnancies. Finally, there is virtually no premarital sex in China. In fact, the simple appearance of sexual impropriety—such as a boy visiting a girl's room at school—can be sufficient grounds for disciplinary action.

Much of the success of the programs seeking to limit population growth is due to the support of the government. Family planning has been given a

102

At a shopping center in Wuhan (Wu-han), schoolchildren view an exhibit on family planning that includes a display of human fetuses at various stages of development. A doctor explains the goals of the government's population-control program.

prominent place in the official bureaucracy. The Family Planning Commission works directly with the various ministries of health, education, industry, youth, and women's affairs. The family-planning programs and the actual distribution of contraceptive supplies are under the jurisdiction of the Minister of Public Health. The commission, however, establishes policies and determines the demographic targets that are to be the goals of the other operating agencies.

Every year each province receives a "growth target" from the central government; the province then allocates the numbers of births permitted to its member counties. A birth-planning committee draws up three- to five-year plans for its community and informs couples when they may have a baby. Plans for marriage must be approved well in advance of the wedding. Once a couple has been authorized to have a child, they are given a planned-birth card; without these formalities a pregnancy is regarded as unplanned. If an eligible couple fails to achieve a pregnancy, their "slot" may be filled by another couple on the waiting list.

A poster shows a proud mother displaying the certificate she has been awarded for pledging to limit her family to one child. Traditionally the Chinese have regarded male children more highly than females, a cultural value that comes into conflict with current policy when a family's first— and presumably only—child is a girl. The appealing little girl on the poster and the mother's obvious pleasure and satisfaction reinforce the notion that female children are now to be held in high esteem.

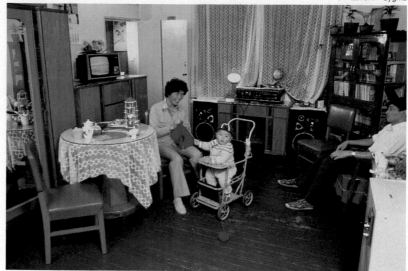

J-P Laffont—Sygma

A system of rewards and penalties is used to reinforce the desirability of the single-child family. Couples who agree to abide by the limit are given preferential treatment, including priority in living accommodations. (Right) This single-child family in Shanghai has a modern apartment, along with a television set and other trappings of economic privilege. In some localities free schooling may be offered for a first, and only, child. Children of factory workers in Beijing attend a residential kindergarten during the week (below left), returning home to their parents on weekends; free nursery schools watch over toddlers (below right) while parents work.

Each of the local authorities is also responsible for establishing its own incentives, which are to be used to achieve the stated goal of the one-child family. Many services and benefits, such as free health care and education, are commonly offered only for the first child. In addition, financial bonuses, as well as a reward for practicing family planning, are given to both the parents and the child of the one-child family. Urban families with only one child may apply for—and usually get—a two-room apartment with its own kitchen and bath, a total of 37 to 56 square meters (400 to 600 square feet). In rural areas single-child families may be given a lower production quota or have a larger amount of land allocated to them.

Compliance: rewards and penalties

Different communities have attempted to stimulate people to accept the one-child-family concept in a variety of different ways. In certain cities the municipal council issues "only-children certificates," which list the mother's and father's names, ages, and places of employment and the name of the child. Before she receives the certificate, a woman is asked to pledge that

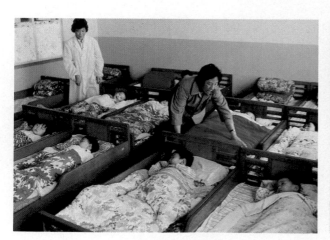

(Left) Black Star; (right) Dennis E. Cox—Click/Chicago

she will not have another child. There are numerous advantages to the certificate. First, it gives the parents priority in living accommodations. It allows the child to attend a residential kindergarten, which provides free room and board during the week, including three meals a day, the child spending only weekends with the parents. This is a particularly desirable incentive when the family's living space is cramped. In addition, only-children families often receive a monthly bonus for the child's food and clothing. And there is also a certain amount of social prestige associated with having a certificate. In rural areas this approach is less popular than in the cities, and only about one-quarter of the families with one child under the age of 14 have agreed to limit their families to a single child.

If a woman who already has one child is found to be pregnant again, an effort is made to get her to accept an abortion. Social pressure is also applied if the particular locality in which the woman lives has already reached the number of births allotted to it for that calendar year. With the birth of the second child, the parents forfeit all previously available free health care and educational benefits, and the family must henceforth pay the usual fees for both children. Should they have a third child, they must pay increased taxes annually until that child reaches the age of 14. If a couple has a second child after being rewarded for making a commitment to the one-child family, 10% of their monthly wages is deducted until the youngest child is 14; the second child is not covered by the family's medical benefits, and the parents, if they are office workers, are denied promotions.

Several factors have contributed to the success of the one-child-family program. In 1980 the Chinese government established a minimum age for marriage of 20 for women and 22 for men. In many parts of the country, however, considerable emphasis has been placed on delaying marriage well beyond these ages. Currently in Beijing (Peking), 25 is the minimum age of marriage for women and 28 for men. There is one exception to this general rule: a young man who must care for younger siblings following the death of his parents may take a wife to help him raise the children.

Different communities have responded differently to the government's family-planning policies. In rural areas, for example, only about a quarter of the families have accepted the one-child-family concept. In addition, not all couples in China are asked to limit their families—exceptions include members of certain ethnic minorities and families engaged in economic activities that require male children for the labor force.

105

Birth control devices and information are free in China, and both are widely available to all married couples. (Above) Doctors offer advice about family planning at an informal sidewalk clinic. Women attending a family-planning session at the Shanghai Maternity Hospital (below) learn about intrauterine devices.

In China women have never been equal to men. However, by virtue of a 1978 constitutional amendment, women now have equal education, equal work opportunities, equal pay, and equal responsibilties within the Communist Party. A marriage law passed in 1980 allows women to retain their maiden names after marriage. While apparently raising the status of women, this provision also eliminates the tradition that a son is needed to perpetuate the family name—further inducement for the parents of a female child to accept the one-child limit.

Chinese culture has always placed great emphasis on large families, and male children have traditionally been far more important than females. It was not uncommon, prior to the revolution, for female infants to be abandoned or drowned, particularly in southern rural areas. In recent years, however, infanticide has become far less common, although it is still occasionally reported in rural China. The traditional bias against female infants had caused a major problem when the first—and only—child was a girl. However, with laws promoting equality for women, the arrival of a female firstborn is being viewed with greater acceptance. Moreover, infanticide is now classified as a serious crime and is punished.

Another change that has facilitated the objective of the one-child family is the increased amount of government-sponsored care available to the aged. In traditional Chinese society, adult children were responsible for the older members of the family. Under the current population policy, it is now possible that one individual may have six elderly people—two parents and four grandparents—to look after. Therefore, the provision of medical care, social services, and financial support to the aged has been of great importance in increasing the acceptance of the one-child concept.

Circumventing the rules

There are some loopholes currently available to certain individuals who wish to go beyond the one-child limit. Members of minority groups who live in the extreme rural parts of China are not limited to one child, and each

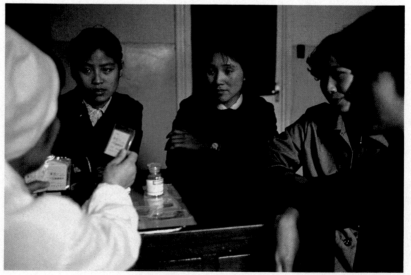

such group may establish its own population policy. In certain mountain and coastal fishing areas, couples are allowed to have a second child if the first is a girl, inasmuch as sons are needed for the labor force.

Throughout the country, however, a second child may be permitted if the first is abnormal or dies, if there has been a divorce or the death of a spouse, or if both parents were the only children in their families. A woman who has no siblings may choose to live with her own family, rather than with her husband's, as is traditional, and she may have more than one child. In the case of a remarriage, where one of the partners has a child and the other does not, another child is permitted. Finally, families in which there has been only one male child for two or three generations are permitted to have a second child, as are men whose brothers are unable to have children.

Another way to get around the one-child limitation has recently been noted. A couple will move from the community where they are registered and take temporary employment elsewhere; they will have another child but, because they are not registered in the new location, the birth will not be recorded. Subsequently, they will return to their original home and claim that the second child was adopted, having been abandoned by its parents, and the child will gradually be accepted as part of the family. A number of means have been suggested to prevent this practice, but none has yet been implemented.

Contraceptives: available upon request

Although various types of contraception were available in limited quantities in China for many years, no consistent efforts were made to promote their use until the initiation of the government's family-planning programs. Currently, contraceptives are distributed free to all married men and women; it has been estimated that 90–97% of couples use some form of contraception. (Because the government has declared premarital sex incompatible with national policy, contraceptive use begins with marriage.)

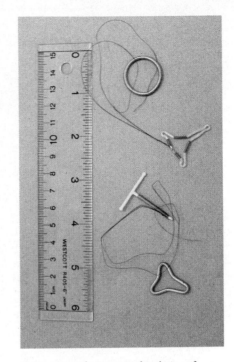

Intrauterine devices are the choice of about 70% of Chinese women using some form of birth control; both the stainless steel spring and copper wire-bearing varieties (above) are popular. An unplanned pregnancy may be terminated by an abortion (below), at no cost to the patient.

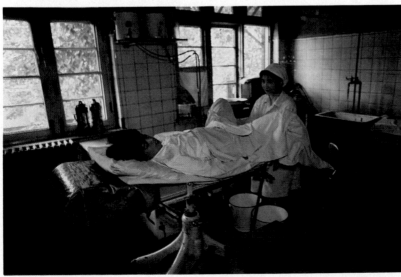

Jim Pozarik—Gamma/Liaison

This Chinese grandmother takes care of her grandchild while the mother is at work—an arrangement that can be expected to become more widespread as women of childbearing age continue to work full time and the proportion of elderly people in the population continues to grow. Taking responsibility for care of youngsters is one way that the elderly make a "positive" contribution to the country's economy.

The low-dose combination formulation of oral contraceptive pills is widely distributed in China. In addition, the Chinese have created a "vacation pill." This is a progestin-only formulation, for use during the month of vacation, which for many couples is the only time of year that husband and wife are not separated by long distances. The pills are taken only during the one-month period when they are together. A yearly progestin injection is also available as a conjugal visit or "vacation" method of birth control. The Chinese have also used "paper pills" (hormones applied to small squares of edible paper) for many years.

Intrauterine devices (IUDs) are used by at least 70% of the women using some form of contraception. Until the past two years, flexible stainless steel ring-type devices have been most widely used. These are available in several sizes. Another type of flexible stainless steel IUD is triangle shaped. More recently two copper wire-bearing IUDs have been produced in China. (The addition of copper metal enhances the contraceptive effect.) One is a Y-shaped steel wire covered with a fine coating of plastic; copper wire is wound around the plastic in several places. The most recently developed IUD to be manufactured in China is a modification of the so-called T Cu 200, or copper T. The Chinese clinicians prefer the copper T to the steel ring because of its greater effectiveness.

Condoms are widely available and widely used. Diaphragms are also available, but because they must be fitted by a trained clinician, they are not as popular as condoms. In addition, the Chinese manufacture another kind of "paper" contraceptive, film containing a spermicide, which is inserted like a vaginal foam or suppository and melts in five minutes.

At the present time the IUD and male and female sterilization account for nearly 80% of contraceptive practice. Between 1971 and 1978, during the third campaign for population control, 94 million IUDs were inserted. More than 20 million Chinese women and 14 million men have been sterilized but, because of the concern about the loss of an only child, the procedure is no longer as popular, and the number of sterilizations appears to have decreased markedly. In fact, in some major medical centers, procedures to reverse sterilization outnumber sterilizations themselves. The reversal of tubal ligation (female sterilization) is fairly successful, and studies are under way to improve the outcome of vasectomy (male sterilization) reversal. Considerable support and research has gone into investigating a male birth control pill made of gossypol (a substance derived from cottonseed), but the process is far from being perfected. Abortion is widely practiced, both as a method of birth control and as a back-up technique in the event of contraceptive failure, and is easily available at no cost to the individual. Both abortion and sterilization allow for a leave of absence from work, which provides an additional incentive.

Problems not yet solved

The stated goal of the Chinese government is to bring the present population growth to a halt around the year 2000, with an anticipated end point of 1.2 billion people. This goal is based upon the premise that total population should be directly related to the ability of society to provide adequate resources and services. It is further planned in the years following 2000 to reduce the population to 600 million–700 million. It has even been suggested that by the year 2000 China may be able to return to the two-child family, as long as the nation's total population remains at the desired levels.

As the result of government pressures and the accessibility of contraception, sterilization, and abortion, the birthrates have again begun to drop. However, despite the fact that the Chinese family-planning program has been both vigorous and successful, it is clear that the population problem is far from solved. Of the present population, 32% are under age 15, almost half are under 21, and 65% are under the age of 30. There are more than 100 million women in the reproductive age group who either have had their one "allotted" child or who, although they have no children, live in areas where the birth quotas have already been attained. All of these women are supposed to prevent pregnancy.

Attempts to make accurate projections of the growth of China's population have been hampered by the fact that it is difficult to get accurate census data. On the one hand, births tend to be reported more accurately than deaths, since birth records are necessary in order to get additional rations, housing, and farmland allocations. On the other hand, the census in 1982 found 3.2 million births—or 15%—that had not been included in the 1981 registration reports. One theory for this large number of unrecorded births is that the underreporting was deliberate—many communities might like to claim that they have achieved their assigned family-planning goals when, in actuality, they have exceeded the allotted number of births. There has also been speculation that some deaths may not have been reported, inasmuch as a death would result in decreased rations and financial allowances.

A number of interesting and important observations can be made on the basis of the age distribution of the Chinese population as determined in the Third National Census, conducted in 1982. China's population is now changing from an increasing to a static number. The proportion of children age 12 and younger is decreasing as the result of family-planning activities. The number of women in the childbearing age and the proportion

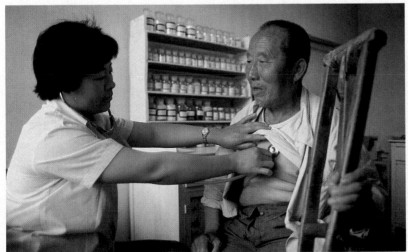

Jim Pozarik

In China, as in other rapidly developing countries, population growth is slowing, people are living longer, and the proportion of elderly people is increasing. The aging population will require increasing resources for its social, financial, and medical support. (Left) A senior citizen receives a medical checkup in a home for the elderly.

of working-age individuals is going up because of the earlier baby boom. Probably of the greatest importance, however, is the fact that the percentage of people middle-aged and older is also climbing. In 1980 the number of Chinese over the age of 60 was estimated to be 80 million, or 8% of the population. Because of the increase in life expectancy, this number is predicted to rise to 11% by the year 2000, and this group may constitute 33% of the total population within 50 years.

Thus, the Chinese population is an aging one and, as in other countries, support for these older individuals is expected to become an increasingly critical social and economic issue. The Chinese government is attempting to deal with this problem in a variety of ways. People employed by the state are guaranteed pensions. In rural areas those who cannot be supported by their families are guaranteed food, clothing, medical care, housing, and burial expenses. They may live in homes set up by the state or in collectives established for older people. On the positive side, this group makes a major contribution to the general economy, as older people have an increasing share of the responsibility for children when both parents work.

The price of progress

China's reemergence into the world and the reopening of its doors to foreigners have wrought many changes. On balance, modernization has brought major benefits to the Chinese people. However, progress has not been achieved without cost. The country's cooperative medical system is being seriously threatened. Formerly, part of the common harvest was allocated to a health fund that provided primary care and health insurance. Now, with each household taking responsibility for its own agricultural produce, this contribution is no longer being made. Many of the newly affluent peasants demand a higher quality of health care, placing the country's higher level medical facilities under great stress. In addition, the number of barefoot doctors is decreasing—in order to earn more money, many have become farmers.

A group of card players who reside in a collective established for the elderly enjoy a leisurely afternoon's game in a sunny room in their shared home.

These robust youngsters make it difficult to think of a time when Chinese children died of starvation or were sold into prostitution. Today in China—as in other countries around the world—children are recognized as the nation's most precious resource.

Even the nature of disease has undergone a major transformation. Perhaps one price the Chinese are paying for modernization is that medical problems are becoming increasingly similar to those seen in the West. Young Chinese men are heavy cigarette smokers, as are the Chinese political leaders. Women do not smoke in the urban areas, but smoking is common among rural women. As a result, while the incidence of tuberculosis has decreased, lung cancer is reportedly on the increase. Furthermore, China is now facing health problems resulting from environmental pollution. Malignancies and cardiovascular diseases—the leading killers in the West—are becoming more common causes of death.

Some parting thoughts

The mingling of old and new, traditional and modern, East and West, yin and yang—all combine to make the first-time visitor to China alternately bewildered and enchanted. The traveler from the United States cannot help but be overwhelmed, and even somewhat intimidated at first, by the vast size of the country, the crush of people in the streets, and the all-pervading sense of antiquity.

Our entire medical delegation (health care professionals from across the United States, including doctors, nurses, educators, and researchers) left China feeling that we had been privileged to witness awesome accomplishments in improving the health and well-being of a vast population. We saw and learned more than we had ever envisioned we would. Our intention had been to "share" medical knowledge with our gracious Chinese hosts (also representatives of the health field). We only hope that we contributed something meaningful that will make a small difference in China's future health care.

111

Penetrating the Mysteries of Human Immunity

by Harold M. Schmeck, Jr.

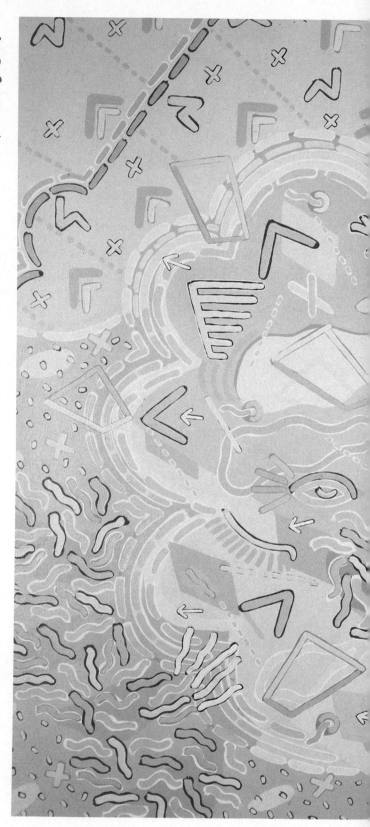

A 28-year-old Filipino woman living in the U.S. had a skin rash, anemia, liver problems, and an overall feeling of weakness, as well as some other, more subtle symptoms. Doctors diagnosed her illness as systemic lupus erythematosus, a serious and sometimes fatal disease of the immune system. A profusion of laboratory tests confirmed the diagnosis. The doctors treated the patient with hormones and anti-inflammatory drugs, but without significant improvement. Meanwhile, other complications developed, including failing kidney and thyroid function. The doctors did more tests, reaffirming the diagnosis, and prepared for a set of more radical treatments used in more advanced cases of the disease.

At this point, however, the patient abruptly left her home in the state of Washington and returned to the remote village in the Philippines where she had been born. Neither her family in the U.S. nor her doctors expected to see her alive again. To the general amazement of all, the young woman returned three weeks later, a picture of health—and she remained so. She explained that the witch doctor in her native village had removed a curse put on her by a rejected suitor. Two years later, according to a case report in the *Journal of the American Medical Association,* she gave birth to a normal, healthy daughter.

The brain and immunity: tantalizing links

Years ago embarrassment would have been the primary response of Western physicians to this apparent triumph of magic over medical science. Today doctors see such events as further dramatic evidence of the links between the brain and nervous system and the body's other most vital and complex instrument—the immune defense system. The brain and the immune system are also the body's two most important contacts with the outside world. Everything we hear, see, feel, or imagine is processed by the brain, whereas the immune system reacts to virtually every virus, bacterium, or other foreign particle that invades the body.

The mysterious power of the witch doctor to effect cures, once seen by medical scientists as a triumph of coincidence, is being reexamined in the light of emerging discoveries about the discipline known as psychoneuroimmunology—the study of the ways in which the brain influences immunity.

Harold M. Schmeck, Jr., *is a science correspondent for the* New York Times.

(Overleaf) "Gris" by Andrew Keating, © 1980, acrylic on canvas, 48 × 68 inches; photograph, Jim Ball

The physician who reported the case wondered what internal immune mechanisms the witch doctor had tapped by his suggestions and just how he had done it. No one knows the answers, but few scientists would doubt that it was somehow the influence of the brain at work on some important immune mechanisms. The growing evidence of links between brain and immune defenses constitutes only one of the frontiers of modern immunology that is being expanded by current research.

Scientists at the University of California at San Francisco, for example, discovered that a long-known brain chemical, substance P, also has links to the immune defense system. They found recognition sites, called receptors, on the surfaces of one of the most important varieties of immune defense cells, the T lymphocytes, to which molecules of substance P would fit like a key in a lock. When substance P finds and attaches to its matching receptor on a T cell, the event evidently acts as a signal, setting off a cascade of reactions that stimulates the immune defenses to extra effort in the part of the body where the signal originated.

There is a logical reason why this seeming link between the brain and immune defense cells could be valuable to the body. Substance P has long been known to play a role in the perception of pain. The existence of pain suggests injury, and the containment and repair of injury usually require the mobilization of the immune defenses.

Derangements of the immunologic system are involved in the group of disorders known as autoimmune diseases; as the name implies, they involve some malfunction of the immune response in which the body's defense system attacks its own tissues. The disease that affected the young woman from the Philippines, mentioned above, is believed to be an autoimmune disorder; so are myasthenia gravis, rheumatoid arthritis, and many others. Even before the discovery relating T cells and substance P, another team of scientists from the University of California at San Francisco had found direct evidence that the same brain chemical, substance P, worsens the damage in arthritic joints.

Another tantalizing link between brain science and immunology was discovered by scientists at the U.S. National Institutes of Health (NIH), Bethesda, Maryland, and the University of Alabama Medical School at Birmingham. Their research used a strategy borrowed from the celebrated experiments of the Russian psychologist Ivan Pavlov, who trained dogs to associate the ringing of a bell with the presence of food and showed that thoroughly "conditioned" animals would salivate at the sound of the bell, even when no food was present.

To test how far brain-immune links could be extended, the U.S. investigators "trained" immune defense cells of laboratory mice to become active on the cue of a signal equally as irrelevant to immunity as the ringing of a bell is to appetite. The mice were exposed to an unusual odor, and some of them were also given injections of a chemical that is known to increase the activity of specific immune system cells called natural killer cells. As expected, the mice injected with the stimulating chemical did respond with a boost in natural killer cell activity. But the remarkable finding was that mice both exposed to the odor and given the injections later showed an increase in natural killer cell activity when exposed to the odor alone, without any injection. It appeared that their immune defenses were exhibiting a conditioned response to a stimulus, in much the same way as Pavlov's dogs had been conditioned to respond to the bell. This experiment clearly seemed to show the brain's influence over immune function.

Comparable experiments had been conducted earlier by a research team at the University of Rochester (New York) School of Medicine and Dentistry.

Although it has been established that certain neurochemicals are able to influence specific components of the immune system, scientists do not agree about the means by which the human brain acts on immune function. In fact, how—or to what extent—an individual's state of mind, emotions, or beliefs affect health and disease is now a matter of heated debate. On the one hand, it is well accepted that stress can alter a person's immune status. In one study of this phenomenon, medical students under pressure at exam time showed a decrease in the activity of natural killer cells, crucial components of the immune system. In addition to academic stress (above), the stress of bereavement has also been demonstrated to affect immunity. More controversial, however, are studies of cancer patients in which the individual's attitude is claimed to influence the course of the disease. A 1985 report of a study at King's College Hospital, London (table left), found a strong relationship between the emotions expressed after mastectomy and ten-year survival rates. Other studies of cancer patients indicate that the severity of the disease, not the individual's attitude, is most influential in predicting long-term outcome. This controversy is likely to continue.

Emotional reaction and survival				
psychological response three months after cancer surgery	after ten years			
	alive, no recurrence	alive, with cancer	dead	total
denial	5	0	5	10
fighting spirit	6	1	3	10
stoic acceptance	7	1	24	32
helplessness/ hopelessness	1	0	4	5
total	19	2	36	57

From Keith W. Pettingale *et al.*, "Mental Attitudes to Cancer: An Additional Prognostic Factor," *The Lancet*, vol. 1, no. 8431 (March 30, 1985), p. 750

In these studies rats were given liquid saccharin to drink; some of the animals were also injected with cyclophosphamide, a powerful immunosuppressive drug (*i.e.,* one that suppresses the body's normal immune responses). Later, when some of the animals were given saccharin alone, their immune response to injections of a foreign substance was impaired. In fact, even before the report of the case of the Filipino woman who had lupus, the scientists in Rochester had used the saccharin-cyclophosphamide conditioning routine to treat mice suffering from the same autoimmune disease.

Autoimmunity as therapy

Although the cause of systemic lupus erythematosus is unknown, the underlying mechanism of the disorder is understood. For some reason, the victim's immune defenses begin to see some of the body's own tissues as foreign and attack them as though they were invaders. In the experiments in Rochester, some of the "conditioned" mice with lupus actually lived longer than other mice who succumbed to the disease, evidently because their trained response to saccharin reduced the virulence of the immunologic attack against their own tissues.

The Rochester research team was most cautious in the conclusions they drew from the experiments, but it is easy enough to see how such a treatment might be applied to some kinds of human illness. Currently, immunosuppressive drugs are used for many therapeutic purposes, notably to treat autoimmune diseases such as lupus and to protect transplanted hearts, livers, kidneys, or other organs from being rejected by the recipient's immune defenses. But these drugs sometimes have devastating side effects. If conditioning of the sort described above can temporarily suppress normal immune responses, could it be used as an alternative to potentially dangerous drug therapy?

The researchers refrained from such conclusions, but they offered as a hypothesis the idea that such a regimen might "be applicable in the pharmacotherapeutic control and regulation of a variety of physiologic systems."

Mind over disease?

Today there is considerable debate on the question of just how much influence the brain exerts on the immune defenses. Can a person's mental state actually alter the course of a disease by affecting the immune system? Age-old experience suggests that a patient's emotional attitude can have an effect on physical disease, and some researchers assert that there is objective evidence to support the idea.

In one study of a group of breast cancer patients, psychologist Sandra M. Levy of the University of Pittsburgh, Pennsylvania, found that women who reacted to their illness with anger and a determination to fight actually lived longer, as a group, than women who had a totally passive attitude. Levy, however, emphasized that a good emotional attitude is no substitute for good treatment. "The most important determinant of cancer outcome is the biology of the tumor and the medical treatment," she said. Nonetheless, other similar studies of cancer patients have also come to the conclusion that the individual's state of mind influences outcome and survival. Yet a

(Top) T. R. Broker—Phototake; (center) Yoav Levy—Phototake; (bottom) Phillip A. Harrington—Peter Arnold, Inc.

1985 editorial in the *New England Journal of Medicine,* citing much evidence to the contrary, concluded that the notion of mind over disease is "largely folklore." There is still considerable debate over which is more important—what kind of disease the patient has or what kind of patient has the disease.

Vital to life

The key characteristics of the immune defense system are its complexity; its incredible facility for recognizing "self," *i.e.,* its own tissues, as distinguished from everything foreign, or "nonself"; and its ability both to remember nonself invaders and to react to them. The person who has once had measles or has been immunized against the disease retains an immunologic memory of the measles virus for years afterward, probably for a lifetime. Years after the original experience, a new assault by the measles virus will be stopped in its tracks. The immune system remembers the virus and mobilizes at once against the remembered enemy.

Immunity is vital to life. An infant born without immune defenses is doomed unless he or she is defended continually against all manner of infectious diseases. Some infections that would be so mild as to pass unnoticed in a child with ordinarily robust defenses would be deadly to a child whose immune system did not function.

David, the Houston, Texas, youngster known to the media as the "bubble boy," suffered from a profound lack of immune defenses. He died in 1984 after 12 years of a life that had to be guarded, from the moment of his birth, with incredible diligence. David's parents, doctors, and nurses kept him alive with liberal use of antibiotics and, more important, by keeping him totally isolated from the world's germs. He lived all of his 12 years in germfree environments that were maintained within plastic tents ("bubbles") and "space suits" that shielded him from every possible source of infection. The heroic efforts that had to be taken to give David even 12 years of life testify to the importance of the immune system that had never developed properly in his body.

Medical science's "most brightly lit domain"

In the past two or three decades, the science of immunology has flowered dramatically. This has occurred partly because of its importance in human health and disease but also because the new tools of molecular biology lend themselves so well to the study of immune processes.

Immunologists were among the first to take up the techniques made available by recombinant DNA research, known popularly as gene splicing. An important related development, the creation of monoclonal antibodies—highly specific antibodies produced in the laboratory—now used for all manner of testing, diagnostic studies, and research, is itself an accomplishment of immunology. Today these special antibodies are an indispensible tool for immunologic research.

According to William Paul of the National Institute of Allergy and Infectious Diseases, a branch of the NIH, "Progress in immunology has been a matter of fantastic technological progress. We have been able to do experiments that, ten years ago, were only dreams." Sir Peter Medawar, the British

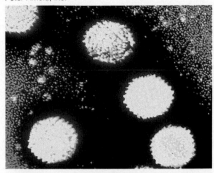

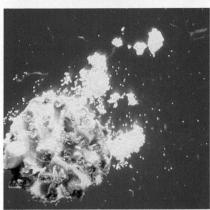

There are literally millions of antigens—substances capable of stimulating an immune response—from disease-causing organisms like the adenovirus (top) to pollen (middle) and house-dust mites (bottom). The human immune system is apparently endowed at birth with the ability to respond to every antigen it will ever encounter.

117

scientist who in 1960 won the Nobel Prize for Physiology or Medicine for his pioneering contributions to immunology, has described that science as "the most brightly lit domain of the medical sciences."

The immune defenses exert their influence on every part of the living body, protecting, regulating, stimulating, as the circumstances require. Cells of the system "talk" to each other continually in a conversation that makes the difference between health and illness, life and death.

Antibodies—various, intricate, and remarkable

To nonscientists the best known components of the immune defense system are the protective antibodies that circulate through the body to combat invasion from bacteria, viruses, and other agents of disease. Antibodies are only one part of the defensive scheme, but their part alone is more various, intricate, and remarkable than early immunologists could ever have imagined.

Immunology embraces two different, but closely intertwined, defense systems. Scientists call them humoral immunity and cellular, or cell-mediated, immunity. Humoral immunity, which relies on chemicals either secreted during the immune response or already circulating in the body, includes the familiar world of the antibodies. These are specially made proteins that act almost like guided missiles, seeking out and destroying foreign invaders such as bacteria and viruses. Actually, antibodies do not ordinarily do the destroying themselves. Instead, they attach themselves to the enemy and call forth a deadly response by other parts of the defense system. Just how this occurs has begun to be understood only in recent years.

The antibodies themselves are particularly remarkable in two respects. First, they exhibit exquisite precision in choosing their targets; it is a commonplace observation that antibodies can easily distinguish the three different types of polio virus. In fact, a single clone (*i.e.*, genetically identical population) of antibodies is so finely tuned that it is able to distinguish one component of such a virus particle from all the others and can make the distinction between two proteins that differ by only one chemical subunit among hundreds. Second, the human body is thought to be endowed at birth with the genetic ability to make every antibody it will ever need in defense against any germ the world can produce. The immense diversity of antibodies and the strategy the body uses to produce them are among the most remarkable aspects of the whole story of immune function.

Keys to the city

Like many other mechanisms of biology, the functions of antibodies depend ultimately on shapes. The part of an antibody that recognizes its destined target does so because its shape fits the shape of a portion of the target, just as a key fits its lock. Almost any substance—the surface protein of a virus, a red blood cell, the complex sugar on the surface of the pneumococcus bacterium—presents one or more shapes that can be recognized by the appropriate antibody and, therefore, can evoke an immune response. By definition, anything that can evoke such a response by antibodies is called an antigen. There are uncounted millions of antigens.

(Opposite page) The human immune defense system has two branches, cellular immunity and humoral immunity, which act together to identify, disarm, and destroy invading foreign particles. Cellular immunity involves many types of cells, including B and T lymphocytes (also called B cells and T cells), accessory cells such as macrophages, and natural killer cells, so named because they have the ability to kill tumor cells. Humoral immunity relies on elements activated during the immune response—for example, antibodies—and substances already circulating in the body. An example of the latter is complement, proteins that combine with antibodies to cause the destruction of antigens.

118

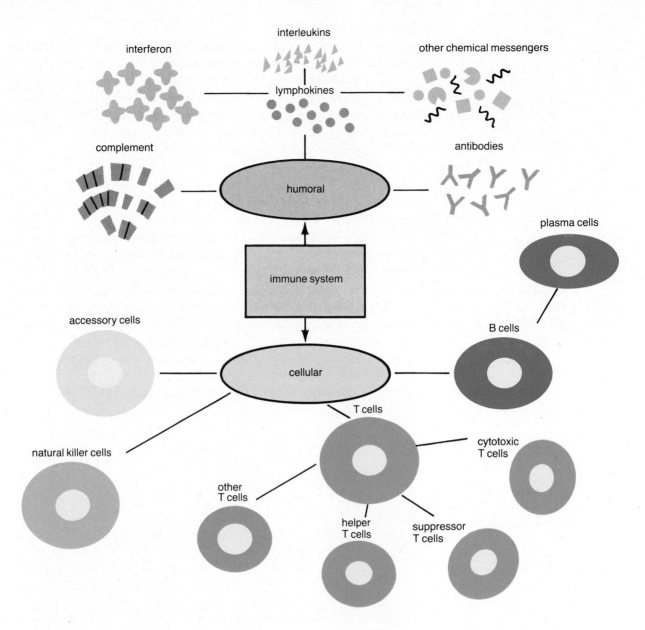

interferon

interleukins

other chemical messengers

lymphokines

complement

humoral

antibodies

plasma cells

immune system

B cells

accessory cells

cellular

T cells

cytotoxic T cells

natural killer cells

other T cells

helper T cells

suppressor T cells

Furthermore, the antibody-making machinery of the human body apparently can make antibodies so profusely and with such variety that one or another will fit any antigen that will ever be encountered—every antigen shape that nature has devised and every one ever synthesized in the laboratory.

In concept it is a bit like giving some favored visitor *all* the keys to the city—except that it is much more than that. The feat of the immune defense system is really comparable to giving that visitor, in advance, not only all the existing keys to the city but every key that the city's locksmiths will ever be capable of manufacturing. Indeed, some immunologists today suspect that the human body carries within it the images of all possible antigens and that this archive might be exploited in the future to create a whole new realm of therapeutic and anti-infectious drugs.

119

Shuffled genes

Much modern research has been devoted to understanding how this seemingly infinite variety of antibodies can be generated. Antibodies are proteins, and the normal rule is that each different protein in the human body is made according to the chemical blueprint carried by a single gene. But the total number of genes in each person's genetic archive is estimated to be somewhere between 50,000 and 100,000. How then does the immune system produce millions of different antibodies? This question has puzzled scientists for decades.

Using the methods made possible by recombinant DNA research, investigators have solved this mystery to the satisfaction of most immunologists. Susumu Tonegawa of the Massachusetts Institute of Technology (MIT) has been a leader in this research. Studies by Tonegawa and others showed that the diversity of shapes in the keylike part of the antibody molecule is achieved by a complex process of rearranging and shuffling genes. This was a revolutionary idea because it had previously been thought that genes were relatively static entities, not capable of being rearranged drastically in the cells where they function. Now it appears that the genes for antibodies are shuffled together and reassorted to produce an incredible variety of shapes at the antibodies' keylike articulating sites, while other portions of

A computer image of an antibody molecule (top right) shows its characteristic Y shape. The molecular subunits of all antibodies are similar. Each is composed of four protein chains (distinguished on the basis of molecular weight)—two identical heavy chains, which extend from the stem of the Y into the arms, and two identical light chains, which are confined to the arms. Each chain has both constant regions (white and yellow in computer image) and variable regions (red), depicted in a highly simplified form in the diagram. At the end of each of the variable regions, a complex folded structure (represented in the diagram as a series of three loops) constitutes the site where antigens bind to the antibody.

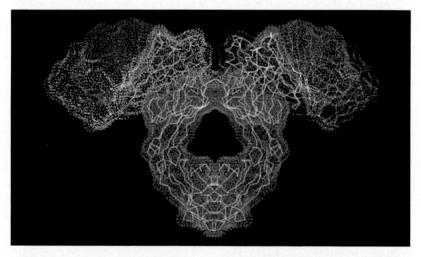

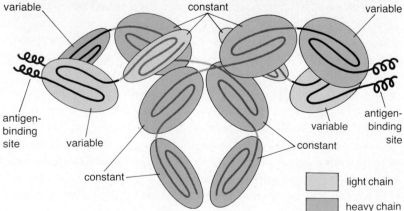

variable · constant · variable · antigen-binding site · variable · constant · variable · antigen-binding site · constant

light chain

heavy chain

Photo and computer graphic model by Arthur J. Olson of the Research Institute of Scripps Clinic. Crystallographic data from the laboratory of David R. Davies, National Institutes of Health. Computer software by T. J. O'Donnell, M. L. Connolly, and A. J. Olson

the antibody structure remain constant. Antibodies are Y-shaped proteins; the flared, opposing ends of the Y contain the variable regions that give antibodies their great versatility.

The antibody-production process has an additional characteristic, according to the MIT researchers, that adds even more possible variety in the products. All genes are subject to random, small changes, called mutations, that occur at a slow, somewhat predictable rate. This slow "drizzle" of random changes into the genetic material, DNA (deoxyribonucleic acid), is the driving force of evolution. In most genes the process is very slow indeed, but in the system that produces antibodies there appears to be a special enzyme—as yet unidentified—that speeds the rate of mutation many hundredfold and adds significantly to the diversity of antibodies.

Cellular immunity

Antibodies are protective proteins that circulate in the blood and lurk in the linings of the nose and intestinal tract to intercept bacteria and other causes of infection. The main purpose of a vaccine is to stimulate the body to produce antibodies against a given disease-causing organism. Vaccination sets up an artificial immunologic memory of the invader and thus arms the body against any future attack.

But antibodies must work in cooperation with the other arm of the immune defense system, cellular immunity. This system involves the white blood cells known as lymphocytes and accessory cells like macrophages. For about 20 years it has been known that there are two categories of lymphocytes, B lymphocytes (B cells) and T lymphocytes (T cells). During the past two decades a wealth of new information has been amassed on the varieties and functions of these defense cells.

All lymphocytes originate in the bone marrow in the form of precursors, called stem cells, from which the more specialized cells evolve. The cells destined to be T cells migrate to the thymus gland, where they are processed in ways that are only partly understood. When the system is working properly, part of the processing appears to eliminate all the clones of cells that would naturally attack tissues of the individual's own body. What emerges from the thymus is a host of cells that are capable of recognizing virtually anything that is foreign but spare the body's own cells and tissues, which are carriers of "self" antigens.

The B cells, the other main category of lymphocytes, are the source of antibodies. Each different population of B cells carries a different antibody shape on the cell surface. When stimulated by the presence of an invading germ, B cells give rise to "factory" cells, called plasma cells, that secrete large quantities of antibodies, each formed in the image of the one carried by the original B cell.

There are at least three fundamental types of T cells: cytotoxic T cells, which kill their chosen targets directly; suppressor T cells; and helper T cells. They act together in complex ways and also interact with other biochemical components of the defense system.

One of the key roles attributed to the suppressor T cells is to limit an immune response, to ensure that it does not go too far. Overreactive im-

121

The body's response to invasion by a foreign substance (antigen) involves the cooperation of several different components of the immune system. First the antigen must be engulfed by an antigen-presenting cell (a), in this case a macrophage. The antigen is processed within the macrophage (b) and then displayed on its surface. Displayed antigen is recognized by a helper T cell (c), which thereby becomes activated. The activated helper T cell then activates B cells carrying the same processed antigen (d). Once activated, B cells proliferate and differentiate into subpopulations. Some of the B cells become antibody-secreting plasma cells (e). The antibodies they secrete bind to the antigen (f), thus targeting it for destruction by other components of the system, including macrophages.

receptor
antigen
activated B cell
plasma cell
activated helper T cell
d
e
antibody
f
a
c
antigen-presenting macrophage
b
processed antigen
macrophage

(Opposite page) A laboratory technician (top) screens samples of serum (the liquid portion of the blood) from blood donors for the presence of antibody to HTLV-III, the AIDS virus, to ensure that the blood does not contain the virus. The test most widely used for this purpose, called ELISA (enzyme-linked immunosorbent assay), relies on a natural immune response, the affinity of antibody for antigen, the antigen in this case being inactivated AIDS virus. In the first step of the process (bottom), a polystyrene bead is coated with inactivated AIDS virus and incubated with a serum sample (a). If AIDS antibodies are present in the serum, they bind to the virus on the bead. The bead is washed, thus removing any unbound material. Next the bead is placed in a test tube with a second antibody that has been tagged with an enzyme (b). If AIDS antibody is present, the second antibody binds to it. The bead is then washed again. Finally the bead is immersed in a chemical solution that will change color if the enzyme is present (c). If the solution changes color, the test is positive for the presence of AIDS antibody.

munity can become a devastating autoimmune disease. Suppressor T cells are thought to prevent this kind of disaster. But functions of this sort are difficult to document because they depend on the absence of an immune effect, rather than on the presence of something easier to observe and quantify, such as the cell-killing properties of cytotoxic T cells. Accordingly, the functions of suppressor T cells are a subject of some debate among immunologists. The majority opinion appears to be that suppressor and helper T cells together are the main regulators of the immune system.

But although the name helper may sound condescending—as if they simply "help out" in various ways—these cells are apparently the crux of the whole immensely complicated system of cellular immunity. Anthony Fauci, an immunologist and the director of the NIH's National Institute of Allergy and Infectious Diseases, describes the helper T cell as the leader of the entire "immunologic orchestra." Helper T cells are usually necessary to aid B cells in the sequence of events that produces a crop of antibodies. They also help the cytotoxic T cells prepare to carry out their mission; activate the scavenger white blood cells, called macrophages, that engulf and digest foreign particles; and secrete a variety of substances called lymphokines that are part of the humoral mechanism and that implement many of the "orchestra leader's" tasks of activation and coordination.

To give an example, the lymphokine called the macrophage migration inhibition factor is one of the most intensively studied of this class of immune substances. This factor has a stimulating effect on macrophages, causing them to be more efficient in engulfing and digesting the germs they attack. In addition, it stops macrophages from migrating through the body, as they usually do; the consequence is that macrophages accumulate at the site where the "invasion" of foreign particles is taking place and destroy the invaders.

122

The potential for practical application

The chemical and cellular details of immunology constitute one of the most fascinating puzzles of biologic research. But the profound interest they hold for some immunologists stems from the practical uses to which they can be put.

Monoclonal antibodies demonstrate both sides of the coin. As the name implies, each species of monoclonal antibody stems from a single clone, and all the antibodies of that clone are, by definition, genetically identical. The technique for making them was developed by César Milstein and Georges Köhler in England about a decade ago for purposes of fundamental scientific research. Until Milstein and Köhler completed the research, they hardly considered practical applications. But once monoclonal antibodies had been made, their potential applications were impossible to ignore. The scientists' first research report on the subject, published in 1975, ended with the now-famous understatement that "such cultures could be valuable for medical and industrial use."

Monoclonal antibodies are now used in biologic laboratories throughout the world. They have applications in diagnostic tests, in treatment of disease, in the search for rare substances of potential importance, and in other processes so various that they fill entire catalogs and, indeed, have generated a commercial industry devoted to their development and manufacture.

Another example of the application of immunologic research—this one a field still in its early stages of development—involves a group of T-cell products, the class of lymphokines that are now known as interleukins. At least four are known, the latest having been discovered in 1986 by Ellis L. Reinherz and his colleagues at the Dana-Farber Cancer Institute and Harvard Medical School in Boston. Named interleukin-4A, it is produced exclusively by helper T cells and stimulates the immune defense system by activating other T cells from an inactive condition called the resting state. The scientists believe interleukin-4A and modifications of it may potentially prove useful in many ways, both as artificial stimulants of immunity and as suppressors of too much immune activity.

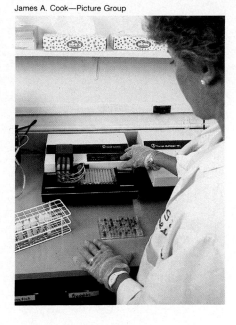

Blood test for AIDS antibody

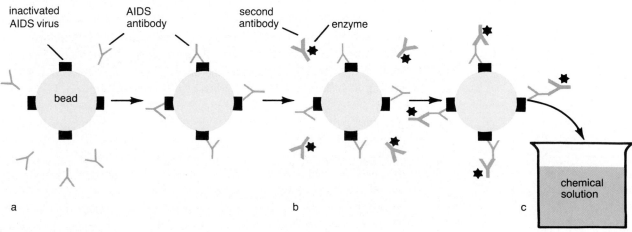

Source: Abbott Laboratories

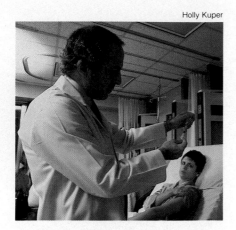

One group of recently discovered immune system products, called lymphokines, shows great promise in the treatment of cancer. In animal experiments the lymphokine known as tumor necrosis factor caused cancer cells to explode, while it spared normal cells from harm. Now researchers such as Jordan U. Gutterman (above), of the M. D. Anderson Hospital and Tumor Institute, Houston, Texas, are testing tumor necrosis factor against a variety of human cancers.

The best known member of the interleukin group, interleukin-2, was originally named T-cell growth factor by its discoverer, Robert C. Gallo of the U.S. National Cancer Institute (NCI). It, too, started out as a problem in basic research: what substance stimulates T cells to grow, and how can it be isolated and used to produce quantities of T cells in the laboratory? But interleukin-2 quickly became a valuable tool for other research. Used to enhance T-cell growth in laboratory cell cultures, it was a key element in the discovery of a human cancer virus, now called HTLV-I, which apparently causes malignant growth of T cells. More recently, interleukin-2 was used as a laboratory tool by the researchers who discovered HTLV-III, the virus that causes AIDS (acquired immune deficiency syndrome).

In 1985 interleukin-2 attracted considerable attention with a report of its use in a new cancer treatment developed by NCI scientists. A research team led by Steven A. Rosenberg developed a system for exposing a cancer patient's T cells to interleukin-2 in an attempt to activate the T cells against the cancer. The treatment, called adoptive immunotherapy, worked so well in laboratory animals that it was subsequently tried in a few carefully selected cancer patients. It worked well in some patients, too, although it produced serious side effects in some of them.

Although cautious about the potential of the treatment, officials of the NCI considered the overall results of these early trials encouraging enough to warrant testing on a larger scale. As a result, the NCI announced that in 1986 six other medical centers would begin experimental trials of the new treatment. Only relatively few patients can be treated at any one time, and each must be chosen with extreme care to provide a fair test of the method as well as maximum hope for the individual.

Immunity and tissue types

On another front entirely, scientists are making important progress in matching a class of white blood cell antigens, the human leukocyte antigens, with individual susceptibility to various diseases. These "self" antigens, known to immunologists as the HLA system, were first studied because they were found to be important determinants of tissue compatibility between donors and recipients of transplanted organs.

Scientists discovered that the spectrum of HLA antigens in any one person's tissues represents a "signature" of the individual's tissue type that is analogous to blood types (which are based on differentiation of the antigens on the surfaces of red blood cells). The HLA tissue types proved to be much more varied and complex than blood types—but fully as important to the success of organ transplantation as blood typing is to blood transfusion. HLA antigens are also helpful in identification and are accepted by the courts of many states as evidence in paternity suits.

Some scientists believe the HLA antigens may have important functions in the regulation of the immune defenses. Continued study of HLA types has also revealed another important aspect of these antigens; certain HLA profiles turn up significantly more often than one would expect by chance in people who have certain diseases. Generally these are diseases in which autoimmunity or some other immune abnormality is a factor. Systemic lupus erythematosus seems to go with one HLA profile, for example, and juvenile diabetes often matches with another. Other diseases that show such links are Addison's disease, a disorder of the adrenal glands; multiple sclerosis, a degenerative disease of the central nervous system; and myasthenia gravis, which affects the muscles. According to two experts on the subject, Paul I. Terasaki and Jawahar L. Tiwari of the University of California at Los Angeles, HLA antigens are associated with disease susceptibility to a greater extent than any other known human genetic marker.

Immunology has made great strides in the understanding, diagnosis, and treatment of many diseases. Advances in tissue and blood typing have made it possible to eliminate diseases that were once beyond the reach of medical science. Rh disease of the newborn, also known as erythroblastosis fetalis, is an important case in point. It is caused by blood type incompatibility between mother and fetus. Today the condition is prevented by routine immunologic treatment of women whose children might be affected. Before this treatment was developed in the 1960s, Rh disease was known simply as a "grave inherited disease" that often killed newborns or fetuses still in the womb.

Vaccines are immunologic weapons against disease. Today new approaches to vaccine design foreshadow a whole new generation of vaccines, more effective and more widely useful than ever before. If vaccination was to be added to the list of achievements credited to the science of immunology, this branch of study might be considered more impressive than any other field of medical science.

Zeva Oelbaum

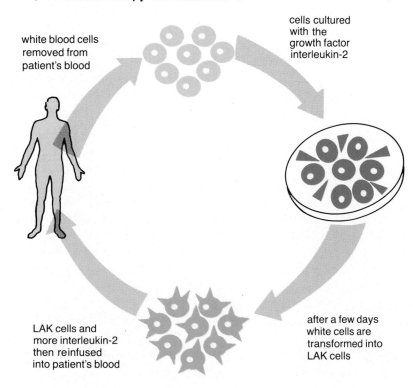

Adoptive immunotherapy with interleukin-2

white blood cells removed from patient's blood

cells cultured with the growth factor interleukin-2

after a few days white cells are transformed into LAK cells

LAK cells and more interleukin-2 then reinfused into patient's blood

A class of lymphokines known as the interleukins activates other components of the immune defenses. One of these immune system boosters is interleukin-2, which causes the body's own tumor-fighting cells to proliferate. In a fermenting vessel (above) bacteria genetically engineered to produce interleukin-2 multiply in a liquid growth culture, producing a sufficient amount of the substance for various research purposes. Investigators at the U.S. National Cancer Institute, Bethesda, Maryland, are using interleukin-2 in a pioneering cancer treatment called adoptive immunotherapy. In this procedure, shown in schematic form at left, some of the patient's white blood cells are removed from the body. Incubated with interleukin-2, the cells are transformed into lymphokine-activated killer cells, or LAK cells, and reinfused into the body along with additional interleukin-2. While extremely promising, adoptive immunotherapy is still in an experimental stage.

Mysteries yet to solve

In addition to its very real and practical applications, immunology remains very much a realm of basic science. Specialists at the cutting edge of this discipline are often occupied with questions so deeply embedded in the intricacies of immune function that their excitement is difficult for the outsider to either understand or appreciate.

William Paul of NIH has noted that, before they are mobilized for defense against a disease-causing organism, none of the many categories of immune defense cells is present in a large enough population to accomplish their defensive task or to lend themselves to study. Much of immunology, therefore, is a study of the selective growth in the laboratory of specific clones of cells and the regulation of that growth in the human body—particularly in the body that is under assault from infection or autoimmune processes.

Another subject crucial to immunology is biologic communication and recognition. The surface membranes of cells are studded with recognition sites—receptors—that are vital to communication. Their function can be compared to that of the earpiece of a telephone; without the receptor the cell does not "hear" the message no matter how loudly its signal is being transmitted.

For years immunologists have known that antibodies themselves are the receptors on the surfaces of B cells; that knowledge helped greatly in elucidating the functions of these cells. But the identity of the receptors on T cells remained frustratingly mysterious. Some scientists described this elusive receptor as the "Holy Grail" of immunology. A 1983 textbook referred to the puzzle as "the T-cell receptor enigma." It might have been logical to assume that the T-cell receptor was also an antibodylike molecule, similar to the Y-shaped protein that serves the B cell as its recognition site. But a great deal of research led to the conclusion that this was not the case.

The mystery was finally solved within the past two years through the combined work of several research teams. The first step in the unmasking of the T-cell receptor was the discovery that it consisted of a protein made up of two chains of amino acids. Even before they could be thoroughly analyzed, they were labeled alpha chain and beta chain. This part of the discovery is credited to research teams led by Ellis Reinherz of the Dana-Farber Cancer Institute, Boston; James Allison of the University of Texas at Smithville; and Philippa Marrack and John Kappler of the National Jewish Hospital and Research Center in Denver, Colorado.

Identifying the genes for the two chains and working out the details of their chemical structure took longer. The first to be elucidated was the beta chain. The gene that serves as the blueprint for the beta chain was identified and was used to grow copies of the chain in the laboratory. This accomplishment is credited to researchers led by Mark M. Davis of Stanford University and Stephen M. Hedrick of the University of California at San Diego, who had previously worked together on the problem at the NIH. A Canadian group, led by Tak W. Mak of the Ontario Cancer Institute and the University of Toronto, worked with human T cells, while the U.S. scientists used those of mice; however, the chemistry of the two proved to be so similar that they were clearly variants of the same thing.

T lymphocytes, or T cells, fight infection on two fronts: they react directly to viruses and play an auxiliary part in the immune system's response to bacterial infection. They are also central in the recognition of "self" and "nonself" proteins and, therefore, are important in the rejection of foreign tissue, as occurs in organ transplantation. Knowing this, scientists also had to assume that the T cell possessed a surface molecule that would act as a receptor, able to bind with specific antigens. But despite years of experimentation, they were unable to locate any such receptor. Recently a series of discoveries contributed to the identification and structural elucidation of the T-cell receptor. The photomicrograph at bottom shows an immature T cell bound to an epithelial cell in the lining of the thymus gland, the site where T cells are processed and differentiate into specialized populations. The dark spots in the photo, more clearly seen in the accompanying schematic drawing, are receptor molecules on the surface of the T cell.

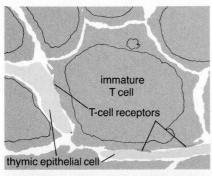

immature
T cell

T-cell receptors

thymic epithelial cell

Photomicrograph, A. G. Farr and S. K. Anderson,
University of Washington, Seattle

126

Photo and computer graphic model by Elizabeth D. Getzoff, John A. Tainer, and Arthur J. Olson of the Research Institute of Scripps Clinic. Crystallographic data from the laboratory of David R. Davies, National Institutes of Health. Computer software by T. J. O'Donnell, M. L. Connolly, and A. J. Olson

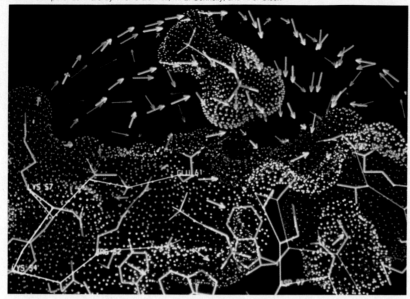

A computer-generated image represents an immune response in progress.

The first to characterize the alpha chain was Tonegawa; he was followed closely in scientific publication by the research teams in Denver and California. With that long-standing mystery solved, Tonegawa added a fresh puzzle. In the course of his research on the T-cell receptor, his group at MIT found a third chain of amino acids that evidently went with the receptor but did not fit its known configuration. There was simply no place in the receptor's structure for a third chain. Tonegawa believes this third chain may function in immature T cells and be replaced later. Further discoveries added even more complexity. In July 1986 scientists from Harvard, Columbia, and Tufts universities reported in the journal *Nature* new evidence suggesting that there is another T-cell receptor, quite different from the one already identified. The functions of this putative second T-cell receptor are still obscure, however.

The scientific community hailed the discovery of the T-cell receptor, or receptors, mainly as a tour de force of basic research but one that will probably have important practical consequences. It may help scientists pin down the number of different kinds of T cells that exist and help to clarify their understanding of how immune responses are regulated. Some experts think detailed knowledge of the T-cell receptor may make it possible one day for scientists to create custom-designed T cells carrying specific traits. This might lead to the development of a whole new class of drugs based on such modified T cells. "Whether such things will become feasible, I don't know," says Paul, "but they could not even have been considered before we knew the structure of the receptor and its genes."

In an editorial comment on the T-cell receptor discoveries, a scientist writing in *Nature* said, "From now on, things will move fast." In fact, things are moving fast in many areas of immunology today, and specialists in this field of research believe that they will continue to do so, for the substantial advance of scientific knowledge and the ultimate benefit of the human condition.

Mirror, Mirror on the Wall...

by Macdonald Critchley, M.D.

As he led the symphony orchestra, he felt himself merging with the sounds that were all around him. Like a giant he bestrode the whole orchestra, looking down and watching the players who appeared in miniature. At times, this feeling was so overwhelming that he believed he was somewhere in astronomical space, gazing down upon the earth, which was like a tiny ball.

—A conductor characterizes his feelings about his body

In an arm-chair, . . . sat the strangest lady I have ever seen, or shall ever see. . . . She was dressed in rich materials—satins, and lace, and silks—all of white. . . . But I saw that everything . . . which ought to be white, had been white long ago, and had lost its lustre and was faded and yellow. I saw that the bride within the bridal dress had withered . . . the dress had been put upon the rounded figure of a young woman and . . . the figure upon which it now hung loose, had shrunk to skin and bone.

—Pip's description, upon first viewing Miss Havisham, in Charles Dickens's Great Expectations, *chapter 8*

The descriptions which many [anorexia nervosa] patients give of their size sometimes make an absurd contrast with how others see them. They deny strenuously that they are abnormally thin, even when they look like walking skeletons.

—Peter Dally, Joan Gomez, and A. J. Isaacs, "Body Image and Mirror Gazing," in Anorexia Nervosa *(1979)*

Three terms—corporeal awareness, body image, and body schema—are used more or less interchangeably to refer to the idea that an individual entertains about the physical properties of his own anatomy. Normally this idea dwells unobtrusively at the fringe of consciousness. With introspection as well as in various physiological and pathological circumstances, it becomes more evident.

Early in the 20th century the otologist Pierre Bonnier, in studying vertigo, described various upsets of the sensory experience—what he called "schematia." More relevant was the later work of neurologists Henry Head and Gordon Holmes, who in 1911–12 proposed the expression schema for the "combined standard against which all subsequent changes of [body] position are measured before they enter consciousness." Over the next decades occurred several pioneering neurological and psychological studies of various aspects of corporeal awareness.

Macdonald Critchley, M.D., is Consultant Neurologist at the National Hospital, London, and President Emeritus of the World Federation of Neurology. In 1962 he was named Commander of the Order of the British Empire. He resides in Somerset, England.

(Opposite page) Photograph, "The Modern Genius at Her Toilet" by an anonymous British artist, 1821; collection, Worcester Art Museum, Worcester, Massachusetts, Samuel B. Woodward Collection

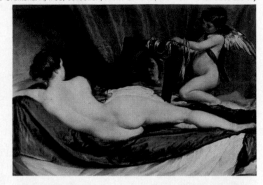

The ideas that an individual entertains about the physical properties of his or her own anatomy are partially gained from gazing in mirrors. But the moment one peers into a looking glass, one adopts an attitude, and the reflected image is thus but an artificial, stylized, and immobile version of one's self.

Development of the body scheme

Early in childhood a coordination of messages (from sense organs and the labyrinths of the inner ear) marks the beginnings of corporeal awareness. A haptic component (related to the sense of touch) comprises stimuli arising within the body from muscles and joints, together with data arising from the surface of the body. One way that the degree of maturity of a child's corporeal awareness is reflected is in his spontaneous drawings of people.

The body image is not a static manikin or homunculus; it may even involve adjacent objects. Thus, the corporeal awareness of a motorist, air pilot, or polo player temporarily includes part of the automobile, the aircraft, or the pony. A surgeon with his probe or a blind man with his white stick is temporarily endowed with an extension of his body. (However, this does not apply to the unskilled apprentice who has not yet attained competence or to the pilot when he is out of his aircraft.)

Visual factors in the developing corporeal awareness include information from exposed parts of one's own body. The face plays a special role,

130

The blind boy without his white stick and the pole vaulter without his pole would feel incomplete because these objects are such vital extensions of their bodies.

being visible to everyone except the owner, whose sole clues come from photographs, portraits, or mirrors. But a reflected image is artificial, for the moment one gazes into a looking glass one adopts an attitude; one does not perceive the little facial mannerisms that others know so well. The mirror reflection is but a stylized and immobile version of what is familiar to all except the one whose face it is. Further, visual information regarding one's own body is never complete, for at any single time some parts (*e.g.,* the top of the head) always are out of sight.

By observing others, one continually gains visual experience. One thus becomes aware of the standards set by the conventional height and stature of others, their features, posture, gait, and gestural habits.

A child born blind develops a body image without the participation of vision, for his chief means of knowing the shape and appearance of himself and others is through the medium of touch. When, therefore, he draws or models a man, odd distortions are displayed, especially if the blind subject is of less than average intelligence. Those parts of his anatomy that are of special significance to him will loom unduly large. Thus, the hand with its sensitive fingers constitutes not only a manipulative tool but also a means of contact with the outer world. When a blind child draws a man, he may exaggerate the fingers and hand to the detriment of the face and body. In clay models created by blind children, the mouth may be prominent, for the blind person not only speaks, feeds, and breathes by way of the lips, tongue, and palate but also at times makes tactual exploration. In the representations of the human figure produced by children of low intelligence who were born blind (collected in the early 1950s by the German neurologist F. G. von Stockert), scarcely any detail exists except for a sphere for the head and a large crater with outturned lips.

Phantom body parts

After the loss of a limb through surgery or trauma, corporeal awareness remains intact, a fact shown by the occurrence of phantom sensations. Thus, an excised or amputated limb is replaced in the victim's mind by a phantom limb. A phantom limb experiences pain and other sensations,

From H. M. Connell, *Essentials of Child Psychiatry*, 2nd ed. (Oxford: Blackwell Scientific Publications, 1985)

A child's sense of the human body—his own and those of others—not surprisingly is reflected in his spontaneous drawings. The picture at left, "My Dad," was drawn by an eight-year-old emotionally disturbed child whose father beat him. Clearly the hand that inflicts the brutal treatment looms disproportionately large in the mind of the child.

(Top) Jean-Loup Charmet, Paris; (bottom) from William A. Cooper,
"History of Radical Mastectomy," *Annals of Medical History*, vol. 3, no. 1 (1941), p. 47

*After the loss of a body part through
surgery or trauma, corporeal awareness
remains intact. Thus, a "phantom" part,
replete with the ability to feel sensations,
replaces the amputated part. Phantoms
can occur with any lost body part—
not just amputated limbs, as was once
believed. Thus, phantom breasts are
common after mastectomy, as are
phantom eyes after enucleation.*

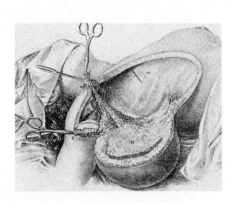

though the phantom tends to fade with advancing years. The phantom
disappears if a stroke supervenes, with resulting paralysis.

Phantom limbs are to be expected in the majority of all amputees unless
the limb is lost in infancy. Phantoms may, however, develop in quite young
children. In one such case an amputee of three and a half years was endowed with quite a vivid phantom image of a limb lost to disease in infancy.
However, in amelic subjects—those born without one or more extremities,
such as thalidomide babies—no phantom limbs occur.

A phantom will be in evidence in any widespread process of impairment
of touch due to the development of polyneuritis (inflammation of multiple
nerves). Feelings of heat or of cold are referred to the missing limb. Itching
due to a skin disorder may also involve the phantom.

When a limb is slowly destroyed through chronic degenerative disease,
no phantom evolves. Thus, necrosis (tissue death) may cause a person
with advanced leprosy slowly to lose his fingers, but no phantom develops.
However, if the arm is subsequently removed surgically, a distinct phantom
of a hand will follow but without fingers.

For some time it was believed that phantom images occur only when
it is a *limb* that has been lost and not after other kinds of surgical abla-

132

tions. However, subsequent experience does not support this contention. Provided the clinical questioning of the patient is adequate, the existence of a phantom may come to light following the enucleation (total removal) of an eye, the removal of a breast, or the resection of the rectum. In the last case the patient may continue to feel as though an anal passage were still intact, ready to transmit feces or flatus.

Being an expression of the body image, phantom sensations may sometimes follow neurological disease. This phenomenon has been noted in cases of paraplegia with gross motor and sensory loss and after severe injuries of the brachial plexus (nerves located in the region of the arm's attachment to the body).

Puppet or actor?

Even more than a percept, or impression obtained via the senses, the body image is a concept—an impression formed in the mind. Thus, the body image is the medium that the individual employs while visualizing himself, both in the past and in the future. Such states of reflection can take place at any time, but they particularly occur in idle moments or while the person is dropping off to sleep.

Just how does the individual visualize himself, and how far does the mental image correspond with actuality? When one conjures up the memory of some past experience, does one "look on" at oneself as if one were a puppet portraying a part? Or is one the actor, once again "looking out" from himself and surveying the scene? When an individual broods over his future movements, such as planning to attend a banquet, make a speech, or meet a friend or colleague, does he look on at, or observe, a future self, or does he experience and act the part in the future meeting?

If in either past or future time he seems to be playing the role of a detached onlooker, what are the details of the visual imagery? What are the spatial components? Is the "puppet" life-size or but a manikin? close by or far away? behind or in front, and directly so or at an angle? Is the puppet a faithful replica of himself as he is now or as he used to be? If the latter, how long ago? Thus, if a fat, middle-aged, bearded man wearing glasses reminisces over his wartime experience, does he visualize himself as being in uniform, young, slender, without spectacles, and clean-shaven?

These are questions of subjectivity versus objectivity. The actual mental image or impression of self largely depends upon remoteness in time as well as other factors, both personal and situational.

The poet Ronald Duncan has described a time in his life when he experienced a sort of compulsive thinking as he dropped off to sleep. In his presleep stage he would experience himself actually bowling; that is, he was not a spectator but a player. In his own words: "Just before I fell asleep I imagined myself bowling at cricket. I would visualize myself running up to the wicket, swinging the ball, then watching it pitch at an unidentified batsman. I would repeat this fantasy for about an hour, by which time I was in a deep sleep. . . . I wondered if the identity of the batsman contained any clue, but though I bowled thousands of overs I never saw his face, nor did he hit the ball. He always disappeared just as the ball bounced on the pitch."

The body image is a concept—an impression formed by the mind—by which an individual visualizes himself not only in the present but also in the past and in the future.

133

The perceived self can take on strange proportions. Though in reality the size or shape of a body part may be quite normal and appear so to others, it is through the disproportionately experienced image that the individual recognizes his physical existence in the world. During the Renaissance, artists used this idea of incongruous proportions in so-called anamorphic pictures. Anamorphosis, derived from the Greek word anamorphoun, *meaning "to transform," is an ingenious perspective technique that shows a distorted image of an object when it is viewed head on, but if the picture is seen from a particular angle or reflected in a curved mirror, the distortion disappears and the image appears normal. The best example is in Hans Holbein's "The Ambassadors" (right). The strange and unrecognizable shape hovering in the picture's foreground is a splayed out skull; it becomes clear that it is a skull, however, only when the picture is viewed from the correct angle. Twentieth-century psychologists interested in perception have given particular attention to anamorphosis.*

In 1924 Swiss psychologist Edouard Claparède speculated that a focus of most vivid imagery lies in a kind of cyclopean (single, unpaired) eye situated between and somewhat behind the orbits—the bony sockets containing the two eyes. This would explain the common experience of thinking of oneself as surveying the world of imagery at eye level. It is uncertain whether this eye-level positioning of the imagery is determined by the stature of the individual or by a tendency to adopt a kind of conformity with the world. Does a midget travel in his dream world always gazing upward at others? Or does he see himself as at the same level as others? Similar speculations surround the corporeal awareness of those whose anatomy is severely distorted by poliomyelitis, Pott's disease, which entails a hunchback deformity, or a congenital absence of limbs. Does the body image correspond with the misshapen reality, or is it rationalized so as to fall in line with the norm?

Aging and self-perception

Considering that corporeal awareness builds up gradually over the years, one can also understand why it usually lags behind reality. On a cognitive plane one is well aware of the signs of middle age—balding, graying, stooping. The information afforded by the mirror, many times daily, is ineluctable. Yet, in one's imagery, the self is usually regarded as younger. Discrepancy between imagery and reality is shown by an increasing dissatisfaction with snapshots. "That's nothing like me," one protests, whereas the family asserts that the likeness is excellent. Then again, there is the

134

An interesting study can be made of artists' self-portraits—especially those in which they do not represent reality. Beatrice Turner always painted herself as voluptuously young and attractive, even when she was actually old and frail, with a withered body, and on her deathbed. The self-portrait (top left) is Turner as a young woman; the portrait at right depicts her in middle age. But she appears, if any different, younger and more radiant in the latter. (Bottom) In his self-portrait at right, Edvard Munch was 76 but appears as a much younger man than in the unflattering earlier painting (left), where he appears unduly old, probably because he was sick at the time and perceived his body in its weakened state as unrealistically decrepit. "Portrait of the Painter in Old Age" (below) is probably the last of Rembrandt's many self-portraits. Though Rembrandt had painted many very fine and sympathetic portraits of persons in old age that conveyed great dignity in maturity, his own portrait emphasizes blotchy, pouched skin and a sad, meek expression.

reunion phenomenon. Meeting an old acquaintance after a gap of many years, one is struck by how much he has aged. The experience is mutual, though probably not expressed.

The common disparity between real aging and specious youthfulness is sometimes betrayed by artists in their self-portraiture. Not always, however. In at least one of his paintings, Edvard Munch depicted himself as looking unduly old. Presumably he was a sick man at the time of painting it. More common is the contrary finding; namely, a representation that is flattering. The latter reached a preposterous level in the case of Beatrice Turner, who throughout her life dwelt in seclusion painting self-portraits in which she always appeared young and attractive. In one of her late self-portraits, she depicted herself as a voluptuous figure in the nude. At the time, however, she was sick, emaciated, and close to death.

Yet another manifestation of this contrast between fact and fancy can be found in the so-called Miss Havisham syndrome. This label applies to those instances where a faded beauty continues to wear the trappings and appanages of youth well into advanced years. (Miss Havisham is the strange and "corpse-like" old lady in Dickens's *Great Expectations*, who continued to wear her bridal costume on her "collapsed form"—"so like graveclothes . . . the long veil so like a shroud."

Body weight and body image

The fat and the thin deserve particular attention whenever the theme of corporeal awareness is discussed. Deviations from the norm cause distress

135

"Portrait of the Painter in Old Age" by Rembrandt, 1669; reproduced by courtesy of the Trustees, the National Gallery, London

to a degree that may seem unwarranted. Those with a "weight problem" often harbor an illusion that they are much fatter and considerably more unshapely than they really are. A few come to terms with their obesity. More, however, betray an anxiety and a dislike of their own body image that may astonish those who are not involved. Numerous studies of people who have lost weight show that they continue to imagine themselves as fatter than they actually are. Even after a massive weight loss, an individual may avoid standard-size seats, such as on a bus.

In certain cultures and among some primitive peoples, adiposity is regarded as desirable, being a mark of beauty. This does not apply to the modern Western woman, to whom "fat is bad, thin is good," according to the anthropologist Margaret Mackenzie. Striving to lose weight sometimes leads to unhealthy eating habits. Starvation regimes may alternate with secret spells of bulimia (overeating to a morbid degree). The victim's body image is often a travesty of the true state of affairs.

Special problems surround individuals with anorexia nervosa—especially adolescent females. A dangerous degree of emaciation bears witness to their delusional state, with food phobias coexisting with fallacious ideas of being too heavy. The thinner they become, the greater the disparity between imagery and fact. An anorexic weighing only 32 kilograms (70 pounds) may continue to reject food, believing that she is overweight and unsightly.

Body enhancement

We expand and contract the postural model of the body; we take parts away and we add parts; we rebuild it; we melt the details in; we create new details; we do this with our body and with the expression of the body itself. We experiment continually with it. When the experimentation with the movement is not sufficient, then we add the influence of the vestibular apparatus and of intoxicants to the picture. When even so the body is not sufficient for the expression of the playful changes and the destructive changes in the body, then we add clothes, masks, jewellery, which again expand, contract, disfigure, or emphasize the body image and its particular parts.

How does the individual visualize himself or herself? How close is the mental image to the actuality? Corporeal awareness is gained gradually over the years, but it often lags behind reality. The mirror and the calendar may say one has aged— grown gray or bald, become stooped and wrinkled, and progressed well into one's seventh, eighth, or ninth decade of life—but those facts have little or nothing to do with what is perceived. One may feel much more like the spritely, able-bodied person one once was, as Honoré Daumier's drawing (below left) of two old men picking up their canes, kicking up their heels, and dancing so clearly suggests. The fat and the thin, too, may not perceive faithful images of themselves, especially if they were once svelte and have grown corpulent or if they have undergone a significant weight loss. The condition anorexia nervosa represents the extreme. A skeletonlike young girl may truly believe she is fat; the more emaciated she becomes, the more she feels the need to starve herself.

(Left) Lithograph by Honoré Daumier; collection, National Library of Medicine, Bethesda, Maryland; (right) Jean-Loup Charmet, Paris

As the Viennese neurologist and psychoanalyst Paul Schilder points out in the foregoing description, many persons have a compulsion to seek kinesthetic pleasure from frequent and unnecessary bodily movements, thus bringing about flexibility in the body image. In part this may represent a sort of play; *i.e.,* the execution of movements for their own sake. The individual may also go to extremes to enhance the body image by utilizing numerous practices that elaborate its visual components. Clothing has already been mentioned in this connection. Utilitarian purposes of protection not infrequently are transcended by outlandish, or even grotesque, adornments.

When women's hats were fashionable, they were said to buoy up morale, especially when they were conspicuous and costly. During the wartime occupation of France, women in Paris reacted against authority by displaying particularly blatant headgear. Fantastic headdresses as a mode of expression have occurred in very different cultures; *e.g.,* among certain primitives, French vaudeville performers, and fashionable cosmopolitan ladies of the 18th century in Europe.

How people perceive themselves has long been reflected in the infinitely varied hairstyles they have worn. Hair has been shaved, plaited, powdered, bleached, teased, waved, waxed, covered by wigs, and adorned with all manner of decorations. Indeed, hairstyles afford enormous potential for asserting personality, age, status, role, and individuality or conformity.

Accentuation of the body image to extents that transcend the more conventional standards of decoration is also brought about by such practices as painting the toenails, wearing jeweled anklets, getting a suntan, and tattooing. Whatever the motives among certain primitive peoples for artificial deformations, *e.g.,* piercing the nostrils with spikes or inserting labrets or wooden disks that penetrate the lower lip or the lobe of the ear, such practices cannot fail to influence corporeal awareness. The same may be said of masks, especially those of gigantesque nature used in ritual dances, processions, and carnivals. In contemporary times we have the cult of the

The neurologist and psychoanalyst Paul Schilder wrote of the way humankind likes to alter and elaborate on the visual components of the body: "We take parts away and we add parts; we rebuild it; we melt the details in; we create new details. . . . We experiment continually with it." Thus, the caricatured woman (below right) prepares to don her padded brassiere, while the man (below left) gets strapped into his corset.

Hairstyles offer a way for people to assert themselves. An American man has his hair "permed"; Masai warriors from Kenya style each other's hair; and a French woman of the 1700s is tended by her personal coiffeur.

punk, replete with elaborately cut and colored hair, sharp metal rings and bracelets, and safety pins that pierce nostrils, ears, or cheeks.

Physiological reasons for body image modifications

Certain regions of bodily awareness assume special importance in various physiological and clinical circumstances. The sphincters, for example, play an important role. To the victim of diarrhea, the anal orifice is obtrusive. A full bladder produces an uncomfortable focus upon the upper pelvic region. Hunger causes the epigastric area to assume importance; thirst fixes attention upon the oral cavity.

Similar shifts in attention may result from physical distress. The writer Spencer Chapman, struggling alone through the tropical jungle, ill with malaria, and very hungry, wrote: "I felt curiously light-headed—as if the top of my skull were a foot higher than normal." Even simple embarrassment causes one to feel "all hands and feet." Sudden alarm may produce an illusory heaviness of the feet rooting one to the spot.

After prolonged immobilization, the parts released may feel unnatural. The writer Orloff de Wet had been in jail for two years with his forearms overlapping and manacled to a waist belt. Of his release he wrote: "One's arms detached, how long they feel! Like caged birds, simultaneously happy and perplexed, what to do with themselves."

In cases of undue introversion with overtones of narcissism, an intrusive body image may assume psychopathological proportions. Hence we find the most vivid body imagery in many intelligent and inward-looking psychopaths.

Morbid states and altered body image

Corporeal awareness may be altered in many morbid states. These changes take three basic forms: (1) enhanced awareness, (2) diminished or lost awareness, and (3) distorted awareness.

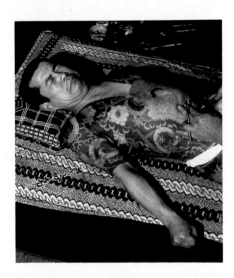

Women from Xingu, Brazil (top), carefully and ritually paint their bodies, while the Japanese man above subjects himself to the excruciating business of having indelible dyes injected into his skin for the sake of having a body decorated top to toe with elaborate tattoos.

The facial scarification on the women (top) is a common body alteration among the Nuer tribe of The Sudan. The man above is a Suya Indian from Brazil dressed for dance; his body is painted, and his lower lip is penetrated by a wooden labret.

Morbid enhancement. Pain, dysesthesia (tingling sensation), or discomfort is liable to cause the affected part to loom large in the body scheme. An accentuation of self-awareness, fragmentary or general (*hyperschematia*), is common in states of disease, organic or psychogenic. In any case of partial paralysis of a limb, the affected segment may seem to be too heavy and too big. After an abdominal exploration, a patient noticed while dozing that his body seemed to consist in a large, painful belly to which were attached tiny limbs and a head, the whole structure floating "like a magnetic mine in the sea." According to a woman with multiple sclerosis, "The left arm and hand often feel of elephantine proportions, and as if sharply outlined . . . as if it had an edge to it."

Some of the most vivid and at the same time bizarre examples of hyperschematia have been described by hypochondriacs. One hypochondriac's description of his unusually accentuated corporeal awareness was as follows: "I have an intense feeling that the right and left sides are interchanged. The right side is too light. Objects feel different in the left hand, there is much more space there. The right hand is much smaller, especially the inner part. When I clench my fist my fingers do not fit my hand."

Lost or diminished awareness. Aschematia (absence of awareness) is the rule when a segment of the body is deprived of both outward (efferent) and inward (afferent) connections. Thus, after transsection of the spinal cord, the victim may feel as if sawn off at waist level. In those rare cases of intense and generalized pain—as during electric shock—the body image may shrink. At exposure to 240 volts: "I felt myself becoming smaller and smaller and squeezed into myself." At 22,000 volts: "My head seemed to enlarge and burst with pain . . . my body, legs, and feet seemed to shrink to nothing until I felt I could stand on a ten-cent piece."

Hyposchematia (diminished awareness) accompanies any condition where the action of gravity is reduced or abolished. Thus, in underwater swimming and in skin diving (perhaps, too, in spacecraft travel), the body and limbs move with ease and freedom, although slowly. Patients suffering from vertigo feel unduly light and seem to float in the air or sink through the bed; they may appear to be rotated by some outside force or jerked violently in one direction or other. Typical is an alarming sense of levitation coupled with an abrupt and illusory transportation through space. The most striking instances of hyposchematia are met with in patients with lesions of the parietal lobe of the brain, and these are of such importance that they will be considered below.

Distortion of corporeal awareness. Examples of distorted body image (*paraschematia*) are met with in drug intoxication. A person under the influence of mescal thought he could both see and feel his thorax consistently growing until it became a garden in which his arms were alleys. Another mescal-drugged subject reported, "I felt my body particularly plastic and minutely carved . . . as if my foot were being taken off. . . . I felt as if my head had been turned by 180 degrees. My abdomen became a fluid, soft mass, my face acquired dimensions, my lips swelled, my arms became wooden, my feet turned spirals and scrolls, my jaw was like a hook, and my chest seemed to melt away."

140

One's corporeal awareness can be greatly affected by states of morbidity. Pain in particular has a tendency to accentuate self-awareness. Thus, the tiniest cut may make the lacerated body part loom enormous (left). The pain of migraine is known to cause sufferers such agony that their perceptions of the world are drastically altered, and often all consciousness becomes focused on the drill-like sensation in the top part of the head. Drawings by patients such as the one below provide some of the best evidence of what migraineurs endure during an attack.

In drug intoxication cases where the substance used was hashish, one person reported, "It seemed that my body had dissolved and become transparent." To another, "The impression was that of wandering out of myself. . . . I had two beings." A third individual described his experience thus: "The sensations produced were those of exquisite lightness and airiness."

The neuropsychologist A. R. Luria, in *The Man with a Shattered World* (1975), described the case of a victim who survived a gunshot wound to the skull that penetrated the left parietal lobe; the victim expressed his subsequent body-image distortion as follows: "I suddenly become very tall, but my torso becomes terribly short and my head very, very tiny—no bigger than a chicken's head."

Paraschematia may also be experienced in semidreamlike states and also in some epileptic auras. And in that rare condition known as ecstasy, gross aberrations in body awareness may be experienced, including an "emancipation of the body image." During strong emotional tension or absorption in music, the body image may be caught up, transported, or exalted.

Paraschematia may attain fantastic proportions in states of depersonalization. One such patient suffered the illusion of being two persons and explained that he did not in fact see or hear his alter ego but imagined it as being outside and beside him as well as slightly in front. He regarded

141

A distorted body image, known as paraschematia, occurs in drug-induced states of intoxication. The woman above has taken MDMA, or "Ecstasy," a recreational drug that became popular in the mid-1980s. When the substance reaches the bloodstream, there is first a feeling of considerable disorientation. This is followed by a "rush"—tingling sensations and sometimes spasmodic jerks. Then, with the person's pupils almost totally dilated, the "high," with its sense of super-sociability, takes over and lasts three to five hours.

one as normal and the other not. The abnormal self would urge him to do foolish things.

The pioneer 18th-century botanist Carolus Linnaeus was a victim of migraine. Just before an attack he would imagine he could see himself seated or standing or walking in such a lifelike fashion as to be deceptive. This symptom was described by the early 20th-century neurologist Charles Féré as a specular hallucination; others use the terms autoscopy or heautoscopy. This sensation has often been mentioned by nonmedical writers, especially the Romantics Goethe, Hippolyte Taine, Alfred de Musset, Gabriele D'Annunzio, Edgar Allan Poe, Honoré de Balzac, Guy de Maupassant, and Axel Munthe.

Heautoscopy has been encountered in many morbid circumstances—drug intoxications, delirium, hysteria, schizophrenia, and "demonical possession." Some people claim they can deliberately release soul from body and, by a willed effort, produce a temporary doubling of the body image. "Negative heautoscopy" refers to the phenomenon whereby a patient loses his reflection in a mirror, or even his shadow. In the so-called *signe de miroir,* one fails to recognize oneself in a looking glass, the reflection being that of a stranger.

Rooted in the brain?

Corporeal awareness, like language, is probably a function of the brain as a whole. As with language, certain cerebral regions seem to be areas of vulnerability in that a circumscribed lesion is associated specifically with an impaired function. Among focal disorders the parietal lobe of the nondominant hemisphere seems often and most blatantly linked with aberrations of the body image. (The parietal lobes are the middle divisions of each cerebral hemisphere and contain an area concerned with bodily sensations.) The explanation for the connection, however, is still a matter of debate.

The modifications of the body image met with in parietal disease (particularly when the minor hemisphere is involved) are variously manifested. Much depends on such things as rate of onset of the lesion, the degree and direction of progression, the coexistence of paralysis, the age of the subject, the influence exerted by others, and the patient's intellectual status.

About a dozen patterns have been tabulated by neurologists. However, these phenomena, described below, are not sharply demarcated. Clinical experience shows that one condition may merge with another, or two of them may alternate. Sometimes in the course of a single clinical interview a patient will display several of these phenomena in an inconsistent, even contradictory, manner.

Unilateral neglect. This is one of the earliest and most characteristic manifestations of an expanding lesion within the parietal lobe, especially of the minor hemisphere. The sign is a subtle one, unnoticed by the patient himself. It is usually transient, and when motor weakness develops, the "neglect" or lack of spontaneity gives way to an inability to move. Typically the patient with neglect is not paralyzed, but he does not use the affected limb even in bilateral activities—those that pertain to both sides of the body—unless his attention is specifically directed to that side.

Many simple clinical tests will demonstrate this neglect. Thus, to the examiner's command "lift up your arms," he raises only one upper limb (usually the right). When attention is drawn to this oversight by such a remark as "What about your other arm?" the patient at once complies and brings up the "lazy" arm to the required position. Or the examiner may place his fingers within the palms of the patient's two hands and request him to squeeze. The patient responds by gripping with one hand only. Again, when the one-sided nature of the response is brought to his notice, the patient immediately grasps with the other hand also. One patient, asked to explain the initial neglect, replied "I didn't want to hurt you."

In the case of the lower extremities, unilateral motor neglect can be shown by placing a pair of slippers in front of the patient and then telling him to slip them on. The patient proceeds to put on only one of the slippers.

Unilateral neglect is usually manifest at a stage when the patient's general sensorium is not wholly clear. Later, when obvious confusion has developed, passive disregard becomes complicated by active neglect. He may eat the food that occupies only one-half of the plate in front of him. He may collide with furniture—always with one side of his body. He may cease to notice half his anatomy and to attend to its hygiene—sometimes letting the neglected side become not only untidy but dirty. He may comb the hair on only one-half of his head or shave merely one side of the face. Female patients may apply cosmetics to only one side of their face and lips and leave their hair unkempt on one side. A striking example of unilateral neglect is shown when such a patient rummages in a drawer. Having found the desired item, he or she then slams the drawer, leaving the left hand entrapped.

Unilateral neglect may also extend outward from the patient's personal space to involve adjacent objects in outer space. This is well shown during the act of dressing. He fails to insert his left lower limb into the appropriate trouser leg or to put on the left sock or shoe, and he may leave the left sleeve of his shirt and jacket empty.

In underwater swimming, as in any action where gravitational force is reduced or abolished, there is a diminished body awareness (hyposchematia). A form of paraschematia (emancipation of the body image) may occur in states of exaltation such as one may experience when absorbed in the raptures of music.

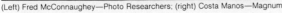
(Left) Fred McConnaughey—Photo Researchers; (right) Costa Manos—Magnum

Victims of gunshot wounds to the skull may experience quite marked distortions of body image. Neuropsychologist A. R. Luria reported the case of one such victim who described a weird state of seeming to become "very tall" while at the same time his torso became "terribly short" and his head "very, very tiny—no bigger than a chicken's head."

Lack of concern. A lack of concern on the part of the patient over the fact that he is paralyzed (*anosodiaphoria*) is another reaction. There is no loss of insight into the existence of a hemiparesis but rather a lack of awareness as to the full implications of the disability.

Unawareness of paralysis. In this characteristic reaction there is a failure on the part of the patient to realize that he is, in fact, paralyzed (*anosognosia*). This happens only if the onset of paresis has been abrupt, as in the case of a vascular accident; *e.g.,* a blood clot in the brain. Though the paralysis is obvious to everyone else, the patient himself does not complain of any weakness. If directly asked, "What is the matter with you?" the patient may reply, "Nothing!" More often he mentions some irrelevant symptom such as headache, cough, or constipation.

Partial realization and fantasies. If the doctor asks (pointing to the paralyzed limb), "Isn't this rather weak?" the patient may almost reluctantly admit that it is but immediately proceed to offer an excuse—an injury, recent or remote, or "rheumatism."

Denial of paralysis. A most abnormal type of reaction may be observed when the hemiplegic goes so far as to deny obstinately that he is paralyzed. The patient has now surrendered himself to a delusional system, and he will probably have to sink still deeper into difficulties in order to discount the evidence of his senses. Other psychiatric features, ranging from a mere confusional state to an actual dementia, will arise.

If the patient who denies that he is paralyzed is called upon to explain why he does not move the limb, he is thrust still further into a world of fancy. He is entrapped within an organic paranoid reaction. Rationalization and confabulations are his only escape. Sometimes these are outlandish. The patient may deny the very existence of the arm, although he can see it lying immobile across his chest. Or he may admit its presence but repudiate its ownership. He may even declare that the paralyzed limb belongs to someone else—real or imagined, living or dead.

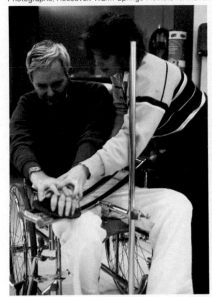 

An example of this adamant denial (*somatoparaphrenia*) is the hospitalized patient who believes that the paralyzed limb is that of the man in the next bed, of the nurse, or of the doctor in attendance. One woman declared that the immobile leg was her brother's, even though he had been dead for 15 years.

Loss of awareness of one body half. This symptom (*autosomatognosis*) consists in a positive feeling of "nothingness" with regard to an arm, or sometimes to the entire half of the anatomy. The resulting impression of an abyss may be frightening. A woman of 57 stated, "My head does not seem to be on my body any more, and the right side of the head is not there. The feeling is as if I were in the air, seeing my body lying in the bed and I say to myself, 'get back there.'"

A woman with right hemiparesis declared that while lying relaxed in bed she felt as though there was something missing on the right side. Another patient was unaware of the existence of the paralyzed left limbs. Whenever he began to write, his paralyzed hand would interfere with the right hand, which held the pen. The patient did not recognize the intruder as being part of himself and would often cry aloud, "Take your hand away."

Exaggerated awareness. In some patients with a long-standing hemiplegia, the paralyzed limbs tend to assume personal significance representing the antithesis of neglect or unawareness (*hyperschematia*).

Personification. Some patients criticize the affected limbs as being heavy, swollen, or inert—*e.g.,* "like a piece of dead meat." One patient complained of difficulty in dressing because "this lifeless block of wood won't cooperate."

More often one finds patients with long-standing and severe left hemiplegia who come to look upon the paralyzed arm as being invested with an existence of its own, like a pet. In this phenomenon of personification the patient refers to the limb in such terms as "old useless," "nuisance," "swine," "dummy," "old stinker," "bloody bastard." Even commoner is the practice of

Modifications of the body image that occur in cases of paralysis vary considerably and sometimes are manifested in quite bizarre ways—e.g., creating wild confabulations about the paralyzed body part (it belongs to the patient in the next bed) or referring to the part with a name such as "Floppy Joe," "swine," or "old useless." With rehabilitation therapy the patient can come to better terms with his or her paralysis. The stroke patient (left) learns how to use a special device to increase voluntary motion and normalize tone of a partially paralyzed arm. (Right) Patients paralyzed because of spinal injury do mat exercises to facilitate use of muscles in the lower extremities and strengthen muscles in the upper extremities.

145

Accentuation of body image to extents that transcend conventional standards of decoration have been seen in every age and culture. In contemporary times there is the "punk" cult.

endowing the limb with a proper name—"George," "Mary Ann," "Dolly Gray," "Hermione," "Toby," "Floppy Joe."

Hatred. Allied to personification is a morbid hatred of the affected arm, which a few patients cultivate (*misoplegia*). Illusory ideas multiply, and the sufferer may describe the limb as "withered," "scaly," "like a bird's claw"; patients have been known to pummel the arm with their good hand to express their loathing. Often they hide the paralyzed arm under the bedclothes or a shawl. Quite often they avert their gaze by turning their head and eyes far over to one side so as not to catch sight of the offending limb.

Phantom supernumerary limbs. Occasionally a hemiplegic feels that his affected hand and forearm occupy a position quite different from actuality. This illusion may come and go. Thus, a phantom "third" arm may sprout from the shoulder region and may lie in an attitude of extreme inward or outward extension at the elbow across the chest. As a rule the phantom is immobile, but in some cases it seems to move of its own accord. Occasionally the patient feels as though, by a willed effort, he could move it.

When the patient is intelligent and introspective, a clear-cut, even vivid, description of this phantom sensation may be possible. If then someone takes the patient's paralyzed upper limb and gently moves it so that it adopts the attitude of the phantom, the illusion of a third arm temporarily disappears.

Inability to specify body parts. In some cases of parietal disease, the patient is unable to point to or name various parts of his body when so requested. This inability (*autotopagnosia*) typically involves both sides of the body. It may, at times, also apply to the bodies of other people or even to inanimate representations, as in the case of a drawing or a statue.

Whether corporeal awareness is a specific function of the parietal lobe is not yet clear. The opinion has been expressed that corporeal awareness is not a consignable function of the brain, even though disorders of the

146

body image are common when one or other parietal lobe is diseased. However, there are dissenting views. Neurologists who currently hold strong localizationalist beliefs about specific brain functions may well assert that the body image is represented within the parietal region of the minor, *i.e.,* nondominant, hemisphere. Others believe that the body image is a function of *both* parietal lobes but that when the dominant hemisphere is implicated, communication becomes difficult.

A rather extreme viewpoint is that pathological neglect of a paralysis on the left side is but an exaggeration of the normal preference for right-handed activities. There is yet another group who remind us that organic repression is a feature of cerebral dysfunction irrespective of the site or sidedness of the lesion, and failure to realize the magnitude of clinical defect is characteristic of a veritable clinical syndrome. A further minority opinion regards the premorbid personality of the patient as the all-important explanation of a body-image disorder.

There remain many such unresolved questions. In any event, the importance of the body image as a whole cannot be overlooked. More and more this recognition is stimulating investigations by neurologists, psychiatrists, psychologists, and others, including philosophers, into the significance of distortions and disorders of corporeal awareness. For example, doctors concerned with physical rehabilitation (physiatrists) are looking at the need for body image restoration for persons who have suffered severe injuries. Psychologists are devising treatment regimens to aid patients who are plagued by intensely negative feelings about their bodies. Some of these studies may be of dubious value. Nonetheless, the body scheme, for all its plasticity, represents an important factor in human thought and behavior. The topic is both a fascinating one and worthy of scientific scrutiny.

147

The Sporting Life

COMPETITIVE SPORTS AND THE GROWING CHILD

Cultivating Young Bodies

by Frank W. Dick

Participation in sport has long been viewed as meeting a broad range of creative, regenerative, and educational objectives for the growing child. The immediate objective is to provide a healthy source of fun, fitness, and learning. Another objective of early sport participation is to develop a competitive advantage for athletic endeavors in postschool years. And, ultimately, youth sport gives a long-term advantage in the establishment of a healthy foundation for life—an active life-style.

These learning experiences not only make youngsters more aware of those values that equip them for life's rough and tumble, such as respect for opposition, for authority, and for the team, but also give them a sense of what personal commitment and pursuit of clearly defined objectives can mean. These early years thus provide education *for* sport and education *through* sport.

Younger, finer athletes

Recently the objectives have changed somewhat, so that greater focus on *achievement* in athletics is occurring earlier. In the past decade the world has seen a remarkable rise in the number of athletic children and adolescents; in the United States, for example, there are presently an estimated two million athletes between 6 and 16 years of age. In 1984 almost 30% of track and field athletes in the Los Angeles Olympics were 20 years of age or under; in Moscow in 1980 the statistic was just over 30%. In some sports the percentage of Olympians under 21 was even higher. This means that preparation for competition at the highest level is starting no later than the early teens.

It might help underscore the dimension of such youthful achievement if these figures were considered in the context of the continuing improvement of world standards. The accompanying table gives the world records for men and women in track and field for 1980, 1983, and 1985 and provides projected figures for 1988 and 1992. The percentage of athletes achieving Olympic standards will not substantially decrease, yet the *standards* will rise to parallel increasing world performance.

Frank W. Dick is Director of Coaching, British Amateur Athletic Board; Chairman, British Association of National Coaches; and President, European Athletics Coaches Association.

(Overleaf) Photograph, Ellis Herwig— Stock, Boston

Growing children *can* accept training loads compatible with producing achievement—levels formerly associated only with mature adults. In these early years children are easily motivated, and the gifted young athlete has many advantages over older competitors in several sports.

Competitive sport is, for the athlete, a vehicle for total personal expression. Seen in this light, a sports performance cannot be considered simply as a feat of strength or merely as a finely executed technique. It is a statement about the performer, who is the product of a unique social capsule—a particular complex of ability and motivation. In drawing the growing child through to high-level achievement in competitive sport, there must be sensitivity on the part of the coach and the parents to the shifting relationship between ability and motivation, a deep understanding of the principles and practice of developing the athlete's abilities, and skillful interpretation of the athlete's motivational climate.

Striking the essential balance: ability and motivation

The young athlete may be considered as progressing through four general stages. Each stage has its own profile of ability and motivation relative to athletic development. The first stage is characterized by ability that is raw and undeveloped, while there is high general enthusiasm (motivation). At stage two ability is developing at a general level, while motivation is variable but generally low. At stage three ability is developing at a special level, while motivation is variable but generally high. Finally, at stage four ability is well developed and sophisticated at a special level coupled with motivation that is high and with a specific focus.

Clearly, the approach of the coach must shift as the athlete progresses from stage to stage. At stage one the coach *controls:* makes all decisions, tempers the athlete's enthusiasm, and designs the appropriate program, then supervises it. At stage two the coach *directs:* makes most decisions,

Competitive sport is, for the athlete, a vehicle for total personal expression, and in some sports the gifted young athlete has many advantages over older competitors. The young gymnast above trains for the U.S. Olympic team.

Photograph, Duomo

151

works to raise the athlete's general enthusiasm and mental resilience, and designs the program and implements it. At stage three the coach *supports:* makes few decisions, works to focus the athlete's motivation on specific objective achievement, discusses and monitors the program, and is available to assist as required. Finally, at stage four the coach *advises:* is available to counsel on decisions, works to keep a "winning" climate of motivation, gives advice on the training program, and ensures that an athlete can "listen" to his or her own body and mind. (Although the approach of the coach is considered here, it should be said that parents and teachers might also review their approach to guiding developing athletes in terms of these stages.)

In light of these developmental stages and the interaction of athlete and coach, it follows that the athlete's objectives at each stage might be identified as follows: stage one, learning to participate; stage 2, learning to compete; stage three, competing to learn; and stage four, competing to win. Ideally, stage four for the athlete should coincide with commencement of the age range at which he or she is at the peak of relevant athletic potential. The first three stages, then, stretch back to the commencement of the "motivational life" in the sport. The starting point will vary for gymnastics or swimming, compared with football or track and field. However, it is clear that stages one through three, at least, will almost certainly run through the athlete's growing years. These developmental stages and their timing have clear implications for those who are involved in talent-selection programs.

Rising standards in track and field

	world records						projected records			
event	1980		1983		1985		1988		1992	
	men	women	men	women	men	women	men	women	men	women
100-m dash	9.95	10.88	9.93	10.79	9.93	10.76	9.88	10.72	9.85	10.70
200-m dash	19.72	21.71	19.72	21.71	19.72	21.71	19.66	21.60	19.60	21.50
4 × 100-m relay	38.03	41.60	37.86	41.53	37.83	41.37	37.75	41.30	37.70	41.20
400-m dash	43.86	48.60	43.86	47.99	43.86	47.60	43.60	47.30	43.50	47.00
4 × 400-m relay	2:56.16	3:19.20	2:56.16	3:19.04	2:56.16	3:15.92	2:55.00	3:15.00	2:54.00	3:14.00
800-m run	1:42.33	1:53.50	1:41.73	1:53.28	1:41.73	1:53.28	1:41.00	1:52.00	1:40.00	1:50.00
1,500-m run	3:31.36	3:52.47	3:30.77	3:52.47	3:29.45	3:52.47	3:28.75	3:50.50	3:27.50	3:49.00
3,000-m run	—	8:27.12	—	8:26.78	—	8:22.62	—	8:20.00	—	8:17.00
5,000-m run	13:08.40	—	13:00.41	—	13:00.40	14:48.07	12:57.50	14:45.00	12:55.00	14:40.00
10,000-m run	27:22.40	—	27:22.40	—	27:13.81	30:59.42	27:12.50	30:45.00	27:10.00	30:30.00
110/100-m hurdles	13.00	12.36	12.93	12.36	12.93	12.36	12.85	12.25	12.80	12.15
400-m hurdles	47.13	54.28	47.02	54.02	47.02	53.56	46.50	52.90	46.00	52.60
3,000-m steeplechase	8:05.40	—	8:05.40	—	8:05.40	—	8:02.50	—	8:00.00	—
high jump	2.36	2.01	2.38	2.04	2.41	2.07	2.45	2.10	2.50	2.15
pole vault	5.78	—	5.83	—	6.00	—	6.10	—	6.20	—
long jump	8.90	7.09	8.90	7.43	8.90	7.44	8.90	7.65	9.00	7.80
triple jump	17.89	—	17.99	—	17.97	—	18.15	—	18.30	—
shot put	22.15	22.45	22.22	22.45	22.62	22.53	22.80	23.20	23.00	23.50
discus throw	71.16	71.80	71.86	73.26	71.86	74.56	72.50	74.70	74.00	75.90
hammer throw	81.80	—	84.14	—	86.34	—	87.50	—	89.00	—
javelin throw	96.72	70.08	99.72	74.76	104.80	75.40	95.00*	77.50	100.00*	80.00
decathlon	8,649	—	8,779	—	8,832	—	9,000	—	9,100	—
heptathlon	—	—	—	6,836	—	6,946	—	7,050	—	7,200

in minutes and seconds (100-m dash through 3,000-m steeplechase)
in meters (high jump through javelin throw)
in points (decathlon, heptathlon)

*new specification javelin

Winners—those in number one spots—are normally higher on natural ability than those in the two through six spots. It is tempting to invest the greatest amount of coaching time and energy on the number one young athletes. However, owing to the fact that the giftedness (ability) of these athletes has exposed them to little or no experience of defeat, they are the ones who often show a lack of resilience (and motivation). This factor costs track and field sports over 60% of these top-level athletes every year. On the other hand, athletes at the school level who are familiar with some disappointment are more likely to have learned by experience the real weight of Calvin Coolidge's words: "Nothing in the world can take the place of persistence. Talent will not; nothing is more common than unsuccessful men with talent. Genius will not; overworked genius is almost a proverb. Education will not; the world is full of educated derelicts. Persistence and determination alone are omnipotent." Therefore, it is wise to "invest" in a wide range and large number of aspiring young athletes.

Vulnerable bodies

Early training should focus on coordination, strength, and mobility work. Each child should then have the opportunity to learn sound basic techniques and improve all-around strength. A comprehensive general training approach for the young athlete should gradually narrow to specialization but normally not before the age of 16–17 years. It is a major error when setting training loads to treat children as scaled-down adults. Indeed, with the increase in

Valerie Brisco-Hooks (opposite), having just accepted the baton from teammate Sherri Howard, proceeds to win the 4 x 400-meter relay in the 1984 Olympics held in Los Angeles. This vibrant young sprinter matched Wilma Rudolph's 1960 U.S. women's record of three gold medals in Olympic track events.

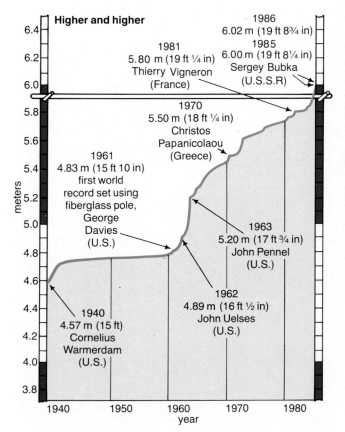

Higher and higher

- 1986 — 6.02 m (19 ft 8¾ in)
- 1985 — 6.00 m (19 ft 8¼ in) Sergey Bubka (U.S.S.R)
- 1981 — 5.80 m (19 ft ¼ in) Thierry Vigneron (France)
- 1970 — 5.50 m (18 ft ¼ in) Christos Papanicolaou (Greece)
- 1963 — 5.20 m (17 ft ¾ in) John Pennel (U.S.)
- 1962 — 4.89 m (16 ft ½ in) John Uelses (U.S.)
- 1961 — 4.83 m (15 ft 10 in) first world record set using fiberglass pole, George Davies (U.S.)
- 1940 — 4.57 m (15 ft) Cornelius Warmerdam (U.S.)

meters / year

(Above) Champion Soviet pole vaulter Sergey Bubka competes in Paris in 1985. Before the 1960s pole vaulters had not catapulted above 4.57 meters (15 feet). In the last quarter of a century, vaulters began using fiberglass poles and have consistently broken records, as the graph (left) indicates. On July 8, 1986, Bubka broke his own record at the Goodwill Games in Moscow with the bar set at 6.02 meters (19 feet 8¾ inches). "Today for me is a good day. I like world records," he said in English. It is expected that the 6.1-meter (20-foot) or even the 6.4-meter (21-foot) mark will be reached.

(Left) Adapted from Charles Siebert, "Vaulting to New Heights," *The New York Times Magazine*, July 6, 1986, p. 20; (above) Vandystadt—All Sport

Nancy Morgan—Sygma

The skeletons of children are highly susceptible to injury because their bones are still growing. Shear force, for example, can cause stress fractures in the lower legs of distance runners. Mary Decker (now Decker-Slaney), right, learned this lesson the hard way. She began running at age 11. At age 13 she set her first record. In 1973, at 14, she entered races against the best women runners in the U.S. With a "hunger to run" she continued to enter and win races until 1974, when she suffered a painful lower leg fracture that forced her to stop competing. She endured several courses of treatment for her injury. Dozens of improperly healed stress fractures up and down her shins meant she had to wear casts for months. Finally she required surgery. Then in 1977 she was injured again in two automobile accidents. Her years of forced absence from competition were probably a blessing: "Wouldn't it be horrible if I'd kept racing and was burned out?" Mary reflected in 1978—the year she finally made her comeback.

younger participants in top-level competition, parallel increases in injuries due to inappropriate loading are occurring.

The skeletons of growing children are highly susceptible to injury because their bones are still growing. Immature bones are some two to five times weaker than bones that are fully grown. Not surprisingly, sports involving rigorous impulse movements (*e.g.,* sprinting, jumping, landing, throwing, striking, and rebounding) can cause a wide range of injuries to immature bodies. Musculoskeletal system damage can be manifested, for example, in "tennis shoulder," or in vertebral injury in gymnasts. A recent long-range survey of gymnasts found that injury rates are strikingly high in young females who train and compete in gymnastics at advanced levels.

Before maturity, bone ends (epiphyses) are separated from the shafts of bones by plates of cartilage—growth plates. Epiphyseal damage—involving the growing portion of bones—can cause knee injuries in young jumpers and elbow injuries in young throwers, for example. A specific cartilage

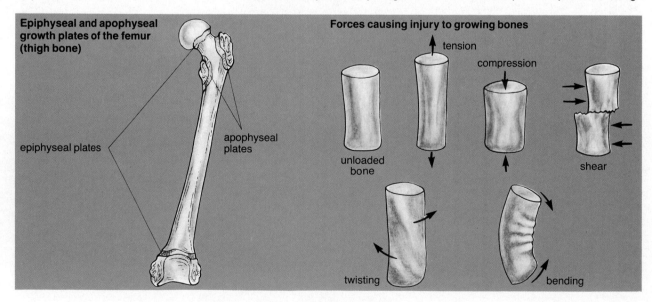

Epiphyseal and apophyseal growth plates of the femur (thigh bone)

epiphyseal plates

apophyseal plates

Forces causing injury to growing bones

tension

compression

unloaded bone

shear

twisting

bending

injury, chondromalacia patellae (softening of the cartilage of kneecaps), is not uncommonly caused by jumping and squatting.

Growth plates also separate bony anchorages (apophyses) of certain tendons from the bone shaft and from powerful muscles. Muscle-tendon junction damage in the form of apophysitis (abnormal protuberance of joints) often occurs in long-jumpers and footballers.

A variety of forces or loads such as compression, tension, and shear force will cause injury to bones (*e.g.,* stress fractures to lower legs in distance runners) and to vulnerable muscles such as quadriceps, hamstrings, and triceps. "Hamstring avulsion" (tearing away of muscle from the pelvis) is sometimes seen in young hurdlers.

Because the skeleton as a whole and growth plates in particular are so prone to damage throughout preadolescent and early adolescent years, it is essential that young athletes not be treated like adults. Committing this error in training may lead to abuse and injuries that can be severe and, in some cases, permanent. Intensive competitive sport training must, then, be geared specifically toward avoidance of the special vulnerabilities of growing athletes' bodies.

With rising standards and increasing participation in international competitive sport, the number of athletes under 21 years of age enjoying success at the top level will only rise. Coaches, parents, commercial sponsors, and sports federations each have key roles in supporting athletes' development through their growing years. They must ensure that this support is aimed at the athlete *as a whole person,* by providing training programs compatible with achievement at each ability/motivation stage, lest these promising young winners be "nipped in the bud" by senseless exploitation.

Participation in sport, in addition to just being fun, can afford growing children important creative, regenerative, and educational advantages. Best of all, youth sport gives a long-term advantage in the establishment of a healthy foundation for an active life. But because growing bodies are so vulnerable throughout preadolescence and early adolescence, it is essential that young athletes be specially trained. Coaches and parents must be sensitive to children's shifting motivations and abilities and to what is and what is not appropriate for them so that their potential to achieve is not nipped before it has had the chance to blossom.

Cultivating Young Minds

by Glyn C. Roberts, Ph.D.

A coveted ideal of the proponents of childhood involvement in sports is that such participation can contribute to personality development and enhance social values. There is good reason—if not much evidence—for the view that sports provide a forum for the teaching of responsibility, conformity, subordination of self to the greater good, the shaping of achievement by developing effort, persistence, delay of gratification, and the like. But the generalization that "sports build character" does not sit well with many who view the consequences of the sports experience as mostly negative. These critics generally focus upon the cost in human relations and the antisocial behavior attributable to an excessive emphasis upon winning, the increase in aggression (and sometimes violence) accompanying competition, and the social stigma of being rejected for nonparticipation. The supportive evidence for such negative views is again largely anecdotal; the true impact of sports upon children remains to be determined.

There is no question that organized sports for children have expanded dramatically over the past few years. Competitive sports organizations have directed much attention to developing competitive sports experiences for children. In one state in the United States, there is even competitive wrestling for four-year-olds! Many attribute this expansion to the impact of televised sports. Estimates of the total number of children involved range up to 200 million worldwide. To the large number of child participants must be added the substantial number of adults (parents, coaches, officials, administrators, etc.) whose involvement takes the form of investment of time and money.

Despite the pervasiveness of athletics—both the increased number of participants and the large segment of the overall society involved—little research has been conducted in this domain. Only recently has sports psychology, as a relatively new and clearly much neglected science, begun to direct attention toward children in sports. Before looking at the findings of sports psychologists relative to children, it is necessary to define sports psychology on a broader scale and to delineate the various roles undertaken by sports psychologists.

What is sports psychology?

Sports psychology is concerned with a facet of athletics that sports scientists, coaches, and athletes themselves have long neglected—the mind.

Glyn C. Roberts, Ph.D., *is a professor in the Departments of Physical Education and Leisure Studies and a member of the Institute for Health and Human Development at the University of Illinois at Urbana-Champaign. He is also General Secretary for the International Society of Sport Psychology.*

(Opposite page) Photograph, Cary Wolinsky—Stock, Boston

Sports participation provides children a forum for learning social values such as responsibility, conformity, and subordination of the self to the greater good—at least so say the proponents.

Young East German athletes such as those training at the College of Sports and Physical Culture at Leipzig (opposite page) are likely to be mentally tough competitors because they learn psychological skills early as part of their total training program.

The field is growing rapidly and is now considered to be an integral part of any sports medicine or sports science program. But much confusion exists regarding the role and function of psychologists within the sports context, and the profession still struggles with a sullied image in some quarters. There have been too many pseudopsychologists who have utilized bizarre and questionable strategies in the quest to enhance performance of athletes. For example, one children's coach in Texas used to bite the heads off of day-old live chickens in order to "motivate" the children to greater intensity in a game they were about to play. A college coach has been known to "punch" a blackboard so that it disintegrates spectacularly just before his charges take the field against an opponent. Whether these tactics work is debatable, particularly in the long run. Such "voodoo" strategies are deplored by serious scientists who operate from a knowledge base that is rapidly expanding and are developing legitimate psychological strategies for athletes. They are focusing on competition and are studying the validity and effectiveness of training programs.

There are two types of sports psychologists. First, there are clinical psychologists (and psychiatrists) who minister to athletes who exhibit abnormal or psychopathological profiles. This is a very important and necessary function within sports. Just as in the normal population, athletes (including elite athletes) can and do exhibit symptoms that demand psychotherapeutic intervention. For example, these practitioners treat anxious or depressed athletes, those who abuse or are addicted to drugs, and those with eating disorders; *e.g.,* anorexia nervosa or bulimia.

But the typical athlete is a normal person who finds himself or herself in abnormal situations of exceptional stress. Take the case of Australian tennis star Evonne Goolagong Cawley, who was notorious for losing her concentration in the middle of games and thus losing matches she should have won. She described what happened as her mind going on a "walkabout" when she was playing. It is the role of the second type of sports psychologist to help athletes in such situations by teaching them psychological skills that they can utilize in order to cope with the stress of the game. These psychologists are typically called educational sports psychologists. Today many athletes are benefiting—and winning—because they have learned psychological skills and developed strategies to prevent collapses of concentration, motivation, and confidence.

There is nothing magical about sports psychology. Nor is it instant in its effect. It is not a "laying on of hands." Psychological skills have to be learned, just like physical skills. The typical skills taught are in the realm of emotional control, attention, mental rehearsal (called imagery by most sports psychologists), and motivation. Just as in the teaching of physical skills, the psychologist begins with basic psychological skills and guides the individual athlete to the level of expertise relevant to his or her needs. The athlete is required to practice the psychological skills every day, just as physical skills are practiced. Ideally the development of psychological skills is part of the total training program. The fact that the East Germans have done this for years is a key reason that East German athletes are so mentally tough—and supremely successful—in competition.

158

The best psychological skills programs give athletes the emotional control, the concentration, the confidence, and the motivation to perform at their best. It goes without saying that athletes use these psychological skills not only to overcome factors that may interfere with performance but to enhance their own performance. For example, golf pro Jack Nicklaus always utilizes imagery to think through each shot before he addresses the ball. In *Golf My Way* Nicklaus wrote:

I never hit a shot, not even in practice, without having a sharp, in-focus picture of it in my head. It's like a color movie. First I "see" the ball where I want it to finish. . . . Then . . . I "see" the ball going there: its path, trajectory and shape, even its behavior on landing. . . . The next scene shows me making the kind of swing that will turn the previous images into reality.

Writer Emily Greenspan has cited the imaging technique that skier Steve Hegg learned at age 19 from the psychologist for the U.S. Alpine Ski Team; he says his mental preparation for competition is "like taking extra training runs." The night before skiing a downhill course that he has skied before, Hegg says, "I sit in my hotel room . . . and see myself making a perfect

Psychological factors can interfere with even the most skilled athletes' games. But by developing special mental strategies, they can overcome potential setbacks. (Above) Evonne Goolagong Cawley (left) has lost many a match owing to collapses of concentration in the middle of a game. Golf pro Jack Nicklaus (center) uses mental imagery to think through each shot in advance; before he raises the club to swing, he actually sees the ball where he wants it to land. Some pro tennis players are known for their emotional outbursts during a game; these may function to shake the rhythm of the opponent or, in John McEnroe's case (right), emotional outbursts probably give him time to regain confidence when his concentration is lagging.

Steve Hegg, a world-class skier and cyclist, learned an imaging technique as mental preparation when he was training with the U.S. Alpine Ski Team for the last Winter Olympics. Though he ended up not competing in the downhill race in February 1984 at Sarajevo, Yugoslavia, the psychological technique he had learned paid off six months later during cycling competition at the Los Angeles Summer Olympics. He "psyched" himself up by "just thinking of the medal ceremony." (Right) Hegg rides to victory; (far right) he proudly wears the gold medal at the victory celebration.

turn in the toughest part of the course." The American ski champions and twins, Phil and Steve Mahre, have also utilized mental rehearsal strategies for years to help them ski better.

There is an assumption widely held by the lay public that the main job of the sports psychologist is to provide the athlete with tactics to disrupt the psychological equilibrium of opponents. This is not so. There are, however, many tactics that individual athletes have developed on their own that they use quite effectively to gain a "psychological advantage." Boxers, tennis players, and track and field athletes often make very confident statements about how they are going to win an upcoming contest. These comments are supposed to charge up the athlete on the one hand and intimidate the opponent on the other. Muhammad Ali is famous for proclaiming invincibility before championship matches with his slogan, "I am the greatest!" During the contest athletes often use tactics designed to gain an advantage—*e.g.,* boxers staring hard at opponents and tennis players keeping opponents waiting. Tennis player Ile Nastase was notorious during a match for having an emotional outburst that was designed to shake the rhythm and concentration of the opponent. It often worked. By contrast, when John McEnroe has an emotional outburst, it appears to be for a different reason. McEnroe rarely displays his well-known "temper" in important matches. Rather, he has his wild tantrums in the early rounds of a tournament. Probably this is because McEnroe uses these outbursts to "psyche" himself up, not psyche out his opponent. When he feels his concentration slipping, he uses a pretext to question the intelligence (or the ancestry) of an unwitting official in order to gain "time out" to recommandeer his waning concentration. Though most sports psychologists do not coach athletes to disrupt games or to be flagrant exhibitionists, they *do* attempt to help athletes find individualized skills to ignore the disruptive tactics of opponents and to increase concentration, motivation, and, consequently, performance.

Some sports psychologists are employed by teams to develop team-wide stress-reduction strategies that promote *physical* relaxation (*e.g.,* low muscle tension, slow respiration and heart rates) and *mental* relaxation (a quietude of the mind). Specific strategies they may utilize are autogenic

160

(Left) David Madison—Duomo; (right) Dennis Stock—Magnum; (below) Adapted from Dale L. Hansen, "Cardiac Response to Participation in Little League Baseball Competition as Determined by Telemetry," *Research Quarterly*, vol. 38, no. 3 (October 1967), pp. 384–388

It is well documented that participation in sports can produce high levels of stress. Studies of Little Leaguers have shown this. The graph below indicates that Little League players' heart rates rose significantly during a game. Anxious children and those who feel pressure to win from parents and coaches are especially likely to perceive the game as stressful; these are also the children who are less likely to do well in competition or to enjoy the game.

training, progressive muscle relaxation exercises, biofeedback, and transcendental meditation.

Psychological skills will not make anyone a superstar. Sports psychologists often have more success with younger athletes. Older, more experienced athletes have often developed their own coping mechanisms, while children have not. In returning to the consideration of children, it is worthwhile to examine the recent research that has aimed to understand the unique perspective of youngsters and then focus on the strategies employed to make the sports experience more rewarding.

What do sports mean to youngsters?

First and foremost, children are not miniature adults. Children do not process information the same way adults do. Participation in sports may have unique meaning to children. For example, athletics may be the key domain in which young boys determine their standing among their peers and consequently determine self-worth. Recent evidence has supported this finding. High school students were asked whether they would prefer to succeed in sports or classroom contexts; both boys and girls preferred to succeed in sports contexts. The only context girls wished to avoid in sports was the individual head-to-head competition with other girls. But it is revealing that girls consider sports contexts (especially team sports) as appropriate contexts in which to succeed against other girls.

When asked whether failure in the classroom or failure in sports was the most aversive, boys clearly could accept their own failing in the classroom but not on the sports field. Girls, on the other hand, even though desiring success in sports, found failure in the classroom to be more aversive than failure on the sports field. This interesting sex difference underscores the different social expectations of boys and girls and how children are socialized toward different achievement interests. But the evidence shows that in Western society, for boys, it is almost impossible to underestimate the importance of demonstrating competence in athletic activities.

But a paradox exists. Despite viewing athletics as a most desirable context in which to achieve, children drop out of competitive sports at strikingly

Anxiety of Little Leaguers

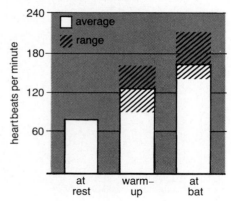

high rates, especially after age 12. Statistics show that 35% of all children involved in sports drop out in any one year, and about 80% of all children drop out permanently between the ages of 12 and 17 years of age. This phenomenon is not peculiar to North America. Australia and Europe show similar dropout trends. But why do they quit?

Research in this area of dropouts has been disappointing. Most of the evidence has been descriptive in nature with researchers either implicating the structure of the sports experience as the cause of high dropout (*e.g.,* adults putting too much pressure on children and/or too much emphasis on winning) or investigators concluding that "conflicts of interest" (*e.g.,* "I have other things to do") are the primary reasons why children drop out. It is not surprising, therefore, that the majority of sports psychologists today are seeking more specific causes to explain the phenomenon. They have been particularly concerned with identifying the sources of stress that appear to influence the decision of the child either to persist or to drop out.

Competitive stress

That participation in sports produces high levels of competitive stress is well documented. For example, in one study the heart rate of children (as a measure of stress) was monitored by telemetry as they were playing Little League baseball. This study found that while the children were fielding in the game, the average heart rate was 128 beats per minute (bpm). The range went from 90 to 161 bpm. A normal or resting rate for an 8–12-year-old boy is approximately 80 bpm. When children were at bat, the average heart rate was 166 bpm, with the range going from 145 to 204 bpm. In one small boy waiting for the ball to be pitched to him, the heart rate was 204 bpm.

Stress can be positive or negative. On the former score it can motivate and energize. Indeed, the ability to maintain performance under stress is as important as physical attributes or skills. But on the negative side perceived undue stress may overwhelm the athlete and stunt performance and self-esteem.

The study of Little Leaguers' heart rates and other surveys have determined that the following elements are implicated in the perception of competitive stress on the part of children. First, children who are anxious about

competitive environments in general perceive high levels of stress. Second, children with low self-esteem experience greater stress than children with high self-esteem. Third, children with lower expectancy of doing well experience greater competitive stress than children with high expectancy of doing well. Fourth, children who worry about the evaluation of their performance by the coach or their parents perceive high competitive stress. Fifth, children who feel great pressure from parents to compete experience competition as highly stressful. And last, children who lose experience greater stress than children who win. Such perception of high stress in competition tends toward the "negative" in this context. In other words, when Little Leaguers or other children perceive athletics as stressful, they are less likely to perform well or enjoy their participation.

Do children perceive that sports are stressful in the same way at all stages of childhood, or is there a developmental facet to the perception? In order to consider this question, it is necessary to look at the information-processing capability of the child at various ages.

Motivation for athletics

We cannot understand the behaviors or perceptions of children unless we understand their goals—*i.e.,* the subjective meaning of achievement for them. If the outcome of sports participation is perceived to afford desirable qualities about the self, such as competence, courage, virtue, and loyalty, then the experience is likely to offer success, and generally little negative stress is experienced. If, on the other hand, the outcome is seen to reflect undesirable qualities about the self, then the experience is perceived to elicit failure, and stress may be significant.

The child is an information-processing organism. This processing affects behavior. The model sports psychologists use in assessing the child's information-processing tendencies is derived from contemporary motivation theory. The basic assumption is that the primary achievement goal of every individual in any case is to maximize the demonstration of high ability and to minimize the demonstration of low ability. Success, then, equals

Winning and losing are part of the game. (Below) Young American participants at a track meet share the pleasure of having won medals; a defeated Australian rugby player is comforted after his team has lost an important game. How athletes react to either situation—winning or losing— depends a great deal on their individual motivations and achievement goals. Are they most interested in performing well by their own standards, in demonstrating they are better than others, or in garnering the approval of others?

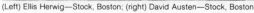
(Left) Ellis Herwig—Stock, Boston; (right) David Austen—Stock, Boston

Social approval can be an important motivator for children in sports. All the effort becomes worthwhile when a coach signifies approval.

ability demonstrated; failure is ability not demonstrated. In sports, ability is assessed in one of three ways, and all have to be considered.

Sports competence. First, ability may be assessed through social comparison processes—*i.e.,* the performer's focus of attention is on how his or her own ability compares with that of others. Athletes constantly evaluate their own, and their opponents', competence. Children generally try hard to demonstrate competence. In competitive contests winning and losing become important criteria. Winning means ability has been demonstrated, and postcompetition stress is low; losing means insufficient ability has been demonstrated, and postcompetitive stress is high. Expecting to win means ability is likely to be demonstrated, and thus precompetitive stress is reduced; expecting to lose means the opposite, and thus precompetitive stress is exaggerated.

Sports mastery. Some athletes are not concerned with demonstrating higher ability than others. These athletes focus upon their own performance based upon their own personal standards. Rather than demonstrating higher capacity than that of others, this child directs attention toward achieving mastery in improving or perfecting a sports skill. In this way high ability is demonstrated when the person exceeds previous levels of performance. These athletes (often described as intrinsically motivated) often become so engrossed in the activity itself that they may lose all concept of the passage of time.

Children who are sports-mastery oriented do not perceive much stress in the competitive sports experience, whatever the outcome. These children perceive stress only if the coach or a significant other criticizes their effort or commitment.

Social approval. One other variable is also of importance. Some athletes are motivated to obtain social approval from significant others, usually parents and coaches. Typically, but not always, children recognize that social approval is dependent upon the demonstration of effort. To these athletes, trying hard to gain social approval is the main goal. This goal is met when the coach signifies approval, but stress is experienced when the coach or significant others fail to signify social approval.

Fluctuating goals

Children are likely to go through several stages in the development of achievement goals. Young children may approach the sports experience because they enjoy the challenge (sports mastery) and are not concerned with the outcome. But as they get older, their goals change. They may want to please others or be rewarded for trying hard (social approval) or demonstrate their ability (competence) to others.

Recently investigators at the University of Illinois's Institute of Child Behavior and Development conducted a study of achievement goals of children (ages 9–14) who were playing baseball or softball or were involved in competitive swimming. The study found that goals emerged at different ages. In the under-12-year-olds they found sports-mastery and social-approval goals. These children were generally unable to differentiate between the relative contributions of effort and ability in determining success and failure.

164

Younger players are unable to assess their own ability accurately; instead, they focus upon effort and believe that effort is ability. These children are particularly sensitive to the comments and criticisms of others, especially the coach. When these young children participate, they quickly recognize that trying hard is an effective means of obtaining favorable comments, and consequently trying hard becomes an important criterion to them. If they are criticized or praised, they are crushed or elated accordingly. This is where adults need to be sensitive to the criteria the child is using for success and failure. Although these children are not focusing on winning or losing, they learn very quickly that winning pleases. One way to please a coach—indeed the *only* way to please some coaches—is to win the game. But young children do not understand that by winning the game they are also demonstrating competence.

Children 12 years old or older were able to differentiate between effort and ability. Evidently it is not until children are about 12 years old that their information-processing ability is such that they understand the relative contributions of effort and ability to success and failure outcomes and recognize that it takes both effort and ability to achieve. This evidence is consistent with other evidence from academic achievement settings, which shows that children go through similar stages concerning what is most important or meaningful to them in terms of classroom performance.

Only when children are able to differentiate between the causes of outcomes are they able to judge their own capacity at the sport. This can be an exciting or a traumatic discovery.

Dropping out

When children do come to recognize their ability—if they perceive they lack valued physical capacities—they may drop out. This may explain why children typically do not drop out of sports until after age 12. As children (boys in particular) regard failure in sports to be very distressing, lacking ability in a valued activity is distressing, and dropping out is one means available of avoiding continuation of an unpleasant or even humiliating experience. One of the most common reasons children give for dropping out of sports is

If children perceive that they lack athletic ability, they may drop out of sports. The experience of failure can cause great distress to youngsters; quitting is a way of avoiding the humiliation of defeat. A British study looking into the question of why young athletes drop out has suggested that drop-out rates are high in the U.S. because the major American team sports are ones in which there is a lot of nonplaying time. Ability-oriented players may become frustrated by spending time on the bench rather than on the field.

165

that they do not enjoy the experience. But the reason for not enjoying the experience may well be that they perceive they have low ability and will be unable to cope. They feel inadequate in the athletic event.

On the other hand, there are children who perceive themselves to have high ability but who may not feel sufficiently challenged. These youngsters are most likely to drop out because of boredom. These are also the players who are typical show-offs. As an immediate means of overcoming their incipient boredom in the sport, they may flagrantly take risks during the play or consciously not try hard.

The major criterion of success and failure that children 12 or older focus on is the outcome—winning or losing. Coaches exacerbate this by evaluating themselves on the won/loss record, and the competitive sports structure focuses upon outcomes with leagues, playoffs, and championships. Thus, society has a system that elevates the importance of winning and losing but recognizes very few teams or players as being "the best."

British researcher Jean Whitehead at the Children's Sport Study Centre of Bedford (England) College of Higher Education views the disturbing loss of ability-oriented players in the U.S. as reflective of the major types of sports (e.g., baseball, basketball, and American football)—all of which involve a lot of nonplaying time. She believes that the youngsters who drop out may not be getting enough opportunity to show ability. These ability-oriented athletes may instead be spending a lot of time "sitting on the bench." She has compared this pattern with that in British athletics, where the typical sports and coaching conditions give children more opportunity to show ability, and she believes that British youth may be staying in sports longer to do just that.

Whitehead has also made the important point that dropping out of adolescent sports is not necessarily "all bad." Rather, children may be taking up many other hobbies and interests, and they cannot pursue all activities into adult life. It is for those who quit sports for negative reasons, such as too much stress, that it is important to minimize adverse effects.

Modifying the sport is one way of making the athletic experience valuable and more enjoyable for children. A good example is the development of minirugby (below right) because overly competitive adult rugby (left) is too difficult and too rough for young players.

(Left) William Meyer—Click/Chicago; (right) Mike Powell—Allsport

(Left) Mary Lou Retton, the newly confirmed best all-around gymnast, is lifted up by her devoted coach, Bela Karolyi, after she received a perfect 10 rating on the vault in the 1984 Summer Olympics. Retton has a unique relationship with her coach, who is remarkably able to fire up his young charge for top-level competition. Not every athlete would be able to bear up to Karolyi's unrelenting standards the way Retton can.

Enhancing athletic enjoyment

If it is believed that the sports experience is a valuable one for children and there is a commitment to their fullest possible development, then an attempt must be made to maintain the motivation of all child athletes, not just those who are the current high achievers. Something is amiss if some are systematically encouraged at the expense of others. Yet this inequality of motivation appears inevitable in a competitive system of organized sports that focuses upon outcomes as the major criterion of success or failure.

In terms of structural change, modifying the sport itself—*e.g.,* smaller playing fields, fewer children on each team, no leagues or championships—can make a great difference. Where they have occurred, such modifications have been successful.

An example is the establishment of the game minirugby in Britain in 1971. This is a game that was devised and adapted to suit the abilities

The type of coaching a child gets can make sports participation grueling or fun. The need for coaches who are attuned to the special physical capacities and emotional makeup of youngsters led to the development of training programs for coaches. In 1981 sports psychologists started the American Coaching Effectiveness Program (below right), which has trained over 25,000 coaches. The ACEP philosophy is "athletes first, winning second."

(Left) Focus on Sports; (right) American Coaching Effectiveness Program

(Above) Girls, ages two to six, take off in a 400-meter (quarter-mile) race in New York City's Central Park, with overeager mothers literally pushing them over the starting line. Too often children are forced into sports to fulfill the parents' needs and in total disregard of the child's desires. When parents push children in this way, the results can be tragic. But a supportive parent (right) whose interest is in the child's enjoyment and not in who wins the game can make all the difference.

of young players. The exceptionally tough and highly competitive game of rugby (established in the early 1800s) was considered too complicated for beginners. The range of skills necessary for playing the original game made too many demands on those new to the game. When young players attempted to play the adult, 15-on-a-side, game, the result was 30 little players hopelessly chasing the ball but little real involvement for most because few players actually got to touch the ball. Consequently, mastery of the fundamentals of the game was nearly impossible. Minirugby thus is a modified game; in the mini version fewer players are involved, and the emphasis is on contact with and skillful handling of the ball. The response to the new competitive youth game has been excellent; minirugby is now widely played in schools in the British Isles.

A very important determinant of a child's enjoyment of the sports experience is the type of coaching he or she receives, since the coach is the key individual in almost any sports program. The coach calls the shots, teaches the skills, and in general makes athletic participation either challenging and fun or grueling and punishing.

Coaching coaches

In North America coaches who were polled about what aspects of athletic performance contribute most to positive outcomes implicated mental factors as ranking high. Both coaches and athletes recognize that mental aspects are important for consistent and enhanced performance. But, ironically, it is the one area that coaches traditionally know least about. In response to the need for well-trained coaches who make sports a positive experience for youngsters, there are now many special programs for coaches, largely developed by sports psychologists. In such programs coaches are being better trained to recognize a wider range of emotions than simply the will to win. One program, the American Coaching Effectiveness Program (ACEP), was started in 1981, based on a philosophy of "athletes first, winning second." More than 25,000 coaches have gone through the ACEP training.

168

They learn that every decision coaches make should be, first and foremost, for the child's well-being. The need for better coaching was especially evident in Little League baseball, the largest sports organization in the world, with at least 300,000 coaches. Little League has been widely criticized for being dominated by overzealous winning-oriented parent/coaches. In 1984 a coaching program was started on a national basis in the U.S. to respond to the great need for healthier coaching methods. It is hoped that such training will go a long way toward altering the tarnished Little League image and making young people's baseball fun again.

It must be recognized that children, despite the best intentions, are going to focus attention on the outcome if they are not helped to focus upon performance goals. Children see sports on television and recognize that all the glory goes to the winner. Children must be encouraged to move away from asking questions such as "Am I better than, as good as, or worse than my opponent?" and toward asking questions such as "How did I play today?" One simple instruction for parents advocated by sports psychologists is for them to ask their children whether they enjoyed themselves rather than asking who won the game.

Sports psychologists recommend a child-oriented approach to setting appropriate goals in order to redefine success and failure. Above all, these goals should be (1) *flexible*—i.e., adaptable to the situation; rigid goals can lead to discouragement; (2) *challenging*—making the athlete apply effort to succeed; (3) *realistic*—not overoptimistic or too easy (girls are more likely to be unduly pessimistic; boys, overoptimistic); and (4) *personally controllable* (children should not feel like they are circus animals). It is also important that short-term, as well as long-term, goals be established because for youngsters even tomorrow can seem a long way off.

Above all, sports are supposed to be a source of pleasure. That is an especially pertinent point, considering that organized sports for children have expanded dramatically in the past several years.

"Hey, watch the child!"

Some of the worst "horror" stories concerning children in sports involve parental pressure. For youngsters the so-called pushy parent syndrome can have tragic results, especially when children's competition is used by adults to achieve their own aims, regardless of whether such aims coincide with those of the child. Indeed, children are exceptionally impressionable beings. Forcing them into sports or imposing pressure to excel can lead to deep physical and emotional scars. In the extreme, children who experience unduly high stress in sports may develop troubling, and sometimes debilitating, physical symptoms such as abdominal pain, headaches, and breathing difficulty. A study reported in 1982 in the *Journal of Psychosomatic Medicine* found a high incidence of stress-induced gastrointestinal complaints in children, which were associated with extreme parental pressure to achieve in competitive sports.

Clearly it is time for adults to stop and ask themselves, "Aren't we supposed to have the interests of the child at heart? Aren't sports supposed to be a source of fun and pleasure?" ("Pleasant pastime" is how the *Oxford English Dictionary* defines "sport.") Just as adults coaching from the sidelines are constantly reminding kids, "Hey, watch the ball!" parents and coaches now must be reminded, "Hey, watch the child!"

The Happiness of the Middle-Distance Runner

by Peter Coe and Sebastian Coe

All agree that physical training should form part of physical education and until the age of puberty it should be less exacting, avoiding too strict a diet and over much work, so as not to hinder growth. The disadvantages of excessive training in the early years are amply proved by the list of the Olympic victors, not more than two or three of whom won a prize both as boys and men; the discipline to which they were subjected in childhood undermined their powers of endurance.

—Aristotle, *Politics*, book viii

In the period from 1979 to 1984 Sebastian Coe broke 12 world records or world bests, acquired two Olympic gold and two Olympic silver medals, and set an Olympic record—even though he had never appeared on a national or world age-best record list until he reached his twenties, and even though his athletic career had begun over a decade earlier. Luckily, in Sebastian Coe's training the profoundly wise advice of Aristotle, dating back 2,300 years, was heeded, rather than more current practices.

Today there is an increasing trend toward putting young girls and boys into endurance running races. The entry of youngsters into such events is mainly the fault of the parents, since no educated or responsible coach would do anything so silly. It is not uncommon to see parents who do not possess any knowledge of physiology or of the principles or practice of good coaching standing on the sidelines of tracks and cross-country courses screaming encouragement at overtired and very strained children. Too often this ill-advised "pushing" is for no better purpose than a parental ego trip. Such behavior is not restricted to "macho" fathers; mothers are there at the sidelines rooting just as vociferously.

There is indeed a very special role for the parents of a young child with athletic interests and aspirations, but the above behavior has no part in it. Good coaching of youngsters in sport is not unlike financial managing; wasting assets for a quick profit and short-term gain is a sure road to bankruptcy. Good managers exploit their assets carefully—for the future; in short, they do not take stupid risks.

Talent: the delicate flower

Having athletic talent does not mean being able to deliver "The Performance" now. It is much safer to consider talent as the ability to deliver great

Peter Coe is Sebastian Coe's father and coach, a retired production engineer, a lecturer in middle-distance running, and Chairman of the British Milers Club.
Sebastian Coe is a world champion middle-distance runner, a member of the Athletes' Commission of the International Olympic Committee, Chairman of the Olympic Review Group of the Sports Council of Great Britain, and an associate member of the Académie des Sports, France; he was made a Member of the Order of the British Empire in 1982. The Coes are coauthors of the book Running for Fitness *(1983).*

(Opposite page) Hugh Hastings

Detail of a Greek vase, 336 BC; the British Museum;
photograph, Michael Holford

*Some 2,300 years ago Aristotle stressed
the inappropriateness of overtaxing the
bodies of young athletes; the wisest
of Greek thinkers was well aware
that Olympic victors were athletes
whose "powers of endurance" were not
squandered in early training.*

*Peter and Sebastian Coe (below) have
been partners in pursuit of athletic
excellence for nearly two decades. All
along the guiding principle of Sebastian's
training has been respect for the whole
body—holism—the absolute necessity of
making slow and careful progress and
always allowing sufficient time before
advancing from one training level to
the next.*

performances later. Unlike music or chess, athletics has no equivalents of child prodigies or juvenile grand masters. A great achievement in athletics is directly related to the physical status of the performer. Sufficient time must be allowed for the whole body to develop to the level of fitness necessary for top-level performances. Yet another metaphor makes the point: talent is a delicate flower. It will not bloom without careful nurturing.

We (father and son/ coach and athlete) have been partners for 17 years in the pursuit of the ultimate in athletic excellence. On the way to world records and Olympic golds, we found that all the lessons learned only confirmed our belief in the absolute necessity of making slow and careful progress.

Sebastian: *Through all the stages from being a smaller-than-average 12-year-old beginner to achieving my ambition of Olympic gold, there was one rule I never broke, that of gradual change. The smooth transition from one phase to the next without abrupt changes was and is my guiding principle—a lesson I learned early from my coach and one which I have maintained ever since.*

In discussing athletes, it is convenient to separate the mental from the physical aspects of training, but the interaction between the two must never be forgotten; it is central to ultimately achieving championship performances. To this end, training must be holistic. A holistic approach not only is morally right but is also a safeguard against excesses in training. Maximizing one's talents, such as they may be, is one thing; winding up as a retired or failed athlete of limited education and intellect is quite another. The aim of anyone involved in guiding young people should be the old Renaissance ideal, the "person in the round"—or, in modern terms, the well-rounded person.

Young bodies: essential considerations

The physical stress of growing, the mental stresses of learning and studying, and the emotional stress of trying to satisfy the demands and expectations of adults soon add up, and it does not take very much for the growing child to be harmed. For good physiological reasons the amount of endurance training that would be necessary for children to succeed even modestly in distance running is totally incompatible with their general health and educa-

Photographs, Hugh Hastings

tion. Endurance running for a child is not just playful expending of energy; it is a severe and draining stress. Thus, one cannot place children, even those with recognized athletic potential, into a highly structured competitive environment and expect them to be happy, integrated individuals.

Holism is needed not only to avoid unnecessary stress but to help the body to develop as harmoniously as possible—a difficult enough task since all parts of the body do not grow at the same rate. For example, between birth and maturity there is only a twofold expansion of the head, while the legs increase their length five times. This is further complicated by the fact that the growth rate also varies with age, a component greatly affecting co-ordination during the adolescent growth spurt. The body has very sensitive internal controls monitoring limb movements, and the brain is "confused" by rapid changes in the limbs' relative positions due to sudden increases in growth. This is the cause of embarrassing adolescent clumsiness.

In growing children an often overlooked factor is the difference between chronological and physiological age. Children are almost always divided into academic and athletic groups according to their age, not their level of development. It may be the only quick and practical way, but it is certainly not a sensible one.

Sebastian: *The photograph of me with my contemporaries at a big interschools meeting illustrates the difficulties that some youngsters have. Had not my father explained that his side of the family, and thus I, were always late developers physically, I might have wanted to go home shouting "No contest"; I certainly could not beat everyone around in those days. He explained that later on my eventual maturity would then be my "ace in the hole." This thought helped me through some of my early disappointments.*

Consider Table I, particularly the last column. These figures show the possible percentage advantage or disadvantage that a child might have in endurance training vis à vis contemporaries and thus how important it is to match training to the individual with great care and patience, especially with young people. As stated earlier, athletic performances are directly related to the physical status of the athlete: the budding but small pianist can put an extra cushion or phone directory on the piano stool; an immature runner has no such aid.

Peter Coe

Sebastian was a "late developer." Above, at age 14, he is with two of his contemporaries at an interschools athletic meeting. A fact that is commonly overlooked is that children grow at quite different rates. Despite the importance of young athletes developing as harmoniously as possible, children are almost invariably grouped in sports according to age. For some late developers such grouping can exact measurable disadvantages, as Table 1 (below) indicates.

Table 1: **Childhood physical maturity**			
chronological age	potential retarded growth (in years)	potential advanced growth (in years)	potential maximum disadvantage (approximate percentage)
8	7.00	9.25	32
9	7.83	10.60	35
10	8.85	11.00	31
11	9.33	12.33	32
12	10.53	13.00	23
13	10.89	14.25	31
14	12.55	15.29	22
15	13.57	16.43	21
16	14.86	17.40	17
17	16.00	18.00	12
18	17.00	19.00	12

Mental readiness is as important in athletic competition as physical readiness. Being able to cope with defeat is essential. Sebastian felt shattered by losing the 800 meter to his fellow countryman Steve Ovett in the Moscow Olympics in 1980 (top left). He managed to overcome his feelings, however, and summoned the mental and physical forces necessary to outrun Ovett in the 1,500 meter (right) and win the gold. As father and coach to Sebastian, Peter Coe (above) always shares emotionally when his son competes.

Mental readiness for competition

The young person also has not had enough time to acquire the necessary mental toughness for coping with the disappointments of defeat in races for which he or she may have great expectations. Yet the athlete's perspective on victory and defeat makes a great difference.

Sebastian: *There are times when the gods do not smile on even the best of us and, believe me, the greater your achievements, the more painful are the defeats. Even more so when as the world record holder, through my own fault, I lost the 800 meter in the 1980 Olympics. I lost it because for the first time in my life I succumbed to the enormous pressure of a major event, and I must say that nothing can exert such pressure as an Olympic final. For those whose expectations are not that high, it must seem like bad sportsmanship to say that settling for an Olympic silver medal was not enough, but that silver was of absolutely no value to me; I felt totally shattered. It was and still is my greatest disappointment. Where did I get my strength from to come back and seize the coveted 1,500-meter gold medal? Some would say character, but character is formed by and draws from many sources, not the least of which is family support. My defeats in my youth were dealt with analytically and truthfully, but I never felt my family lost faith in me. This support, truthful but so warm, is not available from those who scream at you during your early races or make defeat a catastrophe.*

I remember the keen disappointments of my four defeats before I eventually won in an English schools championship. But my father would not change his careful training methods and tactics to those of exploitation for immediate success. He made me realize that it was only later that winning mattered, and I was to be preserved for that day. Dedication and persistence are needed and have to be learned from the teacher, but he must also show the same virtues. Defeats in these prestigious events hurt a lot, and I felt that hurt deeply. It was then that I needed a lot of support.

But young people are not fools. Don't kid them. It is possible to be both truthful and supportive; this is essential for mutual trust and respect. Later, when a lot more experienced, the athlete will know when he was truly beaten and accept it. He will have learned to assess defeat when ill or injured. He won't like it, but he can reconcile himself to it.

Losing to a great athlete like Joachim Cruz in the 800 meter at Los Angeles, viewed in proper perspective, was actually a personal triumph because I had come back with little training after two years of illness. Nonetheless, the effort required to get myself "altogether" for the 1,500 meter was so draining that I hope never to have to face anything like it again.

174

The point of these stories is that children have to be gradually toughened mentally as well as physically to withstand severe disappointments both on and off the track. It is a slow process in which it is easier to "break 'em" than to "make 'em"; however, it is a learning process that must start early.

Coping with setbacks

Learning to cope with setbacks is an essential part of early education for children and especially for aspiring athletes. Most often setbacks in life precede those on the track. In guiding young persons to an athletic career, many adults make the mistake of putting the cart before the horse.

Sebastian: In Great Britain the 11-plus school examination was important because for the great majority the quality of their future secondary education hung on the outcome. My handicap was a nervous disposition and chronic hay fever in the summer that made rural schooling almost intolerable. I failed this examination and, with a very badly dented self-esteem, was sent to a school of lower educational expectations. I was very, very depressed. My father's advice was simple: "You can accept being an educational dropout or get up and really work your way out. If you try I'll help."

Here the application of a "defeated" youngster encouraged by a supportive parent was such that his catching up was swift, followed by his gaining a university honors degree in economics and social history and becoming a postgraduate research assistant. Thus, the foundation of not yielding was already laid before success in sport. In Sebastian's case his scholarship improved with his athletic status. Both father and son, coach and athlete, strongly believe that achieving excellence in one field will have a liberating and enhancing effect upon other activities.

One of the most difficult setbacks for an athlete to overcome is ill health. Injuries, for which there are fairly standard periods of recovery, are usually more easily understood.

Sebastian: My first setback through illness came at a time when I dearly wanted to win a boys' title at 1,500 meters. I was 14 years old, and I was undergoing some orthodontic treatment when my mouth became badly infected. Although I tried hard, I had to concede that trying to compete at that level with a head swollen up like a basketball was just not "on." Recovering from illness was not like getting over a stress fracture of the tibia. The safe way of dealing with the latter is a straight six weeks' layoff and that is it. You just don't try to carry on. Luckily for me, my father stopped me from trying to run with an infection (which is at all times a very dangerous thing to do).

All senior athletes, especially at the top of their careers, feel that they could soon run out of time. Because of my achievements in 1980 and 1981, in which I won an Olympic gold and broke two world records, the years of '82 and '83 were the years of my greatest setback. Not only did I have to deal with the debilitating effects of a heavy infection of toxoplasmosis—a generalized infection caused by a parasite, which is not easy to diagnose in the early stages and is of uncertain duration—but I had to cope with being written off by most of the British press and many in the sport. The actual pain from my swollen glands and the suffering from sore muscles would have caused most men to quit. But 1984 was my annus mirabilis with my second Olympic gold in Los Angeles; I suspect that my extreme jubilation after I crossed the finish line in the 1,500 meter told all.

Partial immunity (it can never be total) to the tremendous stress that an Olympic final can impose is obtained by exposure to very carefully

Peter Coe

One of the most difficult setbacks for an athlete is ill health. At age 14 Sebastian suffered his first setback due to illness (a badly infected mouth after orthodontic treatments) when he had all his hopes set on winning the boys' title in a 1,500-meter race. His father saw that he was not at all well enough to compete, though Sebastian admits he might have run anyway had it not been for his father's guidance and wise respect for his ailing body.

175

Wise and proper training of young athletes requires knowing some of the physiological ways that growing children differ from adults. The younger they are, the greater is the ratio of heart volume to body weight—i.e., aerobic capacity (Table 2, opposite). Young runners may seem like "little aerobic wonders" with unlimited powers of endurance (above left), but this deceptive advantage soon disappears, and growing bodies that have been overtaxed can be seriously harmed.

Children also suffer an "oxygen debt" because before puberty they lack special enzymes that adults have. Therefore, they are not able to race like adults, and they certainly should not race against adults (above center). Another difference is that the breathing capacity of children is about half that of adults. (Above right) During a race in hot weather, the breathing of young runners is both faster and more labored, and they are at high risk of becoming dehydrated and suffering cramps. Overloading the growing skeleton not only can cause severe and sometimes irreparable injury but may also stunt growth. The early results of Linsey MacDonald's shocking training regimen (right) when she was still growing could hardly have been worth the toll it took on her body. MacDonald, from Scotland, "burned out" well before her prime, forfeiting what might have been a great athletic career for the sake of a few early wins.

administered doses of stress very early on. The art lies in the timing and the size of the doses. This is not the spartan method of leaving newborns on the hillside just to see if they survive; rather it is a way of testing and challenging the young with love and care. Loving and caring means being firm and setting hard tasks while being sensitive to the risks of overloading.

Children's physiological limitations

A few basic facts about the exercise physiology of children are essential to understanding wise and proper training of children in athletics. What is known as the cardiac quotient is an important and often overlooked measure of aerobic capacity. This quotient is the ratio of the heart volume (in milliliters) to the body weight (in kilograms). The younger they are, the more relative aerobic capacity children have. (*See* Table 2.) Thus, it would be easy to suppose that distance running and distance racing are ideal pursuits for young children—and the younger, the better. However, it is most emphatically not so. When this marked aerobic advantage later disappears with ensuing age, these children will be left at a great disadvantage—suffering

from overuse injuries. Thus, while it is precisely this high cardiac quotient that allows "little aerobic wonders" to run for such long periods, the effect of prolonged running on the very young is cumulative, and it will emerge as injury and not excellence. Simply put: their small, growing bodies and limbs will not stand up to what their aerobic capacity can tolerate.

In sports training of young children an important distinction must be grasped—that between running and racing. Running as aerobic exercise means that the lungs keep supplying the blood with all the oxygen the muscles need to keep working. This is not so with racing. At some stage racing becomes going as fast as one can to beat others, often coming close to and even reaching exhaustion. This will incur a significant "oxygen debt," which is called anaerobic work. Anaerobic work requires the presence of special enzymes that children do not possess before puberty. Therefore, children are unable to race like adults. This must be emphasized. If children cannot race like adults, why train them the same way?

In distance running the body cannot absorb as much liquid as it loses. This is true even when drinks are supplied. But in children breathing capacity is about 50% less (both shallower and faster) than that of adults; thus, they lose significantly more water vapor and in turn run a high risk of dehydration. At the same time, their fast breathing will blow off proportionately more carbon dioxide; this loss causes cramps to hands and feet. Children need to breathe considerably more air than adults to extract a liter of oxygen; their lungs are also a lot less mechanically efficient. They cannot sweat as freely as adults, and they therefore have greater cooling problems with a greater risk of overheating. These deficiencies do not improve until puberty. Furthermore, the degree of hardship caused by prolonged effort is frequently perceived to be far less severe by children than by adolescents and adults. This renders them prone to "voluntary dehydration." As a precaution against this, it is recommended that young children be given a rest after every 20 minutes of activity.

Overloading can also stunt growth and even deform growing children. Young joints are very vulnerable, and a lot of downhill running, for example, can be harmful to knees. Near the ends of bones are the regions of bone growth, called epiphyseal plates; these are easily damaged by excessive loading. Likewise, the attachment points of the various muscles are easily detached in the young. These apophyseal points do not develop their full strength before maturity and are easily pulled away from the bone—as in Osgood-Schlatter's disease, where the muscle attachment on the shin is torn away just below the knee. Other common overloading problems that occur in young children are a tilted pelvis and lower back problems.

Outline of Sebastian Coe's training (ages 12–16)

age	training
12	joined local running club, participated in a few summer handicap races at 100 m* and the club's 100-m championship for Colts (12-year-olds)
13	*winter:* cross-country (x-c) training runs of around 3.2–4.8 km† on weekends and steady road runs of about 4.8 km on alternate days; occasional race (1.6–3.2 km) *summer:* similar to winter but with one midweek and one weekend track session of light sprint training; racing consisted of some interclub competition at 100 m
14	*winter:* x-c training runs weekends up to 7¼ km over rough terrain; eight to ten x-c races of 3.2–4.8 km each in an interscholastic league over grass courses; training continues to take place mainly on alternate days, with the training distances sometimes as much as 6½ km and at a faster pace *summer:* training on a track two nights a week plus a harder Sunday morning session; interval and tempo training introduced (interval training at well below maximum effort to enhance cardiac output; tempo training at near-maximum effort to enhance resistance to anaerobic fatigue); occasional 800-m and 1,500-m races
15	in essence a repeat of the previous year with a slight increase in mileage (average weekly total over the year: approximately 32 km)
16	*winter:* x-c racing reduced, but the speed of x-c and road running increased; short, hard repetition runs (100 m 20 times) up steep hill introduced and harder fartlek work (in which sprinting, jogging, and walking are alternated) *summer:* training five and six days per week using speed repetitions of 200, 300, 400, and 800 m with short recovery times

*one meter equals 3.28 ft
†one kilometer equals 0.62 mi

Table 2: **Aerobic capacity: children versus adults**

age	height	heart volume	weight	cardiac quotient
8	127 cm (4 ft 2 in)	352 ml	26 kg (57 lb)	13.5
9	132 cm (4 ft 4 in)	353 ml	27 kg (59 lb)	13.1
10	135 cm (4 ft 5 in)	357 ml	29 kg (64 lb)	12.3
30	180 cm (5 ft 11 in)	540 ml	70 kg (154 lb)	7.7

Sebastian has always trained alone. The day he started running was the day his dad started coaching. (Peter Coe has not trained other runners because he does not know them well enough.) Many have noted that Sebastian has an exceptionally smooth and strong stride, and often at the end of a race it appears that he could go on for many more laps. The Coe approach to endurance is, above all, balanced, concentrating on almost every muscle in the body. Unlike many top-level runners, Sebastian avoids racing during training; indeed, holding back has been a unique part of his preparation for major competitions.

The proper conclusion to be drawn is that children must not be made to conform to adult training patterns. People in charge of children's sporting activities should know that while careful loading can promote strength, overloading can severely tax and damage children's growing bodies.

In Great Britain the Amateur Athletic Association (AAA) wisely has limited the distance that children can race to three miles before age 15. Since Britain has produced long-serving athletes who have dominated world-class middle-distance running since 1976, this rule cannot have been too restrictive.

Sebastian: *I started light competitive running with an athletic club when I was 12. Aged 18 years, I took the 1,500-meter bronze medal in the European Junior Championship logging only 28 miles a week. At 21 years, on only 35 miles per week, I again won a bronze medal as a senior in the European Championships and later that year broke the U.K. 800-meter record. The following year I broke three world records on considerably less training mileage than my conqueror in the 1975 Junior Championships. You will not survive to reach the top, never mind staying there, if you start with long, arduous training and racing.*

The lesson here is that the most important aspect of endurance is endurance in the sport, simply staying "whole" long enough to develop full potential—or, as Woody Allen has said, success is 99% just showing up.

Do the same lessons apply to the endurance training of girls, who reach physical maturity earlier than boys? Is this single physiological fact a good guide to real maturity, and is this earlier puberty of any real significance for endurance? It may be in other aspects of their development, such as in the acquisition of learning skills and in development of strength, but *not* in endurance.

The current crop of the female greats in distance running, among them, Marlies Gohr, Marita Koch, Barbel Eckert-Wockel, Tatyana Kazankina, Maricica Puica, Grete Waitz, and Inge Christiansen, are all women who

178

reached their athletic prime as adults—after a careful course of training that did not force them to overtrain as girls and thus wear out early. And they have continued to improve as women whose ages are 27, 35, and more! Tatyana Kazankina was born in 1951 and had reached the age of 25 before achieving her first big win; she then set about slaughtering the world's middle-distance records.

Compare those careers with what happened to a small Scottish lass, Linsey MacDonald. She represents one of the saddest examples of wasted talent. The "training" she endured was not merely misuse but abuse. Her shocking training regimen included wearing a harness and dragging around a heavy car tire while carrying weights in each hand and wearing heavy miners' pit boots! For the price of an Olympic bronze medal in the 4 x 400 relay at Moscow in 1980, she has been cast into total athletic obscurity. One wonders if her coach had read Aristotle.

By observing the following rules, young athletes (girls and boys alike) will gain the best chances for avoiding early "burnout" and for lasting in their sport long enough to profit from proper coaching and training and reach their best:

1. Select intermediate and long-term goals carefully.

2. Plan and train to reach those objectives on the *least* amount of work necessary to achieve them.

3. Do not seek to push on beyond established goals even if they are achieved relatively early—*i.e.*, be satisfied.

4. Look for maximum performances only when it is reasonable to suppose an athlete is at his or her best.

5. Keep the young out of too much involvement in highly structured sport.

6. Do not specialize too early, and do not neglect continual review of the athlete's progress and areas of excellence in a sport.

Endurance training in stages: the Coe approach

In the following approach no differentiation is made between boys and girls simply because there is a slightly different physiological time scale. Performances will differ with sex, as should the loadings, but not the overall direction of the program. In a nutshell, these training stages are as follows:

Both parents in the Coe family have played vital roles in Sebastian's stellar career. While Peter has acted as coach and father, Angela, Sebastian's mother, has always been supremely attuned to his general health and well-being. Both father and son are indebted to Angela for her ability to pick up subtle clues about Sebastian's ups and downs; oftentimes she is the first to see when some kind of alteration is necessary in her son's athletic schedule.

Photographs, Hugh Hastings

Stage I. From the time the child is fairly steady on his feet until the age of seven or eight years, encourage him to be as active and mobile as possible in play—of course, not frenetic and uncontrollable. During this phase simple observation shows, as many parents can testify, that a child will frequently play vigorously, then stop absolutely breathless, then dash about again like quicksilver, and then suddenly succumb to blissful sleepiness. These bursts of energy and exhaustion can be tiring just to watch. But when they are self-paced, young children do not destroy themselves. This phase will taper off between the ages of 7 and 11 years.

Stage II (ages 11–13). Ensure that the child participates in a broad spectrum of games at school with a bias in favor of those games with the longer periods of activity. During this time running potential may be discernible, and the youngster should be encouraged to run. At this stage there should be a balance between what can be called speed work and steady running.

Sebastian Coe: major titles and events up to Los Angeles Olympics 1984

age	class	competition	event		time	finished	record set
14	boy	Yorkshire County state championship	1,500	meter	4 min 23.60 sec	1st	
16	youth	Northern Counties area championship	1,500	meter	3 min 59.50 sec	1st	championship's best performance
		U.K. championship	1,500	meter	3 min 55.00 sec	1st	championship's
		English schools championship	3,000	meter	8 min 40.20 sec	1st	best performance
18	junior	U.K. championship	1,500	meter	3 min 52.00 sec	1st	
		European championship	1,500	meter	3 min 45.20 sec	3rd	
20		U.K. championship (indoors)	800	meter	1 min 49.10 sec	1st	championship's best performance
		European championship (indoors)	800	meter	1 min 46.50 sec	1st	U.K. and Commonwealth
21		Ivo Van Damme Memorial (Brussels)	800	meter	1 min 44.26 sec	1st	U.K.
		European championship	800	meter	1 min 44.80 sec	3rd	
		Coca-Cola U.K. race	800	meter	1 min 43.97 sec	1st	U.K.
22		U.K. championship (indoors)	3,000	meter	7 min 59.80 sec	1st	
			400	meter	46.80 sec	2nd	
		Europa Cup (Turin)	800	meter	1 min 47.30 sec	1st	
		Bislett games (Oslo)	800	meter	1 min 42.33 sec	1st	world
		Weltklasse (Zurich)	1,500	meter	3 min 32.03 sec	1st	world
		Golden Mile (Oslo)	1	mile	3 min 48.95 sec	1st	world
23	senior	Bislett games (Oslo)	1,000	meter	2 min 13.40 sec	1st	world
		Olympic Games (Moscow)	800	meter	1 min 45.90 sec	2nd	
			1,500	meter	3 min 38.40 sec	1st	
24		U.K. championship (indoors)	3,000	meter	7 min 55.20 sec	1st	
		U.K. versus East Germany (indoors)	800	meter	1 min 46.00 sec	1st	world best
		Florence race	800	meter	1 min 41.72 sec	1st	world
		Oslo race	1,000	meter	2 min 12.18 sec	1st	world
		Weltklasse (Zurich)	1	mile	3 min 48.53 sec	1st	world
		Golden Mile (Brussels)	1	mile	3 min 47.33 sec	1st	world
		World Cup (Rome)	800	meter	1 min 46.18 sec	1st	
25		European championship	800	meter	1 min 46.68 sec	2nd	
		London (Crystal Palace)	4 × 800-meter relay		1 min 44.01 sec	fastest leg	world (7 min 3.89 sec)
		U.K. versus U.S. (indoors)	800	meter	1 min 44.91 sec	1st	world best
		Oslo race (indoors)	1,000	meter	2 min 18.58 sec	1st	world best
27		Olympic Games (Los Angeles)	800	meter	1 min 43.64 sec	2nd	
			1,500	meter	3 min 32.53 sec	1st	Olympic

If puberty has any significance for girls in training, it is that there may be sudden increases in weight and lethargy, so a lot of encouragement may be necessary to keep them interested in training. For boys puberty is a time when a tendency to overtrain will surface if they are not properly supervised. On one occasion Sebastian was caught racing the local bus up a mile-long hill!

Stage III (ages 13–15). Even though the emphasis at this stage should be on steady distance training, introduce into every week's training at least a couple of sessions of faster work. Technically speaking, it is important to keep the "fast-twitch fibers" engaged.

Stage IV. From 15 years onward is just one steady progression of balanced training. Training should never be totally continuous, however; all athletes need recovery periods, and teenagers should have at least one rest day per week. At about 16 years the serious aspirant usually can consider higher level competition.

In Britain the first serious tests for youths are the English Schools Championships (intermediates) and AAA Championships, and the age limit for these is 16 years. This makes them benchmarks for many young athletes, although the history of the events shows that even 16 is too early an age for predicting future champions. Not many of these winners go on to greater achievement in running.

Champion in the family

If a family in ordinary circumstances has the privilege of raising a champion, then the whole family has to share the load; some might even say "suffer." Siblings are often expected to make sacrifices; frequently this produces mixed feelings of envy and pride. Often much of the burden rests with the mother. The demands should not be underestimated: special diets, differing and additional meal times, continual need for clean training clothes, new clothes and equipment as the young athlete wears out or outgrows old ones—to say nothing of the transporting to and from practice and competitions and the planning of family vacations around the young athlete's schedule and needs.

The seemingly endless demands raise the question "Should parents coach their own children?" This is obviously not a decision to be taken lightly. In the Coe family both parents have played vital roles and have seen all sides of the problem over the long period from Sebastian's childhood obscurity to recent Olympic fame.

Even when a youngster is coached by an outsider, the parent still has the responsibility for the overall welfare of the child. That is an awesome job in itself. So it follows that taking on the additional role of athletic coach increases the demands and raises inevitable "conflicts of interest."

Hard as it may be, it is vital that a parent/coach wear two very distinct hats and that the young person know this. Thus, when "talking track" we are always Peter/coach and Sebastian/runner—never father and son. The *coach* must always consider strategy and tactics, long- and short-term objectives, if and when the young performer should participate in other sports, when he should specialize, and so forth. In the meantime,

The years leading to the 1984 Olympics were tough ones for Sebastian Coe. He had suffered the effects of a debilitating infection; he was coming back with little training; and he had already been written off by much of the press. Furthermore, Sebastian was worried that his time as a top-level competitor might be running out. When he won the silver medal in the 800 meter, coming in second to Joachim Cruz, he considered it a triumph, but clinching the gold in the 1,500 meter (above) was truly a sensational victory.

181

Though Sebastian cherishes his privacy, he has gracefully accepted his off-the-track role as a public figure.

the *parent* should always be there to support the child through emotional development, academics, and endless life choices not related to the sport.

It is often very difficult to be objective when the victor or vanquished athlete is one's own child. All parents are wont to hedge or give in occasionally to a child's counterproductive wishes—often out of kindness or simply fatigue. In coaching, such expediency in some cases can be fatal to athletic success as well as to the respect and trust that is so vital to the coach-athlete partnership.

The parent/coach must always struggle with the dual role of maintaining the special discipline required by the sport at a time when parental authority is being tested. An intelligent child will soon learn that he or she can play one role against the other. For example, if he is slipping in the classroom, he may blame the "coach" for keeping him away from his studies; or, on the other hand, he might use the training as an excuse for relaxing in his studies and indulge the "coach" for support.

Good parents have invisible antennae that pick up the slightest signals or "vibes" in children's health and general welfare and soon learn to distinguish between what could be serious and what is not. This is a very real ability, more often shown by mothers, as it was in Sebastian's case, though it should not be dismissed as mere "female intuition." It is neither obsessive worrying nor mollycoddling. In the 17 years of Sebastian's training, while Father coached, Mother consistently parented, displaying her special skill in always being attuned to Sebastian's best welfare. This skill has led, and still leads, her to sense when he is overtaxing himself—and not "sparking on all eight cylinders"—a situation that has been enough to bring Father/coach to reexamine the training schedule.

Any parents contemplating coaching their own child should be able to answer "yes" to the following six questions: (1) Do I have the necessary knowledge for this undertaking? (2) Have I got the time to do the job adequately? (3) Have I the patience to suffer the setbacks with fortitude? (4) Am I in good enough health? (5) Do I have enough money for the

In reflecting on all his triumphs, including two gold and two silver Olympic medals, Sebastian says the race that means most to him was the 800 meter in the Bislett games in Oslo in 1979, when he broke his first world record with a time of 1 minute 42.33 seconds. Shortly thereafter, also in Oslo, he broke his second world record in the Golden Mile, with a time of 3 minutes 48.95 seconds. That record had previously been held by John Walker of New Zealand. At right, Coe floats to the finish line of the Golden Mile seeming as if he could go on forever. After the race he jubilantly parades the Union Jack.

"extras" that coaching demands? (6) Above all, do I love the sport with an absorbing fervor?

The pros and cons of undertaking the parent/coach role have to be weighed carefully. "If in doubt, don't" is probably the very best advice. The rewards can be high, but the price of failure can be devastating to both parent and young aspiring athlete. Unfortunately, there are very few success stories in these partnerships.

Some final reflections

Sebastian: *What does life hold now? When you have been as lucky and successful as I have been, you can, without risking the charge of being bigheaded, say, "I have nothing to prove." Although I have represented my country many times, I will still try to turn out for international matches when I am asked, but outside of these events I feel I have earned the right to run only if it pleases me.*

I feel that I still have got some very good races left in me, but when the time comes, when I sense that I can no longer deliver world class performances, or if I am failing to improve, then I will retire.

Off the track, my life is not only athletics, and I do have some private aspirations, but I realize that I have some responsibilities to the sport that I love and that has been good to me. I try to fulfill this duty through my roles with the International Olympics Committee (IOC) and the British Sports' Council. I have chaired the Athletes' Commission on the IOC, and as a member of the Sports' Council I chaired the committee, whose report was submitted to Parliament, for the allocation of funds to various competing sports for the 1988 Olympic Games in Seoul.

In the course of a year I am privileged to meet many from all walks of life. I attend meetings where people from the media, law, business, and politics meet and exchange opinions. I have not as yet settled on a "career" off the track, and the final decision will have to wait until I retire. At any rate, I hope to maintain some role in organized athletics whatever else I may do. This does not mean that I have no other interests.

On a more personal note, I value my privacy most of all, which is not always easy to maintain when the major competitions are on. I have two major sources of relaxation. The fervor with which I support my favorite professional soccer team, Chelsea, is probably more refreshing than relaxing, but I do leave a good match in a happy frame of mind.

The other and much more soothing relaxation is music, nowadays, particularly opera, although my first love was and in some ways still is jazz. My father reminds me that at the end of a superb evening in a jazz club, I once said I would give up all my medals just to play an instrument really well.

Of the many memorable moments of victory on the track, my two Olympic gold medals from Moscow and Los Angeles must stand high on the list. From the first I recall an overwhelming sense of relief after winning the gold; from the second I recall the exaltation of surviving two years of illness and my critics to again become number one.

But perhaps the experience that will last longest in my memory is the almost mystical feeling that I had on a warm evening in Oslo when I broke my first world record in an 800-meter run. I had no particular sensation of speed, and I think I could have run even faster, I wasn't exhausted at all at the end. It was a strange feeling— like being on autopilot; I was mentally outside of what my body was achieving, and it was just beautiful.

Although the rewards have been different for parent/coach and for athlete both in substance and degree, the element that has been unifying has always been the extreme pleasure of mutual achievement. If given the chance would we do it all over again? YES!

Sebastian Coe believes he has quite a few good races left in him. He is not yet sure when he might "retire," but neither is he in turmoil about having to do so when the time comes. He has not yet chosen another career, but because he feels indebted to athletics, he currently serves, and in the future intends to serve, on committees and commissions for organized sports.

Science Sizes Up Cocaine

by Mark S. Gold, M.D.

Despite the fact that it is an addicting drug, cocaine has become the glamour drug of our time. Its "recreational" use in the United States has reached epidemic levels and continues to climb. Surveys estimate that more than 22 million people in the U.S. have tried cocaine and that 5 million to 6 million use it habitually. As use of other illegal substances such as marijuana is leveling off or declining in the U.S., cocaine is attracting as many as 5,000 new users every day. Cocaine has become equally fashionable in many Western European countries. Using police seizures as an indication of the extent of drug abuse, drug enforcement agencies see cocaine as the fastest growing drug in Western Europe. According to UN statistics, worldwide seizures of cocaine in 1982 topped 12 tons, an increase of more than 25% over the previous record. Many factors have contributed to the sudden surge in popularity of this drug. The energy and feelings of competency cocaine temporarily confers, the aura of wealth and power surrounding it, and the widely held but erroneous belief that it is safe and nonaddicting have assured cocaine's place as the "drug of choice" in Western countries.

More precious than gold

Cocaine is one of the alkaloids (alkaline chemical compounds) extracted from the leaves of the coca plant, *Erythroxylum coca,* a shrub that is indigenous to the eastern Andes Mountains in South America. Today it grows largely in Peru and Bolivia but is also cultivated in Central America, Indonesia, and Sri Lanka, among other places.

Smugglers import cocaine in the form of a crystallized powder. Before it reaches the consumer, a series of dealers mix the pure substance with inert adulterants (mannitol, glucose, or inositol) to increase its bulk and thus its profits. In addition, pure cocaine may be mixed with a variety of active ingredients, including lidocaine, procaine, amphetamines, phencyclidine (PCP, or "angel dust"), heroin, or quinine, substances that alter the taste or augment the drug's effects. These latter ingredients also increase the medical risk to the user. By the time it reaches the consumer, the drug contains anywhere from 0 to 50% cocaine. The user usually does not know the percentage or the identity of the adulterants. Currently about 125 tons of cocaine—more than double the amount in 1982—enter the United States from Latin America each year. In adulterated form it sells for $50–$140 a gram, up to

Mark S. Gold, M.D., *is Director of Research at the Fair Oaks hospitals in Summit, New Jersey, and Boca/ Delray, Florida. He is also Founder of the National Cocaine Hot Line, 800-COCAINE.*

(Opposite page) "I want! I want!"—Plate 9 of For Children: The Gates of Paradise *by William Blake (1793). Photograph, reproduced by courtesy of the Trustees of the British Museum*

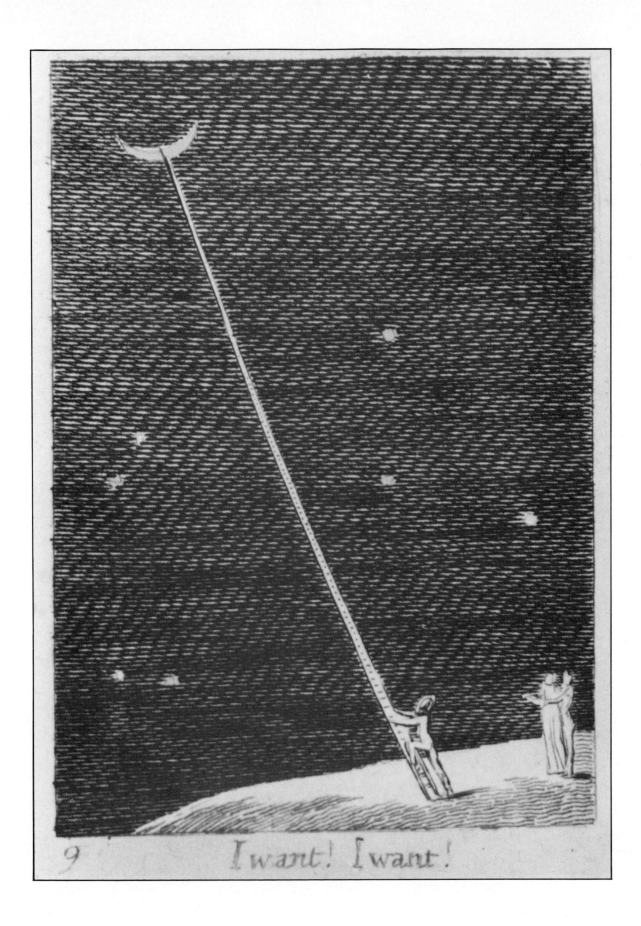

9   I want! I want!

Jean-Loup Charmet, Paris

ten times the price of pure gold. Smuggling and supply are increasing; the price is falling; and the purity of the street form of the drug is rising. Most recently a surge in both drug supply and drug problems has been reported in the U.K., Western Europe, the Caribbean, and Australia.

Although cocaine is also recognized as a topical anesthetic (blocking nerve conduction of pain) and a vasoconstrictor (narrowing the blood vessels and thus acting on the heart and circulatory system, raising blood pressure, and increasing the respiratory rate), its value to so-called recreational users depends on its stimulant and euphoriant properties. While the coca leaves themselves contain many vitamins and minerals, cocaine appears to deprive the body of certain essential nutrients.

From coca to cola

Inhabitants of the South American Andes probably began ingesting coca leaves as food as early as 5000 BC. The use of coca continues to the present time among many Indian peoples in South America, although today it is used for its stimulant rather than its nutrient effect. The "high" produced by chewing on a wad of coca leaves (smeared with ashes, lime, or other alkaline substances to extract the cocaine) is mild, compared with that of the street form of the drug—or even compared with the stimulating effects of a cup of coffee. Nonetheless, the invigorating properties of the coca plant were widely appreciated in earlier eras. The Incas held it sacred and restricted its daily use to the nobility. It "satisfies the hungry, gives new strength to the weary and exhausted, and makes the unhappy forget their sorrows," wrote one observer of the period. Widespread use by the "lower classes" resumed with the Spanish conquest of Peru in the 16th century; with the consequent collapse of the Incas' food economy, the increased ingestion of coca probably also served both a nutritional and a hunger-suppressing function. Today among the poverty-stricken peasants of Peru and Bolivia, coca leaves are still chewed to provide a stimulus to working long hours at high altitudes.

The Spaniards took the coca plant back to Europe, but there was little interest in it until 1860, when a German chemist, Albert Neimann, isolated and extracted the cocaine alkaloid. In 1863 a French chemist from Cor-

Cocaine is an alkaloid extracted from the leaves of the coca plant, Erythroxylum coca *(above), which is indigenous to the eastern Andes Mountains of South America. The cultivation and harvesting of coca, depicted below in a sketch by a 19th-century European traveler in Peru, continues virtually unchanged today. The photograph (below right) shows women picking coca leaves in contemporary Peru.*

(Left) Jean-Loup Charmet, Paris; (right) Vera Lentz—Visions

sica, Angelo Mariani, formulated a tonic consisting of wine with a touch of cocaine. He called it Vin Mariani and sent samples to eminent people throughout Europe and the United States in exchange for their testimonials. Pope Leo XIII, Pres. William McKinley, Thomas Edison, the French sculptor Auguste Rodin, and author Jules Verne were among those who eventually endorsed the elixir for its salutory effects on fatigue, appetite, digestion, numerous diseases, and longevity.

In the 19th-century United States, cocaine was marketed in a variety of formulations—one of which was Coca-Cola, created in 1886 by Georgia chemist John Styth Pemberton. (The cocaine was removed from the popular drink in 1905.) Legitimate medical interest in cocaine was also strong in the 1870s and '80s throughout the U.S. and Europe. Doctors believed the drug to be effective for the treatment of morphine addiction, alcoholism, syphillis, and many psychological problems.

The dark side

In 1884, 28-year-old Viennese physician Sigmund Freud became interested in cocaine's properties, and he began to test the substance on himself in small quantities. His published praise of cocaine eventually led to the development of the drug for use as a local anesthetic. William Halsted of Johns Hopkins University, Baltimore, Maryland, known as the father of

In South America coca leaves have been chewed for centuries for their stimulant properties. The leaves are crushed together with powdered lime, which extracts the active alkaloid. (Below left) A stirrup-spouted vessel from the Mochica culture of northern Peru (c. 200 BC–AD 600) contains one of the finest existing scenes of coca chewing in ancient times. A "rollout" of the vessel's decoration (above) clearly shows three seated figures holding the lime gourds and spatulas used in preparing the coca for chewing. The standing figure holds a bag that would have contained the coca leaves. Another Mochica vessel (below center) shows a single figure with a lime gourd; a wad of coca leaves is visible as a slight protuberance in his left cheek. An actual gourd and spatula, collected from a contemporary Colombian Indian group, are shown in the photograph below right.

Drawing, Donna McClelland

(Left) Linden Museum für Volkerkunde, Stuttgart; (center) Lowie Museum of Anthropology, Berkeley, California; (right) Museum of Cultural History, UCLA; photographs, Dr. Christopher B. Donnan

In the latter half of the 19th century, cocaine could be found in a variety of tonics and patent medicines. Some, such as the toothache remedy advertisement above, capitalized on cocaine's analgesic properties. Other products made more of its stimulant qualities. A lively graphic advertising Vin Mariani (opposite page), a French tonic that combined cocaine and wine, promotes the drink's energizing effects. Testimonials from physicians claimed that Vin Mariani was "well adapted for Children, persons in delicate health and convalescents" and endorsed its use in the treatment of, among others, anemia, asthma, dyspepsia, pulmonary troubles, wasting fevers, sequelae of childbirth, and "tardy" convalescence. In the U.S. a Georgia chemist concocted a cocaine-containing patent medicine he named Coca-Cola. An ad for the popular drink (above right) shows a couple of well-dressed theatergoers enjoying the "pause that refreshes." (The use of cocaine in Coca-Cola was discontinued in 1905.)

(Above left) National Library of Medicine, Bethesda, Maryland; (right and opposite page) Jean-Loup Charmet, Paris

modern surgery, established cocaine's efficacy as a nerve block, permitting different parts of the body to be anesthetized individually. Halsted also became addicted to the drug. By the end of the decade, Freud and several distinguished physicians of the day had begun to report on the dark side of cocaine use, many from personal experience. Reports of toxicity and death due to cocaine abuse became legion.

In the U.S. as the tide grew to stem the use of cocaine, the drug was increasingly blamed for many of the real and imagined ills of society—deterioration of morale in the Army and work force, attacks by black men on white women, and so forth. The states began to restrict its use as early as 1887. After the U.S. Congress passed the Harrison Narcotic Act in 1914, cocaine (although not a true narcotic) could be used legally only with a doctor's prescription. Cocaine was classified as a drug as dangerous as any other addictive substance, a drug that could change people and compel them to act against their own best interests. By World War I—although an illegal market still existed, principally among those with the resources to afford the increasingly expensive product—the first cocaine epidemic in the U.S. had ended.

In the 1960s the flaunting of taboos against illicit drug use paved the way for the return of cocaine. Marijuana smokers of the 1960s and early 1970s eventually provided the core of the market for a much more expensive, and more profitable, product. At the same time, societal values began to shift from '60s-style rebelling and dropping out to making money, succeeding, being aggressive, staying thin, remaining young, and "having it all." Cocaine seemed to provide a fast and stylish means to these goals. It induces a state of euphoria, energy, enthusiasm, mastery, and confidence in sexual performance while reducing the need for food and sleep. It is seen as a formula for success among the rich and famous—jet-set socialites, rock musicians, film stars, professional athletes, and other well-known public figures—many of whom, through the media, openly acknowledge the fact that they use the drug.

Statistics: reflection of cocaine usage

Although cocaine use has now penetrated all levels of U.S. society, particularly the middle class, it continues to be associated with privilege. A 1983 survey among callers to the national cocaine hot line (800-COCAINE) revealed most callers to be between the ages of 25 and 40, with more than 14 years of education. Forty percent earned more than $25,000 a year; 85% were white. Evidence from a later survey of upper-income callers with average annual incomes of $83,000 suggests a direct relationship of drug access and economic factors; they used twice as much cocaine as the $25,000-a-year users on a weekly basis, with corresponding increases in drug-related consequences. Between 1983 and 1985 the percentage of women calling the hot line increased from one-third to nearly one-half of all callers. The typical female user is white, 29 years old, college educated, and likely to be earning $25,000 or more yearly.

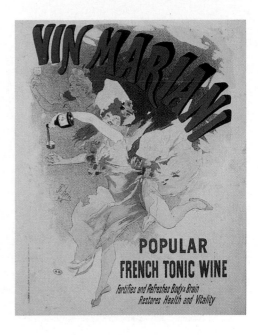

POPULAR
FRENCH TONIC WINE
Fortifies and Refreshes Body & Brain
Restores Health and Vitality

Surveys conducted in the New York tri-state area (New York, New Jersey, Pennsylvania) in 1983 and 1984 reveal other changes in patterns. The 1984 survey shows a higher percentage of lower-income users and a shift toward lower age groups; in 1984 fewer than 50% were earning more than $25,000 per year. While many users are business executives, business owners, or professionals, the 1984 sample includes more students, blue-collar workers, technicians, clerical workers, and housewives than were represented in the 1983 sample.

A further comparison of statistics gathered in 1983 and 1984 shows that in the single year between surveys there was an increase in free-basing (a form of smoking) as the preferred method of use, coupled with a decline in intravenous use. The popularity of intranasal use remained virtually unchanged. There was also an increase in the weekly amount of cocaine used by hot-line callers and a concomitant increase in the use of alcohol or other drugs.

The use of cocaine by teens—and younger children—is growing to epidemic proportions. Cocaine use among adolescents nearly doubled between 1975 and 1983; today about 17% of high school seniors admit having tried it. At the same time, adolescent marijuana use has diminished. The percentage of teenagers who believe that trying cocaine "involves great risk" dropped from 43% in 1975 to 31% in 1980. There has also been a decline in the perceived risk of regular cocaine use. The attractiveness of the drug to young people is enhanced by the image of cocaine users as "cool" and glamorous, in contrast to the picture of the hardened, "degenerate" user of opiate-based drugs. The effect of the role models set by television and sports personalities, as well as by parents, supporting the myth that cocaine is harmless, cannot be underestimated. Forty-one percent of the adolescent callers to the national cocaine hot line report that their parents use marijuana and other drugs—although these same parents generally disapprove of drug use by adolescents.

Matthew Naythons—Gamma/Liaison

Many surveys show that cocaine is the choice of experienced drug users. Of those who have tried cocaine at least once, 98% have also used marijuana; 93% tried marijuana first. The probability of cocaine use increases with the frequency of marijuana use; nearly three-fourths of adults who have used marijuana 100 or more times have tried cocaine. Many people use cocaine and other drugs concomitantly. A 1984 Gallup poll of male cocaine users found that 60% of those in the 25–34 age group combined cocaine with alcohol; 50% combined cocaine use with marijuana.

The addiction controversy

When experts debate the roots of the current cocaine epidemic, they cite medical misinformation as a major factor. Until 1984 the majority of physicians and other drug experts believed that cocaine was not physically addicting—or that it was only psychologically addicting. A drug that is physically addicting, such as heroin or alcohol, produces a demonstrable physiological reaction—withdrawal, or abstinence, syndrome—to the removal of the drug. The widespread conclusion that habitual use of cocaine produced no such syndrome was based on limited, sometimes flawed, medical literature, as well as on poor understanding of the psychophysiological nature of addiction.

Addiction to a drug develops at a certain dose, frequency, and duration of use. During the late 1970s physicians in the U.S. began to encounter undeniable addictive aftereffects of cocaine among entertainers and other celebrities, who could afford its long-term, high-dose use. Despite this "anecdotal" evidence, the reputed safety of cocaine use continued to be upheld by physicians and reported in the media. By 1984, however, most drug experts had changed their opinions. The majority now believe that cocaine is one of the *most* addicting drugs.

According to current estimates, about 125 tons of cocaine are smuggled into the U.S. from Latin America each year. Despite the abandonment of remote jungle refineries like the one in Colombia (right), supplies continue to increase. (Above) Confiscated cocaine is destroyed in Colombia.

El Espectador—Sygma

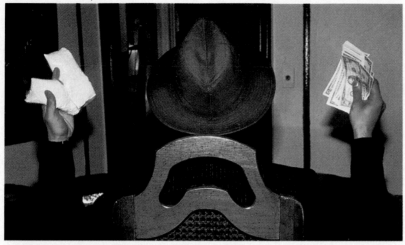

Although the price of cocaine is down, consumption is up—so dealers continue to rake in enormous profits.

Snorting, shooting up, and freebasing

Traditionally, the most popular method of cocaine use has been nasal inhalation of cocaine hydrochloride powder; users sniff, or "snort," it through a straw or a rolled-up dollar bill (or, not uncommonly, a $100 bill). The drug is rapidly absorbed through the mucous membranes that line the nose. Cocaine can also be injected directly into a vein ("shooting up"). The preparations used for smoking may include any part or product of the coca plant—seeds, leaves, coca paste, cocaine hydrochloride or other salts, and freebase cocaine. Freebase, also called base cocaine or simply "base," is cocaine alkaloid that has been extracted ("freed") from its parent compound, cocaine hydrochloride. The traditional extraction process requires heat and a solvent, such as ether.

In the mid-1980s snorting and cocaine injection were becoming less common in the U.S., while freebase smoking was undergoing a dramatic surge in popularity. The sudden increase in the incidence of freebasing appeared to be linked to a shift in cocaine-distribution patterns. Dealers in many areas of the country switched from selling cocaine powder to selling a more potent ready-to-smoke freebase form known as "crack." Crack is a crystalline form of freebase extracted from cocaine powder in a simple procedure using baking soda (sodium bicarbonate), heat, and water (rather than volatile solvents). Unlike cocaine powder, which has a high vaporization point, crack can be readily volatilized into smoke with the heat from a regular match or cigarette lighter. Crack is sold on the street in small plastic holders, each containing a few "rocks." Dealers prefer crack to cocaine powder because of its high addiction potential, low unit cost, ease of handling, and relative safety of processing (as compared with the potentially dangerous methods that use ether or other solvents).

The more rapidly cocaine is absorbed, the greater the so-called rush, the feeling of euphoria for which the drug is fabled. Users describe this sensation with metaphors of energy, power, and sexual orgasm. Snorting produces this effect in a few minutes; injecting, within 30 seconds. When smoked as a freebase, cocaine is rapidly absorbed into the pulmonary circulation and transmitted to the brain in less than ten seconds. Within a few

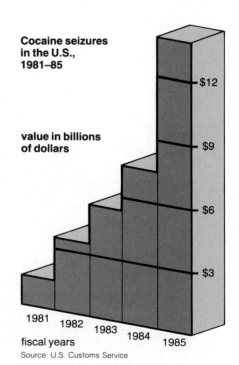

Cocaine seizures in the U.S., 1981–85

value in billions of dollars

$12

$9

$6

$3

1981 1982 1983 1984 1985

fiscal years

Source: U.S. Customs Service

191

In the past few years, nearly every major U.S. sports league has been rocked by cocaine scandals. Athletes are attracted to the drug because of its transitory energizing effect and the initial perception that it improves playing performance. Eventually many find their skills declining; they miss practice, show up late for games, and generally "mess up" on and off the playing field. In 1981 Washington Bullets guard John Lucas (above) stunned his teammates with his admission that he needed help to kick his coke habit. In the summer of 1985, fans were equally stunned when professional baseball, traditionally considered the U.S.'s most "wholesome" sport, was hit by a cocaine scandal. Still, no one was prepared for the tragic deaths of two nationally known sports figures—Len Bias, 22, and Don Rogers, 23—only days apart in the summer of 1986, both attributed to cocaine.

seconds the rush is replaced by a less ecstatic but pleasurable excitability; this state of arousal lasts 5 to 30 minutes, after which the user often begins to feel restless, irritable, and depressed. To maintain the high, even occasional users repeat the administration process, often until the supply is depleted. A prolonged smoking episode, or binge, may extend for two or three days, during which time the user may consume 10–30 grams of cocaine. Other drugs, such as marijuana, alcohol, or heroin, may extend the high and/or ease the "coming down" or "crash" that can result from the removal of cocaine from the system.

Cocaine stimulates the central nervous system and mimics the aroused "fight-or-flight" response to stress. Since the drug first acts on higher centers of the cerebral cortex, users experience psychological effects of arousal first. In actuality the "rush" seems to be little more than the subjective experience of the rapid change in arousal state. Psychological arousal is brief, but physiological arousal—resulting from stimulation of brain centers controlling respiration, cardiovascular function, and heat regulation—lasts up to one hour. The accumulating levels of cocaine in the blood, caused by repeated use to prolong the high, lead to rapid development of toxicity.

After the "rush" is over

Cocaine intoxication can produce a number of effects other than pleasure. Cocaine-induced pleasure states alternate with powerful and unpleasant urges for the drug, forming the underpinnings for continued use. Intoxication can lead to decreased sleep requirement, anorexia (loss of appetite), increased sex drive, and hyperactivity. Paranoia and hallucinations may occur. Aggressiveness, feelings of grandeur, and poor social judgment are common. Physiological signs of cocaine intoxication include cardiovascular arousal (rapid heartbeat), dilated pupils, profuse perspiration, and elevated body temperature.

Chronic use often produces depression, irritability, insomnia, lethargy, fatigue, memory and concentration problems, and sexual disinterest or impotence. These symptoms are the opposite of the effects that originally attracted the user, namely, feelings of heightened physical, mental, and

Photographs, Brian R. Wolff/Time Magazine

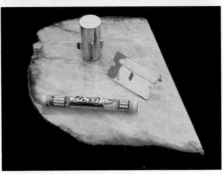

sexual capabilities. It appears that with chronic use, a tolerance develops to the euphoric effects of cocaine; ultimately there is an increase in the speed of onset and duration of the negative effects.

With the development of tolerance, users generally increase the amount of cocaine they take—and/or switch from sniffing to smoking or injecting—in an attempt to regain the high. Increasing dosages invite neurological seizures, which can lead to death; even one such experiment can induce seizures in some individuals. Once this reaction has occurred, less and less cocaine will be required to trigger future seizures. Cocaine use can also cause heart palpitations, angina (severe chest pain), arrhythmia (irregular heart beat), and heart attack.

Overdose and other perils

Cocaine overdose is becoming increasingly common in the U.S. In 1975–76 in New Orleans, Louisiana, cocaine contributed to slightly more than one out of every 100,000 visits to emergency rooms; by 1983–84 that number had climbed to about 185 of every 100,000 visits. Corresponding 1975–76 and 1983–84 figures in other cities were: Miami, Florida, 92.6 and 306.2; Los Angeles, 9.5 and 199.7; New York City, 22 and 144.1. Contrary to popular belief, users can overdose by any route of administration, including snorting. Since cocaine consumers rarely know their lethal dose or the percentage of pure cocaine present in any given purchase, the potential for overdose is always present.

Cocaine overdose is a medical emergency. Those victims who remain conscious often appear sweaty, nervous, and acutely psychotic or manic. They are usually paranoid, panicky, or agitated, although sometimes they are bombastic, exhibiting delusions of grandeur. Physical manifestations may be life-threatening and rapidly progress to death from cardiovascular and respiratory collapse. Deaths from other than direct medical problems have become quite common. Suicide is a risk in the presence of auditory hallucinations, underlying psychiatric illness, and chronic abuse. Driving and work-related accidents and domestic and drug-related violence are also well-known causes of death in cases of cocaine intoxication.

Still other hazards are related to the method of administration. People who snort cocaine commonly have considerable damage to the nasal tissues, some with ulcers of the septum (the tissue separating the nostrils), others with an actual hole in the septum requiring surgery. Sinus, swallowing, and voice problems are common. In some cases damage is permanent.

Risks of intravenous use include hepatitis, skin infections, tetanus, and AIDS (from unsanitary needles). Men are more at risk than women for polyarteritis nodosa, a condition in which medium and small arteries of the kidneys, muscles, gastrointestinal tract, and heart become inflamed and dysfunctional.

Freebasing is extremely hazardous, carrying substantial risks for both accident and toxic reaction. The volatile solvents used to prepare the smokable base form, in combination with the matches and lighters used in smoking, constitute a potential for fire and/or explosion; both have been reported. Accidental chemical burns resulting from contact with materials

Until fairly recently cocaine was regarded as the "caviar" of drugs, the drug of choice of the rich and famous. At a store such as the Beverly Hills (California) Headshop, which deals exclusively in drug-use paraphernalia, gold coke accessories may be purchased for the cocaine user who has everything.

With the advent of "crack," a potent ready-to-smoke form of cocaine, the use of the drug—especially by teenagers and younger school-age children—has grown to epidemic proportions. "Rocks" of crack (left) can be easily prepared from cocaine powder (center), without the volatile, potentially dangerous solvents traditionally used in preparing a smokable "freebase" form of the drug. Crack is commonly smoked in a glass pipe (right). The high produced by crack is intense but short-lived—a 30-second "rush" followed by a few minutes of euphoria.

used in the process of extracting base cocaine have also occurred. The lungs are damaged by deep inhalation of superheated smoke, sometimes coupled with rebreathing exhaled smoke from a balloon. The tremors, lassitude, and fatigue that follow the intense intoxication produced by freebasing often lead to accidental falls, bruises, lacerations, and fires.

The use of alcohol or other drugs that depress the central nervous system taken to offset the typical aftereffects of cocaine intoxication—restlessness, irritability, depression, and overstimulation—can be extremely dangerous. The stimulant effects of cocaine are quick to wear off, and when they do, the user is likely to become instantly stuporous or drunk from the previously ingested depressants; sometimes this transformation occurs when the person is behind the wheel of a car or in some other critical situation. There have been no studies of the health risks of long-term regular cocaine use, so it follows that the effects of cocaine combined with those of alcohol or, say, marijuana are unpredictable and unknown. The possibility of multiple addictions must also be considered.

Popular myths about getting hooked

Clinicians generally agree that cocaine abuse or dependency is characterized by three major features: (1) loss of control over use; (2) craving and

Pattern of cocaine use in 200 addicts

	1983	1984
history of use	3 months–15 years	1 month–12 years
intranasal users	58%	60%
freebase users	16%	27%
intravenous users	26%	13%
grams per week	1–20	5–15
cost per week	$75–$2,000	$35–$1,500
other drug/alcohol use	66%	75%

Source: Mark S. Gold, Arnold M. Washton, and Charles A. Dackis, *Cocaine Abuse: Neurochemistry, Phenomenology, and Treatment,* National Institute on Drug Abuse Research Monograph Series 61: 130–150. (1985)

compulsion; and (3) continued use despite adverse consequences. Other common features include the user's tendency to deny the existence, extent, or severity of the problem, despite expressions of concern by others; an exaggerated level of involvement with the drug, such that a significant part of the user's life revolves around obtaining and using it and recuperating from its effects; a subjective feeling of need for the drug even though functioning has become significantly impaired by it; and a repeating cycle of use, brief recovery, and relapse, with little or no ability to maintain abstinence despite a desire to do so.

One of the most popular myths about cocaine is that snorting cannot lead to severe cocaine dependency and that only freebasing or intravenous users truly have a problem. This notion is challenged by most studies. At least 65% of the cocaine abusers who enter outpatient programs are snorters who do not freebase or inject cocaine. Even those who confine the habit to weekends and others who limit cocaine use to once or twice a week find that they are unable to stop, are preoccupied with thoughts about the drug, and experience negative effects on their health and ability to function. The specific amount and frequency of cocaine use that will cause significant problems seem to be highly individualized and are impossible to predict.

"Acting like a drug addict"

Surveys of callers to the national cocaine hot line reveal that the majority feel and act addicted to cocaine. More than 90% report adverse physical, psychological, and social-financial consequences associated with their cocaine use. In addition, many associate serious personal losses with their habit, including loss of job (25%), spouse (25%), friends (44%), and all monetary resources (34%). They also report drug-related automobile accidents (11%), fighting and violent arguments (59%), and attempted suicide (9%). Thirty-six percent deal cocaine to support their drug habit. Eighty-five percent say that they cannot refuse cocaine when it is made available; 63% think about the drug continuously. Cocaine takes preference over personal grooming and appearance (85%), family (74%), food (73%), friends (70%), and sex (51%). It is clearly seen as a real threat to psychological health (92%), career (76%), family (71%), and physical health (48%), and use continues even though the user believes the drug is causing the problems (90%). Sixty percent of cocaine users acknowledge a clear departure from their precocaine values, yet they report that stealing from friends (51%), familiy (42%), or work (28%) and borrowing with no intent to repay (63%) have become common to them. More than 80% admit to finding themselves "acting like a drug addict." All these findings are consistent with drug dependency and addiction.

Hot-line callers also report symptoms of withdrawal when the drug is not available or when they attempt to kick the habit. Cocaine abstinence states are not as well understood as those of other addictive drugs, but withdrawal is known to produce such symptoms as decreased energy, excessive sleeping, irritability, depression, nausea and vomiting, and retardation of motor and mental function. Until fairly recently, research studies have fo-

Once the province of movie stars, rock musicians, and jet-setters, cocaine is now commonplace in the most conservative settings. In 1985, for example, Chicago police made a series of drug busts in the offices of the city's stock exchange. (Above) Two corporate executives do a few "lines" of coke at a midmorning coffee break.

In a French song, entitled "La Coco" ("Snow"), c. 1914, a woman who has been abandoned by her lover sings of turning to cocaine for solace: "I take cocaine, it clouds my brain, reason disappears, grief flies away, and I go mad."

Jean-Loup Charmet, Paris

cused primarily on the psychological experiences of cocaine abstinence; the physiological signs and symptoms have not yet been adequately studied. If the cocaine abstinence syndrome is more subtle than the constellation of symptoms that typically follows removal of alcohol, opiates, or sedatives, it is no less uncomfortable for the addict, and it provides a significant barrier to ending the use of the drug.

The biologic basis of addiction

All addictive illnesses, whether they involve cocaine, alcohol, heroin, or sedative or hypnotic agents, share certain dynamics and characteristics. Unfortunately, the nature of addiction is often poorly understood, even among medical and psychiatric staff charged with treating addicts.

According to one theory, the establishment of addiction begins with the initial experiences of drug euphoria, which is a "positive" reinforcer of continued drug use. The euphoria, while a subjective state, is a biologic response of the human body, presumably mediated by the activation of systems of reward within the brain. These reward systems reinforce primary survival drives—such as the needs for food and sex—and the use of cocaine becomes an acquired, equally compelling drive.

A similar pattern of cocaine reward is also known to occur in other species, which is consistent with the theory of a biologic basis of addiction. In fact, laboratory animals given unlimited access to cocaine will choose it over food, sex, and water and will readily self-administer the drug, even to the point of severe toxicity and death. Similar behavior is observed among cocaine addicts. Since cocaine intoxication involves pleasure that is far outside the normal range of human experience—it is not a result of love, work, or fulfilling a basic drive—its reinforcing properties far exceed those of other pleasurable activities. Of all psychoactive drugs, cocaine is the one most able to stimulate its own craving and perpetuate its own use. Positive reinforcement is a persistent and powerful motivator, and it explains in part why addicts use cocaine to the point of disability, disease, or death and often relapse even after detoxification.

The repeated use of addictive drugs leads to changes in the brain, which may take the form of abstinence symptoms and drug craving. Just as the intense pleasure of the high serves as a "positive" reinforcer of continued cocaine use, so, in active addicts, do abstinence symptoms serve as physiological "negative" reinforcers. Craving for the drug, which is invariably present in both active and abstinent addicts, persists far beyond the period of acute withdrawal and forms another powerful and insidious negative reinforcer of continued use or, to the abstinent, relapse. Positive and negative reinforcers alternate to form a progressively entrenched cycle of addiction. It is important to note that drug euphoria, drug withdrawal, and, probably, drug craving are biologic phenomena, with psychological effects. The acute and chronic effects of cocaine on nerve systems in the brain mediate the opposing feelings of euphoria and dysphoria that form the biologic basis for compulsive use and dependence.

Addiction also involves a number of psychological dynamics. Treated addicts often return to their old environments and, overcome by the com-

196

bination of craving and easy access, quickly relapse. This classic example of Pavlovian conditioning involves the triggering of intense craving by conditioned stimuli from the environment. The importance of such stimuli far exceeds that of the psychodynamic reasons for drug use, on which psychiatrists and psychologists tend to dwell. Similarly, the effect of the reinforcers, both positive and negative, far exceeds that of physical withdrawal, which in many cases is the sole focus of medical specialists.

The dopamine hypothesis

Cocaine appears to exert its addicting and reinforcing effects through the activation of the so-called pleasure centers in the brain. These might be seen as the afflicted anatomical areas of cocaine addiction, just as the lung is the anatomical site of pneumonia. It is likely that these basic drive-rewarding centers utilize the neurotransmitter dopamine. Recent studies suggest that cocaine causes its mood and many other effects by activation of dopamine systems. Initially cocaine mimics brain reward for fulfillment of a basic drive and comes to be perceived by the user as an equivalent motivator to food, sex, and the others. Soon cocaine becomes more important than these drives and is seen as equal to survival.

Neurotransmitters are fundamental to the brain's communication system. The transmission of information along nerve-cell pathways in the brain is both electrical and chemical; nerve impulses are carried electrically from one end of the cell to the other and chemically from one cell to another. Neurotransmitters are biochemicals that bridge the spaces, or synapses, between brain cells. It is well established that cocaine works to block the reuptake of the neurotransmitter dopamine at the synapses. Reuptake is one mechanism by which the brain removes a neurotransmitter from the synapse once it has delivered its message; reuptake is also a means of replenishing the supply of available neurotransmitter—it is withdrawn back into the cell from which it originated in order to be recycled and reused. The prevention of synaptic reuptake of dopamine leaves an excessive amount of the neurotransmitter in the synapse. In the short term the oversupply produces excessive stimulation. This overabundance of dopamine appears to explain the extreme pleasure that is experienced in acute cocaine intoxication. There is increasing evidence, however, that in chronic use cocaine depletes dopamine, using it up faster than it can be replaced, or inhibits

Reported incidence of adverse physical and psychological effects among 500 cocaine addicts

physical effects	number	percentage
sleep problems	410	82
chronic fatigue	380	76
severe headaches	300	60
nasal sores, bleeding	291	58
chronic cough, sore throat	228	46
nausea, vomiting	193	39
seizure, loss of consciousness	70	14
psychological effects		
depression	415	83
anxiety	416	83
irritability	408	82
apathy, laziness	328	66
paranoia	326	65
difficulty concentrating	323	65
memory problems	287	57
sexual disinterest	265	53
panic attacks	248	50

Source: Mark S. Gold, Arnold M. Washton, and Charles A. Dackis, *Cocaine Abuse: Neurochemistry, Phenomenology, and Treatment,* National Institute on Drug Abuse Research Monograph Series 61: 130–150 (1985)

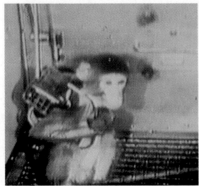 

Photographs, Tom Arma/Discover Magazine © 1985 Time Inc.

Traditionally, cocaine was not considered highly addictive. This myth was dispelled by laboratory experiments in which animals, given control over cocaine administration, killed themselves by overdose. In one such experiment, a monkey (left, pictured on a TV monitor) received an injection of cocaine every time it pressed a lever in its cage. This animal, and others like it, took repeated doses, maintaining a continuous state of cocaine intoxication, until it suffered from drug-induced seizures and died.

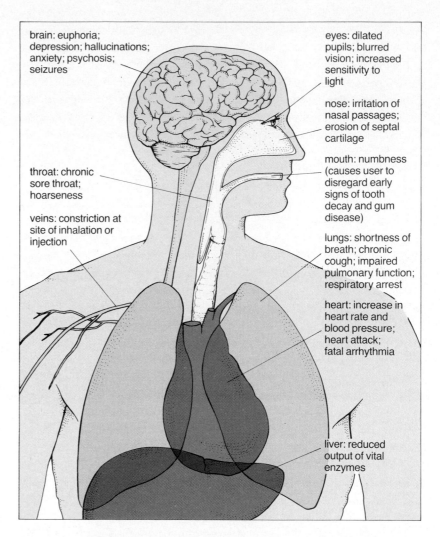

brain: euphoria;
depression; hallucinations;
anxiety; psychosis;
seizures

eyes: dilated
pupils; blurred
vision; increased
sensitivity to
light

nose: irritation of
nasal passages;
erosion of septal
cartilage

throat: chronic
sore throat;
hoarseness

mouth: numbness
(causes user to
disregard early
signs of tooth
decay and gum
disease)

veins: constriction at
site of inhalation or
injection

lungs: shortness of
breath; chronic
cough; impaired
pulmonary function;
respiratory arrest

heart: increase in
heart rate and
blood pressure;
heart attack;
fatal arrhythmia

liver: reduced
output of vital
enzymes

The effects of cocaine on the body are diverse. The results of snorting, for example, range from transitory local irritation of the nasal passages to long-term deterioration of pulmonary function. The possibility of an allergic reaction to unknown adulterants or impurities in the drug must also be borne in mind. Finally, there is the risk of sudden death from cardiac arrest, which may happen to a novice as well as to an experienced user.

dopamine circuits. Dopamine depletion may explain the displeasure side of cocaine, including the "crash" and some of the addictive mechanisms.

The neurochemical basis of craving

Test findings in chronic users indicate physiological dysfunctions consistent with dopamine depletion. For example, in the first week of abstinence, addicts oversecrete the hormone prolactin, which is regulated by dopamine. Consistent with this oversecretion is the high incidence of sexual dysfunction, cessation of menstruation in females, and impotence in males, all of which occur in chronic cocaine use. Cocaine users may also complain of motor problems and may move like people with Parkinson's disease, a disorder associated with dopamine deficiency.

Clinical features of the cocaine crash may also be consistent with depletion of dopamine or of other, related neurotransmitters. These symptoms, such as depression, lack of energy, excessive sleeping, and larger than normal appetite, are generally opposite to those associated with cocaine intoxication. These withdrawal symptoms typically last three to five days, then disappear spontaneously. Along with the intense craving for cocaine,

198

the withdrawal syndrome functions as a significant negative reinforcer of continued cocaine use.

Cocaine craving is described by addicts as an intense, virtually irresistible urge to obtain the drug, regardless of consequences, cost, and danger. It typically persists weeks or months beyond the last use and may easily be triggered by the environmental cues described previously that can stimulate a Pavlovian reaction. The reasoning of the so-called depletion hypothesis is as follows: since chronic cocaine abuse may lead to dopamine depletion, and dopamine circuits are crucial in the reward pathways, the depletion of dopamine may be the neurochemical basis of craving. Decreased dopamine availability at the synapse might be subjectively experienced as cocaine craving, and subsequent cocaine use would correct the dopamine imbalance—albeit temporarily. With continued use, however, further dopamine depletion would develop, leading to renewed craving and a perpetuation of the cycle of addiction.

This neurochemcial cycle might explain why intravenous cocaine users inject themselves several times a day: to maximize the experience of euphoria and to ward off the emergence of intense craving. The depletion model might also explain why regular cocaine abusers often complain that they eventually become unable to experience a satisfactory euphoria from cocaine. These people tend to require more cocaine, more often, in order to achieve the same results. Eventually they may resort to freebasing or intravenous routes. Dopamine potentiation, followed by dopamine depletion, would establish a vicious cycle of addiction, in which continued cocaine use progressively exhausts the brain's internal reward systems, leading to increased reliance on cocaine and decreased enjoyment of life's naturally pleasurable experiences. According to the depletion hypothesis, then, while cocaine acutely activates dopamine neuronal activity, its chronic use inhibits dopamine; this cycle of events may be the basis of cocaine addiction.

The path to recovery

To assure success the goal of treatment must be complete abstinence from all mood-altering chemicals (including alcohol, marijuana, and others) and

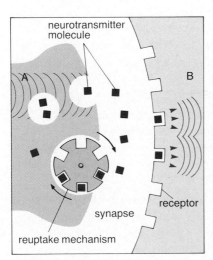 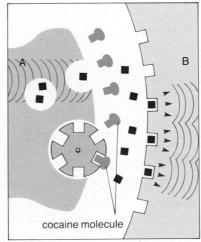

The dopamine hypothesis is a theory that may explain cocaine craving and addiction. Dopamine is a key neurotransmitter in the brain, carrying nerve impulses across the synapse, or space, between nerve cells. The diagram at far left shows how neurotransmitter molecules released by nerve A travel to receptor sites on nerve B. Some neurotransmitters are recycled by a reuptake mechanism for reuse by nerve A. In the second diagram, left, cocaine molecules block the reuptake of neurotransmitters. Prevention of the synaptic reuptake of dopamine causes an excess of dopamine to accumulate in the synapse, producing excessive stimulation. This stimulation is experienced by the user as pleasure. Over the long term, chronic cocaine use may deplete the brain's supply of dopamine. This depletion may account for the dysphoric effects of the drug and the resultant craving for more.

Drug abuse on the job is a dangerous—and growing—problem. In the late 1970s Jim Kelly (above), a former addict, started a drug-counseling program for his fellow workers at Digital Equipment Corp.'s Westfield, Massachusetts, plant. Today the company has similar programs at 24 locations to serve its 70,000 employees, and many other large employers have similar programs.

Cocaine addiction is insidious. Many who are "hooked" manage to deny it until a serious drug-related accident or near-fatal overdose forces them to seek help. In 1980 comedian Richard Pryor (below) was severely burned in an explosion while he was preparing freebase cocaine. Today, in his nightclub act and TV appearances, Pryor uses humor to discourage drug use.

adoption of a drug-free life-style. As noted earlier, most cocaine addicts concurrently abuse alcohol or other sedative or hypnotic drugs. Because these other drugs have usually been associated or paired with cocaine literally thousands of times, their use alone can trigger a powerful urge for cocaine. The addict's hope of being able to return to occasional use of cocaine or other drugs is unrealistic and often leads to relapse. As with other chemical dependencies—alcoholism is a good example—once the line has been crossed from occasional use to dependency, even if compulsive use is infrequent, the ability to return to controlled usage appears to be lost.

Drug-using behavior must be dealt with immediately and directly. The full benefits of psychotherapy, education, and other rehabilitative efforts can be realized only during sustained drug abstinence. Many professionals tend to rely exclusively on psychotherapy to impart to the addict sufficient insight into or understanding of the habit to end it. This approach rarely succeeds; it fails to address the primary presenting problem—drug use—and it ignores the powerful compulsive nature of addictive behavior. Psychotherapy can be very useful in the treatment of cocaine abusers, but only after drug use is stopped.

Hospitalization is necessary only in severe cases. Indications for inpatient treatment include chronic freebase or intravenous use, severe psychosocial impairment, medical or psychiatric complication, concurrent drug dependencies, and inability or unwillingness of the drug abuser to stop cocaine use on an outpatient basis. The early phase of treatment focuses intensively on practical techniques for achieving abstinence. For at least the first two to four weeks, brief, frequent counseling sessions provide the necessary direction, feedback, and encouragement.

One program that has proved successful combines individual and group therapy. The group sessions provide positive role models, a ready-made peer-support network, and an excellent forum for discussing issues that are crucial to abstinence and recovery. In group sessions patients talk about drug urges, addictive thinking, and methods for avoiding potential relapses. Group discussions also focus on thoughts and feelings that may precipitate relapse and nondrug alternatives for coping with stressful situations.

Individual therapy sessions complement the group meetings, focusing more on personal and psychodynamic issues pertaining to relationships, sexual functioning, self-esteem, family problems, and other issues underlying cocaine use. The treatment plan includes couples and family therapy sessions when necessary.

Many outpatient programs have found that urine screening for cocaine and other commonly abused drugs is essential to the success of outpatient treatment. Such screening helps to promote the individual's efforts toward self-control and also serves as an objective monitor of patient progress.

Preventing a relapse

Long years of experience in treating alcoholics have provided the basis for a number of specific relapse-prevention strategies that strengthen and reinforce cocaine abstinence. They teach the recovering cocaine abuser to cope with the trials and perils of abstinent life.

High-risk situations. Cocaine dependence develops within an environment of people and paraphernalia, social situations and particular places. All of these reinforce cocaine use and trigger cravings that can undermine motivation for abstinence. Strategies for recognizing, avoiding, or handling these situations decrease the probability of relapse. To remain abstinent the recovering addict must not only discard any remaining drug supplies and paraphernalia but also end relationships with people associated with cocaine use—these may include many or most of the addict's friends or acquaintances.

Conditioning factors. Conditioned drug urges and cravings inevitably occur during the recovery process; they may be elicited unexpectedly in a wide variety of circumstances. The urge can be short-circuited by one or more substitute activities, from vigorous exercise to calling a supportive friend to talk out the feelings. Knowing the nature of urges makes them less overwhelming. Typically, the person who succumbs to drug urges holds the mistaken belief that such urges will inevitably intensify until they become impossible to resist. This is not true—even very powerful urges are temporary and time-limited. However, "giving in" at the peak intensity of a drug urge serves only to reinforce its strength and its probability of recurrence.

The myth of the "high." Despite the adverse experiences that caused them to seek drug rehabilitation, many patients, once deprived of cocaine, remember only the pleasurable effects of the drug. This selective memory perpetuates the allure of cocaine and heightens the potential for relapse. The tendency of the former user to ignore or forget the negative consequences of cocaine use is especially strong when relapse is imminent. Thus, part of a successful treatment strategy is to repeatedly challenge these glorified views and help patients to arrive at a more realistic appraisal of the way that cocaine use has affected their lives.

The abstinence violation effect. When a person "slips" and violates a period of abstinence, he or she usually suffers intense negative and self-defeating reactions that threaten further progress. Called the abstinence violation effect, the reaction consists of (1) feelings of guilt for having "given in to temptation"; (2) feelings of conflict because the drug use is inconsistent with the hard-won image of oneself as an abstainer; (3) attribution of the slip to personal weakness and lack of willpower; (4) feelings of helplessness, victimization, and a sense that all progress up to that time is now nullified and lost; and (5) feelings of profound failure and the expectation of continued failure. Unless the individual is informed about the abstinence violation effect and how to counteract it, the likelihood that any single slip will escalate into a full-fledged relapse is markedly increased. Through techniques of cognitive restructuring, a process of "unlearning" and "relearning," patients can learn to view the incident as an isolated event from which valuable information can be extracted for use in preventing future relapses.

Stress reduction and changes in life-style. People who relapse almost always feel that they are justified. They rationalize that because they feel stressed, overworked, and deprived, they need the drug for relief from the demands of everyday life. In fact, many cocaine abusers are hard-driving, upwardly mobile "workaholics" whose life-styles are hectic and leave little

Both group and individual therapy have a place in the treatment of cocaine addiction. Group sessions such as the one shown above for teenagers provide important peer support and an open forum for the discussion of issues central to abstinence and recovery.

201

time for relaxation. Often cocaine has been the only form of self-gratification or self-indulgence that they have allowed themselves on any regular basis.

Pharmacological approaches to rehabilitation

While drug rehabilitation programs furnish a number of techniques for reducing craving, a safe means of adjunctive pharmacotherapy—drugs that would help to promote abstinence—would be useful, especially for early stages of treatment when craving and withdrawal are so intense. Some investigators have reported favorable results from one class of antidepressant medication. Drugs that would affect the dopamine system appear most promising, however. Certainly further research into the biologic basis of cocaine addiction promises more refined treatment approaches.

In 1985 one team of investigators reported consistent success in controlling the craving for cocaine by using the dopamine agonist (*i.e.*, stimulator) known as bromocriptine. Daily low-dose bromocriptine therapy has been approved for the treatment of disorders of the pituitary gland, certain cases of infertility, and the tremors and muscle rigidity of parkinsonism. Among recently abstinent hospitalized cocaine addicts, bromocriptine was shown to markedly reduce craving and withdrawal symptoms. Whether bromocriptine can provide a suitable means of treating the later cravings precipitated by environmental cues or life stressors is unknown. If bromocriptine treatment should prove effective, it would further support the role of dopamine in cocaine craving and cocaine withdrawal and could help to refine the understanding of the nature of addiction. Other drug addictions are associated with clinically significant craving, of course, and it is possible that these too might respond to dopamine agonist treatment.

Because drug-induced euphoria constitutes the other major reinforcer of cocaine addiction, the administration of a drug capable of preventing it might have an important role in rehabilitation. Naltrexone, a drug used in rehabilitation of some heroin addicts, provides a model for this strategy; even after intravenous heroin use, addicts taking naltrexone do not experience the heroin high. Such an agent may prevent relapse by serving as yet another impediment to drug use or as a means of limiting the destructive impact of occasional slips during early recovery. Neuroleptic drugs, also

In the first weeks of life, infants born to women who are cocaine addicts show unmistakable signs of withdrawal. Very little is known about the outlook and future of such children, but doctors fear that, like the babies of heroin addicts, they may suffer neurological and developmental problems. Preliminary studies indicate that babies born to coke addicts are smaller than normal and may be at greater risk of sudden infant death syndrome. This 26-week-old neonatal intensive care patient is suffering from typical drug-withdrawal symptoms.

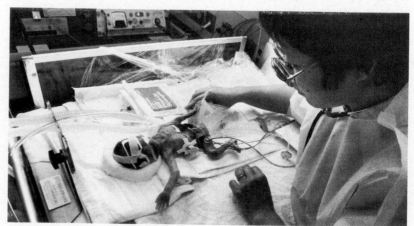

Jack Manning/The New York Times

Much of the recent increase in drug use by teenagers and school-age children has been attributed to the ready availability of crack—it is cheap, easy to conceal, and highly intoxicating. It is also highly addictive. (Left) Worried parents in New Rochelle, New York, calling themselves Mothers Against Crack (MAC), demonstrate their concern.

known as antipsychotics, block dopamine receptors and are known to prevent the euphoria induced by amphetamines ("speed"). However, long-term use of these drugs can cause serious adverse reactions, including tardive dyskinesia, a severe, sometimes irreversible movement disorder. A safe and effective "blocker," which would render a person immune to the effects of cocaine, would be a major breakthrough for both clinicians and patients. Much of what has been learned about cocaine has come from its victims, and new evidence continues to accumulate. Only recently, for example, has it been demonstrated that cocaine use by pregnant women damages the unborn fetus and that cocaine passes from mother to infant in breast-feeding. Whether long-term cocaine abuse causes brain damage in the addict is not yet known but is under investigation.

Cocaine's future

Neuroscientific research will continue to elucidate the adverse effects of cocaine and the mechanisms of drug dependency and addiction and will ultimately lead to sophisticated treatment methods. Nonetheless, drug addiction is a chronic, relapsing, incurable disease. Once a person has become dependent, he or she must be on guard for a lifetime. New treatments will be tested and success rates will increase. Prevention, however, is the only truly successful treatment. Unfortunately, new users continue to believe the mythology—that cocaine is harmless and nonaddictive and that it never fails to make everything better. Until the actual risks of cocaine are widely known and accepted—among members of the helping professions as well as among potential users—the numbers of cocaine users can be expected to increase, and the toll the drug takes will necessarily mount.

It seems to be in the nature of the cocaine experience that the user is compelled to seek that most elusive of all experiences—the ultimate high—which is always just out of reach. Perhaps it would be well to keep in mind the words of the poet William Blake: "If any could desire what he is incapable of possessing, despair must be his eternal lot."

203

The Healing Sea

by George D. Ruggieri, S. J., Ph.D.

Viewed from space, the Earth looks like a blue, watery ball punctuated with islands of land. And well it should, for water covers more than 70% of the planet's surface. The average depth of the ocean is 3,790 meters (12,430 feet), compared with an average elevation of 840 meters (2,760 feet) for the land, while its pressure averages about 410 bars (6,000 pounds per square inch), compared with an atmospheric pressure of about one bar (14.5 pounds per square inch) over most of the Earth's surface.

Because of such physical differences, the oceans offer a range of opportunities for life quite unlike that on land. Water's dimension of depth allows living organisms the option of moving vertically as well as horizontally; on land only birds, bats, and some insects routinely and easily enjoy such freedom. The salty, buoyant waters of the oceans make life possible and easier for the gigantic and the delicate. Although whales possess backbones, no structural support is present in such other giants as squid. Many marine organisms are so exquisitely fragile that they literally collapse when taken from the water. The animal known as Venus's girdle, for example, a graceful, transparent ctenophore, or comb jelly, has a body exceeding a meter (3.3 feet) in length but only a few millimeters (a fraction of an inch) thick. Most importantly, the sea contains all the elements essential to life, and it acts as a buffer, providing its inhabitants with a relatively stable, slow-to-change environment.

The sea and its inhabitants have always piqued human curiosity but never so intensely as now. Only since the mid-1940s, following the invention of scuba-diving gear, has the ocean been opened up to the general scientific community. In addition, more recent technological developments, including robotics, are allowing ship-bound scientists at the surface a vicarious prolonged presence at depths impenetrable just a few years ago. The oceans cover valleys that far exceed the Grand Canyon in size and perhaps in beauty. The ocean floor, once thought the paradigm of absolute dark tranquillity, is now known to be resonant with active volcanoes and earthquakes and to be dotted with hot-water vents that offer precarious homes for a variety of shellfish, shrimps, and giant marine worms.

And if the dominant mode of communication among the life-rich coral reefs were transformed into sound, the water would be filled with an ear-splitting cacophony. Myriad reef animals communicate chemically, attracting

George D. Ruggieri, S.J., Ph.D., is Director of the New York Aquarium and the Osborn Laboratories of Marine Sciences, New York City.

(Opposite page) Earth's watery realm has long aroused human imagination and curiosity, but only since the invention of scuba gear has it been opened to general scientific exploration. Accordingly, the search for medicines from the sea is a relatively recent endeavor. Photograph, Lawrence Gould—Oxford Scientific Films

Bright Prospects

by Herbert J. Cohen, M.D.

Writing about the position of the mentally retarded in society in his book *Christmas in Purgatory* (1966), educator and social reformer Burton Blatt declared that the retarded were "the least of the least; the abused of the abused, the least able to advocate for themselves and the most in need of advocates." Of traditional grim, overcrowded institutional facilities, he later wrote that "to develop such centers is to admit that human abuse exists, is tolerated, is sometimes encouraged, and is frequently legally permissible, and sometimes legally prescribed." Blatt was an expert in special education and, for many years, the director of the division of mental retardation for the Massachusetts Department of Public Health. He was an outspoken advocate of deinstitutionalization. His many books on the conditions of life in U.S. institutions for the retarded and mentally handicapped represent an eloquent plea for change. In recent years—perhaps most of all in the past decade—there have been encouraging signs that such abuses may one day be relegated to history.

The idea of humane care

In any given era, society's dominant perception of the retarded or disabled person has largely determined what types of institutional models were developed. Moreover, since a person's behavior is profoundly affected by the role expectations that are placed upon him or her, when people are viewed as deviant, society's reaction has, more often than not, been to be frightened and to segregate them. Thus, when people are considered sick, the most appropriate treatment is hospitalization in medically oriented facilities. When they are thought to be a menace, a prisonlike environment is provided. When the afflicted are looked upon as objects of pity, segregated but protective care is offered. When they are considered a burden of charity, then food and shelter, but little else, are provided. In the course of history, the mentally retarded and physically disabled have been regarded in nearly all of these ways. Only fairly recently have the retarded been seen as people with developmental potential who, given appropriate training or education, can live productive lives. And only within the past few decades have all disabled people been thought of as having the same rights as other human beings, including the right to the pursuit of happiness.

Herbert J. Cohen, M.D., is Professor of Pediatrics and Rehabilitation Medicine; Director, Children's Evaluation and Rehabilitation Center; and Director, Rose Fitzgerald Kennedy Center, University Affiliated Facility, at the Albert Einstein College of Medicine of Yeshiva University, New York City.

(Opposite page) A music festival at the Camphill village in Copake, New York. Camphill is an international organization of communities in which mentally handicapped people and nonhandicapped live together in an atmosphere that is enriching to both. Photograph, Camphill Foundation; photography by Stephen Rasch

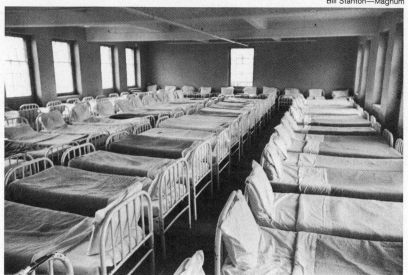

This bleak room with its uniform rows of iron bedsteads is a typical institutional dormitory of the late 19th and first half of the 20th century, when facilities for the mentally and physically disabled served primarily as human "warehouses." Writing about a similar scene in his book Souls in Extremis *(1973), social reformer Burton Blatt said, "It is very difficult to understand how humans can develop in these surroundings and maintain self-esteem, dignity, and social and emotional stability."*

In 1976, aiming to put an end to the kind of institutional inhumanity so graphically portrayed in the works of Burton Blatt, the President's Committee on Mental Retardation issued a report, *Mental Retardation: Century of Decision,* which set forth standards for "humane" care—"to accord dignity to the person served; allow him or his personal representative the determination of his own purposes; acknowledge his privilege of choice, and thereby his independence; permit him to experience shared relationships with others; allow him his own material possessions; and assure him of opportunities for meaningful activity consistent with his wants and needs."

The report further described three broad types of service, namely (1) "developmental," aimed at enhancing the individual's capabilities to the maximum obtainable level of competency; (2) "supportive," aimed at "bridging the gap between attained competency and what is required for normal social independence"; and (3) "protective," in the interest of protecting the person "from excessive hardship, loss of livelihood, sudden disaster, neglect, exploitation, and other threatening circumstances beyond his control."

From these definitions of what "humane" care should be, it is clear that services that would promote more nearly normal life-styles and foster individual growth are the goal. Today most advocates for the welfare of the mentally retarded and severely disabled agree that traditional institutional settings cannot serve these ends. Instead, providing appropriate community services and establishing alternative residential settings are viewed as the optimum means of achieving humane care.

The evolution of institutions

It is quite likely that a majority of the mentally retarded and severely disabled throughout the world have lived in the community rather than in institutions. When they could, most families chose to keep such individuals at home. In Asian countries institutions have never played an important part in the care of the disabled. Little has been written about Eastern attitudes and practices, but it is generally understood that retarded or handicapped

218

(Left) Melwood Horticultural Training Center; (right) Daniel Freeman Memorial Hospital

children who survived in these societies lived at home. In the world of the Chinese peasant, as depicted by Pearl Buck in her novel *The Good Earth,* a mentally retarded child was regarded as an accepted burden, to be cared for as humanely as possible. Under the influence of Western religious thought, parents of such a child were more likely to consider their offspring an object of shame, perhaps even a punishment for past sins. Given such an outlook, it is not surprising that most families opted for secrecy, whether this meant close confinement at home or the relative anonymity of a large, distant institutional facility. The choice was probably determined largely by economic and social considerations and by the availability of institutional care.

Early institutions. In the Western world the practice of establishing shelters to protect the mentally and physically disabled began in the Middle Ages. Virtually all able-bodied people, even those with somewhat limited capacities, were expected to work. Nonetheless, the retarded were generally regarded as helpless innocents—"children of God"—deserving of charity. As a result, some were cared for by churches or in communal facilities; some remained at home and were cared for by families. Others, less fortunate, became beggars or objects of ridicule, buffoons or jesters.

The types of congregate care facilities in which a retarded person might be placed included monasteries, hospitals, prisons, almshouses, pesthouses, and workhouses. Gradually a particular type of institution, the mental hospital, or asylum, came into being. The best known example of the early mental institution is the Bethlehem Royal Hospital in London. This institution, from whose name the word bedlam was derived, has continued to provide care for the mentally disabled to the present day, though descriptions of the initial approaches to treatment make it seem to have been more like a prison than a therapeutic environment.

Except when run for charitable purposes, the institution of earlier centuries tended to have a primitive, punitive character, although periodically social reformers and caring professionals attempted to promote more hu-

Today a majority of the six million mentally retarded people in the U.S. live in the community, not in institutions. They attend school, and many have jobs. Learning work skills is a crucial preparation for productive employment. At the Melwood Horticultural Training Center in Maryland, trainees live in group homes while they learn horticulture, custodial skills, and groundkeeping. Melwood trainees like the young man pictured above (left) work in and around Washington, D.C., tending the grounds of some of the capital's many monuments and public buildings. "Companions," an innovative program at the Daniel Freeman Memorial Hospital, Inglewood, California, pairs developmentally disabled adults with physically disabled older people. (Above) A companion trainee and a wheelchair-bound senior learn together about nutrition, meal planning, and shopping.

219

Jean-Loup Charmet, Paris

mane treatment. At the end of the 18th century, for example, notable improvements were instituted by such reformers as William Tuke, an English Quaker, and the French physician Philippe Pinel. A significant impetus for change in the care of retarded and disabled children came in 1811 as a result of a Napoleonic decree stating that "those infants who cannot be put to board, the crippled and infirm, will be raised in hospitals. They will be occupied in the workhouse at those employments that are not below their age levels." By 1838 the direct supervision of these institutions had been assumed by the French government. In the 1830s and 1840s the Poor Laws in England began to recommend special treatment for those not mentally capable of the usual workhouse activities. This trend led to the establishment at public expense of many so-called lunatic asylums, which housed individuals with a wide range of mental disabilities, and eventually to the founding of special education facilities for retarded persons, who were labeled as "idiots."

A more optimistic view. Until the middle of the 19th century, the generally held view was that people relegated to institutions were incurable. There was, therefore, little incentive to invest resources in this population, although often their labors could be exploited for agricultural or industrial production. Finally, however, in the latter part of the 19th century, the work of the early leaders in the study of mental retardation began to have an effect on institutional practices. In 1801 a French physician, Jean-Marc-Gaspard Itard, published a book about his attempts to educate a so-called feral (savage) child. Influenced by Itard's work, Edouard Séguin—who is often regarded as the father of special education—founded a private residential school for the mentally retarded. The purpose of the program was to train the residents and to improve their mental and social functioning. Séguin was not alone in promoting a program that reflected a more optimistic view of the potential of the mentally retarded and disabled. In many other countries physicians and educators were initiating innovative reforms similar to Séguin's. In Switzerland Johann Jakob Guggenbuhl began a training school for mentally retarded people, especially those suffering from a form of hypothyroidism—or what was called cretinism—the cause of which was unknown at the time. In Germany Carl Wilhelm Saegert founded a successful school for retarded pupils using methods based on his early experience in educating deaf-mutes. In England J. Langdon Down—who first described the signs and symptoms of what came to be known as Down syndrome—and William Wetherspoon Ireland promoted sequential training techniques for the mentally retarded. Influenced by the published works of Séguin, Maria Montessori, an Italian physician, established the Orthophrenic School for the Cure of the Feeble-minded. Montessori attempted to apply educational principles designed to promote creativity and spontaneity; her ideas are well known to educators of the 20th century.

Between 1845 and 1887 residential programs for the mentally retarded proliferated throughout Europe; there were at least 55 residential facilities, ranging in size from one for 10 residents in Riga, Latvia, and another for 20 in St. Petersburg, Russia, to the largest, serving 594 residents, in Earlswood, England. Other countries and localities with institutional facilities

220

included Scotland, Holland, Saxony, Berlin, Austria, Hungary, Denmark, Sweden, and Norway. Most served fewer than 100 residents.

Attitudes in the U.S. The changes in care of the mentally retarded occurring in Europe did not go unnoticed in the U.S. Unfortunately, the harsh Puritan ethic and the acceptance by many people of the practice of slavery did not encourage particularly benevolent treatment of the retarded. Early writings suggest that mentally retarded individuals in colonial America often worked as indentured servants. By the late 18th century Benjamin Rush, a signer of the Declaration of Independence and founding father of psychiatry in the U.S., had begun to promote more humane and inventive treatment techniques for the mentally ill and the retarded. Rush's initial efforts were supplemented by the work of other enlightened persons—physicians, educators, legislators, and social reformers. Samuel Gridley Howe, an 1824 graduate of Harvard Medical School, was among the early U.S. advocates of treatment aimed at improving the functioning of the institutionalized mentally retarded population. These efforts led to the establishment of more progressive residential care facilities. The movement was furthered by the work of Sen. Charles Sumner of Massachusetts, who helped establish the first publicly sponsored residential program for the retarded, and by the efforts of Horace Mann, who promoted special education, and Dorothea Dix, ardent advocate of institutional reform.

Evaluating intelligence

Subsequent periods of enlightenment brought a significant interest in the application of specific techniques for improving the functioning of retarded people and for measuring any resulting changes in their performance. Advances in measuring intelligence were stimulated by the work of the French psychologist Alfred Binet, whose early research led to the development of IQ tests. The Binet-Simon test, developed by Binet in collaboration with his student Theodore Simon, appeared in 1905. This test was revised in 1916 by Lewis Terman, an educational psychologist and head of the Stanford University Department of Psychology. The resulting instrument became

221

widely known as the Stanford-Binet IQ test and, despite later modifications, is still known by that name. Subsequently, several other test procedures were devised. This spate of activity reflected an overall interest in measuring intelligence, in classifying people with subnormal ability into groupings with functional implications or similar prognoses, and in attempting to measure progress, or lack of it, in various aspects of learning. Implicit in these activities was a belief that the abilities and capacities of the retarded could be improved, given appropriate training and education.

Protecting society from the defective

Although the early 20th century represented a time of progress in the fields of psychology and education, which had some impact on institutional practices, other more popular notions about the nature of mental retardation had a greater influence on the treatment of retarded and disabled people. The science of genetics and, more specifically, an interest in heredity as a cause of mental subnormality became the dominant influence on social policies. In turn, these policies became less tolerant and more restrictive. Social control and prevention became the bywords in the first two decades of the century. Mental retardation was viewed as a hereditary disorder and, in some cases, was thought to be a dominant trait, its transmission from one generation to another chronicled in several purportedly comprehensive studies of certain families believed to carry the trait. Few investigators of this era considered the impact of environmental factors on intelligence and ability.

Fearing the "pollution" of the normal population with genes supposedly carrying the trait of retardation, some scientists and social critics felt that eugenics, or controlled "breeding" of human beings, was the only recourse. The tenor of the times was expressed in a 1915 article entitled "The Prevention of Mental Defect, the Duty of the Hour," which declared in favor of strict enforcement measures—"separation, sequestration, and asexualization of degenerates"—deemed necessary to keep the mentally less capable from reproducing. Scientific studies were cited to support legislation that prohibited marriage by any mentally retarded person. State laws calling for

In the 1970s an exposé of the shocking conditions at New York's Willowbrook State School—the largest U.S. facility for the mentally retarded—made the name Willowbrook synonymous with institutional care at its most appalling. Willowbrook was the archetype of the human receptacle, where adult residents passed their days in grim communal rooms (below left) that made no pretense of providing any sort of recreation or domestic comfort. Children, both the physically handicapped and the mentally retarded, were strapped into chairs or carts (below right). A school in name only, Willowbrook provided no training or education, except for a handful of youngsters considered trainable.

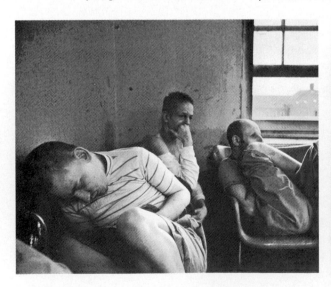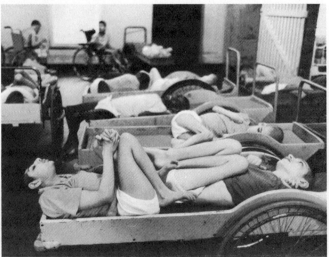

(Left) Bill Stanton—Magnum; (right) Bill Pierce/Time Magazine

Richard Meier

mandatory sterilization for the mentally retarded became common. In fact,
until the 1960s the majority of states in the U.S. still had these laws on their
books, though most states no longer encouraged or formally condoned the
practice of sterilization.

The "warehousing" of people

The benevolent goals of early institutions for the retarded began to give
way in the late 19th and early 20th centuries to regimented facilities that
accentuated deviancy and the need for isolation. The American ethos of
efficiency and the doctrine that "bigger is better" began to be reflected in
the development of very large congregate care facilities that prided themselves on the inexpensive "warehousing" of the retarded and disabled. The
buildings of such institutions tended to have a certain uniform look and
feel about them, a collection of architecturally nondescript brick structures
giving the impression of a cross between a school and a storage facility.
The grounds also tended to be large—hundreds of acres in some instances.
Residents slept in cheerless dormitories, and the sparsely furnished day
rooms offered little recreation, except in more recent times for the ever-
present television set. There were few if any signs of an attempt to simulate
a homelike atmosphere.

New York State's Willowbrook, one of the largest institutions of its kind
in the U.S., was completed around the beginning of World War II. It was
used first as an army hospital and later as a Veterans Administration facility
before being returned to the state in 1951 for its original use. Remarkably,
by 1963 this prototype of the very large institution had more than 6,000
residents in its overcrowded buildings. In fact, at that time a substantial
waiting list existed; families clamored for the opportunity to place relatives in
Willowbrook and similar state facilities. In response to these types of pressures—and because no alternatives were proposed in most instances—
the building of large state institutions continued in many states for several
decades after World War II.

Innovative institutions

In the 1960s those who still believed that institutional care was necessary for most of the mentally retarded began to examine and question the earlier premises about the need for remote or isolated locations and the prevailing notion that large size could be equated with efficiency. Proposals were made to build smaller facilities—500 to 750 beds—that would be "community based"; *i.e.,* designed and scaled to serve a particular local population. One such plan was developed in 1965 in New York State; it resulted in the creation of a network of eight smaller facilities in population centers around the state, four of them in New York City. Perhaps the most unusual was the Bronx Developmental Center, an innovative modern building designed by an internationally known architect, Richard Meier. Nonetheless, to the advocates of humane care, making institutions smaller or more modern did not address the fundamental problem; the institution remained an isolated and restricted environment in which individual autonomy and human potential were inhibited.

The 1960s and '70s: decades of change

In the United States concerns about human rights, civil rights, and the rights of minorities and the underprivileged—including the mentally retarded and the physically handicapped—became important matters of public policy in the 1960s. Internment in large institutions came to be viewed as a violation of rights. Failure to provide adequate programs was seen as a violation of the individual's presumed "right to treatment," or at least "protection from harm," terms that became prominent in litigation to achieve institutional reform.

Another impetus for change in the care of the mentally and physically disabled was the consumer movement. The formation of state, local, and national associations for the handicapped and retarded provided families of these individuals an opportunity to join together to seek common goals. Some groups sought improvement in institutions; others sought alternatives to institutions. Whatever the focus, however, they were able, by joining

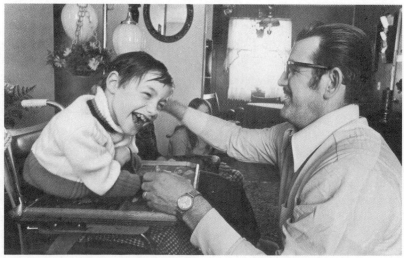

together, to make themselves heard and to bring pressure to bear on lawmakers.

Finally, an important psychological lift was given to the movement in 1961 when John F. Kennedy became president, and the nation learned that the Kennedys had coped with the problem of mental retardation within their family. Kennedy announced that one of his goals would be to seek improvements in the care of the retarded. He appointed an advisory panel and, following its advice, sought legislation to develop research and training centers, to expand the role of community mental health centers, and, by providing incentives to the states, to develop plans for community-based services. This led to landmark legislation in 1963, the Mental Retardation Facilities and Community Mental Health Center Construction Act (PL 88-164).

As noted previously, with the emergence of the civil rights movement, the right to equal protection under the law became the goal for many groups, including the mentally and physically disabled. One key right that was sought was access to services and improved living conditions. PL 88-164 was the first in a chain of important acts that guaranteed rights or access to services. Key among this legislation were three laws: (1) PL 93-112, the Rehabilitation Act of 1973, which included one section that specifically prohibited discrimination by making it illegal to exclude disabled people from any program receiving federal funds; (2) PL 94-103, the Developmentally Disabled Assistance and Bill of Rights Act (1975), which added provisions to safeguard and protect the rights of the mentally retarded and developmentally disabled; and (3) PL 94-142, the Education for All Handicapped Children Act (1975), which mandated free public education in the least restrictive environment for all handicapped children.

Alternatives to institutionalization

Thus, by the late 1970s many influences had come together to decrease the part played by institutions in the lives of the retarded and disabled. Families demanded more and better services for children with disabilities. The law

In the 1960s and '70s a variety of forces converged in the U.S. to change both the way the handicapped and retarded were viewed by others and the number of alternatives available to them. Scientific studies indicated that many mentally retarded people had the capacity for education and training. Federal legislation mandated free public education for all handicapped children. Support groups helped people with specific handicaps— and their families, as well—learn to cope with and overcome their disabilities. As a result of these changes, many parents opted to care for handicapped children at home (opposite page), providing the warmth and affection lacking in even the finest institutional facility. Special education programs were developed for the retarded, like the Down syndrome youngsters (below right), who would once have been viewed as hopelessly defective. And public school classrooms such as the one (below left) in Birmingham, Alabama, were opened to children with special needs.

(Left) EPIC School, Birminghman, Alabama; (right) National Down Syndrome Society

In many countries around the world, community living for the retarded and handicapped has proved to be a happy alternative to institutional life. The Lambs, a 20.6-hectare (51-acre) farm near Libertyville, Illinois, is one such community. The Lambs is home to more than 150 mentally handicapped men and women, who, depending on their degree of independence, live either in group homes or dormitory-style accommodations. Under the guidance of a professional vocational staff, residents work in the many businesses run by the community and patronized by the more than 250,000 visitors who come to The Lambs each year. Some residents care for the animals in the Children's Farmyard; young visitors enjoy petting the sheep (opposite page, top) and being taken for pony rides. Other residents feed and groom the animals that are for sale in the Pet Shop (far right) or wait on customers in the Country Store (right). Residents also run a bakery, a restaurant, and a silk-screening studio that produces stationery and other hand-printed items. The vocational center subcontracts jobs in packaging, assembly, bulk mailing, and similar projects. All aspects of life at The Lambs are aimed at promoting autonomy, maximizing potential, and providing individual fulfillment.

declared that they were entitled to such services and set about allocating funds to provide them. At the same time, scientific research had begun to indicate a more optimistic view of the potential of the mentally retarded. Finally, deinstitutionalization was spurred by the widespread acceptance of concepts intrinsic to the notion of humane care, namely, that institutions, by their very nature, are places where people are deprived of autonomy and dignity and prevented from attaining their full human growth. All of these factors combined to foster a decline in the size of the institutionalized population and an expansion in the availability of alternative care for the mentally retarded and physically handicapped.

In the search for alternatives to traditional institutional care, there has been a considerable degree of experimentation to find suitable arrangements. The most common alternative for children—and for many adults—has been to remain at home with parents or other relatives. Other options include community residences having varying degrees of supervision and whole communities set aside for the disabled. For the more capable and less dependent individuals, fully or partially independent living is sometimes feasible.

Home care. For a child who is mentally retarded or physically handicapped, care in his or her own home is viewed by most contemporary experts as the optimal arrangement; living at home is considered less desirable for adults, who should be encouraged to pursue the normal expectations of adulthood—emotional and physical separation from the family and transition to a more independent life-style. For the child, however, living with the family is a normalizing experience, provided the parents do not infantilize the youngster or foster dependency.

Service planners are pleased with the option of home care because it is seen as less costly than providing a residential bed for an individual. However, if care at home is to be satisfying for the child and the family, a considerable array of services must be provided, and both direct and indirect cost factors must be considered. Direct expenses may include the costs of day treatment or school programs, which may vary with the age

226

of the individual, and transportation to programs; also included are in-home costs for such items as special equipment, medications, clothing, food, medical care—even physical modifications of the home environment and the extra costs of utilities required to power special equipment. Indirect costs, such as time lost from work by parents caring for the child, must also be considered, along with the need for baby-sitting, relief for vacations, or occasional respite—"time off"—from the burden of care. Psychological costs to family members resulting from the normal stresses and frustrations of the situation must also be considered and may require special help.

When a family cannot manage on its own, the best alternatives are foster care or adoption by another family. In some cases the stress of caring for a handicapped child at home is disruptive; some reports indicate increased

Special Olympics Inc.

Competition in the Special Olympics promotes mental, physical, and social development for mentally retarded children and adults. More than 50 countries participate in the games. For the retarded—as indeed for all people—physical fitness enhances confidence and self-esteem.

The National Theatre Workshop of the Handicapped; photograph, Michael Harter

While there are a number of theatrical groups made up solely of disabled people, the National Theatre Workshop of the Handicapped in New York City seeks to provide professional training commensurate with that available to able-bodied students. Since its founding in 1977, the workshop has trained more than 150 handicapped aspirants to careers on the stage and screen.

rates of divorce and separation, increased incidence of abuse and neglect, and increased stress responses in siblings as well as parents. Nonetheless, many families indicate that they have been strengthened by the experience of caring for a handicapped or retarded child and feel that their commitment to help the child has remained unchanged despite any adversity.

Community residences. The concept of "normalization"—enabling the disabled to lead as normal a life as possible—was first promulgated in the 1950s by N. E. Bank-Mikkelson, who, as head of the Danish Mental Retardation Service, brought about significant changes in that country. As a result of the ideological leadership of such people as Bank-Mikkelson in Denmark and Bengt Nirje in Sweden, the Scandinavian countries became leaders in the development of community residential care some time before the idea was widely accepted in the U.S. In Sweden a decentralized network of community facilities, including group homes and boarding homes, was established in the 1960s. A few large facilities have remained, but the clear emphasis has been on smaller residences with single-bed rooms and a range of support services. County councils are responsible for the operation of these residences. In Denmark a similar pattern of smaller residential facilities has developed.

Small homelike settings—primarily of the type known as group homes—have grown rapidly in number in the United States. In the U.S. in 1982 some 57,000 people were reported to be residing in about 6,000 group homes. Programs vary in size, age of residents, and auspices (private nonprofit organization, public agency, or profit-making corporation). More than 90% reportedly are homes with fewer than 15 beds; the average size is about 9 beds. Every state in the U.S. has group homes.

Community opposition to such homes has remained a problem despite active attempts to educate potential neighbors. The entrance into the community of people who are "different" often provokes hostility and fear. Nevertheless, these types of residences are being increasingly accepted, particularly as studies of property values show no decrease in value resulting from the presence of a group home in the neighborhood and as the

In his determination not to let his disability prevent him from taking a long-dreamed-of trip to Europe, John Hessler, a quadriplegic confined to a wheelchair since a diving accident in 1957, enlisted the aid of friends. They drove from Paris to Biel, Switzerland. To reach their ultimate destination, a chalet in the Jura Mountains, the entourage successfully negotiated a steep climb through a dense thicket of trees.

Reprinted with permission of Gazette International Networking Institute (GINI)

Canadian athlete André Viger wins his second consecutive wheelchair championship at the 1986 Boston Marathon, cheered on (at right) by Ted Kennedy, Jr., who is both an amputee and a competitive athlete. People with physical disabilities ask only for the same opportunities open to everyone else— that is, a chance to win, or lose, on their own merits.

presence of disabled people appears less threatening to the public. A more sympathetic portrayal of the disabled in films and on television appears to have had some positive effect on the public's attitude.

Communities for the disabled. One alternative that has proved successful in many different countries is the development of communities for disabled people. In such an environment, individuals can learn to be self-sufficient but, at the same time, have some supervision. In Europe, Africa, and the U.S. the Camphill Foundation has established villages that integrate mentally handicapped people with others who have no disabilities. *L'arche* ("The Ark") is an international federation of communities in which mentally handicapped and normal people live and work together. From its beginning in one house in a small village in northern France, *L'arche* has branched out into other European countries, Canada, the U.S., India, and Africa. As some critics have noted, it is in the nature of such communities that the disabled are somewhat isolated from the mainstream of society; nonetheless, they are permitted a more nearly normal life-style within the restricted setting.

Support services. In order to live comfortably and productively in the community, retarded and physically disabled people need a variety of support services: preschool care; regular school classes; day care for unemployed adults and vocational training for those able to work; transportation; recreational and social activities; medical and dental services, including various rehabilitative and corrective therapies; management and administrative services; and advocacy and case-management systems. A major stimulus to the growth of community programs for the disabled in the U.S. has been the expansion of federal entitlement programs. Of key importance has been Medicaid, which not only pays for institutional care but, as a result of a change in the law in the early 1970s, supports community-based intermediate care facilities. Medicaid also pays for outpatient medical services. The Education for All Handicapped Children Act has helped to bolster educational services for retarded and handicapped children, and Supplemental Security Income payments help to support the costs of care of disabled people who are not institutionalized. In the U.S., federal subsidization of

229

community care has had a significant impact on the services that have become available during the past decade.

Is there a "best" approach?

The transition from a system emphasizing institutionalization to one encouraging community care has raised questions about the most effective means of providing services and improving the lives of the mentally and physically disabled population. It also evokes concerns about what is best for the families of these people and for society at large.

Much of current practice is based on a philosophy of care or an ideology rather than hard evidence that one system is clearly better. Community care is unquestionably more "normalizing." Compared with the institutionalized population, the residents of group homes appear to be better fed and better dressed, and they function at higher levels; society's expectations for them are greater. Fewer regress in such settings. There appears to be less abuse and mistreatment, though problems of high staff turnover, poor staff training, and undue regimentation may occur in group home operations just as they do in large institutions. There is no evidence that the mentally retarded are made "smarter" or the physically disabled more mobile because of a change in their living environment. What community care and normalization offer, however, is the opportunity for individuals to reach their full potential.

From an economic standpoint, there is a strong argument in favor of community care. Average per diem costs in the U.S. in 1982 were $86.25 for care in traditional institutions as opposed to $42.75 in community residences. Foster care costs were $16 per day per person. Investment in educational and vocational training produces long-range savings up to 13-fold by making the mentally retarded and physically disabled less dependent on others for day-to-day care or by providing skills that enable them to be employed and, therefore, taxpayers rather than recipients of public aid.

Given the clear economic benefits, it is likely that budget-conscious administrators and advocates of cost-effective approaches will continue to support community care as a reasonable alternative to care in large institutions. "Bigger is better" no longer makes economic sense and was never a convincing argument from a programmatic standpoint or from a philosophical one.

Looking to the future

Life for the mentally retarded and severely disabled has improved vastly in the past few decades. Large institutions continue to be phased out; many will eventually be closed. Legislation now pending in Congress aims at accelerating the rate of deinstitutionalization and providing fiscal incentives to the states to do so. Similarly, the trend in Europe is toward expanded community services. Though many obstacles continue to impede society's progress toward humane care, it is likely that in the future most people with disabilities will lead better, more productive lives, in warmer, more homelike surroundings, than would have been possible during past eras of isolation, ignorance, and secrecy.

On Having a Heart Attack

by David E. Rogers, M.D.

I have just spent what is for me quite an unusual ten minutes. I have been looking at flowers. Obviously, I have seen flowers all of my life. In recent years my wife's interest in plants has led me to learn more about them. But until right now, I have never really appreciated quite how vivid their coloring is, how intricate their design, how exquisite the shaping of their petals, stamens, and foliage, or just how delicately they are put together. I had never taken the time necessary just to indulge in them. I report that I found it most pleasurable.

So that is the happy ending. I hope it suggests that I am enjoying life—indeed savoring it. But the flowers are a lead-in to my reflecting on something else. As a doctor who has spent much of his professional lifetime trying to listen very carefully to patients and to treat them appropriately, and then to teach others who are becoming doctors how to do it well, I now wish to describe a recent personal experience—to attempt to convey what one very common disease feels like "from the inside" when it starts.

George Gardner

David E. Rogers, M.D., is President of the Robert Wood Johnson Foundation, Princeton, New Jersey. Formerly he was Dean of the medical faculty and Professor of Medicine at the Johns Hopkins University School of Medicine, Baltimore, Maryland. A version of this article was published in The Pharos, *vol. 49, no. 3 (Summer), Copyright © 1986 by Alpha Omega Alpha Honor Medical Society.*

"I have been looking at flowers. . . . I have never really appreciated . . . just how delicately they are put together. I had never taken the time necessary just to indulge in them. . . . I found it most pleasurable."

The disease is myocardial infarction—a heart attack. This peculiarly human disease probably appeared quite suddenly on the historical scene sometime toward the end of the 19th or the early part of the 20th century. After its recognition, it rapidly zoomed to the number one position on the mortality hit list in much of the Western world. In the United States it reached its apogee in 1963. Since then it seems to have been becoming both less common and somewhat more benign.

Clearly, what I have to say here will not add to anyone's understanding of this number one killer of American men of middle age. However, my pedagogical instincts are hard to control, and several young doctors who have quizzed me about what it feels like have suggested I try to put the sensations—not the pathology—into words while the experience is still vivid. I think this suggestion was made, in part, so that they could be spared yet further verbal details from me and get about their more pressing business. However, I promised them I would try, so here goes.

I will omit all the details about what I was doing, or the prodrome—*i.e.,* warning symptoms—(which was classic), but will simply try to describe the episode itself, for soon after its onset I knew precisely what was happening to me, and I had quite an amount of time to think about it.

I have often told medical students that most people I have queried who are having genuine cardiac pain seem instinctively to wish to remain very quiet even when their pain is not particularly severe. Thus, I have generally felt that when patients have told me that they have had to keep "wiggling about" to find a comfortable position or were "writhing with pain" and the like, *their* chest pain was probably noncardiac.

My own experience would certainly confirm this. After the first 15 to 20 minutes, when the sensations were waxing and waning, and I was pretending they were esophageal and popping a few Tums and drinking a glass of milk, the pain certainly told me just what it seems to have told other patients. I felt I must sit down *very, very* quietly. Despite doing so, the pain became a steadily expanding, deep, penetrating ache spreading from beneath midbreastbone, around the sides of my chest, up my neck into my lower jaw, and down the inner aspect of my left arm into my fourth and

Arteriograms of the right coronary artery of a patient experiencing an acute myocardial infarction illustrate the effect of direct infusion of the clot-dissolving enzyme streptokinase. Before treatment (left), artery is completely blocked by a blood clot (a); a preexisting partial occlusion due to plaque deposits is also present (b). After infusion of streptokinase (right), former site of clot is clear (a), although the atherosclerotic narrowing remains (b). Streptokinase can be helpful in salvaging heart muscle only if administered before irreversible damage has occurred. Unfortunately, in the author's case, it was too late.

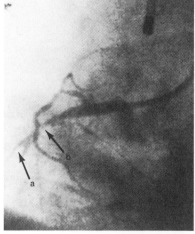 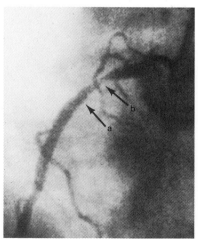

Photographs, Douglas R. Rosing, National Heart, Lung, and Blood Institute, NIH

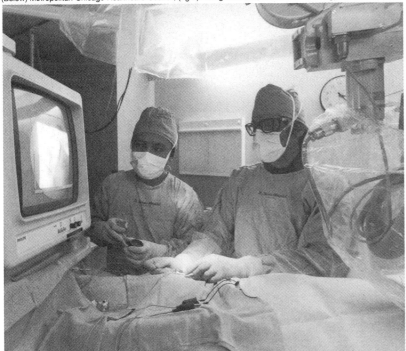

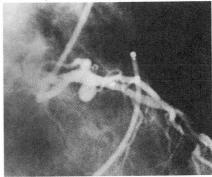

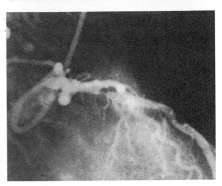

fifth fingers. It would cycle a bit. Sometimes it would seem most dreadful in my chest, then in my jaw and lower teeth, then in my left arm. But it had one clear message. What I felt from the outset and continued to feel through about two hours of what seemed absolutely intolerable pain was that if I remained *absolutely* immobile, not moving even an eyelash, perhaps it would let go of me. I would guess it took about 10 to 12 minutes to build to maximal intensity, and there it stayed. During the entire period I sat absolutely still with my eyes closed, conscious of the fact that I was sweating profusely and that I probably looked very pale and lousy. Although my wife was bustling cheerfully about in the kitchen not 15 feet away, I said absolutely nothing, feeling that even moving my tongue or vocal cords was simply too much. There was no inclination to groan or cry out.

There was another aspect of the pain, which is frequently alluded to by others. There was absolutely no doubt in my mind that I was about to die. As the pain remained, I simply wished exodus would go ahead and happen. The emotion I can recapture regarding this certainty was one not of great fear but rather of anger mixed with sadness; I felt angry because this goddamned thing was happening to me, and because I knew I had done some things—years of smoking and some more recent episodes of handling stress rather poorly—that had provoked it and because I was not going to be able to say goodbye to anybody—particularly my family and close friends and colleagues—or tell them what they had meant to me.

The quality of the pain is as difficult for me to describe as it seems to have been for other observers over the last 70-plus years. It was not the bright, or burning, or well-localized pain one feels with a cut, a puncture, or a burn, from which one instinctively and swiftly retreats. A very different

The photograph (above left) shows a coronary angioplasty procedure, which cardiologists and patient can watch on the monitor. In the procedure a catheter is manipulated to place a balloon in the center of an area that is partially occluded by atherosclerotic plaque. When the balloon has been properly positioned, it is inflated, thereby compressing the plaque and opening the blocked vessel. The above arteriograms, taken during the author's successful angioplasty, show his left coronary artery (top) blocked by atherosclerotic plaque and the reopened artery after the balloon has been inserted and inflated (bottom).

233

set of nerve endings is involved. It was a dreadful, deep, nauseating ache. If you could multiply a hundredfold the kind of ache in your arms you experience after working too long with them trying to screw a recalcitrant light bulb into a ceiling socket that is a little too high over your head to reach decently, you will be close. A stunt I tried many years ago—putting a blood pressure cuff on my own leg above the knee and blowing it up to occlude arterial circulation in order to feel the kind of dreadful pain that affects the calf—is yet closer. (At the time, I was trying to see if I could mimic heart pain.) But what was exquisitely different about that experiment is that I could release the cuff when I felt I could not stand further intensity of pain. In the real instance, there was no such letup.

As to intensity, I keep wanting to use the word unbearable, but obviously this was not true any more than was my certain conviction that I would die. But it was an absolutely monstrously awful sensation, and it was totally untouched by 20 or 30 or 40 milligrams of morphine given me by my doctors over the next two hours. The fact that morphine gave so little relief has made me empathize deeply with the hundreds of patients over the years with the same disease whom I treated with this drug.

So that is what I can best convey about how it felt. Now let me add a few comments about my treatment during the myocardial infarction.

First, having a cardiac catheterization via the femoral artery and vein during an infarction is a piece of cake—almost no discomfort. Further, frequent squirts of dye into one's coronaries (the arteries and veins of the heart), which I could watch on a monitor, are totally painless. It did not improve my morale to see absolutely no dye going into my left anterior descending coronary, which appeared completely blocked, but I already knew that this was probably going to be the case, and all other arteries looked splendid.

One further episode was impressive and of profound relief to me. The cardiologists who were my catheter artisans had maneuvered their catheter

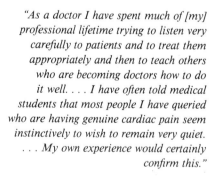

"As a doctor I have spent much of [my] professional lifetime trying to listen very carefully to patients and to treat them appropriately and then to teach others who are becoming doctors how to do it well. . . . I have often told medical students that most people I have queried who are having genuine cardiac pain seem instinctively to wish to remain very quiet. . . . My own experience would certainly confirm this."

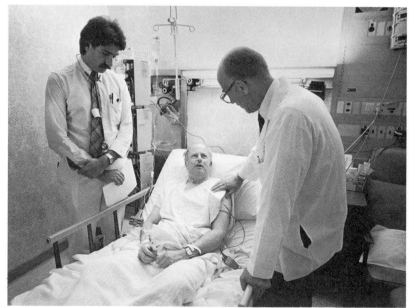

George Gardner

Photographs, George Gardner

into the stumplike orifice of the left anterior descending artery and began dripping in streptokinase (an ancient streptococcal enzyme, which I had used in crude form in patients to dissolve clots in pleural spaces in 1950). Quite suddenly, and after only modest amounts of enzyme, I said—and I think these were some of my first words since the onset of my infarction— "I think you've dissolved it; I've lost my pain." They were quite surprised, but they shot in some more dye, which confirmed part of what I was saying. A thin threadlike squirt of dye could be seen going through a very tight inch-long obstruction close to the origin of the coronary. But the whole artery below the block could be seen looking fat and filled. They continued to profuse the streptokinase, but five to ten minutes later I said, "And now it's clotted off again," for my pain had just then returned in its original intensity. More pictures showed that this indeed was true—no more filling beyond the stump.

Then followed the use of the latest in modern medical miracle technologies. My doctors skillfully threaded a tiny wire through the obstruction, guided a collapsed balloon over it, and positioned it within the ¼-inch-long obstruction. This balloon angioplasty I watched on the monitor with fascination. Then they expanded the balloon, forcing arterial wall, clot, and atheroma outward. Again, swift and blissful relief of pain. Meanwhile, they measured pressures and gradients and fooled around and inflated it again a few times over the next 30 to 40 minutes to make sure the gradient had been eliminated and that it did not clot off again. Subsequent pictures of the coronary looked virtually normal, and I have been pain free ever since.

Let me add just one other thing that my physicians did for me later, for I have felt, in retrospect, that it was a vital factor in speeding my return to full function. Although I had been agitating to get home, I will now confess to some feelings of apprehension about it while still in the hospital. Being

"Being hooked up to all that gadgetry makes one feel surprisingly dependent and fragile and emotionally uncertain about one's ability to function adequately outside the hospital's technological womb. . . . Although I was intellectually sure my heart was functioning splendidly, to have objective proof . . . made me feel totally comfortable about cutting the umbilical cord and striking out on my own again. . . . The residual damage to my heart looks modest and should repair rapidly . . . my priorities have been abruptly, but quite appropriately, reordered."

235

hooked up to all that gadgetry makes one feel surprisingly dependent and fragile and emotionally uncertain about one's ability to function adequately outside the hospital's technological womb. Thus, I had doubts about how I would feel walking up the stairs or up the driveway and the like.

But the night before discharging me, my cardiologists asked if I would like them to run a modified stress test on me before I left, and I agreed with enthusiasm. Consequently, the next morning they hooked me up, stuck me on the treadmill, and proceeded to work me until I thought I would drop. My legs were crying for relief and I was puffing like an aging bull, but my electrocardiogram remained totally unchanged, my blood pressure behaved responsibly, and I had absolutely no chest pain. Afterward, I felt that this was perhaps the greatest gift they could have bestowed upon me as a going-away present. Although I was intellectually sure my heart was functioning splendidly, to have objective proof that it could handle vastly more effort than I was planning for it during the next month or so made me feel totally comfortable about cutting the umbilical cord and striking out on my own again.

So: I have had an experience unheard of until very recently—that of knowing firsthand what having a *massive* myocardial infarction feels like but without the full-blown events actually occurring and without having to live with its crippling aftermath. The residual damage to my heart looks modest and should repair rapidly. My coronary arteries now resemble garden hoses in good condition. And perhaps of equal long-term significance, my priorities have been abruptly, but quite appropriately, reordered. Hence, my leisurely and pleasurable contemplation of flowers.

My last observation: As we continue to struggle to make medical care less expensive without lousing it up, I am obviously going to be thinking hard about the implications of what I have just experienced. I would guess that within a very few years it may be viewed as close to medical malpractice to hospitalize a patient with an acute evolving coronary anywhere but in a hospital with a cardiac unit with catheterization, angioplasty, and backup surgical capabilities unless such a unit is more than two hours away. That, surely, will not reduce acute costs.

But as some of my vintage colleagues and I have since said to each other, we used to care for people like me by slugging them with morphine until their blood-starved heart muscle died and their pain stopped. We would watch fairly helplessly when they developed fatal arrhythmias. We agonized about giving them the drug digitalis when they went into congestive heart failure because of its propensity to produce fatal arrhythmias. Our patients stayed in the hospital for a minimum of six weeks (I stayed ten days), and we created a dreadful number of cardiac cripples who never worked productively again.

One of my colleagues is fond of saying, "Sometimes the best medicine is the most expensive medicine." All I can say is "Amen" in this instance, but over the long haul it seems pretty "cost-beneficial" to me!

ENCYCLOPÆDIA BRITANNICA

MEDICAL UPDATE

Articles from the 1986 Printing of *Encyclopædia Britannica*

The purpose of this section is to introduce to continuing *Medical and Health Annual* subscribers selected *Macropædia* articles or portions of articles that have been completely revised or rewritten. It is intended to update the *Macropædia* coverage of medical and health-related topics in a way that cannot be accomplished fully by a yearly review of significant developments, because the *Macropædia* texts themselves—written from a longer perspective than any yearly revision—supply authoritative interpretation as well as pertinent data and examination of timely issues.

Three wholly new articles have been chosen from the 1986 printing: BURNS; DEATH; and Organ and Tissue TRANSPLANTS. Each is the work of a distinguished scholar, and each represents the continuing dedication of the *Encyclopædia Britannica* to bringing such works to the general reader. New bibliographies accompany the articles as well for readers who wish to pursue certain topics. Because of limitations of space, each article appears here in a slightly abridged version; ellipses are used to indicate where portions of the text have been deleted.

Burns

Burns are a major and unique problem in the field of injury and surgery. In the majority of other injuries or forms of surgery, a person usually remains in a precarious balance between life and death for only a few days and then either recuperates or succumbs. Following deep or extensive burns, the victim's life remains in jeopardy for weeks; and intelligent and unremitting care is necessary. . . .

The problems encountered in the treatment of burns were so great and so unfathomable that until the mid-20th century only a few doctors would devote the time required to caring for burn patients. Probably in no other field of medicine has so little progress been made and treatment been so mismanaged. Only since World War II have there been significant advances in the theory and practice of burn trauma management.

Since ancient times, burns have been mishandled. Emollient preparations with bizarre ingredients were placed on the burn wound as a standard form of treatment. Purgation and bleeding were popular treatments throughout the Middle Ages. Until recently the best form of treatment prescribed consisted of washing the burn wound with soap and water, leaving it exposed to the air, and giving the patient salt water to drink.

In 1607, Fabricius Hildanus recognized three degrees of burns. In 1750 David Cleghorn recognized that purgation was harmful to the patient. By 1905, some physicians were cognizant of the fluid and salt losses sustained by the burn patient. In some medical circles, intravenous salt solutions were prescribed. Greater understanding of the enormous losses of water, salt, and protein was established by the mid-20th century. Although it had been performed earlier, skin grafting came upon a firm basis through the work of Jacques-Louis Reverdin in 1869; Karl Thiersch in 1874; and others in the 20th century.

Local treatments of all types have been tried through the centuries. No local treatment that was not actually harmful was used, however, until Alexander Burns Wallace, Truman Graves Blocker, and Edwin J. Pulaski popularized the exposure method of burn treatment in the late 1940s. This method had previously been described but had been discarded in favour of methods such as treatment with tannic acid, gentian violet, and concentrated silver nitrate.

The Brooke Army Surgical Research Group in San Antonio, Texas, emphasized in 1953 that septicemia (bloodborne infection) was a major cause of death in burns. Probably the most important recent advance in the treatment of burns has been the local application of bacteriostatic agents. The Brooke Army Group also popularized allografting (grafts taken from another person) and xenografting (grafts taken from animals) as a means of temporary physiologic coverage of the burn wound. A deep burn must eventually be covered with the patient's own skin, however, as skin from other people or animals is rejected, just as other transplants tend to be rejected, except among identical twins. (ELI RUSH CREWS, M.D.)

This article is divided into the following sections:

FACTORS THAT DETERMINE THE SEVERITY OF BURNS

The severity of a burn depends largely on the depth of tissue destruction and the amount of body surface affected. Other factors—including the patient's age and prior state of health, the location of the burn wound, and the seriousness of any associated injuries—can also influence recovery from a burn.

In order to appreciate how depth and size of a burn affect the severity of the injury, it is helpful to understand the anatomy and physiology of the skin. Human skin is composed of two layers: an upper layer called the epidermis, and a lower layer known as the dermis (or corium). The largest of the body's organs, skin performs a number of vital functions. Its foremost job is to separate the external environment from the body's interior. The epidermis, the outer surface of which consists of dead, cornified cells, prevents infectious microorganisms and other harmful environmental agents from gaining entrance to the body. The dermis, by contrast, is made up of fibrous connective tissues that prevent the evaporation of body fluids. Embedded within the dermis and opening to the skin surface are the sweat glands. These secrete

Structure and function of skin

perspiration, the evaporation of which helps regulate body temperature. Perspiration also contains small amounts of sodium chloride, cholesterol, aluminum, and urea; it thus plays a role in regulating the composition of body fluids. The dermis also contains all of the skin's blood vessels and nerves, including sensory nerve endings that respond to touch, pressure, heat, cold, and pain. The skin therefore also serves as a sense organ that enables a person to adjust to changing environmental conditions. One final function of the skin is the synthesis of vitamin D, a compound essential to growth and maintenance, particularly of bone. Vitamin D is formed by the action of sunlight on certain cholesterol compounds in the dermis. Destruction of the skin by deep or extensive burns can disrupt all of these functions, subjecting the victim to serious complications.

Depth. Physicians have traditionally categorized burns as first-, second-, or third-degree injuries, according to the depth of skin damage. An accurate determination of burn depth helps predict the subsequent effects of the injury and guides the physician in planning the course of treatment.

By courtesy of E.R. Crews, *A Practical Manual for the Treatment of Burns*, 1st ed. (1964); Charles C. Thomas

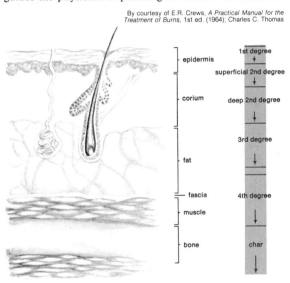

Figure 1: Depth of burn as classified by degree.

In a first-degree burn, only the epidermis is affected. These injuries are characterized by redness and pain; there are no blisters, and edema (swelling due to the accumulation of fluids) in the wounded tissue is minimal. A classic example of a first-degree burn is moderate sunburn. The pain subsides within 48 to 72 hours, and the injury heals without further complications or scarring. Small scales of damaged skin peel off in about a week's time.

The damage in a second-degree burn extends through the entire epidermis and part of the dermis. These injuries are characterized by redness and blisters. The deeper the burn the more prevalent the blisters, which increase in size during the hours immediately following the injury. Like first-degree burns, second-degree injuries may be extremely painful. The development of complications and the course of healing in a second-degree burn depend on the extent of damage to the dermis. Unless they become infected, most superficial second-degree burns heal without complications and with little scarring in 10 to 14 days. In deep second-degree burns, the injured skin may resemble that which overlies third-degree injuries (see below), except that it is usually red or pink. Even an experienced burn surgeon may find it difficult to immediately distinguish a deep second-degree burn from a third-degree burn. Deep second-degree wounds heal slowly, generally over a period of 25 to 30 days; some may take up to 105 days. The healing epidermis is extremely fragile, and scarring is common. In fact, some of the worst burn scars are the result of deep second-degree burns. These injuries cause serious fluid losses and metabolic disturbances.

Third-degree, or full-thickness, burns destroy the entire thickness of the skin. The surface of the wound is leathery and may be brown, tan, black, white, or red. There is no pain, because the pain receptors have been obliterated along with the rest of the dermis. Blood vessels, sweat glands, sebaceous glands, and hair follicles are all destroyed in skin that suffers a full-thickness burn. Fluid losses and metabolic disturbances associated with these injuries are grave.

Occasionally burns deeper than a full thickness of the skin are incurred, as when part of the body is entrapped in a flame and not immediately extricated. Electrical burns are usually deep burns. These deep burns frequently go into the subcutaneous tissue and, at times, beyond and into the muscle, fascia, and bone. Such burns are of the fourth degree, also called black (because of the typical colour of the burn), or char, burns. Fourth-degree burns are of grave prognosis, particularly if they involve more than a small portion of the body. In these deep burns toxic materials may be released into the bloodstream. If the char burn involves only a small part of the body, it should be excised down to healthy tissue. If an extremity is involved, amputation may be necessary.

Extent. The total body surface area (BSA) involved in a burn can be estimated by the so-called "rule of nines." As illustrated in Figure 2, the rule of nines allocates 9 percent of BSA to the head and neck; 9 percent to each arm; 18 percent to each foot and leg; and 18 percent each to the front and back of the trunk. The remaining 1 percent of BSA is accounted for by the perineum. The rule of nines works reasonably well in adults, but it is less accurate for children, whose body proportions differ from those of the adult.

Courtesy of E.R. Crews, *A Practical Manual for the Treatment of Burns* (1967); Charles C. Thomas

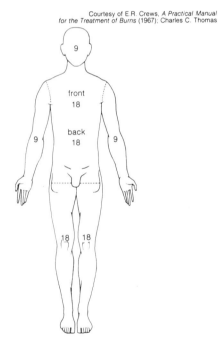

Figure 2: Estimation of percentage burn, rule of nines method.

A more accurate determination can be achieved by using the Lund and Browder charts (Figure 3). The Lund and Browder charts are accurate to within 0.5 percent of BSA and are particularly useful in calculating the extent of burns of children. An accurate estimate of the injured BSA is not only helpful for therapeutic considerations, but it also provides a rough index of patient survival. As a general guideline, the percentage of burned BSA plus the patient's age approximates the percentage of mortality.

Other factors. Mortality rates for a burn of any given depth and extent are significantly higher in patients under two years old and those more than 60 years old. The higher mortality rate in infants presumably is due to the incomplete development of the immune system, a condition that leads to greater susceptibility to infection. In many older individuals, the prognosis for burn injuries is complicated by the presence of chronic illnesses such as cardiac disease, diabetes, or emphysema.

The location of the burn also affects the outcome; for

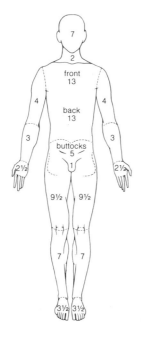

areas variable with age

	birth	1 year	5 years	10 years	15 years	adult
head	19	17	13	11	9	7
both thighs	11	13	16	17	18	19
both legs	10	10	11	12	13	14

areas not variable with age

neck	2	genitalia	1	both forearms	6
anterior trunk	13	both buttocks	5	both hands	5
posterior trunk	13	both upper arms	8	both feet	7

Figure 3: Estimation of percentage burn, Lund and Browder method (see text).

Courtesy of E.R. Crews, *A Practical Manual for the Treatment of Burns* (1967); Charles C. Thomas

example, burns on the hands, face, or perineum present special complications. Electrical and chemical burns, as well as those involving the respiratory tract, also are associated with higher mortality and complication rates.

THE EFFECTS OF BURNS

Local effects.   When examined under a microscope, burns show certain common features. The wound can be divided into three distinct zones. The first is the zone of coagulation, characterized by permanent, irreversible tissue death (necrosis). An analogy can be made between the frying of an egg and the burning of human tissue. The clear, viscous protein (albumin) of the egg coagulates— that is, becomes opaque and hard—after exposure to heat. The protein of human tissue undergoes similar changes after exposure to heat. There is no evidence of capillary blood flow in the coagulated tissue.

An area of damaged tissues marked by sluggish capillary blood flow surrounds the zone of coagulation. This comprises the zone of stasis (stagnation). Stasis can occur shortly after the burn, or it may develop later as the result of further trauma from pressure, infection, rubbing, or dehydration. It is important to avoid such post-burn trauma, as stasis extends the depth of the burn. It is also important to maintain venous blood flow in the zone of stasis, to prevent the death of this tissue.

The zone of hyperemia surrounds the zone of stasis. The tissue of this third zone has suffered nonlethal injury. It reacts with normal inflammatory responses, including the liberation of the chemicals histamine, bradykinin, and serotonin. These chemicals cause increased blood flow and dilation of the blood vessels in the injured tissue, resulting in the leakage of fluids and plasma proteins into the damaged tissue. This response insures that the injured tissue

receives large amounts of nutrients and infection-fighting white blood cells.

Systemic effects.   By destroying a large area of the skin, an extensive burn produces disturbances in fluid balances, metabolism, body temperature, and immune responses. These systemic problems can pose grave threats to the patient.

Fluid losses.   As has been stated, superficial second-degree burns are characterized by blistering. Some of the blisters usually rupture, and fluid oozes from the surface of the wound. This is called a "weeping burn," because fluid continues to seep from its surface for 24 to 36 hours. This visible seepage actually constitutes only a small fraction of the total amount of fluid that is functionally lost. Greater losses occur deep in the wound, where dilation of the blood vessels and loss of capillary integrity cause fluid leakage into the area immediately beneath the burned skin. The fluid is mainly a salt solution, the composition of which approximates that of blood plasma. Fluid losses in the burn wound cease within 36 to 48 hours, and after 48 hours the fluid is slowly reabsorbed. Within about one week, the vascular continuity is restored. The fluid and salt losses from the vascular system are considerable, varying according to the percentage of injured BSA.

There is very little weeping from the surface of deep second-degree and third-degree burns. Capillary damage in these wounds, however, is extensive and results in uncontrollable, rapid, and persistent leakage of salt-rich, plasmalike fluid beneath the burn surface. If the wound is large enough, there may be fluid leakage from remote capillaries in unburned tissues, particularly those of the lungs, thereby exacerbating the fluid losses. The body's immediate reaction is comparable to that seen with acute hemorrhage; there is rapid pulse, generalized constriction of the blood vessels, and increased thirst. If fluid replacement has not been adequately instituted within about an hour, the fluid losses from a large burn begin to impair important organ functions. Signs of circulatory shock— that is, inadequate blood flow throughout the body— become manifest: there is paleness, coolness, restlessness, thirst, rapid pulse with evidence of impaired circulation, and a drop in blood pressure. Without adequate treatment, the body reacts by increased secretion of protective stress hormones, including catecholamines (particularly epinephrine), cortisol, renin, antidiuretic hormone, angiotensin, and aldosterone. Some of these hormones affect the kidneys, causing the retention of sodium and water, thereby helping to compensate for the salts and fluid lost from the circulatory system. Others promote blood vessel constriction and increased cardiac output. These responses, while protective during the immediate shock period, may have an adverse effect once adequate treatment has begun. The magnitude of fluid loss in a large burn is illustrated by the fact that it is not uncommon for severely burned patients to gain 20 percent of their pre-injury body weight during the initial 24 to 48 hours of treatment.

If treatment is inadequate, there will be continued withdrawal of salt solutions from unburned tissues to replace the unremitting losses into the burn wound. There also will be insufficient blood flow to the kidneys, low urinary output, and protracted inadequate circulation throughout the body. The longer this circulatory impairment persists, the more damage to important organ functions will occur. Once a critical level of fluid loss has been incurred, the circulatory shock becomes progressive and nothing can be done to save the patient's life.

Metabolic effects.   Burn victims experience a marked increase in the rates of metabolism and oxygen consumption. In patients with severe burns, the metabolic rate may rise to double its normal resting level. The reasons for the sustained hypermetabolism are thought to be increased catecholamine secretion, evaporative heat loss from the burn wound, and elevated levels of anabolic hormones, including glucagon and cortisol. At first, the increased metabolic activities are fuelled by the breakdown of glycogen, a complex carbohydrate stored chiefly in the liver and the muscles. As glycogen is used up, new sources of energy must be utilized, and the body begins to break down its own protein structures. In burns covering 10 to

Fluid losses in deep burns

40 percent of BSA, the magnitude of late hypermetabolic events is directly related to the size of the burn wound. It is accentuated by the presence of associated injuries and by operations required to care for the wound. The metabolic response reaches a maximum level in burns covering more than 40 percent of BSA.

Heat loss. Normal skin is a very important barrier to evaporative water loss. Following a burn injury, the evaporative water loss becomes grossly abnormal, reaching 300 millilitres per square metre per hour, compared to 15 millilitres per square metre per hour in normal skin. This causes a tremendous heat loss of about 580 kilocalories per litre. Evaporative water loss may be minimized by placing the burn patient in a warm environment, where convection and radiant heat losses are minimized, thereby reducing the metabolic rate to almost normal.

Effects on immune responses. Most burn patients who succumb do so from infection. After many years of investigation, it is clear that the victim is at increased risk from infection because of changes in the immune system following a severe burn. The primary components of the immune system are the B and T lymphocytes and the macrophages. These cells all have specific roles in fighting infection. The B lymphocytes produce immunoglobulins (antibodies), proteins that attack invading microorganisms. The T lymphocytes are responsible for what is called cell-mediated immunity; these cells become attached to the surface of the foreign substances and trigger reactions that weaken or destroy the invaders. Macrophages are large scavenger cells that are capable of digesting microorganisms and cellular debris, a process known as phagocytosis.

Immune dysfunction in burn victims

The serum immunoglobulins A, M, and G are significantly decreased in burn victims; this reflects depressed B-lymphocyte function. T-lymphocyte function is also abnormal, as is evidenced by the prolonged survival of skin grafts taken from unmatched human donors or even from other mammalian species, such as the pig. Such grafts would normally be subject to fairly rapid cell-mediated rejection. Possibly most important is the depression of phagocytic activity of the macrophages following a burn injury. This affects macrophages in the liver, spleen, and lungs. The abnormalities in these macrophages may have a profound negative effect on other components of the immune system and on the ability of the patient to successfully fight a severe infection. As a result of these immune dysfunctions, infections of the burned skin are common, as are infections involving the lungs and bloodstream. The latter two infections carry very high mortality rates.

TREATMENT OF BURNS

The treatment of a burn is, of course, dependent upon the severity of the injury. In general, first-degree burns can be adequately treated with proper first-aid measures. Second-degree burns that cover more than 15 percent of an adult's body or 10 percent of a child's, or that affect the face, hands, or feet, should receive prompt medical attention, as should all third-degree burns, regardless of size.

First aid. Following a first-degree or a small second-degree burn, the best first aid is to quickly immerse the wound under cool tap water. This action will stop the burning process and dissipate the heat energy from the wound. The wound should then be cleansed with mild soap and water and gently blotted dry. After cleansing, the burn can be left exposed, provided it is small and will be frequently washed. If the wound is larger, a dry, bulky, sterile dressing can be placed over it to minimize pain and exposure to the environment. Home remedies, such as butter or petroleum jelly, should *not* be applied to the wound, as these trap heat within the injury and can cause further damage. The application of antiseptics and other irritating substances should also be avoided; a good rule of thumb is to refrain from applying any substance that you would be afraid to put into your eye.

Third-degree burns are true medical emergencies, and the victim should receive professional medical attention as quickly as possible. These wounds should not be immersed, as cool water can intensify the circulatory shock that accompanies third-degree burns. The injuries can be covered with bulky, sterile dressings or with freshly laundered bed linens. Clothing stuck to the wound should not be removed, nor should any ointments, salves, sprays, etc. be applied. Burned feet and legs should be elevated, and burned hands should be raised above the level of the heart. The victim's breathing must be closely watched; artificial respiration should be given if breathing stops.

Outpatient treatment. The majority of burn victims that are brought to hospital emergency rooms are released for outpatient burn care. Table 1 shows the criteria for determining which patients require admission to a hospital and which are eligible for care as outpatients. Before treating a burn victim as an outpatient, however, the physician must have a clear understanding of the home situation and whether or not the family can indeed take care of the burn wound. Also, there is a general tendency to overestimate burn size. If the physician is in doubt, the patient should be admitted.

Table 1: Summary of American Burn Association Patient Severity Categorization

Major burn injury (treat in burn centre)
  Second-degree burn of > 25% body surface area in adults
  Second-degree burn of > 20% body surface area in children
  Third-degree burn of > 10% body surface area
  Most burns involving hands, face, eyes, ears, feet, or perineum
  Most patients with the following:
    Inhalation injury
    Electrical injury
    Burn injury complicated by other major trauma
  Poor-risk patients with burns
Moderate uncomplicated burn injury (may require hospitalization)
  Second-degree burn of 15–25% body surface area in adults
  Second-degree burn of 10–20% body surface area in children
  Third-degree burn of < 10% body surface area
Minor burn injury (outpatient care)
  Second-degree burn of < 15% body surface area in adults
  Second-degree burn of < 10% body surface area in children
  Third-degree burn of < 2% body surface area

Reproduced, with permission, from Lawrence W. Way (ed.), *Current Surgical Diagnosis & Treatment*, 6th ed. Copyright 1983 by Lange Medical Publications, Los Altos, California.

Treatment of the burn wound

Controversy exists about whether blisters need to be debrided (surgically removed). An advantage of debridement is a cleaner wound that is less likely to become infected. A disadvantage is that the wound is more painful. All blisters that involve flexion creases on the hand should be debrided, since limitation of motion is common if these blisters are left intact.

As in first-aid treatment, small wounds can be left open if frequently washed; larger wounds are covered with a dry, bulky dressing. The pain involved in removing the dressing can be reduced by soaking it with tepid water prior to removal or by using a nonadhering dressing such as gauze impregnated with a bland emulsion. The application of topical antibacterial agents in outpatient burn therapy is controversial, and there are no well-controlled studies that demonstrate significant improvement when these compounds are used.

Hospital treatment. *Acute resuscitation.* As indicated above, all patients with severe burns should be hospitalized. The first priority in treating the burn victim is to ensure that the airway (breathing passages) remains open. Associated smoke inhalation injury is very common, particularly if the patient has been burned in a closed space, such as a room or building. Even patients burned in an open area may sustain smoke inhalation. Risk for smoke inhalation is greatest in victims who have injuries to the upper torso or burns of the face, and to those who cough up carbonaceous material or soot. If inhalation injury seems likely, an anesthesiologist or surgeon passes a tube through the patient's nose or mouth into the trachea. This endotracheal tube allows the administration of high concentrations of oxygen and the use of a mechanical ventilator.

Treatment of shock

The next priority is to treat the associated burn shock. This requires the placement of intravenous lines through which resuscitating fluid can be administered; special lines are also placed into the circulation to monitor the resuscitation. A catheter is passed into the bladder to monitor urine output, another index of fluid resuscitation. Most burn centres treat the burn victim during the first 24 hours with intravenous administrations of a balanced salt solution (Ringer's lactate); this solution replaces the fluids lost into the burn wound and from the burn wound into the environment. The administration of blood is not usually necessary, since in most burns blood loss is minimal, and less than 10 percent of the blood suffers hemolysis (*i.e.,* the destruction of red blood cells). This hemolysis of blood, however, can cause serious secondary injuries, particularly to the kidneys; if severe enough, it may even cause the kidneys to fail. This danger can be minimized by rapidly establishing fluid resuscitation and by stimulating urine output with diuretics such as mannitol. A careful medical history is taken, and tetanus toxoid is administered.

After this initial treatment of the airway and resuscitation of the burn shock, a decision must be made as to the disposition of the patient. If the hospital has a special burn centre, the patient should be admitted. If the hospital lacks such a unit, arrangements should be made to transfer the patient to such a centre, in order to continue specialized burn treatment. In most instances this transfer can be achieved over a few hours, during which fluid resuscitation is continued uninterrupted.

Once the patient is admitted to a burn centre, he is usually placed into a special tub, where the wound is cleansed with mild soap solutions. The wound is then dressed. Prior to 1950, it was uncommon for a patient with a burn greater than 30 percent of BSA to survive. With the introduction of antibacterial wound dressings, it has become common for patients whose burns cover up to 50 percent of BSA to survive, unless they have suffered associated injuries or smoke inhalation. The first antibacterial dressing introduced was $\frac{1}{4}$ percent silver nitrate solution; its use dramatically decreased the amount of wound infection and subsequent mortality. Derivatives of sulfa—particularly mafenide—and other antibiotics have since been used with great success in preventing the infection of burn wounds and the subsequent spread of bacteria and toxins through the bloodstream and tissues (sepsis).

Use of anti-bacterial dressings [margin note]

Almost immediately there are other problems that the burn surgeon must address. The patient's ongoing fluid balance must be monitored and regulated, his nutritional needs must be met, pain must be controlled, and the burn wound itself must be repaired. Pain is most problematic in patients with partial or deep second-degree burns and is aggravated by the necessity of frequent dressing changes and physical therapy. In addition, pain leads to increased catecholamine release, which aggravates the patient's nutritional needs and energy expenditure. Burn centres have employed innovative measures to control pain, including the use of morphine intravenously, the administration of incomplete anesthetic drugs at the time of dressing changes, and even the use of general anesthesia during major debridements.

Nutrition can be a particularly vexing problem since the caloric needs are often greater than the patient can consume in a normal fashion. Thus, supplementary feedings administered intravenously or through a feeding tube placed into the stomach are commonplace in treating severe burns. One of the major advances in the treatment of the critically burned has been the use of hyperalimentation, a procedure in which total nutritional support can be provided through a catheter placed into a large central vein. Unfortunately, hyperalimentation involves increased risks of sepsis and of relatively unique metabolic disturbances caused by the lack of trace elements and certain electrolytes (dissolved ions).

Care of the burn wound. The goals in managing the burn lesion are to prevent infection, to avoid further injury to the damaged tissues, and to close the wound as quickly as possible. There are three principal methods of therapy for the burn wound: exposure, occlusive dressings, and primary excision.

Exposure therapy [margin note]

Exposure therapy is indicated for surfaces that are easily left exposed, such as the face. The burn is initially cleansed and then allowed to dry. A second-degree burn forms a crust, which falls off after two or three weeks, revealing minimally scarred skin beneath. Full-thickness burns will not form a crust because of the overlying dead skin, or eschar. The goal of exposure therapy is to soften the eschar and remove it. Exposure allows the eschar to dry. After it dries, saline-soaked gauzes are applied to the eschar to soften it and hasten its spontaneous separation from the underlying tissues. The advantage of exposure therapy is that the patient is not immobilized in bulky dressings. It is particularly useful in burns that cover less than 20 percent of BSA. The chief disadvantage is that the protection against infection afforded by sterile dressings is absent. In addition, pain and heat loss are greater in exposed wounds. Exposure therapy is usually combined with the use of such antibacterial creams as mafenide, neosporin ointment, or povidone iodine.

Use of occlusive dressings [margin note]

Occlusive dressings, usually combined with topical antibacterial agents, are more commonly used in the treatment of extensive burns. The antibacterial ointment or cream may be applied to the patient or to the gauze. The use of occlusive dressings provides a sterile barrier against airborne infection; the dressings also help minimize heat loss and pain. On the other hand, the bandages must be absorptive as well as occlusive and thus are usually bulky and restrictive. Furthermore, the dressings must be changed as often as every eight hours to prevent the growth of bacteria in the warm, moist environment of the covered wound. As pointed out previously, these frequent dressing changes may increase the amount of pain and need for anesthetics.

In both of the above methods of wound treatment, the patient is usually immersed daily in a special tank, where remaining dressings and creams are washed off and loose tissue is debrided. The patient is encouraged to move about to reduce scar formation and subsequent disabling contractures (permanent contractions of scar, muscles, and tendons) over the joints.

Primary excision [margin note]

Primary excision—that is, the surgical removal of necrotic tissues within 24 to 48 hours of the injury—is used to prepare full-thickness burns for grafting at the earliest possible time. This therapy offers two distinct advantages over waiting for spontaneous separation of the eschar. First, by effecting the earliest possible closure of the wound, it helps prevent the development of wound infections that could lead to invasive sepsis and death of the patient. Second, it limits the formation of scars and contractures. Primary excision is particularly worthwhile for deep burns of the hands, where delays in closing the wound often lead to disabling contractures. On the deficit side, surgical removal of dead skin is stressful to the patient, as heat, water, and blood are lost rapidly during the operation. Blood loss is particularly troublesome, and blood transfusions are often necessary. Loss of blood often limits the surgeon's ability to debride the wound fully and to perform subsequent grafting. Another disadvantage of primary excision is that it is difficult to differentiate between deep, partial-thickness and full-thickness injuries early in the post-burn period, and so there is a danger of unnecessarily excising a partial-thickness burn.

Skin grafts [margin note]

After the dead skin has been removed, the surgeon's primary goal is to cover the burned area as rapidly as possible with autografts—that is, grafts of the patient's own skin harvested from uninjured areas of the body. Often, there is a discrepancy between the amount of harvestable skin and the extent of the potential recipient sites. This discrepancy can be addressed by covering the debrided or excised areas with allografts of skin obtained from cadavers, or by treating the burn with porcine xenografts (pigskin), antibiotic solutions, or special plastic dressings. These measures are only temporary, however, and skin autografting is the final method of coverage....

Some burn centres have experimented with growing the patient's own skin on tissue cultures and then grafting this laboratory-grown skin on to the areas of debridement. Despite encouraging early reports, considerable research and clinical trials remain before this method can be widely applied in most burn centres.

Complications. The use of topical antibacterial agents has reduced the incidence of post-burn infection, but infection remains one of the most serious complications of burns. Burn surgeons often obtain cultures of the burn wound and of sputum and other body secretions; these are examined for signs of infection. Early detection and prompt treatment of infection with antibiotics and surgical debridement can minimize its consequences. Acute gastrointestinal ulcers are another frequent complication of burns; they appear as small, circumscribed lesions within the lining of the stomach or duodenum. These ulcers can be detected by endoscopy and are treated with antacids and drugs designed to reduce the amount of acid secretion.

The occurrences of post-burn seizures is a complication unique to children. These seizures may result from electrolyte imbalances, abnormally low levels of oxygen in the blood, infection, or drugs. The cause is unknown in about a third of the cases. Post-burn hypertension is also somewhat unique to children and is probably related to the release of catecholamines and other stress hormones.

A common complication of deep dermal burns and skin grafts is the formation of fibrous masses of scar tissue called hypertrophic scars and keloids. This complication is especially common in brown-skinned races. Reddened, inflamed tissue is biologically active; it has a rich vascular supply, and it rapidly forms collagen, the primary wound protein and major component of scars. Direct pressure on inflamed tissue reduces its blood supply and collagen content, thereby minimizing the formation of hypertrophic scars and keloids. Such pressure can be provided by tailored splints, sleeves, stockings, and body jackets. Skeletal traction may be necessary in special instances.

ASSOCIATED INJURIES

Respiratory tract injuries. Respiratory complications rank as the major cause of death in burn patients. Potentially fatal respiratory complications include inhalation injuries, aspiration of fluids by unconscious patients, bacterial pneumonia, pulmonary edema, obstruction of pulmonary arteries, and post-injury respiratory failure. Direct inhalation injuries, which can lead to other respiratory complications, are especially common. There are three basic categories of direct inhalation injuries: inhalation of dry heat and soot, carbon monoxide poisoning, and smoke inhalation.

Inhalation of dry heat and soot. The inspiration of dry, overheated air can produce burns of the upper airway, which, in turn, can cause swelling of the mucous membrane that lines the upper respiratory tract. If acute, this swelling may block the air passages and lead to asphyxiation. Upper airway burns are particularly common in those who have suffered burns of the face, lips, and nasal hairs. Dry heat inhalation rarely causes respiratory injuries below the level of the vocal cords, because the upper breathing passages cool the hot air before it reaches the trachea.

The temperature inside a burning, smoke-filled room may reach 1,000° C at ceiling level. This extreme heat leads to incomplete combustion and the formation of overheated carbon particles (soot) in the air. If these particles are inhaled, they may directly damage the lining of the trachea and bronchi. In addition, soot particles may carry toxic chemicals, such as sulfur dioxide and nitrous dioxide, into the patient's airway.

Carbon monoxide poisoning. Carbon monoxide is a tasteless, odorless, colourless gas formed as a product of combustion in many fires. Inhalation of this gas does not cause direct pulmonary damage; rather, toxicity results from the combination of carbon monoxide with hemoglobin, the red-blood-cell compound that normally transports oxygen through the bloodstream. If present in significant concentrations, carboxyhemoglobin (carbon monoxide bound to hemoglobin) can impair the oxygen-carrying capacity of the blood to the point of producing asphyxia. Carbon monoxide has an affinity for hemoglobin 200 times that of oxygen. Thus, when excessive amounts of carbon monoxide are present—as is the case in many fires—the risk of carbon monoxide poisoning is substantial.

Diagnosis of carbon monoxide poisoning

Carbon monoxide poisoning must be considered in any patient who was burned in an enclosed space, shows physical evidence of inhalation injury, or has difficulty in breathing. The diagnosis is confirmed by determining the concentration of blood gases—specifically the level of carboxyhemoglobin. Normally, the level of carboxyhemoglobin is below 5 percent in nonsmokers and below 10 percent in smokers. Symptoms of mild carbon monoxide poisoning (carboxyhemoglobin levels below 20 percent) include headache, slight shortness of breath, mild confusion, and diminished visual acuity. Moderate poisoning (carboxyhemoglobin levels of 20 to 40 percent) is characterized by irritability, impaired judgment, dim vision, nausea, and fatigability. In severe poisoning (carboxyhemoglobin levels of 40 to 60 percent), the victim may suffer hallucinations, confusion, ataxia (inability to coordinate voluntary movements), collapse, and coma. Carboxyhemoglobin levels above 60 percent usually lead to death.

The only effective way of detecting carbon monoxide in a home fire is by the routine use of smoke detectors. Tragically, victims suffering from mild to moderate carbon monoxide poisoning often are unable to exercise rational judgment or to remove themselves physically from the environment causing the problem. This emphasizes the need for early detection of home fires and the rationale for installing smoke detectors.

Smoke inhalation. As they burn, many materials give off toxic chemicals in their smoke. Inhalation of these noxious gases causes severe edema of the mucosa (mucous membrane) lining the respiratory tract; this is soon followed by sloughing of the mucosa. Edema rapidly develops around the bronchial tubes and blood vessels in the lung. In the larger airways, the destroyed mucosa is replaced by a membrane that exudes pus and mucus; these secretions may block the air passages. The interstitial lung tissue swells with fluids, obstructing the bronchial tubes and further contributing to their destruction. Within a matter of days, many victims develop bronchopneumonia, a condition that often contributes to sepsis and death.

Toxic contents of smoke

The toxicity of inspired smoke varies according to the source of combustion. The smoke from a kerosene fire, for instance, is fairly harmless. By contrast, the smoke from a wood fire contains aldehyde gases, especially acrolein, which are potent respiratory irritants. Even in concentrations as low as 10 parts per 1,000,000, inspired acrolein causes pulmonary edema. Smoke from the combustion of polyurethane and other newer plastic compounds ranks among the most severe irritants. Burning plastics often give off such potentially lethal gases as chlorine, sulfuric acid, and cyanides. With the increased use of plastics in insulation, furniture, and flooring, these chemicals have become more prevalent causes of smoke poisoning.

Care of respiratory complications. Any patient likely to have suffered inhalation injuries should receive a bronchoscopic examination of the airway. This examination can reveal the degree of respiratory injury and help in planning the appropriate treatment. Constant one-on-one nursing care is often necessary to provide the required pulmonary treatment. In most instances, an endotracheal tube is passed into the lungs and the patient is placed on a mechanical ventilator. By delivering air under constant pressure, the ventilator helps keep the lungs inflated; this aids in the control and prevention of atelectasis (collapse of the air sacs). The ventilator can also be used to reexpand collapsed lungs. In addition, the machine can deliver varying concentrations of oxygen and mists in the inspired air. Patients who have suffered smoke inhalation are given high concentrations of humidified oxygen. Those with carbon monoxide poisoning receive 100 percent oxygen until their blood level of carboxyhemoglobin falls below 20 percent. This generally takes two to three hours. The use of other agents to reduce pulmonary edema is controversial, and the administration of antibiotics to prevent respiratory infection has not been shown to be beneficial.

Electrical injuries. Electrical accidents can cause any of three types of injuries: electrothermal burns from arcing current, flame burns caused by the ignition of clothing, and electrical current injury. Occasionally all three will be present in the same victim.

Electrothermal (flash or arc) burns are thermal injuries to the skin that occur when high-tension electrical current reaches the skin from the conductor. The skin damage is intense and deep, because the electrical arc has a temperature of about 2,500° C—high enough to melt bone. Flame burns from ignited clothing are often the most serious part of the injury. Treatment is the same as for any thermal injury.

Electrical current injuries are characterized by focal burns at the points where the current entered and exited through the skin. These injuries involve more than just burns, however. Once electrical current has entered the body, its pathway depends on the resistance it encounters in the various tissues. The following are listed in descending order of resistance: bone, fat, tendon, skin, muscle, blood, and nerve. The pathway of the current determines immediate survival. For example, if it passes through the heart or the brain stem, death may be immediate from, respectively, ventricular fibrillation or apnea (stoppage of breathing). Current passing through muscles may trigger severe spasms, causing an injury more like a crush than a thermal burn. The force of the spasms can produce long-bone fractures and dislocations. It may also cause thrombosis of blood vessels, which frequently leads to limb amputations. Because bone is so resistant, it becomes a capacitor for storage of the heat energy of the current. This heat energy may then damage the surrounding muscles, leading to the release of the muscle pigment myoglobin into the bloodstream. This, in turn, can cause acute shutdown of the kidneys.

The type of current is also related to the severity of injury. The usual 60-cycle alternating current (ac) that causes most injuries in the home is particularly severe. Alternating current causes tetanic contractions of the muscles; as a result, the patient might be "locked" into contact with the current. Cardiac arrest is common from contact with house current.

The skin burn at the entrance and exit sites of an electrical injury is usually a depressed, gray or yellow area of full-thickness destruction, surrounded by a sharply defined zone of hyperemia. Charring may be present if an arc burn co-exists. All of these entrance and exit wounds must be treated by debridement. Crush injuries and kidney dysfunction caused by the passage of current through the body must also be treated. In general, the treatment of electrical injuries is complex at every step, and after initial resuscitation these patients should be referred to specialized burn centres.

REHABILITATION

Physically and cosmetically debilitating scars are the most common aftereffects of extensive burns. Such scars often require additional plastic surgery—sometimes years after the initial skin grafting. . . .

Many victims of severe burns face years of often painful physical therapy as they work to regain or maintain mobility in damaged joints. The psychological adjustment to disfigurement may be traumatic, and many patients require extended counselling to come to grips with their altered appearance and physical disabilities. Yet, with the help of understanding family, friends, and professionals, even severely injured burn victims can make successful adjustments and lead productive lives.

BIBLIOGRAPHY. SUSAN P. BAKER, BRIAN O'NEILL, and RONALD S. KARPF, *The Injury Fact Book* (1984), provides comprehensive information and statistical patterns for all injuries; THOMAS L. WACHTEL, VIRGINIA KAHN, and HUGH A. FRANK (eds.), *Current Topics in Burn Care* (1983), is a collection . . . from the periodicals *Topics in Emergency Medicine, Critical Care Quarterly,* and *Topics in Clinical Nursing . . . ;* BASIL PRUITT, *The Burn Patient,* 2 vol. (1979), is an analysis of burn complications and therapy; B.C. BLADES, C. JONES, and A.M. MUNSTER, "Quality of Life After Major Burns," *Journal of Trauma,* 19(8):556–558 (August 1979), presents a realistic look at the aftermath of a severe burn injury; A. FEIN, A. LEFF, and P.C. HOPEWELL, "Pathophysiology and Management of the Complications Resulting from Fire and the Inhaled Products of Combustion: Review of Literature," *Critical Care Medicine,* 8(2):94–98 (1980), is an excellent review of inhalation injury. . . .

DONALD D. TRUNKEY. Professor of Surgery, University of California at San Francisco. Chief of Surgery, San Francisco General Hospital. Editor of *Current Trauma Therapy.*

Death

During the latter half of the 20th century, death has become a strangely popular subject. Before that time, perhaps rather surprisingly, it was a theme largely eschewed in serious scientific, and to a lesser extent, philosophical speculations. It was neglected in biological research and, being beyond the physician's ministrations, was deemed largely irrelevant by medical practice. In modern times, however, the study of death has become a central concern in all these disciplines. . . .

Thanatology—the study of death—delves into matters as diverse as the cultural anthropology of the notion of soul, the burial rites and practices of early civilizations, the location of cemeteries in the Middle Ages, and the conceptual difficulties involved in defining death in an individual whose brain is irreversibly dead but whose respiration and heartbeat are kept going by artificial means. It encompasses the biological study of programmed cell death, the understanding care of the dying, and the creation of an informed public opinion as to how the law should cope with the stream of problems generated by intensive-care technology. Legal and medical quandaries regarding the definition of death and the rights of the terminally ill (or their families) to refuse life-prolonging treatments force physicians to think like lawyers, lawyers like physicians, and both like philosophers. In his *Historia Naturalis* (*Natural History*), the Roman author Pliny the Elder wrote that "so uncertain is men's judgment that they cannot determine even death itself." The challenge remains, but if humans now fail to provide some answers it will not be for lack of trying.

This article is divided into the following sections:

THE MEANING OF DEATH

This subject can be approached from a variety of perspectives. It can, for example, be viewed historically, in terms of how popular perceptions of death have been reflected in poetry, literature, legend, or pictorial art. Illustrations of those killed in battle and of their severed parts find particular prominence in ancient Egyptian art. The campaign of the 13th-century-BC Egyptian king Ramses II against the Hittites, in particular the Battle of Kadesh, is recorded in gruesome detail on the battle reliefs of 19th- and 20th-dynasty temples in Upper Egypt. Assyrian art, too, made great play of illustrating cadavers. Those slaughtered by the king Ashurbanipal (flourished 7th century BC) in his campaign against the Arabian king Uate are shown having their eyes plucked out by vultures. These very concrete depictions of the meaning of death seem to have had mainly propagandistic value, boosting the self-confidence of the victors and inspiring fear among the defeated. Deities of the dead were features of many early cultures, but apart from ancient Egypt neither such deities nor those over whom they held dominion were the subject of any significant artistic representation. In Egypt, sepulchral iconography was to reach truly impressive heights, particularly after the democratization of the Osirian cult with its promise of an afterlife for all. Well-known sculptors produced some striking individual tombstones in ancient Greece and Rome, but it was medieval Christianity that gave real impetus to this practice, which can be thought of as an attempt to perpetuate among the living a vivid memory of the dead. The representation of death itself, usually personified in the form of a skeleton, seems to have developed on a large scale only in medieval Christian art.

An alternative approach is to look at the meaning of death in terms of various eschatologies (beliefs regarding death and the end of the world). Human beings have been the only species to bury their dead in a systematic way, often with implements to be used in a further existence. The study of death rites and customs illustrates impressively the relation between religious belief and popular practice in the presence of the dead. Such an approach starts from the meaning of death in those cultures (such as Phoenician, early Judaic, Homeric, Epicurean, and Stoic) in which only a shadowy afterlife or no afterlife at all was envisaged; it analyzes other traditions (such as Sumero-Akkadian) in which ambiguities and contradictions abounded; and it finally searches for death's meaning in those cultures (such as ancient Egyptian, Zoroastrian, Hindu, Orphic, Platonic, Christian, Pharisaic Judaic, and Islāmic) in which a very "physical" afterlife, or the presence of an eternal soul, played central roles.

Both the historical and the eschatological approaches share a common advantage: they need not be preceded by a definition of death. They accept death as an easily determined empirical fact, not requiring discussion or further elaboration. But a conceptual crisis has arisen in modern medicine and biology, a crisis that stems precisely from the realization that the definition of death—taken for granted for millennia—requires reexamination. To approach the subject of death from the biological angle, which is perhaps the most difficult and arguably the most challenging perspective, certainly reflects some of the most pressing needs of modern times.

The difficulty of defining death

Many dictionaries define death as "the extinction or cessation of life" or as "ceasing to be." As life itself is notoriously difficult to define—and as everyone tends to think of things in terms of what is known—the problems in defining death are immediately apparent. The most useful definitions of life are those that stress function, whether at the level of physiology, of molecular biology and biochemistry, or of genetic potential. Death should be thought of as the irreversible loss of such functions.

The remainder of this article first explores the recurrent problems involved in seeking a biological definition of death. It then examines the implications of these problems in relation to human death. In this context, the article raises two major points: (1) death of the brain is the necessary and sufficient condition for death of the individual; and (2) the physiological core of brain death is the death of the brain stem. Finally, the article surveys notions about the meaning of human death that have prevailed throughout history. . . .

THE BIOLOGICAL PROBLEMS

Whether one considers the death of individual cells, the death of small multicellular organisms, or the death of a human being, certain problems are repeatedly met. The physicist may encounter difficulties in trying to define death in terms of entropy change and the second law of thermodynamics. So may the histologist looking at the ultrastructure of dying tissue through an electron microscope. Pope Pius XII, speaking to an International Congress of Anesthesiologists in 1957, raised the question of when, in the intensive care unit, the soul actually left the body. More secularly inclined philosophers have meanwhile pondered what it was that was so essential to the nature of man that its loss should be called death. The questions of what may or may not be legitimately demanded of a "beating-heart cadaver" (in terms of supplying donor organs for transplants or of serving as a subject for physiological experimentation) has given new poignancy to the quip made by the English author Sir Thomas Browne in 1643: "With what strife and pains we come into the world we know not, but 'tis commonly no easy matter to get out of it." Common conceptual difficulties underlie many of these questions.

Death: process or event. The American physician and writer Oliver Wendell Holmes said "to live is to function" and "that is all there is in living." But who or what is the subject who lives because it functions? Is death the irreversible loss of function of the whole organism (or cell); that is, of every one of its component parts? Or is it the irreversible loss of function of the organism (or cell) as a whole; that is, as a meaningful and independent biological unit? To perceive the difference between the two questions is to understand many modern controversies about death. The described dichotomy is obvious, but it is clearly part of a much wider one: civilizations fall apart yet their component societies live on; societies disintegrate but their citizens survive; individuals die while their cells, perversely, still metabolize; finally, cells can be disrupted yet the enzymes they release may, for a while, remain very active.

Death as a process

Such problems would not arise if nature were tidier. In nearly all circumstances human death is a process rather than an event. Unless caught up in nuclear explosions people do not die suddenly, like the bursting of a bubble. A quiet, "classical" death provides perhaps the best illustration of death as a process. Several minutes after the heart has stopped beating, a mini-electrocardiogram may be recorded, if one probes for signals from within the cardiac cavity. Three hours later, the pupils still respond to pilocarpine drops by contracting, and muscles repeatedly tapped may still mechanically shorten. A viable skin graft may be obtained from the deceased 24 hours after the heart has stopped, a viable bone graft 48 hours later, and a viable arterial graft as late as 72 hours after the onset of irreversible asystole (cardiac stoppage). Cells clearly differ widely in their ability to withstand the deprivation of oxygen supply that follows arrest of the circulation.

Similar problems arise, but on a vastly larger scale, when the brain is dead but the heart (and other organs) are kept going artificially. Under such circumstances, it can be argued, the organism as a whole may be deemed dead, although the majority of its cells are still alive.

The "point of no return." To claim that death is a process does not imply that this process unfurls at an even rate, or that within it there are not "points of no return." The challenge is to identify such points with greater precision for various biological systems. At the clinical level, the irreversible cessation of circulation has for centuries been considered a point of no return. It has provided (and still provides) a practical and valid criterion of irreversible loss of function of the organism as a whole. What is new is the dawning awareness that circulatory arrest is a mechanism of death and not in itself a philosophical concept of death; that cessation of the heartbeat is only lethal if it lasts long enough to cause critical centres in the brain stem to die; and that this is so because the brain stem is irreplaceable in a way the cardiac pump is not. These are not so much new facts as new ways of looking at old ones.

Failure to establish beyond all doubt that the point of no return had been reached has, throughout the ages, had interesting effects on medical practice. The Thracians, according to the ancient Greek historian Herodotus, kept their dead for three days before burial. The Romans kept the corpse considerably longer; the Roman author Servius, in his commentary on Virgil, records that "on the eighth day they burned the body and on the ninth put its ashes in the grave." The practice of cutting off a finger, to see whether the stump bled, was often resorted to. Even the most eminent proved liable to diagnostic error. The 16th-century Flemish physician Andreas Vesalius, probably the greatest anatomist of all time, professor of surgery in Padua for three years and later physician to the Holy Roman emperor Charles V, had to leave Spain in a hurry in 1564. He was performing a postmortem when the subject, a nobleman he had been attending, showed signs of life. This was at the height of the Spanish Inquisition and Vesalius was pardoned only on the condition that he undertake a pilgrimage to the Holy Sepulchre in Jerusalem.

Anxieties over premature burial

Fears of being buried alive have long haunted humankind. During the 19th century, for example, accounts of "live sepulture" appeared in medical writing and led to repeated demands that putrefaction—the only sure sign of death of the whole organism—be considered an essential prerequisite to a diagnosis of death. Anxieties had become so widespread following the publication of some of U.S. author Edgar Allan Poe's macabre short stories that Count Karnice-Karnicke, a Russian nobleman, patented a coffin of particular type. If the "corpse" regained consciousness after burial, it could summon help from the surface by activating a system of flags and bells. Advertisements described the price of the apparatus as "exceedingly reasonable, only about twelve shillings."

At the turn of the century, a sensation-mongering press alleged that there were "many ugly secrets locked up underground." There may have been some basis for these claims: instances of collapse and apparent death were not uncommon during epidemics of plague, cholera, and smallpox; hospitals and mortuaries were overcrowded, and there was great fear of the spread of infection. This agitation resulted in stricter rules concerning death certification. In the United Kingdom, statutory obligations to register deaths date only from 1874, and at that time it was not even necessary for a doctor to have viewed the corpse.

The impact of medical technology

The second half of the 20th century has seen tremendous developments in the field of intensive care and the emergence of new controversies concerning the point of no return. Modern technology now makes it possible to maintain ventilation (by respirators), cardiac function (by various pumping devices), feeding (by the intravenous route), and the elimination of the waste products of metabolism (by dialysis) in a body whose brain is irreversibly dead. In these macabre by-products of modern technology, a dissociation has taken place between the various components of death so that the most important—the death of the brain—occurs before, rather than after, the cessation of other functions, such as circulation. Such cases have presented both practical and conceptual problems, but the latter need not have arisen had what happens during decapitation been better appreciated.

"Beating-heart cadavers" were of course familiar to the observant long before the days of intensive care units. A photograph of a public decapitation in a Bangkok square in the mid-1930s illustrates such a case. The victim is tied to a stake and the head has been severed, but jets of blood from the carotid and vertebral arteries in the neck show that the heart is still beating. It is doubtful that anyone would describe the executed man—as distinct from some of his organs—as still alive. This gruesome example stresses three points: it reiterates the fact, admittedly from an unusual angle, that death is a process rather than an event; it emphasizes the fact that in this process there is a point of no return; and it graphically illustrates the difference between the death of the organism as a whole and the death of the whole organism. In thinking the implications through, one takes the first steps toward understanding brain death. The executed man has undergone anatomical decapitation. Brain death is physiological decapitation: it arises when intracranial pressure exceeds arterial pressure, thereby depriving the brain of its blood supply as efficiently as if the head had been cut off. The example serves as an introduction to the proposition that the death of the brain is the necessary and sufficient condition for the death of the individual.

These issues were authoritatively discussed in 1968, at the 22nd World Medical Assembly in Sydney, Australia.

The assembly stated that "clinical interest lies not in the state of preservation of isolated cells but in the fate of a person. The point of death of the different cells and organs is not as important as the certainty that the process has become irreversible." The statement had a profound effect on modern medical thinking. "Irreversible loss of function of the organism as a whole" became an accepted clinical criterion. . . .

The next two sections of this article illustrate these general principles concerning death from each end of the spectrum of living things: from the level of the cell and from that of the fully developed human being.

CELL DEATH

A vast amount of work has been devoted since the late 19th century to discovering how cells multiply. The study of how and why they die is a relatively recent concern: a rubric entitled "cell death" only appeared in the *Index Medicus,* an index to medical literature, in 1979.

Cell necrosis

What most textbooks of pathology describe as cell death is coagulative necrosis. This is an abnormal morphological appearance, detected in tissue examined under the microscope. The changes, which affect aggregates of adjacent cells or functionally related cohorts of cells, are seen in a variety of contexts produced by accident, injury, or disease. Among the environmental perturbations that may cause cell necrosis are oxygen deprivation (anoxia), hyperthermia, immunological attack, and exposure to various toxins that inhibit crucial intracellular metabolic processes. Coagulative necrosis is the classical form of cell change seen when tissues autolyze (digest themselves) in vitro.

Programmed cell death

But cells may die by design as well as by accident. Research in developmental pathology has stressed the biological importance of this other kind of cell death, which has been referred to as programmed cell death. In vertebrates it has been called apoptosis and in invertebrates, cell deletion. Programmed cell death plays an important role in vertebrate ontogeny (embryological development) and teratogenesis (the production of malformations), as well as in the spectacular metamorphoses that affect tadpoles or caterpillars. Such programmed events are essential if the organism as a whole is to develop its normal final form. Waves of genetically driven cell death are critical to the proper modeling of organs and systems. The inflections (curvatures) of the developing mammalian brain and spinal cord, for instance, or the achievement of a proper numerical balance between functionally related cell groups, cannot be understood without an appreciation of how the death of some (or many) cells is necessary for others to reach maturity. Localized cell death, occurring at precise moments during normal ontogeny, explains phenomena as varied as the fashioning of the digits or the involution of phylogenetic vestiges. Several congenital abnormalities can be attributed to disorders of programmed cell death. Cell death occurs spontaneously in normally involuting tissues such as the thymus. It can be initiated or inhibited by a variety of environmental stimuli, both physiological and pathological. Cell death even occurs in some of the cells of untreated malignant tumours, and it is seen during tumour regression induced by X rays or radiomimetic cytotoxic agents. Programmed cell death may also play a part in the process of aging. . . .

CLINICAL DEATH

At the opposite end of the spectrum from cell death lies the death of a human being. It is obvious that the problems of defining human death cannot be resolved in purely biological terms, divorced from all ethical or cultural considerations. This is because there will be repercussions (burial, mourning, inheritance, etc.) from any decisions made, and because the decisions themselves will have to be socially acceptable in a way that does not apply to the fate of cells in tissue culture.

Unless death is defined at least in outline, the decision that a person is "dead" cannot be verified by any amount of scientific investigation. Technical data can never answer purely conceptual questions. Earlier in this article it was suggested that the death of the brain was the necessary and sufficient condition for the death of the individual, but

Human
death
defined

the word *death* was not given much content beyond the very general definition of "irreversible loss of function." If one seeks to marry conceptions of death prevalent in the oldest cultures with the most up-to-date observations from intensive care units, one might think of human death as the irreversible loss of the capacity for consciousness combined with the irreversible loss of the capacity to breathe. The anatomical basis for such a concept of human death resides in the loss of brain-stem function.

Functions of the brain stem. The brain stem is the area at the base of the brain that includes the mesencephalon (midbrain), the pons, and the medulla. It contains the respiratory and vasomotor centres, which are responsible, respectively, for breathing and the maintenance of blood pressure. Most importantly, it also contains the ascending reticular activating system, which plays a crucial role in maintaining alertness (*i.e.*, in generating the capacity for consciousness); small, strategically situated lesions in the medial tegmental portions of the midbrain and rostral pons cause permanent coma. All of the motor outputs from the cerebral hemispheres—for example, those that mediate movement or speech—are routed through the brain stem, as are the sympathetic and parasympathetic efferent nerve fibres responsible for the integrated functioning of the organism as a whole. Most sensory inputs also travel through the brain stem. This part of the brain is, in fact, so tightly packed with important structures that small lesions there often have devastating effects. By testing various brain-stem reflexes, moreover, the functions of the brain stem can be assessed clinically with an ease, thoroughness, and degree of detail not possible for any other part of the central nervous system.

Capacity
for
conscious-
ness

It must be stressed that the capacity for consciousness (an upper brain-stem function) is not the same as the content of consciousness (a function of the cerebral hemispheres); it is, rather, an essential precondition of the latter. If there is no functioning brain stem, there can be no meaningful or integrated activity of the cerebral hemispheres, no cognitive or affective life, no thoughts or feelings, no social interaction with the environment, nothing that might legitimize adding the adjective *sapiens* ("wise") to the noun *Homo* ("man"). The "capacity for consciousness" is perhaps the nearest one can get to giving a biological flavour to the notion of "soul."

The capacity to breathe is also a brain-stem function, and apnea (respiratory paralysis) is a crucial manifestation of a nonfunctioning lower brain stem. Alone, of course, it does not imply death; patients with bulbar poliomyelitis, who may have apnea of brain-stem origin, are clearly not dead. Although irreversible apnea has no strictly philosophical dimension, it is useful to include it in any concept of death. This is because of its obvious relation to cardiac function—if spontaneous breathing is lost the heart cannot long continue to function—and perhaps because of its cultural associations with the "breath of life." These aspects are addressed in the later discussion of how death has been envisaged in various cultures.

Mechanisms of brain-stem death. From as far back as medical records have been kept, it has been known that patients with severe head injuries or massive intracranial hemorrhage often die as a result of apnea: breathing stops before the heart does. In such cases, the pressure in the main (supratentorial) compartment of the skull becomes so great that brain tissue herniates through the tentorial opening, a bony and fibrous ring in the membrane that separates the spaces containing the cerebral hemispheres and the cerebellum. The brain stem runs through this opening, and a pressure cone formed by the herniated brain tissue may dislocate the brain stem downward and cause irreversible damage by squeezing it from each side. An early manifestation of such an event is a disturbance of consciousness; a late feature is permanent apnea. This was previously nature's way out.

Pressure
cone
forma-
tion

With the widespread development of intensive care facilities in the 1950s and '60s, more and more such moribund patients were rushed to specialized units and put on ventilators just before spontaneous breathing ceased. In some cases the effect was dramatic. When a blood clot could be evacuated, the primary brain damage and the pressure

cone it had caused might prove reversible. Spontaneous breathing would return. In many cases, however, the massive, structural intracranial pathology was irremediable. The ventilator, which had taken over the functions of the paralyzed respiratory centre, enabled oxygenated blood to be delivered to the heart, which went on beating. Physicians were caught up in a therapeutic dilemma partly of their own making: the heart was pumping blood to a dead brain. Sometimes the intracranial pressure was so high that the blood could not even enter the head. Modern technology was exacting a very high price: the beating-heart cadaver.

Circula-
tory
arrest

Brain-stem death may also arise as an intracranial consequence of extracranial events. The main cause in such cases is circulatory arrest. The usual context is delayed or inadequate cardiopulmonary resuscitation following a heart attack. The intracranial repercussions depend on the duration and severity of impaired blood flow to the brain. In the 1930s the British physiologist John Scott Haldane had emphasized that oxygen deprivation "not only stopped the machine, but wrecked the machinery." Circulatory arrest lasting two or three minutes can cause widespread and irreversible damage to the cerebral hemispheres while sparing the brain stem, which is more resistant to anoxia. Such patients remain in a "persistent vegetative state." They breathe and swallow spontaneously, grimace in response to pain, and are clinically and electrophysiologically awake, but they show no behavioral evidence of awareness. Their eyes are episodically open (so that the term *coma* is inappropriate to describe them), but their retained capacity for consciousness is not endowed with any content. Some patients have remained like this for many years. Such patients are not dead, and their prognosis depends in large part on the quality of the care they receive. The discussion of their management occasionally abuts onto controversies about euthanasia and the "right to die." These issues are quite different from that of the "determination of death," and failure to distinguish these matters has been the source of great confusion.

If circulatory arrest lasts for more than a few minutes, the brain stem—including its respiratory centre—will be as severely damaged as the cerebral hemispheres. Both the capacity for consciousness and the capacity to breathe will be irreversibly lost. The individual will then show all the clinical features of a dead brain, even if the heart can be restarted.

Evolution of the concept of brain-stem death. It was against this sort of background that French neurologists, in 1958, described a condition they called *coma dépassé* (literally, "a state beyond coma"). Their patients all had primary, irremediable, structural brain lesions; were deeply comatose; and were incapable of spontaneous breathing. They had not only lost their ability to react to the external world, but they also could no longer control their own internal environment. They became poikilothermic (*i.e.*, they could not control their body temperature, which varied with that of the environment). They could not control their blood pressure or vary their heart rate in response to appropriate stimuli. They could not even retain body water and would pass great volumes of urine. The organism as a whole had clearly ceased to function. *Coma dépassé* was considered a "frontier state" between life and death. Ventilation was continued in the vast majority of such cases until the heartbeat ceased, usually a few days later.

In 1968 the Ad Hoc Committee of the Harvard Medical School published a report entitled "A Definition of Irreversible Coma" in *The Journal of the American Medical Association*. This watershed article listed criteria for the recognition of the "brain-death syndrome." It stated that the persistence of a state of apneic coma with no evidence of brain-stem and spinal reflexes and a flat electroencephalogram over a period of 24 hours implied brain death, provided the cause of the coma was known and provided reversible causes of brain dysfunction (such as hypothermia or drug intoxication) had been excluded. The report explicitly identified brain death with death (without seeking to define death) and endorsed the withdrawal of respiratory support in such cases. No evidence was published to legitimize the contention that the coma was

Criteria for
recognizing
brain death

irreversible; *i.e.,* that if artificial ventilation was continued no such patient ever recovered consciousness, and that all invariably developed asystole. There was wide medical experience among the members of the committee, however, and its contentions have since been massively validated. Not a single exception has come to light.

The next few years witnessed increasing sophistication in the techniques used to diagnose brain death, none of which, however, surpassed basic clinical assessment. In 1973 two neurosurgeons in Minneapolis, Minn., identified the death of the brain stem as the point of no return in the diagnosis of brain death. In 1976 and 1979, the Conference of Royal Colleges and Faculties of the United Kingdom published important memoranda on the subject. The first described the clinical features of a dead brain stem, the second identified brain-stem death with death. In 1981 in the United States, the President's Commission for the Study of Ethical Problems in Medicine and Biomedical and Behavioral Research published a report ("Defining Death") and a list of guidelines very similar to the British ones. The commission also proposed a model statute, called the Uniform Determination of Death Act, which was subsequently endorsed by the American Medical Association, the American Bar Association, and the National Conference of Commissioners on Uniform State Laws and became law in many states. International opinion and practice has moved along similar lines in accepting the concept of brain-stem death.

Diagnosis of brain-stem death. The diagnosis is not technically difficult. In more and more countries, it is made on purely clinical grounds. The aim of the clinical tests is not to probe every neuron within the intracranial cavity to see if it is dead—an impossible task—but to establish irreversible loss of brain-stem function. This is the necessary and sufficient condition for irreversible unconsciousness and irreversible apnea, which together spell a dead patient. Experience has shown that instrumental procedures (such as electroencephalography and studies of cerebral blood flow) that seek to establish widespread loss of cortical function contribute nothing of relevance concerning the cardiac prognosis. Such tests yield answers of dubious reliability to what are widely felt to be the wrong questions. As the concept of brain-stem death is relatively new, most countries rightly insist that the relevant examinations be carried out by physicians of appropriate seniority. These doctors (usually neurologists, anesthetists, or specialists in intensive care) must be entirely separate from any who might be involved in using the patient's organs for subsequent transplants.

Stages in diagnosing brain-stem death

The diagnosis of brain-stem death involves three stages. First, the cause of the coma must be ascertained, and it must be established that the patient (who will always have been in apneic coma and on a ventilator for several hours) is suffering from irremediable, structural brain damage. Damage is judged "irremediable" based on its context, the passage of time, and the failure of all attempts to remedy it. Second, all possible causes of reversible brain-stem dysfunction, such as hypothermia, drug intoxication, or severe metabolic upset, must be excluded. Finally, the absence of all brain-stem reflexes must be demonstrated, and the fact that the patient cannot breathe, however strong the stimulus, must be confirmed.

Tests of brain-stem reflexes

It may take up to 48 hours to establish that the preconditions and exclusions have been met; the testing of brain-stem function takes less than half an hour. When testing the brain-stem reflexes, doctors check for the following normal responses: (1) constriction of the pupils in response to light, (2) blinking in response to stimulation of the cornea, (3) grimacing in response to firm pressure applied just above the eye socket, (4) movements of the eyes in response to the ears being flushed with ice water, and (5) coughing or gagging in response to a suction catheter being passed down the airway. All responses have to be absent on at least two occasions. Apnea, which also must be confirmed twice, is assessed by disconnecting the patient from the ventilator. (Prior to this test, the patient is fully oxygenated by being made to breathe 100 percent oxygen for several minutes, and diffusion oxygenation into the trachea is maintained throughout the procedure.

These precautions ensure that the patient will not suffer serious oxygen deprivation while disconnected from the ventilator.) The purpose of this test is to establish the total absence of any inspiratory effort as the carbon dioxide concentration in the blood (the normal stimulus to breathing) reaches levels more than sufficient to drive any respiratory centre cells that may still be alive.

The patient thus passes through a tight double filter of preconditions and exclusions before he is even tested for the presence of a dead brain stem. This emphasis on strict preconditions and exclusions has been a major contribution to the subject of brain-stem death, and it has obviated the need for ancillary investigations. Thousands of patients who have met criteria of this kind have had ventilation maintained: all have developed asystole within a few hours or a few days, and none has ever regained consciousness. There have been no exceptions. The relevant tests for brain-stem death are carried out systematically and without haste. There is no pressure from the transplant team.

The developments in the idea and diagnosis of brain-stem death came as a response to a conceptual challenge. Intensive-care technology had saved many lives, but it had also created many brain-dead patients. To grasp the implications of this situation, society in general—and the medical profession in particular—was forced to rethink accepted notions about death itself. The emphasis had to shift from the most common mechanism of death (*i.e.,* irreversible cessation of the circulation) to the results that ensued when that mechanism came into operation: irreversible loss of the capacity for consciousness, combined with irreversible apnea. These results, which can also be produced by primary intracranial catastrophes, provide philosophically sound, ethically acceptable, and clinically applicable secular equivalents to the concepts of "departure of the soul" and "loss of the 'breath of life,'" which were so important to some earlier cultures.

THE CULTURAL BACKGROUND

Throughout history, specific cultural contexts have always played a crucial role in how people perceived death. Different societies have held widely diverging views on the "breath of life" and on "how the soul left the body" at the time of death. Such ideas are worth reviewing (1) because of the light they throw on important residual elements of popular belief; (2) because they illustrate the distance traveled (or not traveled) between early beliefs and current ones; and (3) because of the relevance of certain old ideas to contemporary debates about brain-stem death and about the philosophical legitimacy of organ transplantation. The following discussion therefore focuses on how certain cultural ideas about death compare or contrast with the modern concept. For an overview of various eschatologies from a cross-cultural perspective, see RITES AND CEREMONIES, SACRED: *Death rites and customs.*

Ancient Egypt. Two ideas that prevailed in ancient Egypt came to exert great influence on the concept of death in other cultures. The first was the notion, epitomized in the Osirian myth, of a dying and rising saviour god who could confer on devotees the gift of immortality; this afterlife was first sought by the pharaohs and then by millions of ordinary people. The second was the concept of a postmortem judgment, in which the quality of the deceased's life would influence his ultimate fate. Egyptian society, it has been said, consisted of the dead, the gods, and the living. During all periods of their history, the ancient Egyptians seem to have spent much of their time thinking of death and making provisions for their afterlife. The vast size, awe-inspiring character, and the ubiquity of their funerary monuments bear testimony to this obsession.

The physical preservation of the body was central to all concerns about an afterlife; the Egyptians were a practical people, and the notion of a disembodied existence would have been totally unacceptable to them. The components of the person were viewed as many, subtle, and complex; moreover, they were thought to suffer different fates at the time of death. The physical body was a person's *khat,* a term that implied inherent decay. The *ka* was the individual's doppelgänger, or double; it was endowed with all the person's qualities and faults. It is uncertain where the *ka* resided during life, but "to go to one's *ka*" was a euphemism for death. The *ka* denoted power and prosperity. After death it could eat, drink, and "enjoy the odour of incense." It had to be fed, and this task was to devolve on a specific group of priests. The *ka* gave comfort and protection to the deceased: its hieroglyphic sign showed two arms outstretched upward, in an attitude of embrace.

The *ba*

The *ba* (often translated as "the soul") conveyed notions of "the noble" and "the sublime." It could enter the body or become incorporeal at will. It was represented as a human-headed falcon, presumably to emphasize its mobility. The *ba* remained sentimentally attached to the dead body, for whose well-being it was somehow responsible. It is often depicted flying about the portal of the tomb or perched on a nearby tree. Although its anatomical substratum was ill-defined, it could not survive without the preserved body.

Other important attributes were an individual's *khu* ("spiritual intelligence"), *sekhem* ("power"), *khaibit* ("shadow"), and *ren* ("name"). In the pyramid of King Pepi I, who ruled during the 6th dynasty (c. 2345–c. 2182 BC), it is recorded how the dead king had "walked through the iron which is the ceiling of heaven. With his panther skin upon him, Pepi passeth with his flesh, he is happy with his name, and he liveth with his double." The depictions of the dead were blueprints for immortality. Conversely, to blot out a person's name was to destroy that individual for all eternity. . . .

The heart played a central part in how the Egyptians thought about the functioning of the body. Political and religious considerations probably lay behind the major role attributed to the heart. Many of the so-called facts reported in the Ebers papyrus (a kind of medical encyclopaedia dating from the early part of the 18th dynasty; *i.e.,* from about 1550 BC) are really just speculations. This is surprising in view of how often bodies were opened during embalmment. A tubular system was rightly said to go from the heart "to all members" and the heart was said "to speak out of the vessels of every limb." But the vessels were thought to convey a mixture of air, blood, tears, urine, saliva, nasal mucus, semen, and at times even feces. During the process of embalming, the heart was always left in situ or replaced in the thorax. According to the renowned Orientalist Sir Wallis Budge, the Egyptians saw the heart as the "source of life and being," and any damage to it would have resulted in a "second death" in which everything (*ka, ba, khu,* and *ren*) would be destroyed. In some sarcophagi one can still read the pathetic plea "spare us a second death."

The anatomical heart was the *haty,* the word *ib* referring to the heart as a metaphysical entity. . . .

The Egyptians were concerned that the dead should be able to breathe again. The Pyramid Texts describe the ceremony of the "opening of the mouth," by which this was achieved. Immediately before the mummy was consigned to the sepulchral chamber, specially qualified priests placed it upright, touched the face with an adz, and proclaimed "thy mouth is opened by Horus with his little finger, with which he also opened the mouth of his father Osiris." It has proved difficult to relate this ritual, in any meaningful way, to specific beliefs about the *ka* or *ba.*

The brain is not mentioned much in any of the extant medical papyruses from ancient Egypt. It is occasionally described as an organ producing mucus, which drained out through the nose; or it is referred to by a generic term applicable to the viscera as a whole. Life and death were matters of the heart, although the suggested relationships were at times bizarre—for example, it was said that the "mind passed away" when the vessels of the heart were contaminated with feces. The only reference that might relate death to the brain stem is the strange statement in the Ebers papyrus (gloss 854f) to the effect that "life entered the body through the left ear, and departed through the right one."

It is clear why the Egyptians never cremated their dead: to do so would have destroyed for the deceased all prospects of an afterlife. Fortunately, there was no question of organ transplantation; in the prevailing cultural context, it would never have been tolerated. Whether the pharaohs would have been powerful enough—or rash enough—to transgress accepted norms had transplantation been feasible is quite another matter.

Mesopotamia. The Mesopotamian (Sumerian, Babylonian, and Assyrian) attitudes to death differed widely from those of the Egyptians. They were grim and stark: sickness and death were the wages of sin. This view was to percolate, with pitiless logic and simplicity, through Judaism into Christianity. Although the dead were buried in Mesopotamia, no attempts were made to preserve their bodies.

According to Mesopotamian mythology, the gods had made humans of clay, but to the clay had been added the flesh and blood of a god specially slaughtered for the occasion. God was, therefore, present in all people. The sole purpose of humanity's creation was to serve the gods, to carry the yoke and labour for them. Offended gods withdrew their support, thereby opening the door to demons. . . . It is not surprising that offerings to the dead were made in a spirit of fear; if not propitiated they would return and cause all kinds of damage.

The Babylonians did not dissect bodies, and their approach to disease and death was spiritual rather than anatomical or physiological. They did not speculate about the functions of organs but considered them the seat of emotions and mental faculties in general. The heart was believed to be the seat of the intellect, the liver of affectivity, the stomach of cunning, the uterus of compassion, and the ears and the eyes of attention. Breathing and life were thought of in the same terms. The Akkadian word *napistu* was used indifferently to mean "the throat," "to breathe," and "life" itself.

Judaism. The canonical writings of biblical Judaism record the relations between certain outstanding individuals and their god. The events described are perceived as landmarks in the unfurling of a national destiny, designed and guided by that god. Jewish eschatology is in this sense unique: its main concern is the fate of a nation, not what happens to an individual at death or thereafter.

Absence of an afterlife in classical Judaism

In classical Judaism death closes the book. As the anonymous author of Ecclesiastes bluntly put it: "For the living know that they will die, but the dead know nothing, and they have no more reward" (Eccles. 9:5). The death of human beings was like that of animals: "As one dies, so dies the other. They all have the same breath, and man has no advantage over the beasts . . . all are from the dust, and all turn to dust again" (Eccles. 3:19–20). Life alone mattered: "A living dog is better than a dead lion" (Eccles. 9:4). Even Job, whose questioning at times verges on subverting Yahwist doctrine, ends up endorsing the official creed: "Man dies, and is laid low . . . . As waters fail from a lake, and a river wastes away and dries up, So man lies down and rises not again; till the heavens are no more he will not awake, or be roused out of his sleep" (Job 14:10–12).

Yet such views were far from universal. The archaeological record suggests that the various racial elements assimilated to form the Jewish nation each had brought to the new community its own tribal customs, often based on beliefs in an afterlife. Both Moses (Deut. 14:1) and Jeremiah (Jer. 16:6) denounced mortuary practices taken to imply such beliefs. Necromancy, although officially forbidden, was widely practiced, even in high places. Saul's request to the witch of Endor to "bring up" the dead prophet Samuel for him (I Sam. 28:3–20) implied that the dead, or at least some of them, still existed somewhere or other, probably in Sheol, "the land of gloom and deep darkness" (Job 10:21). In Sheol, the good and the wicked shared a common fate, much as they had in the Babylonian underworld. The place did not conjure up images of an afterlife, for nothing happened there. It was literally inconceivable, and this is what made it frightening: death was utterly definitive, even if rather ill-defined.

Many were unsatisfied by the idea that individual lives only had meaning inasmuch as they influenced the nation's destiny for good or ill. There was only one life, they were told, yet their everyday experience challenged the view that it was on earth that Yahweh rewarded the pious and punished the wicked. The Book of Job offered little solace: it was irrelevant that the good suffered and that the wicked prospered. One did not pray to improve one's prospects. The worship of God was an end in itself; it was what gave meaning to life. Against this backdrop of beliefs, the longing for personal significance was widespread.

It is difficult to determine when the notion of soul first emerged in Jewish writings. The problem is partly philological. The word *nefesh* originally meant "neck" or "throat," and later came to imply the "vital spirit," or *anima* in the Latin sense. The word *ruach* had at all times meant "wind" but later came to refer to the whole range of a person's emotional, intellectual, and volitional life. It even designated ghosts. Both terms were widely used and conveyed a wide variety of meanings at different times, and both were often translated as "soul."

Emerging ideas of an afterlife

The notion of a resurrection of the dead has a more concrete evolution. It seems to have originated during Judaism's Hellenistic period (4th century BC–2nd century AD). Isaiah announced that the "dead shall live, their bodies shall rise," and the "dwellers in the dust" would be enjoined to "awake and sing" (Isa. 26:19). Both the good and the wicked would be resurrected. According to their deserts, some would be granted "everlasting life," others consigned to an existence of "shame and everlasting contempt" (Dan. 12:2). The idea that a person's future would be determined by conduct on earth was to have profound repercussions. The first beneficiaries seem to have been those killed in battle on behalf of Israel. Judas Maccabeus, the 2nd-century-BC Jewish patriot who led a struggle against Seleucid domination and Greek cultural penetration, found that his own supporters had infringed the law. He collected money and sent it to Jerusalem to expiate their sins, acting thereby "very well and honorably, taking account of the resurrection. For if he were not expecting that those who had fallen would rise again, it would have been superfluous and foolish to pray for the dead" (II Macc. 12:43–45).

Sheol itself became departmentalized. According to the *First Book of Enoch,* a noncanonical work believed to have been written between the 2nd century BC and the 2nd century AD, Sheol was composed of three divisions, to which the dead would be assigned according to their moral deserts. The real Ge Hinnom ("Valley of Hinnom"), where the early Israelites were said to have sacrificed their children to Moloch (and in which later biblical generations incinerated Jerusalem's municipal rubbish), was transmuted into the notion of Gehenna, a vast camp designed for torturing the wicked by fire. This was a clear precursor of things to come—the Christian and Islāmic versions of hell.

Orphic and Platonic ideas also came to exert a profound influence on the Judaic concept of death. These were perhaps expressed most clearly in the apocryphal text known as the Wisdom of Solomon, written during the 1st century BC and reflecting the views of a cultured Jew of the Diaspora. The author stressed that a "perishable body weighs down the soul" (Wisd. Sol. 9:15) and stated that "being good" he had "entered an undefiled body" (Wisd. Sol. 8:20), a viewpoint that was quintessentially Platonic in its vision of a soul that predated the body. Flavius Josephus, the Jewish historian of the 1st century AD, recorded in *Bellum Judaicum* (*History of the Jewish War*) how doctrinal disputes about death, the existence of an afterlife, and the "fate of the soul" were embodied in the views of various factions. The Sadducees (who spoke for a conservative, sacerdotal aristocracy) were still talking in terms of the old Yahwist doctrines, while the Pharisees (who reflected the views of a more liberal middle class) spoke of immortal souls, some doomed to eternal torment, others promised passage into another body. The Essenes held views close to those of the early Christians.

Following the destruction of the Temple (AD 70) and, more particularly, after the collapse of the last resistance to the Romans (c. 135), rabbinic teaching and exegesis slowly got under way. These flowered under Judah ha-Nasi ("Judah the Prince"), who, during his reign (c. 175–

c. 220) as patriarch of the Jewish community in Palestine, compiled the collection of rabbinic law known as the Mishna. During the next 400 years or so, rabbinic teaching flourished, resulting in the production and repeated reelaboration first of the Palestinian (Jerusalem) and then of the Babylonian Talmuds. These codes of civil and religious practice sought to determine every aspect of life, including attitudes toward the dead. The concepts of immortality and resurrection had become so well established that in the Eighteen Benedictions (recited daily in synagogues and homes) God was repeatedly addressed as "the One who resurrects the dead." Talmudic sources warned that "anyone who said there was no resurrection" would have no share in the world to come. . . .

Rabbinic teachings on immortality

Orthodox Jewish responses to current medical controversies concerning death are based on biblical and Talmudic ethical imperatives. First, nothing must be done that might conceivably hasten death. Life being of infinite worth, a few seconds of it are likewise infinitely valuable. Causing accidental death is seen as only one step removed from murder. When a patient is in the pangs of death the bed should not be shaken, as even this might prove to be the last straw. Such invasive diagnostic procedures as four-vessel angiography (to assess cerebral blood flow) would almost certainly be frowned upon. Even a venipuncture (say, for tissue typing) could be conceived of as *shpikhut damim,* a spilling of blood with nefarious intent. In secular medical practice, however, problems of this sort are unlikely to arise. Much more important is the conceptual challenge presented by the beating-heart cadaver. Here it must be stressed that absence of a heartbeat was never considered a cardinal factor in the determination of death (Bab. Talmud, tractate *Yoma* 85A). Talmudic texts, moreover, clearly recognized that death was a process and not an event: "the death throes of a decapitated man are not signs of life any more than are the twitchings of a lizard's amputated tail" (Bab. Talmud, tractate *Chullin* 21A; Mishna, *Ohoioth* 1:6). The decapitated state itself defined death (Maimonides: *Tumath Meth* 1:15). Brain-stem death, which is physiological decapitation, can readily be equated with death in this particular perspective.

Orthodox responses to the beating-heart cadaver

What mattered, in early Jewish sources, was the capacity to breathe spontaneously, which was seen as an indicator of the living state. The Babylonian Talmud (tractate *Yoma* 85A) explained that when a building collapsed, all life-saving activities could legitimately cease on determination that the victim was no longer breathing. The instructions were quite explicit: "As soon as the nose is uncovered no further examination need be made, for the Tanach (Bible) refers to 'all living things who have the breath of life in their nostrils.' "

Apnea alone, of course, does not constitute death; it is a necessary but not a sufficient condition for such a diagnosis. But if apnea is conjoined to all that is implied in the notion of the decapitated state (in terms of the irreversible loss of the capacity for consciousness, for instance), one finds that the concepts of death in the Talmud and in the most modern intensive care unit are virtually identical.

The issue of transplantation is more complex. The Talmud forbids the mutilation of a corpse or the deriving of any benefit from a dead body, but these considerations can be overridden by the prescriptions of *pikuakh nefesh* ("the preservation of life"). The Chief Rabbi of Israel has even argued that, as a successful graft ultimately becomes part of the recipient, prohibitions related to deriving benefit from the dead do not, in the long run, apply.

Hinduism.   Among the collected hymns of the Rigveda (which may date from 1500 BC and probably constitute the earliest known book in the world), there is a "Song of Creation." "Death was not there," it states, "nor was there aught immortal." The world was a total void, except for "one thing, breathless, yet breathed by its own nature." This is the first recorded insight into the importance of respiration to potential life.

Later, by about 600 BC, the *Upaniṣad*s (a collection of searching, intellectually stimulating Indo-Aryan texts) record the quest for a coordinating principle that might underlie such diverse functions of the individual as speech, hearing, and intellect. An essential attribute of the living was their ability to breathe (*an*). Their *prana* ("breath") was so vital that on its cessation the body and its faculties became lifeless and still. The word for "soul," *ātman,* is derived from *an,* thus placing the concept of breath at the very core of the individual self or soul.

The Hindu concept of the soul is central to an understanding of most Hindu practices related to death. In *The Discovery of India,* Jawaharlal Nehru described Hinduism as a faith that was "vague, amorphous, many-sided and all things to all men." The practices that the religion inspires do indeed entail acts that appear contradictory. What is unique to Hinduism, however, is that these are not perceived as contradictions. A common thread unites the most abstract philosophical speculations and childish beliefs in ghosts; a deep respect for nonviolence and the bloodiness of certain sacrificial rites; extreme asceticism and the sexual aspects of Tantric worship. At very different levels of sophistication, these all represent attempts to expand human perception of the truth and to achieve a cosmic consciousness. To the intellectually inclined Hindu, the eternal, infinite, and all-pervasive principle of Brahman alone is real, and the acquisition of cosmic consciousness allows humans to become one with it. The individual soul (*ātman*) is merely a particle of this cosmic principle, the relationship being likened to that between air, temporarily trapped in an earthen jar, and the endless space without; or to that between a particular wave and the ocean as a whole.

The cycle of rebirths

Death practices are probably more important in Hinduism than in any other religion. At one level they derive from explicit religious premises. Each being is predestined to innumerable rebirths (*samsāra*), and one's aggregate moral balance sheet (*karman*) determines both the length of each life and the specific form of each rebirth. Moral attributes are minutely quantifiable causal agents: every grain sown in this existence is reaped in the next. The prospect of innumerable lives is therefore envisaged with dismay. To escape the dreaded rebirths is to achieve final emancipation (*mokṣa*). "Life everlasting" (at least of the type already sampled) is the last thing a Hindu would aspire to. *Mokṣa* can be achieved only by the saintly, or perhaps by those who have died in Vārānasi and had their ashes strewed on the Ganges River. For others, the wages of worldliness is inevitable reincarnation.

Hindu death practices, however, also reflect popular beliefs and fears, as well as local customs. They thus may vary considerably from region to region or from sect to sect, bearing a rather variable relation to religious doctrine. Many practices are derived from the *Dharma-śastra* of Manu, the most authoritative of the books of Hindu sacred law. The alleged author of the book is the mythical sage Manu, who combined flood-surviving attributes (like Noah of Jews and Christians, and Utnapishtim of the Mesopotamians) with law-giving propensities (like Moses and Hammurabi). The book, which grew by repeated additions over many centuries, reflects the evolving interests of a male Brahman priesthood: its prescriptions are overwhelmingly recorded in terms of what is appropriate for men. Women are seldom referred to, and then often in derogatory terms.

Death practices. Hindus hold that a span of 120 years has been allotted to human life, a strange notion in a country where the average life expectancy was under 30 into the 20th century. They have no difficulty with the concept of death as a process. Mythological beliefs involving early Vedic gods held that the god reigning over the ears departed early, as did the gods of the eyes, hands, and mind.

Rituals for the dying

When devout Hindus sense death approaching, they begin repeating the monosyllable *Om.* (This word refers to Brahman and is widely used in religious observance to help concentrate the mind on what matters.) If it is the last word on a person's lips, it guarantees a direct passage to *mokṣa.* When the dying are judged to have only an hour or so left, they are moved from their bed to a mattress on the floor and their heads are shaved. The space between ground and the ceiling is thought to symbolize the troubled area between earth and sky, and those dying there may return after death as evil spirits. A space on

the ground is sanctified with Ganges water and various other ingredients, including cow dung, barley, and sesame seeds. A Hindu should never die in bed, but lying on the ground. As they take their last breaths, the dying are moved from the mattress to ground. Experienced members of the family are usually present to help decide the opportune moment. Water taken from the confluence of the rivers Ganges and Yamuna (at Allahābād) is poured into the mouth, into which is also placed a leaf of the tulsi plant (*Ocimum sanctum*). The forehead is smeared with white clay (*gopi candana*). A woman whose death precedes her husband's is considered so fortunate that her face, and especially her forehead, may be smeared with red. Sometimes, if there is doubt as to whether death has occurred, a lump of ghee (clarified butter) is placed on the forehead; if it does not melt, it is taken as a sign that life is extinct—an interesting but potentially misleading practice in the light of modern awareness of how hypothermia can mimic death. The dead body is wrapped in clean cloth of varying colours that indicate age. In the home the relatives walk clockwise around the body; they will walk around the funeral pyre in the opposite direction.

The body is looked upon as an offering to Agni, god of fire. According to the Vedas, the Indo-Aryans used to bury their dead. Why the Hindus and Buddhists burn theirs has been the subject of much controversy. It has been variously interpreted as a gesture of purification, as the most efficient means of releasing the soul from the corrupted body, as a public health measure with important ecological benefits in a crowded country, or as a symbol of the transitory nature of any particular life and the desire that it should end in permanent anonymity. Fire taken from the deceased's home is transported to the cremation ground in a black earthen pot; this is carried immediately in front of the deceased, and nothing must come between them. For many years women were not allowed to follow the cortege, and only the wives of Brahmans could walk around the pyre. At the cremation site, a lighted torch is handed to the eldest son or grandson, who ignites the pyre, near the feet of the dead woman, at the head of the dead man. While the body is burning the soul is thought to seek refuge within the head. The intense heat usually explodes the skull, liberating the soul; when this does not happen spontaneously, the skull is deliberately shattered by blows from a cudgel. Other traditions hold that the soul passes out through the nose, eyes, and mouth. Some believe it is better still if it leaves through the anterior fontanel, an opening in the skull that normally closes during early childhood. Such theorists hold that if the deceased has practiced yoga or intense meditation, this opening will reopen, allowing free passage to the soul. In some parts of India it is believed that the souls of the really wicked depart through the rectum, and in so doing acquire such defilement that endless purification is necessary.

Cremation

Children under the age of two are not cremated but buried. When dying, they are not placed on the ground; instead they are allowed to expire in their mothers' arms. There are no special death rites; it is felt the child must have been a monster of iniquity in its previous life to have incurred such a terrible *karman.* Infant mortality is clearly attributed to the child's own wickedness and carries a load of 84 *lakh*s of rebirths (*i.e.,* the child has to be reborn 8,400,000 times). The ceremonial defilement of relatives is short, lasting only three days. Among the very high-caste Nagaras, when a pregnant woman dies the fetus is removed and buried, while the mother is cremated.

Ascetics, too, are buried rather than burnt, usually in an upright posture with the body surrounded with salt. Lepers and smallpox victims used to be buried in a recumbent position. Smallpox has been eradicated, and leprosy victims are usually cremated. If a Hindu "breaks caste" by becoming either a Muslim or a Christian, a death ceremony is conducted, the relatives bathe to purge their defilement, and the person's name is never mentioned again. The concept of death clearly influences what is deemed appropriate death behaviour. . . .

Islam. Probably no religion deals in such graphic detail as does Islām with the creation, death, "life in the tomb," and ultimate fate of humankind. Yet the Qur'ān, the holy book of Islām, itself provides no uniform or systematic approach to these problems. It is only in its later parts (which date from the period when the small Muslim community in Medina had come into contact with other religious influences) that problems such as the relation of sleep to death, the significance of breathing, and the question of when and how the soul leaves the body are addressed in any detail. Popular Muslim beliefs are based on still later traditions. These are recorded in the *Kitāb al-rūḥ* ("Book of the Soul") written in the 14th century by the Ḥanbalī theologian Muḥammad ibn Abī-Bakr ibn Qayyīm al-Jawzīyah.

Predestination in Islāmic teachings

The basic premise of all Qur'ānic teaching concerning death is Allāh's omnipotence: he creates human beings, determines their life span, and causes them to die. The Qur'ān states: "Some will die early, while others are made to live to a miserable old age, when all that they once knew they shall know no more (22:5; *i.e., sūrah* [chapter] 22, verse 5). Damnation and salvation are equally predetermined: "Allāh leaves to stray whom he willeth, and guideth whom he willeth" (35:8). As for those whom Allāh leaves astray, the Qur'ān states that "for them there will be no helpers" (30:29). Allāh has decided many will fail: "If We had so willed We could certainly cause proper guidance to come to every soul, but true is My saying 'assuredly I shall fill Jihannam' " (32:13).

In this perspective the individual's fate (including the mode and time of death) appears inescapably predetermined. The very term *Islām,* Arabic for "surrender," implies an absolute submission to the will of God. But what freedom does this allow those predestined to continue in the path of error, or to reject God's will? And if there is no such freedom, what sense was there in the mission of the Prophet Muḥammad (Islām's founder) and his appeal to people to alter their ways? It is hardly surprising that arguments about free will and predestination broke out soon after the Prophet's death. The ensuing tensions dominated theological (and other) controversies within Islām during many centuries.

Nature of the soul

Questions concerning the meaning of life and the nature of the soul are dealt with patchily in both the Qur'ān and the Ḥadīth (the record of the sayings attributed to the Prophet). The Qur'ān records that, when asked about these matters by local leaders of the Jewish faith, the Prophet answered that "the spirit cometh by command of God" and that "only a little knowledge was communicated to man" (17:85). Humanity was created from "potter's clay, from mud molded into shape" into which Allāh has "breathed his spirit" (15:28–29). A vital spirit or soul (*nafs*) is within each human being. It is associated, if not actually identified, with individuality and also with the seat of rational consciousness. It is interesting to speculate on the possible relation of the term *nafs* to such Arabic words as *nafas* ("breath") and *nafīs* ("precious"), particularly in a language where there are no written vowels.

Death is repeatedly compared with sleep, which is at times described as "the little death." God takes away people's souls "during their sleep" and "upon their death." He "retains those against whom he has decreed death, but returns the others to their bodies for an appointed term" (39:42–43). During death, the soul "rises into the throat" (56:83) before leaving the body. These are interesting passages in the light of modern medical knowledge. The study of sleep has identified the episodic occurrence of short periods during which the limbs are totally flaccid and without reflexes, as would be the limbs of the recently dead. Modern neurophysiology, moreover, stresses the role of structures in the upper part of the brain stem in the maintenance of the waking state. Lesions just a little higher (in the hypothalamus) cause excessively long episodes of sleep. Irreversible damage at these sites is part of the modern concept of death. Finally, various types of breathing disturbance are characteristic of brain-stem lesions and could have been attributed, in former times, to occurrences in the throat. Nothing in these passages outrages the insights of modern neurology. The absence of any cardiological dimension is striking.

It is orthodox Muslim belief that when someone dies the Angel of Death (*malāk al-mawt*) arrives, sits at the head of the deceased, and addresses each soul according to its known status. According to the *Kitāb al-rūḥ,* wicked souls are instructed "to depart to the wrath of God." Fearing what awaits them, they seek refuge throughout the body and have to be extracted "like the dragging of an iron skewer through moist wool, tearing the veins and sinews." Angels place the soul in a hair cloth and "the odour from it is like the stench of a decomposing carcass." A full record is made, and the soul is then returned to the body in the grave. "Good and contented souls" are instructed "to depart to the mercy of God." They leave the body, "flowing as easily as a drop from a waterskin"; are wrapped by angels in a perfumed shroud, and are taken to the "seventh heaven," where the record is kept. These souls, too, are then returned. . . .

Muslims accord a great respect to dead bodies, which have to be disposed of very promptly. The mere suggestion of cremation, however, is viewed with abhorrence. The philosophical basis, if any, of this attitude is not clear. It is not stated, for instance, that an intact body will be required at the time of resurrection. It is unlikely, moreover, that the abhorrence—which Orthodox Jews share—arose out of a desire to differentiate Islāmic practices from those of other "people of the Book" (*i.e.,* Jews and Christians). The attitude toward dead bodies has had practical consequences; for instance, in relation to medical education. It is almost impossible to carry out postmortem examinations in many Islāmic countries. Medical students in Saudi Arabia, for example, study anatomy on corpses imported from non-Islāmic countries. They learn pathology only from textbooks; many complete their medical training never having seen a real brain destroyed by a real cerebral hemorrhage.

Attitudes toward transplantation

In 1982 organ donation after death was declared *ḥallāl* ("permissible") by the Senior 'Ulamā' Commission, the highest religious authority on such matters in Saudi Arabia (and hence throughout the Islāmic world). Tales inculcated in childhood continue, however, to influence public attitudes in Islāmic nations. The widely told story of how the Prophet's uncle Ḥamzah was murdered by the heathen Hind, who then opened the murdered man's belly and chewed up his liver, has slowed public acceptance of liver transplantation. Kidney transplantation is more acceptable, perhaps because the Ḥadīth explicitly states that those entering the Garden will never more urinate.

The modern Western context. *The Christian legacy.* The spread of rationalistic and scientific ideas since the 18th century has undermined many aspects of religion, including many Christian beliefs. The church, moreover, although still seeking to exert its influence, has ceased to dominate civil life in the way it once did. Religion is no longer the pivot of all social relations as it once was in ancient Egypt and still is in some Islāmic countries. The decline of the church is epitomized by the fact that, while it is still prepared to speak of the symbolic significance of the death of Jesus Christ (and of human death in general), it has ceased to emphasize many aspects of its initial eschatology and to concern itself, as in the past, with the particular details of individual death. In the age of Hiroshima and Nagasaki, the elaborate descriptions of heaven, purgatory, and hell in Dante's *Divine Comedy,* while remaining beautiful literature, at best raise a smile if thought of as outlines for humanity's future.

The centrality of death to Christianity

Death is at the very core of the Christian religion. Not only is the cross to be found in cemeteries and places of worship alike, but the premise of the religion is that, by their own action, humans have forfeited immortality. Through abuse of the freedom granted in the Garden of Eden, Adam and Eve not only sinned and fell from grace, but they also transmitted sin to their descendants: the sins of the fathers are visited on the children. And as "the wages of sin is death" (Rom. 6:23), death became the universal fate: "Therefore as sin came into the world through one man and death through sin, and so death spread to all men" (Rom. 5:12). Christian theologians spent the best part of two millennia sorting out these implications and devising ways out of the dire prognosis implicit in the concept of original sin. The main salvation was to be baptism into the death of Jesus Christ (Rom. 6:3–4).

Among early Christians delay in the promised Second Coming of Christ led to an increasing preoccupation with what happened to the dead as they awaited the resurrection and the Last Judgment. One view was that there would be an immediate individual judgment and that instant justice would follow: the deceased would be dispatched forthwith to hell or paradise. This notion demeaned the impact of the great prophecy of a collective mass resurrection, followed by a public mass trial on a gigantic scale. Moreover, it deprived the dead of any chance of a postmortem (*i.e.,* very belated) expiation of their misdeeds. The Roman Catholic notion of purgatory sought to resolve the latter problem; regulated torture would expiate some of the sins of those not totally beyond redemption.

The second view was that the dead just slept, pending the mass resurrection. But as the sleep might last for millennia, it was felt that the heavenly gratification of the just was being arbitrarily, and somewhat unfairly, deferred. As for the wicked, they were obtaining an unwarranted respite. The Carthaginian theologian Tertullian, one of the Church Fathers, outlined the possibility of still further adjustments. In his *Adversus Marcionem,* written about 207, he described "a spatial concept that may be called Abraham's bosom for receiving the soul of all people." Although not celestial, it was "above the lower regions and would provide refreshment (*refrigerium*) to the souls of the just until the consummation of all things in the great resurrection." The Byzantine Church formally endorsed the concept, which inspired some most interesting art in both eastern and western Europe.

During its early years, the Christian Church debated death in largely religious terms. The *acerbitas mortis* ("bitterness of death") was very real, and pious deathbeds had to be fortified by the acceptance of pain as an offering to God. Life expectancy fell far short of the promised threescore years and 10. Eastern medicine remained for a long time in advance of that practiced in the West, and the church's interventions were largely spiritual. It was only during the Renaissance and the later age of Enlightenment that an intellectual shift became perceptible.

Descartes, the pineal soul, and brain-stem death. The first attempts to localize the soul go back to classical antiquity. The soul had originally been thought to reside in the liver, an organ to which no other function could, at that time, be attributed. Empedocles, Democritus, Aristotle, the Stoics, and the Epicureans had later held its abode to be the heart. Other Greeks (Pythagorus, Plato, and Galen) had opted for the brain. Herophilus (flourished *c.* 300 BC), a famous physician of the Greek medical school of Alexandria, had sought to circumscribe its habitat to the fourth ventricle of the brain; that is, to a small area immediately above the brain stem. Controversy persisted to the very end of the 16th century.

The departure of the soul from the body had always been central to the Christian concept of death. But the soul had come to mean different things to various classical and medieval thinkers. There was a "vegetative soul," responsible for what we would now call autonomic function; a "sensitive soul," responsible for what modern physiologists would describe as reflex responses to environmental stimuli; and, most importantly, a "reasoning soul," responsible for making a rational entity (*res cogitans*) of human beings. The reasoning soul was an essentially human attribute and was the basis of thought, judgment, and responsibility for one's actions. Its departure implied death. The *Anatome Corporis Humani* (1672) of Isbrand van Diemerbroeck, professor at Utrecht, appears to have been the last textbook of anatomy that discussed the soul within a routine description of human parts. Thereafter, the soul disappeared from the scope of anatomy.

The modern and entirely secular concept of brain-stem death can, perhaps rather surprisingly, find both a conceptual and a topographical foundation in the writings of René Descartes (1596–1650), the great French philosopher and mathematician who sought to bring analytical geometry, physics, physiology, cosmology, and religion into an integrated conceptual framework. Descartes considered the body and the soul to be ontologically separate but interacting entities, each with its own particular attributes.

He then sought to specify both their mode and site of interaction; the latter he deduced to be the pineal gland. The pineal was to become, in the words of Geoffrey Jefferson, "the nodal point of Cartesian dualism."

Before Descartes, the prevailing wisdom, largely derived from Greece, had regarded the soul both as the motive force of all human physiological functions and as the conscious agent of volition, cognition, and reason. Descartes succeeded in eliminating the soul's general physiological role altogether. . . .

Descartes probably was impressed by the central location of the unpaired pineal gland, situated where neural pathways from the retinas converge with those conveying feelings from the limbs. This "general reflector of all sorts of sensation" is, moreover, sited in the immediate proximity of the brain ventricles, from which (according to the wisdom of the day) "animal spirits" flowed into the hollow nerves, carrying instructions to the muscles. In his *Excerpta Anatomica,* Descartes had even likened the pineal to a penis obturating the passage between the third and fourth ventricles.

Descartes proved wrong in his beliefs that all sensory inputs focused on the pineal gland and that the pineal itself was a selective motor organ, suspended in a whirl of "animal spirits," dancing and jigging "like a balloon captive above a fire," yet capable in humans of scrutinizing inputs and producing actions "consistent with wisdom." He was also wrong when he spoke of the "ideas formed on the surface" of the pineal gland, and in his attribution to the pineal of such functions as "volition, cognition, memory, imagination, and reason." But he was uncannily correct in his insight that a very small part of this deep and central area of the brain was relevant to some of the functions he stressed. We now know that immediately below the pineal gland there lies the mesencephalic tegmentum (the uppermost part of the brain stem), which is crucial to generating alertness (the capacity for consciousness), without which, of course, there can be no volition, cognition, or reason.

It is a matter of vocabulary whether one considers the mesencephalic tegmentum either as being involved in generating a "capacity for consciousness" or as preparing the brain for the exercise of what Descartes would have considered the "functions of the soul" (volition, cognition, and reason). In either case, the total and irreversible loss of these functions dramatically alters the ontological status of the subject. Descartes specifically considered the example of death. In "La Description du corps humain" (1664) he wrote that "although movements cease in the body when it is dead and the soul departs, one cannot deduce from these facts that the soul produced the movements." In a formulation of really modern tenor, he then added "one can only infer that the same single cause (a) renders the body incapable of movement and (b) causes the soul to absent itself." He did not, of course, say that this "same single cause" was the death of the brain stem. Some 300 years later, in 1968, the Harvard Committee spoke of death in terms of "irreversible coma" (where Descartes had spoken of the "now absent soul") and stressed, as had Descartes, the immobility of the comatose body. The religious and secular terms seem to describe the same reality.

There have been other neurological controversies concerning the locus of the soul. Early in the 18th century Stephen Hales, an English clergyman with a great interest in science, repeated an experiment originally reported by Leonardo da Vinci. Hales tied a ligature around the neck of a frog and cut off its head. The heart continued to beat for a while, as it usually does in the brain dead. Thirty hours later, the limbs of the animal still withdrew when stimulated. In fact, the elicited movements only ceased when the spinal cord itself had been destroyed. This observation gave rise to a great controversy. Reflex action at spinal cord level was not then fully understood, and it was argued that the irritability implied sentience, and that sentience suggested that the soul was still present. The "spinal cord soul" became the subject of much debate. It is now known that such purely spinal reflex movements may occur below a dead brain. It was shown during the

[margin left] Concepts of the soul

[margin right] Descartes's ideas regarding the pineal gland

19th century that individuals executed on the guillotine might retain the knee jerk reflex for up to 20 minutes after decapitation.

Modern theological concerns

The church is still concerned with the diagnosis of death, but the theological argument has, during the last half of the 20th century, moved to an entirely different plane. As mentioned earlier, in 1957 Pope Pius XII raised the question whether, in intensive care units, doctors might be "continuing the resuscitation process, despite the fact that the soul may already have left the body." He even asked one of the central questions confronting modern medicine, namely whether "death had already occurred after grave trauma to the brain, which has provoked deep unconsciousness and central breathing paralysis, the fatal consequences of which have been retarded by artificial respiration." The answer, he said, "did not fall within the competence of the Church."

Public attitudes. Until about 100 years ago, people had by and large come to terms with death. They usually died in their homes, among their relatives. In villages, in the 18th or early 19th centuries, passers-by might join the priest bearing the last sacrament on his visit to the dying man or woman. Doctors even stressed the public health hazards this might cause. Numerous pictures attest to the fact that children were not excluded from deathbeds, as they were to be during the 20th century.

Changing attitudes toward death

The general acceptance of death was to be subverted by the advances of modern medicine and by the rapid spread of rationalist thought. This led, during a period of only a few decades, to a striking change of attitudes. In the advanced industrial countries, a large number of people now die in hospitals. The improvement in life expectancy and the advances of modern surgery and medicine have been achieved at a certain price. A mechanistic approach has developed, in which the protraction of dying has become a major by-product of modern technology. The philosophy of modern medicine has been diverted from attention to the sick and has begun to reify the sickness. Instead of perceiving death as something natural, modern physicians have come to see it as bad or alien, a defeat of all their therapeutic endeavours, at times almost as a personal defeat. . . .

The development of the death industry (satirized in Evelyn Waugh's *Loved One* and explored in Jessica Mitford's *American Way of Death*) is also a by-product of the technological revolution and of modern attitudes to death. Undertakers have become "morticians" and coffins "caskets." Embalming has enjoyed a new vogue. Drive-in cemeteries have appeared, for those seeking to reconcile devotion to the dead with other pressing engagements. Cryogenic storage of the corpse has been offered as a means to preserve the deceased in a form amendable to any future therapies that science may devise. Commercial concerns have entered the scene: nonpayment of maintenance charges may result in threats of thawing and putrefaction. In a contentious environment, the law has even invaded the intensive care unit, influencing the decisions of physicians concerning the withdrawal of treatment or the determination of death. A wit has remarked that in the modern era, the only sure sign that a man is dead is that he is no longer capable of litigation.

BIBLIOGRAPHY

Biological aspects: The new concept of apoptosis (programmed cell death) is outlined in A. GLÜCKSMAN, "Cell Deaths in Normal Vertebrate Ontogeny," *Biological Reviews of the Cambridge Philosophical Society,* 26:59–86 (1951); A.H. WYLLIE, J.F.R. KERR, and A.R. CURRIE, "Cell Death: The Significance of Apoptosis," *International Review of Cytology,* 68:251–306 (1980); I.D. BOWEN and R.A. LOCKSHIN (eds.), *Cell Death in Biology and Pathology* (1981); and I. DAVIES and D.C. SIGEE (eds.), *Cell Ageing and Cell Death* (1985). The stormy development of the idea of brain death (and . . . the concept of brain-stem death) can be followed in P. MOLLARET and M. GOULON, "Le Coma dépassé," *Revue Neurologique,* 101(1):3–15 (July 1959); AD HOC COMMITTEE OF THE HARVARD MEDICAL SCHOOL TO EXAMINE THE DEFINITION OF BRAIN DEATH, "A Definition of Irreversible Coma," *J.A.M.A.,* 205(6):337–340 (Aug. 5, 1968); JULIUS KOREIN (ed.), *Brain Death: Interrelated Medical and Social Issues* (1978); A. EARL WALKER, *Cerebral Death,* 3rd ed. (1985); PRESIDENT'S COMMISSION FOR THE STUDY OF ETHICAL PROBLEMS IN MEDICINE AND BIOMEDICAL AND BEHAVIORAL RESEARCH, *Defining Death: A Report on the Medical, Legal, and Ethical Issues in the Determination of Death* (1981, reprinted 1983); BRYAN JENNETT, JOHN GLEAVE, and PETER WILSON, "Brain Death in Three Neurosurgical Units," *Br.Med.J.,* 282:533–539 (Feb. 14, 1981); CHRISTOPHER PALLIS, *ABC of Brain Stem Death* (1983), and his "Brain-stem Death: The Evolution of a Concept," in PETER J. MORRIS (ed.), *Kidney Transplantation: Principles and Practice,* 2nd ed., pp. 101–127 (1984); and JAMES L. BERNAT, "The Definition, Criterion, and Statute of Death," *Seminars in Neurology,* 4(1):45–51 (March 1984).

Philosophical and cultural aspects: E.A. WALLIS BUDGE, *Egyptian Ideas of the Future Life: Egyptian Religion* (1899, reprinted 1979 as *Egyptian Religion: Egyptian Ideas of the Future Life*); ANGE P. LECA, *La Médecine égyptienne au temps des pharaons* (1971); ALEXANDRE PIANKOFF (ed.), *Le "Cœur" dans les textes égyptiens depuis l'ancien jusqu' à la fin du nouvel empire* (1930); and HENRY E. SIGERIST, *A History of Medicine,* 2 vol. (1951–61), are useful reviews of the notion of death in ancient Egypt. Mesopotamian concepts are described in J. HACKIN et. al., *Asiatic Mythology* (1932, reissued 1963); and SAMUEL GEORGE FREDERICK BRANDON, *Man and His Destiny in the Great Religions* (1962, reprinted 1963). The latter and F.H. GARRISON, "The Bone Called 'Luz,'" *New York Medical Journal,* 92(4):149–151 (July 23, 1910), also contain much useful information on Judaic attitudes. Hindu perceptions and practices are detailed in PAUL THOMAS, *Hindu Religion, Customs and Manners,* 6th ed. (1975); and NIRAD C. CHAUDHURI, *Hinduism: A Religion to Live By* (1979, reprinted 1980). MUḤAMMAD IBN ABĪ-BAKR IBN QAYYĪM AL-JAWZĪYAH, *Kitāb al-rūḥ,* 2nd ed. (1324); and FRANK E. REYNOLDS and EARLE H. WAUGH (eds.), *Religious Encounters with Death: Insights from the History and Anthropology of Religions* (1977), present Islamic attitudes. More recent developments are discussed in T.S.R. BOASE, *Death in the Middle Ages . . .* (1972); and PHILIPPE ARIÈS, *Western Attitudes Toward Death: From the Middle Ages to the Present,* trans. from the French (1974, reprinted 1975), and *The Hour of Our Death* (1981 . . .). Information about the "pineal soul" is found in RENÉ DESCARTES, *Treatise of Man,* trans. by THOMAS STEELE HALL (1972; originally published in French, 1664); and about the "spinal cord soul" in EDWARD GEORGE TANDY LIDDELL, *The Discovery of Reflexes* (1960). See also GEOFFREY JEFFERSON, "René Descartes on the Localisation of the Soul," *Irish Journal of Medical Science,* 285:691–706 (Sept. 1949); and G. CORNER, "Anatomists in Search of the Soul," *Annals of Medical History,* 2(1):1–7 (Spring 1919). Modern attitudes form the basis of JESSICA MITFORD, *The American Way of Death* (1963, reprinted 1978); ELISABETH KÜBLER-ROSS, *On Death and Dying* (1969, reprinted 1979); and ROBERT M. VEATCH, *Death, Dying and the Biological Revolution: Our Last Quest for Responsibility* (1976). HERMAN FEIFEL (ed.), *The Meaning of Death* (1959, reissued 1965); and JAMES P. CARSE, *Death and Existence: A Conceptual History of Human Mortality* (1980), present excellent overviews.

CHRISTOPHER A. PALLIS. Emeritus Reader in Neurology, Royal Postgraduate Medical School, University of London. Author of *The ABC of Brain Stem Death.*

Organ and Tissue Transplants

A transplant, in . . . this article, refers to a section of tissue or to a complete organ that is removed from its original natural site and transferred to a new position in the same person or in a separate individual. The term, like its synonym, graft, was borrowed . . . from horticulture. Both . . . imply that success will result in a healthy and flourishing graft or transplant, which will gain its nourishment from its new environment.

This article is divided into the following sections:

TRANSPLANTS AND GRAFTS

Transplants of animal tissue have figured prominently in mythology since the legend of the creation of Eve from one of Adam's ribs. Historical accounts of surgical tissue grafting as part of the cure of patients date back to the early Hindu surgeons who, about the beginning of the 6th century BC, developed techniques for reconstructing noses from skin flaps taken from the patient's arm. This method was introduced into Western medicine by the great Italian surgeon Gaspare Tagliacozzo in the 16th century. The flap was left attached to the arm for two to three weeks until new blood vessels had grown into it from the nose remnant. The flap was then severed and the arm freed from the reconstructed nose.

It was found that extremely thin pieces of skin could be cut free and would obtain enough nourishment from the serum in the graft bed to stay alive while new blood vessels were being formed. This free grafting of skin, together with the flap techniques already mentioned, have constituted the main therapeutic devices of the plastic surgeon in the correction of various types of defects. Skilled manipulations of such grafts can produce surprising improvements in the appearance of those born with malformed faces and in the disfigurements resulting from severe burns. Cornea, which structurally is a modified form of transparent skin, can also be free grafted, and corneal grafts have restored sight to countless blind eyes.

Blood transfusion can be regarded as a form of tissue graft. The blood-forming tissues—bone-marrow cells—can also be transplanted. If these cells are injected into the bloodstream, they home to the marrow cavities and can become established as a vital lifesaving graft in patients suffering from defective marrow.

Organ and limb grafts   The chief distinguishing feature of organ and limb grafts is that the tissues of the organ or limb can only survive if blood vessels are rapidly joined (anastomosed) to blood vessels of the recipient. This provides the graft with a blood supply before it dies from lack of oxygen and nourishment and from the accumulation of poisonous waste products.

As can be seen from the examples cited, living-tissue grafts may be performed for a variety of reasons. Skin grafts can save life in severe burns, can improve function by correcting deformity, or can improve appearances in a cosmetic sense, with valuable psychological benefits. Organ grafts can supply a missing function and save life in cases of fatal disease of vital organs, such as the kidney.

A tissue removed from one part of the body and transplanted to another site in the same individual is called an autograft. Autografts cannot be rejected. Similarly, grafts between identical twins or highly inbred animals—isografts—are accepted by the recipients indefinitely. Grafts from a donor to a recipient of the same species—allografts or homografts—are usually rejected unless special efforts are made to prevent this. Grafts between individuals of different species—xenografts or heterografts—are usually destroyed very quickly by the recipient. (The methods used to prevent rejection are discussed in full, below.)

Tissue or organ grafts may be transplanted to their normal situation in the recipient and are then known as orthotopic—for example, skin to the surface of the body. Alternatively, they may be transplanted to an abnormal situation and are then called heterotopic—for example, kidneys are usually grafted into the lower part of the abdomen instead of into the loin (the back between the ribs and the pelvis), as this is more convenient. If an extra organ is grafted, it is called auxiliary, or accessory—for example, a heterotopic liver graft may be inserted without removal of the recipient's own liver.

Grafts are usually performed for long-term effects. Occasionally, the limited acceptance of a skin allograft may be lifesaving, by preventing loss of fluid and protein from extensive burned surface in severely ill patients. The graft also provides a bacteria-proof covering, so that infection cannot occur. When the allograft is removed or rejected, the patient may be sufficiently recovered to receive permanent autografts (see BURNS).

Certain tissues, including bone, cartilage, tendons, fascia, arteries, and heart valves, can be implanted even if their cells are dead at the time of implantation or will be rejected shortly thereafter. These are structural implants rather than true grafts or transplants. They are more akin to the stick to which a rose is attached for support—although their support is essential, their function does not depend on biological processes. In fact, xenografts or inert manufactured devices may often be equally suitable substitutes.

TISSUE TRANSPLANTS

Skin. Most skin grafting is with autografts; the special indication for skin allografts in severely burned patients has been mentioned. Skin allografts seem to be rejected more aggressively than any other tissue.... With autografts, the donor skin is limited to what the patient has available, and sometimes in extensive burn cases this becomes a matter of robbing Peter to pay Paul. If allografts were not rejected, skin from cadavers could be used for coverage of burned areas without the need for subsequent autografting, and many lives would be saved.

Flap grafts. Flap grafts as used by Tagliacozzo are particularly valuable if fat as well as skin has been lost. The procedure of raising a flap and keeping the donor site adjacent to the recipient bed can be complicated and uncomfortable for the patient. The cosmetic results are good, and the fat under the skin contained in the flap can be used to cover exposed bone or to allow movement in a contracted joint or to fashion a new nose.

Full-thickness free-skin grafts. Full-thickness free-skin grafts are the maximum thickness that can survive without a blood supply, and they are therefore in some danger of failure to survive. These grafts produce good cosmetic appearances and are especially useful on the face. The main defect of a full-thickness free-skin graft is that, unless it is very small, the donor site from which it comes becomes a defect that needs to be closed in its own right and may itself need skin grafting.

Split or partial-thickness skin grafts. Split, or partial-thickness, skin grafts are by far the most commonly used grafts in plastic surgery. Superficial slices of skin the thickness of tissue paper are cut with a hand or mechanical razor. The graft, which contains living cells, is so thin that it usually gains adequate nourishment directly from the raw surface to which it is applied, and the risk of failure to take (that is, to survive in the new location) is therefore much less than with full-thickness grafts. Another major advantage is that the donor site is not badly damaged. It is tender for only two or three weeks, and it resembles a superficial graze both in appearance and in the fact that healing takes place from the deep layer of the skin left behind. Split skin grafts can be taken quickly from large areas to cover big defects. They tend to have an abnormal shiny reddish appearance that is not as satisfactory cosmetically as the other types of skin graft.

Other tissue transplants. *Cornea.* There are certain forms of blindness in which the eye is entirely normal

Cornea, blood vessel, and heart valves

apart from opacity of the front window, or cornea. The opacity may be the result of disease or injury, but, if the clouded cornea is removed and replaced by a corneal transplant, normal vision can result. Since cells of the cornea remain viable for some 12 hours after death, a cornea can be grafted if it is removed within that period. Cooling will slow the process of deterioration, although the sooner the section of cornea is transplanted the better. The graft bed to which a cornea is transplanted has no blood supply. Nourishment comes directly by diffusion from the tissues. Because most rejection factors are carried in the bloodstream, the lack of blood vessels permits most corneal allografts to survive indefinitely without rejection. Rejection can occur if, as sometimes happens, blood vessels grow into the graft.

Blood vessels.   By far the most satisfactory blood-vessel transplant is an autograft, similar in principle to skin autografts. Blood-vessel grafts are frequently used to bypass arteries that have become blocked or dangerously narrowed by fatty deposits, a condition caused by degenerative atherosclerosis (hardening of the arteries). Such atherosclerotic deposits in the coronary and carotid arteries are responsible, respectively, for most heart attacks and strokes. If atherosclerosis affects the main artery of the leg, the result is, first, pain in the calves, and then gangrene of the foot, necessitating amputation of the leg. If dealt with early, the effects of the arterial blockage can often be overcome by removing a nonessential superficial vein from the leg, reversing it so that the valves will not obstruct blood flow, and then joining this graft to the affected artery above and below the block—thus bypassing the obstruction. Coronary-artery-bypass grafting has become one of the most common surgical operations in developed countries.

Vein or arterial allografts are far less successful. In time the walls tend to degenerate, and the vessels either dilate, with the danger of bursting, or become obstructed.

Heart valves.   Valvular diseases of the heart can be dangerous, since both a blocked valve and a valve that allows blood to leak backward create a strain on the heart that can lead to heart failure. If the valve is seriously damaged it can be replaced with a xenograft valve or a manufactured mechanical valve. Neither is ideal. Xenograft valves have a normal central blood flow, but after a few years they may become rigid and cease to function. Plastic valves—usually of the ball-valve or trapdoor types—force blood to flow around the surface of the ball or trapdoor flap, and this tends to damage red blood cells and cause anemia.

Bone.   When fractures fail to unite, autografts of bone can be extremely valuable in helping the bone to heal. Bone allografts can be used for similar purposes, but they are not as satisfactory, since the bone cells are either dead when grafted or are rejected. Thus, the graft is merely a structural scaffold that, although useful as such, cannot partake actively in healing.

Fascia.   Fascia, sheets of strong connective tissue that surround muscle bundles, may be used as autografts to repair hernias. The principle of use is like that for skin.

Nerves.   Nerves outside the brain and spinal cord can regenerate if damaged. If the delicate sheaths containing the nerves are cut, however, as must happen if a nerve is partially or completely severed, regeneration may not be possible. Even if regeneration occurs it is unlikely to be complete, since most nerves are mixed motor and sensory paths and there is no control ensuring that regenerating fibres take the correct path. Thus, there will always be some fibres that end in the wrong destination and are therefore unable to function. Defective nerve regeneration is the main reason why limb grafts usually are unsatisfactory. A mechanical artificial limb is likely to be of more value to the patient.

Blood.   Blood transfusion has been one of the most important factors in the development of modern surgery. There are many lifesaving surgical procedures that are possible only because the blood loss inevitable in the operation can be made up by transfusion. Blood transfusion is of value in saving life following major injury, bleeding ulcers, childbirth, and many other conditions involving dangerous loss of blood. Purified blood components can be

transfused to treat specific defects; for example, platelets are used to correct a low platelet count, and clotting factor VIII is given to counteract the clotting defect in classic hemophilia.

Bone marrow.   Diseases in which the bone marrow is defective, such as aplastic anemia, may be treated by marrow grafting. Some forms of leukemia can be cured by destroying the patient's bone marrow—the site of the cancerous cells—with drugs and irradiation. Marrow grafting is then necessary to rescue the patient. There is a tendency for the patient to reject the allografted marrow, and there is an additional hazard because immune-system cells in a marrow graft can react against the patient's tissues, causing serious and sometimes fatal graft-versus-host disease. To avoid these complications, special immunosuppressive treatment is given. The use of monoclonal antibodies (see below *Monoclonal antibodies*) to selectively remove harmful lymphocytes from the donor marrow has produced encouraging results in preventing graft-versus-host disease.

ORGAN TRANSPLANTS

Organ transplants are, for a variety of reasons, more difficult to perform successfully than are most other grafts. Despite these difficulties, kidney transplant has now become a routine operation in most developed countries. Heart and liver grafting have also become established, and promising results have been obtained with pancreas and combined heart–lung grafts.

The kidney.   The surgery of kidney transplantation is straightforward, and the patient can be kept fit by dialysis with an artificial kidney before and after the operation. The kidney was the first organ to be transplanted successfully in humans, and experience is now considerable. Effective methods of preventing graft rejection have been available since the 1960s.

Fatal kidney disease is relatively common in young people. When there is deterioration of kidney function, eventually, despite all conventional treatment, the patient becomes extremely weak and anemic. Fluid collects in the tissues, producing swelling, known as dropsy or edema, because the kidneys cannot remove excess water. Fluid in the lungs may cause difficulty in breathing and puts an excessive strain on the heart, which may already be suffering from the effects of high blood pressure as a result of kidney failure.

Waste products that cannot be removed from the body can cause inflammation of the coverings of the heart and the linings of the stomach and colon. As a result, there may be pain in the chest, inflammation of the stomach leading to distressing vomiting, and diarrhea from the colitis. The nerves running to the limbs may be damaged, resulting in paralysis. Treatment with the artificial kidney followed by kidney grafting can eliminate all these symptoms and has a good chance of permitting the dying person to return to a normal existence. Unfortunately, in most countries only a minority of patients receive this treatment. . . .

Transplantation and postoperative care.   The patient may receive a kidney from a live donor or a dead one. Cadaver kidneys may not function immediately after transplantation, and further treatment with the artificial kidney may be required for two to three weeks while damage in the transplanted kidney is repaired. The patient is given drugs that depress immune responses and prevent the graft from being rejected. Immediately after the operation, for the first week or two, every effort is made to keep the patient from contact with bacteria that might cause infection. The patient is usually nursed in a separate room, and doctors and nurses entering the room take care to wear masks and wash their hands before touching him. The air of the room is purified by filtration. Close relatives are allowed to visit the patient, but they are required to take the same precautions. When stitches have been removed the patient is encouraged to get up as much as possible and to be active, but, in the first four months after the operation, careful surveillance is necessary to make sure that the patient is not rejecting the graft or developing an infection. He may be discharged from the hospital within a few weeks of the operation, but frequent return visits are necessary for medical examination and biochemical

Transfusions (margin note)

Effects of kidney disease (margin note)

estimations of the blood constituents, to determine the state of function of the graft, and to make sure that the drugs are not causing side effects. Each patient requires a carefully adjusted dose of the immunosuppressive drugs that prevent transplant rejection.

Once the dosage of immunosuppressive drugs is stabilized, patients are encouraged to go back to a normal existence. . . . Patients can return even to heavy work, . . . but more often a relatively light job is preferable. Women can bear children after a transplant, and men can become fathers. The course of events is not always so happy, unfortunately. If the patient rejects the kidney or develops a serious infection, it may be necessary to remove the graft and stop administration of the immunosuppressive drugs. The patient must then return to regular maintenance treatment with an artificial kidney but may receive a second or even a third graft.

Data on kidney transplant results. In kidney grafts involving identical twins, in which case rejection is not a problem, recipients have survived more than 25 years. A number of patients who have received kidneys from unrelated cadaver donors have survived more than 20 years, demonstrating that in some patients rejection can be controlled with standard immunosuppressive drugs. There has been a gradual improvement in the overall results of kidney transplants. The patient mortality has declined to around 10 percent per year, death usually being due to infection associated with immunosuppressive treatment; to complications of dialysis in patients whose kidneys have failed; or to other facets of kidney disease, such as high blood pressure and coronary artery disease. Recipients also face an increased risk of malignant growths, particularly lymphomata (growths of the lymphoid system that are probably due to virus infections). Kidney-graft survival has improved since the introduction of the immunosuppressive agent cyclosporine (also called cyclosporin A; see below), and many centres have achieved a one-year survival rate of 80 percent and a two-year rate of 70 percent for patients with a functioning kidney graft from an unrelated cadaver donor. One-year survival rates of 80 to 90 percent have been attained for kidney grafts between parent and child and more than 90 percent for grafts from well-matched sibling donors. As these statistics indicate, the patient who develops permanent kidney failure now has a reasonable chance of good treatment from a combination of dialysis and kidney transplantation. Those fortunate enough to receive a well-functioning kidney can expect complete rehabilitation.

The heart. The heart is a pump with a built-in power supply; it has a delicate regulatory mechanism that permits it to perform efficiently under a wide range of demands. During moments of fear, passion, or violent exercise, the heart rate increases greatly, and the contractions become more forceful, so that the pumping of the blood intrudes on the consciousness; this is experienced by the individual as palpitations. Cessation of the heartbeat has also been, throughout the ages, the cardinal sign of death. Thus, it is perhaps not so surprising that there was an intense public interest when the first attempts were made at transplanting a human heart. The objectives of heart transplantation, nevertheless, are the same as those of other organ grafts.

One of the most important advances in surgery since World War II has been in direct operations on the heart. Heart valves are repaired or replaced with artificial valves, and techniques have been developed so that the heart can be stopped and its function taken over temporarily by an electrical pump. If, however, the muscle of the heart is destroyed, as occurs in certain diseases, the only operation that can cure the patient is to replace the heart with a graft or possibly an artificial heart. Blockage of the coronary arteries and certain other heart-muscle diseases can kill the patient because the muscle of the heart cannot contract properly. A patient with one of these diseases who is close to dying is, therefore, a possible recipient for a heart transplant.

A group of American investigators perfected the technique of heart transplantation in the late 1950s. They showed that a transplanted dog's heart could provide the animal with a normal circulation until the heart was re-

jected. The features of rejection of the heart are similar to those of the kidney. The cells that produce immune reactions, the lymphocytes, migrate into the muscle cells of the heart, damage it, and also block the coronary arteries, depriving the heart of its own circulation. In most experiments it was more difficult to prevent rejection of the heart than of the kidney. Despite this, rejection was prevented for long periods in animals. Based on this experimental work, the next logical step was to transplant a human heart into a patient dying of incurable heart disease. This step was taken in 1967 by a surgical team in Cape Town, South Africa.

In the years immediately following the first transplant, numerous heart allografts were performed at medical centres throughout the world. Unfortunately, many recipients succumbed to rejection of the transplanted organ. Furthermore, the heart is more sensitive to lack of blood than the kidneys are; it must be removed from the donor more quickly and can be preserved without damage for only a short period of time. Because of these difficulties—particularly the problem of rejection—the number of heart transplants performed worldwide dropped considerably after the initial excitement abated. Steady advances in detecting and treating rejection were made throughout the 1970s, however; and the introduction of the immunosuppressant cyclosporine in the 1980s brought even further improvements in the long-term survival rates for heart-graft recipients. Interest in the procedure revived, and many hundreds of heart transplants have now been performed. A number of patients have lived five or more years after the operation. . . .

The liver. Many of the functions of the liver are not known. It is a complicated organ that produces the clotting factors and many other vital substances in the blood and that removes many wastes and poisons from the circulation. It is, in effect, a chemical factory. The two categories of fatal liver disease that may be treated by liver grafting are nonmalignant destructive diseases of the liver cells—for example, cirrhosis—and primary cancer of the liver affecting either the main liver cells or the bile ducts. The liver is extremely sensitive to lack of blood supply and must be cooled within 15 minutes of the death of the donor. The operation can be difficult, since the liver is rather large and of complex structure. Both its removal from the cadaver and its grafting into the recipient are major surgical operations. The operation is more difficult in humans than in animals; particularly, the removal of the diseased liver from the recipient. This may be much enlarged and adherent to surrounding structures so that its removal may result in serious bleeding. Once transplanted, the liver must function immediately or the patient will die. There is no treatment available that is comparable to the use of the artificial kidney for kidney disease. If the liver functions well immediately after transplantation, the rest of the management is similar to that followed in kidney operations, and the same drugs are given. Many early liver transplantation operations failed, but an increasing number have successfully restored dying patients to normal existence. Children do especially well following liver transplantation. The commonest fatal liver disease in childhood is a congenital deficiency of bile ducts called biliary atresia. Several centres have obtained a 90 percent one-year survival in children after liver grafting, although up to 25 percent of these patients may require retransplantation due to failure of the first graft.

The lung. Chronic fatal disease of the lung is common, but the progress of the disease is usually slow, and the patient may be ill for a long time. When the lung eventually fails, the patient is likely to be unfit for a general anesthetic and an operation. The function of the lung is to allow exchange of gases between the blood and the air. The gas passes through an extremely fine membrane lining the air spaces. This exposure to air makes the lungs susceptible to infection, more so than any other organs that have been grafted. Lung infection is one of the commonest causes of death after the grafting of other organs, and it is consequently not surprising that infection has caused failure of many lung transplants. Even a mild rejection reaction can severely damage the gas-exchange membrane, and the patient may die before the rejection is reversed. The actual ventilation of the lungs by rhythmic breathing is a complicated movement controlled by nerves connecting the brain to the lungs and to the muscles that produce the breathing. Cutting the nerves can interfere with the rhythmicity of breathing, and this may be an important cause of the difficulties of successfully transplanting both lungs. Nevertheless, these difficulties have been overcome. If only one lung is transplanted, however, the patient's own diseased lung may interfere with the function of the graft by robbing it of air and directing too much blood into the graft. Further progress may depend on a safer, more perfect control of rejection. Currently, grafting both lungs with the heart is the best method of achieving a satisfactory lung graft.

The heart and lungs. The technique of transplanting the heart and both lungs as a functioning unit was developed in animal experiments at Stanford Medical Center in California. Despite the technical feasibility of the operation, rejection could not be controlled by conventional immunosuppression. With the availability of cyclosporine researchers were able to obtain long-term survivors with combined heart–lung transplants in primate species. Applications to human patients have been remarkably successful. Two-thirds of the patients who received transplants at Stanford are surviving, and other centres have adopted this treatment for patients with severe lung fibrosis and failure of the right side of the heart, which pumps blood into the lungs. Unfortunately, many organ donors have been maintained on ventilators, a process that frequently leads to lung infections; as a consequence, the availability of donor heart–lung units is limited. Furthermore, the lungs are vulnerable to damage from lack of blood, and so transplantation must be performed expeditiously.

The pancreas. The pancreas consists of two kinds of tissues: endocrine and exocrine. The latter produces pancreatic juice, a combination of digestive enzymes that empty via a duct into the small intestine. The endocrine tissue of the pancreas—the islets of Langerhans—secrete the hormones insulin and glucagon into the bloodstream. These hormones are vital to the regulation of carbohydrate metabolism and exert wide-ranging effects on the growth and maintenance of body tissues. Insufficient insulin production results in type I diabetes mellitus, a disease that is fatal without daily injections of insulin. Even with insulin therapy, many diabetics suffer kidney failure and blindness due to the disease's effects on the small blood vessels. There are reasons to believe that a normally functioning pancreas graft will prevent the progression of these complications.

Much effort has been devoted to removing the islets of Langerhans from the pancreas with a view to grafting the separated islets or even the isolated insulin-producing beta cells. Unfortunately, it is very difficult to obtain sufficient islets from the fibrotic human pancreas, and it appears that isolated islets are highly susceptible to rejection. A number of clinical attempts at islet grafting have been made without long-term success. Transplanting the vascularized pancreas has, however, been more encouraging. It is customary to graft the body and tail of the pancreas; that is, half the pancreas is transplanted, using the splenic artery and vein for vascular anastomosis. One of the difficulties with this procedure has been dealing with the digestive juice produced by the transplanted pancreas. A further complicating factor has been the fact that corticosteroids—frequently used for immunosuppression in transplant patients—aggravate diabetes. The availability of cyclosporine has permitted the avoidance of corticosteroids and has prompted renewed interest in pancreas grafting. The procedure is particularly attractive when a patient with diabetic kidney failure can receive a kidney and pancreas graft from the same donor. A technique with encouraging early results has been to insert the pancreas graft very close to the patient's own pancreas in the so-called paratopic position. This allows drainage of insulin directly into the liver, while the pancreatic juice is diverted into the stomach, where the digestive enzymes are inhibited by stomach acid. It is certainly most gratifying to patients who have been undergoing regular dialysis and taking insulin to be free from both these onerous treatments and to be permitted to eat and drink without restriction. The one-year functional survival rate for pancreatic grafts has reached 30 percent; further advances in surgical technique will be needed before the rate matches the results obtained in kidney grafts. It is of interest that the vascularized pancreas probably is less susceptible to rejection than the kidney.

SPECIAL LEGAL AND ETHICAL PROBLEMS

Legal aspects. In most countries, the law on organ transplantation is poorly defined, as legislation has not yet been created to cope with this advance in surgery. The existing framework relating to physical assault and care of the dead has no provision for organ transplantation. It is customary to ask the permission of the relatives, but, because organ removal must take place immediately after death, it may be impossible to reach the relatives in time. It has been suggested that there should be a widespread campaign to encourage persons to provide in their wills that their organs be used for transplantation. An alternative is to provide by law that permission is assumed unless removal has been forbidden by the individual in his lifetime. Such laws have been passed in Denmark, France, Sweden, Austria, and Israel. Compulsory postmortem examination, a far more extensive procedure than organ removal for grafting, is required in most countries after unexpected death. . . .

Ethical considerations. *Defining death.* Transplantation has obviously raised important ethical considerations concerning the diagnosis of death of potential donors, and, particularly, how far resuscitation should be continued. Every effort must be made to restore the heartbeat to someone who has had a sudden cardiac arrest or breathing to someone who cannot breathe. Artificial respiration and massage of the heart, the standard methods of resuscitation, are continued until it is clear that the brain is dead. Most physicians consider that beyond this point efforts at resuscitation are useless.

In many countries, the question of how to diagnose brain death—that is, irreversible destruction of the brain—has been debated by neurologists and other medical specialists. Most of these experts agree that when the brain stem is destroyed there can be no recovery. The brain stem controls the vital function of breathing and the reflexes of the eyes and ears, and it transmits all information between the brain and the rest of the body. Most countries have established strict guidelines for how brain-stem death is to be diagnosed and what cases are to be excluded—for example, patients who have been poisoned, have been given drugs, or have developed hypothermia. The neurological signs of brain-stem death must be elicited by a trained clinician who is not concerned directly with the transplant operation. These signs are reverified after an interval, and, if there is the slightest doubt, further reverifications are made until the criteria are unequivocally met. The guidelines are not seriously disputed, and there has never been a recovery in a case that fulfilled the criteria of brain-stem death.

Shortage of donors. Another area of ethical concern is the dilemma posed by the shortage of donor organs. Advances in immunosuppressive therapy have put increasing pressure on the supply of donor organs, and medical personnel sometimes find themselves having to determine who among the potential recipients should receive a life-saving graft. Furthermore, there is a danger of commercial interests becoming involved with people willing to sell their organs for personal gain, and there is definite risk that organized crime might procure organs for rich and unscrupulous people.

REJECTION

Human beings possess complex defense mechanisms against bacteria, viruses, and other foreign materials that enter the body. These mechanisms, which collectively make up the immune system, cannot, unfortunately, differentiate between disease-causing microorganisms and the cells of a lifesaving transplant. Both are perceived as foreign, and both are subject to attack by the immune sys-

Determination of brain death

tem. This immune reaction leads to rejection, the greatest problem in successful tissue and organ grafting.

Immune responses. In order to understand why rejection occurs and how it may be prevented, it is necessary to know something of the operations of the immune system. The key cells of the immune system are the white blood cells known as lymphocytes. These are of two basic types: T lymphocytes and B lymphocytes. These cells have the capacity to distinguish "self" substances from such "nonself" substances as microorganisms and foreign tissue cells. Substances that provoke an immune reaction are recognized by the presence of certain molecules, called antigens, on their surface.

T lymphocytes are responsible for what is called cell-mediated immunity, so named because the T cells themselves latch onto the antigens of the invader and then initiate reactions that lead to the destruction of the nonself matter. B lymphocytes, on the other hand, do not directly attack invaders. Rather, they produce antibodies, proteins that are capable of initiating reactions that weaken or destroy the foreign substance. The overall immune reaction is exceedingly complex, with T lymphocytes, B lymphocytes, macrophages (scavenger cells), and various circulating chemicals waging a coordinated assault on the invader.

The mechanisms of rejection

Transplant rejection is generally caused by cell-mediated responses. The process usually occurs over days or months, as the T lymphocytes stimulate the infiltration and destruction of the graft. The transplant may be saved if the cell-mediated reactions can be suppressed. Antibody attack of transplanted tissues is most apparent when the recipient has preexisting antibodies against the antigens of the donor. This situation can arise if the recipient has been previously exposed to foreign antigens as the result of pregnancy (during which the mother is exposed to fetal antigens contributed by the father), blood transfusions, or prior transplants. Unlike a cell-mediated reaction, antibody-mediated rejection is rapid, occurring within minutes or hours, and cannot be reversed.

Selection of donor and tissue matching. The factors that provoke graft rejection are called transplantation, or histocompatibility, antigens. If donor and recipient have the same antigens, as do identical twins, there can be no rejection. All cells in the body have transplantation antigens except the red blood cells, which carry their own system of blood-group (ABO) antigens. The main human transplantation antigens—called the major histocompatibility complex, or the HLA (human leukocyte group A) system—are governed by genes on the sixth chromosome. HLA antigens are divided into two groups; class I antigens, which are the target of an effector rejection response; and class II antigens, which are the initiators of the rejection reaction. Class II antigens are not found in all tissues, although class I antigens are. Certain macrophage-like tissue cells—called dendritic cells because of their finger-like processes—have a high expression of class II antigens. There has been much interest in trying to remove such cells from an organ graft, so that the rejection reaction will not be initiated. There has been some experimental success with this approach, although it has not yet been applied clinically.

Histocompatibility antigens

Tissue typing

Tissue typing involves the identification of an individual's HLA antigens. Lymphocytes are used for typing. It is important also that the red blood cells be grouped, since red-cell-group antigens are present in other tissues and can cause graft rejection. Although transplantation antigens are numerous and complicated, the principles of tissue typing are the same as for red-cell grouping. The lymphocytes being typed are mixed with a typing reagent, a serum that contains antibodies to certain HLA antigens. If the lymphocytes carry HLA antigens for which the reagent has antibodies, the lymphocytes agglutinate (clump together) or die. Typing serums are obtained from the blood of persons who have rejected grafts or have had multiple blood transfusions or multiple pregnancies; as previously stated, such persons may develop antibodies to transplantation antigens.

If the lymphocytes of both the recipient and the potential donor are killed by a given serum, then, as far as that typing serum is concerned, the individuals have antigens in common. If neither donor nor recipient lymphocytes are affected, then donor and recipient lack antigens in common. If the donor lymphocytes are killed but not those of the recipient, then an antigen is present in the donor and is missing from the recipient. Thus, by testing their lymphocytes against a spectrum of typing sera, it is possible to determine how closely the recipient and donor match in HLA antigens. As a final precaution before grafting, a direct crossmatch is performed between the recipient's serum and donor lymphocytes. A positive crossmatch usually contraindicates the donor–recipient transplant under consideration.

There is now considerable knowledge concerning the inheritance of transplantation antigens, but, even so, tissue typing is not sufficiently advanced to give an accurate prediction of the outcome of a graft in an individual case, particularly when the donor and recipient are not related to one another. In accordance with Mendelian laws of inheritance, a person obtains one of a pair of chromosomes from each parent. Therefore, a parent-to-child transplant will always be half-matched for transplantation antigens. Siblings have a one-in-four chance of a complete match of the HLA antigens, a one-in-four chance of no match, and a one-in-two chance of a half-match.

The blood-transfusion effect. Since following a blood transfusion some patients become sensitized to the transplantation antigens of the donor, it was expected that prior blood transfusion could only harm the recipient's prospects for a successful organ graft. Careful analysis of results, however, showed the contrary. Specifically, the results of kidney grafting in patients who had received previous blood transfusions without regard to HLA matching were much better than in patients who had never received a blood transfusion. Although a great deal of effort has been expended to determine the mechanisms involved, researchers still do not know how the immune system is modified by prior blood transfusions. Most centres now give blood transfusions before transplantation, though some patients do develop HLA antibodies against a wide spectrum of the population and therefore become very difficult to transplant. This pool of highly sensitized patients is getting larger throughout the world, not only from blood transfusions, but also from patients who have rejected kidney grafts and are back on dialysis, and from women who have had multiple pregnancies.

Donor-specific blood transfusions

A special application of the blood-transfusion effect involves repeated small blood transfusions from a potential donor who is a close relative of the patient. If sensitization does not occur, subsequent kidney-graft results are excellent. Some patients, however, develop a positive crossmatch to donor lymphocytes and cannot receive a graft from that donor.

Immunosuppression. The aim of transplantation research is to allow the recipient to accept the graft permanently with no unpleasant side effects. With current drugs that are used for this purpose, after some months the dosage can often be reduced and sometimes even stopped without the graft's being rejected. In such a case, the patient is no longer susceptible to infections. There would appear to be adaptation of the recipient toward the graft and the graft toward the recipient. The adaptation is probably akin to desensitization, a process used sometimes to cure patients suffering from asthma by giving them repeated injections of small doses of the pollen to which they are sensitive.

Azathioprine. Azathioprine is one of the most widely used immunosuppressive agents; it also has been used to treat leukemia. It can be given by mouth, but the dose must be carefully adjusted so that the blood-cell-forming tissues in the bone marrow are not damaged, which could lead to infections and bleeding. The white-blood-cell and platelet counts need to be determined frequently to make sure that azathioprine is not being given in too large a dose. It is an extremely valuable drug and has been the basis of most immunosuppressive regimens in patients with organ grafts. At first, high doses are given, but eventually the doses may be reduced. Even years after transplantation, small doses of azathioprine may still be needed to maintain coexistence between graft and host.

Corticosteroids. Cortisone and its relatives, prednisone and prednisolone, are very useful in patients with organ grafts. They can be given by mouth, but although not damaging to the blood-forming cells, they do predispose the body to infection, cause stunted growth in children, and have other injurious effects. Persons receiving these substances may develop bloated complexions with swollen faces, may tend to gain weight and become diabetic, and their bones may become brittle. Few recipients of organ transplants, however, can do without corticosteroids, particularly during an active rejection crisis.

Antilymphocyte serum. If rabbits receive repeated injections of mouse lymphocytes, they become immunized and develop antibodies against the mouse cells. The serum from the rabbits' blood can be injected into mice and will often prevent them from rejecting grafts, both from other mice and even, sometimes, from other species. Such antilymphocyte serums can be produced between a variety of species, but in higher mammals, particularly humans, it has been difficult to obtain a powerful immunosuppressive serum without side effects of toxicity.

The activity of the serum lies in its gamma globulin, which contains the antibody proteins. Antilymphocyte globulin is used in humans but contains many proteins that are ineffective and may be harmful. It can be added to standard azathioprine and cortisone treatment without adding to the toxicity of these agents, and it is extremely useful in treating rejection crisis in kidney-graft recipients who have not responded to corticosteroids. Unfortunately, it has been difficult to obtain a consistently effective product, and there are not good methods of assaying the potency of one serum compared with another. Even when they are prepared by exactly the same methods from the same species, one batch may differ greatly from another. The horse has usually been used to produce antilymphocyte serum for the treatment of human patients, but some persons are sensitive to horse proteins and become extremely ill when treated with horse serum. Such patients may, however, be successfully treated with rabbit antilymphocyte globulin.

Monoclonal antibodies. An important development in antibody production followed the discovery that an antibody-forming lymphocyte can be fused with a cancerous bone-marrow cell. The resulting hybrid cell produces the antibody specified by its lymphocyte progenitor, while from the cancer cell it obtains the characteristic of multiplying indefinitely in laboratory cultures. The culturing of the hybrid yields a clone of cells that produce one specific antibody—a "monoclonal" antibody. Such agents are exclusively specific in action and there is no theoretical limit to the number of antibodies that can be produced by different hybrid cell lines. Monoclonal antibodies can be regarded as highly specific antilymphocyte globulin without many of the unwanted materials that are present in the ordinary, polyclonal antilymphocyte serum described above. Some monoclonal antibodies have been produced that appear to be effective as immunosuppressive agents in humans. Further advances in this area are expected.

Cyclosporine. A new type of immunosuppressive agent was found as a natural product of an earth fungus by the Sandoz Laboratories. This material, called cyclosporine, is a stable, cyclic peptide with powerful immunosuppressive activity affecting especially the T lymphocytes. Cyclosporine was found to prevent organ graft rejection in a number of animal species, and when the drug was used in humans the expected immunosuppressive effect was again observed. It has been used in recipients of all types of organ grafts with improved immunosuppressive results. Unfortunately, cyclosporine is toxic to the human kidney, and there is fear that prolonged use of the agent could lead to permanent renal damage. Cyclosporine also increases the growth of hair on the face and body, which can be distressing to female patients. It is a difficult drug to use because, being fat soluble, its absorption is variable and each patient needs to be individually studied to ensure that the dosage is adequate but not excessive.

It is clear that none of the agents so far used to prevent rejection is ideal. No one would use such dangerous agents except as a last resort in a desperate situation. This, unfortunately, is the exact plight of a person in need of a vital organ transplant. Immunosuppression is, however, much more effective and less dangerous than it used to be, and we can expect advances with new chemical derivatives, in particular monoclonal antibodies and nontoxic analogues of cyclosporine.

ORGAN AND TISSUE BANKS

Without a blood supply organs deteriorate rapidly. Cooling can slow down the process but cannot stop it. Organs differ in their susceptibility to damage. At body temperature, irreversible destruction of the brain occurs after more than three to five minutes; of the heart, liver, pancreas, and lung, after 10 to 30 minutes; of the kidney, after 50 to 100 minutes; and of the skin and cornea, after six to 12 hours. Although the shorter the time the organ is deprived of its blood supply the better, the cornea can be removed for grafting at relative leisure, but every minute is of vital importance for a liver transplant. When a kidney is removed from a living donor, it is not necessary to use elaborate preservation techniques. The operations on the donor and recipient are performed at the same time, and the recipient is prepared to receive the graft by the time that the donor organ is removed. Cadaver kidneys are removed as soon as possible after the donor's death, preferably within an hour. Cool solutions are infused into the blood vessels of the kidney, which is then kept at 4° C (39° F) in a refrigerator or surrounded by ice in a vacuum flask. At the same time, the recipient is prepared for operation. Kidneys can be conserved in this simple way for 24 to 48 hours with little deterioration, and during this time they can be moved for long distances. For a kidney to be preserved from 48 to 72 hours, a complicated machine is required to provide artificial circulation. Cool, oxygenated, physiological solutions, with the same osmotic pressure as blood, are passed through the blood vessels of the kidney. The imperfections of the machinery mean that there is a slow deterioration of the organ that does not occur normally in the body. To keep a kidney undamaged for longer than 72 hours is difficult. Blood cells, spermatozoa, and certain other dissociated tissue cells can be frozen to subzero temperatures and kept alive indefinitely. Special preserving fluids will prevent cell destruction by ice crystals, but these fluids have damaging effects if introduced into whole organs such as the kidney.

Long-term storage and banking of organs seem unlikely in the near future. Preservation techniques for the heart, lung, liver, and pancreas have not been so extensively studied as the kidney. The principles are the same, although these other organs will not tolerate such long periods without a blood supply. Grafting is performed as quickly as possible, preferably within eight hours for the liver and pancreas, four hours for the heart, and two hours for the combined heart-and-lung graft. Much research will be necessary before it is possible to keep organs banked in the way that blood can be stored.

Preservation of kidneys for transplantation

BIBLIOGRAPHY. FRANCIS D. MOORE, *Give and Take* (1964), an account of the history of organ transplantation; *Ethics in Medical Progress*, ed. by G.E.W. WOLSTENHOLME and MAEVE O' CONNOR (1966), proceedings of a symposium sponsored by the Ciba Foundation, discussing the ethical aspects of transplantation; ROY Y. CALNE, *Renal Transplantation*, 2nd ed. (1967), a technical account of kidney grafting . . . ; his *A Gift of Life* (1970), a book for the nonspecialist, covering the immunological and clinical aspects and the ethics of organ grafting; RUSSELL SCOTT, *The Body As Property* (1981), a comprehensive examination of the ethical and legal aspects . . . . THOMAS E. STARZL, *Experience in Hepatic Transplantation* (1969), the first full account of the pioneer work on liver grafting; *Liver Transplantation: The Cambridge-King's College Hospital Experience,* ed. by ROY Y. CALNE (1983), a later source on liver grafting; CHRISTOPHER PALLIS, *ABC of Brain Stem Death* (1983), a collection of articles from the *British Medical Journal* . . . ; PETER J. MORRIS (ed.), *Kidney Transplantation: Principles and Practice,* 2nd ed. (1984), a work on theory and methods; ROBERTA G. SIMMONS, SUSAN D. KLEIN, and RICHARD L. SIMMONS, *Gift of Life: The Social and Psychological Impact of Organ Transplantation* (1977), a work based on exhaustive studies.

ROY YORKE CALNE. Professor of Surgery, University of Cambridge. Author of *Renal Transplantation* and other books.

WORLD
OF
MEDICINE

A review of
recent developments
in health and medicine

Aerospace Medicine

In 1985 and early 1986 the National Aeronautics and Space Administration's (NASA's) fleet of shuttle orbiters made a total of ten round-trip excursions to and from Earth orbit. *Columbia, Atlantis, Discovery,* and *Challenger* carried payloads of valuable satellites and invaluable scientific experiments into the weightless environment of space. The voyagers aboard the spacecraft included civilian and military astronauts, national and international scientists from both academia and industry, physicians, a U.S. senator, a member of the House of Representatives, and even an Arabian prince. Hundreds of experiments were performed in the diverse scientific disciplines of astronomy, solar physics, materials science, atmospheric physics, fluid mechanics, and the medical and life sciences.

Medical tests to detect and record bodily changes in shuttle astronauts exposed to weightlessness began in 1982 on the fourth shuttle mission. However, because of limited crew-member time on subsequent flights, many of the experiments scheduled as part of this ongoing program could not be performed.

April 12, 1985, mission

On April 12, 1985, the 16th space transportation system (STS) shuttle mission was launched carrying a test subject whose primary responsibility was to conduct and participate in various medical tests. E. J. ("Jake") Garn, a U.S. senator from Utah, traveled aboard flight STS 51-D, serving both as a subject for medical tests and as a congressional observer.

During launch Garn wore a waist belt that pressed two stethoscope microphones firmly against his abdomen. At main engine cutoff, about 8½ minutes into the flight, he plugged the belt into a portable tape recorder stored in the seat flight bag and began recording his bowel sounds to evaluate early inflight changes in gastric motility. This was yet another attempt to gain some insight into the still unsolved problem of space adaptation syndrome (SAS), a form of motion sickness that affects 50% of space travelers. Garn also wore instruments to measure his blood pressure, heart rate, and other changes in cardiac action during reentry into the Earth's atmosphere and in the event of SAS in orbit.

Echocardiography is a clinical technique that uses very high frequency sound waves to measure changes in heart pump action and size. A 19.5-kg (43-lb) echocardiograph instrument, tested on Garn, was carried aboard 51-D in order to study how the cardiovascular system adapts to weightlessness. Valuable inflight data were obtained, which will be used to develop countermeasures to crew cardiovascular changes (particularly during reentry) and to ensure safety during long-term exposure to weightlessness.

Garn measured his height and girth in orbit and wore a special leg stocking (plethysmograph) to measure leg volume changes that result from the shifting of fluids during adaptation to weightlessness. Space travelers may "grow" up to five centimeters (two inches) when the skeletal system is no longer compressed by gravity.

In a further medical experiment Garn collected saliva specimens for analysis after taking several doses of acetaminophen, a nonaspirin analgesic. This was done in order to determine if medication dosage in space is comparable to that on Earth.

Meanwhile, on *Discovery*'s middeck, an ongoing experiment of great importance to modern medicine was being conducted by payload specialist Charles D. Walker of McDonnell Douglas Corp. He operated the continuous flow electrophoresis system (CFES), which separates and collects quantities of biologic materials for use in new pharmaceuticals. This was the sixth spaceflight on which CFES was tested and the second flight for Walker. The first CFES test unit (on

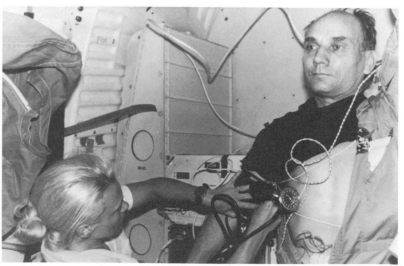

Astronaut Rhea Seddon applies a blood pressure cuff to Sen. Jake Garn on board space shuttle Discovery's *mid-April 1985 mission. Garn served as a medical test subject for a study of how the cardiovascular system adapts to weightlessness, which is of particular concern during reentry into Earth's atmosphere.*

the fourth shuttle mission, in 1982) verified that the process known as electrophoresis, which separates protein materials from their surrounding medium by utilizing an electric field, can, in processing biologic materials in the absence of the effects of gravity, yield 400 times the output and up to 5 times the purity as the same method on Earth.

Recognizing that pharmaceuticals of unprecedented purity can be produced cheaply and efficiently in space by the use of electrophoresis, private industry has invested tens of millions of dollars over the past several years to launch a commercial pharmaceutical production program in space. Just some of the more than 50 anticipated space-produced pharmaceuticals are (1) beta cells of the pancreas, which, when isolated on a mass basis, could provide single-injection cures for an estimated 3.2 million diabetic patients per year; (2) interferon, a substance that provides the body with immunity to viral infections and has shown promise for its role in the treatment of certain cancers; this drug could offer benefits to 20 million persons yearly; and (3) epidermal growth factors in the skin, important for treating burns and facilitating wound healing in more than one million patients each year. Approximately one million additional patients yearly could benefit from other space-made products such as growth hormone to stimulate bone growth in children with deficiencies of this substance, α_1-antitrypsin to limit the progress of emphysema and enhance cancer chemotherapy, anti-hemophilic factors to help control a sometimes lethal blood disorder, and erythropoitin, which modulates the formation of red blood cells and hemoglobin.

June 17 mission

French and Soviet investigators, also intensely interested in echocardiography, flew the French echocardiograph experiment (FEE) on a Soviet Salyut mission in July 1982. The FEE was included in the scientific payload of shuttle mission 51-G, launched on June 17, 1985, as part of a cooperative project with the Centre National d'Etudes Spatiales of France. The June flight, the 18th of the space shuttle program, was distinctively international as NASA flew the first French payload specialist, Patrick Baudry, and an Arabian payload specialist, Prince Sultan Salman as-Saud. Flight 51-G carried in its cargo bay U.S., Mexican, and Arabian domestic communications satellites and three West German small, self-contained payloads known as getaway specials.

On shuttle mission 51-G, Baudry, the French astronaut, carried out biomedical experiments similar to those flown by a French cosmonaut aboard the previous Soviet manned mission. Prince Sultan, in addition to conducting 70-mm photography over Saudi Arabia and photographing a fluids phase separation experiment, participated in parts of a French postural experiment.

Soviet and French cosmonauts Aleksandr Ivanchenkov, Vladimir Dzhanibekov, and Jean-Loup Chretien, above, carried out a series of biomedical tests in 1982 that were continued in 1985 on a joint U.S.-French mission.

The postural tests were a sophisticated series of on-orbit experiments designed to study four areas of human sensorimotor functions: muscular tone, posture, orientation, and movement. Interaction of these functional modes in people permits vertical mobility within the Earth's gravitational field and enables them to maintain their orientation in three-dimensional space. These sensorimotor mechanisms must adapt in space when the physical bias and point of reference normally provided by gravity on Earth are no longer present. A better understanding of this adaptive process not only may help to solve the problem of space adaptation syndrome but also may provide new insights into how these functional modes interact on Earth.

The French postural experiment utilized biochemical electronic sensors, data tape recorders, and a camera to make measurements of muscular activity (electromyography), angular head movements, and involuntary oscillations of the eyes (nystagmus). During in-flight operation, the experiments were conducted by Baudry and Prince Sultan once a day on a noninterference basis with the planned crew activity throughout the mission. Each experimental session required about 65 minutes, including setup and calibration, plus an additional 30 minutes for unstowage and stowage.

October 30 mission

On Oct. 30, 1985, STS 61-A carried aloft the Deutschland Spacelab Mission D-1. Spacelab D-1, managed by the Federal German Aerospace Research Establishment for the German Federal Ministry of Research and Technology, was the first of a series of West German missions on the space shuttle. Used by West German and other European universities, research institutes, and industrial enterprises, the D-1 was designed for scientific and technological research. The experimental facilities were arranged according to scientific disciplines into so-called payload elements. The facilities were provided by the West Germans, the European

On Discovery*'s flight 51-G Sultan Salman as-Saud (left) eats a meal while French payload specialist Patrick Baudry conducts a test involving sensory and motor functions.*

Space Agency (ESA), and NASA. Among the materials included were melting furnaces, equipment for observing fluid physics phenomena, chambers for providing specific environmental conditions for testing living animals and plants, and the so-called vestibular sled.

The vestibular sled is a contribution of the ESA consisting of a seat for a test subject that can be moved backward and forward with precisely adjusted accelerations along rails fixed on the floor of spacelab's aisle. The seat is driven by an electromotor and traction rope. The sled permits tests that investigate the functional organization of the human vestibular and spatial orientation system and the vestibular adaptation processes in weightlessness. These acceleration studies were combined with thermal stimulation of the inner ear and optokinetic stimulation of the eyes in an effort to understand mechanisms of graviperception (how gravity is perceived) in humans.

November 26 mission

The continuous flow electrophoresis system, which had flown aboard *Discovery* in April, was carried aloft again in November 1985, this time aboard orbiter *At-*

lantis*.* Payload specialist Charles D. Walker was in attendance for the third time. The objective of this mission was to separate a sufficient quantity of biologic material for animal and clinical testing of a breakthrough pharmaceutical. Results from mission 51-D in April had shown that preflight levels of cleanliness and sterility could be maintained in the shuttle environment. Walker tested daily for the presence of bacterial contamination by withdrawing small samples of fluid from five locations in his own body and incubating them in vials previously loaded with freeze-dried reactants. He also reconfigured a device to observe the effects that varying sample concentrations have on the efficiency of the process. It was expected that sufficient concentrated protein material would be obtained during this flight to allow the necessary testing to obtain U.S. Food and Drug Administration approval of new, marketable drug products.

A phenomenon of equal interest to the physicist and the medical scientist is the enhanced formation of pure crystals in space. A series of experiments are being conducted to study the possibility of crystallizing biologic materials such as hormones, enzymes, and other proteins. Detailed knowledge of the nature, chemistry, composition, and structure of these materials is extremely important to the ability to manufacture them for medical purposes. However, on Earth it has not been possible to grow crystals of most complex proteins that are large enough to permit their three-dimensional atomic structure to be determined by X-ray or neutron diffraction crystallography. A key objective of the overall protein crystal growth program is to enable rational and specific drug design rather than the present empirical approach to enzyme engineering and the manufacture of most chemotherapeutic agents.

Jan. 12, 1986, mission

A device developed by the Marshall Space Flight Center, Huntsville, Ala., that enabled the growth of crystals in the weightlessness of orbital spaceflight where gravity-driven convection currents do not exist and where the crystals do not sediment but remain suspended while they develop optimum size and configuration was taken on flight 61-C. A protein crystal growth experiment utilized two vapor diffusion crystal growth units and one dialysis unit. Each vapor diffusion unit was 8 cm (3 in) wide, 36 cm (14 in) long, and 1 cm (½ in) thick and contained 24 small crystal growth chambers. Each of the 48 chambers was equipped with a porous liner saturated with a precipitating agent such as alcohol or saline solution. A small drop of protein solution was injected into each chamber shortly after entering orbit. Up to six of the growth chambers were "seeded" by injecting a microscopic particle of crystallized protein into the droplet to form a nucleus for a larger crystal.

The even smaller dialysis unit had an internal cylin-

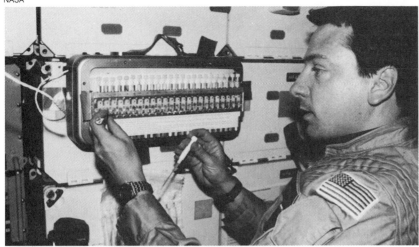

Payload specialist Charles D. Walker of the McDonnell Douglas Corp. conducts a protein growth experiment—one of a series of tests carried on shuttle missions to study the possibility of processing vast quantities of exceptionally pure biologic materials in space for use in pharmaceuticals.

drical cavity containing small glass ampoules of precipitating solution suspended in water. Also suspended in the cavity were three small dialysis ampoules activated by shaking the unit, causing the fragile glass to break and release the precipitating agent to mix with the water. The proteins in the dialysis ampoules were then crystallized out through the dialysis process, which allows this separation of substances. After photographs were taken of the above processes, the units were stowed to allow crystallization to proceed in a vibration-free, gravity-free environment. At the end of the mission, the units were photographed again and prepared for entry, landing, and removal.

U.S. Rep. Bill Nelson (Dem., Fla.) operated the so-called hand-held protein crystal growth experiment as a payload specialist aboard flight 61-C. These operations involved the use of four pieces of equipment designed to grow 60 different types of crystals—12 by dialysis and 48 by the vapor diffusion method.

Nelson also participated in ten detailed supplementary objective studies for NASA's Space Biomedical Research Institute. These included observations of the physiological adaptation of the sensorimotor and cardiovascular systems as well as studies of fluid shifts, electrolyte changes, and pharmacokinetics. The results of these studies will provide additional insight into the effects of weightlessness on the body's systems and will be used in the development of countermeasures against the adverse aspects of physiological adaptation.

Nelson assisted another mission specialist on 61-C, George Nelson (no relation), in monitoring the operations of the initial blood storage experiment. The objective of this experiment was to better understand the factors that limit the storage of human blood on Earth. The experiment attempted to isolate factors, such as sedimentation, that occur under standard blood bank conditions. Whole blood and blood components that had experienced weightless conditions in orbit were compared with control samples stored in otherwise comparable conditions on Earth. The blood samples were housed in four stainless steel drawers placed in two orbiter middeck lockers. With the exception of weightlessness, the conditions for both the flight samples and the control samples on the ground were identical to those in a standard blood bank. Specified temperature levels were maintained by thermoelectric coolers. After the orbiter landed, the blood storage experiment was removed and prepared for shipment to investigators' laboratories in Boston for analysis.

1986: tragedy in space

There were other significant experiments conducted on shuttle flights in 1985. But for all its accomplishments, 1985 was just a prelude to the grand events planned for 1986. The 25th anniversary of manned space and the beginning of an era that might well see humans leave the planet Earth for interplanetary colonization, 1986 was to be the most active and perhaps the most important year in the history of space exploration.

However, the ill-fated flight of shuttle *Challenger* that took the lives of seven American astronauts on Jan. 28, 1986, effectively put the space program on hold. But the program will not be canceled. "We'll continue our quest in space," Pres. Ronald Reagan said after learning of the terrible tragedy. "The future . . . belongs to the brave." The choice to risk one's life, not in the struggle for survival but for purely abstract reasons, is perhaps the most distinctive and most ennobling quality of the human spirit. The men and women of *Challenger*'s crew who gave their lives for just such reasons have left a legacy of scientific and medical knowledge that will ultimately benefit all of mankind. In August 1986 Reagan instructed NASA to build a fourth shuttle but ordered that much of the scientific and commercial program be transferred to private industry.

—*Ralph Pelligra, M.D.*

Special Report
Malpractice in Perspective
by George J. Annas, J.D., M.P.H.

Although physician concern for lawsuits is not new, the public's perception of what is possible in medicine has changed dramatically and in some cases naively. This perception is shared by both patients and their physicians and has been spawned by the arrival of the "new technological age" of medicine. With the landing of Apollo 11 on the Moon, we have come to believe that there is no limit to what we can bend nature to accomplish. As novelist Don DeLillo puts it, technology has given us "an appetite for immortality." We believe that diseases *can* be controlled, and that physicians *should* be able to do something for us when we fall ill. We want to believe in organ transplants, in artificial hearts, in chemotherapy, in genetic engineering, and in psychotherapy. We want to believe that we can have it all, that we can live our lives without regard to physical or mental dangers, and then, like machines, go to the "repair shop" (the hospital) when we suffer a physical or mental "breakdown" and have it fixed. If physicians cannot repair us, it must be because they lack the skill, do not know the latest techniques, or have made a mistake. Therefore, they should be sued for their failures.

Suing doctors

Medical malpractice debates generally pit physicians against lawyers and usually degenerate into unflattering and unconstructive caricatures of the two professions. While these debates have entertainment value, they are pointless from a public policy perspective. It is common, for example, for physicians to quote the famous line from *Henry VI, Part II,* "The first thing we do, let's kill all the lawyers" (Act IV scene 2). It is uncommon to note that the character who spoke these words was an unschooled murderer and anarchist named Dick the Butcher who wanted to overthrow the legal system so that there would be no laws but those that the leader of the rebels from time to time orally decreed. Of course, physicians are not actually calling for the mass execution of lawyers, any more than they really want to overthrow the U.S. Constitution and strip citizens of their rights of access to the courts. But strong rhetoric often obscures real problems, and the medical malpractice insurance crisis, which the American Medical Association (AMA) ranks as the number one issue currently confronting its members, is a case in point.

Physicians have deplored lawsuits against them for almost a century and a half, primarily because the lawsuits are usually decided in public by lay juries. In 1845, for example, physicians indicated alarm at the increase in malpractice lawsuits and suggested alternatives to jury trials, such as committees made up of physicians, to judge such claims. In 1872 the AMA recommended that physicians be appointed as independent arbiters by the court to judge their peers. Physicians also hate the term malpractice, which connotes "evil" or "bad" practice when, in fact, it refers simply to an act by a physician who has not lived up to the customary professional standard set by the "average competent physician" in the same or similar circumstances.

When a patient is injured by the actions of a physician, the patient can successfully sue the physician for the harm done only if the patient is able to prove that the physician was negligent (*i.e.,* that the physician breached a duty owed to the patient) and that this negligence caused the patient harm. For example, if a physician leaves a sponge or clamp in the patient's abdomen after surgery, and this necessitates an additional operation to remove it, the patient can sue for the cost of the additional operation, lost earnings, and "pain and suffering." Our society permits such suits for three basic reasons: (1) to control quality by holding doctors responsible for their actions, (2) to compensate patients for injury, and (3) to give patients an opportunity to express dissatisfaction with the care they have received.

An insurance crisis

In the U.S. in the mid-1970s, there was a "crisis" in the availability of malpractice insurance that physicians and hospitals could purchase. While the cause of that crisis seems to have stemmed primarily from management and investment decisions on the part of insurance companies, the resulting "solution" adopted by 49 of the 50 states was to change the laws to make it harder for injured patients to sue physicians. Some states also formed quasi-public agencies, called joint underwriting associations, to write insurance policies for physicians who could not obtain insurance from private companies. In the mid-1980s the insurance crisis has returned. Now the problem is not availability of insurance but affordability. Underwriters have dramatically increased premium costs, especially in high-risk specialties like obstetrics and neurosurgery, and many physicians are expressing concern over the amount of their income needed to pay the premiums.

Insurance companies argue that the precipitous rate increases are required by increases in the frequency and severity of malpractice litigation. They cite figures indicating sharp increases in the absolute numbers of malpractice suits filed and in the number of jury awards of over $1 million. The companies argue that the U.S. has become an increasingly lawsuit-prone society and that premium increases are needed to keep pace with increases in litigation expenses and unrealistic jury awards. As they did a decade ago, the insurance companies now seek changes in the legal system to make it harder for injured patients to seek compensation from physicians and hospitals.

The AMA's position

The AMA seems to have sided with the insurance companies and has also focused its attention on reforming the tort system. The AMA's four major recommendations for change are (1) limiting jury awards of noneconomic damages ("pain and suffering") to $100,000, (2) requiring deductions in awards for money victims receive from any other source (*i.e.,* eliminating the so-called collateral source rule), (3) using mandatory periodic payments for all awards for future damages that exceed $100,000, and (4) limiting attorneys' fees by modifying the contingency fee (under which lawyers are generally paid a flat percentage of the award, usually 30–50%) to a sliding scale, in which the lawyer's percentage would diminish as the total award grew. Many physicians also believe that the current system actually encourages patients to sue for nonnegligent and unavoidable side effects or inherent risks of their treatments.

The ABA's position

Lawyers, of course, argue that such changes are misplaced. The American Bar Association (ABA), for example, rejected the AMA's recommendations, arguing that the real problem with medical malpractice *is* medical malpractice. Accordingly, the ABA recommends that physicians set up much tougher methods of policing themselves in order to eliminate incompetent and impaired physicians and thereby protect the public. The ABA also notes that changes in the legal system were tried in the 1970s and failed as a method to deal with the problem and that this demonstrates that the real problem is not with the legal system. Alternatively, the ABA argues that if the problem is with the way personal injury suits are handled, then the tort system should be changed across the board, not just for physicians. In this regard there will undoubtedly be more and more proposals for tort changes that will affect all personal injury lawsuits. The chemical industry and manufacturing companies, for example, also have a huge financial stake in limiting compensation for injury caused by their products.

As to specific proposals, trial lawyers generally argue that limiting "pain and suffering" awards to $100,000 is unfair to severely injured victims whom this amount cannot begin to compensate; requiring reduction of awards for outside insurance benefits penalizes those who carry such insurance and is a windfall to the wrongdoer; and radically changing the contingency fee will close the courtroom to the poor and middle class who cannot afford to pay a lawyer out of their own pockets to wage a complex and costly lawsuit.

Consumer groups

Consumer groups, such as Ralph Nader's Public Citizen, see the professional debate between physicians and lawyers as a sideshow. They note that it is the insurance companies who have dramatically raised the rates for insurance coverage and argue that these companies are simply exploiting the fear of physicians in order to make profits. This group notes that the stock market values of the insurance companies more than doubled in 1985, the same year in which these companies drastically increased their premiums.

The St. Paul Cos., Inc., the largest insurance company involved in medical malpractice (with about 20% of the entire malpractice insurance market), is a good example. In 1984 the company suffered its first loss since the San Francisco earthquake of 1906. By drastically increasing its premiums (60% in two years) and cutting its coverage, it made an incredible comeback. Its stock went from $52 to $92 per share in just 12 months, and almost all of this increase was directly attributable to its malpractice insurance business. The company actually pays out more in malpractice claims than it takes in, but it retains the premium money for a long time and makes money by investing these premiums, usually more than enough to both offset losses and make a profit. In 1986 the company had $1.1 billion in its medical malpractice reserves earning investment income at 16% annually.

Others think the insurers are too comfortable and need to be much more closely monitored and regulated. The president of the National Insurance Consumer Organization, Robert Hunter, for example, notes that insurance premiums are much more closely linked to the industry's profit cycle (which is determined primarily by the insurers' return on investment) than to legal liability. He notes that in 1975, the date of the beginning of the last "insurance crisis," the industry earned only 4% on its reserves. Premiums skyrocketed in 1976 and 1977 to make up for this loss. The premium increase brought sharp profit increases (similar to those now being experienced), which attracted a flood of new capital and led to premium price cutting to accumulate more cash to invest at high interest rates. When these rates fell, the industry earned only

2% on equity in 1984. As a consequence, premium rates shot up for 1985–86, essentially repeating the 1976–77 pattern. The only difference was that other insurance lines were affected as well, including liability insurance for day-care centers, cities, and many products. In Hunter's view it is completely implausible to argue that the legal system, as represented by judges and juries, worked perfectly well from 1977 to 1983 and then all of a sudden went out of control with unanticipated high awards in 1984 and 1985.

These consumer groups seem correct. Although the number of million-dollar-plus awards had increased to over 400 in all personal injury cases in 1985, these were awards, not payments or settlements (which are usually significantly lower). Surveys have also shown both that the total number of civil lawsuits is not increasing per capita in the U.S. and that the median jury award has actually remained constant for the past 25 years, at about $20,000.

The economist's view

Economists have found the situation mixed. There is general agreement that the system is inefficient at compensating victims of malpractice but is cost-effective as a method of quality control. The inefficiency at compensation stems from two facts: very few people who are actually injured by malpractice ever get into the system, and there are very high transaction costs that go to the lawyers and insurance companies who

As the U.S. has become increasingly lawsuit prone—with patients suing doctors for negligence and juries granting huge awards—the cost of malpractice insurance for physicians has skyrocketed.

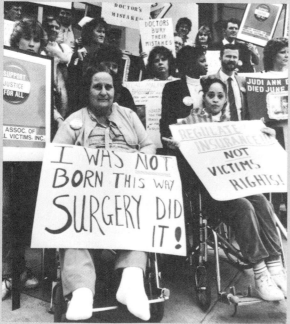

Rob Nelson—Picture Group

get more of the total premiums than injured victims do.

Studies suggest that approximately one of every 100 patients admitted to a hospital suffers an injury due to medical negligence. Nonetheless, only between one in 25 and one in 50 of these injured patients is ever compensated through the current system. But even though the compensation is very limited, as long as the potential for a suit deters any meaningful percentage of negligent injuries, the system will be cost-effective from the patient's viewpoint.

From a system-wide perspective, the scheme is actually very inexpensive. Malpractice premiums for physicians and hospitals combined amount to less than 1% of total expenditures on health care. The alleged added expense due to "defensive medicine," *e.g.,* extra tests that doctors do to protect themselves that do not necessarily benefit their patients, cannot be documented. And although some specialists pay higher rates, the average physician, even in 1986, still spends less than 5% of his or her gross income on malpractice insurance, a percentage that has not changed significantly during the past decade. Nonetheless, there is plenty of room to make the system more cost-effective and more efficient.

What to do?

Some of those concerned with the U.S. malpractice crisis look abroad with envy. Sweden and New Zealand are seen as lands of no lawsuits, and some have urged that the U.S. adopt their no-fault systems, which simply compensate everyone for injury, regardless of cause, by paying their medical bills. What this proposition overlooks, however, is the fact that the countries with no-fault systems, like nearly every industrialized country in the world except the U.S. and South Africa, have a form of national health insurance, in which everyone's medical bills are paid for, regardless of source of injury or illness. Likewise, Sweden has a vast network of social support systems that are government financed and available to all. The United States could adopt the Swedish system for malpractice lawsuits, but first it would have to adopt some form of national health insurance along with government-financed social supports.

In early 1986 the U.S. General Accounting Office issued a report to Congress on "Medical Malpractice." The report's subtitle, "No Agreement on the Problems or Solutions," aptly describes the current situation. In April 1986, the *New York Times,* in a lead editorial, depicted the current crisis in insurance availability (all insurance, not just for medical malpractice) as one with three possible solutions: (1) crack down on the lawyers who manipulate juries to win outlandish settlements and at the same time gain fat contingency fees; (2) crack down on the insurance industry, which has shown itself to be unable to manage its cash flows responsibly; and (3) educate the public with regard to the fact that enormous liability judgments are not cost free. A "fourth" solution—the one promoted by the *Times*—is to adopt all of the above measures.

The *Times* chided the Reagan administration for concentrating only on the first solution in its proposals to reform products liability tort law. "All of the above" is also the best answer when it comes to reforming the out-of-control medical malpractice situation. Specifically, the legal profession must discipline its members who file frivolous lawsuits and pursue untenable claims, and it should do so vigorously. States and the federal government should regulate insurance companies so that accurate data on premiums and claims paid can be compiled and reasonable premium raises can be announced well in advance, limited on a yearly basis, and canceled only with adequate notice.

There are also at least two additional items that should be added to the list: more effective methods of preventing incompetent and impaired physicians from hurting patients, and more effective communication between physicians and their patients. The former will demand a commitment on the part of the medical profession to police its own and on the part of state legislatures to change the composition of medical licensing boards to include larger proportions of nonphysician members. More effective communication between physicians and patients is something everyone can work on now.

Informed consent and malpractice suits

Doctors have been only too eager to support the mechanistic view spawned by this technological age (*i.e.,* patients as machines, doctors as mechanics or repair persons). They have done little to try to explain the limitations of rescue medicine to their patients, and instead promote modern medical technology as something both wonderful and inevitable. They encourage routine screening examinations and replacement of defective organs by real or mechanical ones, and they generally ask patients to put their faith in modern medicine to cure most ailments. Many doctors seem to believe that if people only knew more, they could do almost anything, even live "forever."

As psychiatrist Jay Katz of Yale Law School has pointed out, although most medical diagnoses and treatments are filled with uncertainty, traditional medicine has stressed authoritarianism, and "power and control is maintained not only by projecting a greater sense of certainty than is warranted, but also by leaving patients in a state of uncertainty." He suggests a major effort to promote "shared decision-making" between physicians and patients. But this is not easy.

Can the authoritarian doctor and the submissive patient be brought together? And if they are brought together, can this new understanding of our mortality and the limits of medical intervention have a salutary

effect on the medical malpractice crisis? The President's Commission on Bioethics suggested that the key to a new understanding is taking the legal doctrine of "informed consent" seriously. Specifically, the doctrine requires that patients, before they are asked to consent to invasive or risky medical procedures, be told (1) what the doctor proposes to do, (2) what the risks of death and bodily disability are, (3) what the benefits and the likelihood of success are, (4) what alternative treatments exist, and (5) what the major problems of recuperation are likely to be. If patients are actually given this information by their physicians, and if physicians take steps to ensure that patients actually understand it and share the decision-making burden, both doctors and patients should benefit.

The major cause of malpractice suits has consistently been described as a medically induced injury in the face of an unsatisfactory doctor-patient relationship. What little data we have suggest that patients want to know about potential risks, can handle the information well, and react more positively toward their physicians if fully informed. For example, a nationwide survey sponsored by the bioethics commission in 1981 found that 97% of the public believed that patients should have the right to all the available information about their condition and treatment that they wish. The president's commission also concluded that "when there is a strong pre-existing bond between patient and professional, and when the patient was prepared for the possibility of an adverse outcome, litigation is less likely."

In the wake of the malpractice insurance crisis of the mid-1970s, medical societies persuaded legislatures in about half of the U.S. states to pass laws limiting the scope of the informed consent doctrine as a way to reduce malpractice suits. There is no evidence that these statutes had the desired effect. In fact, insofar as such statutes encouraged physicians to limit the information they gave their patients or to rely heavily on the patient's signature on a consent form instead of upon a candid discussion with the patient, these statutes have probably contributed to the number of lawsuits brought because of unexpected adverse results.

The major problem with medical malpractice insurance is medical malpractice insurance. But unrealistic expectations on the part of patients and ritualistic silence and demands for blind faith by physicians greatly exacerbate the broader medical malpractice problem. Patients who suffer injury at the hands of negligent physicians deserve compensation for those injuries. Negligent and incompetent physicians must be disciplined; many should have their hospital privileges restricted, and some should be removed from the practice of medicine altogether. The malpractice insurance crisis is emblematic of the naïveté of both patients and physicians. One cure is a strong dose of reality.

Aging

There has been remarkable progress in the field of geriatrics—the medical specialty concerned with the clinical problems of the elderly—in the last few years, fulfilling a most urgent need. This "need" has arisen owing to the phenomenal growth of the older population on this planet, growth that will continue. The progress is in the form of research efforts aimed at the unique diseases and disorders of aging.

While geriatrics has an impressive history in the United Kingdom—it was first introduced as a medical specialty in the early 1950s—it is a relatively new discipline in the United States. As recently as 1977, there were only two formal training programs in geriatrics in the 127 medical schools of the United States. Today there are geriatric programs in over 50 medical schools. Yet even this is insufficient. In order to appreciate the scope of the elderly population "explosion" in this century, it is necessary to look back.

At the turn of the century, approximately 4% of the population of Western countries was age 65 or older. Today many Western countries have from 10 to 14% of their population in the over-65 age group—in West Germany 15%, in the U.S. 12%, and in Canada 9.5%. In the U.S. there are some 28 million elderly people, while in China more than 49 million individuals are over age 65. In less developed countries there is similarly notable growth in the numbers of older citizens. However, in countries where birth control is not practiced, such as Egypt and Algeria, the percentage of the population over age 65 remains around 4 or 5%.

Life expectancy and life-span

What is the reason for this pattern? The increases in this century are largely the result of decreases in deaths in infancy and in the middle years of life—resulting in dramatic increases in life expectancy. In the time of ancient Rome, average life expectancy at birth was approximately 25 years. In 1900 average life expectancy was approximately 50 years in the United States. Today average life expectancy is approximately 75 years in developed countries. Thus, life expectancy has increased as much in this century as in the previous 19 centuries combined!

With increased life expectancy, what has happened to life-span—defined as the maximum attainable age by a member of a species? Human life-span has probably not changed and remains about 115 years. While there have been claims for enclaves of longevity in Georgia in the Soviet Union and in Vilcabamba in Ecuador, scientific studies have not supported the claims.

Today there are many books and articles on "life extension," proposing that specific nutrients, vitamins, minerals, food supplements, and drugs can help people break through this life-span barrier. Unfortunately,

A senior citizen competes in a 4.8-kilometer (3-mile) bicycle race in the Maryland Senior Olympic Games. The games include a wide range of events, from walking, swimming, and badminton to square dancing.

none of these claims has any scientific data to support the use of any of the allegedly useful products.

The field of aging research is at its earliest stage. Scientists are just beginning to learn about the nature of aging at the molecular, cellular, and organ level, and indeed it is a burgeoning field of scientific investigation, but as yet not one that has produced clear human applications. In the future, gerontologists may develop effective interventions to slow aging processes. However, since there is still no documented intervention that can extend human life-span, caveat emptor.

The "oldest old"

While maximum human survival may not have changed, unprecedented numbers of individuals are reaching their 9th, 10th, and 11th decades. Today there are 2.6 million Americans over age 85; when the post-World War II "baby boomers" reach this age, there will be 16 million. This group, the "oldest old," presents an important challenge to the field of geriatrics.

Individuals in their sixties represent a relatively healthy group. It is in the late seventies and eighties when the diseases and disorders of aging take their profoundest toll. As a result, the chances of being in a chronic care institution increase exponentially in these later decades. In the U.S. approximately one in four over age 85 is in a nursing home.

Cost impact

The increases in the numbers of elderly individuals have had an enormous impact on health care expen-

270

ditures. In the U.S. the national health expenditures increased from $12.7 billion to $387 billion between 1950 and 1984, from 4.4 to 10.6% of the gross national product. The public sector component of these expenditures increased from 22.4 to 39.6%. The two major public health programs that provide medical care to the older U.S. population, Medicare and Medicaid, accounted for over $100 billion in 1985. It is projected that by the year 2030 those over age 65 will consume over 45% of health care costs.

The unique health status of the elderly

Whereas medicine has traditionally focused on diagnosis, treatment, and cure, geriatrics focuses as well on assessment, evaluation, and functioning. It is rare that an individual aged 80 or older will not have at least one diagnosed medical condition requiring some form of treatment; often individuals at this age have between five and ten. Recently geriatric assessment units in the U.K., the U.S., and some other countries have shown that unnecessary placement of individuals in chronic care institutions can be prevented by thorough evaluation that emphasizes functioning. It is important to point out that geriatrics relies on the team approach with interactions between physician, nurse, social worker, occupational therapist, and physical therapist, all working toward creating the optimum medical and social environment for elderly functioning.

Dementia

Dementia is the most devastating common geriatric disorder. It is manifested by gradually increasing confusion, disorientation, and loss of memory. The memory loss is severe, in contrast to the slight losses of recent memory that typically occur with normal aging. It is crucial that individuals with dementia be evaluated carefully to discern the cause of this condition. There are many treatable medical conditions that cause dementia, including diseases of the blood, thyroid, and brain. One common treatable condition that can simulate dementia is severe depression.

Another condition that can mimic or resemble dementia is drug intoxication. With aging, there are significant changes in the way bodies break down drugs. Certain drugs must be given in lower dosages to older individuals. If too high a drug dosage is ingested or if the individual has a disease of the kidneys, which impairs the elimination of the drug, the drug may accumulate in the blood. If the drug depresses brain function, the individual may appear to be demented. Thus, it is vital that these reversible causes of dementia be discerned and treated.

After all other causes of dementia are eliminated, there remain dementias due to small strokes, called multi-infarct dementia, and Alzheimer's disease. These two conditions often have different clinical courses. The dementia of Alzheimer's disease usually is evi-

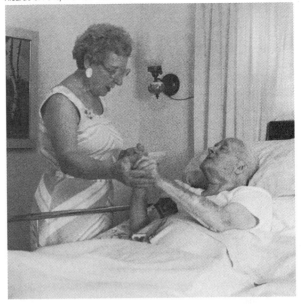

Of the unprecedented number of elderly Florida residents needing long-term care, 70% exhaust their financial resources within a year of entering a nursing home. This bedridden stroke patient is cared for at home by his wife.

denced by a slow, continuous decline in function, while multi-infarct dementia is marked by abrupt changes in function with plateaus, during which there are no apparent changes. Of these two types, Alzheimer's disease is far more common in the U.S., where it is estimated that two million to three million are affected. Less than a decade ago, this irreversible, important disease was not widely recognized. It is now receiving the attention it deserves, attention that bodes well for future solutions.

Recent studies indicate that the prevalence of Alzheimer's disease increases exponentially with aging, reaching as high as one in three individuals in their eighties. If deaths from heart disease and strokes continue to decline and if progress is made in the prevention of and/or cure for cancers, Alzheimer's disease may become the leading cause of death in the 21st century. Research on the cause of Alzheimer's disease has revealed that the levels of several brain molecules called neurotransmitters are diminished in affected individuals. These neurotransmitters are crucial brain molecules that are vital for the communication of brain cells.

Progress has also been made in identifying the abnormal protein molecules that are deposited in the characteristic lesions of Alzheimer's disease. It is hoped that the purification of these proteins will lead to a positive diagnostic test during life for this disease. At this time the diagnosis can be made sometimes by excluding other conditions, but unfortunately the diagnosis can be verified only at autopsy.

Other interesting research has shown that certain unusual viruses, called "slow" viruses because they can lie dormant for up to ten years before causing disease, can cause other rarer types of dementia. Because of the loss of vital cells that is characteristic of this disease, another line of research has focused on transplanting brain cells in animals. This approach is successful with certain types of animal brain cells and may be a future approach for therapy in humans.

Hip fractures

Hip fractures are extremely common with aging. Of the 200,000 such fractures that occur annually in the United States, 160,000 occur in those over age 65 and the majority of these are in women. Factors that place individuals at greater risk include age, gender (female), race (white), and bone size (small-boned). A major factor in the causation of hip fractures is a disease of aging, osteoporosis (the thinning of bone). Research has shown that moderate exercise and adequate calcium intake can slow down age-dependent bone loss. It is recommended that women before menopause consume 1,000 mg of calcium per day and as much as 1,500 mg after menopause. (For reference, the average American woman consumes 500 mg of calcium in the diet a day.) Before taking calcium supplements, women should consult a physician to ensure that they do not have a condition where additional calcium might be harmful, such as kidney stones.

There is increasing evidence that vitamin D deficiency may contribute to the increased risk of older women to hip fractures. Vitamin D also helps the body digest calcium. Therefore, it is vital to ensure that adequate amounts of vitamin D are ingested daily.

Elderly hypertension

Treatment of high blood pressure in the general population has been effective in decreasing deaths from heart attacks and strokes. When physicians refer to hypertension, they usually refer to the lower of the two blood pressure values—the diastolic pressure (e.g., 110 if one's blood pressure is 140/110). Clinical trials have shown that treatment of elevated diastolic blood pressure is effective at all ages. However, with aging there is a significant increase in the systolic blood pressure. At age 80, 20% of the population have elevated systolic blood pressure and normal diastolic pressure; in a typical case of isolated systolic high blood pressure, the value is 180/80. While few physicians treat isolated systolic high blood pressure, studies have indicated that individuals with this condition have a threefold increased risk of dying. Recent studies have indicated that isolated systolic high blood pressure can be effectively treated with very mild medication. A major clinical trial is now in progress to determine whether long-term treatment of this condition will reduce the risk of death.

Slowed sugar metabolism

Research on aging has also provided important insights into the physiology of aging that will be of importance to the practicing physician as well as the public. An example is the change with aging in the way the body manages blood levels of sugar. Ingestion of sugar in a young individual causes an immediate response by the pancreas, which releases insulin into the bloodstream. Insulin is a crucial protein in the body responsible for facilitating the digestion of sugar. With aging, the response of the pancreas is slowed, and the digestion of sugar is also slowed. Since the speed of digestion of sugar is part of the diagnosis of diabetes, it is clear that diabetes must be diagnosed with special criteria in an older individual.

The future

There are many other important age-dependent conditions that have received increased attention with the emergence of geriatric research. These include osteoarthritis (the arthritis of aging), urinary incontinence, hypothermia (abnormally low inner body temperature in response to cold weather), dental problems, and accidental falls.

The field of geriatrics will become increasingly important as our planet ages. Today there are insufficient numbers of faculty in most medical schools to teach this crucial discipline. A variety of federal agencies have programs to increase these numbers so that all physicians in training will be exposed to the special knowledge inherent in the field of geriatrics.

—Edward L. Schneider, M.D.

AIDS

AIDS (acquired immune deficiency syndrome), an apparently new condition, has been likened to an ancient scourge of humankind—the plague. Like the plague that ravaged Europe in the 14th century, AIDS has swept a deadly path and has taken hold of public consciousness. But unlike the plague, AIDS seems to affect a much more limited proportion of the population and is transmitted in a different way, from person to person rather than via an animal vector.

The number of victims and the concern about the syndrome mushroomed in the first half of the 1980s. By late summer of 1986, more than 24,000 people in the United States had developed AIDS; of these, more than 13,300 had died. As many as one million people—some authorities estimate nearly two million—have antibodies to the AIDS virus in their blood, an indication that they have been exposed to the disease. The U.S. Centers for Disease Control (CDC) at first estimated that 5–20% of the people who are seropositive (i.e., have AIDS antibody in their blood) will develop the disease. By 1986 some public health officials had increased this estimate to 33–40%.

Emergence of a new disease

One of the earliest indications that a new disease syndrome was appearing came in the spring of 1981, when an employee of the CDC noticed an unusual number of requests for a drug used to reconstitute the immune system. Slowly the reports started trickling in—a handful of young homosexual men in New York City and California with pneumocystis pneumonia, a fairly uncommon form of pneumonia that usually affects only people with impaired immune systems, and Kaposi's sarcoma, a skin cancer well known in Africa but heretofore rare in the U.S., where it was seen almost solely in older men of Mediterranean extraction. The CDC, which monitors and investigates infectious diseases, reported 168 cases of the new disease in 1981. As the virus believed to be at the root of the immune deficiency spread and physicians began to recognize and diagnose the disease, the number of reported cases soared.

What doctors had begun seeing was the catastrophic result of immune system failure. In addition to the unusual types of skin cancer and pneumonia, patients were mysteriously developing diseases previously seen only in people whose immune systems were impaired by drugs or disease—so-called opportunistic infections that take advantage of the body's immunocompromised status. The individual diseases could sometimes be successfully treated, but they recurred or others developed. The condition was uniformly fatal. AIDS victims died within several months to several years after diagnosis.

The AIDS virus

As the number of people affected by AIDS continued to rise, scientists working to combat the disease considered—and subsequently dismissed—several hypotheses as to its cause. They eventually realized that they were dealing with a disease that was transmitted only through an exchange of body fluids, namely blood or semen, which could occur under several circumstances—through homosexual contact, specifically anal intercourse; through the use of unsterilized needles in intravenous drug use; and via receipt of contaminated blood or blood products. Subsequently, heterosexual transmission to the sexual partners of victims or of people in high-risk groups was added to the list. It was also learned that infants born to women with AIDS (or women exposed to the disease) could become infected in the womb or during the birth process. This pattern of transmission strongly implicated an infectious organism such as a virus as the disease-causing agent.

In April 1983 Luc Montagnier and his colleagues at the Pasteur Institute in Paris isolated a virus they called lymphadenopathy-associated virus (LAV) from the blood of AIDS patients; the following spring U.S. researchers, led by Robert C. Gallo of the National Cancer Institute, announced that they too had isolated a virus, which they called lymphotropic retrovirus-III, or human T-cell lymphotropic virus, type III (HTLV-III). Later, in addition to being isolated from the blood and semen of AIDS victims, the virus was found in cerebrospinal fluid, saliva, tears, breast milk, and cervical secretions.

The viruses discovered by the two research teams were soon found to be essentially identical. They selectively infect a vital cell of the immune system, the T-helper cell, a kind of lymphocyte (white blood cell). As one investigator observed, the effect on the immune system—which is composed of many different cells that must act together to be effective—may be compared to that of an orchestra losing its conductor. In 1985, after some AIDS patients had been observed to be suffering from unexplained neurological disorders, the virus was also found to infect cells of the brain and nervous system.

The AIDS virus belongs to a family of viruses called retroviruses, which are known to cause some human cancers. Retroviruses have a characteristic way of infiltrating and destroying body cells. They use RNA (ribonucleic acid), a molecule similar but not identical to DNA (deoxyribonucleic acid), as their basic genetic material and employ an enzyme, reverse transcriptase, to incorporate themselves into the infected cell's own DNA. Then they subvert the cell's replication process, producing a new generation of viruses that, in turn, infect more cells.

But while the AIDS virus was quickly recognized as a retrovirus, along with other similar agents—among

Two volunteers visit a three-year-old AIDS patient and her mother. In New York City the Gay Men's Health Crisis has established a program to provide comfort and company to lonely youngsters isolated by the illness.

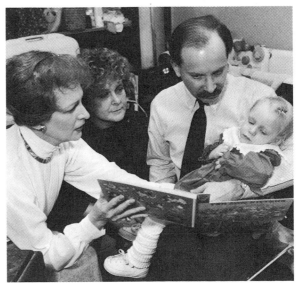

Although scientific studies have demonstrated that AIDS is not spread by casual contact, even among household members, children with the disease are still prohibited from attending classes in many local school districts.

them HTLV-I, which causes human T-cell leukemia, and similar viruses that cause malignancies in animals—scientists later began to see increasing similarities between HTLV-III and the lentiviruses, or slow viruses, a subfamily of retroviruses. This group is known to cause certain diseases in animals, among them a progressive degenerative brain disease in sheep. Evidently, once the AIDS virus takes over the genetic machinery of the host cell (presumably the T cell), it may remain dormant for a period of months or even years. Some time later, then, for unknown reasons, the virus is activated and begins to proliferate. More and more T cells are infected and ultimately die, crippling the body's immune defenses.

The blood test for AIDS

The first major scientific advance from the isolation of the virus was the development of a test to screen donor blood; the procedure was approved by the U.S. Food and Drug Administration in the spring of 1985 and quickly implemented at U.S. and other blood banks. Potentially infected blood was quickly removed from the blood supply, virtually eliminating the threat of contracting AIDS from blood transfusions. However, because blood and blood products are responsible for only 1–2% of all AIDS cases, it remained imperative that broader forms of prevention be instituted.

The ability to screen a blood sample for the presence of the AIDS virus proved both beneficial and controversial. Not long after the test was developed, the Pentagon announced its intention to screen all U.S. military recruits and active-duty personnel, and there were reports that some insurance companies planned to begin screening applicants for health insurance; the companies contended that without such a test, they could eventually be liable for millions of dollars spent for the medical treatment of AIDS victims. It was feared that employers might try to test job applicants or to apply mass screening to all employees. There was also speculation that the U.S. State Department might try to institute screening of all aliens. Because not everyone who tests positive for the AIDS virus has—or will get—the disease, the use of the blood test to deny insurance or employment is still considered highly controversial, and many people worry about the ability of testing facilities to guarantee the confidentiality of the results.

The blood test also proved to be a valuable research tool, however. Using it, scientists were able to analyze blood samples that had been collected in other, earlier studies. They found that AIDS, or some agent capable of producing the same kind of antibodies induced by the AIDS virus, had existed in Africa as long ago as 1972. Examining the virus itself, they found that it was capable of inducing a range of effects, from an asymptomatic state notable only because the blood contains antibodies to the virus (meaning only that the person has at some time in the past encountered the virus), through generalized but relatively mild immune system deficiencies, a condition called AIDS-related complex, or ARC, to the full-blown fatal syndrome.

By 1986 the screening of all donated blood and implementation of other preventive recommendations derived from epidemiological research had begun to slow the spread of the disease. But the number of AIDS patients continued to increase as previously infected people developed the manifestations of the disease. Recent evidence indicates that the virus is more easily isolated before the disease appears; this finding suggests that people with AIDS may be more infectious during early stages of infection and, therefore, prior to diagnosis. Assuming this is so, then even if preventive measures are effective in checking the spread of AIDS among people not yet infected, new cases of the disease may continue to appear for many years.

Recent epidemiological findings

Epidemiologists suspected almost from the outset that the AIDS virus could not be transmitted by casual contact. A study published in *The New England Journal of Medicine* in February 1986, which examined the possibility of transmission among household members, concluded that the disease cannot be spread by casual contact—including hugging or kissing AIDS victims, helping them bathe or dress, and sharing kitchen and bathroom facilities. As noted earlier, symptoms of the disease may not appear for years after exposure; however, antibodies are present in the blood of an exposed person within six weeks to six months. Thus, the researchers looked for the presence of antibody as an early warning sign of the disease. They found no evidence of transmission of the virus in either caretakers or household members of AIDS patients. Investigators in Zaire conducted a similar household survey and arrived at the same conclusion. A French study of young hemophiliacs with AIDS also concluded that casual, day-to-day contact poses no threat of disease transmission.

Only a tiny percentage of health care workers who are not in the identified risk groups have developed AIDS. Furthermore, even most AIDS-related needlestick injuries do not cause infection. In one U.S. study, the health status of 531 health care workers was monitored for more than a year. Of these, 150 had either stuck themselves with a sharp object that had been contaminated with blood or bodily fluids of an AIDS patient or had been exposed to contaminated material via the mouth, nose, or eyes. Only two had positive blood tests.

Despite these reassurances from the medical profession, large segments of the public remain unconvinced, and school systems in the U.S., the U.K., and other countries are wrestling with the question of whether to allow children with AIDS to attend school. Because of the nature of medicine and of epidemiology, researchers cannot give a blanket assurance that casual contact will never cause AIDS, although they do say it is highly unlikely.

There is some evidence that AIDS is transmitted through heterosexual sex. In the U.S. three of the wives of antibody-positive hemophiliacs have documented cases of AIDS, and there are cases of AIDS in men who say they do not use drugs and are not homosexual but have frequented prostitutes. In 1985 blood tests of some prostitutes in U.S. cities showed that a small percentage were antibody-positive, presumably because of intravenous drug abuse. Whether these women may have transmitted the disease to their male partners is still a subject of debate. A woman artificially inseminated with semen from an antibody-positive man is known to have shown signs of infection, and in at least one case an infant contracted the disease from his mother's milk.

Drug treatment

Treatment of AIDS has remained problematic. A battery of drugs is under clinical investigation but, despite occasional—and sometimes premature—reports of success in a few patients, no single drug has yet been demonstrated effective. Furthermore, all of the drugs under consideration may be toxic if used in large quantities or for long-term treatment. Among the agents tested in the past two years are HPA-

23, a drug developed in France, and suramin and azidothymidine, both of which act against the enzyme reverse transcriptase. Antiviral drugs such as ribavirin and acyclovir have shown limited usefulness; acyclovir, used in the treatment of genital herpes infections, eases the symptoms of AIDS but has no effect on the virus itself. Natural substances such as interferon and interleukin-2 are also being tested, and U.S. researchers reported that injections of cortisol (a steroid hormone) have been successful in the management of some AIDS symptoms caused by adrenal insufficiency. In November 1985, based on limited trials with only a few patients, French researchers announced what they termed a major breakthrough—the use of cyclosporine, a drug used to prevent the rejection of transplanted organs. The report was considered premature by most other AIDS specialists, and the French team was widely criticized for raising false hopes.

Most researchers now believe it will take a two-pronged attack to halt or reverse the disease—a drug that can destroy the virus and an agent or process that can reconstitute the victim's devastated immune system. In June 1986 at an international conference on AIDS, U.S. researchers reported some success with a therapy that combined administration of an antiviral drug and bone marrow transplantation. Although only one patient had responded to the treatment, it was the first instance in which an AIDS-impaired immune system had shown signs of recovery. Researchers noted that such treatment would have limited application.

Several aspects of the virus's "life-style" are making the drug search difficult. Once the virus has incorporated itself into the body's T cells, it is difficult to attack without killing the host cells. As mentioned above, the AIDS virus has also been found to infect cells of the nervous system, including the brain. Because the brain is protected by a biochemical barrier that keeps out bloodborne drugs, researchers will have to develop an agent capable of circumventing this barrier.

Vaccine against AIDS?

Developing a vaccine against AIDS has proved as difficult as finding an effective treatment for the disease. Among the many problems encountered by researchers is that the virus itself changes over time, as do the proteins it produces. No two viruses from any two patients are identical. Furthermore, the body *does* produce antibodies in response to the virus. Unfortunately, they are not effective in preventing the development of the disease. So a vaccine cannot simply stimulate the body to produce antibodies; it must induce antibodies strong enough to overwhelm the virus. A vaccine consisting of a disabled or weakened virus is considered risky, as it might trigger the disease itself.

While the creation of a vaccine for general use— *i.e.,* protection of all those considered to be at risk—is not yet in sight, there were some particularly promising developments in 1986. A research team composed of scientists from the U.S., France, and Senegal announced in March 1986 that they had isolated a new virus that is structurally similar to the AIDS virus but even more closely related to a virus that infects the African green monkey. It has been known for some time that several species of primates are susceptible to an AIDS-like disease (simian AIDS, or SAIDS), but this newest discovery may prove to be the long-sought "missing link" between the human and simian forms of the virus. The U.S. researchers, led by Myron Essex of the Harvard School of Public Health, had identified the green monkey virus in 1985 and theorized that it somehow spread to the human population in central Africa. The African patients from whom the new virus was isolated are apparently healthy; they have no symptoms of AIDS. The investigative team hopes that this presumably harmless agent might serve as a natural vaccine, producing immunity in those who are exposed to it.

Another hopeful finding announced in the spring of 1986 was that researchers from Harvard and the National Cancer Institute had succeeded in altering the genetic structure of the AIDS virus in such a way that it becomes inactive. However, it remains to be seen whether the genetically altered virus is truly incapable of causing disease.

Where did AIDS originate?

With the discovery of the apparently harmless AIDS-like virus in the African green monkey, speculation that

The study of AIDS-like diseases in primates may yield a virus structurally similar to HTLV-III that could be used in the creation of a vaccine against the human form of the disease.

Bradford F. Herzog

the disease originated in Africa—a theory proposed earlier in the course of the epidemic—gained renewed credibility. According to this new line of thinking, the AIDS virus originated in monkeys in remote parts of central Africa; the first humans to be infected may have been bitten by these animals or have eaten their meat. At any rate, human emigration from rural to urban areas in Africa carried the virus into more densely populated areas, where it spread from person to person. From Africa the disease may have spread to the Caribbean and western Europe—some early AIDS patients treated in Europe were African-born or had lived for some time in central Africa. U.S. vacationers, homosexuals in particular, are thought to have acquired the disease abroad and taken it home. There is, however, no definite epidemiological evidence to support this theory.

The known and the unknown

Researchers now know—down to the level of atoms—the exact nature of the AIDS virus. They know its genetic sequence, the proteins it produces, and the diseases it causes. But there remains a great deal that is still unknown. Adding to the confusion has been a disagreement over the name. The French prefer LAV, while some U.S. authorities prefer HTLV-III; still others prefer ARV, for AIDS-associated retrovirus. An international committee assigned to come up with a name for the virus decided upon HIV, for human immunodeficiency virus, but whether that will be accepted by the research community remains to be seen. In 1986 U.S. researchers identified a congenital form of AIDS in some children born to women who have the disease or are in high-risk groups. These infants seem to have characteristic physical malformations that identify them as victims of the disease, independent of other symptoms, a discovery that has led some physicians to question the inclusion of the term acquired in the name AIDS and to suggest that congenital AIDS be renamed and classified along with other similar inborn defects of immune function.

More important than the name, however, is the mysterious nature of the virus itself. Why, for example, does it seem to be transmitted to men and women in equal proportions in Africa, whereas elsewhere in the world a majority of the victims are male? Why do fewer infected hemophiliacs, as compared with homosexuals and intravenous drug users, develop the disease? Where exactly did the virus come from, and how did it spread? Why do some antibody-positive individuals develop the disease while others do not? The most important question for the millions more who may have antibodies to the virus is how many of them will eventually develop the disease? And the crucial question for those victims of AIDS who have not yet succumbed to the disease: When will a cure be found?

—*Joanne Silberner*

The Vice of Vodka: Soviet Attack on Alcoholism

by Serge Schmemann

Among the many actions taken to drive the Soviet economy and society out of the doldrums during Mikhail S. Gorbachev's first year in office, probably the most visible was the action launched against drinking. The effort began almost immediately after Gorbachev was named general secretary in March 1985, when the press launched a sustained attack on drunkenness and alcoholism. In May the government announced a package of resolutions and laws that included stiff penalties for alcohol abuse, reductions in liquor production and sales, and calls for a massive campaign against the evils of the "green serpent"—vodka.

War on a pernicious problem

In its resolution "On Measures to Overcome Drunkenness and Alcoholism," the Central Committee of the Communist Party declared that "the overwhelming majority of Soviet people are unanimous in thinking that the use of alcohol does great economic and moral damage and that it is intolerable in the life of our society." Among the measures in the resolution and in subsequent laws enacted by all the Soviet republics, the drinking age was raised from 18 to 21, the sale of liquor before 2 PM was banned, and the production of vodka was ordered to be progressively reduced while production of the cheap, fortified wines that were the staple of hard-core alcoholics was to be halted by 1988. Penalties ranging from 20 rubles (about $26) to 300 rubles (about $390) and various terms of confinement were set for a broad variety of violations—drinking in public places or on the job, inducing minors to drink, speculating in vodka, or drunken driving. The highest fines were for production of home brew, known as *samogon* in Russian; this was evidently a step to prevent the antialcoholism campaign from turning into a bonanza for moonshiners.

The resolution also called for mass public action to deter alcoholism, including sobriety societies, publications, posters, treatment centers and counseling facilities, and improved facilities for leisure activities. Altogether the campaign generated an awesome volume of resolutions, decrees, laws, guidelines, and exhortations. The thrust, however, was relatively simple: the Soviet Union had once again declared war on its most persistent and pernicious problem.

Eduard A. Babayan, the chief addiction-treatment specialist in the Soviet Ministry of Health, emphasized the enormousness of the undertaking: "We have to change life-styles, habits, traditions of interpersonal relations, and rituals; to achieve a psychological breakthrough in the consciousness of tens of millions of people; to develop the material and technical base for carrying out this revolution in manners and morals."

Changes are striking

In the absence of comprehensive official statistics, there was no objective way to measure the progress of the campaign in its first months. But its effects were immediately tangible throughout Soviet life. For example, the number of drunks in Moscow streets declined noticeably.

Meanwhile, long queues became permanent fixtures outside liquor stores toward the 2 PM opening time as the number of outlets for vodka was sharply reduced. Alcoholic beverages were at first banned from 643 retail outlets in Moscow. But authorities relented after social drinkers complained that they were being lumped with hardened alcoholics, and so they permitted general stores to sell dry wines, premier cognacs, and champagne. In August 1985 the price of alcoholic beverages was sharply increased, with the cost of a liter of the cheapest vodka going to 6.20 rubles (about $8). In the first two weeks of June, Moscow police reported closing 21 private stills and arresting more than 1,000 persons for moonshining.

Additionally, as ordered, restaurants ceased serving alcoholic beverages before 2 PM, and alcoholic beverages of all sorts disappeared from official receptions, both in Moscow and at Soviet embassies abroad. Official Soviet hosts, renowned for overindulging their guests in liquor, were suddenly raising toasts with mineral water or Bulgarian fruit juices.

A mass organization known as the All-Union Voluntary Society for the Struggle for Sobriety came into being and within months reported membership in the millions. As the campaign was launched, antidrinking posters proliferated. Drinking scenes were cut from television shows, and movie theaters showed short features on the evils of alcoholism.

Television news carried regular reports about one liquor bottling plant or another switching to production of fruit juices. The new monthly publication, *Trezvosts i Kultura* ("Sobriety and Culture"), combined tales of lives ruined by alcohol with upbeat accounts of happy teetotalers and illustrations of smiling workers quaffing tea. The magazine advocated "dry weddings" and reported on "alcohol-free zones" set up by students in dormitories, workers at their factories, and peasants in their villages.

The antialcoholism campaign was not without its negative side effects. The press reported a jump in cases of poisoning from consumption of perfumes or industrial fluids as die-hard alcoholics sought alternatives to vodka. Restaurant managers and waiters reported a drop of up to 50% in income.

One question on which the press was mum was the impact of the campaign on state revenues. By some estimates sales of liquor had provided 40 billion rubles in annual revenues, or some 10% of the national budget, and there was no indication how the money was being made up.

Yet no one seriously questioned the campaign. By 1985 alcoholism and drinking had simply become too serious. The only question was whether the campaign would prove effective or lasting.

Alcohol's long-standing place in Soviet life

On the social level, drinking in the Soviet Union before the recent campaign had evolved into something of a mandatory ritual at any Soviet gathering. A festive dinner was unthinkable without innumerable toasts, each followed by the downing of a full shot of vodka. Vodka, cognac, and wine flowed freely at offical receptions; not to drink was impertinent. At home a bottle of cognac was the mandatory lubricant for an

Eager shoppers line up in front of a Moscow liquor store before opening time. The sale of liquor is prohibited in the Soviet Union before 2 PM—one of many measures aimed at curbing drunkenness.

Vlastimir Shone—SIPA/Special Features

evening around the kitchen table, and New Year's, a birthday, or most any other holiday was an occasion to get roaringly drunk. There was little social stigma to being drunk—indeed, that was often the purpose of a male get-together, and women were joining in more and more often.

But it was not social drinking, even on this level, that prompted Gorbachev to crack down. Alcoholism and drunkenness had become the major blight on all aspects of Soviet life—the factory, the family, and the streets.

The government stopped publishing comprehensive statistics on alcohol sales after 1963, although addiction specialist Babayan said in an interview in 1985 that per capita consumption of pure alcohol had fallen from 8.7 liters (2.3 gal) in 1980 to 8.3 liters (2.2 gal) in 1982. The figures generally agree with estimates produced by Vladimir G. Treml, the leading American expert on alcoholism in the Soviet Union.

Treml, however, has noted that the salient fact about drinking in the Soviet Union is the high proportion of strong liquor—high-proof alcohol—consumed. He has estimated that between 1955 and 1980, while consumption of all alcoholic beverages, including moonshine, increased only 2.4 times, the consumption of pure alcohol in the form of state-produced beverages increased 3.4 times. The U.S.S.R., according to Treml, had the highest per capita consumption not of total alcohol but of alcohol consumed in the form of strong beverages.

I. A. Krasnonosov, a Soviet sociologist, gave an interview to the newspaper *Sovetskaya Byelorussia* in which he estimated that in 1980, 17 billion liters (4.5 billion gal) of alcoholic beverages with an average strength of 28 proof were consumed in the Soviet Union. This amounted to 63.7 liters (17 gal) per capita, even without the moonshine that is produced and consumed in enormous quantities.

These and other facts and figures that came out in the Soviet press painted a grim picture. Alcoholism, they showed, played a major role in 60% of the larcenies, 75% of murders and rapes, 80% of robberies and armed assaults, and more than 90% of all misdemeanors. In the Russian republic, the largest of the Soviet states, alcohol was responsible for 45% of all divorces, or some 400,000 broken marriages a year.

The accounts showed that the average age of alcoholics decreased by five to seven years over the last decade and that 90% of all alcoholics had begun drinking before the age of 15. Studies in the cities of Moscow, Kirov, and Novgorod showed that 70% of adult women, 80% of boys aged 16 and 17, and 60% of girls in that age group drank.

The drinking took a heavy toll on health. Alcoholism was the third most prevalent disease in the U.S.S.R. after heart disease and cancer, and according to Western experts it was probably a major reason why the

Sensitive issues

What was noteworthy in the press campaign was that the proliferation of horror stories was not matched by studies of the causes of alcoholism, apparently because this touched on ideologically sensitive issues like boredom, loss of spiritual values, social dislocation, shortage of recreation facilities—explanations that might clash with official claims about general welfare. Only a few articles touched gingerly on the subject.

The writer Anatoly Omelchuk noted in *Literaturnaya Rossiya* that a common strand in the stories of alcoholics was the rootlessness of life in the rapidly growing new northern cities, like Novyi Urengoi in the gas fields of northern Siberia: "Each story had some of the same elements: strenuous work with no letup, feelings of restlessness in a new place and the problem of 'killing' free time, which was always solved the same way—with a bottle."

Other accounts found the grimmest scenes in the muddy rural villages. *Izvestiya* told of one rural region with a population of 9,154 where 100,000 to 150,-000 bottles were returned each month—almost all of them liquor bottles. That amounted to something like 20 bottles per month for every person over 17. On Mondays, the paper said, an average of 823 persons were brought into sobering-up stations.

The question of future success

The ultimate success of the campaign will be gauged only in time. Skeptics note that antialcoholism campaigns are not new in Russian and Soviet history. At the outbreak of World War I in 1914, the tsarist regime decreed nationwide prohibition. But in 1925 the Bolshevik authorities lifted the measure, arguing that the population had simply shifted to moonshine, which was often impure and dangerous. Another reason, not listed in Soviet sources, was Stalin's need to raise income for the state.

The dry law was followed by an antidrinking campaign that had some striking parallels to the current one. A decree in January 1929 reduced the production of alcoholic beverages and increased that of juices, and it also banned sales of liquor close to enterprises, educational institutions, and medical clinics. A "Society for Struggle Against Alcoholism" was founded, and its monthly publication, like the recently started publication, was called *Sobriety and Culture.* The magazine ceased in March 1930 after 38 issues.

Many subsequent campaigns were launched, too. But the alcohol problem has survived, apparently because the reasons for drinking survived. Like the earlier campaigns, Gorbachev's stringent new measures will probably show—indeed already have shown—some short-term results. But in time their success is likely to hinge largely on whether the government is willing to look to the causes of the massive, pernicious, and insidious alcoholism problems in the Soviet Union.

"Drunkenness is an evil!" is the translation of the message on the poster above. An all-out attack on alcoholism was among the first and most visible actions taken by Mikhail Gorbachev to drive Soviet society out of the doldrums.

life expectancy of Soviet men had actually declined in recent decades. The growing number of women alcoholics was held responsible for an increase in the birth of brain-damaged children.

The impact in the workplace was tangible. Newspapers said that labor productivity dropped by 15 to 20% after holidays and after the twice-monthly paydays. According to the newspaper *Izvestiya,* "The pernicious consequences of alcohol abuse are largely to blame for the shortage of labor." A sober work force, it predicted, would raise productivity by 10%.

Beyond the percentages and figures were the terrible stories of victims of the "green serpent." On a typical night at the Sklifosovsky First Aid Research Institute in Moscow, the first entry in the register reads: "Despite the resuscitation measures that were taken, we were unable to restore cardiac activity. The patient M., 64 years old, was brought in near death, with chemical burns of the oral cavity, the throat, the esophagus, and the stomach. Essence-of-vinegar poisoning after alcoholic intoxication."

Alcoholism and Alcohol Abuse

Ambivalence, conflict, and guilt mark the historical attitude toward the place of alcohol in many a society. Alcohol has been both valued as part of social custom and banned as a public hazard.

On the one hand, the production of alcohol provides a cornucopia of benefits to the general economy, such as millions of dollars in revenues, employment for millions of people, and billions of dollars in sales. Along with such economic benefits, alcohol also provides health and social benefits, such as longer life and fewer heart attacks, findings that are statistically correlated with moderate drinking. Perhaps alcohol's best known role is as an adjunct to the enjoyment of eating, socializing, and celebrating.

On the other hand, the misuse of alcohol and its consequences are manifold: hundreds of thousands of injuries and deaths, billions of dollars in economic loss, statistical correlations with suicide, homicide, crime, and family breakups. No one can ignore the serious damages inflicted on society by the misuse of alcohol.

U.S. drinking history—in brief

Early in the history of the United States, drinking alcoholic beverages was accepted as a benign and healthful social custom; drunkenness was publicly censured as moral weakness. As the country began to grow in size and complexity, the focus of censure shifted from the user of alcohol to the substance itself. Thus, alcohol was labeled a potentially addictive substance and its wide availability branded a public menace.

In the first half of the 19th century, the shift from censuring the drinker to blaming the substance gave birth to the temperance movement. The temperance movement grew into the Prohibition movement, and after World War I national Prohibition became the law. In 1919 the 18th Amendment to the United States Constitution and the Volstead Act, which enforced it, banned the manufacture, sale, and distribution of alcohol for the next 13 years, from 1920 to 1933. The trying years of economic upheaval and social chaos that accompanied the Great Depression led to a general revulsion against legislating morality. Pres. Franklin D. Roosevelt made alcohol legally available again when, for the first time in history, a constitutional amendment was repealed. The 21st Amendment repealed the 18th in 1933. The country's benevolent attitude toward alcohol and alcohol abuse then spawned the beginnings of the 20th-century disease concept of alcoholism.

For the next 50 years, alcohol experts felt that alcohol did not pose a problem for most people who chose to drink. Demographic studies show that one-third of the U.S. population do not drink alcoholic beverages at all, one-third drink occasionally, and one-third are regular drinkers. However, as alcohol problems increased, it was felt that a minority of people could not use alcohol without succumbing to its potentially addictive properties. Some experts saw alcoholism as a condition caused by a biologic sensitivity, while others saw it as a behavioral and environmental problem stemming from the psyche, society, or combinations thereof.

Alcoholism treatment: an industry

To deal with the growing number of alcohol problems, in 1971 Pres. Richard M. Nixon signed a bill that created the National Institute on Alcohol Abuse and Alcoholism (NIAAA). The institute was mandated to manage, treat, and prevent the nation's growing problem. At that time the number of problem drinkers was estimated at nine million to ten million persons.

With abundant resources for prevention and treatment, alcoholism was now treated and respected as a medical problem. The nonjudgmental climate that bathed the country after World War II was appropriate to the emerging concern with the quality of life.

Thus, during the 1970s and 1980s, the pursuit of a better life and society's compassion for alcoholics spawned one of the fastest growing and newly lucrative segments of the health care industry: the treatment of alcoholism. The change from yesteryear's isolated treatment houses run by recovered alcoholic people to today's nationwide chains of alcoholism treatment centers reaffirmed the radical shift in attitude toward the growing need for treatment and prevention.

Although the new treatment centers offered superior facilities and trained staff, traditional treatment approaches remained—and continue to remain—the modus operandi. In most instances treatment of alcoholism consists of a 28-day in-house program with the goal of total abstinence. Treatment includes detoxification and group therapy based on the principles of Alcoholics Anonymous (AA). The prevailing view among treatment professionals in the U.S. today is that total abstinence is the only reasonable goal for alcoholic people. Almost all treatment efforts in the United States for problem drinkers rely on medically oriented inpatient facilities. Other treatment approaches that contribute to better physical, psychological, and social functioning are given less prominence.

Successful alternatives to abstinence

Other countries, however—Canada and those of Western Europe—endorse the idea that therapy aimed at some degree of nonabstinence is appropriate for some patients. Programs endorsing nonabstinence goals claim better results among young people and with individuals treated in the criminal justice system. Nonabstinence goals have been less successful with people treated in detoxification centers and in-house hospital programs. The abstinence-only approach to treatment, still firmly embedded in a large segment of the U.S. treatment community, is beginning to be questioned.

A significant development in the evolution of the treatment system for problem drinkers has been occurring in the business community. A different kind of recognition and treatment program, the employee assistance program (EAP), helps facilitate the early identification of the problem. An EAP is an early warning and intervention system that offers diagnosis and treatment to "troubled" employees while they remain on the job. Larger companies are able to support their own in-house EAP programs, while smaller ones use a coalition approach. EAPs at the workplace are an example of business at its best: caring, responsive, salvaging, and setting standards for humane care.

In spite of the abundance of resources available to the alcoholic person, information about the possible causes and cures of alcoholism treatment is still scant and conflicting. To help fill this information gap, the alcoholism treatment community has begun to press for answers in genetic research that focuses on biologic sensitivity as cause.

Pursuit of a genetic link

The interest in genetics came from the results of adoption and twin studies that showed that offspring of alcoholic people adopted at birth are three to five times more likely to become alcoholic people themselves, whether or not the adoptive parents are alcoholic. Although there is no scientific evidence to support the thesis that a specific genetic defect can cause alcoholism, many researchers working in this area contend that genetic factors can predispose a person to alcoholism.

Some recent studies report that the offspring of alcoholic people manifest a variety of characteristics that may place them at a higher risk for alcoholism. For example, sons of alcoholic people seem to metabolize alcohol differently than do the sons of nonalcoholic people. The difference in metabolism is based on the findings that show higher levels of metabolic products (acetaldehyde) in the offspring of alcoholic people after drinking. A tendency toward hyperactivity is also reported among children of alcoholic people.

The application of genetic research findings to alcoholism is complicated by an array of conflicting data. Genetic researchers study, examine, and report on clearly definable conditions. But alcoholism is far removed from a clearly definable condition. Moreover, adoption studies fail to account for either the physiological impact of the alcoholic father at conception, *e.g.,* reported temporary breaks in the male chromosomal chain, or the impact on the developing fetus of the pregnant woman's heavy drinking.

Furthermore, recent findings have added to the confusion about the role alcohol plays in heredity. One major study found that sons of alcoholic people reported lower levels of intoxicating effects of a moderate dose of alcohol than a comparison group of

U.S. federal agents pour whiskey down the sewers during Prohibition. The manufacture, sale, and distribution of alcohol were banned by law from 1920 to 1933.

offspring of nonalcoholic people, while another recent study found that sons of alcoholic people report intoxicating effects when given a placebo.

Genetic research can be both appealing and dangerous. On the one hand, the magic of technology holds out the hope that a simple mechanical model might be constructed to solve a complex human and social problem like alcoholism. The search to find evidence that a simple gene might be implicated in the causal factors of an illness is indeed appealing. The danger, however, lies in the public's perception that a genetic predisposition, which increases risk, is fixed and immutable. Such a perception can produce hopelessness and resignation in the affected individual, whereas genetic influences in complex conditions such as alcoholism are highly mutable, especially by environmental influences.

Prevention: successes and failures

In spite of the progress made in providing care for the alcoholic person, including abundant treatment opportunities, industrywide employee assistance programs, and increased research efforts, alcohol problems continue to grow. The number of problem drinkers in the United States increased by 33% in 15 years—from an estimated 9 million in 1970 to an estimated 12 million problem drinkers in 1985. Unfortunately, the goal of prevention continues to be as elusive as the Holy Grail.

In the early 1980s a number of factors contributed toward tempering the nation's benevolent attitude toward alcohol abusers. The factor that captured the world's attention in the 1980s was drunk driving. Public service messages describing the terrible toll ex-

In the 1980s organizations such as Mothers Against Drunk Driving and Students Against Driving Drunk rose up in support of the innocent victims who are killed or maimed by intoxicated persons behind the wheel.

acted from drunk driving reached almost every household. National opinion polls revealed both widespread awareness of the drunk driving problem and the desire to do something to prevent it. Powerful grass roots organizations such as MADD (Mothers Against Drunk Driving) rose up to protect the rights of the victims of drunk driving accidents and their families. These organizations advocated preventive measures, which included the threat of jail terms, stricter punishment, and loss of license for offenders. Other proposed measures included alternative methods affecting the way alcohol is sold, such as warning labels, a national minimum drinking age, responsible alcohol advertising, and server liability.

The most innovative preventive measure that evolved to deal with the problem of drunkenness was more educational than restrictive. National prevention programs such as TIPS (training for intervention procedures by servers of alcohol) sprang up as prevention tools that offered people skills training in the responsible sale and service of alcohol.

Such prevention programs focus on enlisting the aid of the "people around the drinker." People who serve and sell alcohol, concession operators, and even social hosts are trained to recognize and interrupt patterns of abusive drinking, to prevent drunkenness, and to prevent drunk persons from putting themselves or others in the way of harm.

However laudable, preventive measures such as public service announcements, slogans, and pamphlets do not change behavior. Moreover, such messages are directed at the abusive drinkers—the people least likely to retain what they have learned. Thus, an effective prevention plan must bypass the drinker and enlist the help of the people around the drinker.

Although some social observers are predicting another Prohibition, a glance at past prohibition movements shows that society has historically chosen to use alcohol. Flexible treatment approaches, early diagnosis via employee assistance programs, and the prevention of drunkenness by training programs offer the best hope for long-term prevention.

—*Marion C. Chafetz*
and Morris E. Chafetz, M.D.

282

Allergy and Immunology

The human body protects itself against dangers in its environment by using specialized cells and their products; grouped together, these form the host-defense system. One of the disciplines concerned with host defenses is the branch of medicine called immunology, the study of the immune system. Recent discoveries in the field of basic immunology continue to influence the treatment of immunologic and allergic diseases, both common and unusual ones. In the last decade scientists have learned a great deal about specialized cell populations in human tissue and about the products of these cells that are involved in host defense against infection. This knowledge has provided insight into the mechanisms of allergic diseases and thus their treatment.

Host defense system in hay fever and asthma

From an embryological standpoint, the human respiratory tract is developmentally related to the gastrointestinal tract. Therefore, the cell populations and mechanisms for host defense in the respiratory tract are often similar to those in the gastrointestinal tract. For instance, certain specialized cells in the respiratory tract appear to have developed first to defend the body against parasites in the gastrointestinal tract. Two of these cell populations are the mast cells and a specialized white blood cell called the eosinophil. The human respiratory tract contains large quantities of mast cells and can easily recruit eosinophils in large numbers from the bloodstream by means of mast cell products.

Mast cells that make their home in the lining of the respiratory tract have the capability to bind a particular protein known as immunoglobulin E (IgE) antibody, which is found in much greater concentrations in allergic individuals. This antibody "programs" the mast cell for release of its biologically active chemical contents. When the IgE on its surface comes in contact with any substance—*i.e.,* allergen—that it recognizes (for instance, ragweed pollen), chemicals such as histamine are released from storage granules in the mast cell.

These chemicals and others generated from cell membrane phospholipids (a type of fatty acid) cause

(1) contraction of smooth muscle in the respiratory tract, (2) leakage of tissue fluids into the lining of the respiratory tract with resulting swollen membranes, (3) increased mucus production, and (4) the attraction of white blood cells including eosinophils into the lining of the respiratory tract. Eosinophils drawn into the respiratory tract can release toxic chemicals, including a compound called major basic protein, which further damage the respiratory lining. Both histamine and major basic protein are effective in host defense in the gastrointestinal tract against parasites such as roundworms.

If these chemicals are released in the lower respiratory tract, however, narrowing of the airways, wheezing, and shortness of breath that characterize the disease asthma may occur. If the reaction takes place in the nose and sinuses, it can cause the sneezing, runny nose, itching, and nasal obstruction associated with hay fever.

Treatment of asthma

In the United States alone, asthma affects more than six million individuals. Medical science has only recently begun to understand how these immunologic mechanisms and inflammatory cells cause and perpetuate asthma. On the basis of this understanding, new treatment regimens for asthma have been developed. Asthma medications can be classified into three categories: muscle relaxants, anti-mast-cell drugs, and anti-inflammatory/anti-white-blood-cell drugs. Among muscle relaxants the drug theophylline, a compound related to naturally occurring theobromine in cocoa, has long been used in asthma treatment. Long-acting theophylline preparations have now been developed that allow safe, stable blood levels of these compounds. A second medication in this category is the beta agonist, which may be taken either by inhalation or by mouth in pill or liquid form.

In the category of anti-mast-cell drugs is cromolyn sodium, which directly inhibits the ability of mast cells to release the chemicals that cause allergy. It is especially useful in infants and children, as it produces none of the side effects (sleeplessness, abdominal cramps, headaches, nausea) that sometimes accompany muscle-relaxant medications.

Among anti-inflammatory drugs are corticosteroid preparations, which have recently become available for use in the treatment of asthma by inhalation. When given over a long time, large oral doses of corticosteroids can have severe side effects, including fluid retention, softening of bones, and induction of diabetes; however, inhaled corticosteroids in appropriate doses appear to have none of these consequences and to be safe and effective in the treatment of severe asthma.

Besides the increase in understanding of the cellular mechanisms by which asthma occurs, more has also been learned about the mechanisms by which asthma attacks are triggered. This knowledge allows asthmatics to avoid those stimuli that provoke or exacerbate their asthma. It has long been known that house dust can provoke hay fever and asthma in some individuals with IgE antibody to it. The major allergic constituent of house dust appears to be the waste products of a microscopic insect called the house dust mite, which feeds on the contents of house dust and becomes a part of the dust when it dies. Since large quantities of house dust mites are found in mattresses, some patients with hay fever or asthma improve dramatically when they minimize exposure to the insect by encasing their mattresses in airtight plastic covers.

Other factors that may provoke asthma include exercise and exposure to certain drugs, including aspirin, and some preservatives such as the sulfites. Some asthmatics have acute exacerbation of asthma when they eat foods that have been sprayed with sulfite preservatives, antioxidants used to prevent browning of lettuce, potatoes, and fresh fruit. Sinusitis can also trigger asthma and is especially problematic if undetected. Nerve receptors in the sinuses appear to be stimulated by the presence of infection there. The resulting nervous system stimulation can cause reflex muscle contraction and narrowing of airways.

There is a growing consensus that chronic exposure to allergic stimuli induces a condition called nonspecific bronchial hyperreactivity, a state in which airways are easily triggered to constrict by multiple stimuli, including inhaled particles, cold air, cigarette smoke, vapors, fumes, and other environmental pollutants. Patients with this problem frequently complain of episodes of coughing and shortness of breath when exposed to these triggers. Bronchial hyperreactivity may be demonstrated in the laboratory by acute narrowing of the airways (bronchoconstriction as measured by pulmonary function testing) after inhalation of histamine or other bronchoconstrictor chemicals. Decreased allergen exposure or immunotherapy (allergy shots) may help this problem.

Hay fever treatment

The same mechanisms that cause asthma appear to cause hay fever, also known as allergic rhinitis. Hay fever must be differentiated from nonallergic causes of nasal inflammation, including infection. Individuals with hay fever typically have symptoms in the spring and fall.

During the past year several new families of antihistamines effective in the treatment of allergic rhinitis have become available. Moreover, unlike previously available antihistamines, the new ones cause little or no sedation. Some of these compounds can be taken twice a day. One of these new antihistamines that is presently available goes by the generic name terfenadine. The inhaled cromolyn and corticosteroid preparations used in asthma treatment also appear to be safe and effective when used nasally in the treatment of rhinitis.

Hives

In addition to those in the lining of the respiratory tract, mast cells are also present in the skin. When triggered by any of a number of stimuli to release chemicals there, urticaria (hives) may result. Hives are very common; indeed, over 50% of people will experience an episode at some time in life. Several new and interesting types of hives have been described recently.

Some individuals develop severe hives when they exercise and may have associated rhinitis and asthma. This syndrome is called exercise-induced anaphylaxis. It may occur in long distance runners and may be associated with intense dilation of blood vessels that causes loss of blood pressure and collapse. A strange variant of this syndrome, exercise-induced anaphylaxis that is associated with food, may occur when a food such as shrimp or celery is eaten prior to exercise. Individuals with exercise-induced anaphylaxis should seek a physician's advice as to when and how to exercise.

Another strange form of hives is cold urticaria. People with this problem develop severe itching and hives when they come in contact with cold water. Thus, individuals with cold urticaria who jump into or swim in cold water may have attacks of hives so severe that fainting occurs, and sometimes (though rarely) drowning has followed.

Biologic response modifiers

Other cells of the body produce important chemicals termed biologic response modifiers that modify and regulate inflammatory processes. Two families of these substances, interferons and interleukins, are produced by white blood cells called lymphocytes, among other cells. There is a special interest in these compounds as they can now be made in large quantities by using molecular engineering techniques. Interferons have the capacity to "activate" other white blood cells, including cells that may prevent the spread of cancer cells and viruses. In this regard, interferons have been used, with varying degrees of success, to treat viral diseases such as the common cold as well as a variety of malignancies, including Kaposi's sarcoma and malignant melanoma.

Interleukins also have the capacity to regulate immune responses. One of these compounds, interleukin-2, is produced in large quantities by a specialized lymphocyte called the T-helper lymphocyte. This is one of the primary cells that may become infected by the human T-cell lymphotropic virus, type III (HTLV-III), the cause of acquired immune deficiency syndrome (AIDS). If the lymphocyte does become infected, it is no longer able to produce interleukin-2 (also known as T-cell growth factor), and thus T lymphocytes neither grow nor function normally in infected individuals. The lack of normal T-helper lymphocyte function predisposes the patient to viral infections and to a host of other infectious agents. It also puts the patient at risk of cancer.

Hope for the future

Understanding the mechanisms by which immunologic diseases occur has opened new horizons in treatment that hold great promise for patients with these diseases. Long-acting allergen extracts that will al-

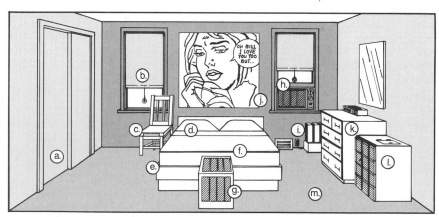

a. Keep closet shut.

b. Use shades rather than curtains or blinds.

c. Have no upholstered furniture; use wood or plastic instead.

d. Use washable synthetic pillows.

e. Keep mattress and box spring in air-tight covers.

f. Wash blankets often; have no wool or down.

g. Air cleaners may be helpful.

h. Air conditioners minimize humidity and mite growth.

i. Close air vents; use electric radiator.

j. Have no cloth wall decorations.

k. Keep furniture dusted; have no exposed books, toys, etc.

l. To prevent mite growth, avoid over humidification in winter.

m. Have no carpets; clean wood or linoleum floors with damp mop daily.

From a study by Andrew M. Murray and Alexander B. Ferguson, University of British Columbia, Vancouver

low immunization against allergens (such as ragweed) should provide considerable relief for allergy sufferers. Newer drugs directed against the specific chemical mediators of allergic reactions also should allow more effective treatment of allergy with fewer side effects. The identification of those compounds that regulate immune responses has made possible the synthesis and production of these regulator compounds in large quantities. Such "immunomodulators" are presently being investigated for their ability to regulate immune responses. In those patients with inadequate immunologic responses, these compounds will allow "turning on" of the immune sytem. In those with inappropriate or ongoing immune responses, which result in disease, other substances may be able to down-regulate these responses.

—*Richard D. deShazo, M.D.,*
and Gillian Fansler Brown, Ph.D.

Arthritis and Rheumatic Diseases

The word arthritis, which is derived from *arthron,* the Greek word for "joint," means inflammation of the joints. Arthritis is not a single disease but a manifestation of many different diseases. While the terms arthritis and rheumatism were once synonymous and are sometimes still used interchangeably, "arthritis" is now ordinarily used when a joint itself is inflamed and "rheumatism" is applied when the soft tissues near joints are involved. The American Rheumatism Association estimates that at least 100 different diseases can cause arthritis or rheumatism. Some of the major recent advances in the understanding and treatment of these diseases are highlighted below.

Genetics and the rheumatic diseases

An important breakthrough in the past 15 years has been the recognition that people inherit a tendency to develop certain kinds of arthritis. Within a person's genetic material are certain genes, called HLA genes, that can be detected indirectly by identifying molecular markers on the surface of blood cells. When individuals with a specific HLA gene develop a disease more often than do individuals who do not have that gene or, conversely, when a specific gene is found more frequently in individuals with a disease than in the population at large, medical researchers recognize that an association exists between the gene and the disease. Four major kinds of rheumatic disease—rheumatoid arthritis, ankylosing spondylitis, Reiter's syndrome, and some forms of chronic arthritis in children—are associated with HLA genes. The most striking is the association between the gene HLA-B27 and ankylosing spondylitis, a disease that usually causes progressive stiffness of the spine. Among whites, for example, HLA-B27 is found in only 8% of the unaffected population but in more than 90% of patients with ankylosing

spondylitis. A white person bearing HLA-B27 is over 100 times more likely to develop ankylosing spondylitis than one who does not. It is not clear how HLA-B27 predisposes to ankylosing spondylitis. Most of the evidence suggests that the disease occurs when an individual bearing a predisposing gene is exposed to an as yet unidentified environmental triggering factor, perhaps a bacterium or a virus.

These findings have had tremendous effect on the thinking of medical scientists. Within the past few years advances in molecular biology have allowed researchers to study an individual's DNA (deoxyribonucleic acid), which constitutes the genes themselves, in a direct way rather than through indirect markers. When DNA is mixed with certain enzymes in the laboratory, it breaks in a predictable way into fragments. When abnormal genes are present, the fragments produced may be of unusual size. Some of these may be found to be associated with diseases. Such differences in DNA fragment length, called restriction fragment length polymorphisms (RFLPs), have been reported very recently in certain rheumatic diseases. If such approaches eventually succeed in identifying genes for disease susceptibility, it may be possible to identify individuals who are likely to develop a particular kind of arthritis. Later, as understanding of possible environmental triggering factors grows, disease in susceptible individuals may be preventable either by vaccination or by instructing them to avoid exposure to those factors.

Autoantibodies and rheumatic diseases

Systemic lupus erythematosus (SLE), or lupus, is an inflammatory disease of the connective tissues that affects many areas of the body including the skin, kidneys, nervous system, muscles, lungs, heart, and blood-forming organs as well as the joints. SLE affects women about eight times as often as it does men. Although it can occur at any age in either sex, it usually appears during the childbearing years. Female hormones, therefore, are suspected of playing a role.

The immune systems of individuals with SLE produce an array of autoantibodies—abnormal antibodies against the individual's own tissues—which appear to cause much of the damage. Among them are antibodies directed against components of cell nuclei—so-called antinuclear antibodies (ANAs). Investigators have discovered ANAs against more than 25 nuclear components including DNA.

New work has demonstrated that ANAs also occur in rheumatic diseases other than SLE, although the specific antibodies found in these conditions generally differ from those found in patients with SLE. Three of these diseases are scleroderma, a chronic hardening and shrinking of the connective tissues; Sjögren's syndrome, in which inflammation in the tear glands and salivary glands eventually leads to dryness of the eyes and mouth; and polymyositis, in which inflammation in muscles causes weakness.

Patients with SLE may have autoantibodies in addition to ANAs. For example, antibodies directed against red blood cells can cause anemia, and antibodies that react with blood platelets can lead to their rapid removal from the blood and produce a consequent tendency to bleed. Non-ANA autoantibodies are found in other rheumatic diseases as well. One of the most important is the so-called rheumatoid factor, an abnormal antibody against immunoglobulins, which are themselves antibody molecules in the blood. Rheumatoid factor is thus an antibody against other antibodies. It is found in about three out of four people with rheumatoid arthritis.

The discovery of autoantibodies in a number of rheumatic diseases indicates that some dysfunction of the immune system plays an important role in many of these conditions. The immune system normally functions to protect the body by recognizing "foreign" substances such as disease-causing bacteria and cancer cells and attacking them. In many diseases that lead to arthritis, especially rheumatoid arthritis and SLE, the inflammatory process probably results from a malfunction in which the immune system mistakenly attacks normal tissues as if they were foreign.

Victims of a number of the rheumatic diseases have immune complexes—antibodies bound to their antigens (the substances against which the antibodies are directed)—circulating in the blood. When these immune complexes lodge in tissues, particularly in the kidney, they may cause inflammation, leading to tissue damage. Immune complexes are thought to be responsible for a number of the manifestations of some rheumatic diseases.

Rheumatic fever

Fifty years ago acute rheumatic fever was a major public health concern in the U.S., largely affecting children and causing not only arthritis but also heart disease. Later in life many individuals who had rheumatic fever as children developed a disease of the heart valves (rheumatic heart disease), which led to serious heart failure and often death. Rheumatic fever is caused by a person's reaction to a throat infection with group A streptococcus bacteria. The capacity of these organisms to cause rheumatic fever is related to socioeconomic factors; rheumatic fever was always more common among the poor than the well-to-do. Studies conducted immediately after World War II demonstrated that rheumatic fever could be prevented by identifying and treating streptococcal infections with penicillin or certain other antibiotics. As the conditions of life have improved in the U.S., and as strep throats have been promptly treated, rheumatic fever has become less and less common, so that today it is quite rare. Similarly the disease is now uncommon in the industrialized countries of Western Europe, such as the U.K., France, Denmark, and Sweden.

In contrast, rheumatic fever still commonly afflicts people in the less developed world. Although reliable statistics are not always available, this disease is known to occur frequently among children in Egypt, Pakistan, India, and the Caribbean. The prevalence of rheumatic heart disease in schoolchildren in affluent countries is between 1 and 5 in 10,000, while in such countries as India, Egypt, Pakistan, and Algeria, the prevalence is between 20 and 200 in 10,000. One survey indicates that as many as 9 of every 100 children in Bolivia have rheumatic heart disease. On the other hand, there has been a decline in the more de-

Although it is now rare in the U.S., rheumatic fever is still common among children in third world countries and is an important cause of heart disease. Susceptibility is related to socioeconomic conditions.

veloped Latin-American countries such as Argentina, Chile, and Uruguay.

Despite the understanding of the relationship between acute rheumatic fever and a preceding streptococcal infection, a number of aspects of the development of this disease are still unclear. Only a small proportion of individuals with streptococcal sore throat develop rheumatic fever, and only a few of these develop heart involvement. Scientists have found that antigenic molecules carried by group A streptococci are shared by human heart cells, suggesting that antibodies directed against the streptococci also attack the heart and are at least partially responsible for the heart damage in this disease. During the past year work continued in efforts to understand more precisely how streptococcal infection leads to acute rheumatic fever and how this scourge can be prevented in those countries in which it is still a major problem.

Crystal-deposition diseases

Two major diseases have been identified as resulting from the deposition of crystals in joints. One of them, gout, has been known for thousands of years. The other disease, calcium pyrophosphate deposition disease (CPPD), was not recognized until 1962.

Although it has been known for about 140 years that individuals with gout have high concentrations of uric acid in their blood (hyperuricemia), the mechanism by which this condition leads to acute arthritic attacks was not understood until relatively recently. Too much uric acid in the blood ultimately results in the deposition of tiny crystals of uric acid salts in the joint lining. Crystals may then fall into the fluid-filled space within the joint, triggering a severe inflammatory reaction, the acute attack of gouty arthritis. Acute attacks of gout are extremely painful, usually begin very quickly, and last a few days to a few weeks. After an attack the joint returns to normal, but attacks usually recur and can eventually damage the affected joints.

A number of different metabolic abnormalities can lead to hyperuricemia; there is no single cause. Genetic predisposition plays a role in some people. Recently it has become apparent that what people consume makes a difference. Both obesity and heavy drinking lead to elevated uric acid levels in the blood. Weight loss and moderation in drinking habits reverse the abnormality. Drugs that lower the concentration of uric acid in the blood to normal levels have completely changed the long-term prospects for patients with gouty arthritis. Such therapy prevents damage to the joints and eventually prevents acute attacks of gout.

Calcium pyrophosphate deposition disease results from crystalline deposits of a certain kind of calcium salt in joints. In some people it may cause acute attacks of severe pain in a single joint, resembling gout; such individuals are said to have pseudogout. In others chronic pain or repeated attacks of pain and

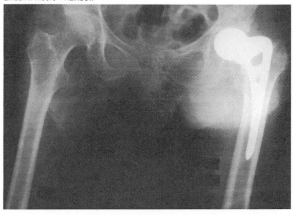

Total replacement of diseased or damaged joints is one of the most dramatic advances in treatment of arthritis. Hip replacement, shown at right in the X-ray above, is among the most successful of these procedures.

swelling may occur over many years. Sometimes people with this condition have coexisting osteoarthritis or other kinds of arthritis. Because both osteoarthritis and CPPD occur in elderly people, the coexistence of these conditions is very common.

Cortisone and beyond

During the late 1940s, following laboratory purification of some of the hormones of the adrenal glands, one of these adrenal corticosteroids, cortisone, was first used to treat people with rheumatoid arthritis, with dramatic results. It soon became apparent that cortisone and related synthetic substances are extremely potent anti-inflammatory agents and are effective in a number of rheumatic conditions. These drugs do not actually cure inflammatory states but merely suppress inflammation. Nonetheless, they have proved to be extremely useful, often lifesaving medications. Because they may have serious side effects, corticosteroids are given primarily to people with severe disease. Over the years the indications for the use of these drugs have become well defined and the proper dosage and duration of therapy better understood.

Doctors try to restrict the use of adrenal corticosteroids because of their toxicity. Until 1953 there was only one nonsteroidal anti-inflammatory drug (NSAID), aspirin. Since then a large number of NSAIDs have become available. Generally much less toxic but more expensive than aspirin, they have contributed substantially to the well-being of individuals with many different kinds of arthritis. In the U.S. one of these drugs, ibuprofen, previously available only by prescription, recently became available over the counter.

At least ten of the newer NSAIDs are in widespread use at present, and more continue to appear. Most rheumatologists feel that they differ little in therapeutic efficacy and toxicity. Periodically claims of enhanced

Sensors located in the ball-shaped head of this partial hip replacement monitor pressures exerted on the joint. This experimental prosthesis is being used to perfect the hip replacement process and enable more effective rehabilitation.

efficacy for a particular NSAID are made, but they have not held up with prolonged experience. Conversely, concerns about unacceptable degrees of toxicity are occasionally voiced; sometimes these have been serious enough to lead to change in therapeutic use. For example, manufacturers of the drug phenylbutazone now warn physicians that it should never be administered casually and should not be employed as initial therapy for any of the conditions for which it is indicated because of the increased risk of bone-marrow damage.

Total joint replacement

One of the most dramatic advances in the treatment of arthritic patients has been the perfection of techniques for total joint replacement, in which plastic and metal alloys are substituted for the diseased bones of damaged joints in selected patients. Availability of the polymer polymethyl methacrylate, which is used as a bone cement, and such modern plastics as polyeth-

ylene and silicone permitted the development of this technique. Because of the dangers of bone infection, total joint replacement surgery is performed in special operating rooms in which laminar airflow prevents bacteria from entering the surgical field.

Application of this surgical procedure to arthritis of the hip has permitted thousands of patients who had previously suffered from severe pain and limited hip motion as a result of rheumatoid arthritis, osteoarthritis, ankylosing spondylitis, or other rheumatic diseases to be relieved of pain and to walk much more freely than would have been possible before. The principles of this technique have been applied to other joints. In general, outcome is related to the skill and experience of the surgeon and his or her team. Total knee-joint replacement is now widely and successfully employed. Considerable success is being achieved at leading medical centers with shoulder- and finger-joint replacement. Techniques for surgically replacing elbows, wrists, and ankles have been developed, although some of them are still in the developmental stage, largely because of problems with attaching artificial materials to bone. Research is focusing on this problem and on developing biomaterials that more closely resemble bone mechanically.

Other areas of current research

Over the years it has been suspected that chronic, slowly developing viral infections may be responsible for rheumatoid arthritis. Interest in possible infectious causes of arthritis was spurred on by the recent demonstration that Lyme arthritis, which occurs following tick bites, was due to infection by a previously unknown member of a group of microorganisms called spirochetes. Recent preliminary evidence implicates a previously unknown virus of a type called parvovirus in the development of rheumatoid arthritis, although this case has not yet been proved by any means.

There is currently considerable interest in the possibility that rheumatoid arthritis may be modified by dietary manipulation. Because of evidence suggesting that inflammatory and immunologic mechanisms may be altered by consuming fish oil, clinical trials in which people with rheumatoid arthritis take fish-oil pills are being carried out. The possibility that arthritis symptoms might be food related and due to a type of allergy has been investigated, but no support for this idea has been found in the vast majority of people tested. Nevertheless, evidence suggests that a small proportion, probably fewer than 5%, have food allergies that could affect their symptoms. Further careful, controlled studies are needed in order to validate this preliminary observation, to discover ways of identifying such people, and to determine how effective any changes in their diets will be. Such studies are currently being undertaken.

—Irving Kushner, M.D.

Awards and Prizes

Prizes for medical research are associated with prestige, money, or both. There are world-renowned prizes of such high honor as the Nobel Prize; additionally, scientific societies have awards, drug companies give honors, university departments name lectureships for former chairmen, commemorative plaques are placed, and hospital wings are named; the list is nearly endless. The types of medical research that garner awards are as varied as the field of medicine itself. Traditionally, honors tend to get heaped on clinical advances or work that directly leads to treatments rather than on pure basic research; this tendency has the effect of giving the public a distorted view of how scientific research actually works. It is usually the work, over many years, of many unrecognized individuals on underlying medical or physiological mechanisms that enables the discoveries or significant clinical advances for which awards are ultimately given. Nevertheless, the representative sampling that follows of major awards given in the calendar year 1985 does point to some of science's major recent successes.

Nobel Prize: 1985

The Nobel Prize for Physiology or Medicine in 1985 went to two researchers who have won most of the major awards in medicine. Michael S. Brown and Joseph L. Goldstein of the University of Texas Health Science Center at Dallas were lauded for their work on how the body deals with cholesterol. The Nobel assembly noted that the two "have through their discoveries revolutionized our knowledge about the regulation of cholesterol metabolism and the treatment of diseases caused by abnormally elevated cholesterol levels in the blood."

While too much cholesterol in the blood clogs the arteries and can cause heart attacks or strokes, the body needs cholesterol to survive. Cholesterol is used in building cell membranes and manufacturing some hormones and digestive acids, and the body makes most of its cholesterol itself.

Brown and Goldstein began on the road to the Nobel in 1973, when they discovered how cells can grab cholesterol from the bloodstream. They discovered that cells have receptors for low-density lipoprotein (LDL), a particle that carries cholesterol in the blood. The LDL sticks to the receptor, which pulls it into the cell, releases it after a series of steps, and returns to the surface of the cell, where it can repeat the process. Meanwhile, the LDL inside the cell is broken down, and its cholesterol is used as a building material. The process primarily takes place in the liver.

Goldstein and Brown found that the LDL receptor is related to a disease called familial hypercholesterolemia. About one person in a million has six times the normal level of LDL in the blood. People in this group generally die of heart attacks by the age of 20; some succumb to heart attacks as early as age 2. A second group, about one in 500 people, have a less severe form of the disease. Their LDL level is twice the normal level. They also suffer heart attacks at an early age, usually beginning at age 35.

At the root of the high blood cholesterol problem is the pair of genes that produce the LDL receptor. The people with the most severe form of hypercholesterolemia are homozygous for it—that is, both of their LDL-receptor-producing genes are defective—and cannot produce any normal LDL receptors. Those with the less severe form have only one defective gene in each cell. They can produce half the normal number of functional LDL receptors. When a person does not have enough LDL receptors, the cholesterol remains in the bloodstream, where it can initiate and exacerbate atherosclerosis.

Brown and Goldstein's work has suggested new forms of treatment for the condition and has explained why some treatments work. They found that the reason drugs that bind to the bile acids lower cholesterol is that the drugs cause an increase in the number of LDL receptors (bile acids are made from cholesterol). The greater number of receptors remove more cholesterol-carrying LDL from the blood, and the person then has a lower blood cholesterol level.

Their work also suggested that people with the homozygous form of familial hypercholesterolemia will not respond to drugs that stimulate receptor formation. As a result of this important finding, liver transplants have been done in people suffering from the disease. The first one was done in 1984 in a six-year-old girl who had suffered several heart attacks. Her new liver, capable of producing LDL receptors and removing cholesterol from the blood, has thus far allowed her to lead a normal life.

Albert Lasker awards

For Brown and Goldstein the road to the Nobel was marked with dozens of other awards for their cholesterol research. Although the information had not been released publicly in October 1985 when the Nobel Prizes were announced, they had already won another of the top medical prizes, the Albert Lasker basic medical research award for 1985. That award was officially given in November.

Bernard Fisher, a surgeon at the University of Pittsburgh (Pa.) School of Medicine, won the 1985 Lasker award for clinical medical research. In the 1950s and 1960s Fisher showed that tumor cells could spread by traveling through the body's lymphatic system. More recently he has run several major clinical trials comparing various breast cancer treatments. Most notable among these was a five-year-long study, initiated in 1976 by the National Surgical Adjuvant Breast Project and conducted at 89 institutions, that compared different degrees of surgery for breast cancer. The findings, welcome news to a great many potential breast cancer victims, showed that in women with small cancers, removing only the tumor and adjacent tissue can be just as effective as removing the breast and underlying muscle.

Lasker awards are also given for public service in the health field. Lane W. Adams, former chief executive officer of the American Cancer Society (ACS), was honored for strengthening the ACS, which stands today as the world's largest voluntary health organization, embracing two million volunteers and providing $250 million a year for research and for cancer prevention and treatment. Eppie Lederer, better known as Ann Landers, also won a Lasker public service award for human relations work she has done through her syndicated newspaper column, translating complex medical information into simple and clear language for the benefit of her readers. Brown and Goldstein shared the $15,000 that goes with their award; the others each received $15,000.

Cancer and immunology awards

Several corporations also present major medical awards. Bristol-Myers Co., for example, has given a $50,000 award for distinguished achievement in cancer research each year since 1978; in 1985 it went to William S. Hayward of Memorial Sloan-Kettering Cancer Center and Philip Leder of Harvard Medical School for their work on the relationship between cancer and genetics.

Cells normally possess a specific gene that has been named the myc gene. In 1980 Hayward discovered that viruses can activate this gene and cause the cell to grow uncontrollably. About 20 such "cancer" genes have been found. Hayward and his colleagues showed that certain viruses can replace the myc gene's normal growth-control mechanism. Leder also studied the myc gene and found that if the gene itself moves to another chromosome, its growth control is disturbed and cancer can result. He and his colleagues found that in a certain kind of cancer (Burkitt's lymphoma), the myc genes had shifted position. Burkitt's lymphoma is the most common childhood tumor in African children residing in a geographical belt of endemic malaria and mosquito-borne infectious diseases.

Another cancer honor, awarded by the Hammer Prize foundation, established and directed by Armand Hammer, went for work with more immediate clinical application, done by Steven A. Rosenberg of the U.S. National Cancer Institute and Tadatsugu Taniguchi of Osaka (Japan) University. The year 1985 was one of substantial public recognition for Rosenberg; in the summer he was part of the surgical team that treated U.S. Pres. Ronald Reagan for colon cancer, and in December he and his colleagues published a paper describing the work for which Rosenberg was awarded

the Hammer prize—a novel cancer treatment that stimulates the immune system to destroy cancer cells.

Taniguchi was honored for isolating and cloning the gene that makes the immune system stimulator that Rosenberg utilized. The factor at the root of both Rosenberg's and Taniguchi's research is interleukin-2, a natural substance produced by the body in minute quantities. Before Taniguchi cloned the gene, only very small amounts of interleukin-2 could be produced. But Taniguchi in 1983 isolated and cloned the gene, making it possible to insert the gene into bacteria, which can then pump out large amounts of the interleukin-2 product.

Rosenberg and his colleagues used genetically engineered interleukin-2 to stimulate white blood cells called lymphocytes that had been removed from cancer patients. The interleukin-2 stimulated the lymphocytes to develop into lymphokine-activated killer cells, which selectively destroy cancer cells. They reinjected the lymphokine-activated killer cells into the cancer patients, along with a booster of interleukin-2. In 11 of 25 patients, previously untreatable tumors reduced in size by at least 50%. The treatment was lauded as a new approach to cancer therapy, inasmuch as it stimulates the immune system to do the work that heretofore had been left to drugs, radiation, or surgery. But the exceptionally complicated treatment is not without side effects, some of which can be severe; they include weight gain and kidney and lung problems and, in at least one case, death.

General Motors (GM) in 1985 gave $130,000 each to a previous Lasker laureate, Paul C. Lauterbur, and to J. Christopher Wagner and Robert T. Schimke. Lauterbur, a professor of chemistry at the State University of New York at Stony Brook, played a key role in the development of magnetic resonance imaging (MRI) and created the first MRI image. MRI (also called nuclear magnetic resonance, or NMR) uses the responses of individual atomic nuclei within an organism to magnetic fields to produce a detailed image; it enables the visualization of soft body tissue often impossible with X-rays or computerized axial tomography (CAT) scans.

Lauterbur worked out the mathematics required to convert the data generated by the magnetic field effects into a three-dimensional image. The process has since proved invaluable in detecting tumors and other disorders. In brain scans it can detect differences between diseased and healthy cells, letting physicians know prior to surgery the precise nature of the problem.

J. Christopher Wagner of the United Kingdom's Medical Research Council pneumoconiosis unit at Llandough Hospital, Glamorgan, South Wales, was honored for being the first to link asbestos exposure to a form of lung cancer and for research into the cancer-inducing potential of other fibers. Wagner discovered that only thin, straight asbestos fibers can cause mesothelioma, a fatal type of lung cancer, and that some types of asbestos are less carcinogenic than others.

The third GM award went to Stanford University's Robert T. Schimke for genetic research into the nature of cancer, specifically, how cancer cells genetically adapt to chemotherapy. Starting with the observation that some malignant cells exposed to an anticancer drug fight to survive by producing more of the vital protein the drug attacks, he found that the cancer cells produced extra copies of the gene that produces the protein, weakening the effects of the chemotherapy.

Immunology research, which is closely linked to current genetic and oncologic investigations, brought Hugh O. McDevitt of Stanford University the $100,-000 Lita Annenberg Hazen award for his research into the genetic control of the immune response. McDevitt found that just as people have blood types, they have tissue types, and people with certain tissue types are more prone to certain diseases. These tissue types are defined by markers that sit on the surface of cells; the markers allow the body's immune system to distinguish self from nonself and are a key factor in the success or failure of organ transplants.

The above prizes and other awards given for medical research and achievements in 1985 recognize the intelligence, training, hard work, and luck that led to significant discoveries; they also set standards of excellence and provide tangible goals to others who are pursuing research.

—Joanne Silberner

Cancer

More than 20 years of research by some of the world's best scientists and the expenditure of billions of dollars have not been enough to slow the rate at which people die of cancer. In the United States, for example, between 1962 and 1982 the total number of people who died from this group of diseases increased 56%, from 278,562 to 433,795. In 1962, 170 out of every 100,000 Americans succumbed to cancer; by 1982 the toll had risen to 185 per 100,000.

These dismal statistics do not tell the whole story, however. Peter Greenwald, director of the National Cancer Institute's (NCI's) Division of Cancer Prevention and Control, in 1986 made the point that improvements in cancer treatment take years to show up in higher survival rates, emphasizing that mortality figures through 1982 reflect progress in the past decade, not the current decade. Commenting on the present status of cancer in the U.S., Charles A. LeMaistre, president of the American Cancer Society (ACS), stressed that statistics alone are misleading; it is important to realize that more has been learned about cancer in the last two decades than in all the preceding decades. In

1986 one-half of serious cancer cases were curable. The half that cannot be cured are better controlled, resulting in longer survival. ACS data reveal that in the 1960s only one out of three cancer patients had any hope of surviving five years after treatment. Today four out of ten people who get cancer will be alive five years after the diagnosis.

Nonetheless, cancer does still kill almost a half million Americans annually. Moreover, the ACS estimates that 472,000 people in the U.S. will die of the disease in 1986, and about 930,000 new cases will be diagnosed.

The number one killer

Lung cancer is, by far, the biggest killer. Of the 472,000 total expected cancer deaths in 1986, it will account for about 130,000; of the estimated 930,000 new cases of cancer diagnosed, 149,000 are expected to be lung cancer. Death rates from this malignancy among white men in the U.S. decreased from 83 per 100,000 in 1982 to 79 per 100,000 in 1983. However, among women deaths increased from 20 per 100,000 in 1974 to almost 33 per 100,000 in 1983. Among black men the 1983 rate was 125 per 100,000.

Smoking habits account largely for these changes. For many years the number of young women who have begun to smoke has risen, and this has been seen as an increasingly alarming trend. For decades breast cancer had been the number one cancer killer in women. As deaths from lung cancer were steadily mounting, it was projected that lung cancer mortality would eventually overtake breast cancer. In 1986 that prediction was realized; deaths from lung cancer surpassed those from breast cancer in 15 states. The ACS anticipates that this trend will spread to all other states.

A person who has smoked for 20 years has a one in 14 chance of developing lung cancer. About 90% of those who contract the disease die within five years, most within the first 18 months. Of those who attempt to quit smoking, fewer than one in ten succeeds in quitting permanently. This led the American Medical Association in 1985 to call for a national ban on cigarette advertising. The ACS Board of Directors did the same in 1986, voting to support elimination of all advertising of cigarettes and smokeless tobacco products in all of the media. The ACS also called for an end to tobacco company sponsorship of sports and other events that attract audiences of young people.

President Reagan treated for two cancers

Colorectal cancer is the second largest cause of cancer deaths in the U.S. The ACS expected 60,000 deaths in 1986, 51,000 from colon and 8,200 from rectal cancer. Public awareness of this toll received a boost when surgeons removed about 61 cm (two feet) of Pres. Ronald Reagan's colon in July 1985. The section contained an adenocarcinoma, the commonest type of colon cancer. The attending publicity resulted in six times the normal number of inquiries about colorectal cancer received by the NCI. The warning signs of this cancer became widely known, and requests for do-it-yourself kits to detect blood in the stool and for sigmoidoscopic examinations by physicians increased dramatically. The ACS now recommends a sigmoidoscopic examination every three to five years after age 50, following two consecutive annual exams with negative results. The experts disagree on whether mass screening of younger individuals will significantly reduce mortality from colorectal cancer.

President Reagan returned to the hospital briefly in August 1985 and again in October 1985 to have cancerous growths removed from his nose. The growths were the commonest, least dangerous form of skin cancer, basal-cell carcinoma—the chief cause of which is overexposure to the sun. Physicians diagnose more than 400,000 cases of this disease each year, in addition to the 930,000 new cases of other, more serious skin cancers. The president's wife, Nancy Reagan, had had the same type of lesion removed from her lip in 1982. There was no connection between the president's colorectal cancer and his skin cancer.

Basal-cell skin carcinomas are usually small, smooth nodules, although sometimes they are red and crusty; they occur most often on the face. In the U.S. one Caucasian in seven will have a basal-cell skin cancer in his or her lifetime. By contrast, blacks rarely develop this type of lesion.

The process that removed Reagan's two skin cancers from his nose is known as curettage and electrodessication. The physician scrapes away the lesion with a sharp circular blade (curette) after local anesthetic is given. Then an electrified needle is applied to the area of the lesion to destroy any remnants of the malignancy. The procedure usually is performed in a physician's office and takes less than half an hour.

With treatment, survival rates for basal-cell skin cancers are 95% or better. But since the chances of developing more lesions within two years are 25–50%, follow-up of patients who have these essentially minor cancers is important.

Reagan drew attention to the major cause of skin cancer when he said that "medicine has been waging a great campaign to try and convince people to stop broiling themselves in the sun." Nonetheless, he admitted that having the skin cancer and thus having to avoid the sun was personally "a little heartbreaking . . . because all my life I've lived with a coat of tan, dating back to my lifeguard days."

In June 1986 Reagan again had small polyps removed from his colon, but these were found to be benign.

Preventive agents

Researchers are attempting to find substances that prevent cancer as well as those that cause it. Since 1982 the NCI has been conducting a program to evaluate substances such as beta-carotene (a precursor of vitamin A), vitamins C, E, and B$_{12}$, folic acid, and selenium. One of the 26 clinical trials the NCI was conducting in 1986, for example, evaluates the effects of wheat fiber and a vitamin C and E combination on development of bowel cancer. Researchers suspect that the vitamins and fiber can reduce the incidence of polyps that become cancerous. Another trial, in Linxian (Lin-hsien), China, involved an attempt to reduce the risk of esophageal cancer with multivitamin and multimineral supplements given in amounts two to three times higher than the U.S. recommended daily

John Durant, president of the Fox Chase Cancer Center in Philadelphia, places a lid on a time capsule in April 1986 at a reunion of 130 survivors of cancer, all of whom had been free of cancer for five years.

requirement. One scientist characterizes these trials as a systematic approach to identifying interventions that may significantly reduce the incidence of cancer.

A study at the Mayo Clinic, Rochester, Minn., has contradicted the widely publicized and controversial assertion of Nobel laureate Linus Pauling that massive doses of vitamin C can extend the lives of people with advanced cancers. The Mayo scientists compared similarly ill patients who took vitamin C with those who did not. They found that large doses of the vitamin did not shrink tumors or allow patients to live longer.

Breast cancer

Breast cancer ranks as the third most common and lethal form after lung and colorectal cancer. The ACS expects 40,000 deaths from it and 123,000 new cases in 1986. Most of these women will be over age 50. Concern had been raised that these numbers are increased by women who take birth control pills. However, at least two recent studies have concluded that for women under 45 years of age, taking oral contraceptives does not increase the risk of getting the disease.

For women of all ages, the sooner the cancer is detected, the better the chance for a cure. According to 1985 ACS statistics, the five-year survival rate for women with localized (*in situ*) cancers is 96%. A recent study done in Sweden of more than 162,000 women found that the death rate was about 30% higher among women who did not get regular X-ray examinations of the breast (mammograms) than among women who did. The ACS recommends mammograms every year for women over age 50; it also advocates monthly self-examination by women 20 years and older and, to detect lumps too small to be felt, a supplementary mammogram every three years. After age 40 mammograms should be done at least every two years.

At one time women who discovered a lump often did not go to a physician because they feared a radical mastectomy, which removes the entire breast, underlying chest muscles, and surrounding lymph nodes. Radical operations dominated until the 1970s, when less-disfiguring surgical procedures became available. The breast-sparing "lumpectomy" procedure removes only the tumor and a very small portion of surrounding tissue. Postrecovery breast-reconstruction techniques are also available today to restore a natural appearance and facilitate the best functional result.

Evidence gathered over many years of testing around the world has established that minimal surgery combined with appropriate drugs or hormones (tailored to the individual patient) offers the best outcome for a large number of women. Moreover, quality of life is enhanced for patients so treated. In 1985 a consensus panel on adjuvant breast cancer therapy, conducted by the National Institutes of Health, made the following recommendations concerning auxiliary drug and endocrine treatments to destroy remaining metastatic

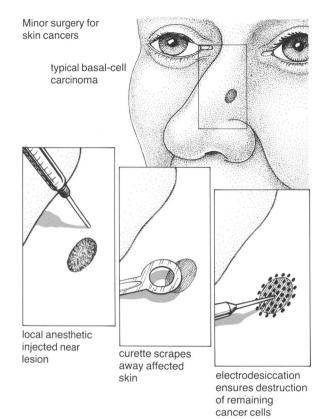

Minor surgery for skin cancers

typical basal-cell carcinoma

local anesthetic injected near lesion

curette scrapes away affected skin

electrodesiccation ensures destruction of remaining cancer cells

disease *after* conservative surgery: (1) chemotherapy using drug combinations for premenopausal women (who make up 25–33% of all breast cancer patients); (2) the antiestrogen agent tamoxifen for women with lymph nodes that test positive for hormone receptors; (3) chemotherapy for postmenopausal women who are not hormone-treatment candidates but who have four or more nodes that indicate the cancer has spread. In 1986, 100,000 women would be appropriate candidates for such management of their cancers.

Prostate cancer

Cancer specialists would like to have the equivalent of a mammogram for easier detection of tumors of the prostate, a gland lying below the bladder. The third most lethal cancer in U.S. males, prostate cancer is expected to kill 26,000 men in 1986. In addition, as many as 90,000 new cases will be diagnosed, according to current ACS projections. A recent Stanford University Medical School study has concluded that tumors of the prostate do not spread to surrounding organs until they reach three to four cubic centimeters (0.18–0.24 cu in) in size. If the tumors could be detected before they grew to this size, then treated by surgical removal or by radiation, deaths from prostate cancer might be dramatically reduced.

Currently, the only way to detect cancer of the prostate at an early stage is through a rectal exam

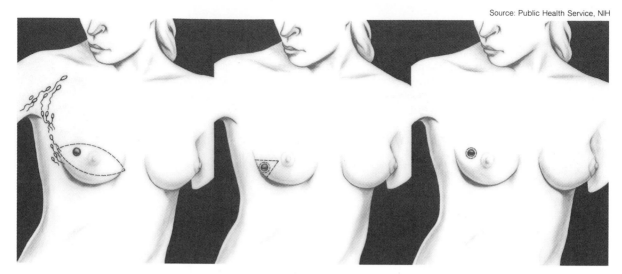

In the 1980s less-disfiguring surgeries dominate breast cancer therapy. (Left to right) Modified radical mastectomy removes the breast, lymph nodes, and lining over chest muscles; partial mastectomy removes the tumor plus a wedge of normal tissue and some of the chest muscle lining; lumpectomy basically removes only the tumor.

and biopsy. Therefore, males over 45 should have a rectal examination yearly. Researchers at the University of Chicago Medical Center have found that when biopsy is indicated, a relatively simple, inexpensive method called fine-needle aspiration is more nearly accurate than the costly conventional method (transperineal core biopsy), which requires hospitalization and general anesthetic. The newer technique takes about five minutes, requires no anesthetic, and causes only minimal discomfort. In a recent comparison study diagnosing 54 men (46 of whom had prostate cancer), the University of Chicago researchers found aspiration biopsy missed only two cases (4%), while conventional biopsies missed nine (19%).

For those whose cancer has already spread, a new drug may offer help. Researchers at several medical centers in the U.S. are testing Zoladex, a drug that interferes with the body's production of testosterone, a hormone needed by most prostate tumors for nourishment. Zoladex may replace diethylstilbesterol (DES), a substance that is sometimes used but causes severe side effects including nausea, fluid retention, and heart failure.

Between 1977 and 1983 clinical trials undertaken by five centers employed neutron-beam therapy to treat patients with locally advanced prostate cancers. Neutron-beam irradiation (which utilizes subatomic particles obtained from atomic accelerators such as those used in nuclear physics) is capable of deep tissue penetration. Technicians are able to direct the beam toward the tumor but spare normal (healthy) tissues as much as possible. The trials demonstrated that such irradiation therapy often can control the growth of prostate tumors, thus positively influencing overall survival of men with advanced, localized prostatic cancers.

A cancer success story

A bright spot exists in the gloomy overcast of cancer statistics. Hodgkin's disease and certain childhood cancers, such as leukemia, pose much less of a threat to life than they did 30 years ago. Moreover, success rates in curing these cancers continue to mount. Most patients with Hodgkin's disease in the 1950s died of their disease; today 88% of them survive. The survival rate for children with leukemia soared from 5% in the 1950s to 68% in the 1980s. For white adults with acute lymphocytic leukemia, five-year survival surged from 3–4% to 42–49% in the same period.

These successes do not show in the overall cancer statistics because leukemia and Hodgkin's disease represent only a small proportion of the total number of cancers. Vincent DeVita, director of the NCI, has noted that 50% of all cures through chemotherapy occur in 10% of cancer patients; that 10% consists mostly of children with leukemia and patients with Hodgkin's disease.

Interferon approved

Researchers also have had success with use of the substance interferon against a variety of rare cancers including hairy-cell leukemia, myeloma (bone marrow cancer), and lymph and blood malignancies. The body produces several kinds of interferon as a defense against viruses and other causes of disease. At first physicians collected it from human blood, but this provided only a small supply, which was frequently contaminated with other blood substances. Recently, genetic engineers learned to make pure interferon by inserting human genes that code for the interferon proteins into bacteria, which then produce copious quantities.

Physicians have used interferon since 1969 to treat hairy-cell leukemia, a rare form of blood cancer that afflicts about 2,000 people annually in the U.S. More than 1,600 out of 1,800 patients in one clinical study experienced remission of their tumors when they received a variety of the drug known as alfa-interferon. The remainder were stablized. This led the U.S. Food and Drug Administration (FDA) in June 1986 to approve the use of alfa-interferon to combat hairy-cell leukemia, the first approval of a genetically engineered substance to fight cancer.

The drug also has benefited some patients with non-Hodgkin's lymphoma (a cancer of the lymph tissue), metastatic (spreading) kidney cancer, and malignant melanoma (a deadly skin cancer). It has been used with some success, too, to treat AIDS patients with Kaposi's sarcoma—tumors that often are malignant. In all cases physicians administered the interferon on an experimental basis. It is expected that the FDA will soon approve interferon for treating these additional cancers on a routine basis. Results of trials giving interferon to patients to arrest lung, breast, and colorectal cancers, however, have been disappointing.

Biotherapy

Genetically engineered interferon is one of a number of new treatments that employ natural substances to fight cancer. This fast-growing biologic arsenal, which offers hope for halting the steadily increasing death rate, includes techniques that utilize the body's built-in defenses. One procedure uses a hormone known as interleukin-2 to bolster the disease resistance of white blood cells called lymphocytes. The body produces this hormone in minute amounts, but genetic engineers have developed ways to mass produce it.

Steven A. Rosenberg and colleagues at the NCI removed lymphocytes from the blood of cancer patients, then added interleukin-2 to the cells. This turned the lymphocytes into "killers" capable of seeking out and destroying cancer cells without damaging healthy ones. Rosenberg's team injected the killer cells into patients, then gave them additional doses of interleukin-2. This induced the killer cells to multiply quickly, increasing their ability to destroy cancer cells. The treatment was given to 25 patients with cancers so advanced that they could not be treated successfully with drugs, radiation, or surgery. Widespread melanoma disappeared in one person, and ten others experienced a partial remission of their tumors. This success startled many experts. However, the treatment involves severe side effects, including fluid retention in the lungs. The fluid, in turn, can lead to breathing difficulties and dysfunction of the kidneys and liver. In fact, one patient whose tumor remitted (not one of the 25) died from the treatment.

Such immunotherapy is experimental, expensive, and time-consuming. However, the NCI has decided that it offers promise to patients with advanced melanoma, kidney cancer, and colon cancer who respond poorly or not at all to standard treatments. Under NCI guidelines, clinical trials involving as many as 300 patients will be conducted at six U.S. medical centers. If these trials prove successful, physicians will have a potent new weapon against certain of the most difficult to treat cancers.

"Magic bullets" with promise

Scientists utilize the disease-fighting capabilities of lymphocytes in other ways. A variety of white blood cells known as B lymphocytes produce antibodies

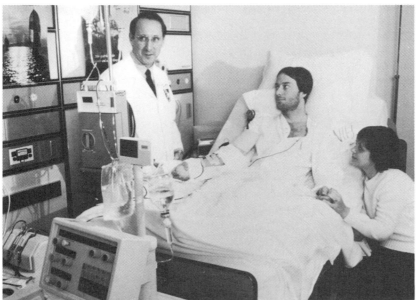

Steven A. Rosenberg (left) is pictured with a melanoma patient undergoing treatment at the U.S. National Cancer Institute. In late 1985 Rosenberg announced the results of his treatment of 25 advanced cancer patients with a highly experimental form of immunotherapy. The treatment utilizes one of the body's potent immune system regulators, known as interleukin-2. In 11 patients tumors shrank by 50% or more. Although these results were extremely promising, most of the patients experienced serious side effects, including fluid retention and breathing problems.

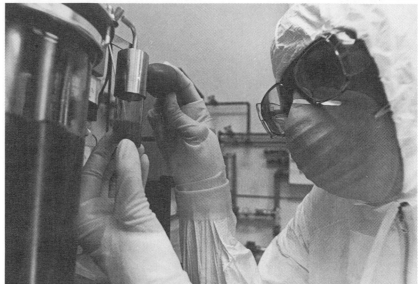

A scientist at Merck Sharp & Dohme draws a sample from a fermentation unit used in the development of the first genetically engineered human vaccine. The new vaccine, which was licensed by the U.S. Food and Drug Administration in July 1986, is designed to protect healthy people against infection by the hepatitis B virus—a major cause of liver disease and a predisposing factor for liver cancer throughout the world.

that seek out and bind to antigens on the surface of tumor cells. These lymphocytes make a variety of antibodies, each of which attacks a specific antigen and no other. However, antibodies produced by one human will destroy antigens in another; even mouse antibodies will work in humans. This provides the basis for a treatment in which antibodies are combined with a radioactive substance or drug. The antibody serves as a guided missile that homes in on a specific type of tumor, and the radioisotope or drug acts as a warhead that increases the antibody's destructive power. Such a combination is popularly referred to as a magic bullet.

Stanley E. Order of the Johns Hopkins Medical Institutions, Baltimore, Md., has treated more than 200 patients with antibodies taken from animals and "armed," or labeled, with radioactive iodine-131. The radioactivity kills tumor cells by shattering their chromosomes. Of 105 people with large, inoperable liver tumors, almost half experienced a 30% or greater decrease in tumor volume. When used on 38 patients with "incurable" forms of Hodgkin's disease, 15 of them showed partial remissions. Of 25 people with a rare form of liver tumor known as biliary cancer, 10 responded well to the treatment. These patients, who had not been helped by surgery, chemotherapy, or radiation, had been given three to six months to live. One has survived for six years.

Order also has tested antibodies linked to yttrium-90, a more effective combination, he believes. Of eight patients treated, one experienced complete remission of metastasizing lung cancer. Other researchers are experimenting with additional types of armed antibodies and with antibodies alone to treat melanoma, leukemia, ovarian cancer, and blood cancers. Results range from complete remission to partial remission to

no response. This inconsistency prompts some experts to predict that antibody procedures will best be used in conjunction with other therapies. One of Order's patients, for example, had a lung tumor removed by surgery; then magic bullets that consisted of antibodies linked to yttrium-90 destroyed the remaining cancer cells.

Several medical centers in the U.S. and Japan are testing another biologic weapon called tumor necrosis factor (TNF). A protein produced in the body by white blood cells called monocytes and macrophages, TNF causes some cancer cells to stop reproducing or to die. However, other tumor cells are unaffected by TNF. Biotechnology laboratories now make TNF in large quantities by genetic engineering techniques. Its availability gives scientists the opportunity to perform experiments aimed at discovering what role TNF plays in the body and how it might be used to treat cancer.

A cancer vaccine

Researchers are always on the lookout for substances that might serve as vaccines against cancer. A new vaccine that is expected to protect people against liver cancer is currently being used. The serum immunizes recipients against infection by hepatic B virus, thought to be necessary for the cancer to occur. According to one of the vaccine's developers, Nobel laureate Baruch S. Blumberg of the University of Pennsylvania School of Medicine, programs are in progress or are planned, involving millions of potential vaccine recipients in Africa, Italy, parts of the U.S., and China.

Hyperthermia

In addition to biotherapy, scientists are experimenting with heat to kill tumors resistent to conventional treatment. In a study coordinated by the Jonsson

Comprehensive Cancer Center at the University of California at Los Angeles (UCLA), 1,170 cancer patients received hyperthermia during a five-year period at nine locations throughout the U.S. Frederick C. Storm of UCLA reported that approximately 80% of these patients had not benefited from treatment with standard therapies. A device called a Magnitrode generates radio energy that, when transmitted to a tumor, applies enough heat (up to 50° C [122° F]) to destroy the malignancy without harming normal tissue. Of 960 patients who completed the treatments, 353 showed tumor reduction. The cancer stabilized in another 313 victims, but in 294 others it worsened. In June 1986 the heating device was under review by the FDA. Until approved by the agency, hyperthermia will remain an experimental treatment.

Early detection

Everyone involved in the war against cancer emphasizes the importance of early diagnosis. The earlier cancer is discovered, the greater the chances of curing it. Scientists believe that the route to early diagnosis lies through so-called oncogenes. Oncogenes, as part of the human genetic makeup, are sequences of deoxyribonucleic acid (DNA) that start out performing essential functions, such as producing proteins for regulating cell growth. But for reasons not yet known, these genes go haywire and make proteins that turn normal cells into cancerous ones. About 40 oncogenes have been found in human cells or in viruses. Researchers want to identify the oncogene proteins, then devise tests to detect their presence. In a further step, they want to find ways to shut off oncogenes gone wrong or to prevent them from malfunctioning in the first place.

The above goal remains on the distant horizon. Closer, however, is a simple, inexpensive way, such as a blood or urine test, to screen people for the suspect proteins. Edsel T. Bucovaz and colleagues at the University of Tennessee's Center for Health Sciences discovered a protein, called B-protein, that appears to be present in all forms of cancer. Its level increases as the cancer progresses. Bucovaz and his team have developed a simple blood test for B-protein raising the possibility of spotting a variety of cancers in the early stages. When given to more than 2,500 patients with a variety of early-stage cancers, the test was 87% accurate in confirming the presence of the disease. Among 4,500 people who did not have cancer, the test was negative in 90 to 95% of the cases. While these results would appear to be indication of a "breakthrough" in cancer detection, much work remains to be done before people can request such a test from their family physicians. Moreover, the NCI cautions against overoptimism, saying that Bucovaz's test must be "rigorously and strictly evaluated to determine its efficacy."

The role of emotions

When someone is diagnosed as having cancer, can a positive mental attitude help that person survive the disease? No, according to researchers at the University of Pennsylvania Cancer Center. They studied 204 people with advanced cancer and 155 patients who had received treatment for breast or skin cancer and, in a widely publicized report, concluded that attitude does not affect either survival or recurrence rate. A supportive editorial in the *New England Journal of Medicine,* which published the study results in 1985, went so far as to dub the idea that attitude induces cancer cures as "folklore." This drew a storm of protest from researchers who believe that they have found evidence to the contrary.

Sandra Levy, a psychologist at the University of Pittsburgh, Pa., wrote to the *Journal* stating that her studies of women with breast cancer strongly suggest that passive patients and those who feel helpless fare worse than those who aggressively fight the disease. Another investigation of breast cancer victims conducted at King's College Hospital in London found that seven out of ten women who reacted with a "fighting spirit" remained alive ten years after a mastectomy. Conversely, 24 out of 32 women who stoically accepted their condition were dead after ten years. Lydia Temoshok, a psychologist at the University of California at San Francisco, followed 40 patients with malignant melanoma for 28 months. The 20 people who died or had widespread metastases during that time scored twice as high on tests that measure tension, anxiety, depression, confusion, and distress. Levy and Temoshok agree that biology and competent medical attention are the most important factors in the cause and treatment of cancer. However, they and others believe that mental state and emotional factors may play a role in survival or remission. What the role might be, no one can say yet. But evidence that stress has a negative influence on the body's immune system and, therefore, its response to cancer continues to mount.

—*William J. Cromie*

Dentistry

Two issues that concerned society in recent months dominated dentistry: acquired immune deficiency syndrome (AIDS) and the liability insurance crisis. Strides in dental research included a new drill-less technique for removing decay material from teeth prior to filling and an artificial mouth for testing dental materials. Owing largely to a nationwide effort by dentists, a law now requires manufacturers of smokeless tobacco to include health warnings.

Health concerns for dentists

Dentists' fears of an increased health risk from AIDS came on top of their already considerable chance for infection with hepatitis B virus (HBV). For the population as a whole, the risk of contracting hepatitis B is about 5%. By contrast, for dentists in general practice it is believed to be three times as high, and for surgical specialists the risk factor rises to six. Although hepatitis B appears to be far more prevalent in the U.S. population than AIDS, dentists have had access to a vaccine against HBV since 1982, while no vaccine is yet available against AIDS.

Dentists run a greater risk of contracting infectious diseases such as HBV and AIDS because of their routine exposure to saliva and blood during dental procedures. Accordingly, the Centers for Disease Control (CDC) and the American Dental Association (ADA) have advised dentists that the same infection-control measures recommended for protection against HBV will work for AIDS. Those measures include the wearing of masks, gloves, and protective eyewear. Interestingly, the oral examinations that may expose dentists to AIDS also give them the unique opportunity to screen their patients for early signs of the disease that manifest themselves orally, among them "hairy" leukoplakia (whitish growths on the oral surfaces), tumors indicating Kaposi's sarcoma (a type of cancer often afflicting AIDS victims), unresolved candidiasis (an oral infection commonly called thrush), and recurrent herpes infections.

As of May 1986 the CDC had reported 29 cases of dental personnel with AIDS. All were members of one or another of the CDC-defined high-risk categories: homosexual or bisexual men, intravenous drug abusers, recipients of contaminated blood or blood products, and individuals who had sexual contacts with persons in high-risk groups. One of the cases occurred in a dental assistant married to a man with AIDS. There were no reported instances of transmission of AIDS from a dentist to a patient or vice versa.

Liability insurance

Dentists, physicians, small manufacturers, cities, towns, villages, and park departments across the U.S. were faced in 1985 and 1986 with tremendous increases in the cost of liability insurance as well as with a crisis in availability. Tort reform laws were proposed throughout the country to remedy the situation. In West Virginia the tort reform legislation passed in March 1986 was viewed as unworkable by insurance companies, who pulled their coverage of professionals in that state. Some dentists contemplated restricting their practices to low-risk procedures, while others said they planned to move to other states should the situation remain unresolved. A special session of the West Virginia legislature was called in May to deal with the problem, and a compromise bill was passed that satisfied the insurance companies' concerns while leaving in a modified version of the reporting mechanism of the earlier bill.

Dental education

Two universities announced the closing of their dental schools in 1985, reducing to 58 the number of dental schools in the U.S. Emory University trustees in Atlanta, Ga., said their decision was due to the declining applicant pool, the cost of running the school, and the improved dental health of the country, which has lessened the need for general dentists. While closing its predoctoral program, the school decided to keep its postgraduate training programs in various specialty areas of dentistry. Emory's last class of general dentists is scheduled to graduate in 1988. Oral Roberts University, Tulsa, Okla., which opened in 1978, graduated the last class of its dental school in 1986. The university said it closed the school because not enough graduates were entering mission work.

The declining applicant pool cited by Emory officials affects all dental schools. While first-year dental school enrollments had decreased by more than 20% from 1978 to 1985, the number of applicants to dental schools decreased by more than 40% during that time. Nationwide the pool had dropped to only 1.2 applicants for every position in freshman dental school classes, according to Emory officials.

Dental research

Considerable publicity surrounded the introduction in late 1985 of Caridex, a system for removing carious (decay) material without the use of the dental drill and without anesthetics. A delivery system similar to an oral irrigator warms and pumps a dilute water-based solution through a plastic tube to a tip resembling a small spoon. The fluid softens decay, working in combination with mechanical scraping action. The product will not eliminate conventional techniques—each case has to be evaluated individually—but it has been recommended by the ADA as an adjunct for caries removal and cavity preparation. In many cases access to the lesions and preparation of the cavity for a filling material will still require drilling.

The removal of dental plaque, a transparent film on teeth that is associated with dental decay and both minor and major gum disease (gingivitis and periodontitis, respectively), continues to be a major area of research. A chemical agent called chlorhexidine, which is under consideration for approval by the Food and Drug Administration for use in the U.S., has been shown in clinical studies to be highly effective in inhibiting plaque formation. There are side effects, however, such as staining of teeth and tongue.

Some toothpaste companies in 1985 began touting their products' abilities to control plaque. While they did not add new ingredients, they showed through clinical studies that brushing with their products—as opposed to brushing without toothpaste—does reduce plaque. Other companies made antitartar claims based on new ingredients in their toothpastes. Tartar, called calculus in dentistry, is a hard deposit that is scaled from teeth and under the gumline during professional cleaning. Although removal of plaque may help prevent gum disease, removal of tartar appears to have only cosmetic benefit.

Implants of artificial teeth are being used increasingly as an alternative to dentures, especially partial dentures. Techniques for surgically attaching the implants to underlying bone are being refined and improved, as are the materials used, which usually include a strong, light metal such as titanium for the anchoring posts. Because the success of the implant depends upon the nature of the patient's oral and general health, the material, and the technique, implants cannot be used as a routine alternative to dentures.

Also gaining increasing acceptance is the use of composite resins (mostly plastics) instead of fillings of silver-mercury amalgam in back teeth. Composite resins can be color matched to the tooth, making the filling more aesthetically appealing. They have drawbacks, however: they have not been shown to last as long as amalgam; they may cost more than amalgam fillings; and they depend much more on proper technique for their success than do amalgam fillings. Today, in a technique called bonding, composite resins are frequently used on front teeth as an alternative to crowns, to correct staining, or to close gaps between teeth. A relatively new material first developed in the 1950s, composite resins are constantly being improved for use in both front and back teeth.

Some dentists gained attention in 1985 for their claims that mercury vapor escaping from amalgam fillings caused health problems and that, after removing amalgam fillings from patients, they had seen improvements in conditions ranging from multiple sclerosis to epilepsy. No reliable scientific evidence, however, has been produced to show any harmful effects from the mercury in fillings, except in the estimated 1% or less of the population that is allergic to mercury. Amalgam has been safely used in dentistry for more than 150 years.

Ten years of research led to the identification at the University of Connecticut in early 1986 of the main ingredient that mussels use to attach themselves to structures underwater. No currently available glue has the right properties to be applied in water, and researchers predict a wide variety of dental and medical uses for the mussel glue. Dentists should be able to use it for pit-and-fissure sealants, in filling cavities, and as an adhesive in bonding teeth. The product is expected to become available for dental use in 1988.

An artificial mouth constructed at the University of Minnesota School of Dentistry is expected to reduce the time and cost of testing dental materials and thereby help speed new materials to the practicing dentist. The device, called artificial resynthesis technology (ART), consists of false and recently extracted human teeth mounted in a flexible base contained in a fluid simulating the oral environment. By means of mechanically driven motions, ART can chew, snap, and grind like a real mouth.

Forensic dentistry

Identification of the remains of the Nazi death-camp doctor Josef Mengele in Brazil in 1985 was accomplished in part through dental records. Forensic dentistry has come increasingly into play in the identification of victims of mass disasters such as major airline crashes. Dentists in the U.S. often work with state and local police as well as the Federal Bureau of Investigation in identifying dead bodies. The first national conference on dentistry and mass-disaster protocol took place in June 1986 in Chicago.

Forensic dentistry also applies to the living. Responding to widespread concern about missing children, a number of companies started producing tiny disks containing identifying information that can be attached to a person's tooth and later removed and read by a dentist if necessary. Recently the American Board of Forensic Odontology established guidelines for bite-mark analysis. Bite-mark evidence is often used to help prove that a suspect committed a crime.

An artificial mouth used to test new dental materials simulates the motions of chewing. Synthetic saliva is produced from ducts while hydraulic pistons move teeth that are mounted on a flexible base.

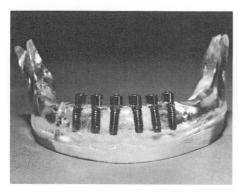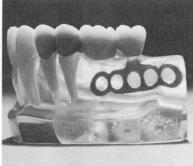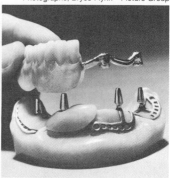

Three alternatives to dentures utilize fixtures that are implanted surgically into the jawbone to serve as anchors for artificial teeth. (Left) Screws are inserted into drilled holes in the jawbone so that tooth caps can be attached. (Center) A metal blade implanted in the jawbone supports three to six teeth cemented to protruding posts. (Right) When the jawbone is badly deteriorated and cannot withstand drilling, a metal frame that grips the bone can be fitted under the gum.

Public health

A hearing in Massachusetts by the state's dental health division in February 1985 was the first step in a nationwide effort by dentistry to place warning labels on smokeless tobacco products such as chewing tobacco and snuff. The Massachusetts hearing led to warning labels in that state on containers of snuff. In January 1986 a National Institutes of Health consensus conference issued a statement that the American public should be warned that the use of smokeless tobacco, particularly snuff when started in childhood, increases the risk of oral cancer. Furthermore, the conference panel noted that use of smokeless tobacco products increases the frequency of localized gum recession and of leukoplakia occurring where the tobacco is placed. By February 1986 Pres. Ronald Reagan had signed a law requiring manufacturers of snuff and chewing tobacco to include health warning labels on packages. In the spring, perhaps heralding a turnabout in the long and visible assocation of professional baseball players with chewing tobacco, the Kansas City Royals canceled its standing order for smokeless tobacco products.

Fluoridation of community water supplies suffered a setback when voters in San Antonio, Texas, narrowly rejected a referendum in November 1985 to fluoridate the city's drinking water. Only about half of the drinking water in the U.S. is fluoridated, despite the fact that fluoridation remains a safe, effective, and inexpensive way to fight cavities.

Fluoridation combined with the use of topical fluorides and dental health education has led to the decrease in decay in the U.S. and other industrialized nations. At the same time, dental decay is rapidly increasing in third world countries, probably because of diets high in refined sugar, lack of fluoridated water, and poor dental health education.

In early 1986 water fluoridation was halted temporarily in some areas because of a shortage in fluoride chemicals—the second time in four years such a situation had occurred. Because fluoride chemicals are a by-product in the manufacture of phosphate fertilizers, fluoride production ceases when fertilizer production stops. A falloff of fertilizer use in the U.S. combined with a decline in foreign exports contributed to the slack in fertilizer manufacture. Some cities were able to store sufficient quantities of fluoride chemicals to sit out the shortage. Dentists were advised to reemphasize the importance of fluoride mouth rinses and toothpastes. Supplementary fluoride treatments were suggested for people in areas where the shortage was prolonged. The CDC estimated that the shortage would last one to three months.

Dental spending

The U.S. Department of Health and Human Services reported in 1985 that Americans had spent $25.1 billion on dental services the previous year; this was out of a total health care bill of some $387 billion. According to the government's Consumer Price Index, the cost of dental services rose by 6.3% in 1985 over the previous year.

The year 1985 was also one of growth for a new form of cost containment in dentistry, the preferred provider organization (PPO). Under PPOs, which originated with hospital and physician services, individual dentists enter contracts with insurance companies in which the dentists agree to offer their services to patients covered by the insurance company for discounted fees. As in the traditional fee-for-service system, insurance companies reimburse either the PPO-covered patient or the dentist. Some dental groups also began promoting direct reimbursement—in which the employer pays directly for the dental care of the employee, thereby eliminating the administrative costs of an insurance company plan—as a way of competing with PPOs and health maintenance organizations.

—*Judith L. Jakush*

Special Report

Child Sexual Abuse: When Wrongly Charged

by Domeena C. Renshaw, M.D.

In the past several years there has been much progress in educating the public through the various media—television, radio, newspapers, pamphlets for schools, and parent seminars—on the subject of child sexual abuse. Indeed an "industry" has sprung up that offers video documentaries and itinerant speakers who visit parent groups, day-care centers, kindergartens, grade schools, and so forth. All states in the U.S. now mandate reporting of suspected child sexual abuse under the Federal Child Abuse Prevention and Treatment Act of 1974. Those states that voluntarily return their end-of-year statistics to the national office receive bonus funds. The intentions behind all of this are certainly laudable. Nonetheless, the time has come for objective scrutiny of the issues and claims that surround the real problem of child sexual abuse.

A sex abuse pandemic?

The 1974 law was designed to protect vulnerable children from exploitation. However, since it defines any act that stimulates a child sexually as criminal sexual abuse, it is so sweeping that it gives great power to any (even an anonymous) accuser and in effect places the burden of proof of innocence upon the one accused. Among reported allegations of sexual abuse, the following acts have been regarded by a plaintiff as criminal: mouth kissing, assisting with soiled underclothes, bathing a baby, and changing diapers. Medical personnel have been accused for clinically examining the scrotum and groin, taking an explicit pediatric sexual history from a 13-year-old girl with lower abdominal pain, performing routine hernia checks in school physicals, and palpating testes.

Allegations of child sexual abuse can be made anonymously to special telephone hot lines but are all to be followed up by obligatory home investigation by a state child worker. In the early 1980s news reports of sexual abuse quoted figures like "a child is sexually abused every two minutes" or "two million children are victims of child abuse." In 1982 the National Study on Child Neglect and Abuse Reporting, conducted by the American Humane Association, reported 1.3 million allegations of neglect and abuse nationwide: 62% neglect, 19% nonsexual physical abuse, 10% emotional abuse, and 7% (about 91,000 cases) sexual abuse. How many allegations came to trial remains unknown. A national review of child abuse (all forms, including sexual) in 1984 determined that some 60% of abuse reports were "unfounded."

For the state of Illinois allegations of sexual abuse rose by 38% (from 5,170 cases in 1983 to 7,134 cases in 1984), but sexual abuse remained proportionally low among total abusive behaviors—4.8% (1983) and 6.7% (1984). Of these allegations 2,736 of the 5,170 sexual abuse charges in 1983 (51%) and 4,122 of 7,134 in 1984 (60%) reached the "indicated" columns—"indicated" taken to mean "possibly founded." "Dropped" cases were, therefore, presumed to be 49% and 40%, respectively. Whether they were pre- or posttrial drops is obscured by the terminology used. These figures, however, do not resemble the 300 to 600% pandemic increase in sexual abuse cases widely and loosely reported in the media.

Divorce and custody weapon

How many of the above allegations were brought in divorce battles is not recorded. However, lawyers, judges, and psychiatrists in divorce-related practices anecdotally report the deplorable prevalence of one parent's making accusations of sexual abuse about the spouse because he or she knows there will be immediate child protection intervention. Unfortunately, what follows may be far removed from the best interest of the child, who almost inevitably suffers greatly. It is not uncommon that after such allegations children are placed in a hospital or foster home, without visitation, and thus lose both parents for weeks or months until the legal machinery lumbers to a conclusion. Both fathers and mothers have been accused by their spouses of sexually abusing a young child—fathers far more frequently accused than mothers. Clearly statistical reports of how often this new legal weapon features in divorces are long overdue.

Sexual abuse allegations when sole child custody is desired by a parent must be especially carefully evaluated to protect the child from being used against the other parent. In a judicial hearing that determines visitation rights and custody, the accused parent must demonstrate that he or she is innocent. The state must prove the crime was committed.

Charging sex abuse: a situation out of control

Charges of sexual abuse of children are not used only by divorcing parents. They arise for multiple reasons in a wide variety of situations. Often headlines cause a rash of reports of sexual abuse. In some cases hearsay evidence (report of a child's report) can be given in some jurisdictions without the accused having the right to challenge it for accuracy. All of these charges may be true and must be rapidly and thoroughly investigated. But many may be false and must be equally thoroughly and swiftly considered and dropped in order to protect the innocent.

Most child welfare workers and police officers (whose jobs are usually at stake) prefer to err on the side of child protection, saying they would rather be safe than sorry. They feel the child must be believed at all costs. It has been widely accepted that children do not lie. The fact is, however, that some children do lie. Nevertheless, the myth of children's innate honesty is now a powerful shield so that child workers or the police may feel less ethically obligated to be scrupulous in obtaining essential details that would make clear whether a report is true or false.

If a child's sexual abuse story is true, all health professionals agree that the child must be protected. But what if it is a false accusation? Does a police apology or a fair hearing undo the falsely accused individual's personal devastation? Is the accused ever the same after the trauma? Does the accuser stop to consider the pain, shame, distress, humiliation, turmoil, and career and family impact on the wrongfully accused?

In some cases, sexual abuse accusations are made by overanxious parents truly concerned about their children, without intent to falsify. However, in bitter divorce and custody battles, false allegations of sexual abuse are not uncommon and may be intended to cause harm to an ex-spouse or his or her new partner or to block parental contact with a child who, unfortunately for all, is sometimes rehearsed to lie. This practice is highly destructive, especially to the child.

How may such contaminated evidence be sorted out? Only by long and careful evaluation of the child witness by a skilled and trained child psychologist or psychiatrist—specialists who are in short supply—can such evidence get a fair evaluation. Explicit dolls or special cartoons illustrating sexual abuse (created for children not old enough or able to communicate experiences in a verbal or coherent manner) do not make an instant child expert out of a caseworker, guidance counselor, police officer, or state's attorney, but the use of such devices by nonexperts is becoming regrettably widespread. Few child workers in the field have had supervised clinical training in child development, child psychopathology, psychiatric evaluation of children, or treatment of children and families. This lack of trained and licensed personnel is presently a serious and glaring gap in the psycholegal system.

Observer bias in any investigation has been well documented for decades. Commonly investigators on each side seek support or evidence by using directive or leading questions—e.g., "Did he touch you down there?" Courtroom objections to such questions are useless when only a videotape is shown, since often a child witness does not appear in court for cross-examination.

In light of this growing problem it is pertinent to ask what recourse anyone has under the law after a wrongful accusation of sexual abuse. Too often the justification for a false accusation is that it is better to protect a child in need of help than to be concerned about the veracity of what is charged. If child protection under the existing law is gained at the expense of injustice to others, then reform of that dysfunctional law is urgently needed.

Remedies

Various corrective measures are now being urged by concerned specialists, who specify that many details of a child's testimony must be considered, especially in light of recent proliferation of "crying" sexual abuse. Following are some of these caveats.

Children are not born knowing right from wrong, truth from untruth. They must be asked, "Is it ever okay to lie?" and also, "Why do people tell the truth?" to establish if they have learned these values directly or indirectly. Some are not taught. Differentiation of true or false recall is very difficult for evauluator or judge. Even with lie detectors there may be reasonable doubt.

A child may not know the meaning of "grown-up" words such as molest, incest, abuse, penis, vagina, or anus. "Do you know what this word means?" must be repeatedly asked by the child evaluator, who must then ask the child to "tell me what it means." Validating the child's answer may easily be assisted with drawings or paper dolls that show anatomically correct genitals.

It must be kept in mind that children are suggestible and compliant, especially with parents and those adults whom they seek to please and protect. Further, children imitate. This is frequently seen in their play after viewing television. Many children have heroes and heroines whom they copy. Children can be taught or rehearsed to say things; this happens daily in school and also at home. Moreover, children, depending on their age and intellectual development, may not understand the consequences of their statements or acts. Nor are they informed of negative consequences when they consent to give a false history as legal evidence to please a parent. Coercion of a child to falsify may be in the form of misinformation (deception), rewards, or threats.

Children take longer to understand questions and to give answers, yet their concentration span is short—before age five it is generally only a few minutes long. The younger the child, the more careful, therefore, the evaluation should be, and it should be done by a skilled professional well trained to work with that age group. A board-certified child psychiatrist may have to be called in as a consultant to comment on a video evaluation or to reexamine a child when there is concern about biased interpretation of a child's history.

Memory of complex events is highly subject to error upon recall. This has been repeatedly shown in studies of the memory of adults on the witness stand. For a child, remembering dates may be impossible, because dates are unimportant to a five-year-old. Yet precise dates may be given by a young child in evidence— *e.g.,* "On June 4 my daddy took off his clothes when we were. . . ." Such a statement should raise immediate concern about the child's having been coached. Memory of an actual event may also be contaminated by the process of being coached and rehearsing lines.

Each child, then, must be carefully evaluated for perception of the words and the questions, perception of the general and the sexual events, perception of the consequences of evidence given, consistency of testimony, fusing or confusing of facts, and understanding of the difference between truth and lies. Obviously, this is no easy task.

Considering the consequences

Although lawyers consider child sexual abuse cases extremely difficult to prosecute, and despite constitutional guarantees of innocence until guilt is proved, accused adults in child sexual abuse cases feel deprived of basic human rights and dignity. The pointed finger often turns into a destructive witchhunt.

A national organization that began in Minneapolis is called Victims of Child Abuse Laws (VOCAL). The group reviews existing laws, brings civil suits in false sexual abuse charges, builds local VOCAL groups for support, lobbies for justice, and highlights the reality of how attempts to do good sometimes cause evil outcomes.

Placing a child in foster care is not treatment. When a father is accused, however, foster care until his trial is the most common outcome. He may be jailed. Foster placement itself may be highly traumatic to a child, who suddenly loses parents, grandparents, home, security, school, and friends. Unfortunately, protection from further sexual abuse is not assured in a foster home. Separation anxiety or depression due to the disruption may follow for the child as well as for deprived family members. Few resources exist for free treatment of the child or family; most state funds are spent on case finding and trials.

The following case illustrates the extent and the kind of consequences that can ensue after a false accusation.

A 39-year-old nursing graduate student was accused by her ex-husband, a physician who had remarried, of sexually abusing their three-year-old son. On weekend visitation he had

taken the boy to a child service facility, where a caseworker, working with dolls, spent an hour interviewing the child on videotape. The father claimed the child had revealed that the mother had abused him sexually.

The father demanded and instantly obtained sole custody. The mother contested this and pleaded innocent, but in disbelief at the accusation she did not immediately retain a lawyer. She demanded to see the videotape, a demand that was at first refused. The presiding judge in the case suggested foster placement for the child, but both parents objected. The paternal grandparents were given temporary custody, although they had not volunteered to provide the child care.

It was two lawyers, numerous court hearings, many months, and several thousand dollars (borrowed from the wife's parents) later (while the father had custody of the boy) that the boy's mother was allowed to see the videotape that had been the sole evidence. The boy had said *nothing* of molestation; rather, the latter was deduced by the unqualified caseworker only because the boy had nodded yes in response to the question, "Does Mommy touch you here?" as the worker pointed to a doll's genitals. (Surely all mothers who bathe a three-year-old child touch him "there"!)

The mother's consequent petition for restored custody was refused. She was allowed only a supervised one-hour-per-month visitation. The mother could not explain her absence to her son, whose new stepmother repeatedly told him *she* was his only "Mommy." The child's temporary and traumatic losses were uncountable: his natural mother, his own bedroom and possessions, familiar surroundings, friends, pets, etc.

After 12 months this case was still unconcluded. Meanwhile, how can the boy's sense of security ever be rebuilt when so unpredictably and suddenly his world has gone to pieces? Can all the king's horses or all the king's men put together again his trust in his father, his stepmother, his grandparents? Can he ever realize the injustice a complex and convoluted system has inflicted on his mother? Can his love for her be restored? Ultimately, what effects will the enormous trauma have on his emotional development?

And what happens to the father and his new wife as false accuser and accomplice? Is he beset by regret, remorse, shame, or guilt? Is she? How do *they* cope?

A particularly unfortunate backlash of the rampant charges of sexual abuse today is a false-charge "phobia." Fathers and grandfathers say they are nervous to hug, hold, or bathe their little ones. Teachers of both sexes in some schools are advised, "Never be alone with a child." Ironically, it is in this century that scientific proof has emerged of the value of abundant touching for physical, mental, and emotional growth— from the cradle to the grave. Indeed, bumper stickers proclaim the importance of physical affection—"Have you hugged your kid today?"—and media personality Leo Buscaglia has become a national "hug idol."

Experts today have many theories about child sexual abuse and its causes and perpetrators. But the fact remains that there have not been adequate studies to answer most of the questions about the reality of sexual abuse. Nor is there an adequate profile of the true offender. At this stage, then, the hyperbolic claim that "a child is abused every two minutes" must be countered with the question, "Is that really true?"

303

Diet and Nutrition

The recommended dietary allowance (RDA) for any nutrient is the amount of that nutrient that must be consumed every day by a person of a given sex and age in order to maintain good health. The values of the RDAs are determined by a panel of U.S. scientists who have special expertise in the fields of diet and nutrition. On the surface RDA would appear to be a simple enough concept—one with which the scientists in charge should have no difficulty. In 1985, however, the tenth edition of the RDAs failed to appear as scheduled because experts chosen by the U.S. National Academy of Sciences were unable to agree on the values for certain important nutrients.

Evolution of the RDAs

In order to understand how this situation came about, it is important to understand how the RDAs originated and how they are being used today. During World War II, in anticipation of food shortages and possible rationing, the U.S. government asked the National Academy of Sciences to determine, where possible, the amount of each of the known essential nutrients that would protect an individual from deficiencies of that nutrient. Thus, the original intent was to determine the minimal amount of each nutrient necessary to maintain good health. These guidelines could then be used in case of food shortages to ensure the best possible nutrition for the U.S. public.

RDA was not a new concept; in fact, British scientists had been determining similar values to protect their country's population. The job for the U.S. scientists was not an easy one, however. The amount of data was limited, and for that reason alone, precise values could not be set. Moreover, new vitamins and minerals were still being discovered during this time; thus, standards set by the committee were nothing more than judgments based on the best available evidence. (Even today there are some nutrients for which reliable, quantifiable data do not exist.)

The first RDAs were published in 1943. It was clear at the outset that they would have to be updated on a regular basis, and over the next four decades a formal revision process evolved. The RDAs were updated periodically as new scientific discoveries were incorporated into the recommendations. Over time, the RDAs began to be used for more and more purposes. Both government-run and privately funded food programs used the RDAs as standards for menu planning. In 1973 the U.S. Food and Drug Administration (FDA) developed a "rounded off" version of the 1965 RDAs, called the USRDAs, for use as a standard in food labeling. The RDAs continue to be revised under the supervision of the Food and Nutrition Board, a standing committee of the National Academy of Sciences. The board appoints a committee of scientists to review

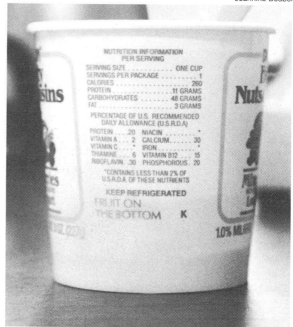

Jeannine Deubel

The RDAs are amounts of vital nutrients determined by a panel of experts to be necessary to good health. A "rounded off" version of the RDAs, called the USRDAs, is used in food labeling.

the existing data and develop up-to-date recommendations. These recommendations are then reviewed by members of the board and other scientists; suggestions are made; and a concensus is reached. Only after this extensive review process are the final values set forth.

RDAs in 1985: no consensus

In 1985, however, the committee proposing the RDAs and the reviewing scientists simply could not come to an agreement over certain nutrients. Several problems arose. First, and probably most important, was the definition of RDA itself. "Good health" is an imprecise term; the words have a general connotation, but to define them is extremely difficult. Does good health mean the absence of disease? Or does it imply lowering of risk for developing certain diseases? Is an adequate diet indicated simply by the absence of signs and symptoms of deficiency? The RDA for any given nutrient differs depending on the definition of good health. For example, to prevent scurvy, the major deficiency disease caused by insufficient vitamin C, only ten milligrams per day are needed. However, the amount needed to maintain the maximum level of vitamin C in blood and tissues is higher. Furthermore, some evidence indicates that even higher levels may be necessary for proper healing after certain injuries. The same is true for vitamin A, which is needed in smaller amounts to prevent night blindness but higher

304

amounts to lower the risk for certain cancers. A similar issue may be raised in the case of calcium. Most people in the U.S. consume enough calcium to prevent signs of overt calcium deficiency, but do they consume enough to prevent the slow, steady loss of calcium from their bones and the osteoporosis that may result? (Osteoporosis is a serious bone-thinning disorder highly prevalent in postmenopausal women.)

The problem is that as scientists change their focus from the amounts of nutrients necessary to prevent deficiency symptoms to the amounts needed to lower the risk for certain diseases, the data base on which they make their judgments shrinks. It is known, for example, that some women need more calcium than others to lower their risk for osteoporosis, but how much more has not been clearly determined. As medical science becomes less specifically treatment oriented and more concerned with health maintenance and prevention of disease, more data on risk factors should become available. At present, judgments must be made from an imprecise data base, and where judgment is concerned, reasonable people may differ. It is this kind of disagreement that interfered with the preparation of the tenth edition of the RDAs.

Another problem had to do with the interpretation of the meaning of some of the available data. In certain instances, based on the same experimental data, the committee preparing the tenth edition of the RDAs came to different conclusions from those reached by the committee that prepared the ninth edition in 1980. Both committees were made up of eminent scientists. Which was right? Once again, interpreting data—unlike collecting data—involves a certain amount of judgment, especially when the interpretation is used as a basis for recommendations. And again, reasonable people may differ in their judgments. Perhaps the best evidence of the imprecise nature of the RDAs—and of the whole process of deriving actual values from judgments—is the fact that the recommendations vary considerably from one country to another. Thus, using the same data, scientists in Canada, the United Kingdom, France, Italy, the Scandinavian countries, and others have come to different conclusions. Scientific "controversies" such as this often exist and almost always, with time, are resolved. In the case of the RDAs, however, there are important practical considerations involved. Many U.S. government food programs, such as the School Lunch Program and the Women, Infants, and Children (WIC) feeding program, use the RDAs as a basis for setting minimum standards and for preparing menus. The USRDAs are used in regulating food-labeling practices. Should such standards be changed on the basis of differences in judgment, or would it be better to wait until conclusive evidence is available? The National Academy of Sciences, the body charged with the ultimate responsibility for making this decision in the U.S., decided that it would be better to wait

until some of these problems could be resolved. As a result, the 1980 RDAs (the ninth edition) will stay in effect until more solidly based recommendations can be made.

Nutrition education for doctors

How much nutrition knowledge do most doctors really have? The fact that this question is being widely asked indicates public concern that the physician—the most highly trained member of the health care team—may not have as much education in nutrition as he or she should have. In 1985 a committee made up of U.S. medical school deans and professors came to the same conclusion. They found that the amount of time devoted to nutrition in the medical school curriculum is inadequate and that the quality of the material taught in different schools varies tremendously. A report prepared by the committee revealed that fewer than half of the U.S. medical schools in a representative sample had a required course in nutrition in their curriculum. The report recommended that all medical schools introduce such a course, and it pointed out that there is no longer any doubt about the importance of nutrition in promoting good health and lowering the risk for certain serious diseases. In addition, the use of special dietary regimens, including intravenous nutrition, has improved care in many serious illnesses. Finally, some of the most serious social and economic issues in third world countries center on the problems of poor nutrition.

The lack of nutrition education in medical schools is not unique to the United States. A recent report by the British Nutrition Foundation revealed that the same problem exists in the United Kingdom. Most medical schools in Canada do not teach nutrition as a separate course. While some countries in Western Europe are beginning to introduce nutrition into their medical school curricula, the quantity and quality of the material taught vary considerably. By contrast, some medical schools in less developed countries appear to be doing a better job, perhaps because the problems of malnutrition and dietary deficiencies are more obvious in these countries. There is some evidence that the situation in the United States and Western Europe may be changing for the better. Medical schools are beginning to introduce required courses on nutrition, and departments of nutrition are being formed within medical faculties.

Health implications of obesity

Obesity remains an important health concern worldwide. A consensus development conference on the health implications of obesity sponsored by the U.S. National Institutes of Health (NIH) in 1985 reviewed many aspects of the problem. The NIH panel noted that obesity is a major contributor to an individual's risk of developing a number of life-threatening dis-

A major study of adult adoptees published in 1986 concluded that genetic factors are more influential than environment in the development of obesity.

eases, including coronary artery heart disease and certain cancers, and that it is increasing in the United States, Canada, and Western Europe. Thirty-four million Americans can be classified as obese (20% or more above their "desirable" body weight as defined in the Metropolitan Life Insurance statistics), according to the panel's report. The conferees recommended that people in this group lose weight in order to lower their risk of developing high blood pressure, high serum cholesterol level, diabetes, and certain cancers. For those who are only 10 to 20% over the desirable weight, weight reduction is indicated if they also have high blood pressure, high serum cholesterol, or diabetes or if there is a family history of these conditions.

Beyond the health implications, the panel recognized that obesity is not simply due to overeating; many factors, including metabolic differences, can result in an excess storage of energy in the form of fat—which is what obesity is. Thus, more than one type of obesity exists; indeed, there probably are many. Already it is clear that anatomical variations in obesity have different causes and varying health implications. For example, the person who has been obese since childhood is likely to have more fat cells, as opposed to larger fat cells, than the person who becomes fat later in life. Weight reduction is much more difficult for the former. The location of fat deposits was cited by the panel as a predictor of the health hazards of obesity; the individual with truncal obesity—that is, with

thin arms and legs, and fat concentrated in the trunk of the body—may be at increased risk of illness and death. And finally, the obese individual under age 50 may be more at risk than his or her older counterpart. Future research must be directed at distinguishing different forms of obesity and defining their specific health risks.

Fat parent, fat child?

The results of an important study by U.S. and Danish investigators, published in the *New England Journal of Medicine* on Jan. 23, 1986, confirmed what many researchers had long suspected, namely, that genetic factors are more important than home environment in the development of obesity. The study population consisted of 540 Danish adult adoptees, chosen from the Danish Adoption Register, which contains the records of every nonfamily adoption granted in that country from 1924 to 1947. Subjects were judged to be in one of four body-mass categories: thin, median weight, overweight, and obese. The researchers concluded that there was no relationship between the weight class of the adoptees and the body-mass index of their adoptive parents. There was, however, a correlation between adoptees and their biologic parents. Furthermore, this correlation was not confined to obesity but was present across the whole range of body builds, from thin to obese. These observations support the notion that genetic factors have a determining influence on all degrees of fatness. The results of this investigation were widely publicized in the popular media, causing the researchers to issue a precaution against overemphasizing the role of heredity in fatness. A person may be predisposed to obesity because of genetic makeup, but this does not mean that he or she will inevitably become fat or that sensible eating habits are of no avail in controlling weight gain.

Weight and pregnancy outcome

During the past decade the importance of proper nutrition during pregnancy has been repeatedly demonstrated. However, it is only during the last year or so that emphasis has been placed on nutrition *prior to* conception as an important factor in the outcome of pregnancy. Recent studies have demonstrated that the prepregnancy weight of the mother is an important factor in determining the birth weight of the infant. Underweight women are at higher risk of delivering low-birth-weight infants than are women who are at, or close to, their ideal weight during pregnancy. Overweight women are in danger of being even more obese after pregnancy. Thus, the underweight woman would be wise to gain some weight before becoming pregnant, while the overweight woman should lose some. In addition, because adequate vitamin and mineral intake are most important in the early weeks of pregnancy (before the woman actually knows that

While doctors have always emphasized proper nutrition during pregnancy, many are now stressing the importance of a woman's prepregnancy weight and nutritional status.

she is pregnant), it is important that any woman who is planning to have a baby begin a varied diet and supplementation with iron and folic acid before she actually becomes pregnant. This is particularly important for women who have been taking oral contraceptives. Some kinds of oral contraceptive interfere with the body's handling of certain vitamins, and it is important that the stores of these vitamins be replenished before pregnancy. Finally, the time to stop consuming large quantities of alcohol and to stop smoking is before conception, not after pregnancy is confirmed—by which time the fetus is already a month to six weeks old. Today many women are planning their pregnancies. Good nutrition prior to conception should be part of those plans.

Calcium: ongoing assessments of need

Calcium is the most abundant mineral in the human body. About 98% is present in bone, and together with phosphorus, it forms a complex compound called hydroxyapatite, a hard material that provides the structure of the skeleton. Even more important, however, is the other 2% of body calcium. This relatively small amount of calcium is essential for proper functioning of virtually every cell in the body. Without calcium, muscle cells cannot contract or relax properly and nerve cells cannot conduct impulses; the brain and the heart and all other vital organs require calcium in order to function. The bones act as a vast reservoir of

calcium, supplying other body tissues when necessary at the expense of their own strength.

The amount of calcium absorbed from the diet determines, to a large extent, whether or not the bones will need to relinquish calcium for use by other tissues. How much dietary calcium is absorbed by the body, in turn, depends on a number of factors, including the amount consumed, the availability of vitamin D (in the proper form needed to enhance calcium absorption), and the amount of phosphorus and protein in the diet. The major action of vitamin D in its active form is to promote calcium absorption from the intestines. In order to do that the vitamin D in the diet or made in the skin from exposure to ultraviolet light must be modified first in the liver and then in the kidney to a compound known as dihydroxyvitamin D, which is the active form. Not only is it important, therefore, to consume enough vitamin D, it is also important for the body to make enough of the active form. Finally, phosphorus, another important mineral, is absorbed by the same mechanisms as calcium. Both are actively transported across the intestinal wall, and they will compete with each other for transport sites. It is just as though there were limited seats on a train; if a seat is occupied by a molecule of phosphorus, there is no room for a calcium molecule. Thus, the more phosphorus consumed along with calcium, the less calcium will be delivered into the bloodstream.

Important balance. It is this careful balance of availability of dietary calcium and calcium in bone that constantly supplies the tissues with their calcium requirement. Because of hormonal differences, women begin to lose calcium from their bones earlier than men, and at menopause this loss of calcium is accelerated. If a woman is not absorbing enough calcium from her diet, she can develop osteoporosis, or brittle bones, due to excessive calcium loss. Whether a particular woman will develop osteoporosis depends on her natural tendency to lose calcium from bone (genetic), her hormonal status (the earlier her menopause, the greater her risk), the amount of calcium already in her bones (women who are small-boned are at greater risk), the amount of weight-bearing exercise she performs (weight-bearing exercise, such as walking, running, jumping, or bicycling, promotes calcium deposition into bone), and the amount of calcium and, to some extent, phosphorus in her diet (the more calcium and the less phosphorus, the lower the risk).

The pregnant woman. Pregnancy is a particularly important time in a woman's overall cycle of calcium balance. The developing fetus requires relatively large amounts of calcium for the formation of its skeleton. To ensure that this calcium will be available, a woman's body makes certain important adaptations during pregnancy. Both the placenta and the woman's kidneys produce dihydroxyvitamin D, the metabolic derivative of vitamin D that draws calcium from the

Inadequate calcium intake is well established as a factor in the development of osteoporosis, or brittle, porous bones, especially in postmenopausal women. Increased calcium intake or calcium supplementation is generally recommended for this condition. It remains unclear, however, whether calcium supplements provide any benefits to people with high blood pressure. Nor has it been confirmed, as some studies have indicated, that calcium protects against the development of colon cancer.

mother's body into the fetus. Pregnant women absorb almost twice the amount of calcium from food that nonpregnant women do. Thus, if the expectant mother consumes a sufficient amount of calcium in her diet, she should be able to provide the fetus with adequate calcium and, at the same time, protect the calcium content of her bones. An obvious question arises: How much calcium is "enough" for a pregnant woman? The RDA for calcium during pregnancy is presently set at 1,200 mg (1.2 g). On the basis of calcium balance studies during pregnancy, this figure appears somewhat low, however, and some physicians recommend that a pregnant woman consume 1.5 g of calcium per day. Eating dairy foods is probably the best way for her to increase calcium intake; if these foods are not tolerated well, a calcium supplement may be indicated.

Calcium and high blood pressure. Recently evidence has been accumulating that hypertension (high blood pressure) may be associated with low calcium intake. This evidence comes from two sources: first, animal studies showing that certain strains of rats can be induced to develop hypertension by restricting their calcium intake and, second, human studies that demonstrate an inverse correlation between calcium intake and hypertension. The lower the intake of calcium in a population, the higher the incidence of hypertension. At present, however, it remains unclear how calcium benefits some people with high blood pressure. In addition, physicians are puzzled by the result of one study that showed calcium supplementation to be associated with significantly higher blood pressure in both normal and hypertensive subjects.

Calcium and colon cancer. Another recent finding about calcium, widely publicized in 1986, was that researchers at several U.S. institutions reported that they had found a link between calcium and the prevention of colon cancer. It was theorized that calcium may

have the effect of preventing cellular changes of the type that predispose to the development of cancer.

In view of these latest findings, and along with what is already known about osteoporosis, some authorities advocate that all women—and some men—take calcium supplements. Others disagree with this recommendation on several counts. First, nothing is yet known about the long-term consequences of too much calcium. Second, there is no evidence that high doses of calcium (above the RDA) will either prevent or cure osteoporosis or hypertension. Finally, calcium is a nutrient and should, therefore, be provided in adequate amounts in the diet. Most physicians are reluctant to advise calcium supplementation for their healthy patients—with the exception of those who do not get adequate calcium from dietary sources.

—*Myron Winick, M.D.*

Drug Abuse

The widespread use of drugs in the 1980s has changed the contours of the drug problem in the United States and many Western European nations where epidemics of abuse have mounted in recent years. The conflict about the acceptability of drug use has escalated; patterns of drug use and abuse have changed; the impact of drugs on work and public safety is coming under closer scrutiny; causes and complications of drug abuse are being investigated; and approaches to treatment have become more diversified and more specific as people with more and different kinds of problems have become involved with drugs.

Acceptability of drug use

Drugs that affect the mind were considered gifts of the gods in many ancient cultures. They were viewed as mediators between the natural and supernatural, as divine nectars with the ability to impart good health and long life, bring luck, deter evil, and cleanse man of sin. In ancient cultures pilgrimages were made to gather the psychoactive plants that were considered sacred. Rites, prayers, songs, and dances were associated with their use. However, drug use was strictly controlled by ceremonial proscriptions and taboos.

The controlled use of drugs found in many ancient cultures is parallel to what is referred to today as the "recreational" use of drugs. Drug users today also make "pilgrimages" to obtain drugs (in this case, to the drug dealers). Also, there are rites and rituals associated with the preparation and ingestion of drugs. The distinction between recreational and compulsive drug use is based on the frequency of use. Many people believe that recreational drug use is unacceptable, while others see this as the only acceptable use. In any case, the recreational and compulsive drug users today are the mainstays of the multibillion-dollar illegal drug industry.

Few would argue about the dangers of compulsive drug use to the individual and to society. However, it is the ambiguous legal, social, and moral status of recreational drug use that is creating much of the debate about drugs and has caused the current stalemate in the "war on drugs."

Evolving patterns of drug use and abuse

Widespread drug use in the United States started in the 1960s; it continued and spread in the 1970s. It may be leveling off in the 1980s, but at a level that is unprecedented in U.S. history.

The opportunity to try marijuana is a commonplace experience. One-half of all youth between the ages of 12 and 17, 85% of young adults between the ages of 18 and 25, and 41% of all persons 26 years of age or older report that they have had the opportunity to try marijuana. The majority of young adults also report that they have had the opportunity to try cocaine.

Epidemiologists have gathered data on the use of over-the-counter drugs, psychoactive prescription drugs, and illegal drugs. They have estimated the incidence and prevalence of the use of these substances and classified them. There are many different drugs in each class, and the drugs are grouped into classes on the basis of their effects.

Depressants include the sedative/hypnotics and minor tranquilizers. Some of the street names of the sedative/hypnotics are goofballs, downers, sleepers, rainbows, yellows, yellow jacks, pinks, red birds, and red devils. The minor tranquilizers are sometimes referred to as tranks; an addiction to minor tranquilizers for a time was referred to as housewife's disease, but this expression is passé.

Narcotics include heroin, a derivative of morphine and the most common narcotic on the illegal market, and methadone, a long-acting narcotic that is substituted for heroin in the treatment of heroin addiction. Meperidine (Demerol) and hydromorphone (Dilaudid) are the two most common prescription narcotics and the ones that are most likely to be abused by hospital personnel.

Hallucinogens include lysergic acid diethylamide (LSD), psilocybin, morning glory seeds, and mescaline. Psychopharmacologists debate whether marijuana and phencyclidine (PCP, or "angel dust") should be classified as hallucinogens. Both have hallucinogenic properties, but they also have other effects and are generally considered in separate drug classes. Stimulants include cocaine, amphetamines, and caffeine. Inhalants are sometimes thought of as a class of drugs, although inhalation refers to a mode of drug administration (which is different from sniffing). Glue, solvent, paint thinner, and amyl nitrite and butyl nitrite ("poppers" and "snappers") have in common the fact that their vapors are inhaled.

Ecstasy: a new drug of abuse

In 1984 a drug called Ecstasy received much publicity. Ecstasy is MDMA (methylenedioxymethamphetamine)—a so-called designer drug. Designer drugs are created by altering the molecular structure of known drugs. Another designer drug—a heroin analogue—has been synthesized in illegal laboratories. It has caused symptoms similar to those that occur in Parkinson's disease as well as injuries and death.

As of July 1, 1985, the U.S. Drug Enforcement Administration (DEA) banned Ecstasy by labeling it with

Reproduced by permission of Johnny Hart and News America Syndicate

Some therapists have considered the chemical substance MDMA a potential pharmacological aid to psychotherapy, claiming it stimulates relaxation and heightens consciousness, intuition, and insight. Recently MDMA, popularly known as Ecstasy, has become a widely abused and dangerous recreational drug, and it is now classified as an illicit substance.

an emergency Schedule I controlled-substance classification—a category reserved for drugs with high abuse potential and no medical uses. The DEA scheduled hearings to determine the permanent classification of MDMA.

In the 1970s MDMA was recommended by a few physicians and scientists who thought that it would be a useful pharmacological adjunct to psychotherapy. It has both hallucinogenic and stimulant properties. It is alleged to produce emotional closeness to others, serenity and relaxation, heightened consciousness, aesthetic enjoyment, intuition, and insight. (This same claim was made for methaqualone—Quaaludes—a few years ago just as, in the 1960s, it had been made for LSD.) MDMA in its pure form is a white powder; on the street its color may range from white to yellow or to brown depending on its purity. The experience that people have when they take it, as is true with most drugs, depends on their expectations and attitude as well as the setting.

MDMA's toxic effects include confusion; fatigue; amnesia of the experience; anxiety; decreased appetite; pupillary dilation; tensing of the neck and jaw muscles; teeth grinding; increase in blood pressure, pulse rate, and body temperature; and dryness of the mouth, throat, and nose. Very harmful side effects include fixed and widely dilated pupils; hyperactive deep tendon reflexes; extreme reflex hyperexcitability to auditory, visual, and tactile stimuli; agitation; hallucinations; delirium; convulsions; coma; and very high body temperature. Respiratory insufficiency produced by chest muscle spasms may cause death.

Drugs in high school

Some trends in drug use and abuse in the 1980s have been examined among U.S. high school seniors. Surveys indicate that 32% (960,000) are currently using an illegal drug. Two-thirds of all young people in the U.S. try an illegal drug before they finish high school.

Approximately 40% have tried drugs other than marijuana. One of every 18 high school seniors (5.5%) smokes marijuana daily; 17% have smoked marijuana daily for at least one month of their lives.

Amphetamines were the second most frequently used drug after marijuana, but their popularity currently may have been surpassed by cocaine. About 0.8% (24,000) of seniors use amphetamines daily, and 0.2% (6,000) use inhalants, sedatives, and hallucinogens daily. The number of high school seniors who have taken a barbiturate (a central nervous system depressant) dropped from 11 to 5% from 1975 to 1983. The percentage of people who tried PCP dropped from 7 to 3% during the same time period. Inhalant use (*i.e.,* aerosols or gaseous fumes, glue, and paint thinner) has remained fairly stable since 1980. In a typical month about 1.5% (45,000) of high school seniors report having used an inhalant. Two of the popular inhalants are amyl nitrite and butyl nitrite.

Polydrug abuse

The use of one or more drugs, or of drugs and alcohol at the same time or at different times, is referred to as polydrug use. Polydrug use is commonplace. When polydrug users experience adverse reactions, it is often difficult to determine which drug has caused the toxic reaction or whether it was the drug interaction. Some 80% of all young adults between the ages of 18 and 25 say that they have used marijuana nearly every time they used a hallucinogen. In every age group the majority of those who have ever used cocaine say that they have used marijuana on the same occasion that they took cocaine. Among young adults more than one-third of those drinking alcohol report that they smoke marijuana. And 43% of young adult cigarette smokers are also marijuana smokers.

Of those in treatment for alcoholism, 43% of women and 20% of men used prescription psychotropic drugs—most commonly the minor tranquilizers and

310

sedative/hypnotics. In this group 25% of the alcoholic women and 10% of the alcoholic men had significant drug problems. Furthermore, 23% of the patients in federally funded drug treatment programs are drinking more than 236 ml (8 oz) of 80-proof distilled spirits per day. Abuse of other drugs and alcohol by methadone maintenance patients was the major reason for introducing urine surveillance into methadone maintenance programs. Any treatment program for alcohol or drug abusers must address the growing general problem of multiple chemical dependency.

Drugs in the workplace

It is estimated that at least 6% of the labor force in the U.S., or at least six million workers, are currently using drugs. Half of current drug users report that they use drugs on the job. There appears to be no difference in the amount of drug use in large and small companies. The younger the worker, the more likely he or she is to use drugs. Marijuana currently is the most commonly used drug at work. Surveys have shown that drug users tend to overestimate the total number of drug users in the workplace. However, drug users' estimates of such drug use among employees are more nearly accurate than nonusers' estimates.

Management has become more aware of the drug problem in the last few years and has been implementing drug screening and testing programs. Since 1982 the percentage of "Fortune 500" companies with drug testing programs has increased from 10 to 25%. In some companies every prospective employee's urine is tested for drugs. If drugs are detected, the applicant is not hired. If drugs are detected in employees' urine during random on-the-job urine tests, action is likely to be taken, the specific action depending on the rules and policy of the company.

There has been a growing decline in the societal punitive attitude toward drug users. In 1969 a survey of executives in "500" companies indicated that 97% of the executives would fire employees found using drugs. By 1971 this percentage had dropped to 22%, and by 1979 to 10%. Some companies have their own assistance programs, and other companies refer their employees for treatment.

Both the practicality and the legality of drug testing in the workplace are controversial. Unions and some lawyers often argue against drug testing. They believe that drug testing must be warranted by probable cause—*i.e.,* widespread random drug testing constitutes an unreasonable search, and employees should be tested only if there are grounds for suspecting drug use.

Techniques used to detect drug possession, use, and trafficking at work include, in addition to mandatory urine testing, undercover investigation, surveillance cameras, and dogs that have been trained to sniff out drugs. The reliability and accuracy of urine testing depends on the analytical methods used and the skills of the personnel using them. Even when the best methods available are used, the results can be difficult to interpret. For example, in chronic marijuana smokers, a metabolite of marijuana is detected in the urine for weeks or months after marijuana use. Even in occasional marijuana smokers, a metabolite of marijuana usually can be detected in urine for up to ten days after the drug has been smoked. It is important to note that the relationship between the amount of drug found in urine and the degree of impairment has not been established. Moreover, the presence of drugs in urine is not sufficient to infer impaired performance.

Drug use during nonworking hours can affect job performance. For example, airplane pilots performed a flight simulation task before and 1, 4, and 24 hours after smoking a marijuana cigarette. Their performance on the task was significantly impaired not only at 1 and 4 hours but at 24 hours after they had smoked a

Adam J. Stoltman—Duomo

Screening employees and prospective employees for drug use is a highly controversial approach to the ever growing problem of on-the-job substance abuse. At left, laboratory technicians test employee urine samples. But random urine testing may not be a reliable method of indicating when drugs have been used or whether a drug taken is likely to impair performance.

single marijuana cigarette. Yet the pilots, in performing the simulated tasks, were not aware of the fact that their performance was impaired.

Causes, complications, and consequences

Drug use starts most often during adolescence and sometimes during childhood. Today there is a generation of children who have observed drug use as an integral part of their parents' lives. The causes of drug abuse and the causes of other psychiatric disorders are both psychological and social; biologic factors may also contribute. However, how much of a contributory role is played by each of these factors is not known and may vary for different individuals.

The factors that make one person more or less vulnerable to the reinforcing effects of drugs are not known. However, once that person is vulnerable, the availability of specific drugs plays a minor role in contributing to drug abuse. If one drug is not available, alcohol or another drug will be used in order to induce the altered state of consciousness that is sought from mood-altering chemicals.

The motivation for drug use may be to alter an unpleasant mood such as anxiety or depression. Drugs may also induce depression. An individual may lose a job or be rejected by friends or relatives because of his or her drug use; these experiences may lead to depression. Drug abuse may also lead to neuroendocrine changes that may in turn lead to psychopathology.

There are many drug abusers who suffer from depressive disorders; drug use may be their attempt to treat their depression. This type of drug use is referred to as self-medication. There are also schizophrenics with both alcohol- and drug-abuse problems. However, the contribution of drug use to schizophrenic episodes is not known. The problem of such dual psychiatric diagnoses has received increasing attention in the past few years. There is a growing recognition of the concomitant and perhaps causal relationship between alcohol and drug abuse and other psychiatric illness.

Who should be tested for drug use?

	good idea	bad idea
high school teachers	64%	33%
airline pilots	84%	14%
police officers	85%	13%
TV, film, and recording stars	52%	42%
high school students	60%	37%
professional athletes	72%	25%
government workers	72%	25%
all other workers	50%	44%

From the Newsweek Poll; © 1986 Newsweek, Inc.

Individuals with dual psychiatric diagnoses must be treated for all of their psychiatric illnesses.

Drug "abuse" refers to drug use that has untoward medical, psychological, social, and/or legal consequences. Drug "dependence" is one complication of abuse. If drug-dependent persons discontinue drug use, they experience a variety of physical and psychological changes—these changes are called withdrawal symptoms. The nature, severity, and duration of the symptoms they experience depend on the drug, the total daily dose, and the pattern of drug use.

The withdrawal symptoms associated with heroin have been recognized for several decades. More recently the withdrawal syndromes associated with the minor tranquilizers such as Valium and Librium have been identified. Withdrawal symptoms emerge three to six days after the last dose of the drug has been taken. Symptoms are agitation, nausea and vomiting, abdominal pain, excessive sweating, tremulousness, irritability, sleep disturbances, dizziness, and loss of appetite. More severe symptoms, which may occur after extremely high doses have been ingested, include abnormally high body temperature, delirium, hallucinations, delusions, muscle twitches, and grand mal seizures. Typical medical treatment for withdrawal from Librium and Valium consists of a progressive reduction of the daily dose of the drug over a period of a few weeks. This treatment can best be accomplished when the person is hospitalized. This procedure reduces the severity of the withdrawal symptoms considerably.

Nicotine and cocaine withdrawal syndromes have been recognized recently. Many heavy smokers experience irritability, weight gain, and sleep disturbances when they stop smoking. These symptoms begin a few hours after the last cigarette and last for up to one week. Some smokers report that they experience withdrawal symptoms for months after they stop smoking. Nicotine chewing gum is being used with increasing frequency to treat nicotine withdrawal. Cocaine withdrawal symptoms include exhaustion, depression, social withdrawal, tremor, muscle pain, eating and sleep disturbances, and craving for the drug. The time course of symptoms is not yet known. There is a debate among professionals about whether hospitalization is necessary for successful detoxification. The necessity of inpatient detoxification depends on the severity of the addiction as well as the severity of other psychiatric and medical problems. The cocaine abuser's environment, motivation, and prior history of detoxification are also considered when a decision about hospitalization is made.

There is currently a debate about whether heavy marijuana smokers experience withdrawal symptoms when they stop smoking. But because the average potency of the marijuana on the street has increased fivefold in the last few years, the presence of withdrawal effects is likely. The marijuana withdrawal syndrome that has been observed in the laboratory is comparable in intensity to mild or moderate alcohol or sedative withdrawal. Relief of withdrawal symptoms is one of many causes of relapse to drug use.

Some of the adverse consequences of drug abuse are the result of using illegally manufactured drugs. Neither the buyer nor the seller is certain of the identity, purity, or potency of the drug being sold. Unknown potency is a major contributor to drug overdose. Illegal drugs may contain unsanitary and/or insoluble material. Infections, tissue damage, viral hepatitis, septicemia, bacterial endocarditis, and acquired immune deficiency syndrome (AIDS) are complications of illegal drug use. It is not clear yet whether the new knowledge about the transmission of AIDS through contaminated needles and cookers has had an impact on drug users' preparation and injection practices.

Treatment today

There are many types of treatment available for drug abusers. They include inpatient and outpatient detoxification—drug-free therapeutic communities in which the drug abuser lives and works in a closed community of drug abusers in a highly structured society. Methadone maintenance is the most common treatment for heroin addicts. The rationale for drug maintenance is that if a drug addict needs a drug, it is best to provide the drug in a medical setting, where the dose of the drug is controlled, the purity of the drug is known, and the contact that is maintained between the addict and treating personnel can be used to promote rehabilitation in other areas of the addict's life.

Drug treatments have proliferated as the number of people seeking treatment for drug abuse has increased. Contingency contracting is a relatively new approach to the treatment of drug problems. In this procedure the therapist enters into a contractual agreement with the drug abuser. The abuser deposits money or something else of value (i.e., a letter addressed to his or her professional licensing board). The terms of the contract provide for what happens to the money or letter if the drug abuser uses drugs. Drug use is monitored through periodic urine surveillance. It is doubtful that this treatment will ever become widespread because there are very few drug abusers who will gamble on maintaining sobriety.

Cocaine Anonymous, Narcotics Anonymous, and Drugs Anonymous (formerly known as Pills Anonymous) are self-help treatment programs that have emerged in the past 25 years. They are fellowship organizations without dues or fees. They are not formally affiliated with the medical or psychiatric profession. Meetings are held in hospitals or churches. There is a basic 12-step recovery program (based on the successful Alcoholics Anonymous program) as well as a sponsorship program in which members of the group who have extended periods of sobriety, or drug absti-

nence, sponsor a new member. These groups keep no records, thus assuring anonymity. Those who relapse to drug use are welcome to return to the program to seek sobriety once again.

The future

The war on drugs that began 25 years ago in the U.S. is still being waged. There has been an increased understanding of the complexity and dimensions of the problem. Progress to date indicates that the war will not end in the 1980s. The magnitude of the problem and the cost to society indicate that the right balance of legal and social sanctions against drug use must be struck. The war must be concerned with attacking the drug supply, on the one hand, and, on the other, finding the best methods of prevention through education, research, and treatment programs.

—Miriam Cohen, Ph.D.

Drugs and Devices

This is an age of high technology development for new drugs and devices. The explosion of knowledge in the fields of biochemistry, biophysics, developmental biology, genetics, bioengineering, molecular biology, and experimental pathology has had a major impact on nearly every field of medicine and science, including cardiology, pharmacology, neurology, and neurobiology. New discoveries in molecular cell biology have stimulated new methodologies for drug development. The use of genetic engineering has permitted scientists to attack not just diseases but the fundamental causes of disease, thus creating a new class of customized drugs. These drugs, however, are not free of the potential to cause adverse effects. By the very nature of the serious diseases targeted for these drugs, toxicity may be associated with use.

In the United States federal regulations govern the conditions under which a new drug or device is studied clinically, how the safety and efficacy determinations are made, and the types of information that are included in the new drug application and in the physicians' package insert for prescription drugs. This control has influenced the new drug research and development process within the pharmaceutical industry. The approval system for new drugs and devices within the U.S. Food and Drug Administration (FDA) was designed to ensure that safety and efficacy issues are fully explored before a drug is marketed.

Another factor influencing new drug development is the trend toward harmonization of regulatory requirements that must be met both in the U.S. and in other countries before a new drug can be released for use. New drugs are being studied for safety and efficacy in clinical trials worldwide under the sponsorship of international pharmaceutical manufacturers who have developed the drugs through painstaking research and development and planning and execution. Regulatory agencies around the world are increasingly in communication about safety issues for drugs that are marketed worldwide. Such communication can protect patients from unnecessary harm.

Selected new drugs

During 1985 there were 53 new chemical entities marketed worldwide, a significant increase over the approximately 40 new drugs introduced annually over the previous three years. In the United States there were 30 new chemical entities approved in 1985 by the FDA—also a new record. But only three prescription drug products were considered to have a major important therapeutic gain over those already in the marketplace. These were somatrem (Protropin), a synthetic human growth hormone; ribavirin (Virazole), an antiviral, anti-infective agent; and amiodarone (Cordarone) an antiarrhythmic.

The human growth hormone, somatrem, was produced using gene-splicing techniques with the bacterial genetic material rDNA. This synthetic hormone enables children with growth defects to reach adult stature. Thousands of children in the U.S. suffer from growth-hormone deficiency caused by the failure of the pituitary gland to secrete enough hormone. Not only is somatrem a significant new tool in the treatment of dwarfism, but its use as one of the first marketed biotechnology products represents a breakthrough for the development of a wide variety of synthetic hormones.

In 1985 a fatal slow-virus infection, Creutzfeldt-Jakob disease, was diagnosed in four people who had been under treatment for growth-hormone deficiency with natural pituitary hormone obtained from cadavers. Future treatment with the naturally derived hormone was then called into question. Thus, the new biosynthetic product means unlimited supplies of hormone can be available without risk of infection.

Ribavirin is one of the few anti-infective drugs that attack viruses. It should be of particular use for the treatment of severe lower respiratory infections caused by the respiratory syncytial virus (RSV), which hospitalizes about 100,000 young children each year. RSV is the most important cause of pneumonia and bronchiolitis in infants and children. It also affects adults—especially parents of young children, personnel in hospital pediatric wards, and the elderly. The drug is administered through a small particle aerosol generator that delivers a fine mist directly to the lungs. Ribavirin is an important new drug since an estimated 5% of affected patients die from the infection, and previously the only available treatment was for symptoms but not for RSV's cause. Approval of ribavirin will soon be sought for use in other viral infections, such as influenza, parainfluenza, and adenovirus. Clinical trials are also being conducted with AIDS patients.

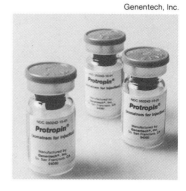

Genetically engineered human growth hormone (Protropin) is a new drug that represents an important therapeutic gain over previously available products. The synthetic hormone enables children to grow to normal height.

Antiarrhythmic agents are classified according to dominant electrophysiological effects. The classes are class I, local anesthetics; class II, beta-blockers; class III, drugs that prolong the action potential duration; and class IV, calcium antagonists. Several cardiac class I antiarrhythmic drugs reached the market in the United States during the 1984–85 period: mexiletine (Mexitil), flecainide (Tambacor), and tocainide (Tonocard). All of these are potent drugs for treating heart rhythm abnormalities. Amiodarone (Cordarone), a class III drug, was originally introduced as an antianginal agent; i.e., to prevent severe chest pain in cardiac conditions. But it is currently being marketed for the treatment of a variety of supraventricular and ventricular tachyarrhythmias (heart rhythm disturbances that result in a resting heart rate of over 100 beats per minute). All of these drugs, which must be used under strict clinical supervision, may have advantages in terms of overall safety and efficacy over previously available ventricular arrhythmia suppressant drugs and thus are welcome additions to the antiarrhythmic armamentarium.

An additional 14 drugs considered to have a modest therapeutic gain over previously available products were also approved by the FDA in 1985. Certain of these new drugs are highlighted below.

Enalapril (Vasotec), a new drug for treating high blood pressure, is the second angiotensin-converting enzyme inhibitor (the first being captopril [Capoten]) to be marketed in the U.S. It inhibits the conversion of a specific body chemical, angiotensin I, to the physiologically active angiotensin II, which is a potent vasoconstrictor; i.e., it causes narrowing of the blood vessels. Partially blocked blood vessels elevate blood pressure as the heart is forced to pump harder. Thus, enalapril, by preventing the production of the angiotensin that causes narrowed vessels, lowers blood pressure in hypertensive patients.

Trientine (Cuprid) was approved for use for the treatment of the relatively rare, genetically inherited Wilson's disease. Named for its discoverer, the English dermatologist Sir William J. E. Wilson, it is a disorder of copper metabolism characterized by neurological symptoms and renal dysfunction. The untreated disease is invariably fatal. The major benefit of the drug is that it can be used primarily in patients who cannot tolerate or who are not responsive to the already marketed product used in Wilson's disease treatment, penicillamine.

A renal enzyme inhibitor and antibiotic combination, imipenem/cilastatin sodium (Primaxin), appears to have the broadest spectrum of activity and the greatest potency of any antibiotic marketed at the present time. It is for treating serious infections that occur in virtually every site in the body and are caused by susceptible strains of all major bacteria. The drug can be used to treat lower respiratory and urinary tract infections; intra-abdominal, gynecologic, bone and joint, and skin infections; endocarditis; and bacterial septicemia. This new antibiotic is likely to be of particular value in treating infections caused by bacterial mixtures—common in hospitals—which usually require treatment with several antibiotics. Life-threatening infections resistant to other antibiotics such as cephalosporins and penicillin have been shown to respond to imipenem/cilastatin.

An oral gold compound, auranofin (Ridaura), was approved for use as an antiarthritic. The availability of an oral dosage form of gold to treat arthritis represents some advantage over the injectable gold product on the market, gold sodium thiomalate (Myochrysine), with regard to ease of administration and reported adverse effects. Gold is a slow-acting "disease-modifying" type of therapy for rheumatoid arthritis—controlling symptoms and delaying progression of the disease rather than providing relief for acute symptoms.

1986 and beyond

Many important and innovative drug products have been approved for use in Europe and are currently under review by the FDA. For example, buspirone (Buspar), a nonaddictive tranquilizer, probably will be approved for use in the U.S. in 1986. This product could possibly replace diazepam (Valium) in the marketplace. Valium is among the most widely prescribed of all drugs.

Significant advances in drug therapy may soon be realized for the complications of diabetes, employing the new drugs sorbinil and tolrestat. These drugs are aldose-reductase inhibitors; *i.e.,* they block the action of an enzyme that causes blindness and kidney and nerve damage in diabetics. Both drugs are presently being evaluated for safety and efficacy in clinical trials.

Cardiovascular agents. Significant advances in drugs to treat cardiovascular conditions are in progress. Milrinone, a cardiostimulant for use in treating congestive heart failure, is under study for long-term safety and efficacy. Atrial natriuretic factor (ANF), a substance produced by heart cells that acts directly on the kidneys, is in the early stages of evaluation in the treatment of hypertension. A fibrinolytic agent (for dissolution of blood clots), eminase, shows great promise

From Tilman Sauerbruch et al.,
"Fragmentation of Gallstones by Extracorporeal Shock Waves,"
The New England Journal of Medicine, March 27, 1986, vol. 314, no. 13, p. 819

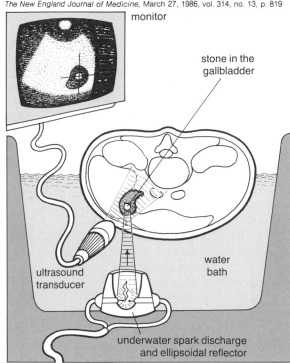

monitor

stone in the gallbladder

water bath

ultrasound transducer

underwater spark discharge and ellipsoidal reflector

West German researchers have successfully treated gallstones by disintegrating them with shock waves. In this procedure underwater shock waves are reflected to a focal point where the stone is positioned.

for dissolving clots in the treatment of myocardial infarction (heart attack).

The long-term efficacy of the currently marketed hypolipemic (lipid-lowering) drug, gemfibrozil (Lopid), in the prevention of myocardial infarction is under study in the U.S. Lipids, including cholesterol, are fatty substances in the blood. High serum cholesterol is considered a risk factor in coronary heart disease. Mevinolin (Mevacor), another new drug, also shows promise for lowering blood cholesterol levels. This drug interferes with a key enzyme system, thus preventing the formation of high blood levels of cholesterol. Mevinolin is being evaluated in human clinical trials. What long-term effect this drug may have in preventing myocardial infarction or artherosclerosis remains to be determined.

Drugs for gastric disorders. Several years ago gastric and duodenal ulcer therapy was dramatically changed with the marketing of cimetidine (Tagamet) in the U.S. and abroad. Cimetidine represents a class of drugs, the histamine H_2-receptor antagonists, which inhibit the action of the body chemical histamine at the H_2-receptor sites on body cells and thereby inhibit gastric acid production. The indications and dosage regimens for this drug are currently being broadened in the United States. The role of H_2-receptor antagonists in nonulcer gastrointestinal disease is also being evaluated. Classification of these drugs for use as over-

Drugs and devices

the-counter (OTC) products is also being explored by drug manufacturers. A longer acting H_2-receptor antagonist drug, famotidine (Pepcid), for the treatment of active duodenal or gastric ulcer disease and pathological hypersecretory conditions, such as Zollinger-Ellison syndrome (an ulcer-producing tumor of the pancreatic islands of Langerhans), was under review by the FDA in 1986, and imminent approval was expected.

Misoprostol (Cytotec) and enprostil (Gardrin), already on the world markets, represent the first of a new class of ulcer drugs, (the cytoprotective prostaglandin derivatives). These synthetic hormonelike substances not only stop the secretion of gastric acid but also promote healing of the stomach lining. Misoprostol was expected to receive U.S. approval for use in patients in 1986.

Another important new drug under development by several drug manufacturers is omeprazole, which reportedly shuts down the cells that produce gastric acid. Clinical trials of omeprazole were to begin in 1986. Assuming that the drug is effective and exhibits an acceptable safety profile, FDA approval is likely later in this decade.

The cochlear implant, by stimulating the auditory nerve, enables some deaf persons to hear sounds. An external microphone picks up sounds that are transmitted to an electrode implanted in the inner ear.

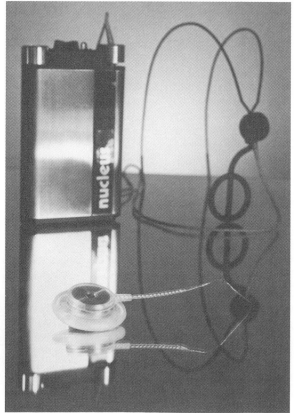

Hank Morgan—Rainbow

Genetically engineered drugs on the horizon

There are many new and exciting genetically engineered products that are becoming available for clinical testing for a variety of diseases. Excess secretion of interleukin-1, which is produced by white blood cells, has been reported as a cause of rheumatoid arthritis. Drugs that block the action of interleukin-1 are under development. Such drugs could become the therapeutic tools of the future for the treatment of arthritis along with the nonsteroidal anti-inflammatory drugs that are currently in use.

For treating cancers, tumor necrosis factor (TNF), which is naturally produced by the immune system and which causes tumor cells but not normal cells to burst, will be evaluated in clinical trials in the U.S., possibly beginning in late 1986.

Monoclonal antibodies, which are ultrapure, highly specific antibodies (sometimes known as "magic bullets"), can be used as homing devices to carry drugs or radioisotopes to kill unhealthy cells. Such antibodies are being tested alone and in combination with drugs, toxins, and radiation as anticancer therapy. Other genetically engineered anticancer substances that may be approved for limited use over the next few years are the interferons and interleukin-2.

Clinical trials are in progress with rDNA tissue plasminogen activator (t-PA) for the treatment of myocardial infarction; t-PA is a gene-spliced protein that stimulates production of an enzyme that effectively dissolves blood clots that block arteries. During 1985 additional clinical trials of t-PA began for four new indications: deep vein thrombosis, pulmonary embolism, peripheral arterial occlusion, and unstable angina.

A synthetic chemical has been designed that blocks corticotropin-releasing factor, a hormone found in the brain. This factor causes the classic response to stress: increased heart rate and high blood pressure. There is also evidence that high levels of this substance are associated with depression, anorexia nervosa, and alcoholism. Research is ongoing to assess the value of the synthetic chemical in these various disease states.

Vaccines are also being developed through genetic engineering. Notable is a recombinant DNA vaccine for malaria that targets the merozoite (blood phase) of malaria parasitic growth rather than the initial sporozoite phase. In such tropical regions of the world as Africa, Latin America, and Asia, both natives and travelers will benefit from this vaccine.

Selected new devices

A large variety of medical devices (implements designed to diagnose or treat medical conditions) have been in use for years, but since 1976 the FDA has required that devices meet standards based on the degree of hazard possibly associated with each device.

Devices in classes I and II comprise approximately 92% of the devices available. These range from simple

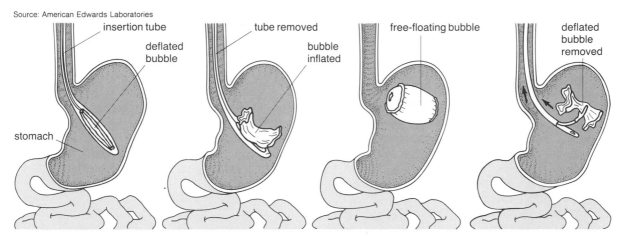

insertion tube   tube removed   free-floating bubble   deflated bubble removed

deflated bubble

bubble inflated

stomach

A new device, used as a temporary adjunct to dieting and behavior modification, has aided some severely obese people in losing weight. A plastic tube is used to insert a deflated polyurethane sac into the stomach. The sac is inflated and the tube removed. The bubble, which expands to the size of a small juice can, apparently aids weight loss by producing a sense of fullness. The bubble is then removed, usually after about three or four months.

ones, such as elastic bandages, to more complicated ones, such as anesthesia machines. The degree of regulation varies from record keeping and registration for class I devices to mandatory performance standards for class II. Class III devices (*e.g.,* artificial organs and intrauterine devices) present the greatest potential hazard and, therefore, require the greatest regulation. They must be thoroughly tested by the developer/manufacturer and approved by the FDA before they are allowed to be marketed.

There are currently on the market 1,700 types of devices and some 40,000 different brands and models. Following are some of the most significant devices to be approved from 1984 to the present.

An agent that will aid in the removal of dental caries is one such new device. An applicator tip can be used in direct contact with the carious lesion and thus significantly reduce or eliminate the need for the dental drill.

An approved ultrasonic kidney-stone-shattering device, called a lithotripter, works by focusing an ultrasonic beam on the stone, thereby pulverizing the material and allowing it to pass down the urinary tract. This device is currently available in a few select locations in the United States. The use of this process reduces the length of hospitalization, the convalescent period, and the cost as compared with surgery for renal stones. A similar device is now being tested to treat gallstones. West German researchers, who have successfully used the lithotripter on patients with gallstones, believe that perhaps 10% of gallstone patients could benefit from this method of treatment.

With FDA approval of the first "bioelectronic ear," called a cochlear implant, it is now possible for profoundly deaf individuals to detect environmental sounds and even conversational speech. The device works by stimulating the auditory nerve.

Obesity in a minority of selected patients can now be treated by a device known as the Garren-Edwards Gastric Bubble. It is a "balloon" that can be implanted in the stomach to provide a sensation of being full. The acid-resistant balloon does not interfere with the digestive process. It is to be used only as a temporary adjunct to diet and behavior modification for individuals with severe obesity. In an Emory University, Atlanta, Ga., study in five hospitals, the device was tested in patients who needed to lose weight for serious medical reasons. Of 20 patients who had the device implanted for 90 days, weight loss ranged from 39.6 to 167.2 kg (18 to 76 lb). Some patients experienced nausea and vomiting at first.

Other important devices recently approved by the FDA include new and better diagnostic imaging devices for detecting diseases in body organ systems, diagnostic laboratory tests that can discover human fetal defects early in pregnancy, and electronic devices that stimulate bone growth when a fractured bone will not heal.

An ever expanding arena

The coverage of drugs and devices presented in this review is by no means comprehensive. Only certain drugs and devices that are considered to be significant additions to the therapeutic armamentarium for the treatment of a wide variety of diseases are included. These agents were developed in laboratories around the world, employing sophisticated scientific research methodologies. New diagnostic and therapeutic devices will enhace health, and the matching of directed research capabilities to the complex cellular aspects of disease should guarantee the continued development of drugs that will be specifically and highly effective in the treatment of acute and chronic disease states.

—*Elizabeth E. Force, Ph.D.*

Special Report

Eruption of Nevado del Ruiz

by Joseph B. Treaster

Late on the warm autumn afternoon of Nov. 13, 1985, flakes of soft gray ash began falling on the prosperous farm town of Armero in a lush green valley in the South American country of Colombia. Soon it started to rain. The ash kept coming. Darkness fell, and a short time later townspeople heard radio reports that the snow-capped Nevado del Ruiz volcano, 46 km (28.6 mi) to the southwest, had erupted. A radio announcer and a priest told listeners there was nothing to fear. Even so, the local Red Cross Committee went into an emergency meeting and established contact with its regional headquarters in the town of Ibagué, 65 km (40 mi) away, by ham radio.

Red Cross officials in Ibagué confirmed that the 5,439-m (17,844-ft) volcano had roared violently to life after nearly 400 years of slumber; it appeared that floodwaters were rushing down the deep, narrow gorge of the Lagunilla River toward Armero. At 10:13 PM Roberto Ramírez, the chief of the Armero Red Cross unit, said into his radio: "The water is here." "That was the last we heard from him," said Guillermo Rueda Montana, president of the Colombian Red Cross.

Natural disaster of stunning proportions

At that moment a towering wall of mud, water, and debris, perhaps four or five stories high, had been sweeping across the town of Armero at a speed of at least 48 km/h (30 mph), overturning cars, shattering houses, and uprooting trees. Many of its 28,000 residents had been asleep or preparing for bed. Most were buried alive in one of the most devastating natural disasters of the century. Thousands of others were maimed, orphaned, or made homeless.

It was a stunning incident that evoked worldwide interest and sympathy and staggered the government of Colombia and the country's relief forces. It brought a rush of food, medical supplies, and rescue equipment from the United States, France, Britain, Spain, Mexico, and several countries in South America, as well as offers of help from numerous expert rescue teams, including some that only weeks earlier had played vital roles in the aftermath of an earthquake that ravaged the heart of Mexico City.

As dawn broke the morning after the eruption, a pilot of a light plane flew over Armero and reported that nothing was left. He saw a few tin roofs glinting

in the early morning sun and some bushy trees whose trunks had been swallowed in the mud and looked like squat shrubs. Otherwise, the pilot said, there was only a smooth gray expanse that reminded him of a beach. That report critically shaped the rescue effort. Rueda, the surgeon who was president of the Red Cross, said that in meetings of the committee in the first 72 hours of the crisis, the sense was that the avalanche of mud had been so overwhelming that "there were very few people alive, and there was no need to rush in."

After 72 hours with volunteers continuing to find people trapped alive, officials began to question their initial assumptions. Foreign diplomats said they had the same impression of the committee's attitude during that period. The government denied that during the crucial early hours, when injured people were suffering in near freezing water at night and then baking under an unyielding mountain sun, it had given the town up for lost. But Alejandro Jiménez, a 23-year-old Argentine surgeon, and a handful of Colombians who set up the main aid station in Armero on a sloping patch of grass overlooking the mud plain, said they had to argue in Bogotá, the capital, for permission to go to Armero. Jiménez said he and the other volunteers got to Armero early Friday morning to begin ministering to victims of a disaster that had occurred on Wednesday evening. They were never reinforced and worked to near exhaustion before being pulled out three days later, in tears, but also worrying that they might be endangered by disease.

The survivors of the tragedy and many others pointed to evidence that scientists had been warning for months that the volcano was threatening to erupt and said that some government experts had even drawn an elaborate "risk map" showing that, in the event of an eruption, Armero and great swaths of the surrounding valleys, some of the richest coffee- and cotton-growing and prize cattle-grazing land in the country, would be inundated.

Only a few Colombian rescue workers ever reached the disaster area. Many said that they had lacked virtually everything needed for a successful rescue operation, including manpower, tents, basic first-aid materials, antibiotics, blankets, and even shovels, picks, and rope. Some international rescue team members said their early offers of assistance had been turned down and that when they belatedly arrived in Colombia, they were hampered by protocol, recalcitrant military officers, and various failures of coordination.

In the fourth day of the rescue operation, with volunteer doctors and aides saying they were still hearing the cries of stranded survivors drifting across the vast plain of gray mud, the Colombian minister of health, Rafael de Zubiría, announced that the search was to end. De Zubiría said, "The stench makes further work in the zone of Armero impossible." After an uproar of complaints from relatives of Armero residents, however, other government officials reversed the health minister's proclamation. But by then supervisors in the field had already started sending rescue workers home.

A relief effort falls short

Indeed, the volcano disaster, in which an estimated 22,000 to 25,000 people were killed, also triggered a torrent of intense and bitter criticism of the government of Colombia that raged for months. In many ways the Colombia volcano disaster provides a case study in what not to do in response to a major calamity. To respond to the volcano disaster, an Emergency Committee with representatives of the armed forces and the nation's relief agencies was called together. The military played the leading role. Pres. Belisario Betancur Cuartas flew over Armero and made inspection tours of some of the nearby towns where refugees had collected. He looked haggard and shaken and spoke emotionally about the loss of life. But Gen. Miguel Vega Uribe, Colombia's minister of defense, said in an interview later that *he* had personally been in charge, he had made the decisions.

The government was slow in getting rescue personnel to the scene, and it never sent more than a few hundred rescuers to cover an area of hundreds of hectares. There were suggestions that the government lacked helicopters and transport planes. But it was possible to get to Armero by car or truck over a mountain road from Bogotá in about four hours. While some rescues had been made early, members of the first medical team to reach Armero said they arrived at least 30 hours after the eruption. General Vega chose not to employ any units of the 100,000-member Army or the 65,000-member police force in the search. He attributed the inability to move troops in the area to "all the mud."

A mixture of military and civilian helicopters searched from the air. The military devoted many aircraft, including several with U.S. crews that the United States Army had rushed in from a base in Panama, to the ferrying of supplies and equipment to aid stations and refugee centers on high ground a few kilometers from Armero. But rescue workers and other civilians in Armero said

No field hospital was set up in Armero, Colombia, after the volcano erupted; thus, thousands of victims were stranded in the mud without help. (Far left) A lucky child who was reached by helicopter is washed after having lain helpless in the mud for hours. But rescue workers failed to devise a way to save 13-year-old Omayra Sánchez (left), who died of a heart attack after being trapped in mud up to her neck for 60 hours.

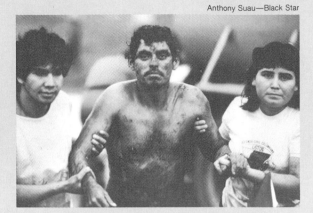

Anthony Suau—Black Star

Many survivors of Colombia's volcano were in a state of shock immediately after the eruption. Months later, those who had lost relatives and their homes bore deep emotional scars.

there never seemed to be many helicopters searching the area and that it seemed that more could have been profitably used. General Vega said that putting more helicopters in the air over Armero would have been dangerous to the airmen.

At the same time, air force Brig. Gen. Alberto Meléndez said it was decided not to put a field hospital in Armero because there was no electricity or potable water there. Meanwhile, dazed victims, caked with mud, most of their clothing shredded or gone, lay on the damp ground in Armero for hours waiting for a helicopter after being hauled out of the morass.

Afterward, at a briefing in the presidential palace in Bogotá, General Vega sketched lines of responsibility on a chart with an assertion of precision and clarity that had not been evident in the disaster area. Mid-way through the mission, for example, General Meléndez, in charge of logistics, had said he did not know who was in charge of the rescue. Majors and captains in the towns near Armero said they did not know either.

General Vega said that by the second day he had ordered that a grid pattern be established over the 19 km (12 mi) of mud that had blanketed Armero and that helicopter pilots be assigned to specific grids to ensure a thorough search and to avoid duplication. Yet on the sixth day a helicopter pilot in Armero was totally unaware of any such scheme and, in fact, said in an interview, "If we had grids, maybe it would be better. Each chopper tries to look in the place he thinks there may be somebody. Maybe the next pilot comes in and tries the same place. We need grids."

Long after the tragedy government officials in Colombia would not concede that they had fallen short in their efforts at Armero. President Betancur and other government officials insisted that the government had done the best it could in a less developed country with grave economic problems and limited resources. Some Colombian officials accused foreign journalists

from developed countries like the United States of exaggerating and failing to comprehend the realities of a less developed nation, ignoring that the specific, detailed criticism had come from Colombian survivors and rescue workers as well as foreign specialists who had studied disasters around the world.

After visiting the volcano and talking with Colombian and foreign geologists, French government volcano expert Haroun Tazieff said flatly that the disaster could have been avoided. "Twenty-one years ago," he said, "we forewarned of a similiar situation in Costa Rica, and there was only one dead person."

When the small team of Red Cross volunteers who had been at the heart of the rescue effort were lifted out of the destroyed town by helicopter a few hours before the health minister's announcement of terminating the rescue, they said they were still waiting for emergency supplies and equipment. In one widely publicized incident, 13-year-old Omayra Sánchez, trapped in water that had risen to her neck, died surrounded by rescue workers who, in 60 hours, had been unable to figure out how to free her. Two hours before the girl died, a water pump that had been requested much earlier arrived. It was broken. Four hours after she died, 18 more pumps reached a nearby town in response to the earlier request.

Months later: emotional scars

Several months after the disaster, tons of the millions of dollars in relief supplies that had poured in from abroad, such as canned food, clothing, and tools, still had not been distributed but were stacked up in customs warehouses with organizations in the capital arguing over who would pay storage and shipping charges.

The government was working on a comprehensive plan to rebuild Armero on another site. But the plan was going slowly and, meanwhile, the thousands of people who had lost everything but their lives in the disaster huddled in refugee camps in tents and cramped one-room cement houses. For months one group camped in a Roman Catholic church in the town of Guayabal, eight kilometers (five miles) north of Armero.

Many of the survivors bear deep emotional scars from the ordeal. According to Doris Amado, a psychologist working at one of the refugee camps, many had turned to heavy drinking, violent family quarrels were frequent, and many suffered from nightmares. The emotional response to the disaster was such that an initial shocked passivity shifted to aggressiveness. Psychologist Amado explained that "the shock of what happened at first made them very passive." But several months after the eruption the people became "demanding, resentful of the outside world." Many refused to accept the disaster, she said. They would not travel the few kilometers to confront the ruins of their town. Some families had forbidden their children to speak of

320

the horrible evening when the mud gushed down on them. It is impossible to predict what the long-term emotional aftermath will be for survivors.

For most of the refugees there was no work, and the atmosphere of listless stupor in the camps intensified. The mayor of Armero, Ramón Antonio Rodríguez, was among those who died in the disaster. The man appointed to replace him during the reconstruction period, army Maj. Rafael Ruiz Navarro, as well as psychologist Amado, spoke of a need to create jobs so that "the people can begin to feel useful again." But even when there was work, some refugees would not take it. Jews in Colombia and the United States set up a brick factory in Guayabal to help the Armero victims. It employed 120 people, but only 40 of them were from Armero. The pay was about $3.30 a day. Oscar Vázuez, who lost his wife and five children in the avalanche of mud, told reporters he was not

Nature Unleashed and Unkind

Natural disasters have claimed hundreds of thousands of lives in the past two decades alone. Volcanoes, earthquakes, tsunamis, and cyclones are probably the most murderous in the sudden force they exert on populated areas. Even advanced rescue and relief strategies and the sophisticated technology of the 1970s and 1980s have been thwarted by such cataclysms.

When disaster strikes, the Red Cross and the country's military personnel are usually the first to act, with aid from other countries and relief agencies, such as CARE (Cooperative for American Relief Everywhere) and UNDRO (the United Nations Disaster Relief Office), soon to follow. Communication, transportation, and organization must be restored amid the destruction. Most immediately relevant: Who is alive? How to find them? How to reach them? Where to transport them? When is it too late to hope for survivors?

Even in the face of these calamitous situations, political relationships have guided decisions. China refused any outside assistance after the 1976 Tangshan (T'ang-shan) earthquakes because of its closed-door policies. At the time of the 1970 cyclone, East Pakistan (now Bangladesh) refused India's helicopters, boats, mobile hospitals, and relief supplies; but a fleet of U.S., French, West German, and Saudi Arabian helicopters was welcomed, as was a four-ship British task force with food, clothing, medicine, water-purification pills, and burial squads.

Environmental circumstances usually dominate planned strategy for rescue and relief. Severed communication lines can prevent the issuing of warnings, curtail efforts to gather estimates of the dead and injured, and make it impossible to transmit information to authorities. Rescue teams are often hampered by blocked roads and toppled buildings, as after the quakes of Guatemala (1976) and Mexico (1985). Helicopter search-and-retrieval efforts can fail because of weather, terrain, and other factors. Although sophisticated ultrasound detectors may locate survivors beneath mud or debris, time may run out before workers can remove the injured and give lifesaving aid, as in the aftermath of the Colombia volcano (1985).

Voluntary medical relief is usually immediate and substantial. For example, at the time of the 1970 earthquake in Peru, hundreds of foreign doctors (112 from Argentina alone) joined Peruvian physicians who had flocked to provide aid. The capital, Lima, was overwhelmed by U.S., West German, French, and other foreign supplies and personnel. But the U.S. ambassador to Peru, Taylor G. Belcher, summed up the predicament, "We don't need personnel, medical or food supplies. We need transport. . . . We just can't move what we have into affected areas." Helicopters had crashed in daring attempts to rescue and transport. Finally, after about a week Canadian Caribou aircraft were able to begin to aid Peru's planes in an organized airlift.

When the injured in Peru could be reached, medical attention focused on multiple fractures, lacerations, internal injuries, gangrene, and shock (as is typical in natural disasters). Two-person medical teams were helicoptered to mountainside points to assess damage and treat injuries, and a field hospital unit and crude air strip were set up on bulldozed areas in the Callejon. Also, typically, rumors of infectious disease caused by decaying corpses were rampant but unfounded; water-purification measures are usually sufficient to curtail epidemics.

For months or years afterward, disaster survivors, homeless and grieving, attempt to rebuild their lives, often with lingering hopes that lost relatives will yet be found. Numbing depression and fears of another disaster are often high, and the memories do not fade.

Scientific prediction of natural disasters and their anticipated destruction has enabled the establishment of evacuation plans for many vulnerable areas. In 1968 the Philippine government safely evacuated 70,000 people from the danger zone of erupting Mt. Mayon. However, communication-cutting disasters that occur at night catch people unaware and unprepared to implement plans. The world's response to such emergencies has been heroic, but hopes are for more specific prediction and preparedness to avert the enormous loss of life.

Death toll—worst recent disasters*

Date	Type	Location	Toll
May 31, 1970	earthquake	northern Peru	70,000
Nov. 13, 1970	cyclone/tidal wave	East Pakistan	500,000
Feb. 4, 1976	earthquake	Guatemala City	24,000
July 28, 1976	earthquake	Tangshan (T'ang-shan), China	655,000
Sept. 19–20, 1985	earthquake	Mexico City	20,000
Nov. 13, 1985	volcano	Armero, Colombia	25,000

*Disaster victim statistics are always estimates; actual numbers reported by different sources often vary by many thousands.

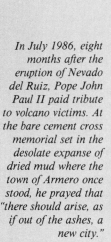

In July 1986, eight months after the eruption of Nevado del Ruiz, Pope John Paul II paid tribute to volcano victims. At the bare cement cross memorial set in the desolate expanse of dried mud where the town of Armero once stood, he prayed that "there should arise, as if out of the ashes, a new city."

interested. "How can a master builder like me reduce himself to working for that?" he asked. So he sat idle, each day becoming more angry.

Humanity shows its darkest side

The disaster also brought out some of the ugliest proclivities of humanity. From a hospital bed in Bogotá, Juan Gaitán, a 31-year-old surgeon who had been visiting his parents in Armero, told a reporter from the *Los Angeles Times* that as he lay trapped in the mud, two men fought their way to him. They stole his watch, his wedding ring, and a crucifix on a gold chain around his neck. "Die, you bastard," they said, and left him bleeding in the mud. Later, Gaitán said, he managed to drag himself over planks and corpses to dry land. Finally, a helicopter came.

In another incident a 25-year-old man was caught trying to rob a group of survivors at gunpoint. There were also numerous reports of looters ripping gold chains and rings from the dead. Months later some people had made a business of sneaking into Armero and digging up furniture, car parts, lumber, and roofing to sell to secondhand dealers. According to the *Miami Herald*, two policemen, who were supposed to be guarding one of Armero's buried banks, were jailed for stealing $170,000. After arresting some thieves they caught breaking in, they had allegedly kept the loot for themselves.

Fear of disease

From the start, rescue workers and health officials in the field and in Bogotá had been concerned that thousands of bodies decomposing in the mud of Armero could cause an epidemic. They worried about the contamination of subterranean water sources and nearby streams, mosquitoes and flies, and even the foul odor

of death that was only slightly tempered by the gauzy green surgical masks that some civil defense workers wore. This fear of disease, which had also troubled the authorities in Mexico after the earthquake, had been one of the elements behind the health minister's premature call to halt the rescue attempts. In the field, army officers and civil defense workers were anxious to begin burning bodies and spraying with lime and other disinfectants.

Within a few days typhoid vaccine began arriving at the field stations in the towns near Armero, and refugees and relief workers were lining up for injections. The same thing had occurred several weeks earlier after the earthquake in Mexico.

But according to Paul H. Blake, the chief of the enteric diseases branch at the U.S. Centers for Disease Control in Atlanta, Ga., the inoculations in Colombia and Mexico were both futile and unnecessary. "Decaying bodies, if healthy," he said, "present no risk to anybody." He referred to mass vaccinations against typhoid in such situations as a "reflex action" to induce the feeling that "somebody is doing something." Two inoculations are necessary, he said, and they do not take effect until too late to be helpful. Further, Blake said the danger of typhoid as well as other waterborne diseases such as hepatitis and salmonella could be eliminated by boiling drinking water or by treating it with chlorine or iodine.

Studies of medicine in disaster areas, which the Pan American Health Organization had conducted for more than a decade, determined that no epidemic is initiated by natural disasters unless there is already an epidemic in the area—for example, cholera. Miguel Gueri, one of the officials of the Pan American Health Organization, is said to have commented that all the material in the mudflow covering Armero could drain into one of the major rivers in the region, "and the only effect would be to fatten the catfish."

Should so many thousands have died?

Shortly after the government officially sealed off Armero and declared it a cemetery park, friends and relatives of the victims held a big outdoor funeral mass in a nearby town. They had heard the official pronouncements in the capital. They felt differently, and they said so with a prominent banner that charged: "The volcano didn't kill 22,000 people. The government killed them."

Months later journalists found the bleak landscape of the ruined town dotted with small white crosses marking the presumed spots where victims lay entombed. In what used to be the main park in Armero, someone had put up a sign listing seven members of the Vargas family lost in the avalanche. There was a message, too. "The disinterest of government officials and the fury of nature," it said, "have destroyed our families."

Emergency Medicine

Emergency medicine continues to grow and evolve as the newest of the American medical specialties. (Emergency medicine officially became a board-certified specialty in 1979.) The importance of this kind of medicine is illustrated by the fact that during 1985 in the U.S. approximately 78 million patients were treated in 5,400 hospital-based emergency departments by some 15,000 emergency medicine physicians. Also contributing their skills were more than 400,000 emergency medical technicians, 27,000 intermediate emergency medical technicians, 35,000 paramedics, 70,000 emergency nurses, and 85 hospital-based helicopter transport services. The American College of Emergency Physicians has 11,200 members, 2,000 of whom have attained fellowship status. Formal emergency medicine graduate education is taught in 65 programs and in 1986 involved about 1,300 residents.

First international conference meets

The growth of the specialty during the past year was exemplified by the convening of the first International Conference on Emergency Medicine in April 1986. The sponsoring organizations were the American College of Emergency Physicians, the Australasian College for Emergency Medicine, the Canadian Association of Emergency Physicians, and the host organization, the Casualty Surgeons Association of the United Kingdom. Of the 400 delegates who assembled in London to discuss issues of common interest, most came from the sponsoring countries. Also present were representatives from many European countries, Japan, Hong Kong, the Middle East, and Africa. Although in the past there had been international medical conferences where emergency medicine was one of many topics considered, the 1986 London meeting was the first conference devoted specifically and solely to emergency medicine. A total of 92 original research papers were presented on a wide variety of emergency medicine topics.

There was a general consensus that the specialty of emergency medicine is a vital component of the worldwide health care delivery system and that the means to fulfill its mission, especially in the prehospital phase, will vary from country to country, depending on local resources, geography, and training. In addition, the delegates recognized that the research base of emergency medicine as a specialty will inevitably involve learning more about the role of emergency physicians in natural disasters, trauma management, environmental and toxicological problems, and the field of resuscitation/reanimation of the critically ill. The latter topic was a subject of considerable interest to those attending the conference, and a number of sessions were devoted to resuscitation/reanimation concepts and recent advances in technique.

The current state of CPR

Throughout the ages people have attempted emergency resuscitation of the dead and near dead. The earliest known techniques included inflicting pain—by whipping the victim's body with stinging nettles or striking the skin with wet cloths—and attempting to restore heat to the cold, lifeless body by applying burning animal excreta to the patient's abdomen. In 1530 Paracelsus used a common fireside bellows to deliver air into the lungs of people who apparently were dead, and this practice became widespread for the next 300 years. Throughout the 18th century many novel methods were advocated to treat the drowned or near drowned, among them rolling the prone victim back and forth over a barrel or draping the body over the back of a trotting horse, causing the chest to bounce up and down. In the 1800s the focus of resuscitation techniques shifted to movement of the chest and, thereby, the lungs; for example, pulling the arms of the supine victim upward over the head for inspiration and moving the arms forward, folded on the chest and pressed against it, for expiration. The early 20th century saw the development of electronically driven devices, such as the iron lung, that alternately compressed and expanded the chest to simulate normal respiration.

In 1960 William Kouwenhoven, an electrical engineer, and his medical colleagues at the Johns Hopkins Hospital, Baltimore, Md., introduced closed chest, or external, cardiac massage to clinical medicine. Shortly thereafter, this technique, also known as chest compression, was combined with artificial ventilation (mouth-to-mouth breathing), and the concept of cardiopulmonary resuscitation (CPR) was developed. In the U.S., through the efforts of the American Heart Association and other such organizations, the practice of CPR has become widespread throughout the medical community and, to a moderate extent, the general public. However, as contemporary emergency medicine has pursued a deeper and more attentive study of the mechanisms of death and resuscitation, many previously believed "truths" are being challenged and newer reanimation techniques developed.

The initial discoverers of CPR believed that during external chest compression the heart was squeezed between the sternum and the spine, causing it to pump oxygenated blood forward to vital organs. This is not clearly the case, and today many authorities believe that the heart acts only as a "conduit," with changes in the intrathoracic and extrathoracic pressures initiating the forward blood flow. Regardless of the mechanism of CPR, there is general agreement that the amount of forward blood flow that results is quite low and will maintain circulation in a pulseless patient for only a short time—approximately 12 minutes. The prospect for recovery is dismal if more definitive therapy is not provided before this time has elapsed. A search for

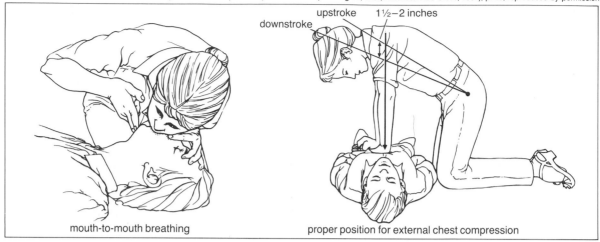

Adapted from *Cardiopulmonary Resuscitation* (Washington, D.C., American Red Cross, 1981), p. 25; reproduced by permission

downstroke upstroke 1½–2 inches

mouth-to-mouth breathing

proper position for external chest compression

New guidelines for cardiopulmonary resuscitation (CPR) published in 1986 recommend that the layperson be trained only in the one-rescuer technique (above), on the grounds that knowing both the one- and two-rescuer methods could be a source of confusion to the individual who must act without help in an emergency situation.

better methods of CPR continues and has included changing the relationship of ventilations (mouth-to-mouth breaths) to compressions, adding intermittent abdominal counterpulsations, developing portable lifesaving equipment, such as a pneumatic vest and abdominal binder, and using military antishock trousers for CPR. To date none of these techniques has improved forward blood flow sufficiently or has proved practical for widespread use; therefore, such methods have not been recommended to replace the type of CPR now in use. In the absence of any substantial advances in resuscitation techniques, the current guidelines for CPR and emergency cardiac care—published in the June 6, 1986, issue of the *Journal of the American Medical Association*—remain basically the same as those recommended in the 1960s.

Advances in defibrillation technology

The purpose of CPR is to maintain breathing and circulation temporarily in a victim of cardiac arrest until more definitive therapy can be provided. Generally, more definitive therapy consists of external cardiac defibrillation—the application of electrical energy (shocks) to the chest so as to convert an abnormal heart rhythm (called ventricular fibrillation) that does not provide adequate blood flow into normal cardiac activity. The earlier defibrillation is provided, the more successful the outcome tends to be. Initially only physicians were considered qualified to operate a defibrillator; later paramedics and intensive care nurses were added to the list of qualified personnel; basic emergency medical technicians are also now trained to perform defibrillation.

The latest development in the attempt to bring this lifesaving treatment to victims of cardiac arrest as early as is possible is the automatic defibrillator. This device

is designed so that after its two electrodes have been applied to the victim's chest, the cardiac rhythm is recorded and analyzed, and if ventricular fibrillation is present, the machine will automatically deliver an electrical countershock. The operator of the device does not need to be trained to recognize specific cardiac rhythms—the machine performs this function itself. Currently, automatic defibrillators are being considered for use in basic ambulance systems and also in the homes of individuals at high risk for cardiac arrest. If these evaluations show that the device does indeed save lives, its use could become widespread—eventually, automatic defibrillators could become as common as fire extinguishers in public gathering places.

Defining organ and tissue needs

All organs and tissues require a certain amount of blood supply in order to function properly, and they are damaged to varying degrees when blood flow decreases or ceases. Animal and human studies of blood pressures and blood flow rates in different parts of the body have been performed for the purpose of defining the different minimal end-organ ischemic (*i.e.*, without blood flow) tolerances and the so-called organ-specific resuscitation requirements. For example, it is now known that a pressure difference between the arterial and venous portions of the circulation of at least 20 mm of mercury is required during CPR to meet the minimal blood flow requirements of the heart that is stopped and cannot provide any of its own blood supply. Thus, newer methods of CPR under consideration have tried to ensure this degree of gradient as a minimal requirement and are attempting to reach even higher values in order to ensure that the heart muscle does not suffer permanent damage prior to or during the resuscitation process.

324

Perhaps the most interesting developments in this area are those associated with reanimation of the brain, the limiting factor for resuscitation. In the classic experiments that defined the extent of brain damage associated with different intervals of cardiac arrest, the upper limit for full recovery of nerve cells was found to be three to four minutes of full cardiopulmonary arrest and eight to ten minutes of localized cerebrovascular arrest (as might occur during stroke). However, more recently scientists have shown in many animal experiments that nerve cells can withstand a complete cessation of blood supply for extended time periods—up to 60 minutes under certain conditions. Currently it is not known why the human brain is so quickly damaged during short periods of cardiac arrest when laboratory studies indicate that the time potential for full recovery of neurons (nerve cells) is much longer. It would seem that irreversible brain death may take some time to fully develop. A complete understanding of the process would yield major advances in clinical therapy.

An important thrust of resuscitation research is now directed toward understanding what happens to the body as a whole when blood supply (perfusion) stops and is subsequently restarted (reperfusion). Researchers are seeking to discover the exact effects of reperfusion of the stomach, intestines, pancreas, liver, and other organs in terms of the overall resuscitation effort and, specifically, complete brain recovery. Thus, CPR has become too narrow a term to describe the effort of reanimation fully, and most scientists now refer to this type of emergency resuscitation treatment as cardiopulmonary cerebral resuscitation.

New approaches to cardiac arrest

Prior to the development of external cardiac massage in 1960, the technique of surgically opening the chest and directly and rhythmically squeezing the heart was widely used in hospitals to treat cardiac arrest. Without question, the amount of forward blood flow is much

Posing with Henry J. Heimlich (right), originator of the emergency technique known as the Heimlich maneuver, five-year-old Brent Meldrum (left) from Massachusetts demonstrates how he saved the life of his friend, Tanya Branden (center), who was choking on a piece of candy.

AP/Wide World

greater with this technique than with external chest compression. But because external methods were initially thought to be very effective, and because the closed-chest technique could be applied anywhere, the invasive surgical method for the most part became extinct. Recently, however, there has been a trend toward reintroducing this type of resuscitation in hospitals in order to improve recovery of patients in cardiac arrest.

Another method of restarting the circulation involves the use of cardiopulmonary bypass technology. Currently this technique is used during open-heart surgery to reroute blood flow from the heart and lungs so that these organs are temporarily bloodless, but the body's metabolic needs continue to be met. The machinery used in cardiopulmonary bypass both pumps and oxygenates the blood—thus theoretically offering a perfect way to provide circulation in the event that both of these vital and essential functions have ceased. It remains to be seen how the brain, abruptly deprived of blood during cardiac arrest, will respond to the sudden reinstitution of normal blood flow by mechanical means.

—*Richard M. Nowak, M.D.*

Environmental Health

The Chernobyl nuclear plant accident in the Soviet Union early in the year dominated environmental health issues in 1986. Several others drew widespread attention as well, including the discovery of high levels of radioactive radon gas in homes in several eastern states of the U.S. and a proposal by the Environmental Protection Agency (EPA) for a ban on the mining, importation, and use of asbestos. The EPA also identified pollution by pesticides as its top environmental risk reduction priority for 1987.

Chernobyl

The accidental explosion at the Chernobyl nuclear power plant in the Soviet Ukraine on April 26, 1986, was a landmark event of the atomic era that would pose serious potential global health consequences for decades to come. By some estimates the radioactive cloud released in the blast and ensuing fire could be responsible for thousands of deaths from cancer in the coming years, mostly in countries neighboring the U.S.S.R. The accident, some 130 km (80 mi) from Kiev, killed more than 25 persons, hospitalized about 300 with radiation sickness, and caused the evacuation of more than 100,000, making it the worst in commercial nuclear power history on many counts. It released radioactive material into the atmosphere that was detected worldwide, causing major concerns in other countries.

Emergency actions at the scene also were unprecedented. Workers tunneled under the Chernobyl plant to place a barrier intended to prevent molten radioactive matter from burning into the ground, contaminating groundwater, and possibly touching off a catastrophic steam explosion. Helicopter crews dumped 5,000 tons of clay, lead, sand, and boron into the reactor to smother the flames and halt escaping radioactivity. By June work had begun to encase the crippled reactor in concrete as a long-term solution to containment.

The accident once again stirred fears about that most dreaded of nuclear accidents, a meltdown, in which a nuclear power plant's radioactive fuel core overheats and melts through the floor of the reactor. Not since the Three Mile Island nuclear power plant accident near Harrisburg, Pa., in 1979 has atomic energy ignited such concerns over nuclear safety. The fire in the fuel core at Chernobyl reportedly reached temperatures of 2,760° C (5,000° F), melting a quantity of uranium oxide fuel. Scientists said they were certain of a fuel meltdown but uncertain whether any of the molten material ate its way through the plant floor and into the ground.

For such an earthshaking event, details of the Chernobyl accident and of the technical characteristics of the reactor surfaced unusually slowly, partly because of the Soviet tendency to deny or downplay unfavorable events. The Chernobyl power plant complex near the town of Pripyat, comprising four 1,000-MW reactors, is one of the largest and oldest of the 15 or so Soviet civilian nuclear stations. The Chernobyl-4 unit, in operation since 1983 and the site of the accident, is of the type known as RBMK-1000, a graphite-moderated reactor that is water-cooled. It consists largely of 1,700 tons of graphite blocks containing 192 tons of uranium fuel in channels drilled into the graphite.

U.S. nuclear experts said the Soviet reactor would not have met U.S. safety standards, in part because it is not encased in a steel-and-concrete containment building intended to prevent radioactive contamination from escaping in a serious accident. Also, approximately 100 commercial power reactors operating in the U.S. as of mid-1986 do not contain graphite, which is combustible and which did catch fire at Chernobyl. Two nuclear reactors in the U.S. do contain graphite.

One is a commercial power plant about 55 km (35 mi) north of Denver, Colo. The other is operated by the U.S. Department of Energy for military purposes in Richland, Wash., and was ordered reviewed for safety.

Chernobyl-4 was operating at low power on April 26 when it experienced a power surge. The sudden rise in temperature created a reaction between the steam inside the reactor and the zirconium pressure tubes and cladding of the fuel, producing explosive hydrogen gas. A hydrogen explosion subsequently blew off the roof of the unit and started a fire that persisted for two days, spewing radioactive debris including iodine and cesium isotopes over the Ukraine, Eastern Europe, and parts of Scandinavia.

The Soviet Politburo in July issued a report stating that the accident had been caused by a series of "gross breaches of the reactor operational regulations." It also said that 28 people had died as a result and that 1,000 sq km (386 sq mi) around the station were contaminated by radiation. A month later, in a report to the International Atomic Energy Agency, Soviet officials detailed the cause as an unauthorized test during which reactor workers had shut down several critical safety systems.

Most seriously poisoned by radiation were workers at the scene, including those who fought the fire despite dangerously high radioactivity levels. Exact levels in the plant were not reported by the Soviets, but high doses are known to destroy bone marrow, which produces the body's red blood cells, the white cells responsible for immune defense, and the platelets involved in the normal blood-clotting process. Bone marrow transplants were performed later on many of the critically ill, most of whom died nonetheless. Two persons were killed directly by the blast.

The Soviet Union was heavily criticized for delays in reporting the seriousness of the accident and in responding to it. An evacuation of more than 40,000 people living near the plant apparently did not begin until 36 hours later. The world was not aware of the accident until Sweden broke the news April 28, after background radiation levels in Sweden and Finland had risen 100 times higher than normal. A week after

A car exposed to radioactive fallout from the Chernobyl nuclear accident is washed at the West German border, and a Polish woman throws away milk given by cows exposed to the fallout.

(Left) AP/Wide World; (right) Laski—Keystone/Picture Group

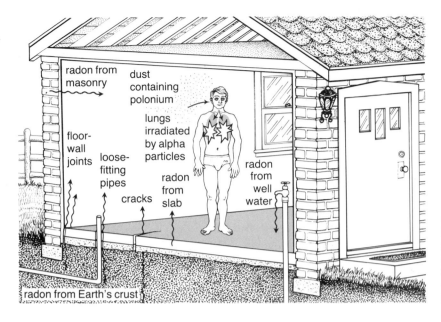

Radon, a naturally occurring radioactive gas, is believed to be responsible for thousands of lung cancer deaths in the U.S. each year. The diagram at left shows how radon enters the indoor environment of a typical house.

Labels in diagram: radon from masonry; dust containing polonium; lungs irradiated by alpha particles; floor-wall joints; loose-fitting pipes; cracks; radon from slab; radon from well water; radon from Earth's crust

the accident the evacuation radius was extended to 30 km (19 mi), and the number of evacuees eventually rose to around 112,000.

The reactor site, 960 km (600 mi) southwest of Moscow, is in the heart of the Ukrainian breadbasket, which produces much of the Soviet Union's food. In May the European Community announced a temporary ban on meat, live animals, and produce from Eastern Europe in an area up to 1,000 km (620 mi) from Chernobyl. Heavy rains fell across Western Europe after the accident, producing significantly higher radiation readings as the rain washed radioactive debris from the skies. Radioactive iodine-131 and cesium-137 were detected in the air, rainwater, and soil and eventually in fresh milk as cows ate contaminated vegetation. The first Chernobyl fallout was detected in the U.S. on May 4. The EPA monitored the country at 68 sampling sites and reported that radioactive fallout from Chernobyl was far below levels of concern to health and safety.

In assessing the likely health implications of the Chernobyl accident, EPA officials felt that the Soviets were going to pay a heavy price for Chernobyl in health. Unsafe levels of fallout were detected in areas populated by about 120 million people in Europe. One expert from the Defense Nuclear Agency, an arm of the U.S. Defense Department that researches the effects of nuclear weapons, expects that "we will see increased cancer deaths of between 5,000 and 50,000 people in the next 30 years, mostly locally in the countries closest to Russia, such as Poland and Scandinavia." The agency said that Chernobyl produced less radioactive fallout than the atmospheric bomb tests of the 1950s and early 1960s, but that fallout from the Soviet disaster was several thousand times worse than that measured in the World War II bombing of Hiroshima, which ushered in the nuclear weapons age.

Indoor radon hazard

At least a million homes in the U.S. were suspected of harboring dangerously high levels of radon, a radioactive gas that is tasteless, odorless, invisible, and believed responsible for thousands of lung cancer deaths a year. In the U.S. the EPA considered radon the nation's leading radiation problem and the second largest cause of lung cancer after cigarette smoking. It estimated that radon causes 5,000–20,000 lung cancer deaths a year, although no studies have confirmed this.

The radon threat was discovered in late 1984 when a worker at a Pennsylvania nuclear power plant repeatedly set off radiation alarms where he worked. The radioactive contamination was traced to his home. Subsequently, high radon levels were detected in homes in parts of Pennsylvania, New Jersey, and New York. Unlike most environmental problems that are man-made, are hard to solve, and pose cancer risks—like toxic chemical pollution—radon is different in many ways. And once identified, the problem can be avoided or corrected. Radon is linked to natural uranium found everywhere in the soil and rock. Uranium decays to radium and then to radon, a gas that is chemically inert and can be carried with the air into homes through basement cracks or other openings and even in well water. Radon can also emanate from building materials like concrete and brick. The danger comes from radon gas levels that build up in basements and upper levels of homes. Radon decays into radioactive elements (e.g., polonium) that are chemically active. If inhaled, they can attach to the lining of the lung, where they emit radiation that causes lung cancer.

Environmental health

The push in the mid-1970s to insulate, or tighten, homes for energy conservation has been accused of causing a new kind of environmental hazard: indoor air pollution, including radon buildup. The EPA suggested that weatherproofing homes for energy efficiency makes them radon traps by stopping the flow of fresh outdoor air that normally ventilates homes. On the other hand, researchers at the Argonne National Laboratory near Chicago and the Lawrence Berkeley Laboratory in California believed that the effect of tightening homes during the energy crisis was being grossly exaggerated in the radon controversy. They pointed out that radon levels seem to vary widely regardless of the uranium content of soil and rock under a home. The researchers said that they suspected that the characteristics of each individual house have a lot to do with it, such as a tendency to draw air from the surrounding soil because of basement air pressures that are lower than those found outside. The solution in such circumstances might be to seal basement cracks where radon enters or to increase ventilation, which can be as simple as opening a window or installing a ventilating system.

Proposed asbestos ban

The EPA early in 1986 announced proposed rules for barring all uses of asbestos because of warnings by health officials that 5,000–10,000 cancer deaths are caused each year by asbestos inhalation. It was estimated that 375,000 workers are still exposed to asbestos on the job. The agency said it would propose an immediate ban on five widely used products—asbestos-containing floor tiles, roofing felts, flooring felts and felt-backed sheet flooring, cement pipe and fittings, and clothing—and gradually eliminate all other products made with the heat-resistant substance over the next ten years. Furthermore, it proposed that all asbestos mining and imports be eliminated over a ten-year period. The new rules would not affect asbestos products already in use. The EPA estimated that the phaseout would cost $2 billion over the next 15 years but would save 1,900 lives.

A widely used insulator and building material, asbestos has been found to cause asbestosis (chronic scarring of vital lung tissue), a form of lung cancer known as bronchogenic carcinoma, mesothelioma (an incurable cancer of the chest and abdominal lining), and other lung diseases and illnesses. As many as 27 million workers in shipyards, power plants, garages, and construction sites were exposed to asbestos from 1940 to 1980. One asbestos manufacturer, the Manville Corp., filed for bankruptcy as a result of more than 15,000 lawsuits by workers. Other companies faced similar challenges. The cost of compensating workers could run to more than $40 billion.

In an earlier move the EPA required school administrators to have their buildings inspected for the presence of crumbling asbestos, which is a hazard because it releases asbestos fibers into the air, where they can be inhaled. The agency estimated that 15 million U.S. children attend schools where crumbling asbestos is present. Not all buildings with asbestos insulation have the crumbling problem and therefore do not pose a risk. EPA rules do not require the removal of such materials, only that parents and teachers be notified of the problem when it is discovered. Asbestos-removal costs in an average-sized school can range from $100,000 to more than $1 million. In addition, the EPA estimated that 700,000 commercial, residential apartment, and federal buildings contain crumbling asbestos.

Toxic chemicals

Late in 1985 the EPA issued a list of 402 toxic chemicals that are "immediately dangerous to life and health" if accidentally spilled and could have "Bhopal-like" consequences if mishandled. The move came as one of the agency's major responses to continuing concerns in the U.S. over chemical safety and environmental health, which were spurred by the catastrophic chemical leak in Bhopal, India, in late 1984. Toxic chemicals and their effect on public health are often portrayed as the most important environmental issue of the 1980s and 1990s.

Checking for asbestos content, a worker takes a core sample (far right) from the insulation of an exposed pipe.

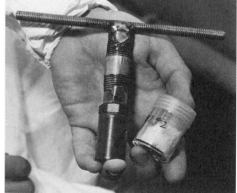

In announcing the agency's voluntary Chemical Emergency Preparedness Program in November 1985, EPA Administrator Lee Thomas said it was intended to help state and local governments better understand the types of hazardous chemicals found at industrial plants operating in U.S. communities and to prepare contingency plans for handling chemical emergencies. The EPA cited a poll showing that two of three Americans believe that within 50 years the U.S. will suffer a chemical disaster of the magnitude of Bhopal. A month later the agency named 402 chemicals that could produce a toxic cloud that might sweep over a nearby community in the event of a chemical plant accident. They included acids, cyanides, solvents, and other chemicals used widely in U.S. industry.

Under the EPA plan, industries that produce or handle such chemicals would notify local governments of their presence. If emergency response plans for coping with a chemical disaster did not already exist, local communities then would be expected to develop them. Responsibility for dealing with such emergencies rests with local authorities, such as fire departments. The EPA offered to provide technical training for such groups in identifying potential chemical hazards and handling them.

In another move related to toxic chemical wastes, the EPA said in June 1986 that it would start within a month to cancel contracts for cleaning up toxic-waste dumps because the $1.6 billion Superfund program had run out of money. The program, adopted in 1980 to address the toxic-dump problem, expired on Sept. 30, 1985, and was awaiting renewal in what has been described as a cliffhanger. The Senate voted to provide $7.5 billion over five years, while the House favored $10 billion. In August the two houses agreed to a $9 billion compromise plan.

Superfund was operating on leftover and stopgap money since its authority expired. Congress provided $150 million for cleanups in April and May while debating renewal of the law. The EPA has named 888 sites on its national priority list to qualify for emergency cleanup funds under Superfund. Since the program started, EPA has fully rehabilitated 13 sites and funded short-term or emergency actions for 623 others. It has been criticized for simply moving the hazardous wastes from one place to another.

Lead in gasoline

The lead content of gasoline sold in the U.S. dropped to 0.1 g per gal on Jan. 1, 1986, under EPA regulations announced in 1984. The agency estimated that leaded gasoline is responsible for about 80% of all lead emissions in the air, which are potentially hazardous. Lead has been blamed for severe health problems, especially in urban black children living in ghetto conditions near congested streets and highways. When inhaled or swallowed, lead causes serious learning and behavior problems. It also damages the kidneys, liver, and reproductive system.

Pesticides

The EPA called pollution by pesticides its most urgent problem, nearly 25 years after Rachel Carson first warned of the danger in her book *Silent Spring*. In its 1987 priority list the agency ranked reducing risks from existing pesticides at the top. It also intended to accelerate the review of existing pesticides through the registration process and to conduct special reviews when the potential for unreasonable adverse health effects was found.

The General Accounting Office (GAO) issued a report in April 1986 saying that most of the 50,000 pesticide products registered for use in the U.S. have not been fully tested for health effects. In 1972 Congress had given the EPA four years in which to reevaluate all older pesticides. The GAO said as of March 31, 1986, that the EPA had not completed a final reassessment of any of the 600 active pesticide ingredients on the market today, although preliminary assessments had been made on 124. The EPA's assessment was expected to extend into the 21st century because of the magnitude and complexity of testing pesticide safety.

The U.S. Congress also began rewriting the Federal Insecticide, Fungicide, and Rodenticide Act (FIFRA), the basic law governing the production and use of pesticides. The 14-year deadlock in rewriting FIFRA came to an end with an unusual agreement between agricultural and environmental groups that would, among other things, put EPA on a strict timetable for reregistering 300 active pesticide ingredients.

—*Casey Bukro*

Eye Diseases and Visual Disorders

Since the introduction of the operating microscope, developed and pioneered by Richard A. Perritt more than three decades ago, there have been continuous and progressive advances in the ever expanding field of microsurgical eye operations. For example, not so long ago it was never dreamed possible that thin, veil-like membranes could be peeled right off the delicate, gossamerlike retina in order to restore useful sight to eyes in which vision had become obscured. (Now such cataract surgery is a commonplace.) Likewise, previously it was impossible to remove a malignant cancer of the eye without removing the entire eye (enucleation). Now a microsurgical procedure can be performed to remove only the cancer; 20 years ago this operation, first performed by Perritt, removed a malignancy but allowed the patient to retain the eye itself as well as full sight—in fact, 20/20 vision.

Clinical research is continuing at such a pace today that with every issue of the various professional journals in the field of ophthalmology, daring new approaches to treating eye problems are described. In addition to advances in surgical treatments, there are new diagnostic tools and new ways of preventing both eye disease and eye injuries. Today recognizing problems early can mean more certainly than ever before that sight can be saved. Indeed, it is now possible to prevent at least one-half of all cases of blindness worldwide and some 500,000 in the United States.

Cataracts

Cataract, a common problem, is one of the conditions that can now be treated surgically with remarkable success. In the United States alone some 540,000 cataract surgeries are performed each year. Of these, 98% are successful. An understanding of what a cataract is is necessary before its removal can be discussed.

The surface of the human eye consists of the cornea, similar to a watch crystal; the pupil; and the blue, brown, or other-colored diaphragm of the iris. Behind these structures is the retina, the sensory membrane that lines the inner eye and receives images. In front of the retina is a transparent lens that focuses clear images on the retina. The lens, however, can grow cloudy and obstruct vision; this is a cataract. When cataracts interfere with a person's lifestyle, surgical removal is necessary. (About 75% of Americans aged 65 and older will have some degree of lens cloudiness upon examination, but in only 15% will consequent vision loss be a handicap.)

Surgical progress. New techniques for cataract surgery and lens replacement have evolved that provide faster visual improvement. In the most common cataract-removal procedure today, a tiny needle about the size of the point of a ballpoint pen is placed into the eye; an ultrasonic beam, vibrating $1/10,000$ of an inch at 40,000 cycles per second, is used to break up the cataract into tiny particles, which are then drawn into the hollow needle and sucked out of the eye. Sterile fluid replaces the amount fragmented out of the eye. Today an added substance called Healon (sodium hyaluronate) is used to protect the fragile tissues of the inner eye from mechanical trauma; it eliminates the need for copious sterile saline solutions. (Some eye surgeons have developed a similar cataract removal technique, performed manually using only a syringe and sterile fluid.)

In most cases today, at the time of removal of the cataract, an intraocular lens is placed into the eye. These lenses require no care and come in a variety of shapes and sizes from which the doctor can choose to fit a particular patient's eye. The power is based on measurements taken by the ophthalmologist before surgery. There have been more than five million of these plastic lenses implanted throughout the world since the first implantation of an intraocular lens in the United States in 1958. Other patients may be fitted

for a normal daily-wear contact lens, which will serve to correct vision after the cataract has been removed.

Lens-replacement innovations. There are many changing techniques and new developments in lens replacement following cataract removal—some already in use either experimentally or in ophthalmological practice, others on the horizon. For example, researchers have developed an injectable silicone gel—a soft material that is injected into the eye and assumes the shape of a normal lens in the same location where a cataract was removed. This gel will be the new lens, replacing the original natural lens of the eye. A second alternative is a folded plastic lens that is placed into a 3-mm (0.12-in) incision and unfolds itself, thus replacing the normal lens that has been removed because of cataract formation.

Recently a kind of "living contact lens" that is attached to the front of the eye has improved vision in adults with cataracts as well as in children with congenital cataracts. These lenses have also been used in correcting malformed corneas and near-sightedness. In this procedure, known as epikeratophakia, a piece of donated human cornea is frozen and shaped to the patient's specifications and is then sewn onto the front of the cornea. Eventually the recipient's own tissue grows into the transplanted cornea; thus, the graft becomes a "living" part of the eye.

A vital new substance. Healon, mentioned above, is also vital at the lens-implant stage of cataract treatment. This recently developed surgical substance was introduced in clinical research in humans in 1980. It is gel-like and made from the rooster's comb. It is nonallergenic, nontoxic, and noninflammatory. Today it is an integral part of all eye surgery—not only cataract surgery. Healon is injected into the eye to move tissue around within the eye and later to prevent adhesions. It helps glide the plastic lens into its proper place, dilate the pupil during surgery, and coat the sensitive inner layer of the cornea. The latter is one of its most important and critical functions because injuries to these cells otherwise can cause swelling and blister formation and gradually diminished sight, often requiring a new cornea to restore sight. Healon is so vital, especially in cataract surgery, that it is now accepted as standard care and used by about 95% of eye surgeons.

New test for blind cataract patients. In patients whose cataracts have already caused blindness and who have also suffered retinal damage, surgical treatment may *not* restore vision, because some degree of retina function is necessary for sight. Previously ophthalmologists were unable to predict which blind patients would benefit from surgery and which would not. Now, however, a new diagnostic device has been developed by ophthalmologists at Johns Hopkins University. Known as a potential acuity meter, it gives the eye surgeon a clearer indication of whether the retina will function well enough after surgery. The device concentrates a ray of light through tiny gaps in a cataract to project a lighted eye chart directly onto the retina. How well the patient reads the chart provides valuable information about future sight potential. Thus far this innovative method of predicting surgical outcome has proved quite accurate and, therefore, should go a long way toward eliminating surgeries that give disappointing results. And most important, the test means patients need not suffer dashed hopes.

Quick recovery. Because of today's lens-replacement innovations, patients have sight restored within days or weeks instead of months and thus are able to resume normal life-style and official duties much quicker. Another important trend in eye surgery today is outpatient operations. Many cataract patients are now happy to go home after surgery to their own surroundings with the family's personal care, without exposure to infection that hospitalized patients face. In the U.S. the number of outpatient eye surgery facilities is increasing annually.

Secondary implants. Since 1954 there have been over 800,000 cataract surgeries with lens implants in the United States alone. Such implants, as described above, involve the simultaneous extraction of the cataract and replacement with a plastic lens. These are known as primary implants.

Since 1984 there have also been over 100,000 secondary implants. Even patients who have had a cataract removed without an implant—some, as far back as 10–15 years previously—are now able to benefit from the recent advances and refinements in lens replacement. Many of these patients could not manipulate or tolerate older varieties of contact lenses. Without a lens, they were virtual optical cripples. They could not see anything without heavy, thick-lensed glasses. Their vision was distorted, objects appeared magnified, and their depth perception was poor, especially when they walked down steps or stepped off curbs. All of these negatives can now be corrected with a secondary lens implant at any time after the cataract-removal surgery. Not surprisingly, these patients are among the most satisfied and grateful because all the previous annoyances are eliminated.

Congenital cataracts. Congenital cataract is a birth defect that affects the lens within the eye and occasionally is associated with other defects within the eye. This type of cataract is usually centrally located, causing nystagmus, or "dancing eyes," which is nature's attempt at seeing around the central blind spot. Surgery must be done early to enable the child to see. The sooner it is done, the better the visual results. These delicate operations are performed even on infants only one week old. The technique is similar to that done for an adult.

The most important aspect after treatment is the parental commitment to remove, cleanse, and replace

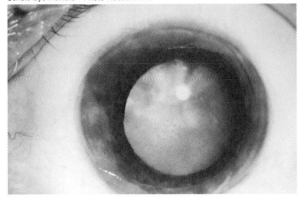

A cataract causes the lens of the eye to become clouded, thus obscuring vision. Advanced surgical techniques and lens replacement can restore sight for most patients.

the contact lens. If the child is older than five years of age, an implant is usually placed in front of the pupil, and if later a lens change is necessary, the previous lens can be replaced with another type when the child's vision has stabilized.

The United States has pioneered in this kind of pediatric eye surgery. Consequently, many children from foreign lands are treated in the U.S. and thus are saved from a lifetime of blindness.

Sunlight and cataracts. Very recent studies by U.S. and Australian researchers have found that in areas with high ultraviolet light exposure, rates of cataracts are higher. Their investigations were of Nepalese villagers and Australian Aborigines. Further work is necessary to confirm the link.

The future. Finally, the increase in the aging population will probably be the most significant factor affecting cataract treatment in future years, according to the American Academy of Ophthalmology (AAO). By the year 2000 the over-65 population will have increased from 28 million (11.8% of the population) to 34 million (13%). By the year 2050 this group will comprise 21.8% of the total population. Among the likely advances that will greatly aid this substantial group is the development of cataract-retarding eyedrops. It is predicted that such drops, which are expected to be in wide use in five to ten years, will halve the population with cataracts requiring surgical treatment.

Glaucoma

Glaucoma is often called "the thief of sight." Glaucoma is a disorder in which pressure of fluid within the eye increases owing to an interruption of the normal internal cleansing and circulation processes. About two million people over the age of 40 in the United States alone are slowly losing sight from glaucoma. Unfortunately, most do not realize that they face blindness.

It is often asked whether blindness from glaucoma can be prevented. While sight destroyed by glaucoma

VISION CONTRAST TEST SYSTEM

A new kind of eye chart called the Vision Contrast Test System uses a series of circles with bars of different contrasts and widths to measure visual acuity more precisely than the standard "E" chart. The test can also measure ability to see under different light conditions and can detect certain visual disorders in their early stages.

can never be restored, if medical treatment is started early, the progress of the "thief" can be controlled. The best defense against the disease glaucoma remains prevention. While there are several theories about cause, certain risk factors are well known. These are age (40 or over); diabetes; race (blacks have a greater chance than whites); emotional states, anxieties, frustrations, and pressures of modern life; family history; congenitally small eyes; drugs taken for gastric distress that affect the pupillary size; and excessive intake of coffee or other fluids. Each one, or a combination of these, may be a factor.

There are four main types of glaucoma. Acute glaucoma strikes suddenly and violently, causing cloudy vision, with severe pain in and around the eye. It requires immediate surgery. The chronic type, open-angle glaucoma, is more common; it progresses slowly and painlessly. The victim is only vaguely disturbed by the symptoms that come and go, often postpones visiting an ophthalmologist, but soon finds that frequent changes of glasses do not improve the vision. Then an inability to adjust eyesight to dimly lighted rooms develops. Loss of side vision may become evident. Blurring or foggy vision and rainbows, halos, or colored rings around lights are additional symptoms. The treatment consists of daily use of medications to reduce the pressure within the eye. Secondary glaucoma, a third type, is due to disease or injury or both and must be treated according to the causative factor. And the fourth type, congenital glaucoma, as the name indicates, is seen in infants at birth. It is commonly said that it affects those "who have large and beautiful eyes." The eyeballs are large and sometimes protrude. The sooner the diagnosis is made of this relatively rare disease, the better chance the infant

has of having sight saved via medication, surgery, or laser treatment. The exact mode of inheritance is not known, but offspring of patients with open-angle glaucoma appear to be at greatest risk.

Topical drugs (eye drops) are a very widely used treatment today. There are several varieties; some constrict the pupil, some dilate the pupil, and the newest type—the beta-blockers—works by lowering intraocular pressure by decreasing formation of aqueous humor without affecting pupil size or visual acuity. However, because the beta-blockers are absorbed into the general circulation, they can cause systemic adverse effects.

Today glaucoma patients will benefit by the following steps: using eye drops according to the ophthalmologist's instructions; returning regularly to the ophthalmologist for reevaluation; consulting the ophthalmologist at once if rainbow-colored halos around lights develop or if the eye becomes painful, vision blurred, or sight further impaired in any way; and avoiding certain medications. (Many new drugs used today in treating other diseases contain ingredients that might increase eye pressure—medications for colds, sinus problems, peptic ulcers, spastic colon, and muscle spasm are some examples.) Finally, having a complete physical examination once a year, maintaining good general health, having adequate sleep, and exercising are also helpful. Glaucoma patients who follow the above rules will probably retain useful sight as long as they live.

A new eye chart

In 1984 a new eye chart was introduced. The chart was developed after 15 years of research by Arthur P. Ginsburg, a biophysicist formerly at the Air Force Aviation Vision Laboratory at Wright-Patterson Air Force

Base, Ohio, where it was first tested on air force pilots and space shuttle astronauts. The new model can measure visual acuity and ability better than the century-old standard "E" chart (the Snellen chart) and has the potential to detect some eye disorders at very early stages. The chart is also able to determine an individual's ability to see in various light conditions. The new chart uses a computer-composed series of circles with bands of different widths and contrasts. Patient responses are plotted on a curve, and the shape of the curve indicates vision disorders.

Sports eye injuries

The most productive area of eye care is prevention. Approximately 50% of all eye injuries are preventable. Increasingly today sport and leisure-time accidents are causing a wide range of injuries to eyes of both children and adults—many of which are quite serious (*i.e.*, resulting in impaired vision or blindness) and most of which are preventable. A recent estimate by the AAO is that 100,000 Americans a year incur recreation-related eye injuries. There are many sources of injury—from carelessness to lack of attention during a game to reckless play to "freak" accidents. An unexpected cause of a surprisingly high number of eye injuries is a seemingly benign piece of equipment that many bicyclists use to strap gear to their bicycles—the "bungee" cord (a stretch cord with hooks on each end). The cords can be accidently snapped into the eye.

In children eye accidents occur during play with sophisticated toys and in many games and sports both at home and at school. Some of the most common childhood injuries are produced by BB guns, pellet guns, and air-powered rifles, which often are sold as suitable toys for children. Each year such guns are the cause of at least 2,000 eye injuries (in addition to a great many more injuries to other parts of the anatomy). Currently few states regulate the sale of these guns; therefore, such needless damage to the eyes of youngsters, particularly boys, is likely to persist.

Other common causes of childhood eye injuries are the bow and arrow, the slingshot, and throwing accidents—the latter including everything from balls to darts to paper missiles.

In adults the most common sports eye injuries occur in racquet sports: racquetball, tennis, squash, handball, and badminton; in hunting; in golf; and in team sports: basketball, ice hockey, baseball, and football. Boxing is now regarded as a risky sport for brain damage and many other injuries, including traumatic retinal injuries and retinal detachment.

Racquet sports account for some 70,000 emergency room or physician visits a year. According to the National Safety Council, racquet sports are the leading cause of sports injuries in men and of *all* eye injuries in women. The velocity of racquetballs or squash balls traveling at high speed is astonishing—more than in

Arthur Shay

A racquetball can travel at speeds well over 160 kilometers per hour (100 miles per hour). Racquetball players can reduce chances of blinding accidents by wearing special protective goggles.

a fired bullet; they have been clocked at speeds well over 160 km/h (100 mph). Even a novice's swing sends the ball traveling at about 130 km/h (80 mph). The average speed of a tennis ball is about 135 km/h (85 mph). Racquet sports injuries damage not only the eye but also the orbital bones. These injuries vary from lacerated corneas to eye hemorrhage with deep cuts of the entire eyeball.

Racquetball players and other racquet sports participants can reduce chances of blinding accidents by wearing special goggles or industrial-quality safety glasses (which are available with prescription lenses as well as with clear ones). Even though most streetwear glasses today are made with impact-resistant plastic or glass, they generally do not provide ample protection. Contact lenses do not protect eyes. Unfortunately, most racquet sports facilities and clubs do not require the wearing of protective eye gear on the court.

Any injury to the head endured in contact sports (especially team sports) may disturb the inner circulation of the eye. A blow or impact frequently causes hemorrhage in the eye. Any injury that causes acute or chronic inflammation of the eye—from a blow to the head or from a severe penetrating foreign body—can result in subsequent development of a cataract, can cause secondary glaucoma, or can lead to complete compression of the globe with loss of function of all the internal eye structures. Even seemingly minor injuries may worsen; thus, the potential of future blindness must always be kept in mind when someone suffers a sports injury to the eye. This is especially true when a child appears to have only a minor abrasion or inflammation.

Eye surgeons today are able to save many sports-injured eyes. Under micromagnification (using the operating microscope) these injured eyes, even those seriously hurt, are being repaired and rehabilitated with extremely fine needles and stitches (finer than a human hair). Such surgery is greatly aided by the use of Healon, which affords protection to all eye structures. Such operations are increasingly being performed on professional athletes, often salvaging careers that once would have been finished. One of the first repairs of a professional athlete's eye was in 1958 for middleweight champion Carmen Basilio after injuries suffered in his championship bout with Sugar Ray Robinson. By removing the blood clots behind the eyeball and reconstructing his eyelids, which were jagged and torn, his eye surgeon, in what was then a dramatic undertaking, was able to restore normal vision for Basilio. In 1982 a severe eye injury caused boxer Sugar Ray Leonard to retire from the ring for several years. But in the spring of 1986 Leonard's eye surgeon pronounced him recovered and able to fight again, his retinal detachment having been fully repaired by surgery and time.

Nowadays eye surgeons are operating regularly on professional players who incur traumatic eye damage during play—for example, in baseball players struck with either a swinging bat or a pitched ball and, recently, in a player whose eye was seriously injured in a fight on the field.

—*Richard A. Perritt, M.D.*

Gastrointestinal Disorders

Research in gastroenterology is proceeding vigorously on many fronts. Previously accepted concepts regarding the causes of certain diseases have been reexamined—and some discarded—as new discoveries are made and confirmed. And more specific, simpler, and often less costly treatments for certain chronic conditions are now in advanced stages of development. It is also becoming increasingly clear that the intelligent layperson must, to a great extent, become an active participant in maintaining digestive health, detecting serious disease at an early date, and becoming familiar with available screening, diagnostic, and therapeutic programs.

Colon cancer: diagnostic concerns

Whenever the illness of an important public figure becomes common knowledge, many people are influenced to seek more information about the disease in question. Pres. Ronald Reagan's surgery for colon cancer was no exception. In July 1985 the president underwent surgery by colonoscope (a flexible fiber-optic instrument for viewing the interior of the digestive tract) to remove a small polyp from his lower colon. During the procedure doctors used the instrument to examine the upper portion of the colon and found, near the cecum, where the colon joins the small intestine, a much larger tumor that had not been detected previously. The following day they performed major

surgery to remove the tumor, which was malignant, and a portion of intestine. The incident not only focused public attention on colon cancer—thousands of people sought more information about the disease in the weeks following the president's operation—it also aroused some controversy in the medical community about the application of available diagnostic measures and spurred further questions about the cost-effectiveness of the diagnostic tests now in general use.

Endoscopy (the visualization of body cavities via flexible fiber-optic tubes) and the newer radiological procedures, such as computerized axial tomography (CAT) scanning and magnetic resonance imaging, have in many ways revolutionized the diagnosis of gastrointestinal disorders, but at a high monetary cost. Many physicians have justifiably questioned whether these new procedures are being overused and whether they are more or less cost-effective than the traditional radiological techniques, such as barium X-ray studies. While endoscopic examination of the stomach and intestines may, in some cases, detect certain significant lesions not found on conventional X-rays, many doctors wonder if the extra cost justifies the routine use of these newer procedures as initial, or first-line, diagnostic studies.

A recent investigation provided some useful insights into these questions. Patients with suspected disorders of the colon were examined by conventional sigmoidoscopy (endoscopy of the rectum and lower colon) and barium X-rays; if there was any indication of colonic polyps, these procedures were followed by colonoscopy (endoscopic examination of the entire colon) and removal of any polyps found. A similar group of patients had colonoscopy alone; any polyps discovered during the process were removed. The differences between cost and treatment of the two groups, considered as a whole, were negligible, and patients who had colonoscopy alone were subjected to fewer diagnostic studies. On an individual basis, however, costs varied widely, since colonoscopy is much more expensive than the other procedures. Thus, a patient having a negative sigmoidoscopy and a negative barium X-ray paid much less than a patient who had a negative colonoscopy. Although medical opinion may appear to be moving in favor of colonoscopy as a first-line diagnostic technique, the results of further studies must be evaluated before any final judgments are made.

Recent findings about peptic ulcers

It has been known for a long while that peptic ulcers are not caused solely by the oversecretion of pepsin and acid and that there must accordingly be some factor that usually resists the action of these substances, which are produced in large amounts in the normal stomach. Were it not for this natural resistive, or cytoprotective, factor, healthy stomachs would digest themselves. During the past 15 years, researchers have shown repeatedly that some members of a class of fatty acids called prostaglandins, which are naturally produced by the body, not only reduce secretion of acid by the stomach but can, in much smaller amounts, protect the stomach from ulceration when it is exposed to agents that usually cause ulcers. Prostaglandins are found everywhere in the body and appear to stabilize cell membranes and thus make them more hardy. It has also been shown that agents such as aspirin and other antiarthritic drugs, which often cause gastric erosions or ulcers in susceptible people, reduce the amount of prostaglandins produced by the mucous membranes, or mucosa, lining the stomach. Recently investigators at the Mayo Clinic, Rochester, Minn., were able to document a direct relationship between the development of gastric damage and a decline in mucosal prostaglandins in volunteers given aspirin or indomethacin (Indocin), another antiarthritic drug. They have thus demonstrated a probable primary mechanism—namely, prostaglandin shortage—for the cause of aspirin-induced ulcers. Furthermore, synthetic prostaglandins, given orally, have been found to be effective in the treatment of some peptic ulcers.

Working on another approach, a research group at the University of California at San Diego has found that patients with peptic ulcers in the duodenum (the first part of the small intestine) secrete significantly less bicarbonate, an alkaline (i.e., acid-reducing) compound, from the duodenal mucosa than do normal individuals, while their production of gastric acid does not differ significantly from normal. This finding challenges older notions that hyperacidity alone causes duodenal ulcers, and it promotes the concept that duodenal alkalinity may be a significant protective factor. In support of this observation is a study from the University of Washington of a new, experimental antiulcer drug, tetraprenylacetone, showing that this medication causes an increase in the secretion of bicarbonate from the stomach and pancreas but has no effect on the secretion of acid.

Cimetidine and ranitidine (Tagamet and Zantac) are two drugs of well-substantiated benefit in the treatment of peptic ulcers. Both drugs function by blocking the histamine receptors on acid-secreting gastric cells and thus preventing the stimulating action of histamine on these cells. Recent studies indicate that both drugs can be given in single, rather than multiple, daily doses with therapeutic effects nearly equally to those of multiple-dose administration and no increase in adverse side effects. The single dose appears to be more effective if taken with the evening meal, rather than at bedtime, as was formerly recommended. Sucralfate (Carafate), the other generally used antiulcer drug, seems both to coat the gastric and duodenal ulcer and to increase the production of prostaglandins. It is quite as effective as the histamine-blocking agents in treating peptic ulcers and, like them, shows promise of preventing recurrences with continued administration at reduced levels after healing of the initial ulcer.

Chest pain not caused by heart or lung disease

Diseases of the esophagus may cause pain beneath the breastbone, or sternum, that is in many respects indistinguishable from true angina pectoris—chest pain due to coronary artery disease. This is particularly true of those diseases caused by strong muscular contractions of the esophagus or by the reflux (backup) of acid from the stomach into the esophagus, the latter condition being a common cause of so-called heartburn. Usually esophageal pain can be distinguished from true angina by the fact that it is not precipitated by effort; esophageal pain differs from the discomfort caused by lung disease or diseases of the pleura (the coating membrane of the lungs) in that it is not aggravated by breathing. However, in some cases these symptomatic distinctions are unclear, and further studies—such as chest X-ray and exercise stress test—are required.

In a large proportion of patients with recurrent chest pain and no evidence of lung or heart disease, it has been shown that the pain may be reproduced by either muscular spasm of the esophagus or acid reflux into the esophagus or by both factors occurring simultaneously. Confirming this finding, a recent study from Belgium reported that more than 60% of patients without heart disease and with repeated attacks of substernal pain may be suffering from disorders of the esophagus. In many cases these disorders are treatable with histamine-blocking agents or antispasmodic drugs.

Gastroesophageal reflux linked to lung disease

There have been numerous suggestions during the past half decade that disorders associated with reflux of gastric contents into the esophagus may lead to recurrent aspiration, or inhalation, of this material into the air passages, usually when the patient is lying down. Asthma and recurrent attacks of pneumonia are the lung disorders most commonly implicated. This impression has now been confirmed, at least in infants and young children, by investigators at the Uniformed Services University of Health Sciences, Bethesda, Md., who found that 18 of 20 patients with recurrent pneumonia had significant gastroesophageal reflux and that the episodes of pneumonia ceased after appropriate antireflux surgery was performed. A group of investigators in Brussels reported that much of the gastroesophageal reflux experienced by asthmatics may be a side effect of their medication rather than a cause of the bronchial disease. This conclusion was based on a study that found a high incidence (45%) of reflux in patients being treated for asthma and a much lower incidence (15%) in untreated asthmatics. Nonetheless, in some asthmatics, reflux may be a causative or aggravating factor.

With regard to treatment of the esophageal disease caused by reflux, two studies, one from West Berlin and one from the United States, have confirmed that, while it does not prevent reflux itself, short- and long-term reduction of gastric acidity with histamine-blocking agents relieves symptoms in about two-thirds of patients and improves the inflammation of the esophagus seen at endoscopy. Therapeutic results in the German study were equally good when a new agent, cisapride, was employed. This drug does not reduce gastric acidity but rather diminishes reflux by increasing the pressure in the esophageal valve, or lower esophageal sphincter, which controls the opening between the stomach and esophagus, and by accelerating the emptying of the stomach into the duodenum. Antireflux surgery, however, remains the most definitive treatment for reflux esophagitis and its complications, and it is usually indicated in extreme cases of reflux not relieved significantly by medication.

Bacterial infection and chronic gastritis

Chronic gastritis (inflammation of the stomach), especially of the antrum, or lower portion of the stomach, is a condition that has been recognized for many years. It is now being diagnosed with increasing frequency, however, because endoscopy is so much more commonly performed today than in the past. While antral gastritis may cause upper abdominal discomfort and belching after meals and occasionally leads to chronic bleeding, it usually causes no symptoms at all. Many gastroenterologists feel that antral gastritis may precede the development of gastric ulcers, and the condition is also associated with duodenal ulcers. The cause of antral gastritis is unknown and, until recently, there were few clues to its etiology. When gastritis accompanies a peptic ulcer, it does not disappear when the ulcer heals in response to conventional treatment. This fact may explain why ulcers usually recur within weeks or months after healing if treatment is completely discontinued.

Over the years pathologists have noted the presence of bacteria in the mucous membranes of lower parts of the stomach removed during surgery or at autopsy. The presence of bacteria in the stomach was commonly ascribed to contamination because it was the general impression of medical scientists that the stomach, because of its acidity, is normally free of bacteria. This opinion has changed recently, however, since an Australian pathologist, J. R. Warren, noted that a specific type of bacterium was found almost invariably in antral biopsies obtained at endoscopy in patients with active chronic gastritis. It was also found less frequently in patients whose gastritis was not "active"—that is, showed little evidence of inflam-

matory cells. In subsequent work with his colleague B. J. Marshall, Warren showed that infection with this bacterium, called *Campylobacter pylorides,* is strongly associated with duodenal and gastric ulcers. The organism appears to withstand the acidic environment of the stomach by embedding itself in the mucous layer of the stomach lining. Its presence provokes an inflammatory reaction in the gastric glands.

Other studies have confirmed the presence of *C. pylorides* in patients with active antral gastritis, even when they are free of symptoms. The bacteria do not disappear in ulcer patients even though the ulcers heal in response to histamine-blocking agents, but another Australian research group has found that *C. pylorides* may be cleared in many cases by the regular use of bismuth-containing compounds for three to four weeks. These compounds and certain antibiotics have also been shown to have a healing effect in some patients with antral gastritis or peptic ulcers. These discoveries may eventually prove that many peptic ulcers and many cases of antral gastritis arise as complications of a unique type of bacterial infection, findings that could point toward new mechanisms of treatment.

Treatment of upper gastrointestinal hemorrhage

The major causes of upper gastrointestinal hemorrhage are peptic ulcers of the stomach and duodenum, linear tears of the mucous membrane lining the upper stomach and lowermost esophagus, acute gastritis (from alcohol, aspirin, or other drugs), and esophageal varices. Varices are enlargements of thin-walled veins in the lower esophagus and upper stomach, produced in response to the increased pressure caused by obstruction of blood flow through a cirrhotic (chronically scarred) liver. Although there are numerous causes of cirrhosis, esophageal varices may form in any type, and their presence carries a great risk of hemorrhage.

Most episodes of hemorrhage due to peptic ulcer, gastritis, and linear tears in the mucosa stop spontaneously or in response to first-line medical treatment. Many other kinds of bleeding, including variceal hemorrhage, do not respond to such treatment and can be life threatening. Until recently surgery was the only second-line treatment for cases of continued or recurrent bleeding. However, with the development of advanced endoscopes that can directly locate the site of the bleeding and probes that can be passed through the endoscope to cauterize the bleeding point, many hemorrhages can now be stopped and recurrences prevented without surgery. In Japan an endoscopic technique employing the injection of an adrenaline solution around bleeding ulcers has also been found to be very effective in staunching (stopping) hemorrhage.

In the case of bleeding esophageal varices, recent investigations in several countries, including South Africa, the United Kingdom, France, and the United States, have clearly demonstrated that bleeding may be controlled and recurrences reduced by means of endoscopic sclerosis, a process in which "hardening" (or obstruction) of the blood vessels is induced medically. The sites of hemorrhage are located with an endoscope and then injected with a sclerosing solution that promotes blood clotting. The injection is administered via a needle-bearing tube passed through the endoscope. Several treatment sessions over a period of many weeks may be required to sclerose the varices completely, but the incidence of fatal hemorrhage can be significantly reduced even though the progress and severity of the underlying liver disease are not affected. Studies have shown that variceal sclerosis can be performed even on patients with very severe liver disease, who would not be considered suitable candidates for the rigorous blood-shunting operations that are generally performed to relieve this condition. Over the long term, however, comparisons of shunting and sclerosis do not show a clear advantage for either treatment. In 1986 a controlled study conducted at San Francisco General Hospital compared endoscopic sclerosis with shunting in a series of critically ill cirrhosis patients. The study showed no significant differences between the two treatment groups with regard to costs of care or total days of hospitalization. This finding was due largely to recurrences of bleeding in the group treated by sclerosis, which might possibly have been prevented by more frequent treatments. A number of studies, emanating primarily from France, have shown marked reductions in rebleeding of varices by the regular use of drugs (propranolol, nadalol) that reduce pressure in the varices; however, other studies have failed to confirm these benefits.

Functional bowel disorders

The most common conditions diagnosed among patients who consult gastroenterologists are not attributed to localized structural disorders. Symptoms consist of varying mixtures of chronic and recurrent bowel irregularities, abdominal pain, abdominal noise, bloating, and often nausea. There is usually much discomfort and loss of time from work but rarely any significant loss of weight. Routine radiological and laboratory studies fail to identify any organic problem, and sigmoidoscopy either shows no abnormality at all or confirms the presence of spastic contractions of the bowel. Traditionally this constellation of symptoms has been called the irritable bowel syndrome or, more generally, functional bowel disorder. The disease is often attributed solely to emotional problems or stressful circumstances. However, recent investigations, particularly in the United States and the United Kingdom, have forced clinicians into rethinking this problem. While it is indeed true that patients with functional bowel disorders tend to be more stressed and tense than others, these emotional reactions may result from the underlying bowel disorder rather than causing it.

It has been found, for example, that the patterns of electrical waves that control the muscular contractions of the intestine are different from normal in many patients with irritable bowels. The ability of the intestine to relax is also reduced, and spastic contractions in response to certain hormonal stimuli are increased. Furthermore, when they consult physicians for reasons other than gastrointestinal problems, these same patients do not appear to be unusually tense.

As a result of these findings, earlier thinking about irritable bowel syndrome has changed. Medical scientists now believe that the condition occurs widely and may be related to abnormal activity in the nervous system that controls intestinal motility, secretions, and absorption. This enteric nervous system, called by some the "brain in the gut," has been shown recently to be in many respects independent of the "brain in the head" and the central nervous system. Its activity may, in fact, instruct the brain as to tastes, appetites, and bodily habits. Considerable research is now being directed toward a better understanding of the enteric nervous system.

—Harvey J. Dworken, M.D.

Genetics

It has now been 20 years since scientists made the first chromosomal study of fetal cells obtained from amniotic fluid. Today more than 200 metabolic disorders, chromosomal aberrations, and congenital defects can be identified through sampling of amniotic fluid. Amniocentesis—withdrawal of fluid via a hollow needle inserted through the mother's abdomen—remains the most commonly used technique for obtaining such a sample. It is usually recommended only in pregnancies where an increased risk of a particular congenital disorder has been identified. Most often amniocentesis is used to check for aberrations in chromosome number or structure. Risk factors include advanced maternal age (over 35 years), the previous birth of a child with a confirmed or suspected chromosomal abnormality, or the knowledge that either parent has a chromosomal abnormality. Testing for inherited metabolic disorders such as Tay-Sachs disease is performed only in cases where risk for a specific disorder has been identified as a result of family history, previous birth of an affected child, or identification of both parents as carriers of a gene defect that, if passed on by both to the child, would result in serious disease.

The introduction of a needle into the amniotic sac to withdraw fluid and fetal cells does pose some risk, both to the mother and to the fetus. Complications such as mild cramping, fetal bleeding, and transient leakage of amniotic fluid occur in about 2% of cases and usually require no treatment. The possibility of directly pricking the fetus with the needle is reduced by the use of ultrasound imaging to guide the needle into the amniotic sac, and if a needlestick injury does occur, it rarely causes serious consequences. In some cases, however, complications following amniocentesis are more serious and may result in premature labor, leading to fetal death and miscarriage. Several large, well-controlled studies, conducted in the mid-1970s in the United States and Canada, examined the risk of fetal death following amniocentesis. These studies found no statistically significant difference between the incidence of fetal loss in women undergoing amniocentesis in the second trimester of pregnancy and the incidence in matched control subjects. On the basis of these and subsequent investigations, most authorities now agree that the fetal loss rate associated with amniocentesis is less than 0.5% and may be as low as 0.2%.

One of the drawbacks of amniocentesis is that test results are not available for two to four weeks after the procedure, because the small number of fetal cells retrieved in the fluid sample must be grown in a laboratory culture to achieve numbers adequate for analysis. At this point in the pregnancy—18 to 21 weeks—the psychosocial aspects of termination are complicated by the fact that the pregnancy is very apparent and its loss will be noticeable. In addition, by this time the fetus can be felt moving inside the womb, an emotional milestone for all expectant parents. These considerations, along with the fact that termination of pregnancy in the second trimester poses some risk to the mother, leads as many as 25% of those eligible for and interested in prenatal diagnosis to refuse amniocentesis.

Chorionic villus sampling

Appreciation of the advantages of a procedure that could be performed earlier in the course of pregnancy has renewed interest in a method of sampling fetal cells during the first trimester, which was first proposed in the late 1960s by Danish geneticist Jan Mohr. The technique involves obtaining a sample of the developing chorionic villi, fingerlike projections of the chorion, the outermost membrane surrounding the fetus. The villi, which are the functioning units of the fetal portion of the placenta, are ideally sampled between the 8th and 12th weeks of gestation, when they are easily accessible and removal of small pieces of tissue does not interfere with their function.

Today the most widely used method of chorionic villus sampling (CVS) is a transcervical approach that combines aspects of techniques developed throughout the world in the past decade. It is similar in principle to Mohr's technique—which included endoscopic visualization of the placenta and retrieval of tissue through the vagina—but incorporates important modifications introduced by researchers in China and the Soviet Union. In the procedure eventually developed in the late 1970s by researchers at University College

Hospital, London, and now employed by most institutions doing CVS, ultrasound imaging is used to guide a small-caliber plastic catheter, or tube, through the vagina to the chorion. When the catheter reaches the sampling site, a syringe is attached and a tissue sample is withdrawn by gentle suctioning. The procedure is done without anesthesia, and patients are able to leave soon after it has been completed.

Unlike amniocentesis, CVS yields enough tissue for direct enzyme assay and studies of the genetic material, deoxyribonucleic acid (DNA). The fetal chromosomes can be immediately examined by microscope for abnormalities in number and major defects in structure. Detection of less obvious, though equally serious, chromosomal abnormalities requires color staining of the chromosomes for more precise definition of structure, a process best done on cells cultured in the laboratory. Culturing the cells takes about a week, and some centers routinely wait for the results of microscopic examination of the cultured cells before reporting the findings to the parents. Even with the delay, results are usually available before the beginning of the second trimester of pregnancy—that is, earlier than the first date at which amniocentesis could be performed.

Safety and accuracy of CVS

Chorionic villus sampling is considered experimental in many countries and is likely to remain so until shown to be safe and accurate by experience at medical centers around the world and by large scientific trials like those currently in progress in the United States. Worldwide, medical centers using the technique have reported more than 10,000 procedures to the chorionic villus registry at the Medical College of Thomas Jefferson University, Philadelphia, and in those pregnancies for which follow-up data are available, diagnostic accuracy has been shown to be excellent. Initial concerns that the genetic makeup of the villi (which are part of the placenta) might not be identical to that of the fetus have proved largely unfounded. In fact, chromosomal analysis of CVS specimens has shown a correspondence rate of better than 99% with the fetus. Occasionally diagnosis is complicated by the presence among the normal cells of a few villus cells with abnormal chromosome number or structure—a condition called mosaicism. However, postnatal followup indicates that most placental chromosomal mosaicisms appear to involve abnormalities in placental tissue in which the fetus is chromosomally normal.

As with amniocentesis, there are risks inherent in CVS. For the mother, hemorrhage and infection are the most serious complications. For the fetus, rupture of the fetal membranes, bleeding, or infection may cause death. Early experience with CVS indicated that the risk of fetal loss might be significantly higher than that associated with amniocentesis. Current estimates

(Left) From Dorothy Warburton,"Current Techniques in Chromosome Analysis," *Pediatric Clinics of North America,* vol. 27, no. 4 (November 1980), pp. 753–769; (right) Victor A. McKusick, the Johns Hopkins Hospital

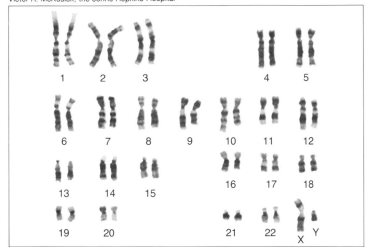

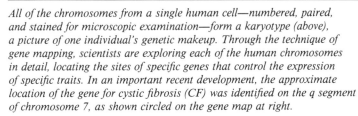

All of the chromosomes from a single human cell—numbered, paired, and stained for microscopic examination—form a karyotype (above), a picture of one individual's genetic makeup. Through the technique of gene mapping, scientists are exploring each of the human chromosomes in detail, locating the sites of specific genes that control the expression of specific traits. In an important recent development, the approximate location of the gene for cystic fibrosis (CF) was identified on the q segment of chromosome 7, as shown circled on the gene map at right.

of risk are lower, however, and appear to improve significantly as institutions become more experienced with the technique. Medical centers with the greatest experience report fetal loss rates as low as 2%— half the spontaneous first-trimester loss rate among women more than 35 years of age, the largest group receiving prenatal diagnosis. Although there have been few reports of significant maternal complications, the potential for introduction of harmful bacteria from the vagina has prompted some research teams to develop a transabdominal method of retrieving chorionic villus tissue. This technique may prove to be an effective alternative to the transcervical approach in some cases.

The roster of genetic disorders that can be identified by means of CVS is constantly expanding and is expected to eventually include nearly all of those detectable by amniocentesis. The major exceptions are neural tube defects, the diagnosis of which depends on the measurement of α-fetoprotein levels in amniotic fluid and maternal blood or visualization of the physical defect with ultrasound. Other diagnostic procedures that cannot be carried out by currently available techniques for CVS include assay of amniotic fluid for the enzymatic abnormalities indicative of cystic fibrosis and detection of potentially harmful infectious organisms, such as the rubella (German measles) virus.

There are important questions still to be answered before CVS can be considered a routine part of prenatal care in cases where there is a known risk of genetic defects. In the light of the obvious advantages of first-trimester diagnosis, CVS may become an op-

tion available to women worldwide if questions on its safety can be satisfactorily answered.

Gene mapping

Parallel to the development of techniques for retrieval of fetal cells for prenatal diagnosis has been an increase in the number of genetic defects that can be detected in the developing fetus. In some cases the defect can be diagnosed by microscopic detection of missing, extra, broken, or rearranged chromosomes or by assay of fetal cells for a specific protein, such as hexosaminidase-A in Tay-Sachs disease. More often, the defect causes a change in the DNA so slight that it cannot be visually detected, and the disease process is so poorly understood that the causative protein is unknown—or, if known, it is not detectable in fetal cells shed into the amniotic fluid. Many disorders can be diagnosed only by detection of the abnormal gene through analysis of the DNA. Before it is possible to diagnose a genetic disease by DNA analysis, a method must be developed of reliably detecting the gene responsible. In some cases the gene itself has been identified and gene defects diagnosed through the use of DNA probes that bind specifically to the normal gene or of enzymes that dissect it.

Identifying a single gene among the nearly 100,000 that make up the entire human genetic "blueprint" has been greatly facilitated by the gradual development of a chromosome "map," a picture of each of the 46 human chromosomes, on which specific genes are being located with increasing precision. Genes identified at specific points on the chromosome serve as landmarks for locating other genes in their vicinity. This technique has resulted in a rapid growth in the number of genes identified and mapped in the last several years. In August 1985 at the Eighth International Gene Mapping Workshop, held in Helsinki, Fin., researchers reported that since 1980 the number of mapped genes had increased from about 400 to more than 900. Another 800 regionally localized DNA segments not known to represent genes have been identified and are expected to aid in further mapping. When the defective gene responsible for a genetic disorder is not immediately identifiable, mapping often locates DNA sequences so close to the gene that they serve as reliable markers of its presence because they are almost always inherited with it. (The smaller the distance between two sites on a chromosome, the less the chance they will be separated during the natural exchange of chromosomal material that occurs in the formation of egg and sperm.) These marker sequences, although not as reliable a predictor as direct identification of the defective gene, are sometimes suitable for diagnostic purposes.

Mapping is soon expected to yield the precise location of the defective gene that causes Duchenne muscular dystrophy, a progressive muscle-wasting disease that starts in early childhood and usually leads to death in the early twenties. This disease is the most common lethal X-linked (*i.e.,* carried on the X chromosome) disorder in humans, affecting one in 4,000 males. All males who have the defective gene are affected by the disease. The sisters of men who receive the gene from their mothers (rather than through mutation) have a 50% chance of carrying the defective gene on one of their X chromosomes. These female carriers are only very rarely affected by the disease, but each of their sons has a 50% chance of inheriting the gene and the disease. The search for the gene itself or a reliable gene marker close to it has been the focus of considerable effort. Those efforts have paid off, and now in many families with Duchenne muscular dystrophy, carrier detection and prenatal diagnosis can be reliably performed by the use of a battery of markers flanking the gene.

Huntington's disease (also called Huntington's chorea), a less common disease than Duchenne dystrophy but no less devastating, may soon yield its mysteries to the detective work of the gene mappers. This degenerative neurological disorder affects specific regions of the brain. The first manifestations usually appear in middle age, with minor disturbances in balance and coordination; the victim is progressively disabled and eventually suffers from dementia. Huntington's disease is fatal within 10–20 years after the first appearance of symptoms. Particularly distressing are the relatively late onset of the disease and its autosomal dominant pattern of inheritance. This means that any individual with one affected parent has a

50% chance of inheriting the disease—and thus an equal chance of passing it on to each one of his or her children—but has no way of knowing if the gene is present until well into middle age, when it may be too late to prevent passing the disorder to the next generation. Essential to the prevention of the disease is a means of genetic screening for people who may be carriers of the Huntington's gene.

In 1983 researchers discovered a marker, called G8, close to the defective gene. Its linkage to the gene for Huntington's disease was established through the study of two families, one in North America and one in Venezuela. In the Venezuelan family, which consists of more than 3,000 descendants of a woman who died of the disease a century ago, G8 is an accurate predictor of the presence of the Huntington's gene in 96–97% of those affected individuals tested. While many researchers would prefer to wait for a marker with at least a 98% accuracy rate before making a screening test available on a widespread basis, pressure from affected families has prompted several institutions in the United States to offer presymptomatic diagnosis for adults, as well as prenatal testing using the G8 marker. Approximately half of those who choose to have the test will be reassured by the results; they will find that they do not carry the Huntington's gene and will not, therefore, suffer from the disease. For the others, the uncertainty, not knowing if they are destined to develop the disease, will be replaced by the anxiety of waiting for the first signs to appear—a stress that some researchers feel makes the test unsuitable for children and adolescents, who may not fully understand the implications.

Use of the test for the presence of the Huntington's gene raises ethical issues similar to those first discussed ten years ago in connection with genetic screening of industrial workers for susceptibility to toxic substances in the workplace. At issue is how to make the test accessible to those who want it while at the same time maintaining the confidentiality of test results. The possibility that a positive test result might lead to difficulties in obtaining health insurance or to discrimination in employment or education is an issue of grave concern. It is the first such diagnostic tool of its kind—a test that predicts the inevitable development of untreatable disease in an apparently healthy person. Thus, many people view its implementation as a test case, likely to lead to national health policy decisions concerning confidentiality of test results specifically and society's approach to genetic disease in general. With predictions that gene mapping may lead to a complete map of the human DNA within the decade, these questions are likely to be viewed with increasing urgency.

Researchers constructing gene maps have also been narrowing the search for the genetic basis of cystic fibrosis, a disorder that affects the sweat, salivary, and mucous glands. Cystic fibrosis is the most common lethal genetic disorder in Caucasians; approximately one in 25 carries the defective gene, and about one child in 2,000 inherits such a gene from both parents and consequently dies of the disease, usually by the age of 30. Despite years of searching, scientists have yet to discover a biochemical characteristic that reliably identifies carriers of the gene, and couples at risk are normally identified only by the birth of an affected child. In late 1985 gene-mapping techniques located the cystic fibrosis gene to a region on chromosome 7. About 80% of families with a history of the disease have diagnostically useful markers closely linked to the gene, and reliable carrier detection and prenatal diagnosis is now available at several medical centers in the U.S. A genetic-screening test for detection of carriers with no family history of disease awaits identification of the gene itself.

Gene mapping is also bringing genetic analysis to the study, prediction, and, perhaps, treatment of conditions such as heart disease, hypertension (high blood pressure), and adult-onset diabetes—disorders that have their origin in a combination of environmental and genetic factors. In the case of heart disease, for example, a person's genetic makeup may increase susceptibility to cholesterol buildup and the development of atherosclerotic plaque that obstructs the coronary arteries. Recently researchers have succeeded in identifying genetic markers associated with defects in lipid metabolism. This development has led to predictions that it may eventually be possible for a simple and relatively inexpensive test to identify individuals who are genetically predisposed to atherosclerosis and for whom preventive measures—early adherence to a low-cholesterol diet, abstinence from cigarette smoking, and a rigorous exercise program—are strongly indicated.

Treatment: bone marrow transplants

While advances in prenatal diagnosis offer the possibility of preventing some genetic diseases, thousands of children are born each year with inborn errors of metabolism, physical abnormalities, and developmental handicaps. Treatment mainly consists of correcting malformation, lessening symptoms of disease, and managing ongoing problems with medication or a special diet. Though a number of genetic diseases may be managed successfully, very few can be truly cured.

There are exceptions, however. Some of these are diseases treatable by organ or tissue transplantation, both of which are playing an increasing role in experimental efforts to treat genetic disorders. Experience is greatest with the transplantation of bone marrow, the source of a self-renewing population of cells that continually replenish the body's supply of oxygen-carrying red blood cells and infection-fighting white blood cells. The first successful use of bone marrow transplantation for treatment of a heritable disease was performed in 1968 to correct a condition known as severe combined immunodeficiency, a disease of the white blood cells. Since then the technique has been used successfully to treat an increasing number of inherited diseases that primarily affect the function of cells derived from bone marrow. More recently its use has expanded to include the treatment of certain enzyme deficiency diseases that affect a variety of cell types in addition to those derived from marrow. Excess enzyme produced by transplanted cells originating from the donor marrow circulates throughout the body, where it penetrates many tissues and fulfills its normal function. Bone marrow transplant can produce remarkable results when it succeeds, but it is a technique associated with a high failure rate and considerable hazard to the patient. In order for organ and tissue transplantation to be completely successful, researchers must gain a thorough understanding of the complex human immune system.

Gene therapy—not yet a reality

Other investigators are exploring strategies that would incorporate the principles of transplantation yet circumvent the problems of tissue incompatibility and rejec-

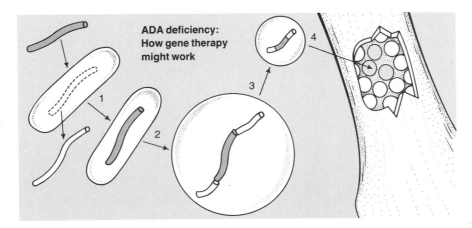

Some DNA is removed from a retrovirus (1) and is replaced with a normal ADA-producing gene. The modified virus "infects" a sample of the patient's bone marrow cells (2); the virus inserts the ADA gene into the DNA of the bone marrow (3). Bone marrow cells, now capable of producing ADA, are reinjected into the patient. They multiply into healthy marrow cells (4), which produce blood cells that provide a sufficient supply of ADA.

This child, a victim of ADA deficiency, leads a life of loneliness, isolated from other youngsters by her extreme susceptibility to infection.

tion of grafted tissue. Instead of transplanting donor tissue, medical scientists envision a way of removing a sample of the patient's tissue and, after correcting the genetic defect in the laboratory, reintroducing these immunologically identical but genetically altered cells back into the body. This technique, called gene therapy, will involve inserting a normal copy of the defective gene into the DNA in such a way that it will compensate for the malfunctioning or missing gene when the cells are returned to the patient's body.

The immediate hopes for gene therapy are concentrated on diseases caused by single-gene defects that could in principle be treated by the manipulation of cells derived from bone marrow. The most likely candidates are adenosine deaminase (ADA) deficiency, a severe hereditary immune deficiency disease so debilitating it can turn a common cold into a killer, and Lesch-Nyhan syndrome, a rare disorder characterized by excessive production of uric acid, neurological abnormalities, and self-mutilation. Both diseases fulfill criteria established early on as basic prerequisites for potential cure by gene therapy as it is envisioned today. Of primary importance is the relative simplicity of the causative defect; both are caused by the malfunction of a single gene. Furthermore, precise regulation of gene activity is not crucial to the success of the therapy in these two diseases because varying amounts of the gene product can bring about a resolution of the symptoms. Cure of heritable diseases caused by defects in more than one gene, or in a single, tightly regulated gene, is beyond the scope of gene therapy today and may require approaches very different from those currently

proposed for cure of Lesch-Nyhan syndrome and ADA deficiency.

How gene therapy might work

In the case of disorders caused by single-gene defects, once the defective gene has been identified and its normal counterpart grown in the laboratory, the effort focuses upon introducing the normal gene into the defective cells. To accomplish this goal, researchers have turned to a type of virus called a retrovirus. Using recombinant DNA technology, scientists can incorporate the normal human gene into the virus's genetic material. Then they rely on the virus's natural ability to enter living cells for the transport of the normal gene into the defective cells. Retroviruses are particularly well suited for this purpose because they are expert invaders of cells and, once inside, actually integrate their genes with those of the host cell. Once integrated into the host DNA, the newly introduced normal gene presumably becomes a permanent part of the genetic makeup of the host cell and its progeny.

While this is an elegant solution to the problem of getting normal genes into cells, there are potential drawbacks to the use of retroviruses as the transport vehicle. Of greatest concern are the ability of various retroviruses to cause certain cancers and, more recently, the discovery that a retrovirus causes acquired immune deficiency syndrome (AIDS). For use as gene carriers in humans, retroviruses must be made completely benign. In one such technique, normal human genes are delivered to the target DNA by means of a retrovirus that has been "disarmed" by having been made unable to replicate. No new virus can be made once it is inside the cell, but the genes of the "remodeled" virus are perpetuated in the infected cells, and no additional cells are invaded.

With development of what appears to be a promising method for getting the normal gene inside the cell and inserted in the DNA, some scientists predict that human trials of gene transplantation for correction of genetic disease may not be far off. While this optimism is understandable, it may be a bit premature. If gene therapy proves successful, it may someday revolutionize the treatment of genetic disease. But the technique is far from ready for widespread application. Many questions about the feasibility and safety remain unanswered. Using current methods, for example, insertion of the gene into the host DNA is more or less random, and the consequences of integration at an abnormal position in the chromosome are largely unknown. The process could trigger activation of previously dormant cancer-causing genes or disrupt the action of essential, properly functioning genes. Ideally, insertion would be targeted to the gene's normal location in the DNA, but this may not be easy to do. In 1986 two teams of U.S. scientists accomplished the first successful targeting of inserted genes to

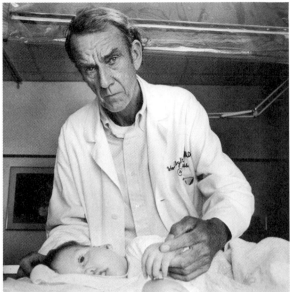

James Caccavo—Picture Group

William Nyhan, a discoverer of Lesch-Nyhan syndrome, examines a child with the disorder. This single-gene defect may one day be treated by means of gene therapy.

their normal chromosomal location in the DNA of test-tube cultivated cells; however, the technique remains inefficient.

The pace of current research leaves little doubt that it is only a matter of time before medical scientists present proposals to perform gene therapy in humans. Therefore, evaluating the potential benefits and hazards of the technique has taken on a new urgency. The assessment of risk is complicated by the fact that there are no known animal models for the enzyme-deficiency diseases that are likely to be the first candidates for gene therapy. Though expression of the inserted gene can be monitored in laboratory tissue cultures and animal experiments, the lack of an animal with the natural symptoms of ADA deficiency or Lesch-Nyhan syndrome makes it unlikely that researchers will be able to demonstrate a clinical "cure" until the technique has been used in humans. Uncertain clinical benefit, along with concern over potential hazards of the use of retroviruses for transport of genes, has limited the prospects of gene therapy to life-threatening diseases for which there is no other cure.

Ethical concerns

In most countries research protocols involving humans are subject to review by local ethics committees or review boards, whose decisions are guided by the general rules for human experimentation stated in the Declaration of Helsinki (1964) and adopted by the World Medical Association in 1975. However, when major therapeutic innovations such as gene therapy are initially proposed, this approach to the development of

guidelines often needs to be supplemented by more detailed ethical and procedural review. During the last several years a framework for the evaluation of human gene therapy proposals has been developed in the United States. Called "Points to Consider in the Design and Submission of Human Somatic-Cell Gene Therapy Protocols," it represents the attempt of a committee of scientists, clinicians, attorneys, and public-policy specialists to identify the areas of greatest concern to the public and professional communities. Written as a series of questions, this document is meant to serve as a guideline for establishing research design, designing a means of risk-benefit analysis, developing standards for informed consent, and guaranteeing privacy and accuracy in reporting results. It also outlines a mechanism of public review of all proposals to perform gene therapy in humans. The only type of gene therapy considered in the document is that intended to affect the patient's body, or somatic, cells, not the reproductive cells. Transfer of genes into egg or sperm cells, which would be passed on by an individual to his or her children, is highly controversial and is unlikely ever to be a reality in humans.

—Jan Hudis

Health Care Policy

With Medicare coverage shrinking, millions of elderly Americans are buying supplemental health insurance in the form of so-called "medigap" policies. Encouraged by fast-talking salesmen and upbeat ads featuring such celebrities as Danny Thomas and Lorne Greene, an estimated 80 percent of the nation's 30 million Medicare beneficiaries have purchased such plans, with annual premiums ranging from $150 to $1,070.

Sadie Molyneaux's family was shocked to find that the elderly woman held almost 50 health-insurance policies when she died in 1981, at age 83. The New Hope, Minnesota, widow had spent about $14,000 on insurance premiums over five years. None of the policies covered the $1,000-a-month nursing-home care Mrs. Molyneaux required for almost a year before her death.

—*Wall Street Journal*
July 29, 1985

Many countries in the world today are enduring health care "crises" because of serious economic problems. In contemporary Europe, for example, the ability to provide cradle-to-grave insurance is severely strained, and many governments are being forced to trim social and health care spending previously afforded by social welfare systems. It is ironic that the United States, as the most productive, freest society in the world's history, is now faced with a seemingly intractable problem in ensuring quality health care to all Americans to an extent that surpasses the crises in most other nations.

Human and economic values in conflict

In the United States health care is now the largest single industry—bigger even than defense—with re-

343

ceipts at around $400 billion, representing 11% of the gross national product (GNP). Because of the rapid growth of costs over the past decade, the medical profession has been forced to retreat from its natural role as the manager of health care delivery systems and give way to the third-party payers, insurance companies and government, who now in the main determine who receives medical care, types of care, and length of care. Thus, health care in the U.S. is rapidly being converted from a social service to an economic commodity, sold in the marketplace to those who can afford to pay for it.

In 1970 the average cost of a day in the hospital was $81, and most patients covered by health insurance could meet the deductibles and patient contribution easily. Traditionally revenue from the paying patients covered the cost of treating nonpaying patients, and this satisfied social and professional ethics in denying treatment to no one. In 1986 the average daily cost was $492, and though most people had major health insurance protection, few left the hospital without owing money and many were in serious debt. A single health insurance plan had become inadequate for most people.

Even after reimbursements, millions of families pay more than 15% of their income on the soaring cost of dealing with illness. Massive health insurance industry advertising, through all the media, is taking advantage of the widespread fear of the consequences of insufficient money to pay for health care.

Because of the intensity of the cost issue, insurers, government agencies, and health care providers have focused their attention on what money should, or should not, be spent rather than what and how much health care needs to be provided. "Our basic problem is that somehow we are going to have to learn to say 'no,'" writes economist Lester C. Thurow of the Massachusetts Institute of Technology—but who will be the naysayers? "Not doctors," says Norman G. Levinsky, chief of medicine at Boston University Medical Center. "Elected officials must decide when limits will be placed on expensive but effective kinds of care."

This new focus has produced bizarre results, which seriously compromise society's ethical values. For example, a proposed "means test" for veterans under the age of 65 and denial of medical services in Veterans Administration facilities to those who are ruled able to pay for private services. Some 85% of the nation's 28.2 million veterans are younger than 65.

Some Medicare patients are being "dumped" from hospital beds before they are well because the amount paid by the U.S. Department of Health and Human Services (HHS) is fixed according to the original diagnosis. This means that a hospital can profit from an early discharge. HHS says that Medicare does not tell doctors or hospitals when to discharge patients, only when benefits have run out.

States across the U.S. are cutting back the coverage for poor people under Medicaid. For example, South Carolina will not pay for more than 12 days a year of hospital care. Tennessee's limit is 14 days; Mississippi's, 15 days. Under federal law all states participating in Medicaid must pay for inpatient hospital services, but states have wide discretion in limiting coverage. Federal courts have generally held that a limit was reasonable if it permitted services adequate to meet the needs of "most of the individuals" eligible for Medicaid, but to say that "most people" can get by with a limit of 15 days a year is irrelevant to a patient who needs 30 days of hospital care to get well.

The insurer Blue Cross and Blue Shield has introduced a program in some states named CostWise, whereby doctors will receive payment from Blue Cross and Blue Shield only if they have an agreement to accept Blue Cross and Blue Shield's maximum allowance for covered services. Nonparticipating doctors will not receive any payment from Blue Cross and Blue Shield, and their patients will receive only Blue Cross and Blue Shield's maximum allowance. The program involves physical therapists and doctors of medicine,

Shorter hospital stays

length of stay in days

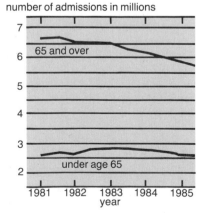

Declining hospital admissions

number of admissions in millions

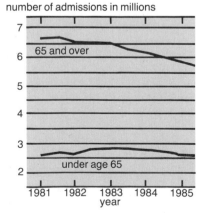

Rising cost of hospitalization

dollars per day

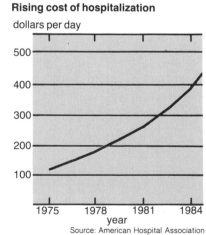

Source: American Hospital Association

chiropody, chiropractic, dentistry, optometry, and psychology. The effect of this program is to pressure medical practitioners into accepting Blue Cross and Blue Shield as the controller of professional fees.

Some state health benefits plans now require a "preadmission certificate" for hospital care. The effect of this is that the medical director of the insurance company, rather than the patient's doctor, determines whether a patient should be hospitalized. If a preadmission certificate is not obtained, the patient incurs severe financial penalties.

Fundamental disagreements exist among politicians, government agency officials, economists, private and public institutions, consumers, and medical practitioners on what policies are appropriate and likely to be effective in solving the dual problems of high cost and individual access to medical care. As a result the United States lacks a health care system as such and has instead a decentralized, fragmented, and uncoordinated set of arrangements, which is increasingly confusing to consumers and professionals alike.

No one wants to lack medical care because it is unaffordable, and few want to see others lack medical care because they cannot afford it either. But if people can afford it, they demand the right to buy whatever medical care they choose. This set of traditional beliefs is now under attack. Economists have suggested that even when a patient can afford treatment, it should be denied in some cases as a way of cutting overall costs. On the other hand, federal and state government cutbacks in funding have resulted in large numbers of poor people denied access to needed medical care.

The results of a 1984 survey sponsored by the American College of Hospital Administrators provided some reassurance to humanists; of more than 1,000 hospital administrators, doctors, legislators, and health regulators surveyed, 98% stated their belief that all Americans deserve at least a minimum level of health care. However, only 12% said that everyone is entitled to the same level of care and that the level of care should not be governed by the individual's ability to pay. In addition, 90% of those questioned predicted a marked decline in access to medical care for uninsured persons, as well as for Medicare and Medicaid beneficiaries.

The ethical issue requires answers to these questions: Does U.S. society have a responsibility to provide needed health care to all Americans regardless of their individual abilities to pay? If the answer to this question is yes, how should this be accomplished? If the answer is no, can society live with the results?

The elderly and the poor

Few Americans are aware of the limits of Medicare's insurance coverage until an elderly relative is hospitalized. First there is a $492 deductible to be paid for the first day. A Medicare patient in a hospital longer than 60 days then pays $123 a day for the next 30 days and $246 a day for the next 60 days. After 150 days, all benefits end.

Since Medicare does not cover nursing home care, it does not provide for long-term illness, to which elderly patients are prone. Patients must pay for long-term care until all their assets are exhausted and they acquire poverty status, which qualifies them for Medicaid. According to a 1985 report from the U.S. government's House Select Committee on Aging, only 13 weeks in a nursing home would impoverish 63% of all Americans 66 and older who live alone.

Poverty in the U.S. has returned to levels that existed 20 years ago. For example, income statistics show that there are 23 million whites among the 35 million people in the United States who are officially classified as poor. This includes elderly widows with incomes below $4,979, adults under 65 living alone with incomes less than $5,400, married couples of working age with incomes less than $6,983, and families of four with incomes less than $10,609.

According to the latest available figures from the U.S. Census Bureau, 20% of all poor families and almost 50% of the poor who live alone do not receive any of the noncash welfare benefits: food stamps, free school lunches, subsidized housing, or Medicaid. The Department of Labor reports 8.2 million people unemployed and a further 1.3 million without jobs but not counted as unemployed because they have given up looking for employment. Further, it has been estimated that between two million and three million people in the U.S. are homeless—a figure offered by advocates for the growing homeless population. The Department of Housing and Urban Development concedes that 300,000 are homeless.

Beyond the officially poor, unemployed, and homeless are a growing group of people, probably around 30 million, whom social analysts call the "new poor." These people earn just enough to pay for food and shelter but not enough to pay for health insurance, since most of them work for employers too small to afford medical insurance for their workers. According to HHS, nearly 30 million Americans have neither public nor private health insurance coverage, and almost 49 million are unprotected against major medical expense. Even those covered by Medicaid are frequently denied needed care except in emergencies.

Under present conditions it is clear that Medicare fails to protect elderly Americans adequately against the cost of covered services and does not provide at all for other needed services such as nursing home care and long-term treatment. Since the elderly are much more likely to suffer long-term illness, they face the likelihood of catastrophic medical costs alone and, without supplemental insurance coverage to close this "medigap," impoverishment. Low-income elderly are already paying one-quarter of their income annually for health care, while high-income elderly pay only 3%. Further, millions of poverty-level citizens and the "new poor" who cannot afford health insurance are without access to adequate medical care except when they can obtain private "charity."

U.S. economic realities

HHS has stated that the status quo (*i.e.,* total costs of $400 billion and 11% of GNP), with its 25% annual increases in private insurance premiums and burgeoning Medicare and Medicaid budgets, is politically unacceptable. The full impact of government policies severely limiting health care financing is yet to be seen, and some results were not intended.

For example, the fixed-reimbursement method encourages hospitals to discharge patients more quickly, and this has occurred. The average length of stay for people over age 65 dropped 7.5% between 1983 and 1984. Thus, what used to be a $3,000 six-day hospital visit could become a $3,000 four-day hospital visit, pushing the daily average costs from $500 to $750 because the formula HHS is required to follow in setting reimbursements and Medicare deductibles is based on average daily costs, not total costs. In fact, the average daily cost of room, board, and routine care in hospitals went from $370 in 1983 to $592 in 1986.

Another example involves intraocular lenses to correct cataracts. Under the fixed-reimbursement method Medicare pays hospitals $1,200–$1,500 for the inpatient operation. Improved technology now allows doctors to perform the operation in hospital-based outpatient clinics. The result is that hospitals and doctors can avoid inpatient limits and receive up to $2,800 for each case. These examples have been characterized by the HHS inspector general as part of a "quagmire of illogical Medicare reimbursement policies" that add significantly to health economics problems.

When Lee Iacocca joined the Chrysler Corp. as its chairman in 1979, he saw that Blue Cross and Blue Shield was Chrysler's largest supplier—annually billing the company more than its suppliers of steel or rubber. At that time Chrysler, Ford, and General Motors were paying $3 billion a year for health insurance. At Chrysler that amounted to $600 million for 60,000 employees—$1,640,000 a day, or about $600 added to the cost of every car and truck produced. This represented about 7% of the sticker price on some of Chrysler's small cars, giving foreign competition a big advantage at a time when the imbalance of payments between the U.S. and Japan was around $30 billion a year in Japan's favor. Chrysler saved itself $58 million in 1984, but only through limiting hospital stays and "unnecessary" surgery for employees.

British versus U.S. systems

A comparison between U.S. and British health care costs is particularly interesting because 98% of health services are provided through publicly owned and operated institutions in Britain, the private sector barely accounting for 2%. Since 1948, when the National Health Service (NHS) was inaugurated, "doomsayers" have been saying that health care costs will cripple the British economy. The facts are that costs are 6% of Great Britain's GNP, compared with 11% in the U.S. And British per capita costs are less than half (41%) of U.S. per capita costs.

Adding to the significance of this comparison are the following factors: (1) Britain has a higher propor-

While public hospitals (right) are struggling to treat the number of patients who have no health insurance and no means to pay bills, private hospitals with low occupancy rates are offering special amenities to the well-to-do. During kidney dialysis (left) a patient enjoys the services of a beautician.

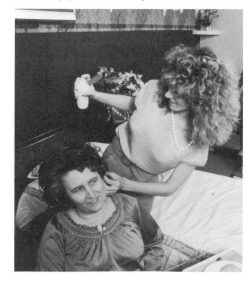 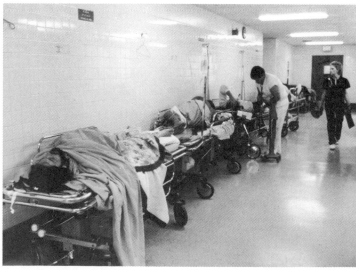

(Left) Andy Levin/Discover; (right) Mark Perlstein/U.S. News & World Report

tion of elderly population—the elderly comprising a group that absorbs a disproportionately high share of health care services (on both sides of the Atlantic); (2) though the total British population growth since 1951 has been only 12%, the level of health care services delivered has almost doubled during the same period when the number of treatments to inpatients and out-patients is used a measure; and (3) the basic concept of the British NHS is to provide a system for people to pay for services when they are well and working so that they can use these services virtually free of charge when they are ill and not working. Thus, access to health care is enjoyed by everyone in Great Britain, and financial considerations dominate neither the health care decisions nor the sick patients' minds.

The extent to which the British public is satisfied with the system may be measured by the small size of the private sector (2% of the total); insurance contributions by employers and employees account for only 11% of total NHS costs, and many more consumers could afford private health insurance premiums if they felt it worthwhile. Over time, the British system, under the NHS, has provided an acceptable health care delivery system to everyone in Britain, and cost containment is effective by any standards.

When Medicare was introduced in 1965, government perceived its role essentially as a "bill payer" for beneficiaries. Provision of needed health care for retired people was made through private institutions under a "reasonable cost" system—which was essentially an open checkbook. With the introduction of Medicaid the following year, it was felt that the needs of the retired and the officially poor were being met.

Unlike the public education system, where public funds remained under public control, however, public funds through Medicare and Medicaid were passed to the private sector, who controlled treatment and costs. This was, in effect, an invitation to indulge in inefficient management, careless financing, greed, waste, fraud, and abuse. During the first six months of 1985, for example, 110 physicians and health care providers were excluded from Medicare and Medicaid for fraud, abuse, and incompetence. There were 31 criminal convictions, and HHS recovered $6.8 million and collected $3 million in fines and penalties during the same period.

Time for change

It is now time for a review of present policies and a return to basics before matters get out of hand. There is a serious question as to whether the current HHS can satisfy U.S. needs through private institutions. For example, Congress in 1984 froze the fees that Medicare pays physicians. The freeze did not have much effect. Only 30% of the nation's doctors agreed to accept those fees as full payment. The rest have continued to charge Medicare patients extra.

It may be that the department will be forced to consider the alternative of federal- and state-owned-and-operated hospitals in order to achieve control over the amount, type, quality, and cost of health care provision. The year 1987 could be the right time for such a move since there is a glut of doctors and large numbers of struggling hospitals are ripe for such a takeover. There could hardly be a more satisfying or humanitarian "basic" than providing a system for people to pay for services when they are well and working so that they can use them free of charge when they are sick and not working, officially impoverished, too poor to pay, or retired. If providing care to the sick and needy is not part of the social "glue" that holds people together, what is?

"Marketing" health care

Patients going to the Methodist Medical Center in Peoria, Illinois, never worry about parking their cars. The hospital started offering valet parking a few months ago. The place also has a doorman. After he swings open the door, patients are handed over to an escort, who shepherds them to their destination.

Hospitals and doctors, faced with competition at every turn, are resorting to the sort of marketing tactics more commonly found in the airline business or the quick-burger industry. One of the more memorable marketing gimmicks was used by Sunrise Hospital in Las Vegas. The hospital staged a lottery that was open only to patients who checked in on the weekend, a typically slack time at hospitals. The grand prize was a cruise for two. Utilization soared by 60 percent in 18 months.

—*New York Times*
April 16, 1984

Though it is acknowledged that the health care market will never function in exactly the same way as the market for consumer products, HHS believes that it should pursue a "market" solution to the cost problem. Characteristics of the health care market make market competition an attractive tool for dealing with the health cost problem. Unlike regulation, which politicizes the issues of how much to spend and where to spend it, the market approach works through mutual consent of buyers and sellers. It is further acknowledged that for the present policies to succeed, it is critical that the *private* sector accept the challenge of slowing the rise in health care costs and that failure to do so will almost certainly lead to heavy-handed regulation of physicians and hospitals, which could in turn pose a serious threat to the quality of medical care that Americans have come to expect.

There are, however, obvious flaws in a market solution to the problems. Buyers of medical services do so under duress. They do not have the knowledge on which to make informed choices and are unable to judge the effectiveness of medical treatment or to decide whether such treatment is necessary. Ignorance, therefore, becomes a source of monopoly power, which, in essence, the medical profession possesses.

In a "free market" environment, institutions will do whatever they have to do to survive, which includes greater selectivity in admissions practices and tight control on the amount of treatment given to Medicare and Medicaid beneficiaries. Consumers will seek the best treatment they can get compatible with available funds. Insurers will adjust their premiums to meet costs and turn a profit. Employers may draw the line on their commitment, but financially able employees will seek to close the gap through supplementary insurance just as financially able Medicare recipients are doing now. The poor will depend on others for what they can get and will turn increasingly to government as the private sector defends itself in a competitive environment.

This leaves government with a social problem that "marketing" cannot solve, since marketing is a mechanism for saying "no" to people without means. In order to survive, even not-for-profit institutions have strict limits on the amount of free care they provide, especially since the emergence of increased numbers of for-profit hospitals that, practicing marketing principles, target the most profitable patients. Supporters of the notion that for-profit business is incompatible with health care needs will have gained some satisfaction from the recent slumps suffered by for-profit hospital groups. The largest one, Hospital Corporation of America, with almost 400 hospitals, enjoyed record earnings in 1984 but declared in 1985 that results will be flat in 1986, ending a decade of uninterrupted quarterly gains. As a result of this and other groups' profit problems, startled Wall Streeters dumped health care stocks and wiped out $1.5 billion of the industry's market value in one day, nearly 10% of its market capitalization. There can be no doubt that government cutbacks in Medicare funding were a major factor in this reversal.

Nevertheless, whatever system is used in a free society to provide health care, there is an appropriate place for the private sector to serve the demands of those who are able and willing to buy something special, just as people now do in education. On balance, the competition between the public and private sectors stimulates improvement both ways. When the public and private sectors become too entangled, as is the case with Medicare and Medicaid, probably the worst side of each follows.

Free-market health care: can it deliver?

According to a recent study, *Health Care in the 1990s,* sponsored by the American College of Hospital Administrators (now the American College of Health Care Executives) and Arthur Andersen and Co., the level of services obtained will be governed by the individual's ability to pay. Also predicted is a marked decline in access to medical care, especially for Medicare, Medicaid, and uninsured persons. One ray of hope offered by the study is that good care will improve by 1995 for those enrolled in health maintenance organizations (HMOs; prepaid health care) and will remain stable for the commercially insured. In the near future, since most people are not conscious of the increase in personal liabilities, it will not be until they are hospitalized and receive their first bill that they will loudly protest.

Harvard University's Center for Health Policy completed a study in 1986. Its recommendation to HHS of heavy cuts in Medicare beneficiary deductibles was among 40 new proposals that, if adopted, would increase Medicare spending by $50 billion in the next 14 years.

HMOs are not a panacea for the same reason that "marketing" is not: only the well-to-do or employer-sponsored person can afford them. However, Medicare is sponsoring a nationwide trial of "social HMOs" exclusively for the elderly. One such plan in the twincities (Minneapolis-St. Paul, Minn.) area provides its members with full home care, including necessary physician visits, nursing care, treatments (*e.g.,* fresh dressings, physical therapy, etc.), and meals if needed. Medicare reimburses each member $175 a month; the members pay only $29.50 a month.

A logical expansion of the "social HMO" concept would be the establishment of a national network of community and teaching hospitals, organized by states and funded by payroll deduction. HHS should establish standards to be maintained, and reciprocation between states should be mandated. Public hospitals would become HMOs. All efforts could be focused upon efficient health care rather than profitable sick care.

The system would provide the means to guarantee health services to all Americans for life, regardless of their financial status. It would establish direct public control over costs, and Medicare/Medicaid would become obsolete.

In this environment the insurance industry and others in the private sector could pursue the "real markets" in the same way the private sector does in education: serving the demands of those who are able and willing to buy something special. Such an approach was described in *American Business* magazine in 1984.

In an effort to lure wealthier patients, Doctors Hospital in Hollywood, Florida, has opened a luxury suite complete with door-to-door limousine service, lobster dinners and champagne cocktails. For $50 to $100 above the regular daily room charge, patients will be driven by limousine to the hotel, where they can recuperate in a private suite, dining on gourmet food served on fine china, quaffing wine from crystal goblets.

The alternative to public control of publicly funded programs is to continue present policies and efforts to control the private sector's treatment of the elderly and the poor. So far, cash savings have come at the expense of reduced care, and the increase in overall costs continues.

—Donald B. Guest, Ph.D.

The Karen Ann Quinlan Case: A Modern Parable

by George J. Annas, J.D., M.P.H.

Chief Justice Richard Hughes, the author of the Karen Ann Quinlan opinion, spoke at a March 1986 conference commemorating the tenth anniversary of his historic decision. He spoke of how the New Jersey Supreme Court had set out to "change the standard of medical practice as a matter of law" so that the physicians caring for Karen Quinlan would honor her parents' wishes to discontinue use of the mechanical ventilator ("respirator"). Karen's parents, Joseph and Julia Quinlan, also spoke at the conference. It was their first meeting with the judge who had authorized their daughter's removal from the ventilator. Julia Quinlan told the mostly medical audience that she hoped their daughter's experience and the court's opinion would help ensure that "we will not become slaves to technology." She said, "When I reflect on her life, I realize she had a purpose far beyond what she could have suspected." What purpose did Karen's life and death serve, and why did the court think it necessary to change medical practice by law?

Karen Quinlan, who died in the summer of 1985, has become part of our language. Many people have voiced their opinions about her state, usually making the point that "if I'm ever like Karen Ann Quinlan, pull the plug." Karen Quinlan has also become a symbol of the mindless use of medical technology. Her story is a modern parable.

The case

On the night of April 14, 1975, Karen Quinlan was rushed to a Denville, N. J., hospital emergency room after she had stopped breathing for at least two 15-minute periods. No one knows exactly what caused these episodes. At the hospital she was resuscitated and placed on a mechanical ventilator, which she needed in order to breathe. After it became apparent that Karen would never regain consciousness, her parents asked the physicians to remove the ventilator and let her die in peace. The physicians were sympathetic but worried about possible criminal and civil lawsuits should they follow the parents' wishes. The doctors therefore told the Quinlans that they would remove the ventilator only if a court approved this action.

The doctors' fear of the law forced the Quinlans into the public arena to fight for their daughter's right to refuse medical treatment. A lower court rejected their plea, but the Supreme Court of New Jersey, in a rare unanimous decision, ruled in their favor. Following the decision, instead of simply discontinuing ventilator assistance, Karen's physicians carefully and slowly weaned her from the ventilator. To the surprise of the judges, but not of the physicians involved, Karen was able to breathe on her own. She continued to breathe, and remained unconscious, for nine more years. She finally died of pneumonia on June 11, 1985, at the age of 31, in the arms of her mother. Her father later said, "She died with dignity."

Much of the attention to Karen Quinlan's case was and continues to be focused on the legal definition of death. But that was not the real issue. She did not satisfy modern "brain death" criteria (she retained some brain function). She survived those nine years in a "persistent vegetative state." This state is contrasted to a coma, in which the patient's eyes are closed. In a persistent vegetative state the patient is awake but unaware, has sleep-wake cycles, but is unconscious and unable to interact purposefully with the environment. While it cannot be said with 100% certainty, there is virtually no chance that such a patient will ever regain consciousness. There are approximately 10,000 such patients in the United States today.

The New Jersey Supreme Court opinion has had such a powerful influence on the American public because Karen's story is so compelling. There is no doubt that her parents wanted only what was best for Karen, and the decision that she would be better off if the mechanical ventilator was removed was one they reached with the greatest reluctance. The court also seems correct in concluding that such a decision would be supported by the "overwhelming majority" of society. This is probably why the court saw its primary purpose as devising a way to change medical practice to get Karen's physicians to discontinue use of sophisticated medical technology.

The constitutional right of privacy

The court's analysis was straightforward, though unprecedented. It determined that if Karen were a competent adult, i.e., if she could have a lucid moment, sit up in bed, understand, and appreciate her situation, she would have the right to refuse further ventilator treatment. Such a decision would be hers alone, and to deprive her of this option would interfere with her constitutional right to privacy (the same right the U.S. Supreme Court had used three years earlier to protect a woman's right to have an abortion, prior to fetal viability, free from state interference).

But, of course, Karen Quinlan was not competent; she was permanently unconscious and would never experience even a moment of lucidity. Therefore, either she lost her right to refuse treatment because of permanent incompetence, *or* the court had to fashion some mechanism for someone else to exercise that right on her behalf. The court decided that permitting Karen Quinlan's father to act on her behalf was proper and that the state could interfere with her father's decision only if it could demonstrate a "compelling state interest."

Four possible state interests were suggested by the court: protecting the sanctity of life, preventing suicide, upholding medical ethics, and protecting others. Since Karen had no children or others dependent on her, the last interest was irrelevant. As for the sanctity of life, the court found that this interest diminished as the "bodily invasion increased and the prognosis dimmed." The court also ruled as a matter of law that the refusal of medical treatment is never suicide because the sick person does not want to die and does not put the death-producing instrument into motion. This makes refusing further treatment different from shooting oneself or taking a lethal dose of pills. As for "medical ethics," the court simply did not believe that her doctors thought it was unethical to remove Karen's ventilator. Instead the court opined that the doctors were *afraid* to remove it because of the fear of law-

suits. Accordingly, the court devised a method to give physicians legal immunity under the circumstances of this case. It said that if a hospital "ethics committee" (more properly termed a "prognosis committee") confirmed there was "no reasonable possibility" of Karen's returning "to a cognitive, sapient state," then the ventilator could be removed and all involved would have legal immunity.

The Quinlan case fallout

The Karen Ann Quinlan case ushered in a decade of litigation about the rights of incompetent patients to refuse treatment. The debate continues today, even though the original opinion's basic structure has been followed by almost every subsequent court. First, courts universally agree that competent adults have the right to refuse treatment and, whether seen as a constitutional or common law right, that the government can interfere with a competent patient's refusal only if it can demonstrate a "compelling reason." Most courts discuss the same four state interests outlined in *Quinlan.* In general, however, it is fair to conclude that unless the patient's refusal endangers the public health or the health of another person, the individual's right to refuse treatment must legally be honored. A popular Broadway play and later a movie, with the apt title *Whose Life Is It Anyway?,* accurately depicts the law on this issue.

Second, courts have followed the *Quinlan* decision in agreeing that individuals should not automatically forfeit their right to refuse treatment upon becoming incompetent. Rather, it can be exercised on their behalf by another person who is acting consistently with the individual's own wishes. This basic notion, that we should honor an incompetent patient's personal

Karen Ann Quinlan's casket is carried to a New Jersey cemetery after her death from pneumonia in June 1985. A court had ruled in 1976 that she could be removed from a mechanical ventilator, according to her parents' wishes. She remained alive, unconscious but breathing, for nine years. The medical-ethical issues that Karen Quinlan came to symbolize were not buried when she was but are still very much alive.

wishes regarding medical treatment, has led to almost 40 states passing "living will" legislation since the *Quinlan* case. Such statutes generally provide a mechanism by which a currently competent adult can write down his or her wishes regarding medical treatment for the time when the individual is no longer able to speak for himself or herself. It is ironic that although "living will" legislation was primarily inspired by Karen Quinlan, it would not have been useful for her if it had been in effect. This is because such statutes generally apply only to terminally ill patients, a criterion Karen did not fulfill. Second-generation living will statutes will not restrict their application to the terminally ill, or to the type of treatment that can be refused, and will permit people to name their own proxy to make treatment decisions on their behalf consistent with their wishes and instructions.

Third, in the event that no one knows what the patient would want, courts agree that decision makers must act in the patient's "best interests." Unlike respecting the patient's wishes, a subjective test, this is an objective one: what would most people feel is "best" for this person? In Karen's case the answer seemed easy to the court, at least after Karen's parents had voiced their decision.

But what about a harder case? What about removing the feeding tubes that kept Karen alive for nine years after she survived the removal of the mechanical ventilator? Karen's parents determined that this would not be in her best interests and continued to have her artificially fed. The artificial-feeding debate now rages. More than a half-dozen cases have reached the courts in which the termination of artificial feeding is and has been debated. Most courts have decided that feeding artificially, usually with a nasogastric tube (through the nose) or a gastrostomy tube (directly into the stomach), is a *medical* procedure. Therefore, they have concluded that the patient should be able to refuse such feeding just as the patient could refuse any other medical treatment. Elizabeth Bouvia, a 28-year-old quadriplegic almost totally debilitated by cerebral palsy, became a symbol of the right-to-die movement in 1984 when she wanted to be allowed to starve to death. She lost that case. But in April 1986 her doctors were ordered by a Los Angeles appeals court to remove feeding tubes, even though the doctors believed Bouvia could not take sufficient nutrition orally to sustain her life.

In 1986 the American Medical Association's council on ethical and judicial affairs ruled that "life prolonging medical treatment includes medication and artificially or technologically supplied respiration, nutrition or hydration." Such life-prolonging treatments, the council believes, can rightfully be removed, based on the patient's wishes, even when, as in Karen Quinlan's case, "death is not imminent but a patient's coma is beyond doubt irreversible." This statement will not persuade those who believe that feeding, even if done technologically, has such a powerful symbolic value in regard to reinforcing the notion of "community and caring" that its withdrawal should never be socially sanctioned. Nonetheless, the trend is to *permit* the removal of such artificial feeding *if* this is consistent with the patient's wishes.

A fourth piece of fallout from the *Quinlan* case is that a "mini-industry" of ethics committees has sprung up. The primary focus of this industry is not to debate "ethics" but to attempt to keep cases like Karen's out of the courts. The courts are viewed by most as inappropriate and clumsy mechanisms that serve to make private decisions a matter of public record and only increase family anguish and expense. This critique has some merit, but the stakes are very high. Only the courts can declare and protect individual human rights, and the role they play in this regard is vital. And, as the *Quinlan* case so well illustrates, courts can catalyze a nationwide debate, build a societal consensus, and help change medical practice to conform to the wishes of patients and the public.

The lingering questions

Where do we go from here? The Karen Quinlan case centers on the proper role of medical technology at the end of life. Must we use medical technology just because it is available? Has medical technology taken on such a life of its own that we are prepared to accord it "rights" of its own? And, if only human beings have rights, how can we protect those rights for the most vulnerable individuals in society, the dying and the permanently unconscious? Karen Quinlan has taught us that modern medical technology can be brutal. To ensure that technology continues to have a useful purpose, we must respect the individual's right to decide if it will be used and when it will be withdrawn. This is a powerful lesson. But many questions remain.

Who should decide for patients who have not made their wishes known in advance through a living will or other written or oral statement? Who should decide for infants, children, or the severely mentally ill or mentally retarded, who never could make their preferences known to us? On what basis should decisions be made for them? What, if any, role should ethics committees play? Is artificial feeding equivalent to other medical interventions? Is it always in the "best interests" of permanently unconscious patients to be kept alive? Should we change our definition of death to include the permanently unconscious? How can we as a culture acknowledge our mortality and face death as an inevitable part of what makes life itself worthwhile?

Julia Quinlan correctly noted that her daughter's case raises "profoundly disturbing questions that do not lend themselves to easy answers." The public debate on these questions is Karen Quinlan's living legacy to us all.

Health Care Technology

Almost daily, technological developments in the health care field are emerging. It is almost impossible to keep up with the vast and varied innovations. They range from miniature TV camera lenses that can be inserted into the body to provide quality color images of human arteries and ducts to an electronic apparatus to inhibit self-injury by autistic children and to three-dimensional computer modeling of the human head that enables surgeons to "design" precise corrections for disfiguring birth defects. Following are just a few of the newest computer and "high-tech" advances in medicine and health care.

Computerizing the patient

At first the role of computers in medicine was limited to management of information such as hospital and patient records. The next step involved the machines in continuous monitoring of patients and in rapid analysis of diagnostic tests. University Hospital, Stony Brook, N.Y., for example, has 400 beds and 300 computer terminals interconnecting all its departments and functions. Nurses obtain results from a laboratory test in four hours or less, which enable physicians to prescribe appropriate treatment at the bedside of patients. In addition the hospital realizes savings in labor and operating costs.

One of the latest computer advances enables computers to gather *all* relevant information about a patient, assist in diagnosis, and give advice to physicians. A system called HELP (Health Evaluation through Logical Processing) takes a patient's medical history with the help of a television screen that displays questions a physician usually asks, such as, "Do you suffer from allergies?" The patient answers by pressing "yes" or "no" buttons. The answer elicits an appropriate follow-up question. The program also suggests tests to obtain missing information, analyzes test results, and offers a diagnosis. In one case at the Latter Day Saints Hospital, Salt Lake City, Utah, HELP processed a routine electrocardiograph and concluded that the patient was in myocardial infarction—*i.e.,* having a heart attack. The computer immediately alerted a technician, and the patient was rushed to an emergency care unit for lifesaving care.

HELP's value goes beyond diagnosis. It comments on a physician's plan of treatment and warns of adverse drug interactions and allergies and other conditions that may affect medical therapies. If, for example, the physician prescribes a drug that, as a side effect, lowers blood levels of potassium, HELP may caution that a particular patient would then be at risk of developing dangerously low levels of potassium (because of another drug he or she is taking). Therefore, a doctor is able to prescribe a potassium supplement. The physician, of course, does not have to accept

352

HELP is a computer system that is used by some hospitals to do everything from analyzing patient test results, "commenting" on treatment, and warning about adverse drug reactions to processing the patient's bill.

the computer's diagnosis or "advice." Systems such as HELP exist to provide information and obviously cannot substitute for the experience, compassion, and intuition of a human.

The HELP system also stores billing and inventory data, processes insurance forms, and holds information about thousands of diseases, symptoms, and drug therapies. It exemplifies the growing use of computer-assisted diagnosis by so-called expert systems. These systems consist of a data base containing medical facts and a knowledge base containing rules for applying the facts. The rules often take an "if-then" form. "Ifs" are facts that, when true, lead to a "then"—an action or conclusion. For example, *if* a patient has difficulty getting air into her lungs, *if* her ability to get oxygen into her blood is below a certain level, *if* her lung capacity exceeds a given value, *then* she probably has emphysema. The above example comes from an actual system, in routine use at the Pacific Medical Center Hospital, San Francisco.

Such expert systems are examples of what is known as artificial intelligence (AI)—computer programs that imitate human reasoning. An AI system in routine use at Stanford Medical Center plans drug therapy for cancer patients. At the University of Pittsburgh, Pa., researchers are developing a program to diagnose more than 650 diseases of internal medicine. Other programs have been used on an experimental basis to diagnose genetic disorders, congenital heart disease, abdominal pain, eye diseases, and other problems. The physician ultimately makes the decisions, but the computer offers helpful suggestions and advice. Specialists in AI point out that such expert systems would be particularly valuable to physicians practicing in rural areas or isolated locations. At present, programs likely to be of greatest help can run only on large computers, but this will change as technicians refine software and companies that specialize in computer hardware build increasingly sophisticated and small desktop terminals.

Medical information in a computer can now be transferred to a credit-card-size LaserCard with the help of laser technology. This card holds the equivalent of 800 pages of data including a digitized photograph of a patient, facsimile of his or her signature, summary of health insurance coverage, representations of an electrocardiogram and chest X-ray, list of medicines being taken, and names of the patient's physicians and the treatments they have provided. To retrieve this information, a hospital or physician needs a laser optical scanner and a computer the size of a typical personal computer terminal. Blue Cross and Blue Shield of Maryland plans to provide its version, the LifeCard, to all its subscribers. Successful use in Maryland could mean much wider adoption of the card.

Robot-assisted surgery

Computer technology also makes possible a variety of new devices for directly treating patients. One of the most startling is a computer-controlled robot arm that assists in brain surgery. At Memorial Medical Center, Long Beach, Calif., the robot arm guides a surgical drill and biopsy needle into the brain to remove samples from suspected tumors. The suspicious areas are found by computerized axial tomography (CAT) scans, which provide the equivalent of three-dimensional X-ray images of the brain. Technicians feed the position of a suspected tumor into the robot's computer memory. The information "tells" the robot exactly where to drill, at what angle to insert the biopsy needle, and how deep the probe should go. "The robot arm is safer, faster, and far less invasive than current surgical procedures"—at least so claims its inventor.

Light that heals

Besides reading LifeCards, laser beams are employed as surgical knives for a variety of purposes—to seal blood vessels, to vaporize tumors, and to remove obstructions in fallopian tubes and arteries. Laser light can be focused to a point smaller than the diameter of a human hair and can reach temperatures of 5,500° C (10,000° F). For certain operations the beams can cut away tissue with less bleeding, more precision, less scarring, and less postoperative pain; tissue also heals faster than in conventional surgery.

In ophthalmology laser light is now routinely used. It can pass through the cornea and thus permit non-invasive surgery inside the eye. One of its first uses was to make surgical removal of cataracts easier by disintegrating the front portion of a tough membrane that surrounds the lens. Following cataract surgery, the remaining part of the membrane may cloud over and block vision. A laser will burst this membrane in

The LaserCard is the size of a credit card but can contain the equivalent of 800 pages of medical data about a patient. The information is readily retrieved on a computer screen in a hospital or doctor's office.

seconds without requiring additional surgery or hospitalization. Ophthalmologists now use the technology in a diversity of other operations such as sealing leaking blood vessels in the back of the eye to prevent blindness in patients suffering from diabetic retinopathy. The eyesight of diabetics also is threatened by macular edema—fluid accumulation in the part of the retina responsible for detailed vision. In a recent clinical trial sponsored by the U.S. National Eye Institute, those who received prompt laser treatment for this malady were half as likely to suffer significant vision loss as those who delayed the treatment for three years.

In another surgical function lasers vaporize unwanted tissue in a highly localized and controlled manner by heating water in tumor cells to the boiling point. This permits removal of benign tumors. Using a carbon dioxide laser that emits infrared (heat) radiation, surgeons can excise tumors from the throats of children, for example. They also employ this type of laser to burn away excess gum growth and to treat mouth lesions caused by smoking and chewing tobacco. Physicians at the University of California at San Francisco use it to vaporize cancerous tissue in the esophagus—a treatment that restores the ability to swallow food. This device also has been applied to removing the beginning of cervical and vaginal cancers. However, these small cancerous areas also can be treated effectively by freezing with a cryoprobe, an established procedure that is less costly than laser surgery.

Along with carbon dioxide lasers, physicians use argon and neodymium:yttrium-aluminum-garnet (Nd:-YAG) lasers to treat certain gynecologic and digestive disorders. Flexible tubes, called endoscopes, carry optical fibers, through which light passes, and these

353

are inserted through the throat, uterus, or abdominal wall. With YAG lasers physicians remove precancerous polyps in the bowel, and they have restored fertility in women by clearing blocked fallopian tubes, allowing eggs from the ovaries to reach the uterus.

There are also many potential applications for future uses of laser light. In addition to direct destruction of malignant tumors, laser light is now used experimentally with a special dye to "poison" cancer cells. Using an endoscope, surgeons inject the dye into the cells, and it reacts with laser light to produce a toxic substance that kills the cancer cells but does not harm normal cells.

Another area generating excitement involves the potential use of lasers to separate improperly joined blood vessels and to remove plaque from coronary arteries. With the aid of endoscopes, surgeons can locate fatty deposits that clog the heart's arteries and cause atherosclerosis. Surgeons believe that heat from a carbon dioxide laser will vaporize the obstructions. Considerable experimental work already has been done, and clinical trials involving patients with both coronary and peripheral artery disease are now under way.

Lasers are already being used to break up gallstones. Based on current research, future applications of lasers may include identifying infectious bacteria and viruses and analyzing tissue damage in burn victims. When researchers aim a polarized laser beam at a material, *e.g.*, a human tissue or a food suspected of containing microbes, the organisms reveal their identity by the way they scatter the light. *Salmonella* bacteria, for instance, produce a pattern of scatter different from that of a herpesvirus. Scientists have begun assembling a library of such light "fingerprints," which hospitals, food inspectors, and public health departments could utilize to identify sources of infection.

Other researchers have found that the amount of light reflected from burned skin depends on how much blood flows in the wounds. This, in turn, predicts which wounds will heal naturally and which wounds have capillaries so badly damaged that aggressive treatment must be applied.

Although laser technology is rapidly expanding and gaining wide acceptance in health care, the light that heals has its disadvantages. The equipment required is cumbersome and expensive, while in many cases the light is slower and less flexible than a scalpel or other surgical tools. Lasers also introduce additional risks; they may cause eye damage, burns, and explosions and have adverse effects on nearby healthy tissue. Some physicians complain that the technology is overused. On balance, however, lasers appear to have a "bright" future in medicine.

Stimulating normal body functions

Advances in other areas of technology, especially microelectronics, also are producing new devices that extend lives and reduce suffering. Fabrication techniques that allow thousands of transistors to be placed on fingernail-size chips of silicon have led to new generations of cardiac pacemakers programmed to adjust the heart rate to a person's activity level. Those who suffer episodes of excessively rapid heartbeat can be treated with a pacemaker that slows a runaway heart and restores its rhythm to a natural rate.

A recently developed pacemaker of another type keeps children with congenital hypoventilation syndrome alive. When the brain fails to signal the muscles of the diaphragm to move in the necessary way for normal breathing, the pacemaker substitutes electric signals to do the task.

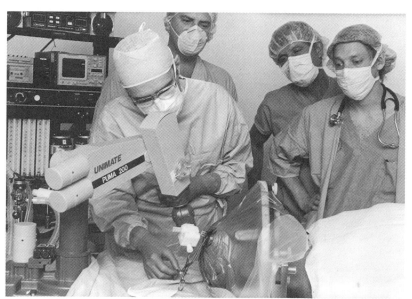

A computer-controlled robot arm assists a surgeon in taking a biopsy of a suspected brain tumor. The robot is able to determine precisely where to drill, at what angle to insert the surgical instrument, and how deep to probe during this delicate operation.

Memorial Medical Center of Long Beach

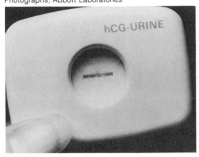 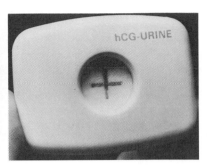

A simple test done at home can tell a woman if she is pregnant even before a missed menstrual period. A small amount of urine exposed to chemicals in a test kit causes a plus or minus sign to appear, indicating whether the pregnancy hormone human chorionic gonadotropin is present.

New body materials

Computer-age electronics are being combined with new types of materials to produce replacements for body parts destroyed by disease or injury. These include electronic ear implants, microcomputer-controlled arms and legs, metal and plastic bones, jaws, knees and other joints, and plastic hearts and blood vessels. If they find the right material, biomedical engineers and surgeons believe it will one day be possible to replace virtually every part of the body.

One of these new body materials is a biodegradable polymer used to stimulate the regrowth of severed nerves. Experiments performed at the Massachusetts Institute of Technology with the polymer have resulted in the regeneration of surgically cut sciatic nerves in rats. If this technology can be transferred to humans, the impact will be enormous in terms of restoring the function of damaged nerves.

The material is made from collagen fibers and a carbohydrate found in cartilage, both of which can be extracted from animals—the collagen from cowhide, the cartilage from sharks. It also has been used successfully to treat burn victims. Placed over the wound, it facilitates the regrowth of skin. The finding that both skin and nerve—two quite different tissues—can be guided toward regeneration by this polymer may be of potential significance in all fields of surgery. Researchers in the field have even speculated that this technique can be used to induce organs such as the liver and pancreas to regrow their lost tissue components in correct anatomical relationship.

Do it yourself

One of the hopes of applying technological innovations to health care is that it will mean lower costs. Diagnostic tests done at home, for instance, are less expensive than the same tests done in a hospital or physician's office. Monoclonal antibodies, produced by genetic engineering techniques, promise a significant increase in availability of such do-it-yourself tests. Monoclonal antibodies respond to proteins associated with specific conditions such as disease or pregnancy. Hormones released during pregnancy, for example, react with monoclonals to produce a color change in urine. Drug companies have taken advantage of this reaction and have marketed inexpensive pregnancy-test kits. Other kits based on this technology are being developed for the detection of gonorrhea bacteria and the genital herpesvirus.

Also under development are small, disposable analytical instruments based on the same microelectronic technology as pocket calculators and implantable pacemakers. One firm plans to introduce kits for diagnosing urinary tract infections and strep throat and for pinpointing the exact time of ovulation.

Do-it-yourself tests based on simpler chemical technology already are widely available. Diabetics can monitor their blood sugar with such kits. Another popular product offers a test for cancer of the colon and rectum, ulcers, hemorrhoids, diverticulosis, and polyps. The latter has been heavily advertised since surgeons removed a cancerous tumor from the colon of Pres. Ronald Reagan in July 1985. Some physicians criticize the test, however, because it does not always detect occult blood in a stool, the symptom that indicates something is wrong. Experts express concern that false readings occur as much as 20 to 30% of the time. This could lead to false optimism and harmful delays in seeking medical attention.

On the positive side, home diagnostic kits make people more aware of their physical condition and more likely to seek professional help. For example, pregnancy tests, say some obstetricians, cause more women to see an obstetrician early for evaluation of the pregnancy and, therefore, to receive better prenatal care.

The number of ways that technology is enabling patients to take more responsibility for their own health increases almost daily. Obviously this is a positive development. However, the fact that patients can increasingly self-diagnose, self-monitor, and self-treat is not an entirely welcome trend. Indeed, technology at best can improve and assist health care. It will not replace professional care. As William H. Foege, special assistant for policy development for the U.S. Centers for Disease Control, has said: "In coming decades the most important determinants of health and longevity will be personal choices made by each individual. This is both frightening and exciting."

—*William J. Cromie*

Type A Behavior
by Redford B. Williams, Jr., M.D.

Type A behavior . . . is associated with an increased risk of clinically apparent coronary heart disease in employed, middle-aged U.S. citizens.
—National Heart, Lung, and Blood Institute's Review Panel on Coronary-Prone Behavior, 1981

Failure to find an association between Type A behavior and risk of coronary heart disease in this sample raises questions regarding the robustness of the Type A hypothesis in its present form.
—R.B. Shekelle et al., American Journal of Epidemiology, vol. 122, p. 569, 1985

Although the exact details have been long forgotten, sometime in the mid-1950s a worker reupholstering the chairs in the waiting room of two San Francisco cardiologists made an interesting observation: the fabric was worn only on the front edges of the chairs. Stimulated by that chance observation, the two physicians, Meyer Friedman and Ray Rosenman, began to pay closer attention to the behavior of their coronary patients. They soon realized that with only rare exceptions these patients had a number of characteristics in common. They were always in a hurry; having to stand in lines tied them in knots. They were very ambitious and involved in their jobs; taking work home was part of their regular routine. And, finally, they displayed high levels of "free-floating" hostility; if the line moved too slowly, they became angry and did not hesitate to express their irritation to those around them.

These observations were intriguing, but they certainly did not prove that this pattern of behavior—which Friedman and Rosenman soon began to call "Type A"—actually caused coronary disease. It could just as easily have been argued that the presence of coronary disease led to the behavior pattern. Realizing this, Freidman and Rosenman mounted a long-term study of healthy middle-aged men—the Western Collaborative Group Study, or WCGS—to determine whether the presence of Type A behavior identified men who had higher than average risk of suffering a heart attack or dying from coronary disease. A similar approach had been used in the well-known Framingham study to show that cigarette smoking, high levels of cholesterol in the blood, and high blood pressure are risk factors for coronary heart disease. (Most research on both physical and psychological risk factors for coronary disease has focused on men, since they are far more likely than women to develop this illness in midlife; hence, the emphasis on male subjects in

this report. It should be noted, however, that all the known risk factors predict increased risk of coronary disease in women, as well.)

When the results of the WCGS were in, after the men had been followed for 8½ years, it was clear that Type A behavior, like the other already identified coronary risk factors, predicted a higher risk of developing the disease. Independently of the other risk factors, those men who were Type A at the start of the study were twice as likely as the Type B men (i.e., those who did not display Type A behavior) to suffer a heart attack, die of coronary disease, or develop angina pectoris (chest pain caused by insufficient blood flow to the heart muscle). With the publication of Friedman and Rosenman's book, Type A Behavior and Your Heart, which has now sold well over 500,000 copies, "Type A" became a part of the American vocabulary. "Don't be so Type A!" one is likely to say to someone who is rushing about frantically, trying to finish too many projects in too little time, and lashing out at all who get in the way.

Type A behavior became an "official" coronary risk factor when a review panel convened by the U.S. National Heart, Lung, and Blood Institute in 1981 reached the conclusion quoted at the beginning of this report. Other studies provided additional support for the Type A hypothesis. Researchers at Boston University, Columbia University, New York City, and Duke University, Durham, N.C., assessed Type A behavior in patients undergoing coronary angiography—an X-ray procedure used to determine the extent of blockage by arteriosclerotic plaque of the coronary arteries, which supply blood to the heart—and found the Type A patients to have more severe coronary blockage than their Type B counterparts. Not only did Type A people appear to be at greater risk of suffering coronary "events"; they also appeared to develop the underlying pathological lesion of coronary disease, the arteriosclerotic plaque, at a faster rate than Type B's.

Contradictory findings

It was at this point that flaws began to appear in the logic of the Type A hypothesis. Not all studies after the first three found more severe coronary artery blockages in Type A patients. In fact, of 11 studies of Type A behavior conducted since 1978 in patients undergoing coronary angiography, 7 have failed to confirm the initial observation of increased arteriosclerosis in Type A's.

Even more troubling were the results of the large-scale Multiple Risk Factor Intervention Trial (MRFIT) study, sponsored by the National Heart, Lung, and Blood Institute. In this study more than 12,000 men who had high blood cholesterol levels, were smokers, and had elevated blood pressure were enrolled in programs designed to reduce the levels of all three risk factors. Based on the growing evidence that Type A behavior is also a bona fide coronary risk factor, the degree of Type A behavior was determined in all of the MRFIT subjects by means of a written questionnaire, the Jenkins Activity Survey (JAS). In addition, more than 3,000 men underwent evaluation by means of a structured interview technique, in which direct observations were made of such Type A characteristics as rapid, explosive speech, emphatic gestures, and frequent interruptions of the interviewer. After more than seven years of follow-up, whether the subjects were assessed by the JAS or the structured interview, the identification of Type A behavior did not predict which of them would develop coronary disease. This failure to confirm the results of the WCGS in an even larger study of similar design led to the conclusion cited above in the second quotation—that the Type A hypothesis might not be as sound as had been thought.

The negative evidence continued to mount. In 1984 an article in the *New England Journal of Medicine* reported that, over several years of follow-up, Type A heart attack victims were no more likely than Type B patients to suffer a second heart attack. In June 1985 an editorial in the same journal went so far as to conclude that the notion that "states of mind" can lead to disease is "largely folklore." These negative evaluations of the Type A hypothesis were widely quoted in the news media, and it is not surprising that many people are now wondering what to believe. First we hear that Type A's are twice as likely as Type B's to suffer a heart attack; then we hear that such statements are no more than folklore. Where does the truth lie?

Hostility: harmful to health?

As originally defined by Freidman and Rosenman, Type A behavior consisted of three components: time urgency ("hurry sickness"), ambitious striving for achievement, and "free-floating" hostility. In all of the research described thus far regarding Type A and coronary heart disease, no distinction was made among these three aspects—that is, all three had to be present before a person could be classified as Type A. In actual practice, research has shown that when the structured interview assessment is used to evaluate subjects, a person who talks fast and interrupts frequently will almost always be called Type A, even if the hostility and ambition components are not prominent aspects of his behavior. The other assessment technique, the

"Is there a place around here where we can get a bite to eat while we're waiting?"

JAS, contains no questions that directly tap the hostility component.

If one of the Type A components is more harmful, or "toxic," than the others and if the studies that fail to find a link between Type A behavior and coronary disease do not adequately assess this component, then one interpretation of the negative studies would be that the Type A hypothesis needs to be refined. That is, not all aspects of Type A behavior are equally bad for the heart; in fact, some may even be beneficial. If a study does not measure the bad aspect, or aspects, reliably and, especially, if the Type A assessment is based too much on characteristics that are not toxic, then it might be evident why some studies fail to support the Type A hypothesis.

There is ample precedent for such a sequence of events. For example, 20 years ago all that was known about cholesterol was that the higher an individual's blood cholesterol level, the greater his or her risk of developing coronary artery disease. Subsequently, biochemists identified different kinds of cholesterol compounds in the blood, high-density lipoproteins (HDL) and low-density lipoproteins (LDL). LDL cholesterol is considered "bad" cholesterol, in that the higher the level of LDL in the blood, the greater the risk of developing coronary disease, and, conversely, HDL is "good" cholesterol, in that higher blood levels of HDL appear to confer protection against development of coronary disease. Consequently, the original cholesterol hypothesis has been modfied; it is now accepted that the higher the ratio of LDL to HDL, the greater the risk of coronary disease.

Could it be that as researchers "fractionate" Type A behavior into its constituent parts and evaluate the contribution of each to coronary risk, a similar modification of the Type A hypothesis will occur? The evidence now available indicates that this is precisely what is happening.

The first clue came when tape-recorded interviews from the WCGS were reanalyzed to identify levels of

Of all of the personal attributes associated with Type A behavior, hostility has proved to be most closely correlated with the severity of coronary heart disease.

the three aspects of Type A behavior in those subjects who had developed coronary disease and in a control group, men who were similar with respect to other risk factors but had remained free of coronary disease. Rather than characterizing the men only as either Type A or Type B, researchers assigned scores based on observations of a wide gamut of Type A characteristics. They found that the most consistent factor in differentiating those who suffered a coronary event from those who did not was "potential for hostility."

Subsequent to this finding, researchers at Duke University, employing the widely used personality test known as the Minnesota Multiphasic Personality Inventory, or MMPI, found that scores measuring hostility correlated with the severity of arteriosclerotic blockages in patients undergoing coronary angiography. The higher the hostility (Ho) score, the more severe the blockages. Although Type A behavior in general was also associated with more severe coronary blockage, when statistical adjustment was made for the relationship between Ho scores and severity of blockage, the relationship of Type A behavior to coronary blockage became much weaker. This finding suggested that some of the relationship between Type A behavior and coronary arteriosclerosis might be due to high levels of hostility among Type A patients. A later study of patients undergoing coronary angiography at Duke strengthened this conclusion. The investigators carefully assessed tape-recorded structured interviews,

evaluating and scoring several components of Type A behavior. Again, "potential for hostility" was found to correlate strongly with severity of coronary blockage. Even more strongly than in the earlier investigation using the Ho scale, this study indicated that any relation of Type A behavior to severity of arteriosclerosis is due to the high levels of hostility that are often present in Type A's.

Another interesting aspect of this study concerned the relation of Type A speech characteristics to severity of arteriosclerosis. When evaluated alone, "explosive" speech was weakly but positively associated with more severe disease. When statistical adjustment was made for the relation of potential for hostility to disease severity, explosive speech was negatively, and significantly, associated with disease severity. In other words, when the increased incidence of arteriosclerosis among patients with high potential for hostility was taken into account, high levels of explosive speech were found associated with *less severe* arteriosclerosis. Similar reanalysis of structured interviews from a study of angiographic patients conducted earlier at Boston's Massachusetts General Hospital confirmed the Duke findings.

These conclusions confirm the suspicion that not all aspects of Type A behavior are equally related to coronary arteriosclerosis. In fact, it now appears that only one, the hostility component, is related to disease severity; and when the relation of hostility to disease is taken into account, the total Type A score is not related to disease. Furthermore, when the hostility-disease relationship is taken into account, Type A speech characteristics appear negatively related to disease severity. These findings prompted researchers to ask this question: Could it be that hostility is analogous to the "bad," or LDL, cholesterol and Type A speech, particularly when motivated by enthusiasm rather than hostility, is analogous to the "good," or HDL, cholesterol?

If so, then the failure of Type A behavior to predict coronary events in the MRFIT study might stem from too much weight's having been given to speech characteristics in the study's structured interview assessments. Reanalyses of the MRFIT interviews now in progress will test this hypothesis. If potential for hostility is positively related to the occurrence of coronary events, this finding would lend additional support to the theory that the hostility component is the toxic aspect of Type A behavior.

Thus far, however, most of the evidence favoring hostility's toxic role has been drawn from patients who already are suspected of having coronary disease. As with Friedman and Rosenman's original observations of high incidence of Type A behavior in coronary patients, the observed association between hostility and more severe coronary artery disease could be simply a reflection of increased hostility as an *effect*, rather than

Redford Williams *et al.*, Duke University, North Carolina

- Do you always feel anxious to get going and finish whatever you have to do?

- What irritates you most about your job or the people you work with?

- Do you think you have as much faith in doctors as your parents probably did?

- When you get angry or upset, do the people around you know it? How do you show it?

On the basis of the structured interview, a set of questions designed to bring out coronary-prone behavior, researchers evaluated test subjects and assigned scores for specific components of Type A behavior. Several of the questions tap into the subject's latent hostility, believed to be a strong predictor of heart disease.

a cause, of coronary arteriosclerosis. To strengthen the case for a causal role for hostility, a long-range study is needed of a population that, initially, shows no sign of the disease in question. Such studies are notoriously expensive (costs of the MRFIT study are estimated to be close to $100 million). Since the Ho scale is part of the MMPI, which has been in wide use for several decades, it has been possible to use previously obtained hostility data to determine whether Ho scores are accurate predictions of coronary events and other health problems.

One such study involved nearly 2,000 middle-aged male employees of a Midwestern company who completed the MMPI as part of a research project 25 years ago. When their health status was evaluated over the ensuing years, it was found that those who had high Ho scores were more likely to have developed coronary disease. Of perhaps equal interest, men who had high Ho scores 25 years ago were 1.5 times more likely to have died from *any* cause. Statistical analyses showed that the prediction of coronary disease and overall mortality by Ho scores was not due to other risk factors, such as smoking, high blood pressure, or high blood cholesterol levels. Another study followed 255 middle-aged male physicians who had completed the MMPI while in medical school (at an average age of 25). Those with higher Ho scores were 4 to 5 times more likely to develop coronary disease and also experienced higher mortality rates from all causes.

From psychology to biology

While the studies cited above enabled researchers to arrive at some important conclusions, at the same time, they raised further questions about the nature of personality traits and their mechanism of influence on the body. What exactly is the psychological characteristic that is measured by the Ho scale? How does it lead to coronary heart disease?

Just as earlier studies attempted to refine the Type A hypothesis, more recent research has sought to refine the understanding of hostility and to identify, if possible, aspects of behavior that, taken together, constitute hostility. Detailed studies of the Ho scale and studies of the potential for hostility, as assessed in the structured interview, suggest that the critical harmful elements of hostility are related to a cynical mistrust of others. People who score high on the Ho scale have the attitude that most other people are basically selfish and inconsiderate and cannot be depended upon to be kind. This attitude leads naturally to increased irritation toward others and, in fact, people who score high on the Ho scale report that they experience anger more frequently than do the low

John Harding

Teaching employees to relax, laugh, and take life a little less seriously is one of the approaches companies are taking to help their workers reduce their risk of heart disease.

scorers. Very recent studies by researchers at Duke and at the University of Maryland at Baltimore suggest that the most severe coronary arteriosclerosis occurs among individuals who harbor both basic mistrust and low regard of others and readily express their contemptuous feelings.

At this time scientists can only speculate about how these particular psychological characteristics might, over time, be translated into the development of severe coronary arteriosclerosis. In the first place, the basic biologic mechanisms whereby arteriosclerosis begins and progresses are not fully understood. The most widely accepted current theory holds that injury to the cellular layer lining the inner wall of arteries leads to the accumulation of cholesterol within the arterial wall; subsequently other factors, possibly derived from platelets that migrate to the site of injury, cause a proliferation of the smooth muscle cells of the arterial wall. Over time, it is believed, the progressive cholesterol accumulation and smooth muscle proliferation impinge upon the arterial passage, reducing the amount of blood flow to the heart muscle and impairing its ability to function. The pain of angina occurs when the blood supply does not meet the heart muscle's need for increased oxygen, as during vigorous exercise. When the discrepancy between the oxygen needs and blood supply exceeds a critical point, a portion of the heart muscle dies—*i.e.*, a heart attack, or myocardial infarction, occurs.

To the extent that the injury hypothesis outlined here is correct, researchers must seek biologic correlates of cynical mistrust and contempt that would contribute to arterial injury. Some promising clues are just beginning to emerge. It has been known for some time that a person's blood pressure rises whenever he or she talks to another person. This is true even of routine, nonthreatening everyday conversation. Now more recent studies show that, in healthy individuals, those who score high in cynical mistrust and contempt respond to interpersonal challenge with larger blood pressure elevations than people who score low on these personality traits. Furthermore, when Type A's are asked to perform challenging mental tasks, they show larger increases in blood levels of such stress-associated hormones as adrenaline and cortisol. In still other studies, people with high levels of cynical mistrust and contempt show more pronounced changes in heart muscle functions when they are given an adrenaline-like drug.

The various kinds of exaggerated biologic reaction, or hyperresponsivity, exhibited by the more hostile, cynical, contemptuous Type A individuals are quite plausible as factors in the promotion of arterial injury, which, in turn, could lead to the initiation and progression of arteriosclerotic lesions. Indeed, studies in animals have already demonstrated that high levels of some of the hormones found to be elevated in the human studies of hostility and Type A behavior are capable of accelerating the development of arteriosclerosis.

Future directions

The research described above, much of it very recent, leads to the conclusion that the original Type A hypothesis was not incorrect; rather, it was, like many hypotheses in science, incomplete—in need of refinement. The nature of that refinement will likely involve still further investigation focusing on the nature of hostility. At present the identification in some Type A's of cynical mistrust combined with readiness to express contempt seems to be a significant step in narrowing the definition of "toxic" behavior. Further research, especially of a prospective sort (*i.e.*, studying a population presumed healthy at the outset) will be necessary to confirm the suspicion of a link between cynicism, contempt, and coronary disease. Equally important will be research aimed at increasing the scientific understanding of the biologic bases and consequences of these behaviors.

One important question remains: What effect will this research have on the lives of those at risk of heart disease? This continues to be the subject of considerable debate. What advice, then, to the man who, mired in traffic, pounds his fists on the dashboard, perspires till drenched, and pours out his contempt for the world on his horn? Should he move to the country? Hire a hypnotist? Get a chauffeur?

As the Type A hypothesis was being tested over the years, some authorities came to the conclusion that the modification of Type A behavior—through changes in habits and education in stress management—was an essential step in reducing the likelihood of heart attack in people predisposed to coronary disease. Cardiologist Meyer Friedman, a self-avowed "reformed" Type A, now listens to music on his car's tape deck when he is stuck in a traffic jam.

But are intervention programs on a mass scale successful in modifying people's behavior? In terms of disease prevention, do they justify the time and money they require? Do they represent the most effective—and efficient—approach to the problem? Many experts in the field say no to all of these questions. They point to new genetic testing that may prove to be the quickest, cheapest, and most definitive method of determining who is at risk of developing coronary disease. They point to new drug therapy that reduces the levels of harmful, stress-induced chemicals in the blood. And they point to the fact that programs directed at changing behavior have not been spectacularly effective—for example, in seven years only 40% of the MRFIT subjects in the active intervention group gave up smoking. It remains to be seen whether these radically different approaches will be reconciled and how the fruits of this research will be translated into new preventive strategies.

Heart and Blood Vessels

Substantial advances in biomedical research in the years since World War II have changed medical practice profoundly; this change has been particularly marked in the medical specialty cardiology. The cardiologist armed only with stethoscope, electrocardiogram, and simple chest X-ray in the late 1940s faced considerable diagnostic uncertainty and treated patients with a limited number of marginally effective drugs. Today cardiologists can draw on an enormous array of diagnostic techniques, many developed only in this decade, and choose from a number of very effective therapeutic maneuvers.

One of the more exciting recent diagnostic advances in cardiology is nuclear magnetic resonance (NMR) imaging and spectroscopy. This emerging technology is beginning to provide images of detailed cardiac structure without costly and uncomfortable catheterization. NMR, which yields sharp images of cardiac anatomic structures without X-ray radiation, will soon provide accurate estimates of the intracellular concentrations of various chemical substances. Such information will undoubtedly provide critically important metabolic information that will facilitate the development of more effective therapeutic interventions.

Recent therapeutic advances in cardiology include more effective drugs for the treatment of angina, heart failure, and heart attack victims; the use of inflatable balloons affixed to catheters to dilate arterial and valvular narrowings; the application of mechanical hearts to permit more time to identify appropriate donors for patients requiring heart transplantation; and the discovery and use of more effective immunosuppressive drugs to prevent graft rejection in heart transplant recipients.

But perhaps the most far-reaching advance in cardiology in recent years has occurred in the treatment of the patient suffering an acute myocardial infarction (heart attack), one of the very serious complications of coronary artery disease. The following discussion details this important development.

Coronary artery disease is a modern epidemic that is most prevalent in industrialized countries of North America and Europe. Often developing silently over a period measured in decades, this disorder leads either to angina pectoris, characterized by recurrent chest discomfort usually caused by exertion and relieved by rest; to myocardial infarction (heart attack), manifest as severe, prolonged chest pain coupled with loss of heart muscle; or to the most feared manifestation, sudden death.

Coronary disease claims over 500,000 lives each year in the United States, with approximately 300,000 due to sudden death. There are an estimated 800,000 patients admitted to hospitals with heart attacks each year in the U.S. Perhaps as many as six million patients have diagnosed coronary artery disease, and a very

large number of middle-aged adults are developing the disease but have not as yet experienced symptoms. These statistics and similar attack rates in other developed countries have led to intense investigative activity designed to develop effective diagnostic, therapeutic, and preventive strategies.

Atherosclerosis, a degenerative disease of large and medium-sized arteries, is the underlying cause of this epidemic. This disorder thickens the lining of arteries, limiting and ultimately depriving heart muscle and various other organs and tissues of nutrient-carrying blood flow. In susceptible individuals and populations, coronary atherosclerosis begins in early adulthood, develops progressively through middle age, and becomes sufficiently far advanced to cause symptoms, angina, heart attack, and sudden death in the fifth and sixth decades of life. The profile of the coronary-prone individual includes advancing age, male sex, cigarette smoking, elevated blood cholesterol, and elevated blood pressure.

It is likely that the coronary disease epidemic will ultimately be quelled by the application of effective preventive measures predicated upon clear understanding of etiology. Until this is achieved, however, physicians must deal with the clinical sequelae of this disease. In this regard a revolution has occurred in the last decade in the treatment of one of these sequelae—the acute heart attack.

Acute myocardial infarction

Three major coronary arteries and their branches supply the heart muscle with nutrients and oxygen and remove metabolic wastes. Closure of a major coronary artery or one of its branches leads to a sequence of progressively more disrupted function in the portion of heart muscle supplied, which ultimately results in

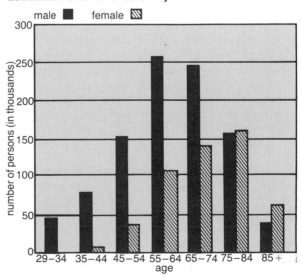

Estimated incidence of coronary attacks

Source: Framingham Heart Study

heart muscle death if occlusion is sustained. In the experimental animal, coronary closure for less than 20 minutes results in no muscle death, whereas occlusion for six or more hours results in necrosis, or death, of virtually all dependent heart muscle. The precise relationship between duration of coronary artery occlusion and death of jeopardized heart muscle is less well known in human heart attack patients, but it is probably quite similar. Thus, there is a window of opportunity for up to six hours after onset of heart attack during which restoration of coronary blood flow can interrupt the process of progressive cell death.

The amount of heart muscle lost during a heart attack is inversely related to the probability of survival, both short term and long term; the larger the heart attack, the worse the outlook. A large amount of heart muscle loss not only decreases the probability of survival but also compromises quality of life. Large heart attacks leave patients with insufficient heart muscle to carry out even routine activities without breathlessness and/or fatigue. Thus, limitation of the amount of heart muscle lost during heart attacks has important practical implications, potentially increasing survival and improving the quality of life.

Heart attack diagnosis and therapy: the past

In the 19th century closure of an atherosclerotic coronary artery by clot (thrombus) was recognized and reported by pathologists at postmortem examination; physicians believed that coronary closure invariably resulted in instantaneous death. In the early years of the 20th century, the symptoms of heart attack were correctly ascribed to coronary thrombosis, and physicians recognized that some patients could not only survive the event but subsequently live fully productive lives. Clear definition of symptoms, findings on physical examination, description of characteristic electrocardiographic alterations, and definition of confirmatory blood test findings had put the diagnosis of myocardial infarction on a clear footing by the late 1950s.

Heart attack victims commonly experience severe central chest pain, which may radiate to neck, arms, and back, with associated nausea, vomiting, sweating, and shortness of breath. An electrocardiogram taken during the next several hours commonly reveals a characteristic change in the electrical activity of the heart. Over the next 12 to 24 hours, blood levels of enzymes released by dying heart muscle confirm the presence of heart muscle death (myocardial infarction).

Conventional immediate treatment of heart attack victims included relief of pain by administration of narcotics, bed rest, and careful monitoring of heart rhythm, vital signs, and physical findings in order to diagnose expeditiously and manage complications such as abnormal heart rhythm, heart failure, and shock. Therapy aimed at heart muscle salvage by pharmacological manipulation of heart muscle oxygen supply or demand was, until recently, limited to animal experimentation and to clinical research efforts.

Thrombolytic therapy: new strategy

Atherosclerotic narrowing of coronary arteries is thought to proceed at a glacial rate, which is measured in years or decades. However, the conversion of a coronary artery that is partially narrowed by decades of slow disease progression to a totally occluded artery can occur precipitously—over seconds to minutes. This precipitous development of total coronary occlusion converts a stable clinical situation, in which a patient may have experienced no symptoms or only mild symptoms, into one of imminent danger that characterizes the acute heart attack. It is this distinct, sudden process that is now a focus of intense investigation.

Coronary arteriography has been used to define the extent and severity of coronary artery narrowing since the mid-1960s. During this diagnostic procedure a thin, flexible tube called a catheter is inserted into the artery at the groin or elbow and advanced to the aorta at a point where the catheter tip lies in the origin of one of the coronary arteries. Injection of radiopaque dye permits X-ray films to be made of the artery lumen, which allow clear visualization of narrowing or closure. Initially this procedure was not applied to patients in the early hours of a heart attack except under exceptional circumstances for fear of causing complications. In the late 1970s definition of coronary artery anatomy by means of coronary arteriography in heart attack victims, followed by direct injection of clot-dissolving drugs such as streptokinase or urokinase, conclusively demonstrated that coronary thrombus, or clot, superimposed on more chronic atherosclerotic coronary narrowing, was often the direct, precipitating cause of the heart attack. Approximately 80% of heart attack victims have total coronary closure, and as many as 70–80% of these occluded vessels open after direct instillation of clot-dissolving drugs. These findings began the current revolution in the therapy of heart attack victims.

Clotting and clot-dissolving mechanisms constitute two of the normal, fundamental processes by which injured tissue is repaired. These two mechanisms exist in delicate balance, their interaction leading to a modulated response of clot formation and clot dissolution during the healing phase of blood vessel injury. Exposure of blood to tissue other than the delicate lining of blood vessels, as occurs during blood vessel injury, elicits the formation of clot, which prevents uncontrolled hemorrhage following injury. Another mechanism opposes the clotting process, the purpose of which is to limit the extent of clotting. If clotting mechanisms were to exist unopposed, excessive clot development might close the vessel and lead to injury caused by the termination of blood flow. Thus, an

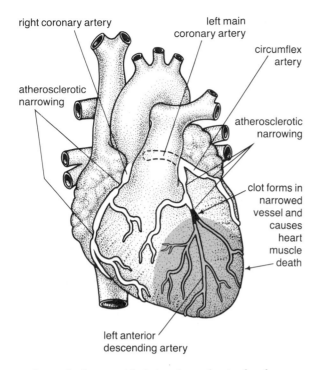

right coronary artery

left main coronary artery

circumflex artery

atherosclerotic narrowing

atherosclerotic narrowing

clot forms in narrowed vessel and causes heart muscle death

left anterior descending artery

When a clot forms suddenly in a heart that is already compromised by narrowed coronary arteries, sudden death is common. A promising new therapy uses clot-dissolving drugs during acute myocardial infarction to prevent death.

exquisitely balanced control system exists to guide the physiological response to blood vessel injury between the twin risks of uncontrolled hemorrhage and blood vessel closure because of uncontrolled clotting.

Both clotting and clot-dissolving processes involve an enormously complex series of usually inactive substances. These are converted to active enzymes by various stimuli. The end result of the clotting process is formation of thrombin, an enzyme that converts fibrinogen, a soluble protein, into fibrin, the insoluble matrix of a clot. The final step in the lytic (clot-dissolution) process is the formation of plasmin, which dissolves fibrin. The key to the normal function of both processes is the limitation of both end products, thrombin and plasmin, to the local area of vessel injury and clot formation. Release of thrombin and plasmin into the general circulation in more than minute amounts can result in catastrophic clot formation, bleeding, or both.

Why a coronary clot develops at a particular time and location, causing acute coronary occlusion and myocardial infarction, is unclear. It is possible that some type of injury develops in vessels predisposed to damage because of atherosclerotic disease, with consequent exposure of clot-inducing material to the bloodstream, resulting in clot formation and abrupt coronary closure. Whatever the precise precipitating cause, relief of coronary artery closure is the immediate treatment goal.

In patients suffering from acute myocardial infarction due to recent clot formation, the normal processes that generate plasmin at the clot surface to restore blood flow by dissolving the fibrin matrix are inadequate. To bolster the body's own antithrombin mechanisms, two standard thrombolytic drugs, streptokinase and urokinase, have been injected directly into the occluded coronary artery. Direct instillation of clot-dissolving drugs by cardiac catheterization as just described imposes a substantial delay in the attainment of coronary reperfusion. Emergency coronary arteriography requires the immediate availability of a highly trained team. Under the most optimal circumstances, arteriography adds a one- to two-hour delay to the initiation of clot-dissolving therapy. During this delay substantial amounts of heart muscle may be lost. Administration of clot-dissolving drugs by vein is more rapid and less costly, but it loses the advantage of regional treatment and may lead to a generalized perturbation of the normal clotting processes. Thus, these drugs activate plasmin not only in the vicinity of the clot but also in the general circulation. An additional problem with intravenous administration of streptokinase or urokinase in patients with heart attack is that very large doses must be used, resulting in reperfusion of only 35–40% of blocked coronary arteries, a success rate that is roughly one-half of that observed when the drugs are given directly into the blocked coronary artery. Furthermore, these large doses magnify the risk of bleeding.

A new generation of drugs, which tend to activate plasmin only on the surface of a clot, includes tissue plasminogen activator (t-PA), prourokinase, and a plasminogen-streptokinase derivative. One of these agents (rt-PA), produced by recombinant DNA technique, has been tested against streptokinase to determine which agent is the more effective in dissolving coronary clots. The new agent appears to be twice as effective, probably because it is chemically drawn to clots. It also results in much less perturbation of the clotting system. This protein is present in the normal circulation in minute amounts. Because it can be synthesized by recombinant DNA technology, it can now be produced in large amounts.

As a result of intense investigative effort in multiple clinical trials in North America and Europe carried out over the last 15 years, it is now clear that intravenous administration of the clot-dissolving drugs, streptokinase or urokinase, reduces in-hospital mortality of heart attack victims. The magnitude of the reduction is approximately 20% and is inversely related to the length of interval between onset of heart attack symptoms and drug administration. The earlier the clot-dissolving drug is given after onset of heart attack, the larger the reduction in hospital mortality. One report notes a 50% reduction in mortality in those patients treated within one hour after onset. This reduction in mortality is achieved with a modest risk of bleeding. The effect of the newer generation of clot-specific drugs on mortality is not yet clear but, given higher coronary clot-dissolving activity, the effect is likely to be more pronounced.

Heart attack treatment: the future

There are both research imperatives and practical implications deriving from the demonstrated effectiveness of intravenously administered clot-dissolving drugs in reducing in-hospital mortality. The new generation of potentially more effective and less toxic clot-dissolving drugs is likely to be approved for general practice soon and will probably result in substantial heart muscle salvage. However, administration of effective clot-dissolving drugs as soon as possible after the onset of pain will require changes in current practice, including provision for immediate electrocardiographic confirmation of diagnosis in patients with symptoms suggestive of heart attack and provision of a means whereby lytic therapy can be initiated without delay. Another barrier to early treatment that must be hurdled is the need to inform potential heart attack victims of the importance of seeking immediate treatment after the onset of suggestive symptoms.

A variety of refinements to thrombolytic therapy for heart attack victims are also being tested, including drugs that may reduce the shock of sudden restoration of coronary blood flow and drugs that may prolong the time during which heart muscle salvage is possible, as well as a variety of medications and surgical maneuvers designed to keep a reopened artery patent.

A major advance has occurred in the therapy for heart attack victims. Properly applied and with refinements currently being tested, it may reduce mortality by as much as 50% and improve long-term outlook of both survival and quality of life. A heart attack is a true medical emergency. If early diagnosis and treatment with thrombolytic drugs followed by appropriate additional therapy are carried out, it seems likely that mortality and morbidity will be substantially reduced in the enormous number of patients who develop heart attack each year.

—*Eugene R. Passamani, M.D.,*
and Stephen E. Epstein, M.D.

Infectious Diseases

The major health problems of the world correlate closely with the state of global development. Although certain illnesses are thought to be characteristic of particular geographic regions, such as those of the tropics, these disease patterns are being redefined according to the state of development of the region. As development occurs, the major infectious illnesses of the region are the first to be reduced in importance; in this way there is a gradual transition from diseases of infectious origin to degenerative diseases and diseases of aging. In general terms the major illnesses of the less developed world are nutritional and infectious, the latter group including diarrheal, respiratory, and parasitic diseases, such as malaria and schistosomiasis. By contrast, the major diseases of the developed world, which includes the United States, Canada, Western Europe, Australia, and Japan, are cardiovascular diseases, cancer, and diseases due to toxic exposures such as those secondary to smoking. Countries in the development stage must of necessity pass through a period of transition in which both categories of diseases will be of major importance until the infectious diseases are brought under control.

The less developed world's infectious health problems today are diseases that developed countries have been rid of for 100 years or more and that, therefore, are of only historic interest to the latter. It is now possible to speed up the process of disease control so that it need not take another century to bring infectious diseases under control in the rest of the world. Technology that is now available but was previously unknown makes it possible to effect dramatic changes at a rapid rate. This has already occurred in such countries as Costa Rica, Chile, Cuba, and China.

A major problem of world development is that of rapid population growth, which is intimately connected to the problems of infant survival and to the incidence of infectious diseases. Some have argued that if the major infectious diseases are controlled, children will no longer die at early ages, and populations in those regions will grow at fast and uncontrolled rates. Recent data have shown that just the opposite is more likely to occur; as children survive, fewer additional children are born into the family, and a significant decrease in population growth occurs, enabling standards of living to rise.

Toll on children

The primary victims of the infectious diseases of the less developed world are small children. About 10–15% of all children born in these areas will die before their first birthday, primarily from diarrheal and respiratory diseases. In some parts of the less developed world, as many as 25–30% of the children do not live to the age of five. This means that of the 15 million infants and children who die each year, almost 95% are in the less developed world. Associated with these infectious diseases are problems of undernutrition in children due partly to a lack of food availability but probably even more importantly to the fact that what they eat is not used adequately by the body.

Children who do survive the difficult first five years of life are then at high risk of becoming infected with many intestinal parasites that arise from lack of clean water and sanitation facilities and lack of adequate hygienic methods of preparing and keeping food. Their life expectancy, however, is not substantially affected, so that, depending on the geographic area in which they live, they will be at risk throughout their lives for developing the most serious parasitic diseases, such as malaria, schistosomiasis, filariasis, onchocerciasis, or other chronic bacterial diseases such as leprosy and tuberculosis—any of which seriously affect their quality of life. Unfortunately, access to medical care is difficult in these areas; immunizations are not readily available; and medicines and doctors' visits, if they are available, are costly.

Major health problems

Diarrhea. Diarrheal diseases of children are one of the two most important causes of death in the less developed world. These diseases, which are caused primarily by bacteria (*Escherichia coli, Shigella, Campylobacter*) and viruses (rotavirus), are spread primarily through fecal contamination of food and water and affect children under two years of age most severely—before they have developed protective immunity to the organisms through repeated exposure. Diarrheal disease is characterized by the passing of loose, watery stool in frequent bowel movements and, if severe, causes dehydration and death, as in the most dramatic of all diarrheal diseases, cholera.

Diarrhea also contributes significantly to the development of malnutrition, since during an epsiode of diarrhea, less food will be consumed and food will not be fully utilized by the body. In many parts of the less developed world, children will have from four to ten episodes of diarrhea each year during the first two to three years of life, and each episode may last for several days to a week or more. These repeated episodes of diarrhea thus may have a marked negative effect on normal growth and development of the child. Fortunately, new, simple techniques (described later) have been developed for the treatment and control of diarrheal diseases.

Respiratory diseases. Respiratory diseases—the other major cause of death of infants and children in the less developed world—include pneumonia, bronchitis, and a large category of upper respiratory illnesses, such as colds. They are caused by many infectious agents, primarily bacterial and viral, and are transmitted largely by the respiratory route—*i.e.,* through aerosolization of respiratory secretions. These illnesses are difficult to diagnose etiologically; therefore, it is often difficult to treat them adequately. Control of respiratory diseases thus will depend largely on improved diagnostic methods that spawn more precise treatment methods, as well as on prevention, with the development of vaccines.

Malaria. There are a large number of important parasitic diseases in the less developed world; malaria is one of the major ones. This disease is found throughout most of the less developed world, especially tropic

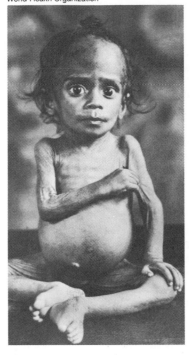

World Health Organization

The infant above is in a state of severe malnutrition resulting from acute diarrhea. In the less developed countries, diarrheal diseases are a major cause of death, particularly in children under two years of age.

regions of Africa, Central and South America, Asia, and Oceania, and it is responsible for an estimated 250 million cases and approximately one million deaths each year. Global attempts at eradication have been made but have ultimately failed to tame this relentless scourge. The disease is caused by the protozoan parasite *Plasmodium* and is transmitted almost exclusively by the bite of female anopheline mosquitoes. Medicines are available for both treatment and prevention, but these must be taken continuously in order to control the disease clinically. The best control measures have focused on decreasing the mosquito populations that transmit the disease, and in many parts of the world this has been done effectively. Unfortunately, however, mosquitoes have become resistant to many of the commonly used insecticides, thus rendering this strategy less effective. One apparently effective new method of controlling the mosquitoes involves introducing fish that consume mosquito larvae into the waters where the larvae grow. Vaccines currently being developed and tested in humans hold much promise for future malaria control. It will be some time, however, before they are ready to be applied in a widespread manner.

Schistosomiasis. This disease, which is prevalent in Africa, South America, the Middle East, the Philippines, and Southeast Asia, is caused by a number of different species of schistosome parasites (trematode worms), which are transmitted in the environment through a complicated life cycle that involves snails. Several hundred million people are estimated to be infected. The diseases produced are chronic and debilitating ones, caused by the adult worms living in pairs in the bloodstreams of the human hosts and producing eggs over a long period of time. Because freshwater snails are a part of the transmission path, the expanding use of agricultural irrigation ditches and canals, which readily support the growth of the snails, has made these diseases increasingly more common and widespread. Unfortunately, there is no adequate treatment of persons who have developed the chronic disease. Control must be thought of in terms of early treatment of infected persons and prevention of the spread of the parasites through water sanitation and control of snail breeding sites.

Onchocerciasis. Although not as widespread as many of the other parasitic diseases, this one is of unusual importance because it results in blindness; it is often called river blindness. The disease is caused by adult filarial worms that live in the tissues of infected persons and release microfilariae that migrate throughout the body, including to the eye. The disease is transmitted by the female biting blackfly, which lives primarily in fast-moving streams. In parts of the less developed world, particularly Africa and Central and South America, whole villages may be uniformly infected, and blindness becomes an inevitable part of growing old.

Recent control measures have been spectacularly effective. These measures involve the spraying of the breeding places of the flies with insecticides, which controls their populations and prevents the disease from spreading. Because of selective spraying, large agricultural lands previously uninhabitable owing to the presence of infection are now being returned to productivity, and children who previously had to anticipate certain adulthood blindness no longer face that threat.

Hepatitis B. While there are many viral diseases of special importance to the less developed world, two that are of particular concern today are hepatitis B and AIDS (acquired immune deficiency syndrome). The former virus causes both an acute and a chronic liver disease, which in some persons leads to the development of liver cancer. In parts of Africa this form of cancer, which is of infective etiology, is one of the most common malignant diseases. In these populations nearly everyone becomes infected relatively early in life; furthermore, a certain percentage of people— as high as 10% in China—may continue to carry the virus chronically after recovering from the acute infection. It is in these chronic carriers of the virus that chronic liver disease and liver cancer later develop. The virus is spread from mother to child during delivery and is also spread by exposure to blood products and through sexual contact. Recently an effective vaccine has become available for the prevention of the hepatitis B virus and the illness it causes. This vaccine holds promise for the prevention not only of the acute and chronic liver diseases but also of liver cancer.

AIDS. Although first described in patients in the United States, it is clear that this infection is also of great importance in certain areas of the less developed world, particularly in Africa. The disease is caused by a virus (LAV/HTLV-III), which seems to be a new virus, although its origin is not known. The virus is spread by sexual transmission primarily, unsterilized needles, and the administration of contaminated blood products. In the United States male homosexuals are the primary population group affected, but in parts of the less developed world the disease occurs throughout the heterosexual community. There is no effective treatment for AIDS, and the development of an effec-

Major efforts are under way to control malaria in the tropical areas of the world, where the disease is endemic. Malaria is caused by a protozoan parasite that is transmitted to humans by mosquitoes. Under development are new drugs, a malaria vaccine, and novel vector-control methods. Female anopheline mosquitoes, attracted to these human hosts, are captured for research.

WHO; photograph, R. da Silva

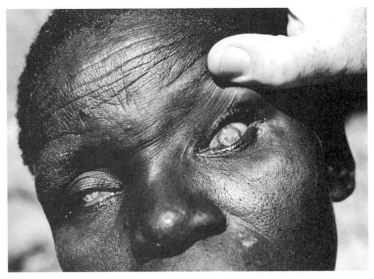

At left, a child leads an adult who has been blinded by the parasitic disease onchocerciasis. Because of a recent successful campaign to control the blackfly vector of the disease, children in endemic areas no longer harbor the filarial worms that cause severe damage to tissues throughout the body, including the eye (above).

tive vaccine is a major priority of research groups now. It is anticipated that such a vaccine will be of major importance in the ultimate control of the syndrome.

The potential of new technologies

Although some of the major infectious diseases in the less developed world are still far from being controlled, there have been effective technologies developed for managing many of them. Some simple, effective, and inexpensive technologies are today being widely implemented.

Oral rehydration therapy. During the past 20 years a simple technology has been developed for the treatment of diarrheal diseases of all types with the use of a simple solution of water, sugar, and salts (sodium chloride, trisodium citrate, and potassium chloride), which can be taken by mouth. Oral rehydration was originally developed for the treatment of cholera, the most severe of all diarrheal diseases, because of the high mortality rate of the disease that occurred when adequate supplies of intravenous fluids, which were crucial to the treatment of patients, were not available. Intravenous fluids, even when available, were expensive, sometimes were contaminated, and required trained medical personnel to administer.

Oral rehydration therapy, or ORT, as it is now commonly known, was based on the observation that the sugar glucose stimulated the small intestine to absorb the electrolyte sodium efficiently; when sodium was absorbed, then water was also absorbed. This mechanism—the stimulated absorption of sodium and water by the small intestine—was sufficient to replace the water and sodium lost in watery diarrheal stools. Therefore, intravenous fluids could be replaced by oral fluids with the same therapeutic effect.

Extensive studies in patients with cholera showed that only those patients with the most severe disease (those already in shock and in whom blood pressure was absent) required intravenous fluids, and then only for a short time to bring them out of shock. The rest of the patients could be treated adequately with ORT alone. This was a remarkable achievement, bringing a simple, inexpensive form of therapy to virtually all patients suffering from cholera and essentially eliminating deaths when used properly.

From these initial studies, ORT was found to be useful not only in cholera patients but in all other patients with diarrheal disease, due to any cause, whether bacterial, viral, or protozoal; furthermore, it could be successfully used in patients of all ages, ranging from newborns to elderly adults. ORT now forms the basis of the worldwide diarrheal-control program of the World Health Organization, whose aim is to make this fluid available to all children of the less developed world with diarrheal disease and thereby decrease deaths due to the disease, as well as the secondary nutritional effects of repeated episodes of diarrhea. At the present time, it is estimated that only about 25% of the world's children have access to ORT, in spite of its low cost and easy distribution.

Breast-feeding. Although breast-feeding is certainly not a new "technology," recent knowledge concerning the medical benefits afforded by it have demonstrated that it is a crucial factor both in the nutritional well-

*A Thai mother gives her child oral rehydration therapy—
a simple solution of water, sugar, and salts—which is a
mainstay of treatment for diarrheal diseases and represents a
remarkable achievement in the prevention of infant deaths.*

being of an infant and in the protection it affords against a variety of infectious diseases, particularly diarrheal diseases. It is therefore now promoted as a major health strategy in the improvement of the health of the children of the less developed countries.

Not only is mother's milk the ideal nutritional food for the infant, but it also contains anti-infective properties from the mother (such as antibodies and enzymes) that protect the child against infection. It is now recommended that infants be exclusively breast-fed for at least the first four or five months of life. Mothers are then encouraged to continue breast-feeding even after weaning foods are introduced into the diet, at least for the first year of life.

In the process of industrialization, breast-feeding has unfortunately often been neglected as an important health intervention. When adequate quantities of high-quality formulas of sanitary cow's milk and other substitutes are provided, along with proper funds, education, and instruction about their proper use, children's health should not be adversely affected. However, when this practice is attempted in areas of the world where mothers cannot afford to purchase adequate quantities of formula, or to provide sanitary means to mix and store the milk, children's health suffers dramatically. Not only may adequate quantities of necessary nutrients and calories be lacking, but contamination of the milk with infectious agents frequently occurs, thus putting the child at great risk for developing life-endangering diarrheal diseases.

Immunizations. In the less developed world few children routinely receive the vaccines that have long been available for the major childhood diseases. Therefore, currently a worldwide effort at immunization is being directed against diphtheria, tetanus, pertussis, poliomyelitis, measles, and tuberculosis.

Bringing these needed vaccinations to the children of the less developed world requires a complex organizational structure because the vaccines have to be given to the same child on several occasions, and the vaccines have to be stored at cold temperatures to keep them from deteriorating. An important goal thus is to develop a "cold chain"—an effective method that will protect the vaccines from the time they leave the manufacturer until they reach the child for whom they are intended, often in remote parts of the less developed countries that lack refrigeration.

Goals of health technology implementation

International agencies, including the World Health Organization, UNICEF, and the United States Agency for International Development, have developed goals for the implementation of health initiatives throughout the less developed world. The major one has been designated "Health for all by the year 2000," which suggests that basic primary health care will be available to all peoples of the world by that date. Other goals are to (1) assure that safe drinking water is available to 85% of the world's population within this decade, (2) provide the immunizations mentioned above to all the world's children by 1990, and (3) eradicate poliomyelitis in the Americas by 1990. All of these goals are clearly within reach with presently available technologies. The limitations are only those of resources (money and personnel) and the vigilance to carry out the necessary implementation.

Travelers' health risks

Persons who have grown up in a sanitized environment have not had the multiple exposures to infectious agents that are routine in the less developed world. Therefore, no immunity has developed in these persons, and when they travel to the less developed world, they are much like the young children of that area; *i.e.,* they are highly suseptible to the prevalent diseases, particularly those that are spread by contaminated food and water. It is important, therefore, that such travelers take certain precautions, which include being immunized against diseases for which vaccines are available and taking appropriate medications to both prevent and treat illnesses that might occur as the result of the travel. Specialized clinics recently have been developed in the United States that provide services for world travelers.

One such facility, the International Travel Clinic at the Johns Hopkins University, Baltimore, Md., provides services through a group of physicians and nurses who have special medical and research interests in diseases of the less developed world, and who have also lived and worked in these geographic areas. At the Johns Hopkins center information on the important communicable diseases of the different countries of the world is constantly updated with reports of recent epidemics and possible changes in vaccine requirements for tourists; this information comes primarily from the World Health Organization in Geneva and the Centers for Disease Control in Atlanta, Ga. The Johns Hopkins clinic and others like it offer travelers appropriate immunizations and medications based on their specific travel itineraries. For example, many countries specify yellow fever vaccination as a requirement of entry, primarily to prevent the importation of the disease into the country. The only other vaccination required by a few countries is for cholera. Smallpox vaccination was required in the past but is no longer necessary, since smallpox was effectively eradicated from the world in 1980.

Other immunizations are of medical importance for protection of the traveler, however; these include immunizations against yellow fever (when not a legal requirement), poliomyelitis, diphtheria, tetanus, and typhoid fever; immunoglobulin for the prevention of hepatitis A; meningococcal vaccine for tourists going to areas of the world where epidemics of disease are known to be occurring; and Japanese B encephalitis vaccine (a new vaccine, not yet licensed for general use in the U.S. but available through special clinics) for persons traveling to China and parts of Southeast Asia in the summertime.

Prophylactic medication to prevent malaria is a must for all travelers to the tropical areas of the world where malaria transmission occurs. Additionally, medications are available for both the prevention and treatment of "traveler's diarrhea," the most common illness experienced by travelers to the less developed world. At international travel clinics advice is also given about general eating habits and ways in which illness may be avoided while traveling. The goal of such clinics, then, is to protect visitors to the less developed countries against many of the illnesses to which they would otherwise be highly susceptible.

The future

The major health problems of the world are changing steadily from those of infectious etiology to those of aging and industrialization. As the important infectious diseases are controlled, the infant mortality rates of the less developed countries will decrease until they approach those of the United States and Europe. As infant mortality rates decrease, population increases should be slowed as well. In the interim, however, the infectious diseases of the less developed world take a huge toll in terms of illness and deaths each year, and major efforts are required by the world community to see that they are brought under control.

—R. Bradley Sack, M.D., Sc.D.

Kidney Disease

There are many substantial recent advances in the treatment of renal (kidney) diseases and their complications and in the understanding of various physiological processes that affect the health of the kidneys. Among these developments are better methods of influencing outcome in kidney transplantation, the possibility of preventing renal disease development in diabetic patients, new approaches to dialysis, a newly discovered natural substance that influences the way the body handles salt, and clearer insights into the severely debilitating bone disease that occurs in many cases with renal failure and into the course of kidney disease once it begins.

Results of kidney transplantation

The advent of the drug cyclosporine, a chemical derived from a soil fungus, has had a substantial effect on the success of organ transplantation. Prior to the availability of cyclosporine in the 1970s, the major drugs used for immunosuppression, i.e., the prevention of rejection of a foreign organ, were cortisone (and its close derivatives) and azathioprine. The success rate of kidney transplantation has substantially increased with the use of cyclosporine, such that cadaveric donor transplants have a one-year survival rate of about 85%, with an excellent chance of continuing survival subsequently, and live donor transplants have a survival rate of approximately 95%.

However, in the early days of the use of cyclosporine, the price paid for a lower rate of rejection was impairment of kidney function due to kidney damage by cyclosporine. This was particularly noticeable in the initial stages of the heart transplantation program, when reports of kidney damage following the use of cyclosporine were widely publicized. Understanding of this complication has made it possible to determine appropriate dosages with a subsequent reduction in toxicity to the kidneys. At present, with the use of lower doses of cyclosporine and with close monitoring of plasma levels of this drug, incidence of kidney impairment after transplanation has been reduced.

Pretransplant blood transfusion

Another important development that has only recently come into use and that is contributing to the improving success rate of kidney transplantation is pretransplant blood transfusion. The blood is obtained from the actual donor in the case of live donors or from random blood donors for potential cadaveric donor recipients. Pretransplant blood transfusions decrease the risk of rejection after transplantation. The precise mechanisms underlying the transfusion effect have not been worked out but probably involve an increase in the number of suppressor cells and the development of antibodies that block the rejection reaction.

Donor organ availability

In the United States one of the ongoing problems affecting kidney transplantation has been a shortage of donor organs. But by mid-1986 that gloomy picture appeared to be changing. Beginning in 1986 many states passed laws that make it obligatory for hospitals to request organ donation from the relatives of patients who are brain dead, unless the patients themselves have expressed unwillingness to be organ donors. New York, California, and Oregon were the first states to pass "required request" laws. By June 1, 1986, 15 states had enacted laws and several additional states were on the verge of doing so. Other states were drafting legislation. The exact form of these laws differs from state to state, but the concept of routine request or routine inquiry seems to have firmly taken hold on the U.S. medical scene.

The initial results of the new laws have been extremely encouraging. In fact, the immediate success has far exceeded the hopes of even the most ardent supporters of the legal measures. Even stronger laws have been in operation in many European countries under which, unless families specifically deny permission for donation, organs can be removed after brain death has been declared.

Other actions that will affect organ availability are proposed federal legislation prohibiting the sale of organs and reducing the number of aliens who may have kidney transplants in the U.S. A quota of no more than 10% of the organs available to various kidney

A donor kidney is rushed for transplantation. In the U.S. new "required request" laws are brightening the outlook for patients awaiting organ transplants.

Enrico Ferorelli—DOT

transplantation programs is being suggested for foreign patients. With the increasing success and safety of transplantation, there is a gradual increase in the donation of kidneys by interested individuals who are not blood relations of kidney recipients—particularly spouses. However, potential abuse of this practice is possible and, indeed, has occurred in some foreign countries where kidneys are for sale.

Renal failure in diabetes mellitus

Diabetes mellitus is the diagnosis in approximately 25% of all patients who enter end-stage renal failure programs (government-paid-for dialysis treatment) in the United States. The gradual increase in the proportion of diabetic patients is partly the result of more liberal acceptance programs that permit almost all who need it to receive dialysis. Of diabetic patients who are insulin dependent (type I diabetics), approximately 40% will eventually go on to end-state renal failure 10 to 20 years after the beginning of the illness. In the older age group, where diabetes is usually insulin independent (type II) and where the disease is controlled by oral agents or by diet alone, only about 6–10% will ever have renal failure.

Recent work suggests that it is possible to identify those patients whose kidneys will fail. At an early stage in the course of their disease, these patients excrete in the urine increased amounts of the serum protein albumin in quantities that are not detected by the usual examination in a doctor's office. Even at the stage in which the excretion of albumin is only slightly increased, these patients may have a slight elevation in blood pressure, compared with healthy people. It is controversial whether continuous subcutaneous insulin infusion will result in a reduction of microalbuminuria (the presence of minute quantities of albumin in the urine) and will slow the rate of decrease in kidney function that occurs in such patients. Different scientific studies showing both a beneficial outcome and no effect have been reported.

However, it does seem very likely that control of high blood pressure may be of substantial benefit in reducing the rate of decline in renal function. Several studies have shown this favorable effect in both the type I and type II diabetic populations. Careful attention to detail and the use of home blood pressure recordings may be valuable in ensuring excellent blood pressure control.

Now that many effective drugs are available, more attention has been given recently to the indirect effects of drugs used to control high blood pressure. For example, while some drugs, *e.g.*, diuretics, reduce the blood pressure and thus the risks of heart disease and hardening of the arteries, they simultaneously may have an unfavorable effect on the serum cholesterol concentration, thus increasing the risk of heart disease. Clearly, in selecting drugs to control high blood

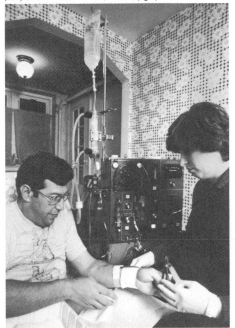
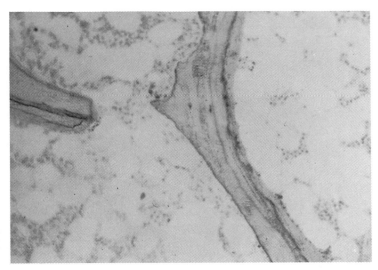

Deposits of aluminum have recently been found in the bones of some kidney failure patients on dialysis. Aluminum, which causes bone to be soft and weak, is sometimes a contaminant of dialysate fluid; it is also contained in drugs taken by renal failure patients. In the X-ray above an accumulation of aluminum is indicated by the dark line.

pressure, concurrent metabolic effects will become increasingly important.

Developments in dialysis

Treatment with the artificial kidney (hemodialysis) is carried out on approximately 70,000 patients in the United States at present. Approximately an equal number of renal failure patients in Europe are kept alive with dialysis. In most instances nowadays the average duration of treatment is about four hours at a time three times a week. The decision as to the amount of treatment to give is often arbitrary. However, a study funded by the U.S. National Institutes of Health concluded that it is possible to define the amount of dialysis compatible with reasonably good health and to define lesser levels of treatment, which were associated with increased hospital admissions, anemia, and a number of other health problems. The study considered such factors as duration of dialysis, blood flow rate through the dialyzer, and the ability of the dialyzer to remove materials. The study also assessed dietary protein intake and the amount of removal of protein breakdown products by dialysis.

Another dialysis development concerns the semipermeable membranes used to carry out dialysis. These are generally made of cellulose and its derivatives. In many patients the membrane interacts with blood components to cause substantial changes in a blood system called the complement system. The complement system consists of a number of proteins in the blood. Activated complement proteins help the body to fight infection-causing organisms. However, activation of this system by the dialysis membrane may cause

adverse effects during dialysis. Recent improvements in hemodialysis include the use of inert membranes, which may not have the same propensity for activating the complement system.

The use of inert membranes combined with very rapid removal of waste products by the artificial kidney may facilitate a reduction in needed dialysis treatment time while providing the same amount of blood cleansing. Clearly this approach is inherently very unnatural since it is performed in three periods of 2–2½ hours a week, compared with what the normal kidney is doing 24 hours a day, seven days a week. The long-term effects of such short-time treatment remain to be investigated, but this treatment represents a substantial benefit to patients who now spend shorter times on their machines.

This method of treatment should be contrasted with continuous ambulatory peritoneal dialysis (CAPD), where treatment is continuous throughout the day. CAPD involves the introduction into the abdominal cavity of a fluid that equilibrates with the patient's own blood, thus allowing very gradual removal of poisons. Some argue that larger molecules akin to those that are excreted in the urine and that may be responsible for some of the toxic effects of kidney failure are removed with peritoneal dialysis, thus making it a more natural method of treatment than the hemodialysis therapy. A benefit of the newer inert membranes described above is that they have large "pores" that permit a loss of larger molecules. Toxic effects—*e.g.,* impairment of brain and nerve function—are not entirely corrected by any method of dialysis but are improved by successful kidney transplantation.

371

Aluminum bone disease

One of the important consequences of chronic kidney failure is bone disease. The pathogenesis of bone disease is complex and is related chiefly to deficiency of a form of vitamin D normally produced by the healthy kidney. A consequent reduction in the absorption of calcium through the gut, retention of phosphorus in the blood (since the damaged kidney has a reduced capability to excrete this chemical), and finally an increase in the activity of the parathyroid gland in the neck play an important role in weakening bone. Before they enter dialysis, the majority of patients have some degree of increased parathyroid function. Unless it is severe, this condition can be detected only by X-rays, by special examinations of the density of the bone, or by pathological examination of bone tissue by a bone biopsy. When the condition is severe, however, bone pain, fractures, and gradual bone destruction may occur.

Many patients in dialysis programs recently have been found to have a different form of bone disease that appears to be related to the accumulation of the metal aluminum. The bone is hard material that under normal circumstances is constantly being "remodeled"; that is, small tunnels are being excavated into the bone by cells called osteoclasts and then filled up again with the matrix of bone (produced by other cells called osteoblasts), which subsequently becomes calcified. Aluminum appears to interfere with the calcification of the matrix, thus resulting in weak, soft bone that easily becomes deformed and leads to severe deformities of the rib cage, vertebrae, and other bones.

The source of the aluminum is twofold. Particularly in the past, aluminum was found as a contaminant in the water used for producing the dialysate fluid used in the hemodialysis procedure. Aluminum is also found in large amounts in the drugs, such as aluminum hydroxide, that are given to patients in renal failure to bind phosphorus contained in food, with the objective of preventing phosphorus from entering the bloodstream after being absorbed by the gut.

In some instances, especially in children, aluminum bone disease is detected previous to dialysis therapy, a fact that confirms that dialysis is not essential for the development of the condition. Once the aluminum is present in the bone, it is not easy for it to be excreted unless a successful kidney transplant (which does result in reversal of the bone disease) is performed.

In recent years a substance called desferrioxamine, which has the property of binding metals such as iron and aluminum, has been used in conjunction with dialysis to form a chemical complex with the aluminum in the patient's blood; the complex can then be removed through the dialysis membrane. Utilization of this approach has resulted in rapid improvement in symptoms and slow but gradual correction of this severely disabling condition.

Insights into sodium excretion

It is common knowledge that a reduction in fluid intake or marked fluid loss from the body results in a reduction in urinary output. Similarly, a reduced intake of sodium in the diet results in a reduced urinary excretion of sodium. The body's mechanisms for conserving water and salt are quite well understood. These include reduction in the blood flow to the kidney and a complex set of hormonal interrelationships involving the adrenal gland and substances formed in the liver and kidney. Substances produced in these organs act in concert to maintain blood pressure partly by helping to conserve sodium by the kidney.

What has not been so clearly understood is the way in which the body responds to the need for *increasing* the amount of sodium in the urine. The recent discovery of a substance termed atrial natriuretic factor, found particularly in the atrial chambers of the heart, has revolutionized the understanding of the excretion of sodium by the body. This substance causes natriuresis—*i.e.,* increased excretion of salt; hence its name. It is probably secreted in response to distention of the atria when the blood volume is increased. For example, heart failure would be a stimulus to the secretion of atrial natriuretic factor. This substance relaxes the blood vessels, blocks the increased secretion of aldosterone (which is produced by the adrenal gland), and inhibits the secretion of renin (produced by the kidney). All this results in sodium being lost in the urine since the mechanisms for conservation of sodium are inhibited. In other words, this natural substance acts in a manner similar to the diuretic drugs used for the treatment of too much salt and water in the bodies of some patients with renal disorders and various other conditions.

The progression of established renal disease

One of the most interesting developments in the last few years in the understanding of kidney problems is the concept that the perpetuation of many kidney diseases, once the initial stimulus or damaging factor has been removed, is the result of increased stress on the remaining units of kidney function. The argument goes as follows: As the result of disease the number of functioning glomeruli (filters of the kidney) is reduced. The pressure usually experienced by a normal number of glomeruli is therefore experienced by the small number remaining, resulting in an increase in blood pressure in each glomerulus. This intraglomerular hypertension (high blood pressure) produces actual physical injury to the cells that line the glomeruli. The physical injury may be augmented by the liberation of cell toxins and by chemicals causing inflammation, with the final result being scarring of portions of the kidney and eventual resultant renal failure.

There is some experimental evidence, both in animals and in humans, that a reduction in protein intake may reverse this phenomenon by reducing the glomerular filtration rate and the intraglomerular hypertension. Much experimental work aimed at testing this idea is under way. Concurrently other investigations are studying the use of drugs that would have the same favorable effect on the pressures in the kidney since, for many individuals, taking medicines is easier than strict dieting.

—*Nathan W. Levin, M.D.*

Lung Diseases

It is an axiom that progress in pulmonary medicine must focus on prevention. The well-established association of smoking tobacco with lung cancer remains a major challenge. But additionally, smoking is responsible for approximately 40% of all cancer because the carcinogens inhaled and absorbed through the lungs also reach other organs. Thus, cancers of the cervix, bladder, pancreas, lip, larynx, and esophagus are now known to be related to smoking.

Genetic protection

At last society has begun to recognize the clear hazards of smoking and the associated consequences of premature morbidity and mortality. One astounding fact to consider is that seven years of life are lost to the average smoker. It is even more persuasive to realize that the time it takes to puff and inhale a cigarette—about 5½ minutes—can cost the smoker *years* in lost health and productivity. Yet, perplexingly, some seem immune.

Why do some people get away with smoking? Why do some *not* suffer the dire consequences? The answer to this critical question is not known. Today theories to explain these differences focus on family history. Both lung cancer and emphysema, another smoking-related disease, cluster in families. Thus, something in the genes may either protect people from or render them susceptible to the damaging effects of tobacco smoke. One theory currently under study at the Webb-Waring Lung Institute of the University of Colorado Health Sciences Center in Denver focuses on protective mechanisms of red blood cells or of lung tissue itself, which appear to be able to ward off the harmful effects of tobacco. The protection is believed to come from antioxidants, substances that oppose oxidation or inhibit reactions promoted by oxygen. Thus, these antioxidants effectively combat the oxygen and other free-radical-related toxic products that occur in cigarette smoke or are released from cells within the lung in susceptible smokers. If this notion is correct, it may help unravel the basic biology of lung cancer, emphysema, and even heart attacks. (About 50% of heart attacks are attributed to smoking.)

Another major line of investigation that involves studying molecular biologic aspects has recently lead to an important advance—the discovery of a fractured chromosome that is present in all patients with the most lethal form of lung cancer. How this broken chromosome allows lung cancer to develop is a fundamental biologic question to be answered by further research. But these studies are likely, one day, to explain the very nature of the smoking-related diseases, which now needlessly kill 1,000 people each day in the United States alone.

Emphysema

Tremendous advances today are being made in the understanding of emphysema, the second most common cause of disability and the fifth most common cause of death in the U.S. Emphysema is a destructive process of the delicate gas-exchange membrane called the alveolar surface and of the small airways that feed this membrane.

Because of oxygen starvation of vital tissues, individuals with emphysema become short of breath with exertion, are forced to limit their physical activities, and may suffer strokes or heart attacks. Emphysema is a disease of older adults. It develops slowly, over many years, and the affected individual generally is not aware of this ongoing destructive process. It has been known for some time that people who smoke cigarettes have a greater incidence of emphysema than nonsmokers. Furthermore, among smokers the risk and severity of the disease increase with the number of cigarettes smoked.

Lung function involves destructive enzymes (proteases) that are released from white cells as well as protective antienzymes (antiproteases). These latter chemical defenders of the delicate air-blood interface become oxidized from the cigarette smoke in susceptible individuals. Within the last quarter century a new

A child with cystic fibrosis is clapped on the back to clear her lungs. Better treatments are extending the lives of cystic fibrosis patients, and a new test enables prenatal detection of genetic markers indicating the presence of the disease.

Sudhir—Picture Group

theory has provided a key to the understanding of the basic mechanism of emphysema. It was discovered by Swedish researchers that emphysema patients lack a certain protein in their blood (α_1-antitrypsin) that has an important antiprotease function. Thus, an imbalance of protease-antiprotease leads to destruction of the lung because of the weak protection function. Recently the protective antiprotease has been synthesized in the laboratory by means of recombinant DNA methods and gene-splicing technology. In particular, scientists are now investigating whether the antiprotease material can be replaced or altered so as to be resistant to oxidative damage.

Though emphysema could be essentially prevented in a smokeless society, the realities of life indicate that such a utopia is some time away. Therefore, in the meantime, the identification of patients who are just beginning to lose lung function is an immediate goal so that they can eliminate the risks of harmful life-styles. It is now known that early identification of emphysema is possible via simple tests of airflow and volume from fully inflated lungs. A simple device called a spirometer, therefore, should be in every physician's office for this purpose. Measuring air volume and flow is no more difficult than typical office measuring of blood pressure.

Asthma

Asthma is another area of major advances. The mechanisms of the disease are now better understood. Asthma is not solely an allergic disease but often is due to other mechanisms that cause bronchospasm and thus perturb air flow through the conducting air passages of the lungs. A new field of biochemistry has emerged to understand these mechanisms. This new chemistry focuses on products of cell membranes called prostaglandins and leukotrienes. Some prostaglandins constrict and others help dilate the air passages of the lungs. The leukotrienes are believed to cause inflammation of the lining of the lungs' air passages and also to increase mucus production. Both are problems in severe asthmatics. Cortisone derivative drugs help combat this inflammation and the excess sticky mucus production. But new and better approaches to both preventing and treating these processes are current directions of study.

Meanwhile, many newer drugs and more effective treatment strategies are helping millions of asthmatics each year. It is not an exaggeration to say that the strategies for the control of nearly every case of asthma are at hand. In 1985 a new metered-dose bronchodilator, bitolterol, became available in the U.S. (marketed under the name Tornalate). Bitolterol is a beta-adrenergic aerosol that triggers the release of active substances known as catecholamines, which have greater effective action on the lung than previously available aerosol drugs such as albuterol, metaproterenol, and terbutaline. This inhaled drug lasts for eight hours or more and is delivered in a simple pressurized cannister for convenience. This is somewhat longer than the duration of activity of older drugs and will add additional convenience for some patients. Moreover, it does not appear to cause any significant adverse affects, nor is it more costly than other aerosols. Two inhalations of bitolterol every eight hours are recommended for prevention of bronchospasm. Somewhat more frequent doses may be needed for control of symptoms.

Cystic fibrosis

Cystic fibrosis, the most common lethal genetic disease in Americans, is on the threshold of solution.

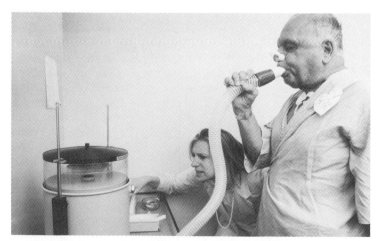

Measuring breathing capacity—the amount of air one can blow out when lungs are inflated—is an important test for patients with lung diseases as well as for healthy individuals. It is easily accomplished in a physician's office (left) or at home with a disposable spirometer (right).

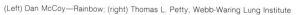

(Left) Dan McCoy—Rainbow; (right) Thomas L. Petty, Webb-Waring Lung Institute

Cystic fibrosis is a hereditary disease of infants, children, and young adults. It is considered the most serious lung-damaging disease affecting infants and children. Cystic fibrosis not only attacks the lungs but can also involve the gastrointestinal tract, liver, and the reproductive organs.

About one out of every 1,500 babies is born with cystic fibrosis. There are an estimated 15,000 to 20,000 cystics in the U.S. at the present time, and an additional 1,000 cases are diagnosed each year. It has been calculated that in the U.S. there are about ten million genetic carriers of cystic fibrosis.

During 1985 the chromosome on which the lethal gene resides was identified. Thus, soon it will be possible to identify patients at risk as well as those who are carriers. Genetic counseling, which can enable couples planning to have a child to take all possible steps to avoid birth defects, should thus enable prevention and will probably result in a significant reduction in incidence of disease. With cystic fibrosis if both parents are carriers, there is a one-in-four chance that their child will be born with the disease. Identification before birth is also now possible, as is identification of the presence of cystic fibrosis in newborns.

New discoveries are leading to treatment strategies to help the child with cystic fibrosis fight the recurrent infections that, if uncontrolled, will finally damage and destroy the lungs. The widespread use of diagnostic and therapeutic techniques already available will considerably improve the outlook for longer life-spans and much better quality of life for cystic fibrosis patients in the near future. Once the biochemical abnormality of cystic fibrosis has finally been fully identified, a cure for this dreaded disease within the next ten years is not unlikely.

Respiratory emergencies

Respiratory emergencies have helped spawn extremely sophisticated technologies and special lifesaving intensive care units in hospitals. Yet serious respiratory emergencies continue to be the scourge of millions of patients each year. Two new syndromes—the adult respiratory distress syndrome (ARDS) and the lethal infections that accompany the acquired immune deficiency syndrome (AIDS)—fall into this category.

Though supportive measures with modern ventilators save many, often even the most sophisticated technological advances are futile gestures that only add a dramatic ceremony to the end of afflicted patients' lives. (ARDS kills some 90,000 people a year and AIDS another 10,000.) Newer approaches to mechanical ventilation, such as high-frequency ventilators that enable air exchange to occur at 100–1,000 breaths per minute at low exchange volumes, are under study. It is hoped that such new approaches offer will alternative strategies in the life support of the most complicated respiratory emergencies.

Reverence for the lungs

The lungs are the body's source of oxygen, which is carried by the blood and pumped by the heart. Oxygen energizes every cell of the body and is key to the energy chain that keeps people alive. A great amount of the oxygen taken in is used to maintain cell and tissue structure. The rest of it is required for muscular activity that is involved in every function of daily living. Thus, a shortage of oxygen affects every organ of the body. This is particularly true of the brain, which has the highest oxygen requirement. The heart also has a fantastic oxygen requirement, compared with the other organs of the body. But all other organs, such as the liver and kidneys, require oxygen for their own function. Thus, in states of oxygen deficiency, in essence, the whole body is robbed of vital energy.

Oxygen is involved in the metabolism of food to create the energy the body needs. A by-product of metabolism is carbon dioxide. This carbon dioxide must be removed by the lungs as blood is returned from the tissues. When the lungs cannot exhale enough carbon dioxide, a buildup occurs. This retention of carbon dioxide causes acidosis, an acid poisoning of all of the cells of the body. The brain and heart and other organs are also impaired by carbon dioxide retention.

If the lungs' function involved *only* oxygen and carbon dioxide exchange, this would be a major enough task. However, the lungs do much more. The lungs are the only organ of the body that receives the entire blood flow with each heartbeat. As blood from the veins flows through the lungs, other changes take place. The lungs process many of the body's chemicals, either inactivating or activating them. One of the key activation processes is the conversion of a precursor hormone to a material that controls blood pressure. Thus, angiotensin I is converted to angiotensin II, which helps regulate the circulation.

The lungs are by far the largest organ in the body. The total surface area is more than 83.6 sq m (100 sq yd). The delicate gas exchange membrane is 1/50 the thickness of tissue paper to allow for the transfer of oxygen and carbon dioxide. This membrane is called the air-blood interface. Millions of tiny capillaries carry the red cells, which are the transporting vehicles for oxygen and carbon dioxide, but red blood cells also protect the body. They contain defense mechanisms against oxidants of cigarette smoke, air pollution, and other noxious materials. Thus, the red cells are not only the servants of every organ and tissue through the oxygen they bring and the carbon dioxide that they remove, but they also defend against lung cancer, emphysema, and other lung diseases. The white cells, which protect against infection, also traverse the lungs. In fact, at any one minute, 17 billion white cells are cruising through the lungs and ready to attack bacteria, viruses, and other infectious invaders that are inhaled every day.

If the lungs are so critical to health and happiness, why do people take them for granted? Population surveys such as the famed Framingham Study—the largest and longest-running epidemiological study of a general population's health, which has focused in particular on heart disease risk factors—has clearly established the importance of the lungs in a person's overall health. The measurement of breathing capacity (*i.e.,* the amount of air that can be blown out of fully inflated lungs), called vital capacity, proved to be one of the most important tests that was done in this large population. The vital capacity was a better predictor of survival than blood pressure, electrocardiograms, or blood tests.

Nearly everyone has his or her height, weight, and blood pressure measured from time to time. Checkups of skin, breasts, and other body organs—by oneself or by a physician—can alert people well in advance of signs of cancer. Yet, unfortunately, few people have regular measurement of their vital capacity. Devices to do this—spirometers—are readily available but are not frequently enough used in all physicians' offices. Nowadays there are as well disposable spirometry devices, which cost less than $2 and can be used by all individuals in their own homes at any time. Indeed, assessing lung health on a regular basis is a priority that could be the first step toward assessment of overall health and longevity.

—*Thomas L. Petty, M.D.*

Medical Education

In the late 1980s medical education will have to respond to dramatic recent changes in medicine and health care delivery. New diseases such as acquired immune deficiency syndrome (AIDS), the emergence of alternative health care systems such as health maintenance organizations (HMOs), and technological advances have all influenced the training of physicians. New disciplines such as medical ethics and decision analysis are finding important places in medical school curricula, and older disciplines such as preventive medicine, occupational health, and chemical dependence are stimulating a resurgence of interest.

Three prominent influences on medical education today include cost of care, treatment of the elderly, and an expected oversupply of doctors. These are examined below.

Cost containment confronts medical education

With almost $400 billion in health care costs per year (approximately $1,500 per person), there is currently in the U.S. a governmental mandate to reduce the proportion of the gross national product that is spent on health. Although many of these cuts focus on reducing reimbursement to physicians, hospitals, and laboratories, medical education will also feel the pinch

of cost containment. These changes will certainly affect the financing of medical education, during both medical school and postgraduate training, but may also influence the structure of academic institutions and the practice of medicine at teaching hospitals.

For medical students the most immediate changes are likely to stem from cutbacks in the availability of loans to support tuition and living expenses while in school. Federally funded scholarships such as those offered through the U.S. National Health Service have already been eliminated, and federal loan money is being progressively limited to economically disadvantaged students. As a result of rising tuition rates and loss of scholarship funding, the average indebtedness of graduating medical students increased from $19,697 in 1981 to $29,943 ($36,417 at private schools) in 1985.

At the postgraduate level the repercussions are more widespread and affect institutional reimbursement for patient care services provided and residents' salaries. Currently approximately 80% of the stipends and benefits of physicians in postgraduate training (residents) are derived from hospital patient care revenue. A large portion of these revenues comes from governmental sources through Medicare (care for the elderly) and Medicaid (care for the poor) programs. In reimbursing the patient care services provided by physicians in training, the federal government has thus far recognized two components—*direct* costs of resident salaries and associated administrative expenses and *indirect* costs, which reflect more costly care provided to patients as a result of the hospital's teaching function. Included in these indirect costs are increased use of diagnostic testing, medical and surgical supplies, and extended length of stay for patients who are treated at academic medical centers. In all, the cost per case at a teaching hospital is estimated to be 13% higher than at a comparable nonteaching hospital.

Recently Medicare's funding of graduate medical education has come under attack because, in essence, health service dollars are being diverted away from patient care to medical education. Opponents of Medicare's funding of graduate medical education argue that the nation already has an abundant supply of physicians and that few of the physicians whose salaries are being funded enter geriatric medicine. Consequently, a cut in federal funding of graduate medical education appears inevitable; reimbursement of both the direct and indirect costs of residency training is likely to be reduced. Specific proposals before Congress for cutting direct costs have included limitation of the number of years of training for which a resident will be funded and a drastic reduction or elimination of reimbursement for foreign medical graduates, including Americans who graduate from Caribbean medical schools. In addition, the rate of reimbursement for indirect costs of medical education is likely to be reduced substantially. Similarly, private payer insurance companies that are attempting to moderate the costs of their commitments to financing medical care are beginning to curb their involvement with teaching hospitals and medical education.

These projected cutbacks have marked implications for many academic medical centers, especially municipal teaching hospitals. These hospitals have been disproportionately dependent on public programs such as Medicare and Medicaid. Furthermore, when compared with nonteaching hospitals they bear a much greater burden of the free medical care and bad debts related to health care. In 1982 the Association of American Medical Colleges' Council of Teaching Hospitals, which accounted for 5.8% of the nation's community hospitals, incurred 31.5% of the bad debts and rendered 51.1% of the country's charity care. Finally, maintaining educational programs to train physicians creates an additional expense for these hospitals. Whether municipal hospitals can absorb these costs without government subsidy or tax revenues remains to be seen.

In addition to these cost-containment measures, which are aimed at institutions, specific programs are being developed to persuade training physicians to curtail test ordering. Several strategies have been developed including reward systems (*e.g.,* free textbooks) and reviewing patients' charts with attending physicians to focus on unnecessary tests. Unfortunately, these plans require extensive faculty time, and the lessons fade quickly when the cost-containment plan has ended. Although results are still preliminary, some investigators are reporting success with physician-designed protocols to provide a standard management plan for certain illnesses. For example, a group of respected physicians would decide the appropriate management of a patient sustaining a heart attack. When a patient was admitted with a suspected heart attack, the management protocol would be implemented, and departures from this strategy would require discussion between the house officer and the patient's attending physician. In this manner lines of communication between faculty and resident are strengthened, and unnecessary tests may be prevented. Presently inves-

tigators throughout the U.S. are designing and testing protocols for a variety of medical conditions to establish strategies that are efficient, are less expensive, and do not compromise patient care.

Cost containment may provide some difficult times ahead for medical education; undoubtedly some institutions will suffer considerably. Nevertheless, academic medical centers are beginning to adopt attitudes and strategies that accept the reality of limited future funding. Preservation of the high caliber of medical education and patient care in the face of these cutbacks remains a challenge for educators and health-policy planners alike.

Educational advances in geriatric medicine

By the year 2000, 12 to 14% of the U.S. population will be age 65 or older, and half of these will be age 75 or older. It has been predicted that these elderly Americans will generate approximately 50% of the work of the medical profession and, consequently, about half of the nation's health care bill. Thus, the need to provide a general background in the care of the elderly for all physicians and specific training of physicians in geriatric medicine has become increasingly important. Research into the physiological changes and diseases that accompany aging has burgeoned and, in its wake, creative approaches to education in geriatric medicine are being pioneered.

Geriatric medicine and its accompanying educational concepts differ from traditional medical practice and education in several ways. Most importantly, the emphasis of health care is on maintaining functional capacity and social role. Specific diagnoses often have little relation to functional status and may lead physicians to overtreat abnormalities without addressing their effect on the patient's independence and activity. Thus, the routine history and physical examinations are augmented by a comprehensive functional assessment, which evaluates the patient's capabilities relative to his or her needs or wishes for independent living. Included in this assessment are evaluations of hearing and vision, postural stability, mental status, and socioeconomic resources. At some academic centers complete geriatric evaluation units have been established to improve diagnostic assessment, therapy, rehabili-

revenue source	1970–71 amount	%	1975–76 amount	%	1980–81 amount	%	1981–82 amount	%	1982–83 amount	%	1983–84 amount	%
federal research	438	25.6	823	24.3	1,446	22.5	1,578	21.9	1,655	20.2	1,820	20.2
other federal	322	18.8	398	11.7	396	6.2	415	5.8	415	5.1	390	4.3
state and local government	323	18.9	808	23.8	1,452	22.6	1,617	22.4	1,784	21.8	1,896	21.0
tuition and fees	63	3.7	156	4.6	346	5.4	413	5.7	482	5.9	545	6.0
medical service	209	12.2	609	18.0	1,850	28.8	2,140	29.7	2,626	32.1	2,980	33.1
other income	358	20.9	595	17.6	935	14.6	1,054	14.6	1,216	14.9	1,378	15.3
total*	1,713	100.0	3,389	100.0	6,425	100.0	7,217	100.0	8,179	100.0	9,010	100.0

Trends in U.S. medical school revenues (millions of dollars)

*totals may not add because of rounding

H. Paul Jolly et al., "U.S. Medical Finances," JAMA, vol. 254, no. 12 (Sept. 27, 1985), pp. 1573–81

Michael O'Brien—Archive Pictures

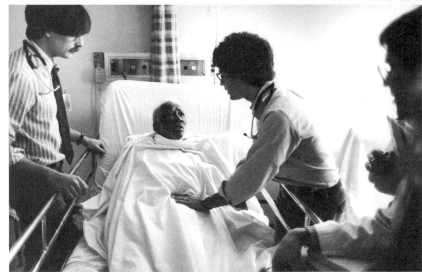

The delivery of health care in the U.S. and most parts of the world is being profoundly affected by the rapid growth of the aging population. By the year 2000 the elderly will require about half of all medical services. Therefore, it is vital for medical education today to focus on understanding the aging process and on developing innovative approaches to treating elderly patients.

tation, and placement services. Early results suggest that these comprehensive centers may lower mortality and decrease the need for nursing home admissions. Furthermore, in one study functional status and morale of elderly patients were significantly improved after a short hospitalization in a geriatric evaluation unit.

In addition to the emphasis on function, geriatric medicine stresses the need for a multidisciplinary approach including physicians, nurses, social workers, nutritionists, podiatrists, and others. There is controversy among experts about what the role of the physician should be in this approach. Some suggest that physicians should be the patient's principal advocate or "case manager," whereas others believe that they should contribute their biomedical expertise but delegate case management to those nonphysicians who are most skilled at coordinating care and social services. All agree that cooperation among different professions is essential, and some institutions have begun pilot programs pairing medical and nursing students together to teach the importance of collaboration in the care of geriatric patients.

Not only is the care of geriatric patients changing, but the setting at which this care is delivered is shifting away from acute care hospitals and toward extended care facilities and nursing homes. Although most elderly persons do not require nursing home placement, the actual number of nursing home beds exceeds that of acute care (hospital) beds. In the 1970s the first truly academic nursing homes were established, largely supported by the National Institute on Aging and the Robert Wood Johnson Foundation. It is anticipated that by the year 2000 each medical school and teaching hospital may have an affiliated teaching nursing home. These facilities will form the core of geriatric medical centers, whose objectives will be to provide better age-specific care for selected patients and their

problems and to lower the cost of medical care. These centers will be staffed with a multidisciplinary team, as described above, and provide ambulatory care as well. Outpatient geriatric units are also being established in European countries and the Soviet Union.

These changes in the approach and delivery of geriatric health care are likely to have a profound effect on the education of medical students and residents. A 1980 survey found that about 60% of U.S. medical schools offered specific undergraduate training in geriatrics, but at the time fewer than 10% of the schools required such courses. Since that time, geriatrics curricula have been developed, and recommendations have been made to make rotations in geriatric medicine mandatory for medical students and residents. Similar recommendations were made in the Royal College of Physicians' report on medical care of the elderly in Great Britain in 1977. In addition to teaching principles of geriatric medicine, these programmatic changes are aimed at creating more favorable attitudes among physicians toward the elderly. Advanced specialty training in geriatrics is also becoming more widespread. The American Board of Internal Medicine recently adopted a policy of offering a certificate of added qualifications in geriatric medicine, thus providing formal recognition of internists who are specially skilled in the care of the elderly. By doing so, the board encourages postresidency training in geriatric medicine.

As geriatric medicine becomes an increasingly important component of the health care system, the understanding of the aging process is leading to new approaches and settings for the care of the elderly. These innovations are becoming integrated into medical education at all levels of training to improve the health care of the rapidly expanding population of elderly persons.

Too many doctors?

In the mid-1960s in the United States, a perceived physician shortage and a strong push toward equal health care for all citizens prompted federal and state officials to provide funds for increasing the supply of physicians. As a result the number of United States medical schools increased from 88 to 127 and the number of graduates per year doubled within a 15-year period. In addition, many foreign medical graduates were employed in the U.S. Currently approximately 17,000 students receive medical degrees each year. By 1990 nearly 600,000 physicians will be practicing, one-third of whom received training in the 1980s. Even the most conservative estimates forecast that the number of physicians generated has more than compensated for the projected shortage; it is predicted that by the next decade there will be a surplus of at least 70,000 physicians. Similar excess numbers of physicians are present or projected in many European countries, especially Belgium, The Netherlands, and West Germany. In the United States general surgery and virtually all of the surgical subspecialties, obstetrics-gynecology, cardiology, pulmonary medicine, and most other subspecialties of internal medicine are likely to be oversupplied. In spite of these projected physician surpluses, graduating physicians continue to opt for training in these oversubscribed fields. Moreover, in some subspecialties that have large excesses, such as infectious diseases and pulmonary medicine, the rate at which graduates are selecting these fields is actually increasing.

Although most experts estimate that the current health care needs are best met by a ratio of 70 to 80% generalists and 20 to 30% specialists, the current ratio is almost exactly reversed. Only about one-quarter of physicians in the United States are functioning as generalists, much fewer than in many European countries, where the proportion of generalists ranges from 40 to 75% (40% in The Netherlands and 75% in the United Kingdom). Generalists are those physicians practicing in the three primary care disciplines of family practice, pediatrics, and general internal medicine. (Obstetrics-gynecology is also sometimes considered a primary care specialty.) Collectively these physicians handle almost two-thirds of all outpatient visits, treating patients for the 15 most common problems encountered in office practices. Within primary care, family practice constitutes the largest share of generalists (about 12% of all practicing physicians) and figures most prominently in managing outpatient problems. Although internal medicine has a higher number of residents and physicians in practice, many of these are not practicing as generalists at present. In fact, over 60% of internal medicine graduates are pursuing subspecialty training, and by the turn of the century the number of subspecialists will exceed the number of generalists practicing internal medicine.

This imbalance between generalists and subspecialists is likely to further increase as HMOs and other managed systems of care continue to grow. In staffing these health care delivery systems, the optimal ratio of generalists to specialists is approximately 3:2, as opposed to the 1:3 ratio that currently exists in private practice. As these organizations progressively employ generalists, more and more subspecialists will enter the already saturated private sector. Increased competition for patients and more intensive (and expensive) care are likely consequences of this surplus.

What can be done about this projected surplus and maldistribution of generalists and specialists? In addition to the provision of better career counseling to medical students, several proposals have been suggested. Since career choices are directly tied to residency training, many possible solutions are linked to the funding of graduate medical education. There is growing support for eliminating the entry of graduates of foreign medical schools (including U.S. citizens). Competency requirements are likely to be more stringent, and funding for support of foreign medical graduates' residency salaries may no longer be available. Additional suggestions include limiting the duration of federal support of funding for each resident to three years, which is precisely the length of training needed to achieve board eligibility in family practice, pediatrics, and general internal medicine but far short of that required for surgical and medical subspecialty training. Expenses for further years of training would have to be funded either by hospitals or through professional fees generated by academic departments. One leading medical educator has proposed that 70% of all training positions be offered in primary care specialties. Of these, half would be in general internal medicine, about 20% would be in family practice, and the remainder would be distributed among pediatrics and obstetrics and gynecology.

Countries other than the U.S. have responded to the projected oversupply and maldistribution of physicians as well. For example, The Netherlands has recommended reducing the number of new first-year students by about 50%, while Belgium has recommended decreasing the availability of specialty residency positions and relying on market forces.

The various proposed sanctions clearly seem restrictive to medical students who are about to embark on careers, but considerable evidence suggests that the problems of oversupply and maldistribution of physicians will not resolve spontaneously. Medical schools are not substantially decreasing enrollment, and graduating students continue to select oversubscribed specialties. Unless some correction of physician supply to rneet projected societal needs is made, the practice of medicine is likely to be more competitive and less satisfying for all physicians.

—*David B. Reuben, M.D.*

Special Report
Doctors on the Witness Stand
by George D. Lundberg, M.D.

In many countries a trial is the decisive culmination to any civil or criminal legal action. In the trial the parties involved present evidence in a concentrated and specific fashion to support their points of view. They present such evidence generally through testimony of witnesses. In such a trial (or hearing) verdicts may be rendered by juries or by judges alone. Attorneys represent the various sides involved. In criminal cases these are called the prosecution and the defense; in civil cases, the plaintiff and the defendant.

After jury selection the attorneys for each side begin the trial with opening statements, which outline the nature of the case and what each attorney hopes to prove. The trial then moves to the phase of calling witnesses. Most of the information provided at the trial is presented through witnesses who testify under oath as to what they know or believe to be the truth as it applies to the case. This testimony first is guided under direct examination by the attorney who requested that witness to testify; then the attorneys representing the other side cross-examine the witness. Following the testimony of witnesses, the attorneys for each side present closing arguments to the court. The judge then instructs the jury about the appropriate and applicable laws to consider, and the jury (or the judge if there is no jury) retires to deliberate in private to reach a decision (verdict), which is subsequently announced in court. In criminal cases in which there is a verdict of guilty, another phase of the trial may determine the sentence to be applied.

Witnesses are generally of two types: those who are a party to the case and those who are not. Those who are a party to the case have knowledge relating to specifics of the case by virtue of their own involvement in the circumstances of the case. The witnesses who are not a party to the case have been brought into the case because of expertise they have that may be of value in resolving the points of issue. These are called expert witnesses, and they are there to help guide the court, the judges, and the jury to the truth.

The expert witness
In the United States, as a general rule, expert witnesses are sought by attorneys representing one side

of a case or the other. These individuals are consulted by the attorneys, and if the attorneys believe that their testimony would be beneficial to their case, they are brought to the witness stand. They provide testimony to the court first through direct questioning by the attorney who brought the expert, after which attorneys representing the other side cross-examine the expert witness.

In addition, it is within the inherent power of a court to appoint expert witnesses directly. Most states in the U.S. and the federal judiciary have adopted specific provisions for the use of impartial expert witnesses. These experts may be used to perform court-ordered examinations of a party prior to presenting testimony. Impartial experts appointed by the court report to the court and not to the counsel for either party and thus serve as officers of the court and not as partisan witnesses.

The question of impartiality
Many critics have suggested that the system by which expert witnesses are retained by both sides in court proceedings could result in the expert's becoming an advocate rather than being an unbiased interpreter of the truth. In general, the first step in the process is that those who are retained as experts consult with the attorneys in developing the case for their side.

It is, of course, the job of the attorneys to represent their clients to the very best of their ability. Thus, if the information provided and the position taken by any particular expert during the phase of consultation is unfavorable to the position of the attorney's client, the attorney obviously would not bring that expert to the witness stand. If, however, the information and opinion of the expert is favorable to the case the attorneys are attempting to make, the expert probably will be put under oath to testify either at the deposition (fact-finding under oath in advance of the trial) or in the trial itself.

Information developed from such consultation is supposed to be shared among attorneys. If the information is in writing, it often is shared; if it is not in writing, however, such information may not be shared with the other side's attorneys. Since it is only "human" for consultants to tend to become partisan easily, the expert witness in consultation with an attorney may well become an advocate for the attorney's client's point of view.

The deposition is a commonly used procedure in the discovery phase of investigation prior to proceeding to court. In the deposition a witness is sworn to tell the truth. Attorneys for both sides are present and ask questions of the witness, following normal court procedure, and a court reporter records all statements. But neither a judge nor a jury is present. Sometimes the deposition may be videotaped as well. The entire deposition, or parts of it, may be presented later in court without the witness's having to reappear. Or, alternatively, the deposition may be used mainly for fact-finding to guide the attorneys to their next steps in the case and as a basis of comparison against which to judge subsequent testimony by the witness in court.

Testimony from doctors

The trial of a lawsuit is traditionally an adversarial proceeding. Attorneys representing the opposing parties have a duty to present the issues in the most favorable way for their client by every ethical and lawful mechanism available. When doctors are called as expert witnesses, it is their ethical duty not to become advocates or partisans in the trial. Physicians have a responsibility not to withhold, conceal, or distort information, and they should not slant or twist their medical opinions. They should maintain scientific objectivity.

For some doctors, because of their "human" biases or because of the nature of the case, maintaining objectivity may not be easy. However, it is essential for the administration of justice and for the maintenance of the honor and dignity of the medical profession. The American Medical Association and most smaller medical societies and organizations endorse the use of doctors in court trials as impartial experts, but with strict stipulations that the above ethical practices be upheld.

As long as there are differences of medical and scientific opinion on significant issues, there will be instances in which testimony of differing points of view will be presented in good faith by honest expert witnesses. Because of real concerns that expert witnesses may turn out to be partisan, independent impartial expert witnesses are increasingly being appointed at the discretion of the court. Such important expert witnesses report directly to the judge and may be used to perform examinations of a party ordered by the court prior to presenting testimony, or they may simply examine the records and materials and make judgments based upon such evidence. When such an impartial expert is called to testify during the trial, this expert, although considered an officer of the court and not a partisan witness, nonetheless, is subject to cross-examination by attorneys on both sides.

Specialist consultants

Medical specialists of all kinds may be asked to serve as consultants and may be called upon to give expert testimony. The nature of the case determines which sorts of physicians will be involved. For example, in cases involving surgical operations (e.g., a hysterectomy), a surgeon knowledgeable in the most up-to-date gynecologic therapies and practices most likely would be involved.

Psychiatrists are very commonly involved in criminal court proceedings for such things as the determination of whether the accused was legally sane or insane at the time of the alleged criminal act. In some instances the psychiatrist may examine parties prior to a trial. In others he or she may become involved at the stage of a trial after the defendant has been found guilty and in which the determination of a proper sentence is at issue.

Toxicologists very often testify in court about the validity of analyses they have performed on bodily fluids and confiscated materials to determine whether drugs are present and, if so, what drugs and how much. The testimony of a toxicologist on the level of alcohol in the blood may be critical in determining whether a defendant was indeed driving under the influence of ethyl alcohol.

Forensic pathologists frequently testify in court, especially those who are employed as coroners or medical examiners. Their testimony pertains to the cause and manner of death of an individual. And forensic pathologists give evidence relating to a crime, such as the path of a bullet or the character of a knife wound. Pharmacologists, as well, occasionally testify in court describing unexpected and adverse effects of drugs when they are administered under proper clinical circumstances and in proper dosages.

Doctors against doctors

Very frequently litigation in a court trial is against a doctor—in particular, in malpractice cases. The physician specialists most frequently finding themselves defendants in court action include those in high-risk practices such as neurosurgeons, orthopedic surgeons, obstetricians, and anesthesiologists. In such circumstances it would be usual for experts in the same field as the physician being sued to be called upon for consultation or as actual witnesses.

One of the key ethical considerations that confronts doctors as courtroom witnesses is whether they should participate at all. Most physicians prefer to practice medicine; very few enjoy being involved in courtroom activities. Court is not a natural environment for a physician, and the adversary procedure is foreign to the educational background and experience of the average physician. The treatment of patients is a cooperative procedure rather than one of an adversarial nature. Yet society lives by a "government of laws and not of men." Thus, it is not only appropriate but essential that physicians with knowledge in important areas make themselves available to consult with attorneys and to serve as impartial experts on the truth for the court.

Many years ago physicians as a group were accused of participating in a "conspiracy of silence," in which, it was alleged, they would not report on inappropriate activities of other physicians and would not appear in court against one another. Those times are long since gone. The peer review process that functions in virtually all aspects of medical practice requires physicians to judge each other's credentials and performance in an ongoing, critical way. Similarly, physicians are often called upon to testify to the truth in cases in which medical professional liability is under examination. The key point in this entire process is that such experts should be readily available and must provide honest and correct consultation and witnessing under oath to "the truth, the whole truth, and nothing but the truth."

The question of true expertise

One of the principal problems concerning doctors on the witness stand is the determination of who is in fact an expert. In the U.S. the various states have sharp differences in their laws regarding what constitutes an expert in the eyes of the court. It is well known that many physicians and other professionals from time to time behave in an unprofessional manner, providing alleged expert testimony in cases in which they truly have little or no bona fide expertise. Individuals functioning in this manner incur great disrespect from others and are often termed whores or hired guns. This kind of circumstance seriously complicates the system of attempting to find the truth and administer justice.

Nonexperts, of course, should not "pose" as experts (primarily for high fees), testifying to very different findings and conclusions than legitimate expert witnesses would. Many believe that justice would be far better served if the expert witnesses were no longer representing both prosecution and defense (or plaintiff and defendant) but rather were identified by the court as true experts from an impartial panel of authoritative leaders in the particular field involved. Such experts would serve as witnesses for both sides, and their fees would be paid equally by both sides, thus rendering them totally impartial. The judge and the attorneys for both sides would question them, and the jury would be better able to arrive at a just decision.

Fees for testimony

In the current ethical practice of medicolegal consultation and courtroom testimony by physicians, it is perfectly proper for fees to be paid. Such fees are usually based upon the amount of time involved in studying the cases, making reports, and appearing for deposition or in court. Most such payment thus is determined

on a prorated hourly basis and is completely independent of which side the witness is working for or what the ultimate verdict or settlement happens to be.

As a general rule, the contingency fee basis used as a method of compensation by many plaintiff attorneys is not used by physician experts. In some states such an arrangement may be illegal, and in most settings it is considered generally unethical. It is perfectly obvious that paying the expert witness on the basis of a contingency fee determined by the verdict and basing that fee upon the size of the award could provide a strong motivation for the expert to testify convincingly for his side whether or not the testimony represented truth.

Predicting future violence in criminals

Some other interesting side issues arise in this area of the doctor in court. Psychiatrists often are asked to predict long-term behavior of convicted criminals and others. They are asked to say whether a given individual is likely to become violent and if so when and against whom. They are also requested to make definitive comments regarding the prognosis of certain mental illnesses. Actually, psychiatrists have great difficulty predicting short- or long-term behavior on the part of many mentally ill people. This is especially true of persons who are prone to becoming violent. Psychiatrists often cannot predict with any degree of certainty who is likely to attack another and when, or who is unlikely to do so.

The unpleasant truth

There is some question as to the humanism and propriety of physicians serving in open court providing completely honest and candid information regarding such things as the exact details of homicides to the families in attendance. Such evidence shown to the family in attendance may put them once again through the grieving process long after they have mourned the loss of a loved one. This is unfortunate but sometimes necessary. In a court of law the facts must come out exactly, although one does attempt to deal with them in as tasteful and kind a way as possible. For example, in many courts black-and-white, rather than color, photographs of homicide victims are provided as evidence, since the former may seem a little less vivid to families who must be in attendance as well as less inflammatory to the jury.

It is very important to society that in this "age of litigation" individuals and courts be provided full access to the highest level of expertise possible to assist in adjudicating charges against criminal defendants and judging claims in civil cases. Physicians as experts swear to tell the truth and are subject to direct examination and cross-examination. It is essential that the members and leaders of those two old and honorable professions, law and medicine, work together to the fullest extent possible as colleagues.

Medical Ethics

From high technology medicine to animal research, from cost-cutting measures to the care of dying adults and disabled newborns, medical ethics in 1985 and early 1986 ranged over wide territory. Following are summaries of six medical-ethical issues that have been topics of particular concern and focus at the Hastings Center, Hastings-on-Hudson, N.Y., a pioneering institution established in 1969 to grapple with the troublesome moral issues and controversies that cloud the practice of medicine in today's world.

The morality of animal research

Over 100 million animals are being used for research worldwide for purposes that range from the diagnosis of disease and the development of new drugs to the testing of the toxicity of cleansers and cosmetics. Because of growing pressures from animal rights groups about animal misuse, the U.S. National Institutes of Health (NIH) has issued regulations stipulating that institutions receiving federal funds must establish animal care and use committees; committee members must include at least one nonscientist and one person not affiliated with the institution.

In July 1985 the NIH suspended funding for animal research in a unit of the animal research facility at the University of Pennsylvania where animals are experimentally subjected to head trauma. While acknowledging the importance of the research, the agency expressed concern about a failure to comply with U.S. Public Health Service policy on the care and use of laboratory animals.

A recent report from the U.S. Office of Technology Assessment, which considers the ethical dimensions of animal research, maintains that "animals are morally entitled to be treated humanely; whether they are entitled to more than that is unclear." The report concludes that for most areas of scientific research, fully replacing animal use with nonanimal methods is unlikely in the near future.

On the theoretical front, philosophers have led the debate, creating what Jerrold Tannenbaum and Andrew Rowan described in "Rethinking the Morality of Animal Research," an article in the *Hastings Center Report* (October 1985), as a new phase in the ethical controversy. This involves "a moral reevaluation of the status of animals, a biological and philosophical examination of the nature of pain and suffering, and an analysis of the benefits of different types of knowledge." Tannenbaum and Rowan categorize the various ethical positions that form the basis for the debate as follows: (1) ethical skepticism—in which there is no right or wrong but only what people desire; (2) ethical relativism—in which right and wrong exist but depend on what a group or society values; (3) absolute dominionism—in which there are no moral restraints at

AP/Wide World

Protesters outside the National Institutes of Health in Bethesda, Maryland, claim victory after the government suspended funding of a research project that was inflicting head injuries on laboratory baboons.

all on the use of animals; (4) anthropomorphic consequentialism—in which mistreating animals is wrong because of its effect on human beings; (5) reverence for life—a view held by Albert Schweitzer, in which all life exhibits a "will to live" and thus deserves society's moral concern; (6) human beneficence—a view held by traditional animal welfare societies that human beings must not cause animals needless pain and distress but that animals may always be killed painlessly for legitimate human purposes; (7) utilitarianism—a view that weighs the animal's pain and distress against the prevention or cure of disease (philosopher Peter Singer, sometimes called the father of the animal rights movement, maintains that only a tiny fraction of animal research produces any significant benefit and most produces significant pain or distress to animals); and (8) abolitionism—a view in which it is inherently wrong to use common laboratory animals in research, since most mammals over one year of age are mentally on a par with some retarded and comatose people who have moral and legal rights.

Tannenbaum and Rowan maintain that any acceptable view of animal research must take into account qualities of animals (such as self-awareness and the capacity to experience pain and pleasure and to reason). Other essential considerations are the nature of animals themselves and their interaction with human beings, as well as the potential benefits and differing moral weights of research and the value of the research enterprise itself.

383

Medical ethics

Frozen embryos and surrogate mothers

While artificial reproduction in its many forms has proved a boon to many childless couples, it raises questions for society about the nature of parental responsibility and what constitutes the best interests of children. Lately two issues have dominated the ethical landscape: embryo freezing and surrogate motherhood.

Improved techniques of freezing, thawing, and implanting embryos have focused attention on whether and how to protect embryos stored outside the body. Are they property that can be disposed of at the donor's will, or do they have a right to life of their own? This question first arose in 1983, when Mario and Elsa Rios died in a plane crash, leaving behind in Melbourne, Australia, two frozen "orphan embryos." For two years a committee debated whether the embryos should be destroyed, maintained, or implanted in another woman. Now the Australian state of Victoria has passed the Infertility Act, which stipulates, among other things, that the minister of health should instruct the hospital to make the embryos available for donation to another woman who wants them.

Philosopher David Ozar in "The Case Against Thawing Unused Frozen Embryos," *Hastings Center Report* (August 1985), defends this outcome as the ethical way to proceed. If one believes that an embryo has rights, Ozar says, then it has a right not to be thawed unless it is placed in the only environment in which it can survive—a woman's womb. But even if it has no moral rights of its own, there is a moral obligation to protect it from harm, provided that can be done with relatively little cost and effort.

George Annas, professor of health law at Boston University School of Medicine, expresses a different view. Acknowledging that the human embryo is a "powerful symbol of human regeneration," he believes it should have legal recognition, though not legal rights. Annas stresses the importance of informed consent of both gamete donors in deciding to freeze embryos. When pregnancy is achieved, or when both donors are dead, he says, the remaining frozen embryos should be destroyed.

Yet a third view was expressed by Britain's Warnock Commission in its Report to Parliament, July 1984. The commission would allow the storage facility to dispose of unused frozen embryos as it sees fit, subject to licensing laws.

Surrogate motherhood—in which a woman agrees to be inseminated with the sperm from the husband of another couple in order to conceive and bear a child for that couple—has been the subject of much debate because of its commercial aspects and the potential impact on both surrogate and child. Is surrogacy a form of baby selling? Are women who become surrogates being exploited? Who is responsible for an unwanted child born to a surrogate?

While surrogacy is still being debated in the U.S., other nations have taken or are considering action. In The Netherlands a scientific board of the Dutch Health Council has issued interim guidelines on *in vitro* fertilization that also forbid surrogacy. In Canada the Ontario Law Reform Commission has recommended that surrogate motherhood be legalized and regulated, subject to prior court appeal. In Britain commercial surrogacy has been made a criminal offense, and the British Parliament is considering making it illegal for British agencies to offer services outside the country. Finally, commercial surrogacy has been banned in the state of Victoria, Australia, where the Infertility Act makes it a criminal offense punishable by up to two years in prison.

Caring for elderly parents

More than 20 years after the passage of Medicare and Medicaid in the U.S., federal and state governments would like to reduce their financial commitments to ailing elderly people. With medical costs continuing to climb and more people living into their eighties and nineties, thoughts are turning to the role families should play in supporting and caring for elderly parents.

In 1983 the Reagan administration announced that states under Medicaid could legally require adult children to contribute to their elderly parents' care. Also in that year, Rep. Mario Biaggi (Dem., N.Y.) introduced a bill in Congress to allow family members to claim a tax credit for housing a dependent over age 65.

Sherry King (left) joyfully bore a child for her infertile sister, Carole Jalbert (right). But as surrogate motherhood is becoming more common, not all such arrangements are turning out so amicably.

AP/Wide World

While neither effort made much headway (Biaggi's bill died, and few states took up the administration's invitation), such moves have provided an occasion to examine an underlying moral question: in an age when parents and children pride themselves on leading independent lives, what are the special obligations of adult children to their aging parents?

As philosopher Daniel Callahan, who is the director of the Hastings Center, has said, "The moral ideal of the parent-child relationship is that of love, nurture, and the mutual seeking for the good of the other." Still, Callahan recognizes that "many children do not find their parents lovable." For their part, "many parents are not happy with the way their children turn out . . . and do not seek to remain intertwined with them." Given the contrast between reality and the moral ideal, what is the nature of the parent-child bond?

Callahan has identified several sources of family obligation, which may operate under different circumstances. These include friendship, gratitude (for a parent who has done far more than is morally necessary), and the "utter need" of the elderly person. However, the relationship remains oddly elusive, requiring a moral phrase that catches the notions of duty and affection in one concept.

Callahan believes that some claims on children have moral priority over others. Most important, children should visit, phone, or write letters, since affection is what parents desire most. But the principal financial obligation of adult children is to their own children. "Adults with elderly parents ought not to be put in the position of trying to balance the moral claims of their own children against those of their parents or jeopardizing their own old age in order to sustain their parents in their old age," says Callahan. And further, "Though such conflicts may at times be inescapable, society ought to be structured in a way that minimizes them."

In the U.S. the dependence of elderly people generally follows a long period of financial and social independence. But in nonindustrialized countries that may not be so. Anthropologist Nancy Foner points out that in countries where there are no social welfare benefits, people rely on their families during hard times throughout their lives. We tend to think of family relationships in such countries as being very close and loving, but Foner cites evidence to the contrary. Adult children often resent their responsibilities and fulfill them grudgingly. Sometimes they act out of love and gratitude, but they also perform their duties in exchange for property or because they fear disinheritance or community disapproval.

The final Baby Doe regulation

On May 15, 1985, the U.S. federal government's final Baby Doe rule went into effect. The rule is the culmination of three years of intensive political controversy that has pitted the rights of severely ill newborns against the judgment of families and treating physicians.

The controversy erupted in 1982 when a baby with Down syndrome and a defect of the esophagus was deprived of treatment with the approval of the Indiana courts. The baby—known only as Baby Doe—died of starvation after his parents followed their doctors' advice and refused permission for corrective surgery that would have allowed their baby to eat. In a series of moves designed to prevent such infant deaths, the federal government moved swiftly to curtail the decision-making powers of doctors and parents. Regulations were first drafted by the Department of Health and Human Services under Section 504 of the Rehabilitation Act of 1973; these were subsequently struck down on the grounds that the law did not apply to handicapped infants, a decision that was upheld by the U.S. Supreme Court. Congress then proceeded to pass the Child Abuse Prevention Amendments of 1984 and published regulations to implement the law.

The Baby Doe regulations have now undergone several revisions in response to criticism by physicians, ethicists, and the six senators who sponsored the original amendments in Congress. The final version specifies that each state's child protection agency must have in place a mechanism for investigating instances of "medical neglect" or otherwise forfeit federal child-abuse-prevention funding. Withholding treatment (other than food, water, and medication) is permissible only if—in the treating physician's "reasonable medical judgment"—the infant is chronically and irreversibly

The final Baby Doe regulation that went into effect in the U.S. in mid-1985 stipulates that withholding treatment from severely ill or handicapped infants is permissible only if treatment would be inhumane and futile.

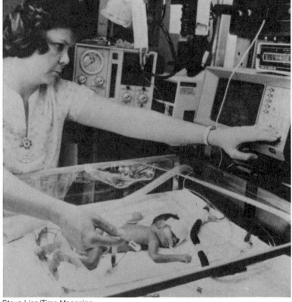

Steve Liss/Time Magazine

comatose; treatment would prolong dying or otherwise be futile in saving the infant's life; and treatment would be inhumane.

The impact of the final rule is being watched closely. Is it a powerful symbol of society's concern about disabled newborns, or is it unwarranted and dangerous interference in a private sphere that is leading to cases of overtreatment?

Thomas Murray, a social psychologist at the University of Texas Medical School at Galveston, believes that the rule, in conjunction with the larger public debate that has gone on simultaneously, has lead to the articulation of the "best interests of the infant" standard. He expresses confidence that the language that was incorporated into the final rule gives physicians the flexibility they need to decide which infants to treat. A similar view is expressed by William Weil, chairman of the bioethics committee of the American Academy of Pediatrics. The academy fought long and hard for less-rigid language in the final rule.

Philosopher John Moskop and pediatrician Rita Saldanha disagree. They argue that, whatever the language of the final rule, it has made doctors fearful of legal consequences and hence far more likely to overtreat babies ("The Baby Doe Rule: Still a Threat," *Hastings Center Report* [April 1986]). Moskop and Saldanha believe that the rule will force physicians to violate the Hippocratic principle of "do no harm" by providing treatment that has no compensating benefits. They are critical of a policy that will require already overcrowded newborn intensive care nurseries to devote ever larger proportions of their beds—at the expense of children who might benefit from treatment—to some children who may never recover.

Withholding food and water from dying patients

When, if ever, is it permissible to withhold or withdraw artificial nutrition (in the form of tube feedings) from dying patients? Debates among scholars and recent court decisions have been inconclusive, but a consensus is gradually building toward the time when not being fed will most probably become standard "treatment" for all patients who are permanently unconscious or are suffering from severe, irreversible dementia.

Among those who argue that food and water may be withheld in carefully limited circumstances are Joanne Lynn, a physician, and James Childress, a philosopher. Lynn and Childress believe that medical nutrition and hydration have more in common with other medical procedures than with typical human ways of providing nutrition (offering a sip of water, for example). In their view feeding, like any other medical procedure, may be stopped in the rare instances when the burdens for the patient outweigh the benefits.

Others take issue with that view. Hastings Center director Callahan sees feeding, even by medical means, as the "perfect symbol of the fact that human life is inescapably social and communal." While he acknowledges the "moral licitness" of Lynn and Childress's position, he expresses a revulsion at the stopping of feeding even under legitimate circumstances and fears the practical consequences. Once we allow feeding to be discontinued, he asks, will we take the next step and say that it must be discontinued because it does the patient no good and wastes money?

During 1985 two important court decisions sent mixed messages. In the case of Paul Brophy, a 48-year-old fire fighter who has been in a persistent vegetative state since March 1983, a Massachusetts probate court permanently enjoined the hospital from removing the feeding tubes, despite testimony that Brophy had told his wife, "No way do I want to live like that." The judge based his decision on his belief that feeding tubes are categorically different from other forms of treatment, such as mechanical ventilators.

But the New Jersey Supreme Court—the same court that ruled a decade ago that Karen Ann Quinlan's respirator could be disconnected—came to the opposite conclusion. In the case of Claire Conroy, an 84-year-old nursing home patient who died before the opinion was handed down, the court ruled that artificial feeding, like mechanical ventilators, could be discontinued, provided certain carefully spelled-out procedures were followed. The court also established a state ombudsman to consider future requests to discontinue feeding for nursing home patients.

In March 1986 the judicial division of the American Medical Association issued a statement that will make it easier for physicians to withhold food and water. The AMA's guidelines state: "Even if death is not

Elizabeth Bouvia, a quadriplegic cerebral palsy patient, is pictured with an unwanted feeding tube in place. Bouvia fought for—and in April 1986 finally won—the legal right to refuse food and water.

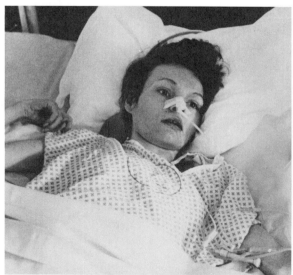

imminent but a patient's coma is beyond doubt irreversible and there are adequate safeguards to confirm the accuracy of the diagnosis and with the concurrence of those who have responsibility for the care of the patient, it is not unethical to discontinue all means of life prolonging medical treatment." Life prolonging medical treatment is defined as including "medication and artificially or technologically supplied respiration, nutrition or hydration." In September 1986 the highest Massachusetts court ruled that the fire fighter Brophy could have his feeding tube removed.

DRGs and the quality of care

Since 1983 hospitals across the United States have been phasing in so-called diagnosis-related groups (DRGs), the federal government's new method of paying for Medicare costs. Under this prospective payment plan, hospitals are no longer reimbursed for the cost of the services they provide to Medicare patients. Instead they receive a predetermined amount for each patient's stay, based on the average cost of treating a particular condition.

Initial indications are that DRGs have succeeded in reducing the length of hospital stays, and some say they have done so without harming the quality of care. But DRGs have also been criticized by physicians, patient advocacy groups, and others who maintain that such things as access, quality of care, medical progress, and the autonomy of hospitals run the risk of being sacrificed in the name of efficiency.

Those upholding this view cite evidence that hospitals are turning away poor patients and patients who seem likely to require longer-than-average hospital stays and are devising strategies to woo DRG-profitable patients. For patients who are admitted to hospitals, some tests and therapies will be eliminated. At many hospitals nonmedical support staff have already been reduced. And some patients are being discharged earlier than they might have been otherwise.

DRGs may also have indirect costs. They are likely to impede medical progress because hospitals have less incentive to buy or develop costly tests or technologies. And they may reduce local autonomy by forcing independent hospitals to join large chains.

DRGs are also altering the doctor's relationship to patients. Since each hospital now bears the cost of the doctor's medical decisions, physicians face a conflict between their traditional allegiance to patients and their loyalty to the hospital. "Ultimately," writes philosopher E. Havvi Morreim, "the conflict pits the interests of the current patient against those of future patients whose health care will one day suffer if hospitals are fewer in number and less well equipped" ("The MD and the DRG," *Hastings Center Report* [June 1985]). While Morreim believes that doctors have to work with their hospitals to control costs, she sees a danger in strategies that some hospitals are adopting. Hospitals

should not penalize doctors for high spending patterns or offer them financial rewards for holding down costs. Nor should physicians make cost-cutting decisions at the bedside. Instead, Morreim says, they should collectively revise the informal protocols that guide clinical decision making while they strive to maintain the quality of care.

In February 1985 the U.S. General Accounting Office submitted a preliminary report to the Special Committee on Aging of the U.S. Senate indicating that patients are being discharged earlier and sicker today and that there are insufficient nursing home beds to accommodate them. Concerned about the trend toward premature discharge, consumer groups have lobbied successfully to persuade the Health Care Financing Administration to require hospitals to inform Medicare patients of their discharge rights, in writing, at the time of admission to the hospital.

Looking ahead

Unquestionably, further discussion of these issues can be anticipated in the near future. Many other medical-ethical issues are also of continuing concern to patients, philosophers, clergy, physicians, lawyers, social scientists, and society at large.

Specific topics that have arisen in the past few years are represented by the case of Baby Fae, the infant who died in November 1984 at Loma Linda (Calif.) University Medical Center shortly after undergoing surgery to replace her defective heart with the heart of a baboon; by the case of Elizabeth Bouvia, a woman with virtually no motor function who fought a series of court battles in California for the right to refuse food and water as a hospitalized patient; by the ethical issues relating to AIDS—blood screening, public health dilemmas, epidemiology, clinical care, research, public policy, and public education; and by temporary and permanent artificial heart implants and the impact of the technology on individual patients and society's health care priorities.

Further, the dangers and potentials of gene therapy are very much on people's minds as scientists prepare to treat single gene defects in human beings. In the U.S. closer scrutiny of medical ethics at the federal level can be expected from the newly created permanent Biomedical Ethics Board and Biomedical Ethics Advisory Committee, established by Congress under the Health Research Extension Act of 1985. The board, first proposed by Senators Edward Kennedy (Dem., Mass.) and Albert Gore (Dem., Tenn.), will report to Congress annually on ethical issues in health care delivery, biomedical and behavioral research, and genetic engineering. Among its charges, the advisory committee has been asked to study the ethical implications of changing the risk standard in the federal regulations governing fetal research.

—*Joyce Bermel*

Special Report
Children of Divorce
by Edith T. Shapiro, M.D.

Jane S. recently made an appointment with a psychiatrist for her 17-year-old daughter, explaining, "Kay is supposed to go away to college next fall, something she's always wanted. But she's been deeply depressed lately and now says she doesn't want to go. Also she is involved with a boy I hate—a real nothing. I'm sure our divorce (even though it was ten years ago) and Kay's father's behavior ever since are at the root of the trouble."

Whether she is correct or not, Jane is expressing a prevalent worry. Roughly 50% of marriages end in divorce, and in the United States the number of children who must cope with the separation or divorce of their parents increases by 1.1 million each year. From another perspective, it is estimated that a decade from now half of all the children in the United States will be living in one-parent homes (because of increased illegitimacy rates as well as disrupted marriages). Psychiatrists and other mental health professionals, the legal establishment, and the media are now actively studying and reporting on these children.

The current consensus is that children of divorce are more likely than other children to suffer from emotional problems; more such children are appearing in psychiatric clinics than children from two-parent homes, and teachers report that the former are less socially competent and have lower educational and social strivings. It also appears to some observers that disturbances such as neurotic symptoms or undesirable personality characteristics may persist into or first appear in adult life in children of divorce more frequently than was previously recognized. Recent studies suggest that the physical health of children is also impaired by divorce.

As is often true in studies of human behavior and emotional responses, much that is reported is impressionistic rather than scientific, and all conclusions about cause and effect must be treated with skepticism. The fact that certain symptoms are seen in children after divorce does not necessarily implicate divorce as the sole cause. Most of the research that has been done thus far does not meet stringent scientific criteria—not because researchers are careless or incompetent but because the phenomena studied are so complex. In 1984 psychologists Korrel W. Kanoy and Jo Lynn Cunningham, who surveyed the scientific literature on children and divorce, found contradictory results. However, they concluded that more uniform answers would come from improved research methods. They pointed to three major sources of error: (1) the questions the researchers asked were often colored by their beliefs, which in part determined the answers; (2) random samples were difficult to define and obtain; and (3) frequently parents and other adults were interviewed rather than the children themselves, and they may have reported their own feelings rather than those of the children. The media play a major role in popularizing premature conclusions. Unfortunately, parents and lawyers who are involved with the process and possible consequences of divorce are more likely to get information about the burden of divorce on children from popular rather than scientific sources.

How deep is the hurt?

Currently, specialists from diverse disciplines are in agreement in at least one area: for children who had a previously "normal" family life, divorce—at least in the short run—is a calamity. Beyond that, most of what can be said now is at best speculative.

According to a developmental thesis, children are immature organisms needing stable and predictable parenting in a consistent setting as a foundation for normal adult personality. Optimally they need parenting from both parents (who, incidentally, need not be the biologic parents). Thus, children become adults through a kind of unconscious copying of adult models, the formation of emotional bonds, and the experiencing of feelings of reciprocity. Both the sense of self and self-respect evolve in this way.

Parental discord disorganizes and confuses children, and younger children are more profoundly affected. Older children with more stable personality organization—with stronger egos—cope with divorce better than the very young, although even adult children may react to parents' divorces with symptoms of psychiatric distress. One such adult, Joe G., went to a psychiatrist at the age of 35 complaining of depression and an impulse to quit his job and terminate his own marriage, although he previously had been satisfied with both. He denied that the recent divorce of his parents was a factor, and only after months of psychotherapy did his feelings of rage, disappointment, and fear of abandonment produced by the parental separation emerge.

In the 1960s and '70s there was an emphasis on individualism and self-fulfillment of both partners in a marriage and consequently an increase in solving marital discord through divorce. At the same time, observed effects of divorce on children were minimized as short-term crises.

Child psychiatrist E. James Anthony is among those who support the view that divorce is a short-term crisis for most children. He has noted that children tend to idealize predivorce home life. While they need help from friends and family to cope with the immediate situation created by the family breakup, professional intervention, he has found, is not usually necessary. In his view children who suffer long-term effects were probably already vulnerable to manifesting emotional instability.

Other researchers, however, have found that some children who appeared to be well adjusted after divorce voiced the cynical idea that divorce was all right because all relationships were fragile and none could last. Some older children who said that they "approved" of their parents' divorce (younger children rarely claimed to approve) were able to understand that divorce had been desirable for their parents, but none felt that it had benefited them. Thus, though children may appear to have "accepted" divorce, they may really not have accepted it at all and may harbor strong feelings of distress. New York University child psychiatrist Stella Chess and others studied individuals from birth through their twenties and concluded from their research that ongoing parental conflict is more harmful to children than divorce per se.

Kay's case

Few among the professionals dealing with divorce now disagree that divorce has an immediate, disruptive, and painful effect on offspring of all ages. The debate is still mainly about long-term or delayed effects. Kay, the young woman referred to above, can serve to illustrate some of the acknowledged short-term as well as the possible long-term effects.

In Kay's case the parents divorced when she was six years old, after an acrimonious three-year separation characterized by the father's virtual abandonment of Kay, although he was said to have adored her. Shortly after the divorce he remarried, moved to another state, and made no effort to see the child. He did continue to send money punctiliously, although according to Jane, Kay's mother, it was never enough. She took him to court to try to force him to pay for Kay's tuition at a private college.

In psychotherapy a psychiatrist customarily works backward: the patient states the current problem, and the psychiatrist traces its origins by reconstructing the history. Kay at first spoke mainly about her symptoms and only later brought up recollections of her parents' divorce and her feelings about it then and since.

In her recounting to the psychiatrist, Jane provided important information. According to Jane, when the father left the household for the first time, Kay was a charming, precocious three-year-old. At first she asked about her father, but when told that he was gone she stopped asking. Around that time she began to wet her bed and to cling to her mother in ways she previously had not. The father, who was already involved with another woman, paid a few visits; he took Kay out but usually brought her back early, saying that her behavior was "wild." His visits ceased completely for two years following an argument between him and Jane. After the divorce and the father's remarriage, there was one more contact, which ended disastrously when Kay panicked at staying with her father and his new wife and telephoned Jane, who fetched her home.

Kay's behavior as described by Jane coincides with the recent observations of Judith S. Wallerstein and Joan Berlin Kelly, California researchers who studied 60 divorced middle-class families during the first 18

It is becoming increasingly apparent that children suffer acutely when parents divorce. They may do poorly in their schoolwork, and in class they may exhibit emotional insecurity, anger, sadness, or guilt. "The Divorce Club," an innovative program run by teachers at an elementary school in Ypsilanti, Michigan, gives students with divorced parents a chance to talk about their struggles.

Peter Yates

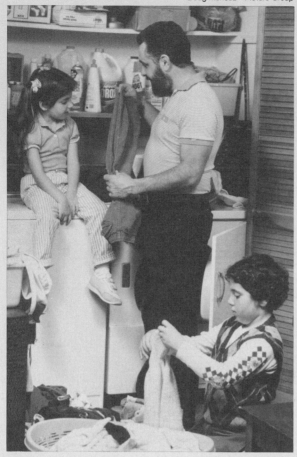

At least one study has shown that after a divorce, fathers may be better equipped than mothers, financially and emotionally, to provide the best home for and to have legal custody of the children.

months after separation and again after five years. They reported that in the first 18 months after separation preschool children spoke little but in play therapy acted out the chaos and confusion in their lives.

Emotions in these children were often out of kilter, and impulsive outbursts were common. Psychologically children could not grasp that their parents were distinct from themselves and felt guilt and responsibility for the divorce. Older children with stronger ego structures understood separateness better and tended to show depression, a more adult symptom, which was noted in Kay when she was in her mid-teens.

Over the years Kay expressed alternately indifference and anger toward her father. She aligned herself with Jane and became her mother's support and confidante. When Jane remarried, Kay "adopted" her stepfather, who was affectionate and loving toward her.

Kay showed great concern about money, which was a constant topic of conversation in the household—usually in the context of the penuriousness of her nat-

ural father. She worked as a sales clerk, an actress, and a model throughout her high-school years. She was an excellent student, independent and mature—a paragon in all respects—until she met her boyfriend at age 15.

Around this time, in a joint therapy session with her mother, Kay appeared to be her mother's peer in manner, dress, and conversation, which were extremely mature. Kay's mother assured the psychiatrist that there were no secrets between them and that everything could be discussed freely. But the psychiatrist, who was by then in Kay's confidence, knew that this was a maternal self-deception. In fact, Kay had always been protective of her mother, withholding distressing and important information, and had told her nothing of the immediate antecedents that precipitated the crisis.

Wallerstein and Kelly described fluctuations in behavior similar to Kay's in children at corresponding ages. Their conclusion was that precocious maturation after divorce is often unstable—a coping response to the diminished parenting capacities of parents. They point out that parents on the average are ineffective as parents for some 2½ to 3½ years after divorce, when they are largely preoccupied with their own problems. They concluded that children of divorce are caught in a role reversal; *i.e.*, they must be "parents" to their parents—as Kay was to Jane. In their book, *Surviving the Breakup: How Children and Parents Cope with Divorce* (1980), Wallerstein and Kelly state their finding that such children are "overburdened, overwhelmed, and deprived of the generational distance necessary for normal development." Sometimes very young children are suddenly expected to care for themselves, while older children often become advisers to parents—in particular, to mothers who have custody.

University of Massachusetts sociologist Robert Weiss has reached a somewhat different conclusion. In an article on the experience of growing up in a single-parent household, entitled "Growing Up a Little Faster," published in the *Journal of Social Issues,* he noted that in divorce some children gained substantially in maturity and independence, participated with parents as coequals in everyday tasks, and enjoyed friendship and communication with them. "Being the parent's anchor in a time of turmoil is a flattering role to some children," he contends.

In many studies girls of all ages are said to fare better overall than boys when parents divorce. Researcher E. Hetherington, however, discovered that the superior adjustment of girls was not sustained and that frequently girls showed disturbances later on in their relationships with men. Indeed, such symptoms did surface with Kay.

In therapy Kay told the psychiatrist that she did not know whether to go away to college or to comply with her boyfriend's ultimatum to stay home or lose him. She had not told her mother about the boyfriend's threat. Indeed, Kay revealed much to the psychiatrist that her mother was unaware of; Kay described her boyfriend as immature, selfish, jealous, manipulative, and unfair, confirming her mother's estimation that he was a "nothing." She also revealed that he had a criminal record for dealing in drugs. He was in academic trouble and espoused a "macho" orientation that went against all Kay's convictions. Furthermore, unbeknownst to Jane, Kay and the young man had been sexually intimate for two years, and six months previously Kay had undergone an abortion (which the boyfriend paid for while at the same time refusing to accompany her to the clinic, causing her great hurt and humiliation).

Kay said that she had forgiven him and also that she both loved and hated him. She volunteered that she had recently been thinking more and more about her father. Jane had told Kay that her father had been "no good" and that she had given him an ultimatum to "shape up" and face his responsibility, but instead he had left. Kay was distressed by her parents' money quarrel over her college tuition and wondered whether she was the responsibility he had not been able to face at the time of the divorce.

Against this background one sees that there is literally nothing that Kay would not put up with from her boyfriend to avoid the pain of yet another rejection and loss. Furthermore, she was adamant about not repeating her mother's mistake and driving away a man by making demands. On a deeper level, the psychiatrist discovered that Kay believed she did not deserve better treatment. She seemed to consider herself as unworthy of respect since her own father thought so little of her.

Only after weeks of therapy did Kay acknowledge that she always had felt responsible for the divorce— that she was the root of the failed marriage. Kay divulged all this to the psychiatrist rather than to her mother because she was not willing to add to Jane's burdens. "I'd rather die," she said dramatically.

Kay is a patient who has shown what appear to be both short-term and long-term effects of divorce— an abnormally stressful childhood with symptoms of emotional turmoil immediately after her parents' disunion, followed by precocious maturity. As a teenager she became attached to a boyfriend and began to engage in regular sexual activities. Then her unsatisfied dependency needs became increasingly manifest. She was angry and defiantly independent while feeling lonely, needy, and fearful. By the time she entered therapy, she had little expectation that people would treat her with sensitivity, love, or kindness. Her self-esteem especially as a woman was so low that she was willing to pay a high price for what she perceived as love from her boyfriend.

Many of Kay's symptoms that plunged her into therapy ten years after her parents' separation do seem to have roots in the divorce. University of Michigan psychologist Neil Kalter has noted what he calls "time-bomb" symptoms in children who appear to be coping. Drug abuse and sexual promiscuity are not uncommon manifestations years after a family has broken up. Yet many professionals would still be reluctant to say Kay's problems were unique or typical of children of divorce.

The nature of childhood

Several widely debated issues concerning divorce and its effects on children are unresolved. Should children be protected from parental discord or exposed to it? Can they handle the burden of failed marriages and grow and mature from the experience, as sociologist Weiss maintains? Or is the hurt inevitable and exposure to divorce decidedly harmful for children, as many other specialists are saying?

The late French social historian Philippe Ariès, in an exhaustive historical account entitled *Centuries of Childhood,* pointed out that only since the 18th century has childhood been viewed as a unique state entitled to special protection. Throughout the rest of the history of Western civilization, it had been only a way station to adulthood, and children were not accorded special treatment. One reason for this was the extremely high death rate of children; adults avoided excessive attachment, knowing that the probability of children's survival into adulthood was very low. By the 18th century major breakthroughs in science and medicine were greatly improving survival rates; by the 19th century the Western world was child centered.

More recently a study of hundreds of American children in different communities led Marie Winn to conclude in *Children Without Childhood* (1984) that because of disruption in family life, high divorce rates, and numerous other factors reflective of contemporary society, childhood as a unique state (as her title would suggest) had ceased to exist.

New attention to the child's best interests

Another of Ariès's observations was that the family is a hardy institution that has survived assaults throughout the ages. He believed that while more permissive attitudes toward divorce had indeed weakened the institution of marriage per se in contemporary society, marriage as an *ideal* continued to thrive.

Some recent trends, including the augmented interest in children of divorce, may be supporting his view. After three decades of soaring divorce rates, there appears to be a possible leveling off. After two decades of minimizing the impact of divorce on children when individual partners in a marriage were largely preoccupied with asserting their individualism, the importance of the marital unit for children is being newly acknowledged. While few in contemporary society question the appropriateness of divorce as a remedy for serious marital distress, staying together for the sake of the children if at all possible is an old idea gaining new respectability.

When Wallerstein and Kelly followed up their study of 60 middle-class families (chosen in an effort to isolate divorce as the pivotal effect and to minimize the impact of poverty, social class, race, and lack of education), they found, after five years, that major upheavals had taken place in the children's lives to a degree that made it extremely difficult to identify divorce as the principal variable. Among other things, in the wake of divorce the majority of households slipped a notch on the socioeconomic scale. Also, children were exposed to at least twice as many babysitters as children in two-parent homes; this meant additional adjustments and attachments were called for, which diluted the impact of particular adult models, who are so crucial for personality formation.

In recognition of these factors, parents, therapists, and the legal establishment are experimenting with tactics that are aimed at stabilizing the environment for children caught in a divorce. Some psychiatrists and others in related professions recommend that all divorcing families enter some form of therapy to explain to, reassure, and support the children. Children's advocates are impartial observers—usually from the mental health profession—appointed by the courts to recommend, for example, custodial arrangements that are best suited to individual children.

Some in the legal establishment have urged that children be represented by their own attorneys in contested divorces. Divorce mediation and joint custody are other new ideas. Joint custody is an ambiguous term that can mean anything from shared responsibility for decisions regarding children to shared physical custody. It is meant to give both parents equal rights, hence equal interests, in child rearing and ideally to give children unlimited access to both parents. Divorce mediation attempts to mollify or preempt the effects of the usual adversarial system of divorce, where children often become "spoils" of an ongoing war between parents. Divorce mediation and joint custody in carefully selected situations can work well. Unfortunately, these strategies have gained premature support with their seductive but unrealistic and unrealized promises of painless divorce.

Because children spend a large portion of their time at school, many of their feelings about their home life are acted out there. Children of divorce are often easy to spot; there are predictable academic declines and sudden shifts in behavior—anger, guilt, insecurity, and sadness are common. Consequently, a few school systems have been experimenting with courses and counseling programs to help teachers deal with the problems of children of divorce in their classes.

Historically mothers have been considered to be uniquely suited to care for their children, and men were given custody only if the women were considered unfit. Richard A. Warshak of the University of Texas Health Science Center at Dallas has studied custodial fathers and concludes that "preference for maternal custody is unwarranted" and that in certain situations children are better off with the same-sex parent. Furthermore, after divorce men are usually better off financially and can provide more for the children. Custodial fathers seem better able to maintain discipline and have better relations with noncustodial mothers than vice versa.

Health risks, too

Psychologist John Guidubaldi of Kent (Ohio) State University and coresearchers designed a scientific protocol to test the hypothesis that divorce leads to impaired physical health of all parties in the divorce, including children. School psychologists nationwide were selected at random to study 699 children, again chosen at random, 341 of whom came from divorced families. The parents of the children were asked to rank the children's physical health on a scale from poor to excellent. In addition a battery of psychological tests was administered to all family members to elicit other variables.

The conclusion was that divorced parents did report poorer health for their children and that poor health was correlated with diminished school performance and with emotional problems. The physical toll was manifested in lethargy ("no pep"), weight changes, and sleeplessness, among other symptoms.

Minimizing the hurt

Children of divorce suffer acutely in the short term, and a large percentage of children continue to have problems five years later and beyond. While research on best coping methods is being conducted in many academic centers, some tentative recommendations have already emerged from the work completed to date. If divorce is inevitable, parents should contrive by every means possible to minimize the conflict between them and to isolate the children from it since conflict is clearly destructive for children.

After divorce it is crucial to allow children free access to both parents, but how that is accomplished should be decided on an individual basis. Abstaining from criticism of the other spouse is vital, since children, who have internalized parts of both parents in the process of personality formation, are put into the position of having to hate parts of themselves. (The patient, Kay, had mentioned early in her therapy that she had seen some old home movies of herself with her father and had been very disturbed by her physical resemblance to him.)

Perhaps the last word here should be left to one little boy whose enlightened family sought counseling prior to divorce. During a discussion about who hurt the most, the child said, "We all hurt as much as possible."

Mental Health and Illness

Anxiety and depression are painful emotions that almost everyone has experienced. Both can occur as normal emotions that are part of the human condition. Faced with danger, one feels the fear, apprehension, and tension that are characteristic of anxiety, along with typical physical sensations that come from increased heart and respiratory rates and increased sweating. Following a significant loss, depression (experienced as feeling sad or "blue") is an important part of normal grief. In both instances the painful emotions serve adaptive functions, and the absence of anxiety or depression in those circumstances is abnormal, usually reflecting the presence of other psychological problems. However, anxiety and depression can occur as symptoms in the course of a wide variety of both physical and mental disorders and also as core features of specific syndromes that deserve careful diagnosis and treatment. Among the key new developments in the field of psychiatry are several important advances in the understanding of such disorders that have spurred new treatments and reevaluation of old treatments.

Panic disorder and agoraphobia

One of the most important recent developments in psychiatric diagnosis has been the recognition of a syndrome characterized by recurrent spontaneous panic attacks. This syndrome usually starts in early adulthood, when a previously healthy individual begins to experience episodes of the sudden unexplained onset of severe feelings of panic accompanied by a variety of physical symptoms including heart palpitations (a sensation that the heart is racing or skipping beats),

sweating, dizziness, trembling, hot and cold flashes, and shortness of breath. Chest pain may also occur, and the panic attack commonly includes powerful fears of dying, losing control, or going crazy. The attacks usually last for a few minutes at a time but sometimes can persist for several hours. The frequency of occurrence varies from every few weeks to several times a day, with the frequency often increasing after a few widely spaced initial attacks. These subjectively devastating attacks understandably cause the individual to seek medical attention at an emergency room or physician's office. The results of a routine physical examination and electrocardiogram are usually normal, except that the pulse reading may indicate an increased heart rate.

Although this syndrome of recurrent attacks of panic associated with typical physical symptoms is certainly not a new disease (in the past such symptoms were sometimes referred to as neurocirculatory asthenia, "soldier's heart," or anxiety neurosis), official recognition of the disorder in the psychiatric nomenclature, under the label of "panic disorder," occurred only in 1980, and the previously neglected and often misdiagnosed syndrome has received intensive investigation since then.

The disorder is very common; a recent large-scale community survey disclosed a current prevalence of about 1% in the general population. The cause of panic disorder remains unknown, but there are some interesting leads currently under scrutiny. Although the initial attacks commonly occur during a period of stressful life circumstances, specific psychological precipitants are usually not found. In the past the physical symptoms occurring during panic attacks were thought to be due to the disturbances of internal acid-

Frequency of symptoms with panic attacks

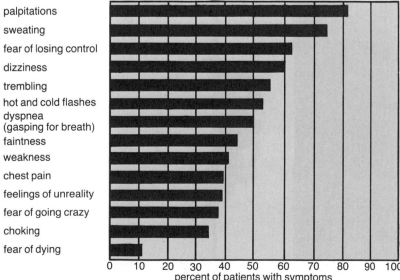

Data from D. A. Katerndahl, "Panic Attacks: Psychologic Response or Mental Illness?" *Postgraduate Medicine*, vol. 75, no. 8 (June 1984), p. 262

A recently recognized psychiatric syndrome is characterized by recurrent panic attacks. Those most often afflicted are previously healthy young adults. The syndrome is manifested by a variety of physical symptoms and powerful fears.

base balance resulting from hyperventilation (rapid overbreathing). Patients were sometimes advised to "breathe into a paper bag" during a panic attack in order to decrease the amount of carbon dioxide lost from the blood due to hyperventilation. However, many panic disorder patients do not hyperventilate during their attacks, and voluntary hyperventilation of room air rarely produces typical panic attack symptoms. The paper bag technique probably served mainly as a distraction while the panic attack resolved naturally.

Several lines of evidence suggest that biologic mechanisms are important in causing panic disorder. First of all, panic attacks can be triggered by several types of biologic challenges, which include infusion of lactate (a naturally occurring by-product of muscle metabolism) as well as several other specific chemicals. These substances generally produce panic attacks in panic disorder patients but not in normal persons. The precise mechanism of action is not yet known, but animal studies indicate that some of the panic-inducing chemicals increase the discharge of neurons in an area of the brain called the locus ceruleus. Other animal studies have shown that stimulation of the locus ceruleus elicits anxietylike behavior. Thus, "dysregulation" or hypersensitivity of the locus ceruleus may play a role in panic disorder. In any case, panic disorder patients appear to have an unusual sensitivity to the subjective sensations produced by these biochemical "triggers."

Second, there is a high rate of panic disorder among the relatives of panic disorder patients, and the possibility of a genetically transmitted vulnerability is supported by twin studies showing that the concordance rate for panic disorder (i.e., the rate of both members of a twin pair having the disorder) is much higher for identical twins, who have the same genetic endowment, than it is for fraternal twins.

Another biologic connection for panic disorder is its association with mitral valve prolapse (MVP), a malformation of the valve between the left atrium and left ventricle of the heart. Mitral valve prolapse is a common condition occurring in about 5% of the general population. The diagnosis of MVP is often based upon echocardiography, a relatively new technique that uses sound waves to evaluate the structure and function of the heart. Mitral valve prolapse usually does not have an adverse effect on heart function, and most persons with MVP have no symptoms from it. Several studies have found that as many as 50% of panic disorder patients also have MVP, although not all investigations confirm it. The meaning of this association is being investigated, but it is very unlikely that there is a causal connection between the two disorders, since many panic disorder patients with typical recurrent panic attacks do not have MVP, and most persons with MVP do not have panic attacks. This is also an important point regarding treatment, because chest pain and palpitations without panic attacks, the main symptoms

when MVP does become symptomatic, often respond well to beta-adrenergic blocking drugs such as propranolol. However, beta blockers have shown little benefit for panic attacks.

One disorder that does appear to be causally connected to panic disorder is agoraphobia. Often misunderstood as meaning a fear of open spaces, the term agoraphobia literally means "fear of the marketplace" and presumably came into use because those suffering from this disorder fear crowded situations such as shopping places. However, the essential feature of agoraphobia is a more general fear of being in any situation from which escape might be difficult or help not available in case of sudden incapacitation. Fear and avoidance behavior cause increasing constriction of normal activities and usually dominate the afflicted individual's life. Many agoraphobics are unable to leave the security of their own home unless accompanied by someone they know and trust, and some agoraphobic patients become completely homebound. Agoraphobia is thus distinguished from simple phobias (irrational fears of some specific object or circumstance such as insects, closed spaces, or heights) by the widespread and generalized nature of the fear and avoidance and also by the fact that agoraphobia usually occurs as a complication of panic disorder. The typical history is that the individual lives quite normally until the recurrent panic attacks begin. Subsequently, the sufferer begins to avoid travel and crowds because of the

PET scans of cerebral blood flow—one biologic mechanism under study—in persons susceptible to panic attacks have revealed abnormal patterns. The dot in the right hemisphere below indicates an area of abnormally high blood flow.

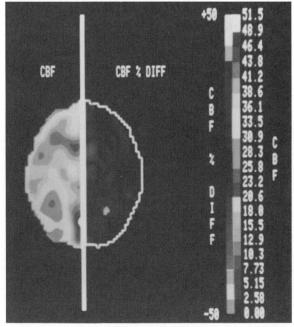

Marcus E. Raichle, Washington University School of Medicine

fear of having a panic attack, with the avoidance then becoming increasingly extensive. The fear and avoidance behavior may persist even if the panic attacks remit after a period of time. The question of why some panic disorder patients develop this complication and others do not is an area of current interest, with some studies finding that the patient's attitudes and cognitions (thoughts) about the initial panic attacks play an important role.

Even without the life-dominating complication of agoraphobia, panic disorder is a devastating condition. Since panic disorder symptoms are similar to those of heart disease, hyperthyroidism, and some adverse drug reactions, those conditions need to be ruled out when the initial attacks occur. Once a diagnosis of panic disorder has been established, patients benefit greatly from an explanation of the disorder, including the fact that it is not "imaginary."

Research over the past several years has shown that several drugs are beneficial in reducing the frequency and severity of panic attacks, sometimes eliminating them completely. The drugs that have been found to be effective in controlled studies include imipramine and phenelzine, both of which have previously been successfully employed as antidepressants, and also alprazolam, a newer drug that is also used for nonpanic anxiety. Achieving adequate dose levels is essential for effective treatment. For patients with agoraphobia, behaviorally oriented psychotherapy involving gradually increased exposure to phobic situations is often helpful in enabling patients to "unlearn" their patterns of fear and avoidance, since phobic anxiety will usually gradually extinguish with increasing exposure to the phobic stimulus. The combination of drug treatment with behavior therapy makes particular sense for the agoraphobic patient who is continuing to have frequent panic attacks.

Anxiety and depression: a newly established link

The distinction between anxiety disorders and depressive disorders is important for diagnosis and treatment, but recent evidence also indicates important areas of overlap. Panic attacks can occur during episodes of major depression (a very common syndrome of persistently depressed mood associated with sleep and appetite disturbances, loss of interest and energy, feelings of self-reproach and worthlessness, and recurrent thoughts of death or suicide, all lasting for at least two weeks).

Understandably, patients with panic disorder may also become depressed, but careful histories indicate that, in addition to such "secondary" depressions, a substantial minority of panic disorder patients (more than would be expected by chance alone) have had episodes of major depression even before their panic attacks started. In addition to this evidence for co-occurrence, the fact that some medications previously

Will McIntyre—Photo Researchers

A patient is given anesthesia and muscle relaxants in preparation for electroconvulsive therapy (ECT). For many severely depressed patients, ECT may be faster, safer, and more effective than drugs or psychotherapy.

thought of as "antidepressants" (e.g., tricyclic drugs such as imipramine and monoamine oxidase inhibitors such as phenelzine) can be effective in treating panic disorder has also raised the possibility of a similar biologic disturbance underlying both disorders. However, these drugs have a number of different effects on various areas of the brain, and there are some treatments that are effective for depression (e.g., electroconvulsive therapy and bupropion, a new antidepressant drug) but not for panic anxiety. Pending further data, it seems reasonable to conclude that panic disorder and major depression are distinct disorders with a substantial degree of co-occurrence and a possibly shared vulnerability in some patients.

Consensus on a controversial treatment

A number of treatments with documented efficacy for clinical depressions are now available. These include several classes of antidepressant drugs and several types of psychotherapy. Combinations of psychotherapy and drug treatment are frequently more helpful than either treatment alone. Drugs containing salts of the element lithium are often effective for prevention as well as treatment of bipolar disorder, a condition previously called manic-depressive illness and characterized by recurrent episodes of both depression and mania (abnormally elevated mood with irritability and extreme hyperactivity). Recent studies indicate that carbamazepine, an anticonvulsant drug, can benefit bipolar patients who do not respond to lithium.

Unfortunately, these rather well-accepted treatments are not always successful. There are some patients whose medical conditions preclude the use of some treatments and others whose lives are threatened if their depression persists for the four weeks required for an adequate trial of a drug. Patients with such

395

severe depressions are often unable to participate in psychotherapy. In those situations electroconvulsive therapy (ECT) needs careful consideration.

Although it has been in use for over 45 years, ECT remains the most controversial treatment in psychiatry. To evaluate its current status, the U.S. National Institute of Mental Health convened a Consensus Development Conference on Electroconvulsive Therapy in June 1985. (The results were published in the *Journal of the American Medical Association,* Oct. 18, 1985.) Although the depiction of ECT as an abusive technique of behavioral control (such as in the popular novel, play, and film *One Flew over the Cuckoo's Nest*) may have some basis in past misuses, such frightening imagery does not reflect the reality of current medical use of ECT. Rather, a number of studies have shown that ECT is an effective treatment for severe depressions, where it is often faster and safer than antidepressant drugs. ECT may also be helpful for some patients with acute schizophrenia or treatment-resistant mania.

In modern use ECT treatments are administered after the patient has been put to sleep with a short-acting anesthetic. The use of muscle relaxants and ventilatory assistance during the anesthetic period have all but eliminated the risks of fractures and inadequate oxygen. Treatments are given several times per week, and a course of 6 to 12 treatments is usually effective. The degree of improvement occurring in a severely depressed and suicidal patient can be dramatic. The biologic mechanisms responsible for the effectiveness of electrically induced brain seizures have not been established, but some studies have indicated that ECT leads to changes in the functioning of specialized neuronal receptor sites in the brain that are similar to those induced by antidepressant drugs. There is no scientific evidence of brain cell damage from ECT, but some loss of memory for events occurring several weeks before, during, and after the course of treatment has been documented. Objective testing has not documented that ECT causes more extensive memory deficits. Confusion and memory loss during the course of treatment can be decreased by the use of unilateral ECT (both stimulus electrodes placed on one side of the head), although this technique is not as effective for some patients as bilateral electrode placement.

The consensus panel gave careful consideration to the issue of informed consent for ECT, a process that is often complicated by the unfortunate stigma surrounding this treatment. Patients and their families may erroneously believe that ECT produces "zombies" rather than a return to normality. Regarding legislated prohibitions on the use of ECT, the panel concluded that "such absolute bans are unduly restrictive and make treatment impossible for patients who might obtain more benefit, at acceptable levels of risk, from ECT than from alternative treatments."

Turning a light on seasonal depression

During the past two years, a new subcategory of depressive illness has been proposed: seasonal affective disorder—sometimes dubbed SAD. This is a condition characterized by regularly recurring depression in the winter, frequently alternating with elevated mood in the summer. During their winter depressions such patients usually oversleep, overeat, experience a strong craving for carbohydrates, and are generally slowed down. To qualify for a diagnosis of seasonal affective disorder, these seasonal mood swings must be much more pronounced than the normal responses to changes in climate and must not be accounted for by seasonally changing psychosocial variables such as work or school stresses.

Based on patient reports that winter depressions can be dramatically improved or prevented by travel to sunny climates close to the Equator, psychiatrist Norman Rosenthal and colleagues at the National Institute of Mental Health postulated that the decreased length of daylight in the winter months might play an important role in seasonal affective disorder. In a set of intriguing experiments, they have shown that extending the length of day by means of artificial light

People who experience severe depressions in the winter months may have the condition known as seasonal affective disorder. Exposure to extremely bright artificial lights appears to be an effective therapy.

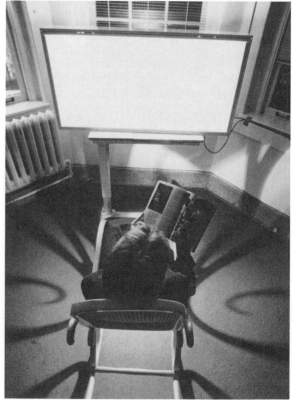

Rich Frishman

several times brighter than ordinary indoor lighting can produce a marked improvement after just a few days in patients suffering from the characteristic winter depressions.

Several hours of bright light treatment in both the morning and evening seem to be most effective. Light of the intensity of ordinary room light is not effective, and removal of bright light treatment leads to relapse within a few days. The mechanism of action of light therapy is not known, but it may involve alterations in melatonin, the pineal gland hormone that mediates a number of light-dependent seasonal biorhythms in animals. Although seasonal depressions often respond to antidepressant drugs, light therapy has the advantage of being essentially free of side effects. Further implications of this unusual new treatment modality, including the question of whether it might benefit non-seasonal depressions, are being actively investigated.

—*Richard M. Glass, M.D.*

Neurology

Recent developments in neurology have been marked by some surprising new discoveries, as well as by continuing progress in some stubbornly difficult areas. With the observation of unexplained neurological disorders in patients suffering from AIDS (acquired immune deficiency syndrome), a disease previously believed to directly affect only the immune system, researchers in 1985 isolated the AIDS virus from the brain tissue and cerebrospinal fluid of some patients. Thus, it became clear that the AIDS virus not only makes the central nervous system vulnerable to organisms that are harmless to the normal immune system but also appears to invade the nervous system directly. Viral particles have been found at autopsy in the brains of a majority of AIDS victims; the virus is evidently responsible for the progressive mental deterioration and brain atrophy seen in these patients.

In another recent finding, clinical trials of plasmapheresis in Guillain-Barré syndrome have shown that the technique can shorten the duration of the disease. Guillain-Barré syndrome is an infection, probably viral, of the nerves emerging from the spinal cord; it causes quickly progressing generalized weakness that can lead to total paralysis. Recovery is painfully slow, often taking many months. Plasmapheresis is a procedure in which whole blood is removed from the patient, the plasma (the fluid portion) is removed by centrifugation from the cellular components, and these components are reinfused into the body in fresh plasma. In several steps all of the patient's blood is removed, treated, and reinjected. The benefit to Guillain-Barré patients is thought to result from the removal of abnormal immune complexes from the circulating plasma. The process is time-consuming and expensive, but it appears to hasten recovery from this debilitating condition.

Progress in preventing and treating cerebral vascular disease remains heartbreakingly slow. In recent years one approach to preventing stroke—or lowering the risk of recurrence in stroke victims—has been surgical alteration of the arteries that provide blood to the brain. One such technique is the grafting of arteries on the scalp to arteries within the skull, a procedure known as extracranial-intracranial (EC/IC) bypass. In this way narrowed blood vessels in neck or brain areas inaccessible to surgery can be bypassed and blood flow to their terminal branches improved. The technique was developed in the 1960s in Europe by surgeons and has been widely practiced in the U.S. According to one estimate, about 3,000–5,000 EC/IC bypasses were being performed annually at U.S. hospitals. However, the results of a multimillion-dollar international trial published in 1985 showed no reduction in stroke rate or improvement in survival in patients who received this type of bypass, compared with similar patients who did not. Thus, what appeared to be a promising technique was suddenly called into question. The operation is costly—about $15,000 in the U.S.—and without proof of its effectiveness, it is likely to be strictly curtailed until the procedure can

Rats with a form of Parkinson's disease turn in circles when their brains are infused with a chemical that stimulates movement. Scientists are using this animal "model" to study new drugs for human Parkinson's patients.

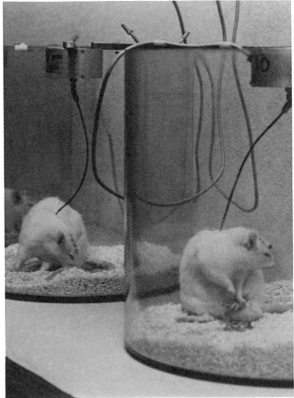

National Institute of Mental Health, NIH

be thoroughly reevaluated. Some researchers suggest that more careful selection of candidates for EC/IC bypass could improve the results.

New insights into Parkinson's disease

Parkinson's disease, or parkinsonism, is one of the commonest diseases of the aging nervous system, affecting about 1% of those over 50 years of age. It mainly affects the ability of the victim to move normally. The person with Parkinson's disease typically walks with a slow, shuffling gait; all movements are difficult for the patient to initiate. A characteristic tremor of the hands or body is often present. These symptoms are slowly progressive and can eventually cause complete disability.

In spontaneously occurring Parkinson's disease, all of these symptoms appear to be due to the gradual deterioration of a tiny group of nerve cells, or neurons, in the base of the brain, called the substantia nigra. The cause of the disease is unknown, but current theories include premature aging and death of these nerve cells, exposure to an environmental toxin, or infection by a slow-acting virus.

Certain drugs are also known to cause symptoms of Parkinson's disease. Many of them, such as haloperidol (Haldol), chlorpromazine (Thorazine), and fluphenazine (Prolixin), are commonly prescribed for serious psychiatric disorders such as schizophrenia. Parkinsonism caused by these medications is usually readily reversible when the drugs are stopped. Exposure to unusually high amounts of certain naturally occurring toxins can also cause parkinsonism. Prolonged exposure to the metal manganese, which may occur in manganese miners, can produce permanent neurological symptoms including those of parkinsonism. Carbon monoxide poisoning, as occurs in suicide attempts or certain industrial accidents, also can produce parkinsonism. In rare cases carbon disulfide poisoning does the same. In all of these toxicities, however, parkinsonism is usually only part of a more fully developed picture of neurological injury.

Drug treatment can blunt the effects of naturally occurring parkinsonism, particularly in the early stages of the disease. Trihexyphenidyl (Artane), benztropine mesylate (Cogentin), and, most recently, levodopa (L-dopa; Sinemet) and bromocriptine (Parlodel) can often enable an otherwise crippled Parkinson victim to walk and move about normally. But because symptoms of the disorder become more difficult to control as the disease progresses, research into both causes and treatment has continued to have a high priority among neuroscientists. These investigations have been hampered by the fact that parkinsonism does not occur spontaneously in animals. In laboratory animals certain drugs can be used to induce symptoms similar to those of Parkinson's disease, specifically, abnormalities of movement that respond to L-dopa or

other antiparkinson medications. But no "animal model" identical to the human disease is known.

In 1982 several young heroin addicts in California suddenly developed clinical signs of full-blown parkinsonism. They were discovered to have taken an impure heroin substitute manufactured for street sale by a local "kitchen chemist." Analysis of the substance revealed the presence of a contaminant called 1-methyl-4-phenyl-1,2,3,6-tetrahydropyridine (MPTP), probably an inadvertent by-product of the drug-manufacturing process. Researchers subsequently discovered that MPTP readily produced parkinsonism in rhesus and squirrel monkeys. The addicts who had taken the drug responded to treatment with L-dopa and other antiparkinson drugs, but the MPTP appeared to have caused permanent injury to their central nervous systems.

Examination of the brains of monkeys given MPTP, and of one person dying of MPTP poisoning, has revealed destruction of neurons in the substantia nigra, just as is observed in spontaneously occurring Parkinson's disease. Moreover, unlike manganese or carbon monoxide toxicity, MPTP poisoning appears to cause a relatively "pure" Parkinson syndrome. Thus, MPTP poisoning appears to have provided a new, impressively accurate model of Parkinson's disease, and scientists now have an animal model of the disease to study in hopes that discoveries about the chemistries, cell behavior, and response to therapeutic agents in MPTP toxicity may apply to naturally occurring human Parkinson's disease. For example, MPTP can be labeled with a radioactive marker so that its natural distribution in both animal and human brains can be studied. Such studies have revealed the affinity of MPTP for areas of the brain rich in a naturally occurring enzyme called monoamine oxidase (MAO). It is this enzyme that may effect the breakdown of MPTP, producing a chemical that actually causes the neuronal injury underlying parkinsonism. The fact that the amount of MAO present in the brain increases naturally with age may explain why Parkinson's disease is a disease of the elderly.

Some researchers have postulated that other, as yet unidentified, environmental toxins may be involved in the cellular injury behind Parkinson's disease, and the study of MPTP may enable new discoveries in that direction as well. At any rate, the MPTP story demonstrates that a tragic occurrence for a small group of people may eventually lead to important therapeutic advances that may help thousands.

Improved outlook for herpes encephalitis

Encephalitis, literally "inflammation of the brain," usually refers to an infection of the cerebral hemispheres. In its mild form encephalitis may produce only headache, fever, and a flulike syndrome. When it is severe, however, it may be fatal. Most encephalitis is caused by viruses. These viruses vary considerably in type and behavior, as well as in the extent of illness they may cause. Some, like arboviruses—arthropod-borne viruses—are transmitted to people from horses or other mammals via mosquitoes, fleas, or ticks. These kinds of encephalitis may have a seasonal variation or may occur in epidemics, as in wet summers when heavy rains and standing water have contributed to an especially high mosquito population. Other viruses, usually those with unknown transmission routes, cause sporadic unpredictable brain inflammation in humans at any time of year.

Herpes simplex encephalitis is the most common form of sporadic, fatal encephalitis in the United States. The herpesvirus is one of a family of viruses called varicella. One of its members causes smallpox; another, chickenpox. Another herpesvirus, herpes zoster, causes shingles, a painful nerve inflammation. Two types of herpes simplex viruses may cause disease in humans. Both are widespread. The most common manifestation of herpes simplex type 1 (HSV-1) is the cold sore, a painful but transient ulcer usually located on the lip or inside the mouth. HSV-1 infection is often a recurrent condition. Herpes simplex type 2 (HSV-2) is the cause of genital herpes, a sexually transmitted disease that may also be stubbornly recurrent.

The cause of herpes encephalitis is almost always the type 1 virus. The first symptom of the disease usually occurs abruptly, but the manifestation may be a subtle one, such as an alteration in behavior or personality. In some cases the change may be extreme, so that the first consultation is with a psychiatrist. Within days to a week or so, however, it becomes evident that a very serious physical disease is present. The patient may have seizures or become paralyzed. Fever is common, and rapid prostration and coma usually ensue in untreated cases. Untreated herpes encephalitis is fatal in 70% of the cases; of the 30% who survive, many suffer severe permanent neurological injury such as intellectual deterioration, paralysis, or loss of speech.

Diagnosis of the condition can be difficult, especially early in the course of the disease when symptoms may be relatively nonspecific. Eventually the course is so devastating that the presence of an aggressive encephalitic process is clear, and vigorous therapy is begun. The computerized axial tomography (CAT) scan, electroencephalogram (EEG), and lumbar puncture (spinal tap) all play an important role in diagnosis. The ultimate diagnostic tool is brain biopsy. The tissue sample obtained through biopsy may reveal characteristic cellular changes directly caused by the virus, or it may confirm the diagnosis when it is subjected to immunologic tests specific for herpes simplex.

Finding effective drugs to combat viral infections has proved difficult, and most common viruses (for example, those causing the common cold) play out their natural course in humans and are then killed or neutralized by the body's immune system. Until recently, few specifically antiviral drugs existed. The first important blow against herpes encephalitis came in 1977, when vidarabine (Vira-A) was shown to reduce the mortality of the disease to 44%. But in order to be effective, the drug had to be given intravenously early in the course of the disease. Furthermore, vidarabine was found to cause serious adverse side effects, and it failed to help many victims of herpes. A brain biopsy was usually performed before vidarabine treatment in order to confirm the diagnosis and to spare the patient inappropriate exposure to the drug.

Recently, however, a relatively new antiviral drug, acyclovir (Zovirax), has changed the outcome of herpes encephalitis for many victims. Acyclovir has now been well tested in clinical trials and represents a firm step forward in therapy. Recent trials comparing acyclovir to the best known previous therapy, namely vidarabine, show that it can reduce the number of deaths due to herpes encephalitis even further—to 28%. Almost equally important, acyclovir has fewer dangerous side effects than vidarabine; thus, brain biopsy is no longer be demanded by all physicians before they decide to start drug treatment of possible herpes encephalitis. Sober consideration of the survival figures indicates that treatment of herpes encephalitis still is not fully satisfactory. Early diagnosis probably remains crucial, since viral destruction of brain tissue is never reversible, but new pharmacological approaches are needed and are being sought.

Alzheimer's disease and Down syndrome: clues to a possible link?

Alzheimer's disease is not a new disease. It has long been recognized as a cause of senility or senile dementia. It is only lately, however, that Alzheimer's disease has come to be recognized as the most common cause of intellectual deterioration in the elderly and middle-aged population. Once symptoms of Alzheimer's disease appear, they increase inexorably until death. The disorder has therefore been regarded with interest by neuroscientists and the general public as well, both because of its devastating effect on the lives of victims and their families and because no effective therapy is known. The major obstacle to the development of successful treatments for Alzheimer's disease is ignorance of the cause of the disorder. Many theories have been offered, proposing origins ranging from environmental aluminum toxicity or viral infection to genetic abnormality or premature aging of the brain. Thus far, no hypothesis fully explains the circumstances, course, and cellular pathology of the disease.

Although it is a disease of later life, Alzheimer's disease has recently been linked with Down syndrome, a disorder stemming from the very beginning of life.

The observation of certain similarities between the two disorders may shed light on the true origins of Alzheimer's disease. Down syndrome, or mongolism, as it is sometimes known, is the result of genetic malfunction at the very inception of human life. Cells of the human body have 46 chromosomes, 23 from each parent, which direct the proper growth, development, and function of the body from the very instant of the union of egg and sperm. The person with Down syndrome has an extra chromosome number 21 in each cell, three of this chromosome rather than a pair (for which reason the disorder is sometimes also called trisomy 21). The extra chromosome produces profound alterations in normal development; people with Down syndrome have a distinctive physical appearance, are mentally retarded, and have shorter than average lifespans. Other abnormalities have been observed in Down syndrome patients, including an unexpectedly high incidence of leukemia and deficits in the immune system. They also have a remarkable propensity for the development of Alzheimer's disease. Two recent studies found symptoms of Alzheimer's disease in about 25% of Down syndrome patients.

Just as significant, perhaps, is the fact that when the brains of adults with Down syndrome are examined microscopically, the tissue often shows cellular abnormalities apparently identical to two characteristic abnormalities seen in the brains of victims of Alzheimer's disease—structures called neuritic plaques and neurofibrillary tangles. Both formations appear to be the result of degeneration of nerve cells, with the neurofibrillary tangles representing the result of chemical alterations in the normal internal fibers within the cells. Another minor but intriguing similarity between the two conditions has also been reported. People with Down syndrome show a preponderance of certain patterns of fingerprints. The same fingerprint patterns have been found in an unexpectedly large proportion of people suffering from Alzheimer's disease.

What is the significance of these similarities? There are several speculations. For one, people with Down syndrome show alterations in certain cells of the immune system that mediate normal responses to infectious agents. Similar alterations occur as part of normal aging. Therefore, in aging people and in people with Down syndrome the development of Alzheimer's disease may represent an abnormal susceptibility to an unknown infectious agent. A slow-acting virus or viruslike infection is thought by some to be involved in the genesis of Alzheimer's disease. Another possibility is that the neurofibrillary tangles seen in both Down syndrome and Alzheimer's disease may reflect an abnormality of the minute internal fibers or filaments within nerve cells. If this is a widespread cellular malfunction, it might be related to trisomy 21 itself, causing erroneous distribution of chromosomes by cellular fibers in early cell division. The cellular malfunction may also be related to the high rate of occurrence in Down syndrome of certain leukemias that are accompanied by an abnormal chromosome number in the leukemia cells.

Finally, Alzheimer's disease itself is thought by some researchers to have a genetic component. A minority of people who develop Alzheimer's have close family members with the same condition. Such familial occurrence suggests that, at least in some cases, Alzheimer's disease is a genetically determined disorder. (However, not all Alzheimer's disease shows familial clustering, so there may be different types of the disorder.) All of these possibilities are matters of conjecture. Someday, however, these observations may provide some of the pieces needed to solve the puzzle of the cause of Alzheimer's disease.

—*Donna Bergen, M.D.*

Nearly every Down syndrome adult over age 30 develops the typical brain lesions of Alzheimer's disease. Brain tissue from an adult Down syndrome victim (far right) shows these characteristic signs, neurofibrillary tangles (arrows) and neuritic plaques (P's), along with normal nerve cells (N's). The 55-year-old woman with Down syndrome at right has suffered the mental deterioration, memory loss, and dementia that are typical of Alzheimer's disease.

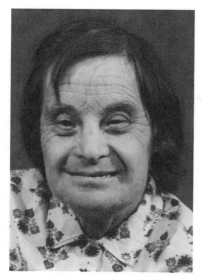
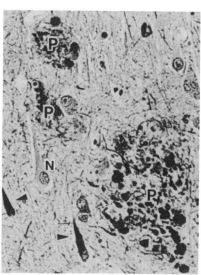

(Left) Krystyna Wisniewski; (right) National Down Syndrome Society

Nursing

A nurse practitioner in rural Missouri conducts breast and pelvic examinations; nurse-midwives in Africa and Asia train and supervise traditional birth attendants; a nurse in Finland gives diet and exercise advice to persons susceptible to heart attacks; a Michigan nurse serves on a hospital ethics committee; a nurse in Texas conducts research into the relationship between nausea and vomiting and the time of day at which chemotherapy is given to cancer patients; a nurse in England comforts a child after eye surgery. The scope of nursing practice is broad; these are only a few examples of the work of nurses who are currently practicing in hospitals, clinics, extended care facilities, schools, churches, factories, and homes. Today approximately 4.5 million nurses are working to promote health and to provide health care services.

Health promotion and disease prevention

While changes in the forms and settings of nursing practice have been rapid in the 1980s, the roots of nursing in the imperatives of humanitarian service have continued to influence ideas about what nurses should be and do. The essence of nursing continues to be *caring*—offering comfort and support, giving assistance and treatment, and promoting health—but a shift is occurring toward increased emphasis on health promotion and disease prevention.

The widespread use of "primary nursing" in the United States offers nurses increased opportunities to stress health promotion. Although cost-cutting policies in the United States over the past several years have resulted in fewer nurses caring for sicker patients in hospitals, the dominant movement has been toward more qualified nursing staffs and toward the use of primary nursing, in which one nurse is responsible for the 24-hour nursing care of specific clients. (Many nurses now prefer the term client so as to deemphasize the passivity that "patient" implies.) When a primary nurse is off duty, other nurses follow the primary nurse's plan. Primary nursing clearly identifies one nurse as a client's own—*i.e.,* a nurse who is fully knowledgeable about his or her condition and so can answer questions, coordinate care, and teach the client how to reduce health risks. Primary nursing is well suited to the nearly unanimous view in nursing today that nurses should serve as client advocates who support persons in ways that enhance their well-being, dignity, and efforts to care for themselves.

Interest in promoting health and lessening disability while controlling health care costs has also caused an increase in the number of nurses practicing outside hospitals. For example, the number of community psychiatric nurses in Great Britain increased by 60% in five years, paralleling a national policy of closing large mental institutions and providing psychiatric care to persons in their communities. Most of Britain's community psychiatric nurses care for elderly psychiatric patients who, with the support of these nurses and others, now manage to live at home.

The worldwide shift of nurses toward becoming "primary providers" of health care, especially in areas where doctors are scarce, is one of the more important ways that nurses are attempting to promote health and prevent disease. The International Council of Nurses (ICN) has recently stressed primary health care through workshops in Colombia, Botswana, Thailand, Senegal, Jamaica, Cyprus, and the Philippines. Nursing leaders from 75 countries have attended these workshops, and the council has planned a similar program in Europe.

Demand for academic preparation

To meet the need for nurses who are well prepared to practice both in nontraditional settings and in hospitals, nursing schools throughout the world are changing their curricula. Three basic models in nursing education have influenced modern nursing practice: the two and a half year French model, which stresses nursing skills and medical pathology (seen primarily in Latin-American countries and in regions influenced by French colonization); the three-year British model, in which students are paid employees primarily preparing for hospital service (seen throughout the world because of extensive British colonization); and an American or academic model, which is based in institutions of higher education (well established in the United States and seen increasingly in Europe, Asia, Africa, and South America).

While the first two models are similar, the academic model deviates markedly both in emphasis on health promotion and in preparing nurses to practice in a variety of settings, such as home, workplace, and hospital. The academic model stresses the development of independent thinking and the importance of a problem-solving scheme commonly termed the nursing process. Clinical learning experiences for students occur both inside and outside of hospitals.

The need for a general academic as well as a professional education for nurses is increasingly evident worldwide. Sociological and technical-medical changes require that registered nurses be prepared to work with a wide variety of people, from tiny infants to the very old—people with diverse customs, desires, health problems, living conditions, and resources. Not only do contemporary nurses provide traditional nursing care, engage in health teaching, and work with physicians and others in sophisticated treatment programs, they must also make diagnostic and therapeutic decisions. By 1984, in recognition of the critical importance of expert clinical nursing judgments, 23 states in the U.S. used the words diagnosis or nursing diagnosis or similar terms in their nursing practice acts.

Nurses in Burma (right), like nurses in many areas of the world where physicians are in short supply, are serving a vital role in the prevention of disease and the promotion of health as the primary providers of care.

Problems, however, plague the nursing profession as its members struggle to agree on the basic educational preparation nurses should have. In the U.S., for example, for 30 years student nurses have been able to prepare in two-year community colleges (associate degree), three-year hospital programs (diploma), or four-year colleges (baccalaureate degree). In seeking to solve the problem of multiple entry levels to nursing practice, in 1985 the American Nurses' Association adopted a policy that urges states to establish the baccalaureate degree with a major in nursing as the minimum educational requirement for licensure to practice professional nursing as a registered nurse (RN). The policy also urges that states establish the associate degree with a major in nursing as the educational requirement for licensure to practice technical nursing as an associate nurse. Such legal changes, when enacted by various states, would apply to new nurses seeking licensure to enter nursing practice in the United States.

The British nursing profession is also confronting the need for academically well-prepared registered nurses to meet the daily challenges of modern nursing practice. In 1985 the Royal College of Nursing of the United Kingdom published a report urging change in the traditional basic preparation of nurses from the hospital worker model to a college model that would focus more intensely on academic preparation.

Paralleling the demand for increased academic preparation in basic nursing programs, significant numbers of nurses are seeking certification to signify that they meet a level of professional competence exceeding that required for licensure as RNs. A certified nurse is one who meets a prescribed standard of excellence through education and experience and who demonstrates that excellence through examination. In

the United States 16 organizations offer 35 separate certification programs in nursing specialties, such as those for nurse anesthetists, critical care nurses, emergency room nurses, operating room nurses, and family nurse practitioners. More than 85,000 nurses are currently certified.

Many nurses see the necessity for specialized education if they are to be certified and practice in an advanced practice role like that of a clinical nurse specialist. Each year over 4,000 nurses enroll in master's level advanced clinical practice programs in the United States. Emphasis upon increased educational preparation also extends to the doctoral level. In 1985, 34 university departments of nursing in the United States offered doctoral programs.

Also accompanying contemporary emphasis on academic preparation in nursing is a recent trend in leading U.S. colleges of nursing for faculty members to offer their services in clinical practice in addition to performing their traditional duties as faculty members. These faculty members are practicing in a variety of institutions—providing care as primary nurses in hospitals, managing health centers, working with the elderly in clinics, and participating in interdisciplinary faculty practice in primary care. Faculty practice offers opportunities not only for improving clinical instruction but for engaging in clinical nursing research.

High priority on nursing research

Nurse researchers, usually unknown to those benefiting from nursing care, continue to transform nursing into a scientifically sound profession that helps improve people's health. A classic example of the benefits of nursing research is a 1970s Wisconsin study, which showed that patients who were methodically taught various deep breathing, coughing, and bed exercises before surgery had significantly improved recoveries and shorter hospital stays than surgical patients who had not received such structured lessons. A replication of the Wisconsin study in Canada not only supported its conclusions but showed that people who had received structured preoperative instructions returned to work earlier than those who had not. When the effects of this kind of patient teaching became known to thousands of nurses who worked with preoperative patients, changes in preoperative nursing practices undoubtedly benefited many people.

Research in nursing is not a new idea or practice; Sigma Theta Tau, the U.S. honor society of nursing, has been funding nursing research for more than 50 years. But the high priority that nurses and others in the 1980s place on nursing research is notable. In 1983 two reports on national studies of nursing, one by the Institute of Medicine and one by the National Commission on Nursing, included statements on the importance of nursing research.

Most nurse researchers concentrate on studies of nursing practice. For example, a recent research proposal submitted to Sigma Theta Tau was to study women's experiences of infertility. Another proposed to study blood oxygenation after endotracheal suctioning, a task commonly performed by nurses in critical care settings. Papers that nurses presented at a recent ICN congress also reflected the contemporary focus upon nursing practice and included, for example, a Swiss study on "deranged" elderly patients, a Brazilian study on breast-feeding, a Swedish study on elderly persons disabled by a stroke, and a British study on measuring patient dependency and quality of care.

Nurses are also examining traditional nursing procedures and finding that certain of them should be changed. A clinical nurse specialist in cardiovascular physiology recently reported a study that concluded that in many cases heart attack patients should use, not the dreaded bedpan, which has been in hospital use for more than a century, but a bedside commode; its use is no more strenuous and is much less disagreeable for a patient. If such a timeworn practice is to change, however, the study will have to be replicated and publicized.

Low status and restrictions

A major problem nurses face is that nursing worldwide continues to be a low-status woman's field— a situation that is perhaps underscored symbolically by the fact that only four nurses serve on the entire headquarters staff of the World Health Organization (WHO) headquarters. If salary is used as a standard, even expert nurse specialists, such as nurse anesthetists—who provide 50% of anesthesia services in the United States—fail to enjoy a recognized high status; physician anesthesiologists receive salaries four times higher than those of nurse anesthetists. In part

because of nursing's low status, recruitment problems plague the profession around the world—from the U.S. to China.

Nurses are taking legal steps to change the practice of paying women less than men, although such a change may be very slow. Nurses in the United States recently lost two legal bids for equity in salary payment. A nurses' suit in Illinois that focused on the issue of sex discrimination was based on findings that employees such as nurses who work in female-dominated jobs are paid less than employees such as electricians and auto mechanics who work in male-dominated jobs. The Justice Department ruled that most of the nurses' claims were based on the theory of "comparable worth," rather than resulting from discriminatory job situations in which male and female jobs "were identical or substantially so," and were thus not covered under the Civil Rights Act of 1964. In another suit a federal court ruled on appeal in 1985 that the state of Washington did not have to pay women employees, including nurses, equal salaries for jobs

Nurses traditionally have accepted low pay and low status. (Below) Nurse anesthetists, though specialists, are paid four times less than anesthesiologists yet provide 50% of anesthesia services in the U.S.

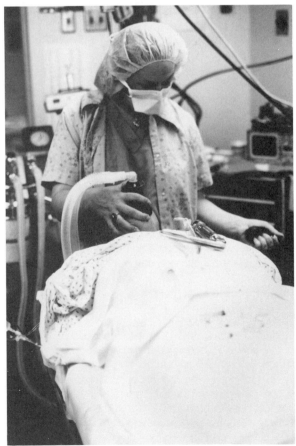

Dan McCoy—Rainbow

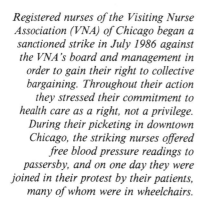

Registered nurses of the Visiting Nurse Association (VNA) of Chicago began a sanctioned strike in July 1986 against the VNA's board and management in order to gain their right to collective bargaining. Throughout their action they stressed their commitment to health care as a right, not a privilege. During their picketing in downtown Chicago, the striking nurses offered free blood pressure readings to passersby, and on one day they were joined in their protest by their patients, many of whom were in wheelchairs.

of comparable worth. Later in the year, however, the employees' union and the state government signed an accord, subject to approval by the legislature and a federal court, that would give affected state employees a compensatory pay raise. Australian nurses are also fighting to gain equal pay for comparable worth. As in the United States, the average salary of an Australian woman is only about two-thirds that of a man.

Not only are nurses plagued by low salaries and low status, but in many parts of the world they are hampered by policies and laws that restrict them in their attempts to provide health care. In South Korea, for example, nurse practitioners, nurses who work in an expanded role as primary care providers, are permitted to practice only in remote villages. In the U.S. the first nurse practitioners began practicing about 20 years ago, and they now number about 24,000, approximately 2% of the nation's registered nurses. But it has taken years of effort by the nursing profession to begin eliminating legal restrictions; in 35 states nursing practice acts now allow expanded practice, but in only 18 states can nurse practitioners write prescriptions, and in only 15 states can they be paid directly by third parties such as insurance companies and Medicare.

Nurses awaken politically

In the 1950s an American leader in the field of nursing said that the U.S. nurse was "like a sleeper"—*i.e.,* too apathetic to take action to improve working conditions. In the 1980s a nursing education leader used a similar metaphor, that of a "slumbering giant," to describe the potential nurses have for political action, especially action required to change laws and policies affecting patients' health care.

Only recently have substantial numbers of nurses begun to awaken politically. As diverse as nurses are

in geographical location and nursing practice, they are united by their concern with helping people improve their lives—improve how they are born, how they live, and how they die. Nurses increasingly recognize that if they are to help people in significant and lasting ways, they must take political action and must form political coalitions with other groups that also work to improve health care.

The recent success of the Nurses' Coalition for Action in Politics (N-CAP), the political arm of the American Nurses' Association, is evidence that nurses are translating their concern into real political influence. In the 1983–84 election cycle N-CAP raised over $300,-000 (an amount placing it in the top 3% of successful fund-raising political action committees for that period), and 88% of the candidates N-CAP supported were elected. The new name for N-CAP is American Nurses' Association-Political Action Committee (ANA-PAC).

Nursing as a social force

In 1985 Halfdan Mahler, director-general of WHO, said, "After some years of doubt, WHO has now grasped the significance" of nurses' potential to help achieve the goal of WHO, "Health for All by the Year 2000." He acknowledged that nurses "hold the key to an acceptance and expansion of primary health care because they work closely with people, whether they are community health nurses in the Amazon rain-forests or intensive care nurses in a heart transplant unit." He also explained that change cannot occur "without an accompanying reappraisal of the policies on health manpower" and that now is the time to involve nurses in decision making.

Undoubtedly, nurses are more than ready to respond to Mahler's call. In June 1985, 3,000 nurses at the 18th Quadrennial Congress of the International

Council of Nurses focused on how the profession affects the quality of people's lives throughout the world. The theme of the congress, "Nursing as a Social Force," underscored the social impact of clinical nursing practice as well as the role of nurses in health care legislation and policy formation.

But the practical, political, and moral challenge for nurses to take a leading role in the effort to achieve "Health for All" is great. Nurses daily face problems concerning people's access to health care and the quality of that care. They also face issues concerning women's equality and restrictions upon nursing practice, especially upon nurses engaged in primary care. Reflecting on these and other issues at the close of the 1985 ICN congress, Nelly Garzon, the newly elected president, announced the new watchword that should guide nurses in their concern for health care and social action in the following four years. That watchword is justice.

—Joy Curtis

Occupational Health

Occupational medicine, as a branch of preventive medicine, focuses on the prevention of disease related to work and the work environment. Although long recognized in Europe, it is only in the 20th century that it has developed as a specialty in the United States—with much of that development coming in the past two decades. Today fewer than 3% of all U.S. physicians practice either full- or part-time in the area of occupational medicine; thus, most medical care related to injury and illness in the workplace is delivered not by specialists in occupational medicine but by primary care physicians. The American College of Physicians, the nation's largest organized group of internal medicine specialists, recently reviewed the status of occupational medicine as practiced by internists and concluded that there was an essential role for them in this branch of medicine. A survey conducted in 1980, and subsequently reviewed in 1985, showed that U.S. medical students have little training in occupational medicine. While it was encouraging to note that the percentage of medical schools requiring some training in this field rose from less than 50% to more than 50% during the five-year period, the average time for required study in the area of occupational medicine continues to total only about four hours in the four years of medical school. Several current developments— a growing emphasis on prevention, the increasing percentage of salaried physicians, and better public appreciation of work-related health hazards—will undoubtedly have profound effects on this specialty.

Problems old and new

Within occupational medicine, some old problems persist, while new ones continue to be recognized. Ongo-

ing research focuses on problems such as workplace-related cancers, chemically induced neurological disorders, lead poisoning, and occupational lung diseases. In the U.S. alone more than $1 billion is spent each year in benefits for coal miners and their families as a result of black lung disease—a totally preventable disease and one of only two ailments for which the federal government pays for treatment (the other is advanced kidney disease, requiring costly dialysis). The prospect of such categorical government reimbursement for the victims of other occupational disorders is not foreseen at the present time, although legislative efforts are under way to fund treatment for workers with byssinosis (or brown lung, a disease that results from exposure to cotton dust) and those suffering from asbestos-related diseases, such as asbestosis and lung cancer. Compensation for disabled asbestos workers continued to be a subject of litigation in the private sector. In August 1985 the Manville Corp., once the world's largest producer of asbestos-containing products, announced a proposal to establish a $2.5 billion trust fund for the payment of claims of victims of asbestos-related diseases, including several thousand former Manville employees.

Among the newer problems being recognized in the workplace are those experienced by professional artists, art teachers and therapists, and art students. A number of the ingredients in paints, inks, fixatives, and other such chemical products are toxic in themselves or when used under certain conditions—for example, in small, poorly ventilated spaces. Ceramists and sculptors face risks from inhalation of a variety of disease-causing dusts. The Center for Occupational

Artists, who often work in poorly ventilated spaces, are exposed to many health hazards—visible and invisible— among them, chalk dust and fumes from ink, paint, glue, and chemical fixatives.

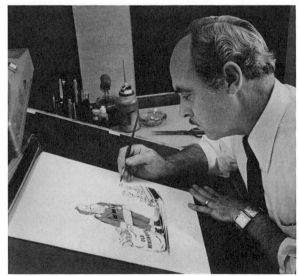

Michael Hayman—Stock, Boston

Hazards, a New York City-based institute established in 1977, concentrates specifically on identifying the health hazards in artists' materials and publishing information on the prevention of disease in the studio.

Threats to reproductive health

Reproductive hazards in the workplace continue to be an area of concern. In 1985 the agricultural pesticide dibromochloropropane (DBCP), which has been determined to be a cause of male sterility, was ordered to be phased out of use by the U.S. Environmental Protection Agency (EPA). DBCP had been widely used in the pineapple fields in Hawaii. Various health hazards to hospital workers, especially those working with anesthetic agents, have been well documented, but recent concern has focused on better documentation of reproductive health problems among nursing personnel who handle antineoplastic drugs. These powerful anticancer agents have been linked with higher than normal fetal loss among pregnant women who handle such drugs in the course of patient treatment.

In an attempt to alert U.S. physicians to the occupational hazards faced by pregnant women, an advisory panel on Reproductive Hazards in the Workplace, sponsored by the American Medical Association, issued a report on the subject in June 1985. The panel reviewed the effects of 120 chemicals, chosen on the basis of widespread use and/or inherent toxicity. The substances investigated included pesticides, solvents, dyes, and chemicals used in the manufacture of plastics, metals, and other industrial products. For each chemical investigated, the panel prepared a description of the substance and its uses, the known reproductive effects—based on animal studies and, where available, human data—and a summary statement indicating whether the available evidence confirms a possible reproductive risk.

The indoor environment

While blue-collar jobs have generally been accepted as carrying a potential for injury, white-collar employment, previously regarded as "safe," is increasingly being recognized as a source of possible health problems. Among these is a fairly recently recognized phenomenon called "tight building syndrome." This condition is caused by the buildup of indoor air pollutants; for example, plasticisers and formaldehyde gases from upholstery and other furniture components, asbestos and glass fibers from flooring and insulation, chemicals used in copying machines, cigarette smoke, and carbon monoxide from indoor garage facilities or from vehicles idling near air-intake vents. These substances tend to accumulate in newly constructed or renovated buildings as a result of heavy insulation and inadequate air circulation. Many such buildings are sealed against outside air with windows that do not open. In order to conserve energy, air is heated and cooled in a central system and continually recirculated. In addition to producing headaches, breathing problems, fatigue, and dizziness, these conditions have also been responsible for documented episodes of infectious diseases disseminated to building residents by means of central air systems. Legionnaires' disease is one such example. The health hazards of air in the home are also a subject of ongoing interest. Consumer products such as paints, cleansers, propellants, plastics, and various building materials have been cited as chief sources of home pollution, along with cigarette smoke.

Another phenomenon increasingly being reported in the medical literature is that of epidemic psychogenic illness, also called mass hysteria. In a typical episode there is an outbreak of complaints among co-workers that, upon examination, cannot be traced to either a physical or a chemical problem. It appears that complaints by one or two workers can travel rapidly

The agricultural pesticide DBCP, which has been widely used in Hawaiian pineapple fields, is now being phased out because there is evidence that it causes male sterility.

through the workforce in a given building and can lead to numerous complaints of physical illness—sometimes even to the evacuation of the building.

Video display terminals

A newly developing area of concern in the workplace is the potential for a variety of health problems associated with the use of video display terminals (VDTs). Complaints vary from eyestrain and muscular aches to psychological stress due to changes in patterns of personal interaction. The science of ergonomics—that is, the study of the relationship among people, machines, and the environment—has shown that musculoskeletal problems (*e.g.,* wrist, arm, neck, and back pain) and other related discomfort can be eliminated by redesign of the work space and equipment to make them adaptable to individual needs and requirements. Some adjustments can be made to alleviate eyestrain and other vision problems related to lighting and glare, and the scheduling of frequent rest breaks is known to have a beneficial effect on worker comfort. The concerns about long-term problems, however, are more difficult to evaluate—for example, the reports associating an increased risk of cataract development as a result of long-term use of VDTs. Even more difficult to evaluate are the claims about the effects of VDTs on human reproduction. There have been several reports—in the U.S., Canada, and Europe—of clusters of problem pregnancies among VDT operators, and there are unsubstantiated claims that the nonionizing radiation emitted by VDTs can cause miscarriage or birth defects.

The problems related to job stress are more difficult to study than are specific allegations about physical disorders. The output and efficiency of an employee at a computer terminal can be monitored continuously, creating within the office an assemblyline sense of pressure to produce. The patterns of personal interaction and communication may be drastically changed when workers are confined to self-sufficient individual workstations, thus minimizing human interaction during the workday.

It is estimated that by 1990, 40 million workers in the U.S. alone will be using VDTs at the workplace. From a public health and preventive medicine viewpoint, it is crucial that more be learned about the potential health hazards of this equipment. In May 1986 a major international meeting on the subject of VDTs was held in Sweden, reviewing the current state of knowledge in this area and suggesting the direction of future research.

Industrial accidents

In addition to concerns about occupational health, accidents and accidental death are of major concern in the workplace. After some years of a continuing decline in the number of on-the-job accidents and fatal-

Workers at video display terminals commonly complain of eyestrain and muscular aches and pains. Some of these problems can be solved by improvements in the design of office equipment and adjustments in lighting.

ities in the U.S., figures most recently collected show a rise in such accidents. The first documented worker death associated with an industrial robot was reported in Michigan in July 1984. Despite a thorough course in safety precautions and physical barriers specifically designed to prevent such an occurrence, the worker was able to circumvent safety barriers and suffered a cardiopulmonary arrest as a result of sustained pressure of the robot against his chest. The incident provoked a reexamination of safety training and precautions in automated industries.

Nuclear power hazards

The matter of worker safety with regard to nuclear materials remains problematic. Of all the developments following the 1979 accident at the Three Mile Island, Pa., nuclear power plant, the question of worker training and education in the operation of such facilities probably received the most attention. In the interim it has become clear that even in the case of a nuclear accident that can be contained, there remains the problem of protecting workers involved in the cleanup operations.

On the other hand, as was demonstrated by the explosion and radioactive-dust release at the Chernobyl nuclear power plant in the Soviet Union in April 1986, risks to workers can occur as the direct result of a nuclear accident, the immediate radiation exposure giving rise to acute radiation sickness. Furthermore, because of the accident at Chernobyl, there now will be a need to monitor a large population of people for the rest of their lives, including plant workers, fire fighters, and other rescue personnel who were exposed. In addition to those at the power plant (which is to be encased in concrete and will remain "hot" for many hundreds of

407

years), people employed nearby in settings, such as agricultural workers and their families, will likewise be at increased risk for cancer over their lifetimes.

Worker training and understanding of potential danger were also at issue in the January 1986 radioactive gas leak at a Gore, Okla., plant that processed uranium for use in nuclear power plants. One employee was killed and some 30 other workers and local residents hospitalized when workers heated an overfilled storage tank containing uranium hexafluoride in the mistaken belief that heat would cause some of the tank's excess contents to evaporate. About 100 people in the immediate vicinity sought medical treatment; they were suffering from radiation exposure, chemical burns, and respiratory problems. What was evident at the time of the accident was that what had occurred was in clear violation of plant safety rules; even more disturbing, however, was the fact, subsequently revealed, that such violations had apparently occurred at the same plant many times before. A special investigative team appointed by the Nuclear Regulatory Commission to look into the incident was unable to assess the potential long-term health effects of worker exposure to uranyl fluoride, a weakly radioactive substance, because some plant employees had been subjected to levels for which there are no reliable data relating to human exposure.

Legal and ethical issues

In the U.S. new federal laws regarding "right-to-know" information for manufacturing workers became effective in 1985. These regulations required that the sellers of potentially toxic materials have information available that details the possible health and safety hazards of such materials. As of 1986, users of such substances—for example, owners of manufacturing facilities and chemical plants—were required to make such information available on request to employees working with hazardous substances. The federal law was interpreted as applying only to workers who might be directly endangered as a result of exposure during the manufacturing process; however, state and local governments were continuing their efforts to extend such right-to-know information to a wider audience. In the state of New Jersey a law was enacted mandating the sharing of such information outside of the manufacturing setting, making it available both to other workers who might use or come into contact with hazardous products and to the general public. The tragic accident at Bhopal, India, and the many similar, but smaller-scale toxic gas leaks in populated areas have pointed up the close connection between the manufacturing site and the environment around it. Even if toxic ingredients are closely guarded in the manufacturing plant, the waste products of the manufacturing process almost inevitably affect the physical environment and the community at large.

As an extension of health and fitness programs increasingly being offered by employers are assistance programs to help workers with health-related problems such as substance abuse. In the past year the question of drug testing at the workplace has come to occupy a prominent role in corporate medical planning. Many companies have instituted pre-employment drug screening, and others are wrestling with the legal and ethical difficulties involved in the development of drug-testing programs for employees already on the job. Similar thorny problems surround the issues of workers who have AIDS (acquired immune deficiency syndrome)—or who are suspected of having the disease.
—*Arthur L. Frank, M.D., Ph.D.*

Pediatrics

Infant mortality rate—the number of infant deaths per 1,000 live births—is a universally agreed-upon indicator of public health. Therefore, it has been a source of discomfort to health officials in the United States that the current U.S. rate compares poorly with that of many other developed countries, including Finland, Japan, Sweden, France, Canada, West Germany, and the United Kingdom. In 1979 the U.S. Public Health Service (PHS) set a national goal: to reduce the infant mortality rate to 9 deaths per 1,000 live births by 1990. By 1984 the rate was 10.6, a decrease of 2.8% from the previous year's figure but still not good enough to satisfy the officials and not falling as fast as they had hoped. In fact, the rate of decline had slowed.

Most of the progress made in the reduction of infant mortality between 1960 and 1980 can be attributed to improvements in obstetric and newborn care—that is, technological advances. But almost 7% of the babies born in the U.S. are low-birth-weight (LBW) infants, and more than two-thirds of the deaths in the neonatal period (the first month of life) occur among LBW infants. Other developed countries do not have comparably high percentages of LBW infants. Even within the U.S. the rates differ in different populations—black women are more than twice as likely to deliver LBW infants as are white women. To date, research studies have been unable to account for this discrepancy on the basis of socioeconomic or educational factors or differences in medical care.

While the ultimate goal of physicians and health officials is the prevention of prematurity, until more is known about the causes and prevention of low birth weight, the immediate objective is better prenatal care, especially better nutrition, avoidance of smoking during pregnancy, and postponement of pregnancy until, at the very least, late adolescence. With a few exceptions, *e.g.*, Belgium and Israel, the countries with higher infant mortality have greater proportions of mothers younger than 20 years of age. There is good evidence that decreasing the number of teenage moth-

Pediatrics

Comparison of infant mortality in 24 countries with populations over 2.5 million

country	number of births, 1983	infant mortality rate 1984	infant mortality rate 1983	% births to mothers less than 20 years old, 1983*
Finland	67,023		6.2†	5.0
Japan	1,508,687	6.0†	6.2	1.1
Sweden	91,780	6.3†	7.0	4.4
Switzerland	73,900	7.1†	7.6	4.6
Denmark	50,878		7.7†	3.3
Norway	49,937		7.9†	6.8
The Netherlands	170,111	8.4†	8.4†	2.9
Canada	373,689		8.5	7.8
France	748,790		9.0†	4.3
Singapore	40,585		9.4	3.5
Australia	243,202		9.6‡	7.6
Spain	509,685		9.5	6.9
Ireland	66,815		9.8	4.8
United Kingdom	720,319	9.6†	10.2†	8.9
West Germany	593,112		10.3	5.2
East Germany	233,756	10.0†	10.7†	14.2
United States	3,638,933	10.6†	11.2	14.8
Belgium	117,080		11.3†	7.4
Austria	89,662	11.5†	11.9†	11.8
Italy	600,318	11.6†	12.4†	11.7
New Zealand	50,474		12.5	10.2
Israel	98,724		14.4	5.4
Greece	134,000	14.1†	14.9	12.3
Czechoslovakia	228,701		15.6†	11.1

data from United Nations Statistical Office
*data for 1983 or latest available year
†provisional data
‡data for 1982

balanitis (infection of the foreskin) and prevention of cancer of the cervix in the female sexual partners of circumcised men. Opponents of circumcision describe it as unnecessary "mutilation," question the data that circumcision protects against cancer, and maintain that simple hygienic practices can prevent balanitis. Moreover, they point to the infrequent but serious surgical complications of circumcision. Cutting away too much or too little of the foreskin is one cause of fairly minor complications. Accidental burns caused by the electrocautery procedure can have much more severe consequences. In at least one case, surgical reconstruction of the penis was necessary; in another, the penis had to be removed and a sex change operation performed. Such accidents inevitably become the subject of well-publicized litigation and exacerbate the controversy over the medical justification of routine circumcision.

The latest evidence in favor of circumcision comes from two recently published reports conducted by the neonatology service of a large U.S. Army hospital. A survey of more than 400,000 infants showed that male infants who had not been circumcized were ten times more likely than their circumcized counterparts to develop urinary tract infections during the first year of life. The investigators speculate that, because the foreskin is not usually retractible in young infants, accumulated bacteria are not easily removed from the meatus (the external opening of the urethra) and thus can ascend into the bladder, producing infection. This new information is unlikely to settle the controversy over the advisability of circumcising male infants, but it will probably stimulate new studies.

The choking child

The Heimlich maneuver has long been accepted as the first-aid procedure of choice for an adult choking on a foreign object. In the U.S. it is now mandatory for restaurants to display drawings showing how to perform the maneuver—a strong "hug" that sharply compresses the diaphragm—to prevent "cafe coronary," the typical choking that occurs when an object, such as a piece of meat, is lodged in the trachea. But for a long time, children were considered too fragile for the maneuver, which, although lifesaving, can result in fractured ribs or other injury. Recently, however, a conference on the subject of choking brought adult medicine and pediatrics specialists together. In the summer of 1985, based on a comprehensive review of anatomic and physiological data, representatives of the American Heart Association (AHA), the American Academy of Pediatrics, the American Red Cross, and the American College of Cardiology agreed on the following recommendation:

A choking child (more than one year old) should be treated with abdominal thrusts (the Heimlich maneuver). If the child is small, he should be placed on his back, with the rescuer

ers will decrease infant mortality. In the meantime, it is not clear whether the U.S. will meet the PHS goal—and the infant mortality rate of 9 per 1,000 births—by 1990. A report issued by that agency in May 1985 was not optimistic. Some critics of U.S. health-funding policies charged that reductions in government spending had contributed to the lack of progress in lowering infant mortality; the Reagan administration, however, refused to authorize a study of the relationship between federal appropriations and infant mortality.

Circumcision: ongoing debate

The practice of circumcision (removal of the foreskin of the penis) for medical reasons has become increasingly prevalent in the U.S. in recent decades. This surgical procedure is now usually performed on male infants within a few hours to a few days after birth. The physician may use a scalpel or similar cutting instrument or a form of electrocautery.

Circumcision originated in antiquity as a religious or cultural ritual. It is still performed for this reason, as well as for health reasons, in many parts of the world, especially in tropical countries, where poor hygiene quickly results in skin irritation. Medical claims for its benefits include the prevention of penile cancer and

409

From *JAMA*, vol. 255, no. 21 (June 6, 1986), p. 2959; copyright 1986 American Medical Association

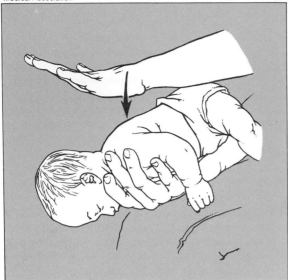

The recently revised recommendations for treatment of a choking infant instruct the rescuer to deliver light back blows while holding the infant face down on the forearm, as shown above.

kneeling next to him and placing the heel of one hand on the abdomen for these thrusts. If an infant is choking, back blows are recommended. These should be administered with the heel of the hand high between the shoulder blades while the infant is face down on the rescuer's forearm. If the obstruction is not relieved, rapid chest thrusts should be delivered over the front of the chest.

Treating growth deficiency

The distribution of natural human growth hormone for the treatment of growth deficiency in children was halted in the U.S. and several other countries in 1985 because of the possibility that the hormone transmitted a fatal slow-virus disease known as Creutzfeldt-Jakob disease. The action followed the discovery that four children treated with the hormone in the 1960s and 1970s later died of this disorder, which is extremely uncommon in young people.

Several hormones are important in assuring normal human growth: growth hormone (made by the pituitary gland), thyroid hormones, insulin, and the sex hormones, androgen and estrogen. Human growth hormone, administered over a period of several years, is used to prevent severe dwarfism. The hormone used for this purpose was extracted from pituitary glands taken at autopsy from accident victims. In the U.S. the collection, purification, and distribution of growth hormone was controlled by a government agency, the National Hormone and Pituitary Program. Because of the nature of the process, the supply of natural growth hormone was limited and unpredictable. In 1985, when production was stopped, about 2,500 U.S. children were depending on the program for their treatment.

A potential crisis was averted in late 1985 when the U.S. Food and Drug Administration (FDA) approved the marketing of somatrem (Protropin), a biosynthetic growth hormone, for the treatment of children with growth hormone deficiency. The production process—in which recombinant DNA techniques are used to produce human growth hormone in bacteria—ensures the availability of this important agent for all who need it. In fact, now that the supply is virtually unlimited, there is speculation that the biosynthetic hormone may eventually be approved for treatment of children of short stature who are not hormone deficient.

Controversy over cholesterol

In late 1984 a consensus development panel met at the U.S. National Institutes of Health to discuss the relationship between blood cholesterol and heart disease. This panel recommended a fat-restricted diet for all Americans over the age of two. Earlier the AHA had set forth its own guidelines for fat consumption. The AHA recommendations called for restricting dietary fat to no more than 30% of total caloric intake. (The average American currently derives 40% of total calories from fat.) Cholesterol intake was to be limited to 300 mg per day. In August 1986 the AHA issued revised guidelines, slightly more stringent, calling for dietary fat to be restricted to less than 30% of total calories, with cholesterol intake limited to less than 100 mg for every 1,000 calories (and not to exceeed the 300-mg-a-day limit). These guidelines were to apply to people in every age group, with the exception of infants.

While many physicians approve of these restrictions and believe that they are beneficial for people of all ages, many pediatricians disagree. They take issue with the recommendations on three main grounds. First, they cite the fact that U.S. deaths from coronary heart disease have already declined significantly, presumably in part because of present dietary practices. Second, they point to flaws in the evidence that atherosclerosis ("hardening" of the arteries) begins in childhood; specifically, they disagree with the theory that the microscopic fatty streaks found within the arterial linings of most adolescents are really precursors of the fatty plaque that typically accumulates in atherosclerosis. Among other reasons for this viewpoint, pediatricians point out that such fatty streaks are found in *most* adolescents and, therefore, are not predictive of adult disease. Third, and perhaps most important, pediatricians are concerned about the possible hazard of fat restriction in the diets of growing children. Foods that are high in fat and cholesterol—meat, eggs, dairy products—contain high-quality protein and iron, calcium, and other minerals essential for optimum growth and development. On the basis of these considerations, the American Academy of Pediatrics recommends an overall "prudent life-style" as the best means of preventing heart disease in adult life. This life-style calls for varied diet, establishment of regular lifetime exercise habits, avoidance of obesity, and refraining from cigarette smoking.

Childhood obesity

A National Institutes of Health workshop held in March 1986 considered the problem of childhood obesity, a condition that has increased by 54% among 6–11-year-old U.S. children and by 39% among 12–17-year-olds in the past 15 to 20 years. One question that was considered: Is television a contributing factor in the rising prevalence of obesity in youngsters? Every five years the U.S. Centers for Disease Control (CDC) conducts a national survey to characterize the nutrition and health status of the country's population. Data from the CDC's most recent Health and Nutrition Examination Survey indicate that TV viewing is a strong predictor of obesity. The combination of inactivity and snacking while watching television evidently makes for fat children, and this is especially true if the parents are also fat. Since 40% of children who are obese at the age of seven become obese adults—at increased risk for heart disease and other serious health problems—the workshop concluded that childhood obesity is definitely unhealthy and attempts should be made to prevent it.

Smokeless tobacco

The popularity of "smokeless" tobacco (snuff and chewing tobacco) among young children and adolescents—possibly fanned by aggressive advertising

U.S. health authorities are alarmed over the growing use of smokeless tobacco by youngsters. Dentist Greg Connolly (above), a Massachusetts health official, led the drive for mandatory warning labels on such products.

WARNING: THIS PRODUCT MAY CAUSE MOUTH CANCER

Seth Resnick—Picture Group

techniques—is a growing phenomenon. It is estimated that there are at least ten million users in the United States, of whom three million are under the age of 21. In some areas there has been a threefold to sixfold increase in the use of smokeless tobacco by teenagers. A Colorado study showed that more than 25% of male high school students regularly used snuff or chewing tobacco; the mean age of users was 16.7 years. Very young children, eight- to nine-year-olds, perhaps influenced by television advertisements featuring professional athletes, have taken up the habit; in one study 11% of those surveyed said that they used smokeless tobacco.

Chewing tobacco and snuff are recognized carcinogens, producing various cancers of the mouth as well as causing periodontal and other dental disease. Marvin Sean Marsee, an Oklahoma high school track star, died at age 19 of tongue cancer after having used snuff for six years. Major sporting events are regularly sponsored by tobacco companies, which also sponsor collegiate scholarships. In an attempt to curb advertising aimed at young people, a new law, the Smokeless Tobacco and Health Education Act, was passed by the U.S. Congress in 1986. This law, which became effective in September, bans electronic media advertising (radio and TV) and requires health warnings on smokeless tobacco products.

AIDS in children

Scientists studying the transmission of acquired immune deficiency syndrome (AIDS) found conclusive evidence in 1985 that the AIDS virus can pass through the placenta, carrying the disease from mother to fetus. A pregnant woman infected with AIDS may run as much as a 65% risk of passing the infection on to her unborn child. In addition, because pregnancy sometimes has an immunosuppressive effect on a woman's body, becoming pregnant increases the risk of disease in women who carry the AIDS virus but have no symptoms.

As of mid-August 1986, 349 (1–2%) of the AIDS cases reported to the CDC had occurred in children under 13 years of age. However, the incidence in children may actually be higher, because the CDC criteria for the diagnosis of AIDS in adults may not be appropriate for children. The CDC definition of AIDS requires a positive serological test (*i.e.,* a blood test confirming the presence of the AIDS virus) plus confirmed evidence of additional diseases, such as Kaposi's sarcoma (a rare malignancy), that are known to accompany AIDS. Children with AIDS-related complex (ARC)—a condition characterized by tender, swollen lymph nodes, fever, weight loss, and fatigue—do not meet the CDC criteria and, therefore, may not be counted in the official statistics. There is some evidence that infants born with AIDS may have a marked appearance of disease as notable as that associated

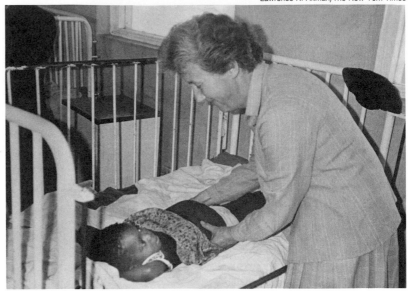

Pediatric cases of AIDS are growing in number around the world. Most infant victims of the disease are born to AIDS patients or have parents who are members of high-risk groups. A few youngsters have contracted the disease from transfusions of contaminated blood or blood products. (Right) A doctor in Lusaka, Zambia, examines a young AIDS patient.

with other recognized congenital disorders and malformations. In 1986 a research team at the Albert Einstein College of Medicine of Yeshiva University, Bronx, N.Y., found that many children born with AIDS and ARC have clearly distinguishable physical characteristics, including growth retardation, microcephaly (a small head), a prominent boxlike forehead, hypertelorism (greater than normal distance between the eyes), and a flattened nasal bridge. The identification of a congenital AIDS syndrome could be helpful in identifying infants with AIDS even before the appearance of clinical symptoms of the disease.

The issue of school attendance of children with AIDS, or those with the milder condition, ARC, has aroused intense controversy. Present studies indicate no risk of transmission of the disease from child to child or from child to caretaker, except after prolonged and intimate contact with bodily fluids. A generally overlooked fact is that there may be a serious health risk for the child with AIDS who attends school and is thus exposed to a variety of infections that his impaired immune system is powerless to fight.

New weapons against childhood disease

A new vaccine against *Hemophilus influenzae,* type B (Hib), became available in 1985. Hib is a major cause of serious bacterial infection in young children, responsible for meningitis, pneumonia, osteomyelitis (an inflammation of bone and cartilage), and other severe diseases that kill about 1,000 children every year in the U.S. alone; about 10,000 cases of meningitis due to Hib are reported every year. For reasons not thoroughly understood, the new vaccine is much more effective in preschool-age children, two years and older, than in infants. Unfortunately, many of the most serious Hib infections occur in children six months to

two years in age. Research is therefore in progress to develop an improved vaccine for infants. Many of the children who survive Hib infection have serious neurological damage.

A new vaccine against varicella, or chickenpox, has been tested in children with leukemia, lymphoma, and other malignancies, among whom this viral infection can be fatal. The varicella vaccine seems to be safe and effective, and it may soon be licensed for use in young cancer patients and normal children as well. Another promising vaccine, still in the research stage, will protect against rotavirus, the leading cause of viral gastroenteritis in infants. Rotavirus is the most common cause of diarrheal disease in children from six months to three years old, especially in winter, and is a particular problem in day-care centers because it is highly contagious by the fecal-oral route. One rotavirus vaccine has been tested at the University of Maryland; others are also being studied. Researchers are also experimenting with a vaccine to prevent cytomegalovirus (CMV) infection. In most adults this virus causes mild, subclinical infection, but it is of special concern to pregnant women and others of childbearing age because it can cause fetal damage, spontaneous abortion, stillbirth, and serious disease in the newborn. CMV also causes complications in patients receiving immunosuppressive drugs (*e.g.,* transplant recipients, children with leukemia).

Continuing concern about the rare but sometimes severe neurological effects of the whole-cell vaccine against pertussis (whooping cough) have spurred the search for an improved vaccine. Several less toxic vaccines are on trial in Japan, Sweden, and the U.S.; it is not yet clear whether they will adequately protect against the disease.

—*Jean D. Lockhart, M.D.*

412

Reevaluating Modern Obstetrics: A Study from Vienna

by Alfred Rockenschaub, M.D.

Average life expectancy is probably the most nearly accurate single measure of the quality of life in a given society. It summarizes in a single number all of the natural and social stresses that operate upon the individuals in that society. Seen from this point of view, life expectancy has become the standard against which a nation's health and social policy can be evaluated.

In the developed countries more individuals die during the first year of life than in any other single year up to 65. On a statistical basis, for every one-year-old and 65-year-old who die in the same recording period, an average life-span is reduced to 33, thus lowering the overall standard of longevity. The infant mortality rate, therefore, has a crucial influence on average life expectancy and is of major concern to public health authorities. (Infant mortality rate is officially defined as the number of deaths per 1,000 live births occurring in the first year of life.) Consequently these authorities are interested in the practice of obstetrics—and particularly in the management of labor, which has a direct effect on fetal outcome. Because of their vested interest in producing favorable statistics, health authorities are liable to be influenced by biased obstetric research and to inflict the consequences of such bias on society. The findings of such research quickly become translated into new equipment or procedures viewed as absolutely necessary for routine care, and they often form the basis for a significant commercial enterprise—as has been the case of sophisticated technology and the process of childbirth.

In the view of the modern obstetrician, the standard of obstetrical performance is not the health of the individual infant but the overall rate of perinatal mortality (*i.e.,* infant deaths occurring around the time of birth). The perinatal mortality rate, calculated per 1,000 deliveries, includes all stillborn infants weighing more than 1,000 g (2.2 lb) and deaths of liveborn babies less than seven days old. Obstetricians are anxious to improve the perinatal mortality rate. In this regard a successful delivery consists of getting the fetus out of the uterus alive and keeping it alive until the seventh day of life. Toward these ends, therefore, sophisticated methods for fetal monitoring have been developed, as have ways for "programming" or controlling the progress of labor and supporting the life of the premature baby.

The routine use of intensive fetal monitoring in labor and the increased use of medical induction or augmentation of labor have caused a significant rise in the number of operative deliveries, which includes cesarean sections and deliveries aided by forceps.

The cesarean-minded physician

Cesarean section is the delivery of a baby from its mother's uterus by a surgical incision through the abdomen. Even today cesarean section carries with it a considerably higher maternal risk than does a vaginal delivery. Present-day obstetricians tend to be cesarean-minded, however, and they hold those who disagree responsible when an infant dies at birth. But when asked to defend their own failures, they resort to the excuse that candidates for cesarean section are, by definition, a high-risk population. In fact, the latter contention can be as little disproved as it can be proved; nonetheless, the physician who attempts to limit cesarean delivery exposes himself to the increased possibility of malpractice litigation. Moreover, physician prejudice in favor of the cesarean section dovetails neatly with the common superstition that surgical delivery most effectively relieves maternal suffering and/or fetal distress.

Electronic monitoring: better than the stethoscope?

The original clinical criteria for the diagnosis of fetal distress were laid down in 1893 by Franz von Winckel, a leading professor of obstetrics in Germany. In 1959 Norman Walker, a South African physician, reported a study of routine monitoring using these criteria and demonstrated that monitoring increased operative intervention in delivery but did not improve the perinatal mortality rate. In 1960 Nicholson J. Eastman, a prestigious obstetrician in the United States, disputed the significance of the various signs of fetal distress. Eastman looked to electronic monitoring to provide indisputable indications of fetal distress. In 1965 Louis M. Hellman, a pioneer in electronic fetal monitoring, suggested that despite the increasing use of high technology equipment, little more information was being obtained than had been available from the use of the simple stethoscope.

At a meeting in 1966, West German obstetricians discarded the prevailing standard of obstetrical performance—the maternal mortality rate—as the criterion of success; the incidence of maternal death had become so small that it no longer served as an adequate parameter. Instead they established perinatal mortality as the standard, an action that promoted the use of fetal-monitoring equipment and the concomitant increase in interference with natural labor and birth. At the same time, some physicians saw the beginning of a decline in humanitarian concern in obstetrics, a trend that led to an almost casual attitude toward maternal well-being, combined with a zealous concern for saving the fetus at all costs.

In the city of Vienna, the use of electronic fetal-monitoring equipment, which had been increasing since 1966, was spurred by government funding in 1975. (The appropriation was attached to a liberalized abortion law, which, although denounced by the predominant Catholic Church of Austria, was favored by the Socialists, who held political power.) The professors of obstetrics in Vienna managed to convince every practitioner in the city to use sophisticated monitoring during labor. Thus, since 1980 there have been 61 cardiotocographs (CTGs; machines that register uterine contractions and fetal heartbeats) at hand for the city's daily average of 39 deliveries.

Abandoning "modern" methods

The medical staff at the Semmelweis-Frauen-Klinik Wien (SFKW), the biggest maternity unit in Vienna, decided to register their opposition to the prevailing trend in obstetric management. Indeed, physicians at the SKFW had long been concerned about the direction that obstetric practice was taking. They decided to abandon the principles of "modern" obstetric management and return to the methods of their early teachers, knowing well that their policy would be open to serious criticism and would need to be validated at every step.

The major premise of the argument was that the decrease in the Viennese stillbirth and infant mortality rates since World War II was the result of the considerable improvement in the health of the population rather than the introduction of sophisticated fetal-monitoring equipment. A corollary to the basic premise was that the mother's health is the determining factor in fetal outcome. Over the years since 1965, when the new policy was initiated, with the increasing awareness of their success, doctors at the Semmelweis Clinic became increasingly radical in their opposition to certain modern obstetric practices. The last step in their reinstatement of conservative methods was spurred by the publication of Robert C. Goodlin's "History of Fetal Monitoring" (*American Journal of Obstetrics and Gynecology*) in 1979.

At the height of its success, the Semmelweis Clinic's policy of conservatism yielded a cesarean section rate of 1% and a forceps delivery rate of 2.3%. Such low rates of operative intervention seem unbelievable to most modern obstetricians. The overall cesarean section rate in the U.S. and Western Europe amounts

A 20-year study by obstetricians at a Viennese maternity hospital confirmed the belief of those physicians that modern innovations in obstetrics do not significantly improve fetal or maternal outcome. They concluded that the "high tech" approach to childbirth so prevalent in Western countries today provides few if any advantages over more traditional practices.

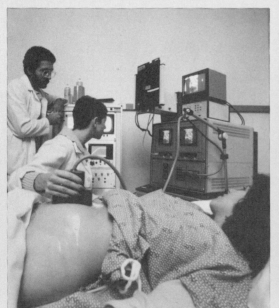 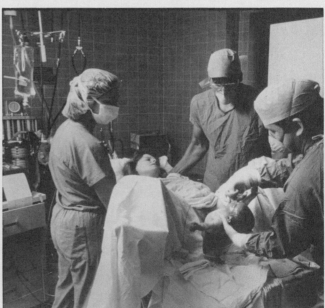

(Left) Kenneth Garrett—Woodfin Camp, Inc.; (right) Southern Illinois University/Peter Arnold, Inc.

easily to 10%. Most of these operations are said to be indicated for prevention of fetal death. Thus, much time was devoted to the discussion of unavoidable versus avoidable operative interference in labor by all members of the SFKW clinical staff.

The first step in the Semmelweis Clinic study was a study of the prewar literature on cesarean section for the purpose of adjusting the old clinical criteria for contemporary medical conditions. On this basis researchers decided that the cesarean section rate must not exceed 1.5% of all deliveries if it is to be statistically conclusive of a conservative approach. Likewise, the forceps delivery rate must not exceed 3%. Therefore, cesarean section was performed only if vaginal delivery was impeded and its enforcement seemed to imply a maternal risk higher than that associated with cesarean section.

Generally, cesarean section was considered a serious maternal shock that should be avoided. The only fetal indication for cesarean was prolapse of the umbilical cord (in which the cord falls into the vagina, where it may be compressed by the pressure of the baby's head). Forceps delivery was undertaken only if labor failed to progress but the fetal head was deeply engaged in the pelvis, a situation appropriate for low forceps delivery. All breech (buttocks first) and foot-first presentations were regarded as suitable for vaginal delivery insofar as there was no inherent maternal indication for cesarean section. All operative intervention was carried out under general anesthesia. (Clinic patients who had vaginal deliveries, on the other hand, rarely had or asked for anesthesia for relief of labor pain.)

A key to the conservative management of labor and delivery is maternal involvement and cooperation. It was therefore important that the women who were to give birth at the Semmelweis Clinic knew that there was going to be a difference in their treatment compared with that offered at the other maternity units in Vienna. The clinic thus started a program of maternal education, inviting the active participation of the patients. Clinic physicians evolved a policy of close antenatal (*i.e.*, before birth) supervision, rigorous preparation for childbirth, and minimal interference in the progress of labor. The mothers were encouraged to attend childbirth preparation classes. Careful clinical checks were made on the condition of the mother and fetus; the common minor complaints of pregnancy were dealt with; and much time was given to the discussion of the pregnancy. There was an attempt to reduce as much as possible the hospital atmosphere and to eliminate obtrusive clinical interference, such as routine vaginal examination and shaving of pubic hair. Episiotomy (an incision to enlarge the vulval opening) was performed in about 35% of deliveries. The future mothers were prepared to look after their babies on their own, even if the baby was underweight but

healthy. Distressed newborns were transferred to one of the neonatal centers in Vienna.

The outcome of the study

Details of all births in Vienna, 99% of which occur in hospital, are collected centrally by city council authorities. These cases were used as a control group. Vienna has a fairly homogeneous population, and the number of patients classified as high-risk cases proves very much alike for Vienna as a whole and the SFKW. However, the frequency of such cases is difficult to assess and depends to a great extent on which of the many vague definitions is used.

In the 20-year period from 1966 to 1985, there were 42,514 deliveries at the SFKW. There were three maternal deaths associated with labor and delivery. Three patients died of complications of diseases existing before the onset of pregnancy.

In the years from 1966 to 1970, there were 11,806 deliveries at the SFKW, and the cesarean section rate was 1.5%. At that time the SFKW record was compared with the results of a Swiss maternity unit, the Frauenspital Basel (FSB), that had a cesarean section rate more than six times as high (9.7% of 11,816 deliveries, 1966–68). Excluding all liveborn infants of less than 1,000 g, the FSB had one stillbirth fewer per 1,000 deliveries than the SFKW and one more infant death in the first week after delivery. Thus, the perinatal mortality of both facilities was practically equal, although the cesarean section rates were widely divergent. This discrepancy prompted the doctors at the Semmelweis Clinic to subject to further scrutiny the possible advantages of obstetric sophistication. By 1974 electronic fetal monitoring had become widely available in Vienna, and the newly appointed Austrian minister of health looked on the obstetric advance with approval. In Austria, as in other industrial countries, there is strong faith in perinatal medicine. Modern fetal monitoring and treatment are generally assumed to be superior to a comprehensive social approach—or, at least, to compensate for the neglect of humanitarian concerns.

Interestingly, the perinatal mortality rate for all of Vienna in 1974 (based on 16,196 deliveries)—the city's single best year (*i.e.*, lowest perinatal mortality rate) during the period 1966–75—was no better than the average rate of the SFKW during the entire ten-year period (19,567 deliveries). As in the comparison with the FBS in 1966–70, the SFKW had a higher stillbirth rate but a lower rate of death of liveborn infants during the first week. During the period from 1966 to 1975, the cesarean section rate of the SFKW was 1.5%; that of Vienna for the year 1974 is not known but is supposed to have been relatively low.

Ferdinand Sator, an Austrian sociologist and pediatrician, was working on a study of social indicators and infant mortality, examining in detail all infant deaths

415

recorded in Vienna in 1976. In cooperation with him, doctors at the SFKW were able to follow up on cases of postperinatal mortality, learning of all Viennese infants born in 1976 at the SFKW who had died more than a week after birth. (Postperinatal mortality is number of infant deaths per 1,000 live births in the first year of life, with the exception of those that occur in the first week.) In the meantime, electronic fetal monitoring was fully established at all obstetric facilities in Vienna. The cesarean section rate of Vienna as a whole was about 7–8%; that of the SFKW, 1.1%.

In comparison with the average number of the SFKW in the period 1976–80, the lowest annual perinatal mortality rate in Vienna as a whole, recorded in 1980, showed a continuation of the previous trend: there was one stillbirth fewer for every 1,000 deliveries in Vienna in 1980, compared with an equally lower first-week mortality rate at the SFKW during the five-year period. Researchers at the Semmelweis Clinic were puzzled by the fact that the clinic's postperinatal mortality rate was clearly below the Viennese average, but they hesitated to draw any conclusions because the size of the sample was still too small.

The detailed analysis of the clinic's study group of 1976–80 indicated that the mothers of stillborn, premature, and underweight babies might not have had sufficient prenatal care, particularly regarding psychological problems. Therefore, the childbirth preparation classes were intensified and a full-time psychologist was engaged to deal aggressively with psychosomatic problems of the expectant mothers. The medical indications for cesarean section were even more strictly limited. In the last ten-year study group, 1976–85 (22,-947 deliveries), the cesarean section rate dropped to 1%. In 1984 health authorities in Vienna recorded the city's lowest perinatal and infant mortality rates of the period (14,523 deliveries). In that same year, however, the cesarean section rate was no less than 10%.

It is striking to note that in 1984 Vienna reported four more postperinatal infant deaths per 1,000 live births than the SFKW recorded during the last phase of the study, from 1976 to 1985. Thus, the Viennese figures for postperinatal mortality were nearly 90% higher than the SFKW average. The perinatal mortality rate, as earlier, was about equal. The difference between the postperinatal mortality rates and cesarean section rates is significant.

The case for conservatism

The steady improvement in primary health care in postwar Vienna has been accompanied by a continuous linear decrease in the stillbirth and infant mortality rates. The introduction of sophisticated fetal monitoring equipment in 1975 coincided with a drop in perinatal mortality, a fact that would seem to suggest a significant improvement in perinatal management. Yet the infant mortality rate did not decline proportionately;

while this would seem to reflect a lag in the improvement of postperinatal infant care, in fact, it shows a failure to improve prenatal care.

More than 42,000 deliveries have taken place at the Semmelweis Clinic since the staff adopted a conservative attitude toward technological and operative intervention in the process of childbirth. Since 1965, when the conservative policy was adopted, the perinatal mortality rate at the clinic has improved in accordance with the figures of Vienna's other obstetric facilities, while its postperinatal mortality rate has been lower than that of the city as a whole. The consistent improvement in fetal outcome, associated with a low level of maternal death, would seem to be a sufficient reason to question the value of surgical intervention in childbirth, based on the use of modern fetal monitoring equipment. Even with the sophisticated electronic devices now available, there is no form of monitoring that can accurately and consistently detect true fetal distress in time to justify cesarean section. Furthermore, the equipment now in use yields many false-positive indications of fetal distress—and it would appear that this inaccurate information accounts for most decisions to interfere with the normal course of labor.

There is, as the SFKW study demonstrated, no evidence that routine fetal monitoring has a positive effect on the outcome of labor. On the other hand, it would seem that the more widespread the availability of intensive fetal monitoring, the greater the incidence of delivery by cesarean section—a situation that clearly should raise concern.

In the U.S. as well as Austria, objections to the growing number of cesarean births are periodically voiced, along with cautionary remarks about the difficulties of distinguishing necessary intervention from the unnecessary. The increase in cesareans in the U.S., from an overall rate of about 5% in 1970 to more than 15% in 1980, was addressed by a National Institutes of Health consensus panel in a report published in 1981. The panel concluded that the number of cesarean deliveries could be reduced without jeopardizing fetal or maternal safety. A December 1984 editorial in the *Journal of the American Medical Association*—responding to the charge that U.S. physicians were not actively trying to reduce the cesarean rate—noted that "Breech birth and fetal distress are clouded issues." The author went on to emphasize that there is no "ideal" cesarean birth rate. On the other hand, U.S. obstetricians, like their European counterparts, cannot help being influenced by trends in malpractice litigation, which have had the effect of increasing operative intervention in childbirth.

The results of the SFKW study suggest that it is time to reverse current trends in obstetrics. And special attention must be given to reevaluating the indications of and response to fetal distress, with increased emphasis on respect for maternal health and well-being.

416

Skin Disorders

The skin is the largest organ of the body. It weighs three to four kilograms (six to nine pounds) and covers about two square meters (20 sq ft). The skin's important functions include acting as a barrier to prevent the loss of bodily fluids from the inside and the entry of noxious agents from the outside environment, regulating the body's temperature, and acting as a sensory organ. The skin also serves important psychological and social functions, for it is the first thing people see when they look at themselves and the first thing other people see. In the 1980s there have been several new advances in understanding and treating disorders of this important organ.

Acne: dangers of potent new drug

Nearly everyone has acne to some degree during their lifetime. Some patients develop a severe form of acne in which cysts and nodules develop that may leave permanent scars even after the acne has resolved. In September 1982 a new drug, isotretinoin, was introduced into the United States as an effective treatment for this type of acne. Isotretinoin is also known as 13-*cis*-retinoic acid and is marketed in the U.S. under the trade name Accutane. Isotretinoin is recommended for scarring types of acne that have not responded to conventional therapy such as oral antibiotics and topical agents. It is the only drug available to date that changes the course of the disease and often produces a prolonged remission. Isotretinoin is generally taken for only 16–20 weeks, in contrast to other therapies for acne, such as oral antibiotics, which must be taken continuously—usually years—as long as the acne is active.

There are several disadvantages and adverse reactions to isotretinoin, however, which must be considered carefully before the drug is taken. First, it is quite expensive. The cost of the medication alone will range from $300 to $500 for one course of therapy, depending on the dose given and length of treatment.

A recent finding is that isotretinoin causes severe and often multiple birth defects if taken by pregnant women. Women of childbearing capacity, therefore, *must* ensure that they are not pregnant (by having a negative pregnancy test and a normal menstrual period) before starting the drug and *must* use an adequate form of contraception while taking the drug and for at least one month after discontinuing the drug.

Blood testing is required before and during Accutane therapy to monitor the effects the drug may be having on the blood fats, liver function, and blood cells. The drug should not be used in young children since it causes premature cessation of bone growth. Additionally, approximately 25% of patients who take the drug may develop small calcium deposits along the spine. These deposits produce no symptoms, and their ultimate significance is unknown. Isotretinoin has many other common and uncommon side effects, which should be discussed thoroughly between the doctor and patient before therapy is initiated.

Baldness: a new treatment

A patterned loss of scalp hair, known as androgenetic alopecia (pattern baldness), is a common feature of the normal aging process. This process results in receding

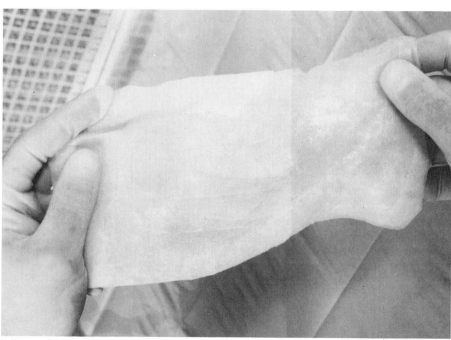

Researchers at Shriners Burn Institute in Boston have devised a method of growing large sheets of skin in the laboratory (left) from cells of severely burned patients. In July 1983 they successfully used cultured skin grafts to treat two young brothers, both of whom had massive burns covering their entire bodies.

Ira Wyman—Sygma

of the hairline along the temples and loss of hair on the top of the scalp in men. It can occur as early as the second decade in some men, and as a more diffuse hair thinning starting later in life in women.

The observation that excessive hair growth occurs in most patients who are treated for high blood pressure with the drug minoxidil (Regaine) inspired several investigators to treat male pattern baldness by applying a solution of minoxidil directly to the scalp. While topical minoxidil will make some hair grow in most balding patients, the number of patients with cosmetically acceptable hair growth (enough hair growth to cover bald or thin areas), is quite small (only 17% in one study). In some patients hair that at first grows in response to minoxidil falls out while a course of therapy is still continuing, and in most patients the hair falls out when topical therapy is stopped. The use of topical minoxidil appears to be safe. Only small amounts of the drug are absorbed through the skin, and systemic side effects have not been encountered. The drug only rarely causes local irritation or allergic reactions. The few reports of sudden death occurring in patients using topical minoxidil were probably unrelated to minoxidil use.

Alopecia areata is a less common form of hair loss in which a few or many round bald spots appear on the scalp. Alopecia areata may on rare occasions produce total baldness and even loss of hair of the eyebrows, face, and body. Spontaneous regrowth of hair in bald spots often occurs. Minoxidil has been used in patients with alopecia areata. Results of clinical trials published to date have shown that cosmetically acceptable hair growth occurs in up to 50% of patients with mild disease but in only 6% of patients with extensive involvement. Topical minoxidil therapy is expensive ($20 to $100 per month, depending on the concentration of minoxidil used), and its ultimate role in treating hair loss awaits further study.

Human skin grown in the laboratory

Scientists have labored for the past decade to grow human skin cells in tissue culture. Prominent among these researchers is Howard Green of Harvard Medical School. In Green's laboratory enough skin to cover the entire body has been grown in only three weeks from a postage-stamp-size piece of skin. A biopsy specimen can grow to around 10,000 times its original size in that time. This technology was used at Shriners Burn Institute in Boston to cover much of the burned surfaces of two small boys, ages five and six, who had burns involving more than 95% of their bodies. These brothers had suffered burns when a paint solvent they were using burst into flames. Such extensive burns are often fatal, but thanks to this experimental therapy, which used tiny patches of their own skin taken from the underarm area to produce large enough quantities of graftable skin, these two children survived.

Cultured human skin has also been used to cover chronic leg ulcers in several patients. Considerably more experimentation will have to be conducted before laboratory-produced human skin is an available and proven therapy for burn patients and patients with other skin conditons.

Skin disorders in AIDS

No health-related subject has captured more attention in the public press and the medical literature than acquired immune deficiency syndrome, or AIDS. AIDS is now known to be caused by a virus known as the human T-cell lymphotrophic virus, type III (HTLV-III) and/or the lymphadenopathy-associated virus (LAV). Interestingly, AIDS was initially recognized by the occurrence of an unusual skin lesion, known as Kaposi's sarcoma, in young homosexual men. Kaposi's sarcoma is a malignant tumor of blood vessels that appears as a reddish purple lump or spot on the skin. Kaposi's sarcoma occurs in 30% of patients with AIDS. Lesions may be in any location and are often widespread. It is now apparent that many other rashes are commonly

An Australian poster stresses that people who have moles should not ignore them. Moles that are irregularly shaped or colored or present at birth may increase the risk of developing melanoma, a life-threatening skin cancer.

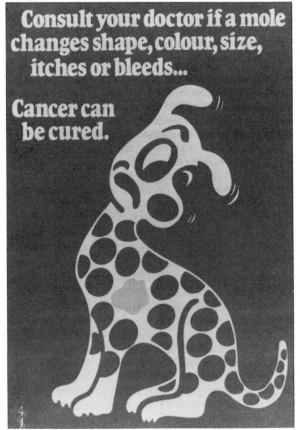

Queensland Cancer Fund, Australia

associated with AIDS, among them severe seborrheic dermatitis, herpes simplex infections, herpes zoster infections (shingles), and yeast infections of the skin and mouth. Cutaneous infections seen in AIDS patients also can be quite extensive and persistent.

Lyme disease

Researchers at Yale University Medical School, headed by Allen Steere, have clarified understanding of a rash that has puzzled dermatologists for decades. Erythema chronicum migrans (ECM) is an eruption that looks like a red ring with a clear center that expands in diameter over hours to days. A patient may have multiple lesions. Steere and his colleagues have clearly demonstrated that this rash is often the earliest and most characteristic sign of a newly recognized disease known as Lyme disease, after the town in Connecticut where it was first detected in 1974. Lyme disease is now known to be caused by a special bacterium known as a spirochete, which is introduced into the body by the bite of ticks from infested deer.

ECM occurs 3 to 30 days after the bite and may be accompanied by fatigue, headache, fever, stiff neck, joint aches, and swollen glands. If it is untreated, neurological symptoms, cardiac symptoms, and arthritis may develop. In the later stages the disease is easily diagnosed with available blood tests. However, in the early stages when ECM is present, the blood tests may be negative in up to 50% of patients. Recognition of ECM and its association with Lyme disease is important since therapy of the skin rash with tetracycline can prevent later complications.

Moles and skin cancer

The risk of developing melanoma, a malignant and potentially life-threatening form of skin cancer, is greater in those patients who have a family or personal history of melanoma or who have large (greater than 7 mm [0.3 in]), irregularly shaped, irregularly contoured, or multicolored moles. These patients should be examined periodically to detect any atypical moles or melanomas that may develop while they are in an early and, therefore, curable stage.

Patients who have congenital melanocytic nevi (moles present at birth) may also have an increased risk of developing melanoma both within the congenital nevus and elsewhere on the body. There is considerable debate among dermatologists about whether all congenital nevi should be removed in order to prevent later malignant change. Most dermatologists agree, however, that congenital nevi should either be removed or closely observed to detect changes suggestive of malignant melanoma.

Aging skin

It is now well established that prevention can play an important role in dermatology. Aging of the skin (*i.e.*,

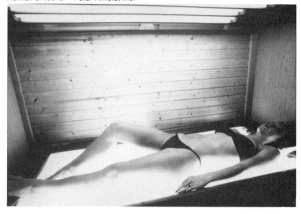

Tanning beds in salons have been widely promoted as safe, but the ultraviolet light delivered may in fact cause burning, itching, and rashes and have adverse effects on the body's immune system.

wrinkling, laxity, thinning, and prominent small blood vessels) is not just due to the passage of time but instead represents the results of cumulative absorption of ultraviolet irradiation. People can protect their skin from these aging effects and from the most common types of skin cancer, basal-cell carcinoma and squamous-cell carcinoma, by avoiding excessive ultraviolet light exposure. Avoiding ultraviolet irradiation is most important for fair-skinned individuals who sunburn easily and tan poorly or not at all. Avoidance may be accomplished simply by wearing a hat, wearing long sleeves, and using sunscreens during the sunny parts of the year. Intentional sunbathing, sunlamps, and tanning salons should be regarded as unhealthful and avoided even if the short-term color and glow seem desirable. Tanning now means paying later.

Salon tanning

Recent evidence suggests that the long-wave-length ultraviolet light (UVA) sources used in most tanning salons—a popular new trend in urban areas—provide poor protection against sunburn, can have adverse effects on the body's immune system, and may be associated with bothersome side effects including sunburn, itching, and rash. Though they claim to provide tanning with UVA, salons may use sunlamps that emit a mixture of UVA, medium-wave-length ultraviolet rays (UVB), and visible light. UVB is 1,000 times more potent in inducing sunburn and is also more potent in inducing tanning. The sunburn, itching, and rash observed after salon tanning may, in part, be due to the presence of small amounts of contaminating UVB. UVA penetrates skin more deeply and causes cumulative harm. Thus, the "safe" tans promoted by salons are not so.

—*Michael Bigby, M.D., and Kenneth A. Arndt, M.D.*

419

Smoking

Tobacco use has long been a part of American culture, dating from the time of Columbus's early voyages nearly 500 years ago. The use of cigarettes, however, has a much shorter history than other tobacco products, spanning only the last hundred years.

Evolution of tobacco use in the U.S.

In 1900, of the more than 3 kg (7 lb) of tobacco consumed per adult, over 2.7 kg (6 lb) was in the form of chewing tobacco (1.9 kg [4.1 lb]), pipe tobacco (0.7 kg [1.63 lb]), and snuff (0.15 kg [0.32 lb]). Cigars and cigarettes accounted for the remaining pound of tobacco used, with cigars being the predominate form of the two. As a nation, the U.S. consumed approximately 2.5 billion cigarettes in 1900, or about 54 cigarettes annually for every person aged 18 and over. In contrast, today cigarettes account for nearly 90% of all tobacco consumed, not only in the U.S. but in most countries around the world. In 1985 Americans used approximately 600 billion cigarettes, or about 3,400 cigarettes per capita.

Two seminal events have occurred that significantly altered the U.S. smoking scene. The first was in 1884, when the first cigarette-making machine ran successfully for a full day in the cigarette factory of W. Duke and Co. Prior to the introduction of this unique invention, most cigarettes that were produced were of very poor quality and consumer acceptance of them was low. Most men preferred a good cigar or smoked a pipe. Others preferred smokeless tobacco, usually chewing tobacco.

The second major event in the history of cigarette use occurred in January 1964, when U.S. Surgeon General Luther L. Terry issued the now-famous *Report on Smoking and Health,* which concluded that "Cigarette smoking is a health hazard of sufficient importance in the United States to warrant appropriate remedial action." For the first time in the U.S., an official government statement received widespread public attention. Smoking was judged to be a cause of lung cancer in men and was suspected of being so in women. It was deemed the most important cause of chronic bronchitis and was found to increase the risk of dying from emphysema. Smoking was also found to be associated with other sites of cancer and increased probability of developing coronary heart disease.

If the first event ushered the country into the era of the modern cigarette, the second surely changed forever the way society viewed smoking. At the time the surgeon general's report was released, well over half of the males in the United States were using cigarettes regularly. Female use of cigarettes was around 30% of all women and growing. Few smokers actually had quit by 1964. However, this pattern quickly changed. A significant decline in male smoking occurred, par-

Source: Office of Congressional Technology

Estimated cancer deaths caused by tobacco: U.S., 1985

site	total deaths	Excess deaths attributed to tobacco number	percentage
cancer, males			
lung	87,000	79,170	91.0
oral—includes pharynx, larynx, or esophagus	15,950	11,962	75.0
bladder	7,300	4,110	56.3
pancreas	12,500	5,025	40.2
other specified sites	110,500	5,500	5.0
unspecified sites	15,700	6,814	43.0
total males	249,000	112,600	45.0
cancer, females			
lung	38,600	29,876	77.4
oral—includes pharynx, larynx, or esophagus	6,100	2,623	43.0
bladder	3,500	1,032	29.5
pancreas	11,700	2,972	25.4
other specified sites	137,300	1,400	1.0
unspecified sites	15,800	2,370	15.0
total females	213,000	31,950	15.0
total males and females	462,000	140,448	30.4

ticularly in the period immediately after 1964. The decline in male smoking rates continued over the next 20-year period. The smoking pattern of women has been different; use of cigarettes by women actually increased until about 1970 but began to decline soon after that, although not nearly to the extent observed among men.

Currently in the U.S., adults have a cigarette-use rate of around 30%. This translates into about 50 million adults classified as current regular smokers who consume an average of slightly more than 30 cigarettes each per day. While this decline in the percentage of the adult population who smoke is encouraging, one must be aware that because of the increased population over this time period, there is approximately the same absolute number of smokers today as 20 years ago.

A world pandemic

While smoking is to various degrees on the wane in many of the industrialized nations of the world, it is increasing in less developed nations to the extent that the World Health Organization has deemed the third world "tomorrow's disaster area."

Tobacco is one of the most widely distributed crops in the world, and now multinational cigarette companies have begun to inundate less developed countries with their products. The most alarming aspect of this new marketing is that cigarettes are being promoted without warning of the dangers.

Smoking and health today

Today the scientific base linking smoking to a number of chronic diseases is overwhelming, with a total of nearly 50,000 studies from dozens of countries. There is no longer doubt that cigarette smoking is the leading cause of premature death and disability in the developed world. The U.S. Public Health Service estimates that cigarette smoking is responsible for over 300,000 *excess* deaths annually. In the United Kingdom the death toll is 100,000 a year, which is predicted to be maintained through the present century unless drastic measures are taken.

The effects of smoking on human health are now well established and well known, though every year substantially more is learned about the health toll. Cigarette smoking is responsible for slightly over 30% of all cancer deaths annually, is recognized as a major risk factor for coronary heart disease, and is the major cause of deaths from chronic obstructive pulmonary diseases, which include chronic bronchitis and emphysema. In addition, smoking by a pregnant woman can adversely affect her pregnancy by causing a lower birth weight, premature delivery, and neonatal death. Smoking is also recognized as the single largest cause of residential fire deaths in the United States each year. Tragically, many of these latter victims are not the smoker.

The number of cancer deaths that were associated with chronic tobacco use for 1985 was estimated at 140,000. This far surpasses all other known causes of cancer mortality, including occupational and environmental agents. For some cancers, such as lung cancer, cigarette smoking is *the* major cause of the disease; it is responsible for an estimated 90% of all such cases.

The death rate for cancer of the lung among women has increased 300% since 1950, whereas the death rate for cancer of the breast has changed little. The American Cancer Society now estimates that lung cancer will displace breast cancer and become the leading cause of cancer mortality for women, as it has been for men since the mid-1950s. Whereas the cause of breast cancer is still unknown, lung cancer deaths are almost entirely preventable.

Smokeless tobacco

Recently public concern has mounted over the health effects of smokeless tobacco use, particularly the long-term use of snuff. Total consumption of smokeless tobacco products, both chewing tobacco and snuff, increased approximately 40% from 1972 to 1985—from 44.5 million to 63.1 million kg (98 million to 139 million lb). Between 1970 and 1985 the percentage of adult males using these products increased slightly, from approximately 5.2 to 5.8%, but because of the increase in the male U.S. population that occurred between 1970 and 1985, there are now 1.5 million

Soldiers take a quick drag between classes in a specially designated smoking area at Fort Belvoir, Washington. In 1986 the U.S. Army adopted a stringent new policy to reverse the long-held tradition of soldiering and smoking.

additional users of these products. Several studies have noted that use of smokeless tobacco, particularly snuff, results in an increased risk of oral cancers, especially cancers of the cheek and gum—the sites where most users of such products tend to keep the tobacco for prolonged periods of time.

Recent U.S. congressional actions

Soon after the release of the 1964 report, Congress required all cigarette packages to carry a health warning: "Caution: Cigarette Smoking May Be Hazardous to Your Health." This first labeling measure was considered by many health authorities to be very weak. Experts now contend that it probably has helped the tobacco industry more (in product liability suits) than it informed the public about the true hazards of cigarette smoking.

In 1969, after new medical information became available about the health consequences of smoking, Congress strengthened the warning measure on cigarette packs to "Warning: The Surgeon General Has Determined That Cigarette Smoking Is Dangerous to Your Health," and in 1984 new legislation was passed that now requires a series of health warnings on cigarette packages and in advertising—four warning statements that are rotated quarterly. (Sweden has 16 rotating warnings.) The new U.S. warnings state: (1) SURGEON GENERAL'S WARNING: Smoking Causes Lung Cancer, Heart Disease, Emphysema, And May Complicate Pregnancy; (2) SURGEON GENERAL'S

Smoking

WARNING: Quitting Smoking Now Greatly Reduces Serious Risks to Your Health; (3) SURGEON GENERAL'S WARNING: Smoking By Pregnant Women May Result in Fetal Injury, Premature Birth, And Low Birth Weight; and (4) SURGEON GENERAL'S WARNING: Cigarette Smoke Contains Carbon Monoxide.

In February 1986 Congress approved and the president signed similar legislation affecting smokeless tobacco products. These products will now also be required to carry rotating warning statements, and advertising of them will be banned on radio and television. A similar ban on use of electronic media was enacted for cigarettes in 1970.

Despite some restrictions, cigarettes and other tobacco products are still the most heavily advertised and promoted consumer products in most countries of the world. In 1984 the U.S. Federal Trade Commission estimated that expenditures for advertising and promotional activities for cigarettes alone exceeded $2 billion. The American Medical Association, American Cancer Society, American Heart Association, American Lung Association, and others recently called for a complete ban on *all* advertising of tobacco products from *all* media. U.S. Sen. Bill Bradley (Dem., N.J.) recently introduced legislation that would prohibit tobacco companies from claiming advertising and related expenses as a tax deduction.

Environmental tobacco smoke and the nonsmoker

In the 1970s scientists increasingly began to turn their attention to the possible health effects of so-called passive smoking. Tobacco smoke contains over 4,000 known constituents; some five dozen are known carcinogens, tumor promoters, or tumor intiators. A partial listing of some of the substances found in tobacco smoke that have been identified by the U.S. Toxicology Program as being either carcinogenic or reasonably anticipated to be carcinogenic includes benz-[*a*]anthracene, benzo[*b*]fluoranthene, benzo[*a*]pyrene, cadmium and certain cadmium compounds, dibenz-

Steve Sack; reprinted with permission from the Minneapolis Star

[*a,h*]acridine, dibenz[*a,h*]anthracene, 7*H*-dibenzo-[*c,g*]carbazole, dibenz[*a,j*]acridine, dibenzo[*a,h*]-pyrene, dibenzo[*a,i*]pyrene, indeno[1,2,3-*cd*]pyrene, 2-naphthylamine, *N*-nitrosodiethylamine, *N*-nitrosonornicotine, *N*-nitrosopiperidine, *N*-nitrosopyrrolidine, and 2,3,7,8-tetrachlorodibenzo-*p*-dioxin.

Researchers have also found that many of these as well as other health-compromising substances are found in sidestream smoke in higher concentrations than are found in the mainstream smoke that the smoker inhales. Sidestream smoke is that which the nonsmoker is exposed to either from a smoldering cigarette or from the part of the smoke that the smoker exhales into room air. Thus, tar, the fraction of tobacco smoke that is usually associated with the cancer process, is 1.7 times greater in sidestream than in mainstream smoke. Carbon monoxide is 2.5 times greater, ammonia 73 times greater, benzopyrene 3.4 times greater, and nicotine 2.7 times greater. Even though many of the constituents found in tobacco smoke are found in higher sidestream concentrations, it is important to remember that sidestream smoke is released into the ambient air, and therefore is diluted. Nonsmoker exposure is also dependent upon the amount of smoke generated, the volume of ambient air, and the type and amount of ventilation of the particular space occupied.

In 1981 three studies were published that examined the question of whether passive smoking increased nonsmokers' lung cancer risk. These studies, one each in Japan, the U.S., and Greece, found that nonsmok-

A nonsmoker's exposure to cigarette smoke

respirable suspended particulates
(measured in micrograms per cubic meter)

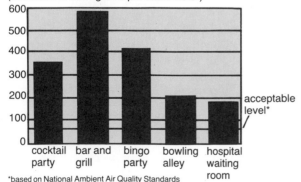

*based on National Ambient Air Quality Standards

J. Repace and A. Lawrey, "Indoor Air Pollution, Tobacco Smoke, and Public Health," *Science,* vol. 208, no. 4443 (May 2, 1980), pp. 464–472; copyright 1980 by AAAS

ing wives of smoking husbands experienced higher lung cancer death rates than wives of nonsmoking husbands. In two of these studies (Japan and Greece) the differences in lung cancer rates between exposed and unexposed nonsmokers were significant. In the past several years many additional studies have been published. Currently in the scientific literature only 3 of 15 studies on passive smoking and nonsmokers' lung cancer risk do not show a positive correlation. The majority of these investigations indicate that nonsmokers have an elevated risk of developing lung cancer because they either live with or work with tobacco smokers. The most recent study conducted by the American Cancer Society found that wives whose husbands reported using a pack or more per day in the home experienced a lung cancer risk that was double that of women whose husbands were nonsmokers. A dose-response effect—*i.e.,* the more the husband reported smoking, the greater the degree of risk for his nonsmoking spouse—was also found.

Although there is considerable evidence of adverse effects for nonsmokers, it should be emphasized that smokers continue to have a lung cancer risk that is substantially higher than that of nonsmokers. The lung cancer mortality risk for a heavy smoker is 20 to 30 times greater than that of a nonsmoker.

Tobacco smoke in public places

Contaminants from tobacco smoke are found wherever people are permitted to smoke. In one study high levels of particulate matter (tar) from tobacco smoke were found in every one of 19 different environments where smoking was taking place, including restaurants and a wide range of other areas open to the public. These concentrations exceeded the National Ambient Air Quality Standards (NAAQS) used by the U.S. En-

Survey of attitudes toward smoking					

Should smokers refrain from smoking in the presence of nonsmokers?

	yes		no		no opinion	
	1983	1985	1983	1985	1983	1985
current smokers	55%	62%	39%	37%	6%	1%
nonsmokers	82%	85%	14%	15%	4%	0%
former smokers	70%	78%	22%	22%	8%	–
all adults	69%	75%	25%	24%	6%	1%

Should companies have a policy on smoking at work?

	assign certain areas for smoking	totally ban smoking at work	no company policy	no opinion
current smokers	76%	4%	19%	1%
nonsmokers	80%	12%	6%	2%
former smokers	80%	9%	10%	1%
all adults	79%	8%	12%	1%

Source: American Lung Association

vironmental Protection Agency as a means of gauging the quality of outside air.

In the early 1970s increased concern about the potential health effects of tobacco smoke emitted into room air became an important issue to scientists who were concerned that nonsmokers may suffer some of the same ill effects as do active smokers. As published reports began to show correlations, particularly for lung cancer, resulting from such exposures, nonsmokers began to voice strong disapproval at being subjected to tobacco smoke in public places. Today in the U.S. approximately 40 states have enacted legislation limiting smoking in many public places. Some states—Minnesota, for example—have very comprehensive laws, while in others the regulations are much weaker. Ten states currently have legislation that addresses control of ambient tobacco smoke in the workplace as a means of reducing nonsmokers' exposure. Some 40 cities in California have adopted local measures aimed at restricting smoking in public.

Because expressions of public opinion on the issue of nonsmokers' rights have increased substantially during the last couple of years, a survey on the subject, sponsored by the American Lung Association, was recently conducted by the Gallup Organization. The results showed that a large majority of the public believes that smokers should refrain from smoking in the presence of nonsmokers and that companies should have a policy governing smoking at work. Even a majority of smokers favor such actions.

Tobacco industry interests are concerned about such changing social patterns. The R. J. Reynolds Co. has placed a number of ads in many national magazines as well as newspapers questioning the scientific evidence linking passive smoking to adverse health effects in nonsmokers. While more than nine out of ten persons now acknowledge the health hazards of smoking, tobacco companies still do not publicly admit that cigarettes are harmful even to the smoker, despite the fact that their products must carry warnings.

Obviously, the tobacco industry is concerned that restrictions on public smoking, as they become more widespread, will have a negative effect on how society views not only smoking in public but smoking in general. As more and more legislation is enacted at the national, state, and local levels to restrict smoking in public, it is likely that cigarette smoking will be increasingly regarded as unacceptable social behavior.

One may calculate what such legislation would mean to the tobacco industry in purely economic terms. If, because of restrictions on public smoking, each smoker had to forgo smoking only one cigarette per day, total cigarette sales would decrease by over $900 million annually. And, of course, the long-term concern of the tobacco industry is that as smokers find they can do without one or more cigarettes, they may find they can do without them entirely. Thus, the very existence of the tobacco industry as we know it is threatened.

—*Donald R. Shopland*

Sports Medicine

In a field that embraces such a wide variety of areas and involves scientists and others from so many different professions, it is natural to expect many new developments and controversies each year, and for sports medicine 1985 was no exception. The principal problems appeared to be increasing numbers of civil actions for liability against health and other professionals and against manufacturers of exercise and sports equipment. Major concerns related to increased evidence of exercise-induced amenorrhea; the accumulation of evidence of osteoporosis in older persons, especially women but also in men; and the apparent increase of sports-related spinal cord injury. Controversial subjects included the advisability of introducing strength training to prepubescent children and the prophylactic use of lateral knee braces in football players. New findings were the occurrence of serious eye injuries in the practice of war games and evidence of pathogenic weight-control behaviors in some female athletes. New procedures included improved techniques of managing fractures of the jaw in athletes and a very accurate method of determining proportionate body composition.

Legal actions

For many years actions alleging civil liability regarding products used in sports and physical education have been brought against manufacturers with varying results. In the United States recent increases in their number and in the sizes of the financial claims made and awarded resulted in 1985 in substantial increases in premiums for insurance against such liability. Football helmets have been favorite targets for such actions, and one result is that there are only three manufacturers of these helmets continuing to produce them in the U.S. In many cases insurers simply stopped writing contracts for this coverage. As a result there has been action in some state legislatures to place limits on the amounts of the judgments that could be awarded for such intangibles as pain and suffering.

The liability of physicians attending athletic events has become such a serious concern to the medical profession that recently many physicians have refused to volunteer their medical services. In the U.S. all 50 states have some form of Good Samaritan laws that are designed to encourage voluntary rescue by ordinary citizens of persons who are in danger. If harm should result in the process of attempting to help or save the life of someone who is stricken, the rescuer is protected from potential civil liability. In the event that

the rescuer is a physician, he or she is not protected against acts or omissions that can be interpreted as constituting gross negligence. Good Samaritan statutes provide protection only for emergency care. Since physician volunteers customarily attend athletic events where emergency treatment is very likely to be needed, the treatment situation in which a physician acts may not be regarded as an emergency, and thus the physician is not necessarily protected and may, in fact, be sued.

Three states (Kansas, Missouri, and Tennessee) have expanded their Good Samaritan laws to include athletic events. Six states (Arizona, Arkansas, California, Florida, Ohio, and Oregon) have enacted qualified immunity laws to protect medical practitioners who attend sports events so that they are available when the emergency occurs. The Florida law, however, does not exempt the physician from liability for ordinary negligence as distinct from gross negligence. All of these laws, however, require that the emergency care be rendered in good faith and without compensation. They do not necessarily protect against secondary care given away from the site of the injury, as in the locker room or at a referral center such as a medical office or hospital. Finally, the laws do not offer protection to the physician regarding the important decision as to whether the injured athlete may return to play on the same day.

The liability situation that doctors currently face in the sports arena is exacerbated by the fact that physicians' personal liability insurance has risen drastically for many specialties during recent years. Indeed, the current insurance-malpractice crisis is so extreme that some older physicians have decided to retire rather than to add the exorbitant costs to their already heavy office expenses.

Menstrual changes in female athletes

The associations between strenuous exercise and oligomenorrhea (scanty menstrual periods) or amenorrhea (temporary cessation of menses) in many women have long been noted and attributed to several possible mechanisms. Recently there has been a much greater appreciation of the significance of these conditions, of the secondary effects that may be related, and of the importance of distinguishing those instances that may not be related solely to exercise and providing appropriate treatment.

Not all exercising females develop irregular or absent menses; the average occurrence is estimated to be about 50%, but among elite athletes it is even less. In the case of any individual who has not menstruated for two months or has irregular, especially heavy bleeding, it cannot be assumed without a thorough medical examination that this is due to exercise. Nor can it be assumed that it is due to weight loss or emotional stress. Examinations should include evaluations of the blood and urine for changes in hormone and other blood chemical levels.

The occurrence of a luteal phase (postovulation stage in the menstrual cycle when there is hormonal preparation of the uterus to receive a fertilized egg) shorter than 12 days, accompanied by decreased production of progesterone, may lead to infertility. Anovulation (failure to ovulate) is evidenced by the continued secretion of estrogen without progesterone and can cause overstimulation of the endometrium (lining of the uterus), leading to pathological change. Precancerous conditions and several types of cancer (including breast cancer) may be associated with anovulation in athletes. Premature ovarian failure, with decreased estrogen, creates an increased risk of osteoporosis (thinning of the bones) at any age in spite of the favorable effect of exercise in preventing a loss of bone density. Both anovulation and premature ovarian failure can be corrected by supplying the missing substance—in the former case progesterone and in the latter estrogen and calcium.

An important consideration for athletes who have irregular periods or amenorrhea is that they must use contraception if they do not want to become pregnant. A cessation of periods that at first is due to exercise may shift to a lack of periods that is pregnancy-related without a woman's being aware of the change.

Osteoporosis in men

Although physicians have been aware for some time of the increased risk of fracture due to osteoporosis in older women, more attention has been given recently to the similar but somewhat less severe risk in men. The beneficial effect of exercise on their skeletons recently has been emphasized as well as the finding that many older men need an increased intake of calcium, without which the exercise alone will be less effective.

Spinal cord injuries in sports

Injuries to the spine with associated spinal cord damage previously had been regarded as a relatively uncommon category of sports-related injury except in diving accidents. A number of recent surveys, however, by a team of researchers from Toronto have noted that over the past 25 years there has been an ever rising trend in acute spinal cord injuries resulting from recreational and sports accidents. Whereas such injuries made up only 15% of all acute spinal injuries in two Toronto hospitals between 1948 and 1973, in the period 1974–79 the proportion was 22%, and from 1980 to 1983 it was 28%.

From 1980 to 1983 diving accidents were responsible for as many of these injuries as all other sports-related causes. Diving injuries have continued to be due to diving into shallow water, and the number of these injuries occurring in swimming pools has been steadily increasing.

Spinal injuries due to ice hockey increased from zero in 1948–73 to 3% in 1974–79 and 11% in 1980–83. Spinal cord injuries due to football declined over these periods, while those due to tobogganing, bicycling, swimming, and fishing showed slight increases.

A further cross-Canada survey in 1982 that uncovered 42 spinal injuries between 1976 and 1982 in ice hockey players found that most of the injuries were fracture dislocations affecting the middle to lower cervical region. Of these, the spinal cord was injured in 28, 12 of which resulted in total paralysis; the others resulted in lesser grades of neurological damage. The majority of these injuries in ice hockey were due to a forceful impact against the player's helmeted head as a result of being checked from behind or being pushed into the boarded wall surrounding the rink.

Consensus on strength training for children

Strength training for prepubescent boys and girls has long been decried as ineffective (because of a lack of the hormone testosterone) and as dangerous (because of slender bone structure, relatively weak epiphyses, *i.e.*, the ends of long bones, and poor coordination). A policy statement of the American Academy of Pediatrics (AAP) in 1983 regarding weight training and weight lifting for prepubescents recommended that such training be carried out very cautiously or not at all. The National Strength and Conditioning Association (NSCA) in the U.S. issued a position paper on this subject early in 1985 defining the terms resistance training, weight training, weight lifting, power lifting, and strength training. The last was described as the use of progressive resistance methods to increase one's ability to exert or resist force. It said further that free weights, the individual's own body weight, machines, or other devices might be used for this purpose but that the training sessions must include timely progressions in intensity to stimulate strength gains greater than those associated with normal growth.

Studies completed in 1985 at the Center for Sports Medicine and Health Fitness at St. Francis Medical Center in Peoria, Ill., at Children's Hospital in Boston, and at the Laboratory of Applied Physiology at Wright State University in Dayton, Ohio, all showed significant strength gains in forearm flexion and knee extension with concentric contraction exercises in prepubescent boys compared with controls of the same age group. All were in early stages of growth. The experimental group in the Illinois study showed that strength training paid off in performance manifested by significant increases in the vertical jump and standing broad jump.

Partly as a response to these studies, the American Orthopaedic Society for Sports Medicine (AOSSM) sponsored a conference on strength training in August 1985. Participants included representatives from the AAP, the American College of Sports Medicine, the National Athletic Trainers Association, the NSCA, the

President's Council on Physical Fitness and Sports, the U.S. Olympic Committee, and the Society of Pediatric Orthopaedics. The following guidelines were recommended for prepubescent strength training:

Equipment. Strength-training equipment should be (1) of appropriate design to accommodate the size and degree of maturity of the prepubescent; (2) cost effective; (3) safe, free of defects, and inspected frequently; and (4) located in an uncrowded area free of obstructions with adequate lighting and ventilation.

Program considerations. (1) A preparticipation physical exam should be mandatory; (2) the child must have the emotional maturity to accept coaching and instruction; (3) there must be adequate supervision by coaches who are knowledgeable about strength training and the special problems of prepubescents; (4) strength training should be a part of an overall comprehensive program designed to increase motor skills and levels of fitness; (5) it should be preceded by a warm-up period and followed by a cool-down; (6) emphasis should be on dynamic concentric contractions; (7) all exercises should be carried through a full range of motion; (8) competition should be prohibited; and (9) no maximum lift should ever be attempted.

Prescribed program. (1) Training is recommended two or three times a week for 20- to 30-minute periods; (2) no resistance should be applied until proper form has been demonstrated (6 to 15 repetitions equal one set; one to three sets per exercise should be done); and (3) weight or resistance should be increased in 0.5- to 1.4-kg (1- to 3-lb) increments after the prepubescent does 15 repetitions in good form.

Football players' knees

The use of lateral braces to protect the knees of football players who have not already suffered from a disabling knee injury is a new and controversial practice that is becoming more and more widespread. In 1980 George Anderson, head trainer for the Oakland Raiders (now the Los Angeles Raiders), developed a brace that was helpful in protecting the injured knee of quarterback Ken Stabler. Anderson then used knee braces on more injured players and gradually on uninjured offensive and defensive linemen and linebackers who were at the greatest risk of knee injury. Knee braces reduced the number of complete tears of the medial collateral ligament among the Raiders to one in five years, as compared with 22 in the five years preceding their use. This use of protective lateral knee braces on uninjured players then spread to other professional football teams and then university teams. By 1985 some high school teams were using the braces. On some teams only players in certain positions used them, but on others all used them, either by choice or by mandate, for both practice and games.

The experience with the use of these braces has not been uniformly favorable; some teams experienced more medial ligament injuries with the braces than without them. Of even greater concern, several found more injuries to the anterior cruciate ligament with the braces. The Sports Medicine Committee of the American Academy of Orthopedic Surgeons held a conference in 1985 that was attended by some brace users and representatives of two brace manufacturers; at the conference it was concluded that the available evidence did not show that such braces would prevent medial ligament injuries. In November 1985 the board of directors of the AOSSM issued a statement warning football coaches, team physicians, and athletic trainers that lateral knee braces may not prevent or reduce the number of knee injuries sustained by football players.

Unfortunately, there is a lack of published data documenting specific testing of these braces to show the strength of the brace relative to that of the normal ligaments. In one series of bench tests on cadaver knees, the intact ligaments were stronger than the brace; the brace itself would bend before the medial ligament would tear. Another problem was that braces are constructed for a knee with normal anatomical alignment, providing a standard amount of built-in valgus bending. But the fact that not all knees have the same amount of valgus positioning can result in preloading of some knees, increasing the force that is applied to the medial and internal ligaments when they are stressed. There are also unresolved questions about the proper designs for braces, the best type of hinge, and the correct placement of the brace on the knee.

At present most team physicians and orthopedic surgeons favor the use of knee braces but stress that further investigation is needed and correct determinations for use need to be established.

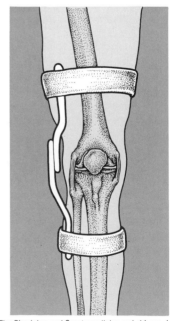

At right is an anterior view of a knee fitted with a brace. In recent years lateral knee braces have been widely used in football to protect players' knees even if they have not previously sustained injuries. But the practice is controversial. In players without normal anatomical alignment, the braces may stress, rather than protect, the knee joint.

Adapted from *The Physician and Sportsmedicine*, vol. 14, no. 4 (April 1986), p. 111

War games and injured eyes

Concern about preventing eye injuries and permanent loss of vision in racquet sports such as tennis, racquetball, and squash has increased in recent years. Now the wearing of shatterproof spectacles or eye shields is becoming more common for certain of these sports and has begun to reduce the serious toll. Eye and face protection is present at all levels of ice hockey except the professional, where it is not mandatory for those veterans who joined the professional ranks before it was mandatory for all amateur players. Just as serious eye injuries have been reduced in these sports, a new sport has appeared in which serious damage to eyes is now occurring regularly.

In the United States and Canada in the past few years, war games that go by various names have become popular. In the games, which combine sports and military activity, two teams try to capture their adversary's flag in a large wooded area. The players dress in combat fatigues and use compressed-gas guns that shoot paint-filled, high-velocity plastic bullets. The bullets explode when they hit and mark the victim's camouflage attire, thus designating a "kill." The players usually wear plastic goggles. But a survey in Quebec in 1984 revealed that 13 cases of eye injury from this sport had occurred, 6% of all sports-related eye accidents there.

None of the injured persons in the Quebec survey wore goggles or any other type of face protection. Nine required hospitalization, and six suffered decreased visual acuity. As these games gain in popularity, the importance of always wearing protective eye gear will have to be stressed.

Pathogenic weight control by female athletes

Excess weight can handicap athletes by diminishing speed, flexibility, endurance, and relative strength. This can be a problem especially in the young female who may normally have about 20% body fat. Ballerinas, gymnasts, long distance runners, and skiers often have body fat percentages of less than 10%. Unfortunately, they may achieve that level in ways that can be described as pathological.

A study at Michigan State University published in 1985 reporting results of a questionnaire administered to 182 female collegiate athletes showed that 32% overall manifested at least one pathogenic weight-control behavior. Self-induced vomiting occurred in 14%; other common methods of achieving low body weight were the use of diet pills (25%), laxatives (16%), and diuretics (5%). Eating binges more than twice weekly occurred in 20%, while 8% lost more weight than they had intended.

There was no relationship overall to a history of obesity, and the majority indicated that their concern was primarily for improved performance, not personal appearance. The greatest number of pathogenic be-

Michael Neveux

In war games paint-filled explosive bullets are aimed at opponents to mark their camouflage uniforms. Players who do not wear face protection risk serious eye injuries.

haviors was in gymnasts and field hockey players; the least in basketball players, swimmers, and golfers.

Jaw fractures

Sports-related mandibular (jaw) fractures make up only about 3.5% of all those treated for mandibular fractures, but new methods of treating these fractures are benefitting athletes who suffer jaw injury. Dentists Joseph E. Van Sickels and David P. Timmis of the University of Texas Health Science Center in San Antonio reported in 1985 on their largely successful management of these fractures.

Displacement of the fractured mandible depends on the direction and impact severity of the blow that caused the injury. Emergency treatment is usually to wire the teeth and support the mandible. Bleeding must be controlled by local pressure or ligation. In some mandibular fractures, the anterior muscle support of the tongue may be lost, so the tongue must be pulled forward to prevent it from occluding the airway.

Simple undisplaced fractures can be treated by placing wires around four teeth on each side of the mouth to make a splint. More elaborate wiring techniques and pin and bar fixation of the fragments may be desirable in certain of these fractures. So-called maxisystems that involve rigid immobilization with two bone plates allow primary healing, while the patient can open his or her mouth to eat. Minisystems use screws to place flexible plates through only one cortex of the bone and cause compression of the fragments in the tension band area of the bone. Most of these plates are removed six months to one year after implantation.

Such newly developed intraoral fixation systems are technically difficult to install but avoid scarring and

(Left) Jean-Pierre Laffont—Sygma; (right) adapted from W. D. Ross and R. Ward, *The O-Scale System* © 1984

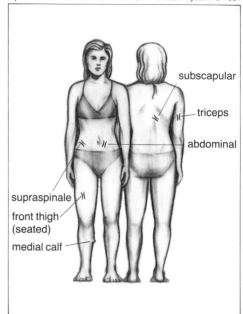

subscapular

triceps

abdominal

supraspinale

front thigh
(seated)

medial calf

A new approach to assessing body composition requires the accurate measurement of six skinfolds (far right). Unlike previous approaches, the O-Scale System is able to assess the body's nonfat component (muscle and bone) and recognize that those who are "overweight" may not be "overfat"— bodybuilders, for example.

possible damage to the facial nerve. They permit better function and adequate nutrition in the early course of treatment and also allow the preservation of otherwise intact teeth.

Assessing body composition

Of all new developments in sports medicine that became available for general use in 1985, the one that may have the most lasting influence is still relatively unknown to many of those who are likely to find it most useful. A new approach to the assessment of human body composition was designed by a team of physiology specialists at Simon Fraser University, Burnaby, B.C., in conjunction with colleagues from the Free University of Brussels. It is a result of 18 years of work and study, including thousands of measurements of children and young adults as well as studies using cadavers.

There are more than 100 formulas that have been in use for determining body fat percentage based on skinfolds, but the lack of reliability of these systems when applied across different populations has made it apparent that a better method was needed. The new method, known as the O-Scale System, requires the accurate measurement of weight, height, six skinfolds, and three limb girths to permit comparison of the individual data to appropriate age and sex norms. A system for determining chronological age in decimal years is used, and all physical measurements are adjusted to a common stature and a proportional body weight rating related to a norm for the subject's age and sex. The sum of skinfolds with a size adjustment for age and sex is given an adiposity rating. A proportional weight is obtained from a similar size adjustment to the gross nude body weight.

Each category measured produces a number (from one to nine) that represents the percentile in which an individual falls, compared with the standard for the same age and sex. An adiposity rating of five would be between the 40th and 60th percentiles; a rating of eight or nine defines moderate to extreme obesity. An adiposity rating of one could apply to an extremely lean, highly trained athlete but could also apply to someone with anorexia nervosa. The interpretation of the data depends on clinical observation as well as physical measurement.

What this system does to counteract the inconsistencies of other methods is to recognize that although the fat component of the body has a reasonably constant density, the nonfat component, which is chiefly muscle and bone, does not. It is possible to be overweight while not being overfat. Adipose tissue is 14% bulkier than the equivalent weight of muscle. A weight trainer, for example, has large, bulky, extremely highly developed muscles but very little fat.

The density of bone varies considerably depending on age, proportional body size, and other factors. Although skinfold thicknesses, if measured accurately, are real data, the formulas that have been used to predict body fat percentage are not reliable because they do not take into consideration the nonfat component. Therefore, unacceptable conclusions, *e.g.*, that some subjects had only 1 to 2% or even negative body fat or that very lean body builders are obese, may result. According to the O-Scale System, there is no "ideal" weight or adiposity standard; rather, measurements give a realistic appraisal of physique status.

—*Allan J. Ryan, M.D.*

Addicted to Exercise
by Connie S. Chan, Ph.D.

As a result of the fitness craze that began a little over a decade ago, recreational athletes took to the roads, pools, aerobics classes, and racquet courts in their quest for health. Indeed, large numbers of people made strong personal efforts to initiate and maintain a regimen of regular physical activity through running and other forms of aerobic (endurance) exercise. Because aerobic fitness requires consistent practice (at least three times a week) and discipline (maintaining one's heart rate at 60–80% of maximum output), the individuals who were able to maintain a consistent exercise routine found themselves not only becoming more physically fit but also experiencing new feelings. They found that there were some major psychological benefits; it improved their self-esteem, elevated their mood, made them feel more relaxed, and helped them to cope better with stress and tension. Not surprisingly, researchers who studied the effects of exercise found a strong correlation between physical fitness and mental health. Because beneficial mental health effects were repeatedly shown (in several studies among diverse populations), some clinicians even began to prescribe exercise programs as a means of treating symptoms of depression and anxiety in patients.

From getting fit to getting "hooked"

As more recreational athletes discovered both the physical and the psychological benefits of aerobic exercise, they became more consistent in their routines and also more dependent upon the salutory effects. Many individuals reported the need to exercise daily and for longer periods of time to achieve the same feelings of relaxation, achievement, and satisfaction that less exercise had previously produced. Road races, marathons, triathlons, and other forms of intense competition became the new goals for many recreational athletes, and all of this required more exercise and more time spent in training. For some, exercise had become an *end* unto itself rather than a *means* to physical fitness.

The push for more mileage, more strenuous and more frequent workouts, and more time devoted to exercise meant that athletes who started out as recreational exercisers became *overly* dependent upon, or in fact "addicted" to, exercise. (A dictionary definition of "addiction" is "to devote or surrender oneself to something habitually or obsessively.")

In 1976 William Glasser wrote *Positive Addiction*, in which he characterized running and other forms of aerobic exercise that become a daily requirement as an addiction. "Addicted" runners, he maintained, are dependent upon this activity as their primary method of coping with stress. Glasser classified addicted runners as similar to smokers and alcoholics who require consistent use of cigarettes or alcohol to get through the day. He asserted, however, that unlike cigarettes and alcohol (which have no redeeming qualities and only adverse health effects and thus are negative addictions), running is a *positive* addiction.

The majority of the recent research on addiction to exercise supports Glasser's theories about the positive aspects of intensive exercise but has also begun to focus upon the potential negative effects of such addictions. In 1979 psychologist William Morgan described the most convincing negative symptom of exercise addiction—*i.e.,* that a running addict will continue to run even when it is medically, vocationally, or socially contraindicated. A true addict gives a daily run or exercise routine higher priority than personal health, jobs, family, or friends.

A widely publicized and controversial study conducted by psychiatrist Alayne Yates and colleagues at the University of Arizona in 1983 compared "obligatory" male runners to anorexic women. According to the investigators, compulsive runners often suffer from the same pathological drives as patients with anorexia nervosa. The resemblances they found were in family background, socioeconomic class, and certain personality characteristics (*e.g.,* repressed anger, excessively high self-expectations, tolerance of physical discomfort, denial of serious debility, and a tendency to suffer from depression). Critics of the study charged that the conclusions were unsubstantiated and that the study had been based on extreme cases and male runners only.

Who is addicted?

Whether the running-anorexia comparison is valid has yet to be substantiated, but the concept of exercise addiction is now fairly well accepted. Runners and other aerobic athletes can be considered to be addicted if they meet several of the following criteria: (1) the need to run or exercise on a daily or near-daily basis to reach an equilibrium, or baseline level of functioning; (2) the experience of minor withdrawal symptoms, such as irritability, feelings of guilt, tension, and anxiety, when unable to exercise for several days; (3) the experience of major symptoms of withdrawal, such as symptoms of depression, lack of interest in other activities, loss of self-confidence and self-esteem, insomnia, weight loss or gain, lack of energy, and overall mood disturbance when unable to exercise for longer periods of time; (4) exercising even when it is contraindicated by physical injury; (5) the prioritizing of exercise to the point where it is placed above job or family obligations; (6) organizing one's life around exercise and exercise-related activities.

Exercise addicts can be found in almost any sport. However, since endurance exercise provides greater physiological as well as psychological rewards with consistent and intensive training, the highest incidence of addicts occurs in the aerobic sports.

Profile of the addicted exerciser

Individuals who are addicted to exercise are not by any means limited to the professional, world-class, or elite athletes who earn their livings through competition. Instead, they tend to be casual recreational athletes who participate for personal satisfaction and benefits. They are individuals who may possess only average athletic ability but above-average desire and achievements.

Some runners are so dependent on their daily exercise that it becomes their number one priority—over job, health, family, and friends.

Kirk Schlea—Berg & Associates

The "typical" exercise addict is between ages 20 and 60, female or male, and began exercising in adulthood as a way to lose weight and to become more physically fit. As these individuals improve their heart rate, lose weight, and feel better physically, they also begin to feel better about themselves. They develop a sense of control over their bodies—something they had been unable to do through dieting—and this feeling of control generalizes to a sense of control over their lives. In other words, they feel more powerful and more self-confident.

Being able to exercise and participate in athletics (both in and outside of competition) gives them a feeling of quantifiable, measurable achievement. For example, they can now run ten kilometers (six miles) in a road race, do aerobics for an hour, or swim 1,830 m (2,000 yd), all of which are measures by which they can keep track of their progress or compare their performances with others.

Running and other forms of aerobic exercise often develop into obsessions among individuals who already demand high standards and achievements for themselves in other spheres of their lives. Instead of serving as a coping mechanism, running and exercise can become additional stressors creating yet another requirement for the day's already demanding agenda and providing another arena to compete in.

"Richard" is an example of an addicted runner. He has been running for three years and averages 11–13 km (7–8 mi [60–80 minutes]) of running daily. He reported:

I simply cannot exist any longer without a daily run. Sometimes my work schedule becomes so hectic that I have to be in the office from 8 AM to 7 PM. So I began to run after work, but then I didn't get home until 9 PM, and I never saw my children. Then I began running before work, at 6:00 AM, but it was so dark, and I was so stiff that I pulled a muscle one cold morning. So now I try to sneak away at lunchtime, but my boss wants me to entertain clients at that time. I don't know what I'm going to do. When I run, I feel very energized, proud of myself, and have more confidence. If I don't run, I feel like a slob, lazy, heavy, and tired. I won't last long at my job if I don't spend the necessary hours there, but if I don't run, I won't be any good at it either. . . . Running is my life. It makes me feel like a complete person, and I need to do it every day.

Consequences of exercise deprivation

When those who are addicted to exercise are unable to pursue their usual exercise routine, what happens? Do they suffer withdrawal symptoms? Are they able to substitute other activities to achieve the same benefits?

In 1985 psychologists C. S. Chan and H. Y. Grossman designed a research study addressing these questions concerning the psychological effects of being prevented from running. They compared a group of 30 "prevented runners," unable to run for at least two weeks owing to a minor running-related injury, with a comparable group of 30 "continuing runners" who ran without interruption. The groups were compared on three standardized psychological scales—Profile of Mood States (POMS), Rosenberg Self-Esteem Scale, Zung Depression Scale—and a Running Information Scale. They found that the "prevented runners" group displayed significantly greater symptoms of psychological distress, including depression, anxiety, confusion, overall mood disturbance, lower self-esteem, and greater dissatisfaction with their body image, than did the "continuing runners" group.

The psychologists concluded that as an addiction, running can have both positive and negative aspects. Consistent runners clearly demonstrated psychological benefits by maintaining their running regimen, scoring significantly above the norm on measures of psychological well-being (such as self-esteem, body image, and positive mood states), a fact that supports the positive aspects of their dedication to running. However, when prevented from running, subjects expressed withdrawal symptoms such as depression, overall mood disturbance, and decreased self-esteem. These findings suggest that a deprivation of running can result in withdrawal symptoms of psychological distress for consistent runners who are dependent upon the psychological reinforcement of running.

The exercise "high"

In addition to psychological benefits from aerobic exercise, there has been evidence indicating that there are physiological, or biochemical, benefits from consistent aerobic activity. A number of researchers have theorized that running and other strenuous aerobic exercise produce specific biochemical effects that may, at least in part, account for the positive psychological benefits and the "runner's high" (described by athletes as a pleasurable feeling of relaxation and euphoria sometimes experienced after an hour of exercising).

The substances suspected of producing these feelings of exercise-induced euphoria are endorphins, or endogenous morphines—naturally occurring opiumlike compounds. These compounds seem to be neurotransmitters of the nerve pathways in the brain that process information about pain, emotions, and other opiate-affected body processes. Beta-endorphins, when injected into the brain through intravenous means, tend to cause analgesia, a state of insensibility to pain without loss of consciousness. Although the evidence is still inconclusive, the discovery of these kinds of effects has led researchers to speculate about a cause-effect relationship between the production and release into the body of endorphins during strenuous exercise and the so-called exercise high.

Several studies have demonstrated an increase in the levels of plasma beta-endorphin—i.e., the surge of endorphins in the circulatory system—during and after running and other strenuous exercise. In one study

D. B. Carr and associates (1981) found that as length of training and fitness increase, there is a stabilization or decline in acute beta-endorphin production, suggesting an interaction between fitness level and beta-endorphin production. Carr theorized that the more physically fit an individual becomes, the less beta-endorphin is needed in response to the stress of exercise. If it is found that production of endorphins is in some way responsible for runner's high, then this conditioning effect on endorphin production could help to explain exercise addiction. In other words, an athlete may need to run or exercise longer, harder, or faster to maintain antidepressant and antianxiety effects.

It has been further suggested in a study by Solomon H. Snyder that endorphins seem to have a tolerance effect and may lead to physical dependence just as the drug morphine does. However, other research has raised questions about the role of endorphins. E. W. Colt and his associates have suggested that an increase in intracerebral endorphins—i.e., within the brain—must be found in order to connect these substances with the runner's high, since pain relief and related effects originate in the brain. Since there is no evidence thus far to indicate that endorphin is able to penetrate the blood/brain barrier once it enters the circulatory system, further research is necessary to prove that endorphins are responsible for the exercise high.

Symptoms of withdrawal

To what extent exercise addiction is physiological in origin has not been determined, but the withdrawal

Athletes should have alternative forms of aerobic exercise to which they can turn, especially if for some reason they cannot pursue their main sport.

symptoms that occur with deprivation from exercise are well delineated. An individual who is prevented from participating in his or her daily exercise activity may demonstrate short-term withdrawal symptoms. These symptoms are similar to those experienced during withdrawal from addictive drugs: fatigue, feelings of guilt, change in appetite, irritability and edginess, difficulty concentrating and working, distorted body image (feeling his or her body is falling apart), and feelings of disappointment at being "human" and not invincible. These short-term withdrawal symptoms have been reported by consistent exercisers when unable to exercise for even two to three days, but they generally surface within a week. The symptoms can be lessened by participating in whatever kinds of exercise can be done, such as swimming, biking, or brisk walking, to replace their usual physical activity, although exercisers report that the replacement exercise is not nearly as satisfying as their regular activity.

More severe psychological effects can develop for those athletes who are prevented from participating in their customary exercise regimen for longer periods of time. These long-term effects may include a loss of interest in other activities, a lack of energy, insomnia, change in appetite, a preoccupation with not exercising, major distortions in body image resulting in eating disorders such as anorexia or bulimia as a consequence of trying to control body weight, loss of sexual drive, exaggerated fears of losing hard-won physical conditioning (feeling that the positive effects of exercise will be reversed), feelings of loss of control over their lives, extreme tension and irritability, and loss of self-confidence and self-esteem. In addition, symptoms of depression and anxiety are generally accompanied by restlessness, insomnia, and generalized fatigue. Decreased or increased appetite and constipation may occur. These long-term withdrawal symptoms have been reported by consistent exercisers when unable to exercise for more than two weeks.

Coping with the need to excercise

When recreational athletes find that they *need* to exercise on a consistent basis and are arranging their lives around meeting that need, they are at risk of addiction. Since athletes who are addicted tend to increase the amount of exercise they do to achieve even greater benefits, they are at the highest risk of overtraining. Overtraining, in turn, frequently leads to overuse injuries caused by stress to muscles, bones, and joints from repetitive activity inherent in aerobic exercise. Overuse injuries are common in aerobic sports such as running (shin splints, stress fractures, tendinitis), aerobic dance (knee, ankle, and foot problems, back problems, shin splints), bicycling (knee and back problems), racquet sports (elbow, shoulder, knee injuries), and sometimes swimming (tendinitis, muscle strains). Such overuse injuries, which are frequently chronic in nature, may require anywhere from one to eight weeks to heal and usually require athletes to cut back or discontinue their particular aerobic exercise until recovery is complete.

Some obvious preventive measures will reduce the likelihood of suffering from exercise-addiction effects. Since injuries resulting from overtraining account for the majority of forced layoffs from aerobic exercise, athletes are advised to restrict their activity level, perhaps by cutting back on mileage or time, or by taking a day off per week. An athlete should be aware that he or she could be at risk of becoming dependent upon the psychological and physiological benefits of physical activity. The dangers of "putting all their eggs in one basket" if they rely upon one type of aerobic activity to meet their physical, emotional, and social needs should be recognized. These athletes are encouraged to develop other means of coping with stress and to diversify their physical activity.

Athletes who are able to substitute other forms of aerobic exercise (such as swimming for runners and bicycling for dancers) suffer fewer withdrawal symptoms and are able to maintain their aerobic conditioning. Therefore, as a preventive measure, devoted athletes are advised to develop proficiency in another sport *before* they become injured and are prevented from participating in their usual activity.

Managing addiction to exercise involves both preventive measures and treatment for the loss of the activity if it occurs. Since withdrawal symptoms are distressful, athletes who are temporarily prevented from pursuing their usual exercise routine are advised to participate in *whatever* exercise they *can* do as a means of keeping active, maintaining conditioning, and coping with stress. In more severe cases and when injury is such that *all* forms of exercise must be curtailed, injured athletes may need to seek professional help for depression or distress. Symptoms of psychological distress should not be ignored, and appropriate treatment should be provided.

What can be gained from the present knowledge about addiction to exercise? Since preventive measures are successful, athletes are advised to adjust their training methods to ensure that they do not push their bodies beyond their capabilities. In addition, coaches should be able to recognize symptoms of addiction among athletes and to advise them in their training so as to avoid "burnout" and overuse injuries.

As more recreational athletes participate in aerobic exercise, a number of them will become dependent upon the physical and psychological benefits they achieve and will become addicted to exercise. The awareness that obsessively overdoing it can cause physical injuries as well as profound psychological distress should help make prevention a high priority. Diversified aerobic activity is thus important from the beginning of developing an excercise program.

Transplantation

The death in August 1986 of William J. Schroeder, the longest-surviving recipient of a permanent artificial heart, marked the end of a chapter in the history of artificial heart implantation. Much earlier, however, it had become clear that the device, at least in its present form, was marred by serious design flaws. Furthermore, the very idea of permanent implantation of a mechanical heart was under attack by critics who felt that the device should be used only on a temporary basis, to keep a critically ill patient alive until a human heart was available for transplantation. At the time of his death, Schroeder was the only survivor of the five patients who had received permanent Jarvik-7 artificial hearts. However, more than 20 people worldwide who had received artificial heart implants as a temporary measure—to keep them alive until a human donor heart became available—fared better. Survival of the latter patients and others who received transplants of heart, kidney, liver, lungs, or pancreas increased dramatically in 1985 and 1986, mainly because of cyclosporine—a relatively new and important immunosuppresive drug that successfully combats rejection of foreign organs. This positive development was tempered by a growing shortage of donated organs. In the United States, however, attempts to alleviate the problem, in the form of federal and state legislation and physician education programs, were showing progress.

The first implantation of an artificial heart took place in 1982. The patient, Barney B. Clark, survived for 112 days. Schroeder, the second artificial heart recipient, was a 52-year-old retired government employee. Surgeon William C. DeVries implanted Schroeder's Jarvik-7 heart (named for its inventor, Robert K. Jarvik)—at the time the only such device approved by the U.S. Food and Drug Administration (FDA)—on Nov. 25, 1984, at Humana Hospital-Audubon in Louisville, Ky. The patient subsequently suffered three stokes that left him partly paralyzed, impaired his memory, and resulted in slow, slurred speech. Schroeder recovered sufficiently to be moved into a specially equipped apartment near the hospital in April 1985, and he was able to visit his home town of Jasper, Ind., later in the year. In November, however, another stroke left him bedridden. At his death on Aug. 6, 1986, Schroeder had lived 620 days with the artificial heart.

The FDA had given DeVries permission to implant the Jarvik-7 into seven people. The third candidate for the procedure was Murray P. Haydon, a 58-year-old retired auto worker, who received a Jarvik-7 heart on Feb. 17, 1985. Haydon also suffered a stroke following the implant, but he recovered without permanent brain damage. Other major complications occurred, however. Haydon's kidneys failed temporarily, and a small hole in the remaining chambers (atria) of his natural heart produced internal bleeding. (The Jarvik-7

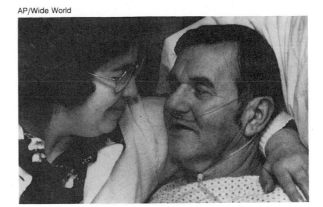

William J. Schroeder, the longest-surviving artificial heart recipient, is shown above with his wife, Margaret. Schroeder died on Aug. 6, 1986, having lived for 620 days after the implantation of his Jarvik-7 heart.

replaces only the pumping chambers, or ventricles.) Surgeons corrected these conditions, but Haydon had continued breathing problems and eventually suffered kidney failure as a result of long-term drug therapy. He died in June 1986.

On April 7, the same day that Schroeder became the first artificial heart recipient to leave the hospital, surgeon Bjarne K. H. Semb, at the Karolinska Institute, Stockholm, performed implantation surgery using a Jarvik-7 heart. The patient, Leif Stenberg, a 52-year-old businessman, then suffered a stroke and severe cerebral bleeding. Stenberg also suffered from preexisting kidney and liver problems. Nevertheless, his condition improved to the point where physicians thought he might be strong enough to undergo transplant surgery. Before a donor heart could be located, however, Stenberg suffered another stroke and died on Nov. 21, 1985.

In April 1985 with three of the four people to receive the Jarvik-7 heart remaining alive, DeVries went ahead with his fourth implant. The patient was Jack C. Burcham, a 62-year-old retired railroad engineer. To prevent strokes, believed to be caused by clots forming in the plastic heart and traveling to the brain, physicians gave Burcham four different anticoagulant drugs. These drugs were believed to have played a role in permitting leakage of blood from vessels connected to the artificial heart. The blood filled the patient's chest, and blood clots pressed against the left atrium of his natural heart, shutting off blood flow. Other problems worsened the situation. Burcham died ten days after the implant. His death brought a halt to use of the Jarvik-7 as a permanent heart replacement.

A bridge to life

An alternative view of the artificial heart, as stated by Jack G. Copeland, a Tucson, Ariz., heart surgeon, was that such devices should be used only as a "bridge to life"—to keep a patient alive until a human heart could be transplanted. Copeland had performed a natural heart transplant on Thomas Creighton, a 33-year-old mechanic, in March 1985, but the organ failed immediately. To keep the patient alive, Copeland took the drastic step of implanting a type of artificial heart not approved by the FDA for human use. The device, which was designed by Phoenix, Ariz., dentist Kevin Cheng, was still undergoing testing in animals. The Phoenix heart, as it became known, was rushed to the University of Arizona Medical Center in Tucson, where Copeland and his team work. Surgeon Cecil Vaughn implanted the device in Creighton on March 6, although it was too big to fit into his chest, and physicians had to leave Creighton's chest open, the pump covered with a sterile dressing. He survived in this condition for 11 hours, when Copeland transplanted a second human heart. Altogether, Creighton received three hearts (two human transplants and the Phoenix heart) to replace his own but died of respiratory failure a few hours after the last transplant surgery.

Copeland encountered severe professional and public criticism for the unauthorized implant. But the FDA took no action beyond a mild rebuke, excusing Copeland's action on the grounds that he, as a physician, was not wrong to make every attempt to save a life. The agency later granted him the first authorization to implant a Jarvik-7 heart on a temporary basis. An appropriate recipient was found in August 1985. Michael Drummond, a 25-year-old store manager, was the youngest person to receive an artificial heart. Drummond suffered mild strokes seven days after the implant, but he recovered sufficiently to undergo transplant surgery in September, when a human heart became available. Despite a life-threatening lung

Michael Drummond, 25, pictured below with his surgeon, Jack G. Copeland, was the youngest artificial heart recipient and the first to receive the device on a temporary basis before receiving a human heart transplant.

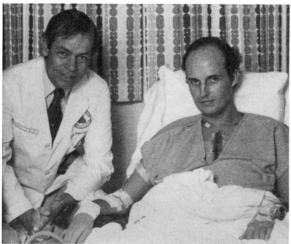

University Medical Center, Tucson

condition, Drummond survived. Tests on the Jarvik-7 device removed from his chest showed that clots had formed in the left pumping chamber at the point where the device had been connected to the aorta, the body's main artery. It was believed that crevices and ridges in this connecting portion may have caused the clots.

Heart models

The pumping chambers of the Jarvik-7 heart consist of rigid plastic sacs, each fitted with a rubber diaphragm. Air pumped into the chambers from a compressor outside of the body expands the diaphragms, pushing blood into arteries that carry it to the lungs and through the body. In the diastolic part of the air-driven heartbeat (in which the cavities of the natural heart dilate), the diaphragms collapse, drawing in blood from the atria. Metal valves prevent backflow. The Phoenix heart contains no diaphragm. Instead, the chambers themselves, made of flexible plastic, expand to collect blood and contract to pump it out, much like a natural heart. Compressed air provides power.

Researchers at Pennsylvania State University's Milton S. Hershey Medical Center at Hershey developed a third model, the so-called Penn State heart. Although it is similar to the Jarvik-7, it was designed as a temporary rather than permanent heart replacement. Ventricles in the Jarvik device consist of two-piece sacs, coated within so that the seam between them does not interrupt the smooth surface. Bioengineer William S. Pierce made the Penn State heart from the same type of plastic (polyurethane) as the Jarvik-7 but cast each sac as one piece. He reasoned that a seamless inner surface would reduce clot formation.

The FDA approved the Penn State heart in March 1985. Surgeons implanted the first one in Anthony Mandia, on October 18 of that year, when physicians believed that his natural heart was close to failing. Mandia, a 44-year-old recreation director, suffered some neurological injury two days later, but his speech and vital signs returned to normal in about one hour.

On October 24, while the Penn State device was still keeping Mandia alive, surgeons at the University of Pittsburgh's Presbyterian-University Hospital gave a Jarvik-7 heart to Thomas J. Gaidosh, a 47-year-old factory worker who was waiting for a human donor heart. Gaidosh was suffering from cardiomyopathy (degeneration of the heart muscle) and became so ill that his doctors believed he would die without the artificial device. Because of his size, Gaidosh needed a large heart. When the heart of a large male donor became available, a medical team rushed it to Mandia's physicians, in Hershey, but the heart was too large for Mandia's chest. Physicians quickly flew it across the state and transplanted it into Gaidosh on October 28. The same day, a smaller female heart became available, and surgeons transplanted it into Mandia. Gaidosh survived his transplant and was still alive in

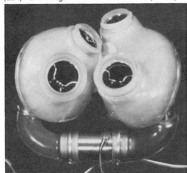 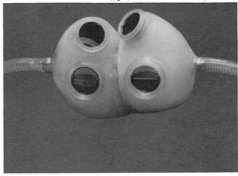 

Three artificial heart models have been implanted by U.S. surgeons—the Jarvik-7 (left), the Phoenix heart (center), and the Penn State heart (right). They are constructed of similar materials—various combinations of plastic, rubber, and metal—but differ in design of the valves and structure of the chambers.

the late summer of 1986. Mandia, who had been kept alive for 11 days by the Penn State heart, died of complications after receiving the human heart transplant.

Meanwhile, Jarvik, working to improve the device he pioneered, made a model 30% smaller than the original and capable of fitting the chest of a relatively small person. The FDA gave physician Lyle Joyce, who had assisted DeVries with his first implant, permission to use the smaller model in humans on a temporary basis. In December 1985 Mary Lund, 40, the victim of a sudden and rare heart infection, became the first woman to receive an artificial heart. Lund required a second operation to check internal bleeding but remained alive with the Jarvik implant for six weeks, at which time physicians decided that the virus that had attacked her natural heart had been eliminated. She received a human heart, from a 14-year-old girl, on Jan. 31, 1986.

Implants curtailed

By October 1985 all of the surgeons involved with implantation of the Jarvik-7, with the exception of DeVries, had agreed that they would not use it on a permanent basis until design changes had reduced the probability of strokes and internal bleeding. Copeland's opinion was that the air-driven pump produces significant damage that gets worse with time. Heart surgeon Denton A. Cooley, who had implanted two temporary artificial hearts in 1969 and 1981, stated that the quality of life of a patient with a mechanical heart is too poor for long-term use. The patient remains connected to an air compressor via two 1.8-m (6-ft)-long plastic tubes. The compressor, air tanks, and monitoring system weigh hundreds of pounds and fill a wheeled cart about the size of those used in supermarkets.

The concensus of most experts was that the artificial heart should be used as a temporary measure to enable patients who might otherwise die to recover to the point where they become candidates for a natural organ transplant. DeVries disagreed with this view. He

announced that he was prepared to use the Jarvik-7 again as a permanent heart replacement as soon as a suitable patient came along, but the FDA prevented him from doing so. On Jan. 8, 1986, the agency declared that DeVries could not perform a permanent implant unless he received FDA approval on a case-by-case basis. He remained the only surgeon authorized to implant the Jarvik-7 as a permanent heart replacement, but he could no longer proceed without prior approval, even in an emergency. The FDA also prohibited implantation of the smaller Jarvik-7 pump until its safety could be ascertained. Furthermore, the agency ruled that it had to approve research to modify the artificial heart before such a device could again be implanted on a permanent basis.

Transplants versus implants

According to South African surgeon Christiaan N. Barnard, who performed the first successful heart transplant in 1967, the quality of life is much higher for those who receive human hearts than for recipients of artificial hearts. Jarvik countered that not enough donor hearts become available to meet the need, a prime reason for developing the artificial replacement. The organ shortage was aggravated by the fact that survival rates among transplant patients have increased dramatically. By 1985 more than 80% of heart transplant patients remained alive after one year; 67% remained alive three years after the surgery. At Stanford University Hospital the world's largest heart transplantation center, surgeons also transplant heart and lungs together, not on an experimental basis but as therapy for those whose heart and lungs can no longer keep them alive. In such cases the two-year survival rate has reached 57%.

Other organ transplants

The one-year survival rate of kidney transplantees almost doubled—it went from 45 to 84%—in the period from 1963 to 1983, according to a study conducted by the Veterans Administration Medical Center, Nashville, Tenn. George L. Ivey, who headed the study, concluded that kidney transplants offer a safe, effective, and financially sound alternative to long-term dialysis treatment.

Survival rates continue to improve as a result of cyclosporine, often hailed as a transplant wonder drug. Cyclosporine was approved by the FDA for human use in November 1983; without completely disarming the body's capacity to fight infection, it suppresses that part of the immune system that attacks transplants. A five-year Canadian study compared cyclosporine with the drug previously considered a standard for transplantation, azathioprine. The one-year survival rate among kidney transplant patients jumped from 86.4 to 96.6% after the introduction of cyclosporine. Optimism about the drug, however, is tempered by suspicions that its long-term side effects may include kidney damage and the development of lymph cancer.

For the short term, however, the most significant side effect of the increased success of transplantation procedures is exacerbation of the organ shortage. Agencies concerned with procurement claim that no more than 19% of the U.S. population have volunteered to donate organs. If, as estimated by the national Task Force on Organ Transplantation, 20,000 people suffered brain death in 1985, the small percentage of willing donors means that 16,400 functioning hearts, livers, pairs of lungs, and pancreases, together with 32,800 kidneys, were unavailable to those who needed them. As many as one-quarter of the people in need of transplants die waiting for organs, according to the task force.

Because of the problems involved in matching the sizes of donor and recipient livers, children in need of liver transplants stand to benefit from the recent success of operations using only part of the adult organ. In January 1986 surgeons at the University of Chicago Hospitals and Clinics transplanted a portion of an adult liver into a three-year-old. Hepatitis had destroyed the boy's liver, and physicians had been unable to find a liver small enough to keep him alive. The surgeon, Christoph Broelsch, who had successfully performed a segmental liver transplant in West Germany in 1983, estimated that about ten such procedures had been performed in Europe, about half of them successful. For long-term success the segment must grow along with the child, ultimately developing into a fully functioning organ. Should the procedure prove successful in the long run, it opens up the possibility that one liver could be used for two transplants—enough to treat one adult and one child. There is also the possibility that part of a liver from a healthy parent or other family member may be used to save a child.

Deriving two liver transplants from a single organ would help to ease the shortage of organs available for transplantation, but it would not close the wide gap between those who actually commit themselves to be donors and those who say that they are willing to do so. In the U.S., for example, 19% of the population carry cards willing their organs to others; yet in a recent survey, 50% of those asked said that they would be organ donors. The study, conducted by the Battelle Human Affairs Research Centers, Seattle, Wash., also found that 53% of those surveyed stated that they would be willing to donate organs of close relatives who die. To increase the actual number of potential donors, organ-procurement officials have advocated public education, donor statements on driver's licenses, and laws requiring physicians to request organ contributions. Public education efforts, such as the American Council on Transplantation's

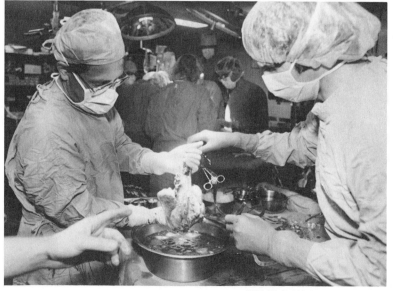

The surgical team at Presbyterian University Hospital, Pittsburgh, Pennsylvania, prepares a donor heart and lungs for a rare double-organ transplant. Although only a few U.S. medical centers are performing the procedure, the success rate is fairly impressive—more than 50% of heart-lung recipients are still alive two years after the surgery.

Donor Awareness Week, have not raised the number of willing donors above 4,000 a year—about 20% of the estimated availability. In the U.S. all states except Delaware and Pennsylvania and the District of Columbia give the holders of driver's licenses and those with nondriver identification cards the option of indicating that they will donate all organs, specific ones, or the entire body. But the Task Force on Organ Transplantation maintains that very few donor organs are generated by this system. By late 1986, 15 states had laws requiring hospitals to ask families for organs in cases of brain death. Similar legislation was under consideration in another 28.

Organ-procurement agencies believe that these laws, combined with education of physicians and hospital staffs, could go a long way toward solving the problem. In one survey almost 90% of 2,613 physicians, nurses, and administrators who were questioned voiced a need for more information about procedures for obtaining donor organs. When this information was provided at the Henry Ford Hospital in Detroit, and the staff of the intensive care unit was obligated to propose organ donation to all families of brain-dead patients, the number of donors tripled—from an annual high of 6 to 18 in 1985—yielding 32 kidneys, 3 hearts, 2 pancreases, and 1 liver.

The U.S. National Transplantation Act of 1984 authorized a nationwide procurement and transplantation network. This federally sponsored network, along with increased education of physicians and laws that make it easier for hospital personnel to request donations, is expected to improve the availability of organs. The improvement, it is hoped, will be enough to narrow significantly the gap between those who give and those who say they are willing to give—and between those fortunate enough to receive and those who die waiting.

—William J. Cromie

Veterinary Medicine

Veterinary medicine has entered the high-technology era, and pets, food animals, zoo animals, and wildlife are benefiting from the scientific advances made by the profession. In the U.S. and other developed countries, particularly in the Western Hemisphere, animal health and productivity have been major beneficiaries of the advances in biotechnology.

About 80 million people in the U.S. are pet owners. The health needs of their pets are being met by approximately 23,000 veterinarians, of whom slightly more than 1,000 are members of recognized specialties. These specialists use modern techniques and instrumentation that were once almost exclusively the province of human medicine. Some 6,000 veterinarians are responsible for the nation's millions of food animals. Another 1,500–2,000 veterinarians look after the

health of the 12 million riding horses and racehorses in the U.S. The care of racehorses in particular requires special expertise to meet the challenges of stress and exercise physiology, scientific breeding, and prevention of reproductive diseases. About 3,500 of the veterinarians in the U.S. are involved in education and research; 2,500 are employed by federal, state, and local governments, with responsibilities ranging from public health to military veterinary medicine. The remainder, about 5%, are employed in private industry, such as pharmaceutical and cosmetic firms, to look after the health of test animals.

The human-animal bond: new dimensions

The benefits of companion animals to human health and well-being—for example, increased survival rates among heart attack victims and improved response to therapy of both the mentally and physically handicapped—are now well documented. Pet-facilitated therapy has been successful in numerous incidences of assisting a withdrawn, uncooperative, or uncommunicative patient to change into a more alert and responsive person.

The decision to use pets in therapy or as social catalysts depends on the type of condition being treated, the ability of the patient to relate to pets, and the mental alertness of the patient. One of the most recent medical applications is the use of animals in dealing with child abuse and in stemming the wave of teenage pregnancies. The underlying common denominator is the need for a love object, and researchers postulate that puppies, kittens, and other small animals may be able to fill this emotional gap.

The significance of the human-animal bond is perhaps most profoundly evident when the bond is broken as a result of a pet's death or separation of pet and owner. In the U.S. guidelines have now been formulated to allow pets to be kept in certain types of federally funded housing and health care facilities, thus removing one barrier that has traditionally separated the sick and the elderly from their animal companions.

Modern diagnosis of animal ailments

The rapid acceptance by the veterinary profession of cross-country telephone transmissions of electrocardiograms has improved diagnostic and therapeutic approaches in the cardiovascular diseases of animals. Currently under consideration is further refinement of the system, with the development of video transmission of X-rays by telephone. Tele-X-ray will allow veterinarians to transmit views of a segment of an animal's body or images of entire body systems to a distant point where the image can be interpreted by a board-certified radiologist.

The application of ultrasonography to veterinary medicine is expanding rapidly. Although ultrasound units provide an up-to-the-minute internal view of cer-

A puppy brings delight to a 90-year-old nursing home patient. New U.S. government guidelines allow residents of certain federally funded housing and health care facilities to keep their well-loved pets.

tain organs, many of them have the capability of continuous monitoring, if indicated. An ultrasound image provides baseline data for future ultrasound readings; comparisons of pictures taken at different stages also help veterinarians learn more about the progress of certain disease conditions. The confirmation of pregnancy in breeding stock is one of the most popular veterinary applications of ultrasound, but there have been major advances in several other physiological and medical applications. For example, with modern, real-time equipment, veterinarians can watch the beating of an animal's heart, identify the presence of fluid within the chest cavity, detect an aneurysm in an intestinal artery that may result from a parasitic infection, and determine the progress of certain liver and kidney diseases that are often characterized by anatomical changes.

A new generation of powerful diagnostic imaging techniques has broadened the veterinarian's capability to make earlier and more accurate diagnoses. Nuclear medicine, utilizing radioisotopes, has been helpful in identification of internal cancers and abnormal function of body organs; it is also used to identify the probable cause of lameness in horses. Computerized axial tomography (CAT) scans produce pictures of both soft tissue and bone; in some procedures, contrast dyes are used to highlight certain body structures. A new harmless and noninvasive procedure called magnetic resonance imaging (MRI) produces detailed cross-sectional images of any part of an animal's body. MRI uses magnetic fields, radio frequency waves, and sophisticated electronics to accomplish its results. Thus, it eliminates the potential dangers of harmful ionizing radiation emitted by conventional X-rays and CAT scans and in many instances avoids the need for more costly invasive procedures.

Treatment advances

Laser surgery uses a controlled beam of light to cut tissue and also coagulate or cauterize the surgical site. The beam provides precision along an identified cell line without disturbing normal cells in close proximity. Veterinary applications of laser therapy are primarily for pain control, wound healing, and stimulation of atrophied or degenerating tissues. As the laser is directed over open wounds, the process of healing is accelerated. If the surgeon desires to assist healing and eliminate pain and swelling, the laser can be used to radiate the surgical site. Utilizing the concept of acupuncture, the laser can target a light beam to stimulate a point on the body without the use of needles. This technique appears to be more effective than classical acupuncture in treating animals' paralyzed limbs, herniated disks, and atrophied muscles. There are also indications that laser beams are effective in managing animal pain associated with chronic degenerative disease such as osteoarthritis.

Hyperthermia is the heating of tissues to higher than normal body temperatures. While its therapeutic application is recent, the concept itself is not new; in the early 1900s it was observed that cancer patients who developed high fevers would occasionally have unexpected remissions. The administration of heat has now been studied scientifically, and indications are that cancer tissues must be heated to approximately 43° C (110° F) for 30 minutes for optimum results. The structure of the tumor determines the effectiveness of the procedure. Tumors in general have a poorly organized blood supply that limits oxygen and results in undernourished cells. As heat is applied to a tumor, the lack of an adequate blood supply prevents the cooling that would be effected through normal blood flow; the result is the death of cancer cells.

438

A unique device that uses ultra high-frequency sound to destroy cancer cells is being evaluated at the University of Illinois College of Veterinary Medicine. This hyperthermia unit uses computer-controlled beams of ultrasound to heat tumors deep within an animal's body. Its temperature monitor and computer, which controls 16 independently regulated ultrasound emitters, allow it to selectively heat cancerous tumors without seriously burning surrounding healthy tissues.

The ultrasound applicator is a water-filled box on the end of a movable arm that allows the applicator to be positioned against the animal's body above the tumor. Stretched across the face of the box is a thick rubber membrane. Inside the box are 16 ultrasound emitters arranged in a four-by-four array. The water serves to transfer the soundwaves from the emitters through the rubber membrane into the animal's tissue. Tiny heat-sensing devices called thermocouples are inserted into the tumor and the surrounding tissue. A monitor connected to these probes records the temperature of the different tissues and sends this information to a computer.

The computer rapidly adjusts the output from each of the 16 ultrasound emitters. The ability to control and change the intensity and pattern of ultrasound emission enables the device to maintain a killing temperature in the entire tumor without causing unacceptable damage to surrounding tissue. This flexibility allows the operator to heat odd-shaped tumors selec-

Sophisticated imaging devices developed for use in human medicine are now being applied to veterinary practice. This goat at the Animal Health Center of the Bronx Zoo is undergoing examination by ultrasound.

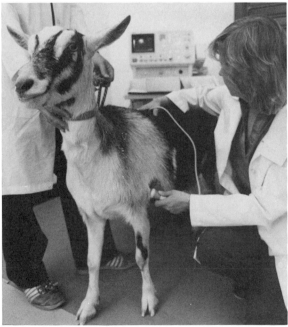

Sara Krulwich/The New York Times

tively and even provides the ability to differentially heat parts of the tumor that require higher temperatures than others.

Further advances in this exciting new therapeutic approach to a dreaded disease include a phased-array ultrasound emitter that can electronically aim ultrasound beams with considerably more precision than is currently possible. The beam of energy from these emitters is focused and swept electronically over the target tissue with great precision. The ultimate goal is a system that will allow delivery with much greater accuracy and minimal harm to normal tissues.

Biotechnology

Reproductive medicine, one of the fastest growing specialities within veterinary medicine, is based on the application of techniques developed for human reproductive disorders. In the search for methods of improving livestock production, the art of embryo transfer has been developed and perfected. Further research has resulted in development of methodology for freezing, splitting, and subsequently implanting the embryos sired by champion bulls into specially selected breeding cows. Similar efforts have been used to improve breeding stock in the swine industry. The current economic plight of farmers in the U.S. will inevitably be accompanied by a drastic reduction in the number of farms with livestock. However, owing to new methods and technologies, those remaining will be able to be more efficient in addressing the industry's production and management needs while providing an adequate supply of meat for consumers. The racehorse industry has not yet accepted embryo transfer, but the breeders of quarter horses and Arabian horses are using it selectively to improve their herds.

Genetic engineering is an exciting and rapidly evolving component of the biological sciences. Veterinary medicine and agriculture—and human medicine, as well—will change dramatically as scientists perfect and extend the use of molecular and cell culture techniques into many aspects of these broad sciences. The microbial production of human insulin and human growth hormone and the production of a safe, effective vaccine to protect food animals against foot-and-mouth disease are current examples of genetic engineering at work.

The explosive worldwide development of cytogenetic laboratories engaged in veterinary research and diagnosis had its origin in 1964, when a team of Swedish researchers discovered a specific chromosomal abnormality that was responsible for impaired fertility in cattle. The defect was subsequently identified in more than 30 breeds of cattle worldwide and has since been largely eliminated from the breeding stock. Similar chromosomal abnormalities that cause small litter size have recently been found in pigs. Sophisticated cytogenetic techniques are now routinely used in several countries in the selection of breeding animals.

At present, little is known about the genetic background of several of the economically most devastating animal diseases. If genetic techniques were available to increase resistance to these diseases, production efficacy would be enhanced, and the consumer would benefit from lower food costs. Additional economic benefits could be realized if diagnostic tests could be developed to predict the susceptibility to disease of the offspring of affected animals. Examples of some of these diseases in cattle include cystic ovaries, metabolic diseases, and the inability to express normal external estrus (female hormone cycle) symptoms. Some of these disorders have complex genetic backgrounds that may also be influenced by environmental and managemental factors. New biotechniques, including gene manipulation and identification of genetic markers, would make for healthier animals and enhanced production.

Immunology

The history of advances in human immunology, immunization, pathophysiology, and tissue transplantation has been intimately linked with the history of veterinary medicine. The British surgeon Edward Jenner (1749–1823), for example, discovered that exposure to a disease of cattle—namely, cowpox—could protect human patients from smallpox. The animal studies of Claude Bernard (1813–78), a French physician, contributed to his development of the concept of homeostasis of the internal environment, which became the cornerstone of virtually all studies of biochemistry, metabolism, and the various feedback mechanisms by which physiological equilibrium is maintained. More recently R. R. A. Coombs, a veterinarian from Cambridge, England, solved the unexplained problem of

hemolytic disease of the newborn; he clearly showed that it was due to Rh incompatibility between the conceptus and the mother.

Perhaps the most dramatic change in immunological thinking took place when Bruce Glick, a U.S. poultry scientist, demonstrated that a structure found in chick embryos, the bursa of Fabricius, controlled the humoral aspect of the immune response, which was clearly distinct from cell-mediated immunity. Thereafter the division of the immune system into two pathways, namely the bursa, or bone-marrow, derived system versus the thymus-dependent system, was born. Today immunologists have postulated "bursa equivalents" in the mammalian system by analogy to Glick's avian model.

Veterinary medicine specialists have continued to lead the way in the development of vaccines. The most significant among these includes an irradiated vaccine against cattle lungworm, the only vaccine of significant efficacy against a parasitic worm disease. Recently another breakthrough occurred when the Institut Mérieux in France developed and marketed a vaccine against canine babesiosis, the first such weapon against a protozoal disease. Researchers working on the prevention of foot-and-mouth disease pioneered the development of the most advanced genetically engineered, synthetic vaccines for this important disease of livestock. This model provided the impetus for the development of other vaccines for diseases such as human malaria, rabies, and pseudorabies.

New developments in infectious diseases

A new rickettsia organism, the causative agent of Potomac horse fever, was isolated at the University of Illinois in 1984. This organism was named *Ehrlichia risticii* after Miodrag Ristic, for his outstanding contributions in the field of rickettsial and protozoal dis-

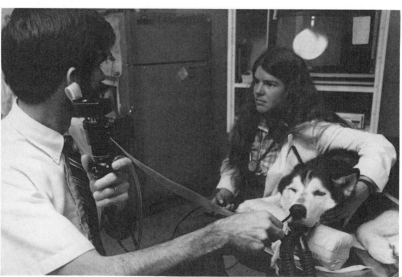

A veterinarian examines a dog's upper respiratory tract by using an endoscope, a flexible fiber-optic viewing device, passed through the animal's nose.

College of Veterinary Medicine, University of Illinois at Urbana-Champaign

Distribution of U.S. veterinarians in federal, local, and private sectors

	estimated number	percent of total	percent male	female
private practice				
large animal exclusive	1,555	5	93	7
large animal predominant	4,691	16	95	5
mixed animal	3,003	10	89	11
small animal predominant	4,333	15	87	13
small animal exclusive	14,089	49	82	18
equine	1,383	5	88	12
other than private practice				
college or university	3,432	38	81	19
federal government	2,313	25	94	6
state and local government	776	9	94	6
armed forces	587	6	93	7
industry and other	1,992	22	88	12

Adapted from AVMA Office of Economics, 1985, with permission

The vast majority of veterinarians in the United States are engaged in the practice of treating small animals, primarily pets.

eases of humans and animals. Since its identification as a clinical entity in Maryland in 1979, Potomac horse fever has spread across the entire U.S. It generally occurs during the warmer months and is characterized by fever, violent diarrhea, colic, and death. The discovery of the causal organism has facilitated diagnosis and treatment, and the availability of the agent in laboratory cell culture now provides a potential for the development of a vaccine. Rickettsial organisms have also been identified as disease agents in other animals and are well recognized as the cause of Rocky Mountain spotted fever in human beings.

Another agent, *Borrelia burgdorferi,* transmitted by a tick, has been identified as a cause of certain signs of disease in dogs and humans. In dogs the major signs appear to be fever and lameness associated with arthritis; in humans fever, headache, arthralgia (joint pain), and a characteristic rash are followed by neurological and cardiovascular symptoms.

For centuries malarial organisms spread by mosquitoes have been responsible for worldwide disease in humans and in several species of animals. The major symptom is a relapsing fever that leads to death in many cases. Authorities at the U.S. Centers for Disease Control estimate that one million people, mostly children, die of malaria each year. The majority of deaths occur in the third world countries of Africa, Asia, and South America. Veterinarians and other scientists in collaborative efforts are on the threshhold of producing a vaccine for humans against the mosquito-borne phase of malarial infection.

Certain viruses, known as retroviruses because they reverse the common method of viral replication, are known to cause malignancies in humans and animals. One retrovirus is known to cause a fatal leukemia in cats. Another, called HTLV-III, causes AIDS (acquired immune deficiency syndrome). Myron Essex, a researcher at the Harvard School of Public Health, is known for pioneering work on feline leukemia and other retrovirus-caused diseases in animals. Recently Essex and his colleagues provided some interesting findings on the HTLV-III virus that may provide the key to the prevention of AIDS. They are now working with a simian virus that appears to be closely related to the etiologic agent for AIDS.

Future perspectives

Continuing progress in molecular genetics and genetic-engineering techniques will help veterinarians understand disease control and increase productivity in livestock. Rapid, accurate diagnostic procedures will allow professionals to implement mass screening programs that will more thoroughly monitor animal diseases. The addition of genetic material to embryos will allow scientists to improve production traits at all levels. Even more spectacular is the possibility of producing strains of animals with genetic resistance to specific diseases.

Veterinary education will have to undergo changes in order to meet the demands of consumers and to provide understanding of scientific advances. The basic science background of veterinarians will have to be strengthened to allow the next generation of graduates to enter the many important nonpractice areas of veterinary medicine—specifically, information in epidemiology and statistics will be a necessity as veterinarians deal increasingly with population medicine. Postgraduate training will be emphasized at all levels, with increased emphasis on, for example, herd health management, reproductive medicine, laboratory animal medicine, and aquaculture. Graduate training in molecular and cellular biology, immunology, and other sciences will serve as the basis for modern research in both basic and clinical veterinary medicine.

Veterinary medicine is approaching the 21st century with an increased ability to serve the needs of the consumer, the pet owner, and the animals themselves. The number of pet owners continues to grow, and as people become better informed about health care in general, they will insist on the best care for their animals and the most up-to-date training for those who provide it.

—Erwin Small, D.V.M.

HEALTH INFORMATION UPDATE

Instructive and practical
articles about common
health concerns

New Dads and New Babies

by Tom D. Naughton

Not long ago it was accepted that during the birth of a child the father's place was in the waiting room. Other than drive his wife to the hospital, he was expected to do little more than pace the floor, flip through old magazines, and chain-smoke while waiting for good news to come through the delivery-room door.

Nowadays the father is more likely to be found inside the delivery room, dressed in surgical clothes and coaching his wife through the motions of birth. In fact, the role that fathers play in all phases of pregnancy and child rearing has expanded.

Viewed from a historical perspective, the increased involvement of fathers in childbirth today may be seen as more of a return to older customs than as the beginning of a new one. Throughout most of history, when human societies were composed primarily of large hunting or farming families, childbirth and child rearing were family affairs. The Industrial Revolution, however, took men away from farms and into factories or offices. As a result, child rearing became the exclusive domain of women. As families moved into cities, women began having their babies in hospitals instead of at home. While hospital deliveries had definite advantages, such as lower death rates for mothers and infants, there was a major disadvantage as well: giving birth soon became equated with undergoing surgery. Mothers were anesthetized for delivery, and the father's presence became viewed as unnecessary—and perhaps even a hindrance—during these highly technical births.

Expectant parents today

In recent years women have been rebelling against this technical approach to childbirth for several reasons. The feminist movement encouraged women to take more responsibility for what happened to their bodies. At the same time, there was a growing back-to-nature movement. Women began to point out that mothers have been delivering for thousands of years without drugs and without having an obstetrician pull the baby out.

This does not mean that most women have abandoned all medical intervention or even hospital deliveries. They understand that some complications require immediate attention from a doctor. But women today realize that most deliveries occur naturally—that they, not the doctor, deliver their babies. Today's women do not want to be in an anesthetic stupor when they

deliver their babies; they want to be conscious so they can appreciate and remember the moment their child came into the world. Likewise, they want their husbands to be present and to share in the experience.

These couples can choose from a variety of natural-birth techniques, but the most popular is the Lamaze method. In this system women learn to regulate their breathing to reduce the pain of delivery. Women who use the Lamaze method usually need much smaller doses of drugs, if any at all. By timing her breathing according to the frequency and intensity of her uterine contractions, the woman can somewhat control the delivery.

An advantage of the Lamaze method is that the woman's husband is no longer considered a hindrance; instead he plays a valuable role as his wife's breathing coach. Most Lamaze couples start attending classes about two months before the expected birth. Through films and lectures, they learn about the physiology of birth and the role that breathing plays. The woman practices altering her breathing for the different stages of labor, and her husband practices coaching her through them. Women who have delivered using the Lamaze method often report that during the confusion and excitement of birth, their husband's coaching helped them concentrate on the proper breathing pattern—and added a much-needed element of reassurance.

The involvement of fathers has spread from being present at the birth to other activities concerning pregnancy and child rearing. At one time there was great emphasis on the need for mothers to prepare their bodies for pregnancy but little emphasis on the father's health. Today doctors recognize that a man's physical condition affects the quality of the sperm he produces; men who are attempting to impregnate their wives are therefore given some of the same advice their wives receive: to stop smoking, to stop drinking alcohol, and to get some exercise.

Once his wife is pregnant, today's father-to-be is more likely to accompany her on her visits to the obstetrician. Only a decade ago fathers were not expected and often were not welcome at these sessions. Most hospitals now allow fathers in the delivery room even if they are not actively participating—a

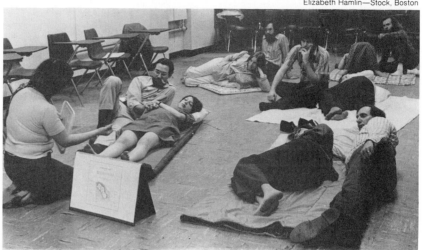

The most popular birth-preparation training that couples participate in together is the Lamaze method. Parents attend classes starting about two months prior to the baby's due date. A main feature of Lamaze is learning special breathing techniques that the woman uses at different stages of labor to reduce pain and, in most cases, to eliminate the need for anesthetics. The husband coaches his wife's breathing from the first labor contraction to the moment of birth.

complete turnaround from the days when most hospitals would not allow the father past the waiting-room doors. Some hospitals allow a woman's husband to remain in the delivery room even if she must undergo a cesarean section, believing that his presence will be comforting to her. Other hospitals, however, still insist that no nonmedical personnel should attend what is essentially a surgical procedure.

New life for new dads

Largely because of the women's movement, the roles that fathers play once mother and baby are home are changing as well. Many women today expect their husbands to be equal partners in feeding, diapering, and bathing babies. And many men, regretting a lack of closeness with their own fathers, are anxious to be more involved with their children. Some businesses have even altered their maternity-leave policies and

included paternity leaves as well, allowing new fathers to take up to 18 weeks away from the job to care for their newborns.

Today's woman is likely to have a career, which she may not want to give up. Many businesses now allow their employees to work on flextime or to divide the duties of a full-time job between two part-time workers. In this way new parents can work out a schedule that allows one of them to always be able to care for the baby though both continue working.

While married fathers today are clearly searching for ways to spend more time with their children, it has often been assumed that the substantial number of unmarried, teenage fathers want nothing to do with their offspring. But results of a project partially funded by the Ford Foundation have indicated that many young, unmarried fathers are both willing and eager to help. The project offered vocational counseling and parent-

There are many emotional rewards afforded by the father's participation in, rather than exclusion from, the baby's birth. Many hospitals today allow—indeed encourage—fathers to be present alongside the obstetrician and delivery-room nurses.

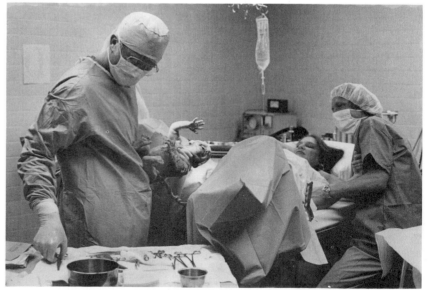

ing classes to nearly 400 teenage fathers in eight major cities. After two years a study of the program found that 82% of the fathers kept in daily contact with their children, 74% contributed financial support, and 90% maintained a relationship with the mother even though few couples got married.

Many teenage fathers grew up without a father to serve as a role model; when faced with a pregnant girlfriend, they may have no idea what a father should do. Many times they find themselves treated like outsiders by a welfare system geared toward helping mothers, and so they become absent fathers themselves even though they may want to be with their children. The Ford Foundation program indicated that, given advice and opportunity, they will jump at the chance to keep their own offspring from being raised fatherless.

Emotional reactions to pregnancy and a new baby

The reevaluation of the roles fathers and mothers play has prompted a better understanding of the emotions they both experience during pregnancy and childbirth. Some fathers, as an expression of their need to feel recognized as expectant parents, even experience physical symptoms—"sympathy symptoms"—that mimic the physical changes a woman goes through in a pregnancy. These symptoms may include bloating, nausea, appetite loss, and weight gain. Later a father may have postpartum blues, sharing his wife's feelings of sadness and fatigue.

Couple woes. Almost immediately, both partners undergo a change in their feelings about sex. The mother-to-be may find that morning sickness, which often occurs at night, and mood swings decrease her sex drive. Although this stage will likely pass and she may find sex enjoyable again, late in her pregnancy she may find sex uncomfortable or fear that she is

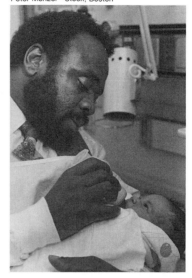

Just like new moms, dads may need to learn how to care for the new member of the family. There are special programs and books that help fathers get over fears about mishandling the baby and instruct them on how to attend to the infant's many needs.

unattractive to her husband. The husband, for his part, may take his wife's mood swings or lack of desire as a personal rejection. Through talking and sharing their feelings, both partners can work out these troubles.

Some couples, especially later in the pregnancy, fear that sex may harm their baby. Unless there are physical problems such as bleeding or a broken amniotic sac, intercourse can safely be continued until the final few weeks before the baby is due. Some women, however, find that they need to alter their customary positions during sex to avoid discomfort.

Mom's woes. After the baby is born, one emotion many new mothers feel is stress caused by time pressures. A mother may feel that all the baby-care tasks and household responsibilities cannot fit into 24 hours. She may also get "cabin fever," feeling that she is

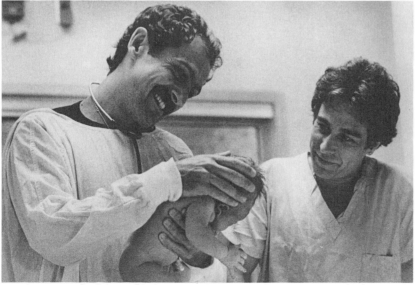

Today's dads share in the joyous moment of birth and in the all-important "bonding" process.

stuck at home because of the baby, and that her at-home life makes her boring to others. She may feel herself resenting the baby's round-the-clock needs—and then feel guilty over her resentment. All these emotional pressures, along with the hormonal changes her body is going through, can lead to postpartum blues, feelings of sadness and depression.

An involved father can help his wife overcome these pressures by helping with baby care and housework. By being understanding and talking with his wife, a husband can help keep her expectations reasonable and assure her that she is still interesting and attractive to him. He can also help by assuring her that he is pleased with his role as a father—especially if the child is the first. Studies have shown that a woman's satisfaction with her new role as mother is strongly influenced by her opinion of her husband's satisfaction with fatherhood.

Dad's woes. An emotion often experienced by men approaching fatherhood for the first time is self-doubt. They may begin dwelling on their perceived faults and worry that they will pass these traits on to their children. They may question their ability to be good fathers. They may, despite feminism-inspired concepts about male-female roles, feel increased pressure to be a good provider.

Expectant fathers used to have nowhere to turn when they felt these doubts. They were often afraid that expressing their feelings would upset their pregnant wives. Now that the role of fathers is better understood, there are many books available to help them understand their feelings and overcome their doubts. An expectant father may even join a discussion group with other fathers-to-be.

Another emotion commonly experienced by new fathers is jealousy. Before the birth he may feel that all the attention is focused on the mother. The old doctors-only deliveries only added to this problem. After the birth the husband may feel that his wife's attention is concentrated on the baby. By assisting in the delivery, a father can feel that he *is* needed and appreciated. Likewise, by becoming more involved with the baby-care responsibilities, a father can feel that he and his wife are working as partners in raising the child. It is important for both mother and father, however, to set aside some time for themselves when they talk about something other than their baby.

Active dads: rewards for all

The mother, the father, and the baby all benefit when a father plays an active role in pregnancy, childbirth, and child rearing. A pregnant woman often feels burdened both physically and psychologically. Some hospitals now offer classes in which an expectant father can learn to understand and anticipate his pregnant wife's emotions and mood changes so that he can provide the emotional support she needs.

Husbands may also learn how to give their wives massages to ease the aches and pains of pregnancy. When her husband becomes involved in her pregnancy, the woman is less likely to feel that an awesome responsibility has been thrust completely upon her shoulders. And, of course, a husband's physical presence during delivery offers a woman important psychological support during what can be an otherwise emotional, painful, and frightening experience.

Perhaps the most satisfying benefit fathers receive from their increased involvement is a closer relationship with their children. Psychologists now believe that a baby forms strong emotional bonds through skin-to-skin and face-to-face contact. This "bonding" may begin to take place in the first moments after birth. Fathers can now be with their children from the beginning. By participating in the feeding and bathing of their children, fathers can establish the kind of emotional closeness that was once thought to be reserved for mothers.

Of course, children benefit from this closeness as well. A good relationship with both parents is important to a child's emotional adjustment. Psychologists say that girls who are close to their fathers while growing up tend to have more stable relationships with their own husbands.

Young children almost invariably think of their fathers as big and strong. They perceive a father as someone who can banish monsters and otherwise relieve childhood fears. A close relationship with a father is thus a strong source of security for a child.

Finally, when mother and father are both actively involved in a child's upbringing, the child experiences two styles of parenting. In this way the child comes to an early understanding that people are different and that differences are healthy and natural. This is a lesson that will help a child form successful relationships throughout life.

FOR MORE INFORMATION:
COPE (Coping with the Overall Pregnancy-Parenting Experience). 37 Clarendon Street, Boston, MA 02116. Provides guidance for new parents through support groups, classes, and printed materials.
The Fatherhood Project. Bank Street College of Education, 610 W. 112th Street, New York, NY 10025. A national clearinghouse of information on support resources for fathers.
MELD (formerly Minnesota Early Learning Design). 123 W. Grant Street, Minneapolis, MN 55403. A growing network that offers support and education programs for first-time parents.
Also check the library or a bookstore for one of the many new books written by fathers for other fathers. These cover everything from dealing with the sight of blood in the delivery room to how to burp a baby.

Dental Plaque
by Sebastian G. Ciancio, D.D.S.

Dental plaque is a soft, sticky deposit that accumulates normally on the surfaces of teeth and dental restorations (fillings, crowns, bridges, dentures). It is composed of approximately 75% bacteria and 20% organic and inorganic solids; the remainder is water and a variety of cells. The bacteria in dental plaque—although present to some extent in all healthy mouths—are responsible for tooth decay and gum disease. The bacterial population is in a continuous state of change and is affected by the individual's age, oral hygiene habits (*i.e.,* frequency and thoroughness of brushing and flossing), diet, and the location of the deposits on the teeth.

The amount of plaque formed is about the same in men as in women, but many dentists note that women tend to remove it better and, therefore, have less accumulated plaque on their teeth. The plaque that forms in children's mouths is different from adult plaque in that it contains more of the *Streptococcus mutans* bacteria, which are a primary cause of tooth decay. The type of plaque that forms in the adult mouth is usually associated more with gum disease than with decay.

Prior to the formation of plaque, pellicle, a thin film derived from saliva, attaches to the surface of the tooth. Pellicle contains no bacteria and forms within seconds after teeth are cleaned. Subsequently, bacteria become attached to the pellicle and accumulate on the tooth surface. Eventually, unremoved dental plaque can become calcified, forming hard, porous deposits on the teeth, called tartar or dental calculus. Components of saliva and food contribute to the formation of tartar deposits, which are visible to the naked eye. Once formed, tartar cannot be removed by brushing, flossing, or other self-care measures; professional removal is necessary. The surface of tartar serves as an excellent base for further bacterial colonization, thus promoting the accumulation of plaque.

Plaque-forming bacteria

At birth the human oral cavity is sterile. Within the first ten hours of life, however, bacteria from the infant's environment can be found in the mouth. More complex bacteria appear as early as ten days after birth, and by the time the first baby teeth erupt, such complex forms are present in the mouths of all infants. These bacteria are derived initially from the external environment, ingested with food or on objects placed in the mouth, including the infant's own thumbs and fingers.

Once bacteria begin to accumulate in the mouth, large numbers thrive on the surface of the tongue, teeth, and, to a lesser extent, the oral mucous membrane. During periods of reduced salivary flow—for example, during sleep or when the mouth is dry as a result of medication or stress—the number of bacteria in the oral cavity increases. A decrease is seen after eating certain foods and following brushing and flossing. In the adult mouth microscopic counts of bacteria average more than 750 million per milliliter.

Types of plaque

Dental plaque is classified according to its location in relation to the gum margin. Above the gum margin it is called supragingival plaque and below the margin, subgingival plaque. Subgingival plaque is wedged between the gum tissue and root surface and is attached to both. The area it occupies is called the gingival crevice.

Supragingival plaque. Supragingival plaque is the first to form. In the early stages it is invisible. However, as it accumulates and the bacteria begin to multiply, supragingival plaque becomes slightly visible, varying in color from pale yellow to grey. As the plaque mass increases, teeth begin to feel less smooth to the tongue; some people say that their teeth feel "fuzzy." The plaque deposit increases as a result of multiplication of existing bacteria, the addition of new bacteria, and the accumulation of dead bacteria, products of bacterial metabolism, and components derived from the diet. The process of bacterial formation and growth is affected by age, diet, tooth position, systemic disorders, and a variety of related, so-called host factors, including composition of saliva. Most of these host factors have not yet been identified, and research is under way to determine why a few people form minimal amounts of plaque.

Supragingival plaque attaches to all tooth surfaces, fillings, crowns, dental appliances, and dentures. It has a predilection for rough areas, tooth surface cracks, and poorly contoured restorations. The attachment of bacteria to pellicle is more readily accomplished by some bacteria than by others. Certain bacteria, particularly S. mutans, contain an enzyme capable of decomposing dietary sugar into a sticky material that facilitates the attachment of other bacteria to the tooth surface. Once these initial attachments have occurred, subsequent bacteria adhere more readily, and colonies are formed, which then grow and mature.

Following a thorough tooth cleaning, a measurable amount of bacteria, consisting of growing bacterial colonies, remains on the tooth surface; within 12 hours the colonies multiply into organized masses that cover most tooth surfaces. The rate of colony formation and the location of colonies vary among individuals, from area to area on the same tooth, and from one tooth to another in the same mouth. By 24 hours after cleaning, plaque is well organized and highly tenacious. For this reason it is incorrect to assume that once-a-day brushing and flossing will adequately remove plaque. Instead, plaque should be removed at 10- to 12-hour intervals, or twice a day, as it is more vulnerable to mechanical action at this time. A thorough once-a-day cleaning will, however, help to break up colonized plaque, which is the most harmful.

Subgingival plaque. Subgingival plaque, although an extension of supragingival plaque, contains some bacteria not found beyond the gumline. Since the gingival crevice (the area below the gumline) can serve as a protective hiding place for bacteria, the bacteria are less subject to removal by routine daily oral cleaning. Because of the protective nature of the gingival crevice, bacteria that thrive in areas having no free oxygen (anaerobic bacteria) can accumulate and thrive. Also, microorganisms that cannot adhere easily to a surface above the gumline may accumulate more readily in this protected area. Because these bacteria are in intimate contact with the inner aspect of the gum tissue, they can derive nutrition from this tissue more readily than their supragingival counterparts.

Plaque and tooth decay

Supragingival plaque is the main factor responsible for tooth decay (caries). Not all bacteria in plaque are involved in the initiation and progress of caries, how-

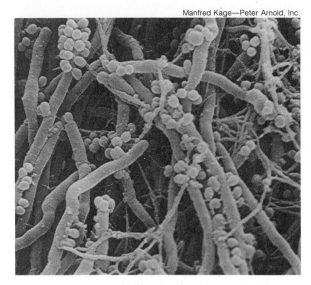

Manfred Kage—Peter Arnold, Inc.

Dental plaque, the sticky film that forms on tooth surfaces between brushings, is composed primarily of bacteria. These organisms are responsible for both tooth decay and gum disease.

ever, and those responsible for the decay process can differ depending on the surface involved. Decay-causing bacteria produce an acid that breaks down the tooth structure. Prior to age 50 the main surfaces that are affected are the crevices on the biting surfaces of the back teeth, the flat surfaces between teeth, especially at points of contact between teeth, and the area along the gumline. After age 50 the decay process shifts to the root surfaces, with different bacterial types predominating.

Plaque and periodontal disease

Various types of periodontal disease are associated with specific bacteria that differ from those usually found in the healthy gingival crevice. As the numbers of bacteria in supragingival and subgingival plaque increase, the gum tissue becomes inflamed. As this inflammation, called gingivitis, increases, plaque bacteria can be found not only on the surface of the tissue but within it, progressively going deeper as the disease process becomes more severe. The base of the gum tissue attached to the tooth is disrupted; the gum slowly recedes; and less tissue is attached to the root of the tooth. Gradually the space between tooth and gum tissue becomes wider and deeper, facilitating the continued movement of bacteria into the soft tissue and, eventually, into the bone. As bone loss occurs due to the destructive action of bacteria, the gingivitis becomes periodontitis, a term denoting that both hard and soft tissue around the tooth are diseased. The word is derived from the Greek *peri,* meaning "around," and *odont,* meaning "tooth." Although supragingival plaque plays a role in this process, subgingival plaque and its associated bacteria are essential.

In spite of extensive research in both animals and humans, it has been difficult to identify those bacteria in plaque that are most responsible for the various gum diseases. It is scientifically accepted that the metabolic products of plaque bacteria—acids, ammonia, hydrogen sulfide, amines, enzymes, and other substances that can destroy body tissues—are toxic to gum and bone around teeth. Some of these plaque products also contribute to bad breath. The harmful effects of plaque bacteria can sometimes be overcome by the body's defense mechanisms. Even in the healthiest person, however, these mechanisms can be overwhelmed if the bacteria are not routinely removed by correct oral hygiene procedures. Certain systemic diseases, including diabetes and some blood disorders, weaken the body's ability to overcome the effects of plaque.

Bacteria also contain proteins and carbohydrates that can activate immune mechanisms in gum tissue. As these mechanisms are activated, the body produces antibodies in response to bacterial antigens, forming an immune reaction that can cause tissue destruction.

Plaque control

The best control of plaque is accomplished by mechanical procedures, which include brushing, flossing, and professional prophylaxis. A professional cleaning is recommended at least twice a year to remove plaque and tartar, both above and below the gumline. Also, it is important for the dentist or hygienist to evaluate the effectiveness of the patient's home hygiene procedures and to make appropriate suggestions for their improvement.

Brushing. A recent survey of brushing habits in the United States showed that only 60% of the public follow a strict brushing regimen. Clearly, motivation and education are needed in this area.

For the average adult, a soft brush with rounded bristles is most efficient in removing plaque from supragingival tooth surfaces (with the exception of these surfaces between the teeth). Most bristles are made of nylon, although hog-bristle brushes are still manufactured. Both are equally effective in plaque control. Subgingival plaque can be removed only to a depth of a few millimeters. For patients with a highly developed gagging reflex, a child's toothbrush often overcomes the problem of gagging. In addition, these patients sometimes find that placing a small amount of salt on the tongue is helpful in checking the desire to gag.

Studies of toothbrushing methods indicate that thoroughness is more important than technique. In the United States the most widely used technique is one in which the bristles are directed into the gingival crevice at a 45° angle, and a gentle jab-jiggle action is used. The motion is elliptical, rather than a back-and-forth scrubbing. Electric toothbrushes are of value for

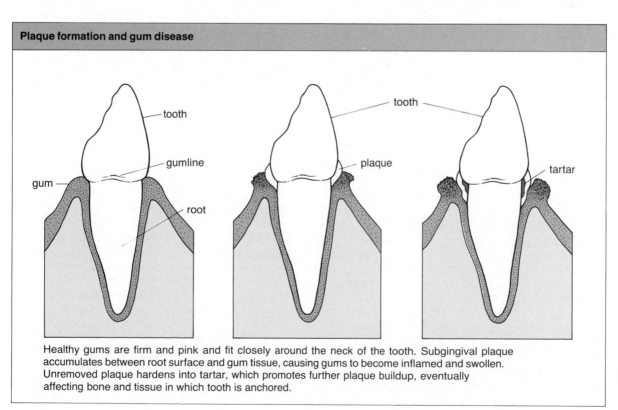

Plaque formation and gum disease

Healthy gums are firm and pink and fit closely around the neck of the tooth. Subgingival plaque accumulates between root surface and gum tissue, causing gums to become inflamed and swollen. Unremoved plaque hardens into tartar, which promotes further plaque buildup, eventually affecting bone and tissue in which tooth is anchored.

people who have motor coordination problems or difficulty in properly removing plaque by manual brushing. For children the novelty effect of the powered brush is sometimes of motivational value.

Flossing. In the survey referred to above, it was found that only 25% of the population questioned use dental floss regularly. Flossing is essential for removal of plaque from the surfaces between teeth and under the gumline, where the toothbrush does not reach. Because plaque has a propensity to build up in these areas, some dentists feel that flossing is actually more important than brushing.

To prevent damage to the gum tissue in the process, proper flossing requires instruction by a dental professional. For patients who do not have the manual dexterity to use dental floss, there are various types of dental floss holders. Dental floss is available in waxed, lightly waxed, or unwaxed varieties. Most dentists feel that a lightly waxed or unwaxed type is more efficient in plaque removal. If the floss shreds or splits during use, this may be a sign of decay between the teeth or a defective filling margin.

Disclosing agents. Disclosing agents are dyes similar to those in food colorings that, when introduced into the oral cavity, color the supragingival plaque and make it easily visible. Various dyes are available in both liquid and tablet form. They are used in the dental office and at home both to increase the patient's awareness of plaque and to demonstrate where self-care has been ineffective in removing it.

Toothpastes. The majority of toothpastes advertised as specially formulated to control plaque contain (in addition to fluoride) a foaming agent and a mild abrasive, both of which facilitate plaque removal. However, no such product currently available is accepted by the American Dental Association (ADA) as possessing an active ingredient with proven ability to prevent or control plaque formation and prevent gingivitis. Toothpastes claiming to be "more effective" against plaque are simply more effective than brushing without any toothpaste because the use of toothpaste motivates people to brush longer and more thoroughly. In fact, it is mainly the mechanical action of brushing that removes plaque.

There are some relatively new products that claim to be effective against tartar and that contain ingredients on which this claim is based. However, these products are most useful after professional cleaning, and because they prevent the reformation of tartar only *above* the gumline, the ADA considers such products to have cosmetic rather than therapeutic value.

Toothpastes are effective as vehicles to deliver fluoride to the tooth surface, and although fluoride may have some effect against plaque bacteria and their enzymes, its major effect is to make the tooth surface more resistant to destruction by plaque bacteria. Many toothpastes are accepted by the American Dental As-

sociation for their fluoride content and effectiveness against tooth decay.

Mouthwashes. Of the many mouthwashes available without prescription, only a few contain chemical agents that have some ability to kill plaque bacteria. These products have some value as adjuncts to mechanical cleansing procedures. A limitation of mouthwashes is that, because they can reach subgingival plaque only to a depth of a few millimeters within the gingival crevice, they are most effective against supragingival plaque. Preliminary studies suggest that use of a mouthwash with plaque-reducing properties in an oral irrigating device may have a more profound effect on subgingival plaque. At this time no nonprescription mouthwashes that claim to reduce plaque are approved for that purpose by the ADA; some prescription formulations are being developed.

The effect of diet. Supragingival plaque comes into contact with food more than subgingival plaque does; therefore, diet has more of an effect on supragingival plaque. The consistency of the diet affects the rate and amount of plaque formation: soft, sticky foods favor plaque formation; hard, crispy foods do not. Sugar, easily metabolized and utilized by plaque bacteria, is an excellent nutrient for these organisms. Certain carbohydrates and fats also are supportive of plaque bacteria. Because the length of time that sugars and carbohydrates are present in the mouth, or available to bacterial plaque, is important, the frequency of ingestion is as important as the amount. People who eat high-protein, low-fat, and low-carbohydrate diets accumulate less plaque.

Other aids. A number of devices aid in the removal of plaque from surfaces between teeth, between exposed roots of multirooted teeth, around bridgework, and in other areas that are difficult to reach. The limitation of many of these devices is that they are effective for control of supragingival plaque but, at best, can remove subgingival plaque only to a depth of a few millimeters. Therefore, they are of minimal value against subgingival plaque located deeper within the gingival crevice, as is the case in gum disease.

Various oral irrigators on the market remove some loosely attached plaque and particles of debris present around teeth and dental appliances, including braces. Because they are not effective in removing attached plaque, they are not substitutes for brushing and flossing; rather, they should be used as adjuncts to these procedures. In addition, oral irrigators are limited in their ability to reach subgingival plaque. Some studies have suggested that irrigators may alter plaque composition by flushing out noxious materials, but these data are not well substantiated. Patients with badly inflamed gum tissues should be cautioned to use irrigators at low pressures to guard against tissue laceration, which may aggravate the existing problem.

450

Coronary Bypass

by Marc K. Effron, M.D.

Coronary artery bypass surgery has become a common procedure for the treatment of atherosclerotic heart disease. In the United States coronary operations number over 180,000 per year and cost approximately $25,000 per case. Each year this number of middle-aged and elderly individuals is added to the burgeoning ranks of cardiac patients who have undergone this major operation and major life experience.

A coronary surgery patient is subjected to a great personal challenge. This may entail becoming aware of a life-threatening illness for the first time. Then the patient may face fear of the illness and of the treatment, an intense recovery phase immediately following the operation, and a period of readaptation to life's demands after the surgical wounds have healed.

Pathophysiology

Coronary artery disease is a very common cause of illness or death among citizenry of developed nations in the Western world. Despite large-scale attempts at prevention, the major causes of coronary artery disease remain prevalent. Cigarette use, hypertension, elevated blood cholesterol, diabetes mellitus, and genetic tendencies all contribute to the formation of atherosclerotic plaque. This plaque obstructs blood flow in the coronary arteries that supply the muscular chambers of the heart. Severe narrowing or total occlusion of these critical vessels may compromise or permanently damage the heart muscle.

An early symptom of coronary disease may be angina pectoris, a transient chest pain or discomfort occurring during periods of diminished blood flow to the heart muscle. Some patients may initially experience the sustained chest pain of myocardial infarction, indicating permanent cardiac damage. Others may die suddenly, without the warning of a prodromal chest pain syndrome of any type.

Treatment of coronary disease includes attempts to modify the causative factors by termination of cigarette use, control of high blood pressure, and lowering of serum cholesterol. Medications can reduce the risk of thrombosis of the coronary arteries and augment the balance of oxygen and nutrients in the heart muscle. Currently risk factor modification and pharmacological treatment probably cannot reduce atherosclerotic plaque that has already formed in the coronary arteries.

No two patients with coronary disease are anatomically identical. Each individual has a unique developmental pattern of the coronary arteries with different numbers or sizes of vessel branches. The distribution of coronary artery narrowings due to deposition of atherosclerotic plaque also varies considerably.

Nonsurgical treatment

If one or two of the three major coronary vessels are severely narrowed, short-term prognosis is usually good. Most such patients will undergo a careful trial of antianginal medications to control symptoms and prevent myocardial infarction or death.

If patients do not respond favorably to medical treatment, a procedure known as percutaneous transluminal coronary angioplasty may be applied to stretch open the narrowed vessels by means of a small balloon. This relatively new procedure is usually performed under local anesthesia; through a small incision at the groin area, the angioplasty balloon catheter is positioned, with fluoroscopic guidance, across the narrowed arterial segment.

Indications for surgical treatment

If medication has not been helpful and coronary angioplasty is not technically feasible, then patients with one or two diseased vessels may be considered candidates for coronary bypass surgery. The operation can very effectively relieve angina.

Some patients have significant narrowings of all three major branches of the coronary system. Fewer than 10% of coronary patients have a narrowing of the essential left-main coronary artery. Such patients with three-vessel or left-main coronary disease are often offered coronary surgery as an early treatment modality.

Survival of patients with left-main disease is clearly improved by surgical treatment. A survival advantage also may be obtained in patients with three-vessel disease, particularly if part of the cardiac muscle has already been permanently damaged. Thus, some patients have coronary disease of such severity that the

451

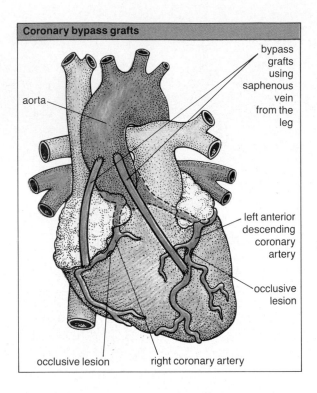

Coronary bypass grafts

aorta

bypass grafts using saphenous vein from the leg

left anterior descending coronary artery

occlusive lesion

occlusive lesion

right coronary artery

risk of a cardiac death remains high despite the use of medication. Surgical treatment is thus offered to these seriously ill patients not only to relieve angina but also to extend life.

The presurgical setting

Prior to the actual coronary operation, the patient has been confronted with the diagnosis of coronary disease and has undergone coronary arteriography, the invasive diagnostic catheterization procedure that details and visualizes the extent of an individual's disease. When bypass surgery has been decided upon, some patients' operations are performed on an elective basis. These patients are generally quite stable and comfortable during the days preceding surgical treatment.

Other patients are nonelective or emergency cases and may be clinically unstable as they enter the operating room. Preceding days or hours are physiologically and psychologically stressful as attempts are made to adjust intravenous medications intended to stabilize the angina. In elective cases there is time to contemplate the benefits and risks of surgical treatment, but the emergency setting does not always permit such contemplation and understanding.

The bypass procedure

The operation itself is performed with general anesthesia and therefore is not within the direct experience of the patient. During a three- to six-hour period, the cardiac surgeon performs a sternotomy, splitting the

breastbone and dissecting to the great vessels and surface of the heart. The great vessels are cannulated—*i.e.*, small tubes are inserted—and connected to a pump oxygenator device in order to perfuse the body with oxygenated blood while the heart is stopped. Segments of the chief superficial (saphenous) veins of the legs are removed for use as graft material and are anastomosed—*i.e.*, utilized as interconnecting conduits—between the proximal aorta and the coronary arteries. One or both internal mammary arteries may be dissected free from the chest wall and distally connected to the coronary arteries, providing particularly long-lasting grafts with a patency rate (*i.e.*, they remain unobstructed) that is superior to that of vein grafts.

Recovery in hospital

Upon awakening in the intensive care unit (ICU), a patient has an endotracheal tube in place and is connected to a mechanical ventilator. Multiple intravenous and intra-arterial catheters are in place, and large tubes exit from the chest to provide drainage of blood and fluid. A cardiac catheter may be in position to monitor pressures in the heart chambers. Temporary pacemaker wires have been placed on the cardiac surface and exit the chest to be connected to an exterior pacemaking device. Doctors and nurses closely monitor and control cardiac rhythm and function. Some medications are administered continuously by infusion pumps. Pain is controlled by intravenous narcotics, and the recovery process begins.

Most patients have the endotracheal tube removed and are stable without the support of potent intravenous drugs by 24 to 48 hours following the operation. By 72 hours after the operation, most patients have been transferred to a floor of the hospital with

Immediately following the operation, the coronary bypass patient faces an intense recovery phase in the hospital before the major transition of returning home.

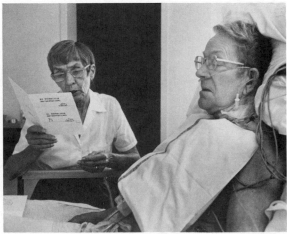

Maureen Fennelli—Photo Researchers

452

radio-transmitted monitoring of cardiac rhythm and have begun the second phase of in-hospital recovery. Physical and dietary activity progresses over six to eight days until the patient is ambulatory and capable of doing well at home.

Complications of bypass surgery

Several complications of coronary surgery may appear during or immediately following the operation. Death due to myocardial infarction, or other serious problems, is observed in 0.5 to 1% of surgical cases in major cardiac centers. The operative mortality is higher in patients with severe prior damage to the heart muscle or other serious concomitant medical problems. Major nonfatal complications include myocardial infarction, renal failure, stroke, or vascular occlusion of an extremity. Postoperative bleeding from tissue at or around the heart surface may require therapy with clotting factors or a repeat operation to control blood loss.

Other complications include heart rhythm disturbances, fluid in the pleural space adjacent to the lungs, pneumonia, and injury to the brachial nerves at the shoulder region, causing weakness of the arm.

Wound infections are now very infrequent. Patients with preceding lung disease may experience a transient deterioration of their pulmonary condition. Diabetes may temporarily worsen following the operation. Elderly individuals particularly may display a diffuse cerebral injury with memory loss and mild delirium related to cardiopulmonary bypass with the pump oxygenator. This cerebral deficit usually improves gradually over days or weeks, but some patients may require several months before mental capacity fully returns to normal.

Recovery at home

Return to home is a major transition for the coronary surgery patient. Cardiac monitoring systems and observant nurses in the hospital environment provide safety and assistance. Dependency on this environment is broken upon discharge from the hospital. The transition may be triumphant or frightening. Medications for mild anticoagulation and heart rhythm stability are prescribed for use at home.

Activities progress at home as in the hospital. Ambulation is the major exercise, with gradual progression to at least 30 minutes walking daily over the first two to three weeks at home. Some patients may be enrolled in formal cardiac rehabilitation programs in which exercise is directed daily and supervised. The goal of either a home- or institution-based rehabilitation program is to resume normal activity gradually over the month following surgery.

The last physical restriction often applies to use of the upper torso musculature. Lifting and arm work such as driving an automobile are restricted until up to six weeks following the operation. This is rec-

Joseph A. DiChello, Jr.

Aerobic exercise such as jogging or vigorous walking is an essential part of life after coronary bypass. Many hospitals have cardiac rehabilitation programs that provide exercise training and supervision.

ommended to ensure good healing of the sternum. Sexual activity may be resumed in correspondence to other physical activities at home. Return to work may be advised at between one and two months following the operation. This decision depends on the progress during recovery, any complications of the operation, and the occupation of the patient.

Late complications

Some complications of coronary surgery typically appear or become important only following discharge from the hospital. Because the saphenous vein has been excised from one or both legs, mild venous insufficiency may lead to ankle swelling or edema, which may appear when the patient is more frequently upright and ambulatory at home. The phenomenon is usually transient and can be treated by leg elevation and wearing of special compression hosiery.

The chest wall may be a continuing source of chest pain despite healing of the sternotomy incision. The sternum or adjacent cartilage and ribs were stressed and repositioned during the operation. Some patients experience weeks or many months of anterior chest wall pain. Anti-inflammatory drugs may be offered to ease the discomfort. With such pain, diagnostic distinction from recurrent angina is important.

Postpericardiotomy syndrome is observed in a small minority of coronary patients. Days to weeks after the surgical treatment, an inflammatory reaction may appear at the pericardial lining of the heart and at the pleural surfaces of the lungs. Chest pain, fever, and localized collections of fluid are common findings, which may abate with administration of anti-inflammatory drugs. A rare patient experiences episodic recurrences of the postpericardiotomy syndrome when suppressive drug therapy is withdrawn.

Mental depression may result from any major medical illness. It is particularly common in coronary patients following myocardial infarction or coronary surgery. During surgical recovery the patient may focus on his or her own physical limitations and mortality. For some individuals the clinical decision to operate occurred on an abrupt emergency basis; thus, full contemplation of what may be perceived as a medical dilemma may occur only after discharge from the hospital. A sense of helplessness may accompany this delayed recognition of illness. The helplessness is intensified when chest wall pain and general weakness cause dependency on family members at home.

The patient's predicament is usually well publicized to family, friends, and those at the workplace. This means that the individual's privacy is lost or severely compromised during the profound medical illness. The patient is continually vulnerable to the scrutiny of others and may have to bear the social implications of having a "weak heart." The classic coronary patient is the middle-aged working male, now reduced to convalescence with doubts about his future health.

Depressive symptoms are usually brief, but some patients may require several months to acclimate psychologically to their new medical condition and the real or imagined social implications of that condition. In some cases spousal relationships may be challenged during this period. Consultation with the physician, formal psychological counseling, or a group cardiac-rehabilitation program may all be of assistance.

Limitations of surgical treatment

Surgical treatment of coronary disease may stop angina, prevent myocardial infarction, and sustain life, but not indefinitely. Up to 15% of venous grafts occlude and are nonfunctional by the first year after the operation. Graft patency declines at a much slower rate subsequently. Yet by eight to ten years after coronary surgery, many venous grafts are not functioning well. Survival rates approach equivalency when medically and surgically treated patients are compared a decade following the operation. These findings are not unexpected, considering the gradual progression of vessel disease during this period and the lack of permanence of the saphenous vein grafts.

Coronary surgery improves blood flow to cardiac muscle, but it does not strengthen the contraction of previously damaged portions of the muscle. Late-onset congestive heart failure and cardiac arrhythmias, despite intervening surgery, may occur in cases where there is myocardial scarring from prior infarction. Coronary surgery can minimize the progression of cardiac damage but cannot remove previously incurred injury. Although some patients may have an excellent prognosis after surgery, others are left with enough dysfunction of the ventricular chamber to warrant a guarded prognosis and careful observation for future problems.

Preventive measures after surgery

Patency of the coronary grafts can be enhanced by use of platelet-inhibitory agents. Drugs such as aspirin and dipyridamole can prevent platelet thrombus formation and perhaps prevent damage to the endothelial lining of the vein segments.

Risk factors contributing to progression of atherosclerosis must be actively modified after coronary surgery. Every effort must be made to prevent progression of coronary disease in the native vessels distal to the surgically grafted interconnections. Otherwise, the utility of the grafts will be lost. Cigarette use must not be resumed. Blood pressure should be controlled by weight loss, salt restriction, and/or medication. Cholesterol levels must be minimized by a low-saturated-fat, high-fiber diet and, if necessary, use of lipid-lowering drug therapy.

Aerobic exercise should become a regular habit. Walking, bicycling, and swimming are excellent aerobic activities that are unlikely to cause orthopedic disability. Jogging may or may not be recommended following coronary surgery. This depends on the patient's weight, degree of myocardial dysfunction, and enthusiasm for this form of vigorous activity, as well as the estimated degree of revascularization achieved at operation. Exercise can assist with weight loss, improve the profile of favorable and unfavorable serum lipids, provide general cardiovascular conditioning, and augment the psychological rehabilitation.

Rather than being a cure, coronary bypass surgery is a palliative procedure that relieves symptoms and prolongs life. For many patients it is a beginning in the treatment of atherosclerotic heart disease. The causative factors must be modified after surgery in order to prevent progression of the disease.

Regular follow-up visits to the cardiologist are required for monitoring of the cardiac condition as well as bringing blood pressure, cholesterol levels, and contributory habits under control. The dramatic surgical experience of the patient with atherosclerotic heart disease should serve as a strong incentive for attention to personal health and improvement of lifestyle, which can, like the operation, favorably alter the course of this common disease.

Hoarseness
by Edward L. Applebaum, M.D.

Hoarseness is a vocal change resulting in a harsh or discordant quality of the voice. Natural changes in the human voice take place throughout life. During the years of growth, as the larynx, or voice box, enlarges and responds to hormonal change, the voice gradually deepens and becomes more resonant. This change becomes pronounced in boys at puberty. As a person ages, the muscles controlling voice production lose tone and weaken, and the voice gradually becomes weaker and harsher. Although these normal voice changes sometimes cause alarm, they are natural occurrences and require no special diagnostic studies or treatment. On the other hand, rapidly developing hoarseness often causes concern and may indicate the presence of serious disease. Therefore, it is important to know when to seek medical attention for hoarseness.

Normal voice production

There are several components to voice production. When the lungs are compressed by the diaphragm and chest wall, a column of air is sent up the windpipe, or trachea, to the larynx. In the larynx the vocal cords interrupt the column of air to produce a coarse sound that is the basis of the voice. This coarse sound is modified as it ascends through the oral cavity, tongue, and lips and becomes formal speech. The voice is given further resonance by the chambers of the nose and sinuses. Abnormalities in any of the components of voice production can change voice quality, and all of these components must be considered when evaluating hoarseness. Additionally, the brain exerts control over the entire process of voice production, and the nervous system must also be investigated at times as a possible cause of hoarseness. The larynx itself is of most concern, however, since its abnormalities are the most frequent causes of hoarseness.

The larynx

The larynx is situated in the front of the neck; sometimes the protrusion of the frontal portion of the larynx produces a noticeable bulge—the so-called Adam's apple. In addition to its role in voice production, the larynx also functions as a protective device, preventing ingested solids and liquids from entering the lungs. Strong reflexes are stimulated whenever anything touches the sensitive mucous membrane that lines the inner cavity of the larynx. These reflexes are part of the protective mechanism familiar to anyone who has swallowed something "the wrong way." Spasmodic closure of the larynx, coughing, and gagging occur when liquids or food touch the laryngeal lining.

Within the larynx are the vocal cords, two bandlike structures that meet at the front of the larynx, dividing it into an upper and lower compartment and forming a V-shaped aperture through which the respiratory air column passes. At the back of the larynx each vocal cord is attached by means of a rotating joint, which allows the cords to swing inward, toward each other, and outward. The actual movement of the vocal cords is produced by muscles within the cords themselves and other muscles in the larynx. During breathing, muscles hold the vocal cords apart to allow free passage of air. During speaking the vocal cords move together, and the space between them closes, becoming a very narrow slit. Vibrations of the vocal cords, acting on the air column passing through this slitlike opening, produce sound. This sound is the critical basis of voice production, and even the slightest abnormality of vocal cord structure or movement can cause hoarseness.

Three basic mechanisms can cause hoarseness from laryngeal disease: (1) mechanical factors that prevent the free edges of the vocal cords from meeting (approximating) properly; for example, a benign or malignant growth on or near the vocal cords or traumatic injury to the larynx; (2) infections that cause swelling of the vocal cords, resulting in impaired vibration; and (3) abnormalities of the brain or of the nerves supplying impulses to the laryngeal muscles, resulting in weakness, paralysis, or uncoordinated movements of the vocal cords.

455

When vocal nodules occur in a professional singer, the hoarseness that results can be devastating to the singer's career. In this case a speech pathologist or professional voice coach is usually needed to train the person to sing without undue abuse of the vocal cords. Hoarseness and vocal damage are common in rock singers, usually as a result of lack of training in vocal technique.

In almost all instances, vocal nodules and the hoarseness they produce will resolve gradually after the habitual abuse of the voice stops. In a small number of cases, vocal nodules are persistent and resist conservative measures to resolve them. In such cases the nodules must be surgically removed. The surgery is done through a hollow tubelike instrument called a laryngoscope, which is inserted through the mouth and allows the surgeon to visualize the vocal cords. The vocal nodules are removed either by cutting them from the vocal cords with delicate instruments passed through the laryngoscope or by vaporizing them with a laser beam, sparing the underlying normal tissue.

Vocal cord polyps

As a response to the irritation of chronic cough, smoke inhalation, voice abuse, chronic bronchitis or laryngitis, or other causes, the vocal cords sometimes develop areas of localized thickening called polyps. They cause chronic hoarseness by interfering with the vibration of the vocal cords. Polyps are formed by accumulation of fluid in the vocal cord tissue. They may develop on one or both vocal cords. Unlike nodules, polyps are soft in consistency. If the underlying irritation can be eliminated, the polyps will sometimes resolve. However, they frequently persist and must be removed surgically. Strict voice rest is often advised for the first week or two following surgery so that healing can take place without the trauma that occurs when vocal cords strike each other. If both of the vocal cords are involved, they may be operated on separately, the two procedures being several weeks apart. This prevents excessive scar tissue from forming between the raw surfaces from which the polyps have been removed. Vocal cord polyps tend to recur if the underlying causes are not eliminated. For this reason periodic examination of the larynx may be suggested following surgery.

Vocal cord paralysis

Either one or both vocal cords may become immobile if trauma or disease interferes with the nerves supplying them. A penetrating injury to the neck or neck surgery (such as thyroidectomy) may result in a severed nerve. A malignant tumor in the neck may engulf a nerve and prevent it from functioning normally. The nerve that supplies the left vocal cord courses through the upper part of the chest on its way to the larynx. (Its counterpart on the right follows a different course.)

Therefore, diseases of the chest, such as lung cancer, may produce paralysis of the left vocal cord. In rare cases a vocal cord may become paralyzed for no apparent reason. The great operatic singer George London suffered this devastating complication at the very peak of his career.

Paralysis of one vocal cord produces hoarseness because the mobile cord cannot reach the paralyzed one. In some cases the mobile vocal cord strengthens with the passage of time, so that eventually it can reach the paralyzed cord. When this compensation takes place, the voice returns to near normal. If the mobile vocal cord does not compensate, the voice can be restored by surgery. Teflon or other inert substances can be injected into a paralyzed vocal cord to enlarge it, thus moving it closer to the mobile vocal cord and allowing the two to meet.

Paralysis of both vocal cords may have little effect on the voice if they are very close to each other. But while proximity of the cords may allow good voice production, the failure of the cords to separate during breathing usually causes severe airway obstruction. Surgery is usually needed to restore an adequate air passage. Unfortunately, if the surgery is successful in restoring the airway, the resulting separation of the vocal cords will make the voice hoarse.

Cancer of the larynx

Cancer of the vocal cords or other sites in the larynx causes chronic, persistent hoarseness, which may be the only symptom of laryngeal cancer for many months before the onset of the associated symptoms of pain, difficult swallowing, and weight loss. If a biopsy confirms the presence of malignancy, radiation therapy, surgery, or a combination of these treatments is initiated. Early diagnosis of laryngeal cancer is important. Tumors discovered in early stages can be treated quite successfully with either radiation therapy or limited surgery, both of which can preserve voice while eradicating the tumor. The vast majority of laryngeal cancers occur in cigarette smokers, many of whom are also heavy drinkers. In this respect laryngeal cancer is probably one of the most preventable cancers.

Miscellaneous causes of hoarseness

Arthritis can affect the joints on which the vocal cords rotate. In some patients with rheumatoid arthritis, these joints may become so severely damaged that the inward and outward movement of the cords is impaired or even prevented entirely, thus causing hoarseness. An underfunctioning thyroid gland may result in thickened vocal cords; in this case hoarseness improves with the administration of thyroid hormone. Chronic infections such as tuberculosis and syphilis can involve the vocal cords and produce hoarseness, but the other symptoms of these diseases are usually prominent.

Confronting the Computer: Help for Eyes

by Robert C. Yeager and
Weylin G. Eng, O.D.

Poet William Blake called eyes the windows of the soul, and some psychologists suggest that eyes may be a clue to personality—linking dark eyes to imagination, impulsiveness, and energy and lighter eyes to rationality, patience, and steadiness. But most people treasure their eyes for what they most obviously are: the irreplaceable biologic instruments with which they view the world.

Since the 1970s the eyes of many people have confronted something new—namely, computer display monitors—and that confrontation has not always been salubrious. Computer screens, or video display terminals (VDTs), as they are often called in the workplace, are blamed for ailments ranging from backaches to birth defects. In the United States workers in one state even claimed their exposure to VDTs caused angina, an extreme form of heart pain.

Though research is continuing, thus far studies by the U.S. National Institute for Occupational Safety and Health, the National Research Council's Committee on Vision, the American College of Obstetricians and Gynecologists, the American Academy of Ophthalmology, and other U.S. and foreign health organizations and agencies have not substantiated contentions that display monitors emit excess radiation or dangerous microwaves. Nearly all researchers, however, have documented widespread worker complaints of VDT-related headaches, burning eyes, and other forms of eye irritation, including chronic eyestrain and blurred vision.

Most of these symptoms have been reported by people who use the screens at least several hours a day. (An estimated 10 million to 14 million American workers now use VDTs, according to a 1985 U.S. House of Representatives Subcommittee on Health and Safety report.) But eye problems also can affect anyone who uses a home computer for long periods of time. The impact on home users of personal computers (PCs) is especially worrisome because such machines often are operated in undesirable lighting and are connected to inherently inferior display devices, such as household television sets.

Faced with mounting public concern over the health implications of VDTs, more than 25 U.S. states and several other nations have considered or issued legislative guidelines for their use. This should not be surprising when it is realized that Americans who work in offices far outnumber those employed in auto plants, steel mills, and other traditional heavy industries. Within a decade, one out of every two Americans is expected to be using a VDT on the job.

Luckily, a few relatively simple precautions may eliminate or reduce the severity of many vision problems related to VDT use. These precautions include choosing a quality VDT and heeding the principles of good lighting and proper furniture placement. Further, following simple exercise routines for the eyes, based on a few well-established techniques of vision training, can alleviate many problems.

The eye's anatomical systems

Vision fitness is particularly important for people who use computers for long periods. Display monitors strain the main operating systems that govern normal binocular vision—those systems that control the eye's refraction, muscular movement, and lubrication.

The refractive system. The primary anatomical parts of the eye's refractive system are the cornea, iris, pupil, lens, and retina. Like a clear outer "skin," the cornea permits the passage of light; the iris reflexively responds to light, shrinking and expanding the size of the pupil (an adjustable opening that controls the volume of light progressing through the eye); the disk-shaped lens consists of a series of transparent layers of tissue that allow for changes in focus; and, at the back of the eye, the retina, a light-sensitive plate of nerve endings, registers images before these images are sent on to the brain.

The muscular system. Separate external and internal muscle systems permit normal binocular vision. Six external oculomotor muscles hold each eye in place and move it up and down and from side to side. When properly functioning, these muscles, fastened to the outside, or white, of the eye, allow the eyes to follow moving objects and to work together as a unit. Internally, the ciliary muscles attach to the edge of each lens like a web of rubber bands. By contracting and relaxing, these muscles control the shape of the lens and thereby the eye's ability to bring objects into focus.

Confronting the computer: help for eyes

by the American Optometric Association as a way of improving depth perception, peripheral sight, and focusing ability. The practices of Japanese shiatsu (finger massage, or acupressure) and Indian yoga include workouts designed to improve eyesight. In China millions of factory and government workers, schoolchildren, and shopkeepers practice daily a centuries-old eye-training regimen, which combines acupressure and massage to relax, tone, and strengthen the eyes.

Vision training cannot reverse the effects of aging or overcome preexisting defects caused by disease, retinal damage, or physiological malfunction. But three simple exercises, which can be practiced by those who work with VDTs without even leaving their seats at the terminal, can alleviate many common complaints. Each should be performed regularly, twice a day. The only equipment required is a sharpened pencil. Eyeglasses, if worn, should be left on.

Jump duction exercises. These exercises tone the ciliary muscles and are especially suited to combating the effects of prolonged near-point focus. They will enhance the flexibility of the eyes' internal and external muscles and, thereby, the ability to focus smoothly and quickly over a wide range of distances.

1. Hold pencil in one hand, arm extended to its greatest length. Bring the pencil point into focus with both eyes open.

2. Shift eyes ("jump") to a target such as a clock, calendar, or sign that is between 4.6 and 7.6 m (15 and 25 ft) from where you are sitting. Bring this target into focus.

3. Now jump the focus of the eyes back to the pencil tip and refocus. Repeat ten rounds of jumping between target and pencil.

Pencil pushups. These exercises work on the external muscles called the medial and lateral recti muscles, which control the eyes' ability to converge and diverge, respectively, while staying focused on near and far objects. This ability is especially important in computer tasks that require tracking (*i.e.,* involving eye movements that sequentially follow lines of text or numbers from left to right)—as is encountered in word processing.

1. Hold pencil in one hand, arm extended. Bring the point of the pencil into focus with both eyes open.

2. Slowly move the pencil toward nose, keeping the tip in focus as long as possible.

3. Continue moving the pencil toward nose until you see it as doubled. Then extend the arm holding the pencil to full length again. Repeat ten times, trying to keep the pencil in single focus as long as possible.

Binocular coordination exercise. This exercise concentrates on the eyes' internal and external muscles. Binocular coordination refers to the synchronous movement of both eyes as a team. Such movement, which should occur quickly, easily, and automatically, can be crucial to the scanning and/or jumping movements re-

quired to search the computer screen—for example, when working with or preparing a spreadsheet.

1. With the arm extended, focus on pencil tip with both eyes open.

2. Using the pencil tip, trace a large imaginary *H* in front of you. Follow the pencil with both eyes as far as you can without moving your head.

3. When you have completed the *H,* switch to a circular pattern by tracing a large imaginary *O.* Perform 10 repetitions of each letter, alternating between them (20 letter tracings in all).

One should note the time elapsed between starting and finishing each exercise. An entire typical workout of all three routines should take from three to five minutes to perform—less as visual skills improve.

Gauging eye health

Vision training can aid the individual in evaluating his or her own eye health. A noticeable decline in the ability to focus on the far target during the jump duction exercise, for example, could indicate increasing nearsightedness or astigmatism. Though some minor soreness in eye muscles may be experienced early in the practice of such exercises, one's ability to perform the workout should improve markedly after one or two weeks. If one is or becomes visually unable to perform any of these exercises, professional help should be sought.

The important visual skills achieved by conscientiously following a vision-training program will greatly aid the computer user. But eye exercises and vision training are not a panacea.

In most cases they cannot improve visual acuity, compensate for the loss in near-point focusing due to age (usually experienced by the early forties), or reverse preexisting ocular dysfunction. In all probability, among current computer users there are many who are working, despite discomfort, with undetected eye problems.

Thus, thorough vision analysis and examination should be the first requirement for anyone contemplating prolonged exposure to computer display screens. This is particularly true for wearers of contact lenses and bifocal glasses and to a lesser degree for wearers of ordinary vision-correcting spectacles.

Some manufacturers are now producing prescription eyeglasses specifically designed for the unique strains and stresses on eyes that occur with use of computers. The idea that special glasses might be advisable for computer users should seem no more surprising than the fact that blacksmiths don heavy aprons or that telephone linemen wear safety belts. To the extent that they encourage the use of proper equipment, periodic eye examinations, and regular vision training, computers can be transformed into strong allies of healthy eyesight.

The Vulnerable Knee

by Tom D. Naughton

The knee is the largest and most complex joint in the body. Much more than a simple hinge, it has a complicated configuration of bones and ligaments that allows it to bend through a range of 150 degrees, rotate, pivot, and angle from side to side. However, the knee is not quite an engineering masterpiece. The same structure that gives the knee its freedom of movement also leaves it highly vulnerable. As a result, the knee is one of the most frequently and most severely injured joints. Athletes especially dread knee injuries, because "trick knees" or "Joe Namath knees" can end an otherwise promising career. Likewise, weekend joggers and fitness buffs often find that knee pain can prevent them from enjoying their favorite sports or exercises.

Structure of the knee

The knee is prone to injury because of its unique anatomy and its position in the body. In most other joints the bones fit together to form a stable structure, such as the ball-and-socket structure of the shoulder. Some joints are also protected by surrounding tissue; the shoulder joint, for example, is buried under layers of muscle. The knee, however, lacks both inherent bony stability and protective tissue. Structurally, the knee could be described as resembling two flat-topped sticks held together by rubber bands.

Specifically, the femur (thighbone), sits atop the tibia (shinbone) to form the knee joint, which is protected by the patella (kneecap). A synovial membrane behind the patella secretes a fluid to lubricate the joint.

The femur and tibia are held together by four tough, fibrous ligaments. The medial collateral ligament provides support on the inner side of the knee; the lateral collateral ligament provides support on the outer side. The anterior (front) cruciate ligament and the posterior (back) cruciate ligament form an X within the knee and help control its backward and forward movements.

The femur and tibia are kept slightly apart by two triangular wedges of cartilage, the medial and lateral menisci. The menisci serve two purposes: they add cushioning to the joint and, at the same time, they increase its stability. The femur has a more rounded end than the tibia, which is nearly flat. The cupped shape of each meniscus helps these bones to fit snugly together during movement of the knee.

The joint is operated by the muscles and tendons of the thigh—the hamstrings in back and the quadriceps in front. Because the knee depends on all these muscles and ligaments for its stability, injuries to any of them can have a profound effect on the functioning of the entire joint.

Athletic injuries

Knee injuries can be sudden and traumatic, or they can result from a series of microtraumas over time. Sports understandably account for the largest share of traumatic injuries, with football, basketball, and skiing topping the list. Football alone causes so many injuries that orthopedic surgeons are employed as regular consultants and practitioners by all major league teams. Many such physicians hold seminars for players during training. Professional conferences expressly on "football knees" are held for orthopedic specialists regularly.

Sports-related knee injuries usually occur when a running athlete plants his foot on the ground and then suddenly changes direction, causing a twisting within the knee that strains the ligaments. Other ligament injuries are caused by blows to the knee. In football, for example, a blocker or tackle may throw his body into another player's knee, forcing it out of its range of motion. Twisting within the knee also can also occur during jumping motions.

When a ligament—most commonly the medial ligament—is damaged, the injury is called a sprain. Doctors grade sprains according to their severity. In a grade-one sprain, the ligament has been stretched. The knee will probably require wrapping and a few weeks of rest to heal. In a grade-two sprain, the ligament has been partially torn. The knee will probably require a brace or cast and several weeks' rest. In a grade-three sprain, the ligament is completely torn and cannot hold the bones together. Surgery may be required. If the anterior cruciate ligament is torn, surgery will almost certainly be necessary to reattach it, and the knee may never return to full function.

To make matters worse, about half of all ligament injuries are accompanied by a torn meniscus—another injury likely to require surgery, and one that athletes

463

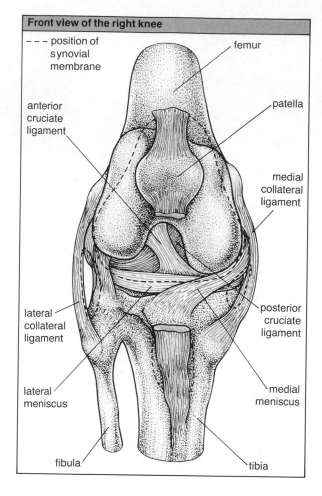

Front view of the right knee

- - - position of synovial membrane

femur

anterior cruciate ligament

patella

medial collateral ligament

lateral collateral ligament

posterior cruciate ligament

lateral meniscus

medial meniscus

fibula

tibia

especially dread. Depending on where it occurs, a tear in a meniscus may be permanent. The outer third of the meniscus has a good blood supply, so it can usually be surgically reattached and eventually will heal. But the inner two-thirds of the mensicus receives no blood—so once that portion is torn, it cannot heal and simply stays torn. If torn bits of the meniscus are left in the knee, they can scratch the surface of the surrounding bones and interfere with other ligaments, leading to painful arthritis. Generally, the surgeon treating this type of injury has no choice but to remove the torn section. When this is necessary, the knee will be left with reduced stability and shock-absorbing capacity. Patients who have undergone this procedure—known as a meniscectomy—must accept that their knees are not normal and cannot be put through the rigors of some sports.

Weekend fitness buffs do not usually subject their knees to as much twisting and pounding as professional athletes do, so they are not likely to face such drastic injuries or treatments. However, some aerobic or endurance exercises involve small, repetitive stresses to the knee and can lead to a number of overuse ailments.

Doctors have seen more of these ailments during the last decade because of the renewed emphasis on fitness. While ever increasing numbers of people have taken up running and aerobic dancing in the quest for cardiovascular health, many are paying with their knees. When a person runs, his knees absorb a force equal to two or three times his body weight with each step, and a run of just one mile (1.6 km) involves more than a thousand steps. The knee also tends to twist some with each step, and if a person has a malalignment—*e.g.,* if he is bowlegged or knock-kneed—the twisting is exaggerated, resulting in increased stress to the knee.

One common runner's ailment that can be produced by this stress is patella-femoral syndrome, or tenderness and pain around the kneecap. Doctors are not sure exactly how this syndrome develops, but one possibility is that the constant pounding in the knee causes the meniscus to lose its elasticity. Further shocks to the knee—such as those generated by running—would then be transmitted to nerve endings within the bones, causing irritation. Women are about twice as likely as men to develop pain around the knee, because their wider pelvises tend to add stress to the joint.

Miscellaneous causes of injury

Of course, not all traumatic knee injuries are caused by participation in professional athletics or recreational sports or exercise. Falls, automobile accidents, and any number of other home or industrial accidents can cause knee injuries. Occupations that involve working in a kneeling position or constantly lifting heavy loads can lead to overuse ailments, such as tendinitis within the knee. This kind of damage involves stiffness and swelling around the knee and is often referred to as "carpet-layer's knee" or "housemaid's knee."

In addition to stress-induced injuries, knee functioning can be affected by diseases, most commonly the pain and swelling of arthritis or bursitis. However,

The Los Angeles Lakers struggled through repeated losses during the middle of the 1985–86 season while star player Earvin ("Magic") Johnson nursed an injured knee.

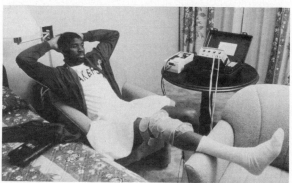

464

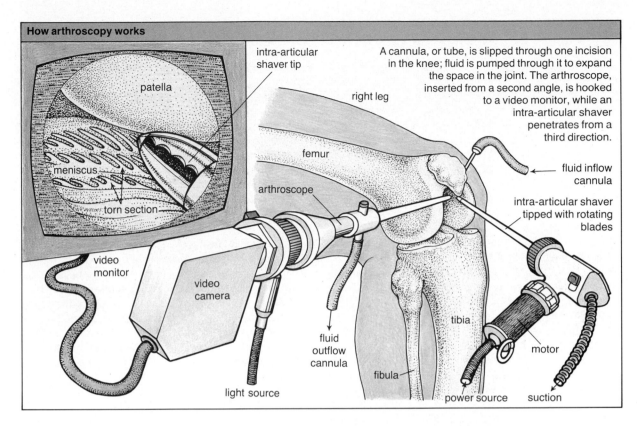

How arthroscopy works

patella

meniscus

torn section

intra-articular shaver tip

right leg

femur

arthroscope

A cannula, or tube, is slipped through one incision in the knee; fluid is pumped through it to expand the space in the joint. The arthroscope, inserted from a second angle, is hooked to a video monitor, while an intra-articular shaver penetrates from a third direction.

fluid inflow cannula

intra-articular shaver tipped with rotating blades

video monitor

video camera

fluid outflow cannula

tibia

motor

fibula

light source

power source

suction

these conditions are usually the result of earlier tissue injuries.

Avoiding knee injuries

Because so many knee injuries occur in competitive sports, it is important for athletes to wear appropriate kneepads to cushion blows to the joint. In many junior-league sports, kneepads are mandatory equipment. Those who participate in recreational activities that are likely to involve falls onto the knee—skateboarding and ice skating, for example—should also wear kneepads.

Good physical conditioning will help prevent many injuries to the knee. Exercises that strengthen the hamstrings and quadriceps may help reduce the chances of injury by adding extra stability to the knee joint. Gently stretching the leg muscles and tendons before and after exercise may help prevent torn ligaments. If the tissues have more give, they are less likely to snap under stress. Also, athletes who are not conditioned for their sport or who play when overtired or ill are more likely to make mistakes that result in injury. But being in great shape is by no means a guarantee against injuries—if it were, college and professional athletes would not suffer so many injuries.

The most important aspect of avoiding overuse injuries is to train gradually. The musculoskeletal system will respond to the added stress of exercise by producing stronger, more durable tissues. However,

this process of adaptation takes place very slowly. Fitness enthusiasts who exceed their bodies' abilities to adapt—who do too much too fast—will suffer tissue injuries over time. It is important that runners and

Arthroscopy has had stunning results in many world-class athletes. Six weeks before the 1984 Olympics, it appeared that 16-year-old gymnast Mary Lou Retton would not realize her dreams of Olympic glory. But arthroscopic surgery enabled her to be back in training the next day, and she went on to win a gold medal.

Jerry Cooke/Sports Illustrated

aerobic dancers do not ignore pain. Discomfort in the knee during exercise is a sign that the joint is being overstressed.

Runners and aerobics enthusiasts can prevent some of this stress by wearing good shoes with thick, shock-absorbing soles. Athletic shoes should also provide good heel control—otherwise, the foot will turn inward and throw the knee out of alignment, causing further stress.

People who are knock-kneed or bowlegged may simply have to accept that their knees cannot handle the stress of running. They are likely to be better off participating in other endurance exercises, such as cycling and swimming, that do not involve pounding with the legs.

Advances in treatment

At one time just finding out what was wrong with an injured knee could sideline an athlete for weeks. To diagnose some injuries, orthopedic surgeons had to cut the knee open to look inside. The surrounding tissues were often so damaged in the process that weeks of rehabilitation might be necessary.

Fortunately for the world's athletes and other knee-injury victims, advances in medical technology have changed that. Now orthopedic surgeons can look inside the knee through a small instrument called an arthroscope: a long, thin tube that contains flexible fiber-optic elements. The optical fibers cast light inside the knee, then allow the light—and thus the images from inside the knee—to be bent.

The first arthroscopes were strictly diagnostic tools, and somewhat limited ones at that. The flexible tubes, measuring only 5 mm (⅕ in) in diameter, were inserted into the knee, and surgeons peered into an eyepiece to assess the injury. If they decided surgery was necessary, the knee still had to be opened up for the actual operation.

Now, however, arthroscopes have made it possible for surgeons to operate through a 6-mm (¼-in) incision, about the size of a shirt buttonhole. The arthroscopes are attached to video cameras that transmit video images to a monitor, allowing surgeons to get an enlarged view of any damage. Using the arthroscope's images as a guide, surgeons can perform delicate operations without cutting the knee open.

To perform arthroscopic surgery, the surgeon first makes a small incision in the knee. Saline solution is injected to flush away loose tissue and distend the joint. A second small incision is then made, and the arthroscope is inserted. After viewing the knee and deciding the precise surgical procedures necessary, the surgeon makes a third small incision and inserts tiny surgical instruments. Using a variety of shavers, hooks, and clippers, and guided by the enlarged video view of the knee, the surgeon can then cut away and remove torn bits of meniscus and cartilage.

Arthroscopy offers several advantages over open-knee surgery. The enlarged view allows surgeons to diagnose microtears they might otherwise have missed. Because surgeons can see exactly where the damage begins and ends, they can avoid removing more tissue than is necessary. Most importantly, arthroscopy does not require that the skin, muscle tissue, and ligaments surrounding the knee all be cut open to expose the inner joint.

Whereas traditional knee surgery required at least a week in the hospital and several weeks of rehabilitation afterward, arthroscopy, being a "buttonhole" procedure, allows for precise repairs within the knee with little damage to surrounding tissues. Because there is so little peripheral damage, patients can usually undergo surgical arthroscopy on an outpatient basis; at most, they may spend one night in a hospital. Instead of needing weeks of rehabilitation, some patients can walk the next day, and most are back to normal in less than two weeks. Because of these advantages, arthroscopy now accounts for 90% of all knee surgery performed in the United States. More than 600,000 such procedures are now performed each year. Recently, however, orthopedic surgeons have become concerned that this important form of microsurgery, which has been a great boon to athletes and many others, is being overused. As a result, some patients may be left with unrealistic expectations of what it can do.

Arthroscopy has been a boon to injured athletes because they can often return to competition within a week. In 1984 Mary Lou Retton, the Olympic gold-medal gymnast, underwent surgical arthroscopy to remove a piece of torn cartilage in her knee. The next day, she was back in training. Marathon runner Joan Benoit had similar surgery, resumed training within two days, and also went on to win a gold medal a few months later.

For knee injuries too severe to be treated with arthroscopy or traditional surgery, technology is providing other answers. When ligaments are torn and fail to heal naturally by growing back together, some surgeons now insert tiny lattice structures made of biodegradable tissue. The lattice then helps support the ligament as it grows back together. Still other surgeons are experimenting with artificial tissues that could completely replace ligaments damaged beyond repair.

Artificial knees, metal structures held together in many cases by a patient's own tissue, have been in use for some time; about 30,000 are inserted annually in the United States. Someday perhaps even these will not be necessary. Orthopedists and genetic engineers are now working on what may be the ultimate cure for injured knees—new joints, grown across lattices, using the patient's own cells for tissue.

Toys: Hazardous to Health?

by Nancy Seeger

Throughout the world, in nearly every culture, play is an expected behavior, perhaps synonymous with the definition of childhood. The length of childhood and the expectations for behavior may differ within specific societies, but in most cultures the years from birth to, or through, adolescence are considered to be a crucial preparation for adulthood. Play is the way in which children learn to imitate the world around them. Toys and games help children develop large and fine motor coordination, use their imaginations and intellectual skills, and interact socially with others.

Toys have been used by children throughout history. Toy animals and dolls have been found in the pyramids of Egypt and in the burial mounds of ancient Crete and Persia. During the 18th century miniature medieval knights and silver rattles were popular. The first dollhouses, invented by the Dutch, served to teach young girls about decorating and maintaining houses. In the United States toys are used in households, schools, day-care centers, and hospitals. Their use has wide application in other social settings as well.

Play can begin once infants are able to focus on objects and certainly when they can handle them. As a child's vision improves, colorful objects placed in a crib or within his view help to stimulate the baby's imagination and perceptions. As the baby becomes more mobile, usually at about three to four months of age, he gains greater dexterity. At this stage especially, toys can help the infant interpret and adapt to the surroundings he will soon explore. By one year of age, most children move about easily and can control objects fairly well. When they are toddlers their confidence increases, and they explore more and learn quickly. This increases the importance of play and toys.

Children's choices of toys change as they mature and as new and different items are introduced, but toys are usually a vital part of play into early adolescence. At age five a boy may play with trucks, action figures, or building sets, but by age ten he may select bikes, skateboards, and video or computer games as his playthings. Similarly, a 5-year-old girl may play primarily with dolls or modeling clay, but her 11-year-old sister may choose a telescope or a chemistry set.

Potential problems

Although consumers often assume that any toy on the market is safe, the facts show that this is not always true. Toys and games can be hazardous, and toy safety is a critical factor in child rearing. In the United States approximately 150,000 toys and games are currently available to consumers, and about 4,000 new toys are introduced each year. The majority of toys produced by the U.S. toy industry are well designed and adequately tested for safety, yet some have caused injuries and death, particularly to infants and toddlers.

According to the U.S. Centers for Disease Control, it was estimated that in 1984, 588,700 children under the age of 15 were treated in hospital emergency rooms for toy-related injuries; there were 31 toy-associated fatalities. These numbers included injuries involving bicycles, skates, sleds, and skateboards.

Product design, quality of materials and construction, the child's age and maturity, the presence of adult supervision, and combinations of these factors and others must be taken into account by those who monitor toy safety. Production of safe toys begins with complicated and thorough testing of designs and materials long before assembly begins. Once products are manufactured, they must be accurately age-graded and honestly labeled so consumers can understand the specific requirements for their safe use. Setting quality standards for such a variety of products is

On June 2, 1986, the U.S. Consumer Product Safety Commission called for the Piglet Crib Gym (right) and two other varieties of crib toys sold by Johnson & Johnson Baby Products Co. (Soft Triplets and Triplets Marching Band) to be recalled and for future sales of the items to be barred. The commission believed that the more than 1.6 million such crib toys on the market posed a serious hazard and should be removed at once from all cribs and playpens. Two babies had strangled on these toys or strings used to tie them across their cribs.

difficult, and the manufacturer's standards may not always encompass the imaginative use—and abuse—to which the products may actually be subjected.

Toy-related accidents and deaths

Even the most carefully designed and the safest toys can be hazardous if improperly used. Toy trucks, cars, or blocks scattered on a sidewalk, stairway, or floor have been known to cause serious falls, unrelated to the quality or purpose of the toys themselves. Children also may have access to toys not designed for youngsters their age; if children lack the physical or emotional maturity to handle the toys safely in an unsupervised setting, accident potential increases. Of the 16 toy-related fatalities reported in the U.S. in 1983, 9 involved incidents that could have been prevented by adult supervision, and most involved objects not usually considered hazardous; for example, a balloon or a beach ball.

In some cases of toy-related deaths, specific products have been incriminated. In 1984 an infant died of strangulation caused by a crib "gym." For two years preceding the fatal accident, Edward Swartz, a leading toy-safety advocate and liability lawyer, had criticized that particular toy. It is also alleged that three children between the ages of six months and two years recently choked to death when small, doll-like figurines they were playing with became lodged in their throats. A 14-month-old suffered severe brain damage while playing with the same kind of toy. The figurines involved in these accidents are still on the market and have not been redesigned.

As children grow up, their capabilities for assuming responsibility increase, and they usually are less vulnerable to the dangers of choking and strangulation and other typical causes of harm to infants and toddlers. The concern for toy safety does not fade away, however; it simply changes form. An older child can be seriously injured while skateboarding, bike riding, kite flying, or experimenting with a chemistry set. These kinds of injuries are common.

Psychological harm from toys

Toys may be damaging to children in ways other than the strictly physical. Many toys and games currently available are considered by some people to be unsuitable for children because they may have undesirable psychological impact. For example, should children play a board game based on the subject of nuclear war? Supporters of the game argue that because nuclear war is possible, the game is appropriate and, perhaps, even educational. Critics claim that the subject is disturbing and negative, and that the game is inappropriate for play. Likewise, for many years the propriety of toy guns and other weapons has been debated. Some critics focus on the physical danger posed, while others feel that serious ethical and political considerations are involved.

Similar discussions are raised about video or computer games that appear to condone violence and war toys and "action figures" that glamorize combat. Even dolls—for example, the well-advertised and popular Barbie doll—have raised concern. Barbie's critics claim that she promotes a sexist image of women, one that fosters an outdated and chauvinistic attitude. Her supporters say that she is pretty and fun and that little girls can engage in imaginative play with her different costumes, enhancing their own creativity and maturity and pleasantly anticipating the time when they too will be grown up.

Tables from Good Housekeeping Consumer Research Department surveys

Problems with toys
(on a scale of 1–10)

they are too expensive	8.2
they break too easily	7.7
parts get lost	7.3
they do not live up to expectations	7.2
they do not hold the child's interest	6.7
the storage containers break	6.3
the advertising is misleading	6.1
they are not educational	5.3
parts are missing from original package	4.7
they are not safe	4.6

Regulation of the toy industry

The U.S. Consumer Product Safety Commission (CPSC), the National Safety Council (NSC), Toy Manufacturers of America, Inc. (TMA), and the American Society for Testing and Materials are among the varied U.S. groups that attempt to ensure that toys available to the public are safe and to warn consumers of

The Rambo doll, modeled after a popular movie hero and armed with high-tech weapons, was one of the best-selling and most controversial toys on the market in 1986.

Marilynn K. Yee/The New York Times

hazardous misuse of playthings. Various federal laws regulate the toy industry. The Federal Hazardous Substances Labeling Act of 1960 was first amended by the Child Protection Act of 1966 to include toys and was at the same time renamed the Federal Hazardous Substances Act to indicate a broader scope. The Child Protection and Toy Safety Act (1969), the Consumer Product Safety Amendment (1981), and the Toy Safety Act (1984) also amended the original 1960 legislation. The latter two define and expedite recall procedures available to the CPSC in the event that a dangerous product must be removed from store shelves and no longer marketed.

Special regulations about toy safety are found in Title 16 of the Code of Federal Regulations, which defines the items within its purview as any "toy, game, or other article designed, labeled, advertised, or otherwise intended for use by children." These regulations specify that toys must be tested for their abilities to withstand impact (dropping), flexure (bending), torque (twisting), tension (pulling), compression, and biting or chewing. According to the regulations, the objective of safety tests is to simulate "normal use" of toys and to anticipate as much as possible damage or abuse to which they may be subjected. Essentially, the test methods are developed to assure that normal use or abuse of toys will not result in a hazard.

The tests required for a specific toy vary according to the age group for which the toy is intended. There are three age categories: 18 months of age or less, over 18 months but not over 36 months (three years), and over 36 months but not over 96 months (eight years). If labeling on a toy does not clearly specify a particular age group, the toy must undergo the most stringent testing, regardless of the age group for which it is intended.

Federal regulations for toy safety include the following objectives: (1) toys and other articles intended for

What influences the decision to buy a toy
(on a scale of 0–10)

the quality of the toy	9.2
the safety aspect of the toy	9.1
the play value of the toy	8.9
the belief that the child would enjoy the toy	8.9
the creative value of the toy	8.9
the educational value of the toy	8.7
the child's request for the toy	8.1
the physical activity the toy would involve	8.1
the price of the toy	7.8
the advertisement of the toy in a magazine	7.4
the fact that the toy was on sale	6.4
the name of the toy's manufacturer	6.1
the style of the toy	5.6
the newness of the toy	3.8
the packaging of the toy	3.6
the color of the toy	3.5

children under eight years must not have sharp points or sharp glass and metal edges; (2) toys intended for children under three years must not have small, removable parts; (3) pacifiers and rattles must be large enough that they cannot become lodged in an infant's throat, and they must not separate into small pieces; (4) minimum standards must be adhered to regarding noise the toy makes, lead content of the paint used, flammability, durability, and toxicity; and (5) instructions and warning labels must accompany chemistry sets, model rocketry sets, model airplane fuel, and other such products that by their nature have harmful chemicals and are designed for older children.

A more stringent standard that applies to all aspects of toy design, function, engineering, and production for children up to 14 years of age has been established by the Toy Manufacturers of America (TMA), the United States trade association for producers of playthings and holiday decorations. Product Standard 72-76 (PS72-76) was initially developed in 1976 by the TMA, in conjunction with the National Bureau of Standards of the Department of Commerce. It is continually being developed under the auspices of the American Society for Testing and Materials.

The TMA claims that its 250 members are responsible for approximately 90% of the industry's total sales, and that most of them adhere to the standard. However, this is a voluntary standard, and toy manufacturers may ignore or exceed it if they choose.

Not covered in PS72-76 are bicycles, playground equipment (these have separate standards), skateboards, art materials, craft sets, model kits, rockets, sporting goods, air pistols, and rifles. In 1984 the industry developed a voluntary safety standard for toy chests—which have been involved in several serious incidents—requiring that all toy chests with hinged lids have special supports to keep the lids from closing on a child's head or neck.

The existing regulations and testing procedures are extensive; however, there is no single standard that covers all toys. There are also many ways by which manufacturers can alter the rules, as when products are labeled for an older age group so the restrictions on small parts can be ignored. The Consumer Product Safety Commission claims it does not have a large enough staff to completely monitor an industry that produces almost 4,000 new toys a year.

Some guidelines for toy buyers

The Consumer Product Safety Commission, the National Safety Council, and the Toy Manufacturers of America make the following suggestions for toy safety.
● Buy toys that have the manufacturer's name and address on the packaging.

● Read labels carefully for information stating that paints are nontoxic and that fabrics are nonflammable.
● Explain to children how to use toys properly and safely.
● Teach children to put toys safely away on shelves or in a toy chest after playing, to prevent tripping.
● If a toy chest has a vertically opening hinged lid, make certain that it uses a lid support that will hold the lid open in any position in which it is placed. If the container used to store toys does have a free-falling lid, completely remove the lid or install a lid support that will hold the lid open in any position. For extra safety, make sure the toy chest has ventilation holes for fresh air. Watch for sharp edges that could cut and hinges that could pinch or squeeze.
● Look for labels that give age recommendations, and take heed.
● Avoid hand-me-down toys with small parts for children under three years of age.
● Avoid toys that shoot objects that can injure eyes. Arrows and darts used by children should have blunt tips made from resilient materials such as rubber or plastic suction cups. Avoid those dart guns or other toys that might be capable of firing articles not intended for use in the toy, such as pencils or nails.
● Avoid toys with long strings, cords, loops, or ribbons for infants and very young children. Never hang such toys in cribs or playpens where very young children can become entangled and, possibly, strangled.
● Make sure that toys used outdoors are stored after play. Moisture can rust or damage toy parts, creating hazards.
● Examine toys periodically for sharp edges and points that may have developed. Repair broken toys and discard toys that cannot be fixed.
● Do not buy stuffed toys with parts that can pop out or be swallowed.
● Make sure that electrical toys carry the Underwriters Laboratories (UL) mark or that of another recognized testing agency.

FOR FURTHER INFORMATION:
American Academy of Pediatrics, 141 Northwest Point Road, Elk Grove Village, IL 60007.
U.S. Consumer Product Safety Commission, Washington, D.C. 20207.
National Society to Prevent Blindness, 70 Madison Avenue, New York, NY 10016.
National Safety Council, 444 North Michigan Avenue, Chicago, IL 60611.
Toy Manufacturers of America, Public Information Department, Room 740, 200 Fifth Avenue, New York, NY 10010.

The Epstein-Barr Virus

by Stephen E. Straus, M.D.

The Epstein-Barr virus (EBV) is the major cause of acute infectious mononucleosis, a common syndrome characterized by fever, sore throat, extreme fatigue, and swollen lymph glands. While more is generally understood about specific diseases than their causes, the opposite is true of the Epstein-Barr virus and its associated disorders. More is known of the biology of this virus than of the diseases it provokes.

The virus

In 1964 British scientists M. A. Epstein, W. M. Barr, and B. G. Achong reported finding viruslike particles in cells grown from tissues involved with a newly described lymphatic cancer. In the two decades since that observation this virus, named for two of its discoverers, has been shown to be a herpesvirus. It is the fifth and most recently described human herpesvirus (*see* Table 1).

Among viruses the herpesviruses are relatively large and complex. They are too small to be seen with the light microscope, but with an electron microscope it can be seen that the herpesviruses are about 1/100,-000 of an inch in diameter. The virus is composed of an inner core and an outer skin or envelope. The viral envelope derives from protein-containing membranous elements of cells in which the virus had grown. The core is assembled from several different proteins and a chromosome. The viral chromosome is a large double-stranded molecule of deoxyribonucleic acid (DNA), the material that carries the hereditary traits of all cells. The more than 160,000 pairs of nucleotides, the individual chemical units that this DNA comprises, are linked end to end. The order in which they are linked provides the code for all of the proteins that are necessary for the manufacture of the virus within cells. The DNA code of EBV has been determined recently, a scientific feat that could not have been accomplished even ten years ago. While this DNA coding sequence is known, scientists remain uncertain as to the functions of most of the proteins it encodes.

The Epstein-Barr virus is known to be able to infect only two different types of cells in the body: some salivary gland cells and one special type of white blood cell. The salivary glands are located in several sites around the mouth and secrete saliva to help with swallowing and digestion of food. Virus that grows in the salivary gland cell is carried into the mouth in the stream of saliva. Saliva is the only bodily fluid that has been proved to contain infectious EBV particles.

A white blood cell called the B lymphocyte can also carry Epstein-Barr virus. These highly specialized cells manufacture antibodies to help fight infections. No matter what the antibody is directed against, the B cell can be infected with EBV. The type of infection that EBV initiates in these cells is very different from that which occurs in the salivary gland cell. In the salivary gland the infection is termed a *productive* one because the growth cycle of the virus in salivary cells is completed and infectious virus particles are generated. The virus growth cycle in B lymphocytes, however, is an *abortive* one. Only some of the first stages in the virus development occur. Late steps that could result in assembly of infectious virus particles do not occur. Epstein-Barr virus persists in the B lymphocyte in a partially replicated state for the life of the cell.

Although intact virus is not made in the B cell, the lymphocyte is altered by the infectious process. B cells that carry EBV genetic material are permanently transformed; *i.e.,* they take on growth characteristics that resemble those of cancerous lymphocytes. It is believed that continuous surveillance by the human immune system is necessary to keep these cells in check. In special settings in which the immune surveillance is ineffective, these B lymphocytes can multiply excessively to produce a cancer of the lymphatic system. This may explain the high rate of such cancers in patients who receive organ transplants and drugs that reduce the immune system's activity in order to control rejection and in patients with the acquired immune deficiency syndrome (AIDS).

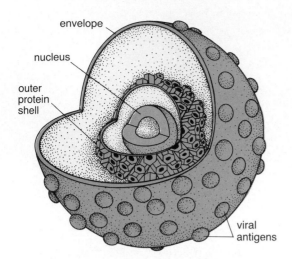

envelope

nucleus

outer
protein
shell

viral
antigens

The Epstein-Barr virus is composed of an inner core and outer envelope. The envelope can fuse with certain body cells, enabling the virus to invade and cause infection.

In most people the immune system is properly balanced to control EBV infection of lymphocytes. However, the immune system cannot rid bodies of all the infected cells. This virus, like all other herpesviruses, persists in the body for life. Small numbers of virally infected B cells can be detected in the bloodstreams of totally normal individuals. Similarly, virus can be recovered intermittently in the saliva for years following EBV-associated infectious mononucleosis. Thus, the presence of virus in the saliva or of infected cells in one's bloodstream does not indicate disease. Lifetime carriage of Epstein-Barr virus seems to be of no consequence for most people.

Infectious mononucleosis

Infectious mononucleosis may be a relatively new disease. In medical literature spanning the centuries, there are excellent accounts of tuberculosis, measles, typhoid, plague, herpes, and many other classical infectious disorders. But there were no reports of illnesses similar to infectious mononucleosis until the end of the 19th century. An illness called Drüsenfieber (glandular fever) was reported to be characterized by malaise, fever, sore throat, and enlargement of the lymph nodes, liver, and spleen. It had features of then newly recognized lymphatic leukemias and lymphomas, but glandular fever appeared to be infectious and self-limited.

In the early 1920s American physicians noted that unusual, or atypical, forms of white cells can be found circulating in the bloodstream of patients with glandular fever. The white cells are of the mononuclear class—they possess only a single nucleus, the inner core of the cell. Thus, the disease came to be termed infectious mononucleosis.

In the 1930s J. R. Paul and W. Bunnell discovered another curious anomaly in the blood of some patients with this syndrome. They noted the presence of antibodies against parts of the red blood cells of certain animals. Antibodies are proteins that help rid the body of foreign substances including infectious organisms. To this day it is not known how such antibodies arise, but it is a well-known observation that the serum of 75–90% of people with acute infectious mononucleosis possesses antibodies of this diverse, or heterophile, specificity.

Until the end of the 1960s the diagnosis of infectious mononucleosis depended largely upon the patient's complaints and findings on physical examination and the detection of large numbers of atypical lymphocytes in the blood and heterophile antibodies in the serum. Today the diagnosis is still usually made this way, but in the interim it has been learned that such a method of diagnosis may not be totally accurate. Many conditions can cause the symptoms and signs of infectious mononucleosis (*see* Tables 2 and 3). A variety of infections or reactions to drugs can lead to the development of atypical lymphocytes and low levels of heterophile antibodies.

EBV-mononucleosis connection

Acute infectious mononucleosis is a syndrome—*i.e.,* a clinical picture that can result from a variety of different causes. Studies done in the late 1960s, however, prove that the Epstein-Barr virus is the most common cause of this syndrome, accounting for about 90% of all typical cases. The less typical the case, the less likely that EBV is the cause.

Table 1. **Relation between Epstein-Barr virus and other human herpesviruses**

virus	usual age of infection	% infected by age 40	major associated diseases
herpes simplex 1	childhood	50–70	herpes sores of the mouth, eye, or skin
herpes simplex 2	adolescence to adult	20–50	herpes sores of genitals and adjacent skin
varicella-zoster	childhood	80–90	chicken pox, shingles
cytomegalovirus	all	50–70	hepatitis, mononucleosis, congenital infections
Epstein-Barr	childhood to adolescence	80–100	infectious mononucleosis

Table 2. **Symptoms of infectious mononucleosis**

symptom	percentage
sore throat	82
malaise	57
headache	51
loss of appetite	21
muscle aches	20
chills	16
nausea	12
abdominal pains	9
cough	5
vomiting	5
joint pains	2

Table 3. **Physical signs of infectious mononucleosis**

sign	percentage
enlarged lymph glands	94
inflamed throat	84
fever	76
enlarged spleen	52
enlarged liver	12
rash	10
jaundice	9

Adapted from R. T. Schooley and R. Dolin, "Epstein-Barr Virus (Infectious Mononucleosis)," in G. L. Mandell _et al._ (eds.), _Principles and Practice of Infectious Diseases_ (1979)

How did that realization come about? Not long after Epstein and his colleagues described the virus, scientists Werner Henle and Gertrude Henle working in Philadelphia made a fortunate but accidental observation that linked this herpesvirus with infectious mononucleosis. The Henles were studying the same type of lymphoid tumors as Epstein and his colleagues. They noted that the serum of patients with this cancer contained antibodies to a virus protein that was being made in the tumor cells. They chose to test the accuracy of their results by also examining in each experiment the sera from normal individuals who lacked antibodies to the protein. Fortuitously, one such healthy subject developed acute infectious mononucleosis during the course of the scientific studies, and serum specimens later taken from this subject were found to react with the tumor cell proteins. Rather than neglecting such an important clue, the Henles and several other investigators quickly studied other individuals with acute infectious mononucleosis and proved the general association of Epstein-Barr virus with this syndrome.

Today the strategies for confirming that an EBV infection has occurred are similar to those used by the Henles and their colleagues. It involves detecting the appearance of antibodies to some of the virus proteins in the serum of patients. Another test for EBV infection involves the recovery of virus from the throat of patients. The patient is asked to gargle with a special solution that is then added to susceptible white blood cells, usually those harvested from human um-

bilical cords otherwise discarded with newly delivered placentas. The virus infects the umbilical cord blood B lymphocytes and transforms them into continuously growing colonies of cells, which can easily be recognized and tested for the presence of virus proteins. Throat cultures for EBV are not widely utilized because they are expensive and time-consuming. But probably more importantly, finding the virus does not indicate how recently the infection began because virus can continue to be shed into the saliva for months and even years.

With the development of specific tests for diagnosing EBV infection, it became possible to test samples from patients with a variety of other conditions of unknown cause. In those tests, several very remarkable things were learned about Epstein-Barr virus. First, it quickly became apparent that most people acquire such infections, even though they may be unaware of it. In the less developed nations these infections occur in almost all children before age five and are not associated with any symptoms, or certainly none typical of infectious mononucleosis. In industrialized nations about half of the people successfully avoid EBV infection through their late teens or early twenties. When Epstein-Barr virus infection is delayed until the teenage or early adult years, the body seems to respond to it differently. In about two-thirds of cases, the infection is still asymptomatic or very mild. But in one-third of cases such EBV infections induce the symptoms and physical findings of acute infectious mononucleosis. Epstein-Barr virus is thus another one of several viruses that cause more serious illness in older individuals than in the young child.

It is currently believed that most of the symptoms of acute infectious mononucleosis are provoked by an excessive response by the body's immune system. The swollen lymph glands, liver, and spleen are engorged with reactive lymphocytes that have multiplied in an effort to help fight the virus infection. The atypical lymphocytes in the blood are also of this type. The atypical lymphocytes are not themselves infected with the Epstein-Barr virus.

Link with other illnesses

In addition to acute infectious mononucleosis, a number of other rarer disorders have been associated with Epstein-Barr virus. The African lymphoid cancer Burkitt's lymphoma, named for its discoverer, Denis Burkitt, is characterized by unchecked growth of Epstein-Barr-virus-transformed B lymphocytes. Recent data suggest that other cancer-causing genes may be active in these cells as well, ones whose activities may be enhanced by Epstein-Barr virus. It is therefore unclear whether EBV alone can cause this cancer. A cancer of B lymphocytes that is similar to Burkitt's lymphoma is seen in the United States but is generally not associated with the EBV.

A cancer of the nasal sinuses and throat that is common in China and Southeast Asia, nasopharyngeal carcinoma, has also been associated with the Epstein-Barr virus. As in the case of Burkitt's lymphoma, evidence for the presence of the virus in the cells exists, but its role in initiating the cancer is unknown. It is possible that the virus is an innocent bystander to the malignant process.

Certain uncommon but severe neurological illnesses, including encephalitis (inflammation of the brain) and paralyses of various nerve groups (Bell's palsy, for example), can occur with EBV infections. Sometimes these neurological disorders complicate acute infectious mononucleosis, but in other instances they occur without any of the other usual symptoms of infectious mononucleosis.

The defense systems of patients with other rare disorders in which the lymphocytes are impaired (immune-deficient patients) may fail to control EBV infections properly. In some cases the immune impairment results from toxic drugs prescribed for cancer treatment or to prevent rejection of transplanted organs. In these individuals discontinuation of the treatment usually allows the immune system to regenerate sufficiently to make the lymphoid tumors regress. In other cases the rapid multiplication and spread of the virus-infected B lymphocytes is fatal.

Chronic EBV infection

Within the past few years scientific evidence has mounted that suggests that some individuals who develop EBV infection do not recover within the usual time frame of days to weeks that is typical of acute infectious mononucleosis. They might partially recover from infectious mononucleosis but continue to experience fatigue, intermittent sore throats, tender lymph nodes, and feverishness. Upon examination they appear completely normal. For those few in whom the symptoms wax and wane or persist for years, the inability to document that something is actually wrong with them leads physicians to suspect hypochondriasis and leaves patients frustrated and angry.

There are two reasons to consider the Epstein-Barr virus as cause of this disorder. First, the chronic fatigue and associated symptoms begin in some cases with acute infectious mononucleosis. Second, some of these individuals possess higher than expected levels of antibodies to EBV proteins, in amounts and patterns suggestive of relatively recent or active infections.

On the other hand, there are several reasons to consider that Epstein-Barr virus is not the cause of many or most such chronic fatiguing illnesses. First, the illnesses usually do not begin as acute infectious mononucleosis and lack many of the features of that syndrome. Second, some individuals who lack antibodies to EBV, and who therefore have never been infected with the virus, can have the same symptoms. Third, some normal individuals can also have high levels of serum antibody to EBV. Thus, the antibody tests are not specific enough.

The association of a chronic fatiguing illness with Epstein-Barr virus is still a hypothetical one. It is far more likely that many disorders of immune, infectious, and psychological origin can look sufficiently similar to be confused with chronic EBV infection. To date there are no certain ways of discriminating among these likely causes.

Treatment

There are no specific treatments for any forms of Epstein-Barr virus infection. Chemotherapy and radiation therapy are helpful in treating Burkitt's lymphoma and nasopharyngeal carcinoma. But such aggressive therapies as these are not indicated for acute infectious mononucleosis or other EBV-associated disorders. Physicians still recommend the time-worn remedies of rest, fluids, mild painkillers for sore throat, and aspirin or related drugs for fever. In very unusual cases of this infection in which there are seriously enlarged tonsils or spleen or certain other complications, steroid hormones can be used briefly. They temporarily dampen what may be an excessive immune response, but they have no direct effect on the virus itself.

Antiviral drugs are now available for treatment of some other herpesvirus infections. In early trials the most potent of these, acyclovir, seemed inadequate to significantly alter the course of Epstein-Barr infections. It may be necessary to await the development of more potent compounds or to combine acyclovir with other medications to effect a substantial amelioration of the disease.

Prevention

Epstein-Barr virus is a ubiquitous virus. Sooner or later it is shed in the saliva of just about every human being. Thus, it is hard to avoid. But it is also hard to spread. Only a small percentage of susceptible household contacts of individuals with acute infectious mononucleosis develop the infection. Nonetheless, individuals with acute infectious mononucleosis should avoid spreading their saliva through kissing or sharing of utensils. Current data indicate that patients with a chronic fatiguing illness that may be associated with the Epstein-Barr virus seem to be no more likely to spread this virus than anyone else and need not worry about contagion.

There are currently no vaccines for Epstein-Barr virus. Several different strategies are being explored for EBV vaccine development, but it is unlikely that any will be proved safe or effective until well into the 1990s.

Sexual Dysfunction: Causes and Cures

by **Domeena C. Renshaw, M.D.**

Most children learn customs and beliefs regarding the proper time and situation for expression and control of most natural bodily functions and feelings, but often they are left in the dark about sexual ones. Sexual interest and concerns, however, are as old as the human race. Ancient art and earliest recorded history testify to such preoccupations.

What is new in the past 30 years is that there has been careful study of human sexual responses. The result is that people now feel entitled to effective sexual functioning. Women, for example, want more from sex than passive compliance because they now know there *is* more. A recent development is the emergence of "sexual medicine" as an important and serious subspecialty.

The modern study of the basic mechanisms of male and female sexual response was pioneered by William Masters, a gynecologist at Washington University School of Medicine in St. Louis, Mo., and behavior therapist Virginia Johnson. Their findings have since been replicated and validated at other centers in the U.S. and in Europe.

In 1959 Masters and Johnson opened the first clinic for the treatment of sexual disorders. The treatment pioneered by Masters and Johnson was both innovative and controversial. The basic premise was to treat couples—focusing on the relationship rather than on the sexual dysfunction. In therapy sessions couples learn sensual and communicative techniques that they then "practice" as "homework." Masters and Johnson's work encouraged hundreds of therapists to adopt and modify their methods, which are effective in about 80% of cases they treat. In the U.S. the American Association of Sex Educators, Counselors, and Therapists has certified some 4,000 sexual therapists, most of whom are nonphysicians.

In 1964 the Masters and Johnson Reproductive Biology Research Foundation—which still functions as an active center for the ongoing scientific study of human sexual response—was established in St. Louis. Much has been learned; much has yet to be discovered about the basic human function sexuality.

Private sexual preoccupations

While the range of normal sexual behaviors is wide, complex factors affect what is appropriate and acceptable. For many, inhibitions, moral beliefs, and sexual ignorance cause persistent shame and anxiety about sexual function. Masturbation, or self-stimulation to orgasm, for example, is a prevalent and generally secret concern. Myth and misconception have long surrounded it; madness, evil, and disease have been associated with it. But masturbation is neither perverse nor depraved. In fact, it is normal in development and a healthy form of sexual release.

Perhaps the biggest question about sexual functioning in most people's minds is: Am I normal? There are also a host of other preoccupations: Is it normal to have sexual fantasies? Why don't I feel what others say they feel? What is the right age to have sexual interests? Why are my sexual feelings so strong? Is this feeling sexual or is it love? Will I be rejected? Even after many years of sexual intimacy, there are sexual worries: Is masturbation for a married person normal? Is it normal to have intercourse with my spouse only once a month? Is it normal to feel sexual urges when I sleep? Is oral sex natural? And so forth.

Persistent fears about closeness, performing poorly, contracting infections, and being rejected or hurt may cause sexual problems. Thus the question arises: Is there a physical reason for the problem? The answer is usually no. The majority of problems are reversible or transient. In a marriage or a committed partnership, compatibility in or out of the bedroom may cause fluctuating sexual dysfunctions; partners usually can recognize these as conflict-related. If a sexual dysfunction is pervasive or persistent, however, then it should be checked out.

Today a systematic workup—physical and psychological—by a specialist in sexual disorders, or sometimes by a team of specialists that may include internist, endocrinologist, urologist, gynecologist, neurologist, psychiatrist, psychologist, and social worker—can usually get to the root of the problem. Once the cause of a sexual dysfunction has been determined, appropriate treatment can follow.

Sexual dysfunction: causes and cures

A useful definition

What are sexual dysfunctions? Clinicians specializing in sexual medicine generally define dysfunctions as impaired, incomplete, or absent expressions of normally recurrent human sexual desires and responses. When difficulties with pleasurable climactic resolution of appropriate sexual arousal occur, they may be transient or recurrent; they become problematic or symptomatic only when there is subjective discomfort related to the dysfunction. In some cases one partner's dissatisfaction with sex may precipitate awareness of the dysfunction for the first time.

In the 1980s many are seeking help from their physicians or from sexual dysfunction clinics. Even in cases of unconsummated marriages of up to 21 years' duration, partners have sought and received help. In men the most common sexual dysfunctions are impotence and premature ejaculation. Men less commonly seek help for delayed or absent ejaculation. In women anorgasmy (not having orgasms), dyspareunia (pain on intercourse), and vaginismus (spasm of the lower vagina) are the predominant complaints. For both sexes loss of sexual desire is an increasingly common reason for seeking help.

In these times of widespread alcohol and drug ingestion, sexual dysfunction symptoms are often associated with their use. In some cases needed medications cause distinct sexual problems. In men chemicals can cause loss of libido or interfere with erection or ejaculation. In women drugs can reduce desire and inhibit orgasm. Prescription drugs such as antihistamines, tranquilizers, antihypertensives, antidepressants, diuretics, sleeping pills, and some medications for cardiac conditions can have sexual side effects and can be the cause of temporary sexual dysfunctions. Often the patient is uninformed about the potential side effects when a drug is prescribed. Multiple drug use can also create temporary dysfunction.

If there has been long-standing alcohol use, blood tests for liver damage are needed. A complication of heavy use of alcohol is interference with testosterone metabolism, and there may be resultant softening of the testes. Marijuana, too, can have several negative

effects on sexual performance and drive despite myths that it is an aphrodisiac. Heroin and other street drugs may cause ejaculatory difficulties.

The medical workup and trial therapy

Diagnosis of sexual dysfunction is individualized, but there are general steps that are usually taken in order to unmask a problem. Step one is for an individual or a couple to determine that there is a problem. Step two is to seek help from a physician who has had some training in sexual medicine. It is best for sexual partners to go for diagnosis together.

The doctor will first ask for a thorough and explicit history of the sexual complaint and both partners' reactions to it. A routine medical, personal, family, and marital history is taken next. Then a thorough, top-to-toe physical and genital examination for both partners is needed to carefully exclude overt physical problems. Visible or palpable genital abnormalities, the strength of male peripheral pulses, and local causes for vaginal or pelvic pain may be diagnosed during such an examination. If the problem is not found from such examination, further tests might be needed.

The next step may be a trial of sex therapy—*i.e.*, sex education, relationship therapy, and engagement in sexual activities at home. This may occur at the same time that further investigation is in process. At home the couple engages in prolonged nongenital foreplay (sensate focus), which allows them to learn to relax, discover how highly erotic the skin is, and enjoy this loving foreplay while they delay intercourse. Both are encouraged to be open and honest and to use sexual fantasy to stimulate erections and vaginal lubrication. The woman is often helped by such arousal since a woman's response on the average takes four times longer than a man's. This approach relieves the male of performance and penetration pressures. Over several weeks he gains confidence as he becomes adept at controlling his erections, which are deliberately unused in intercourse.

With cooperative patients who take the time at home for playful touching, kissing, sexual surprises, laughter, showering together, and having enjoyment in

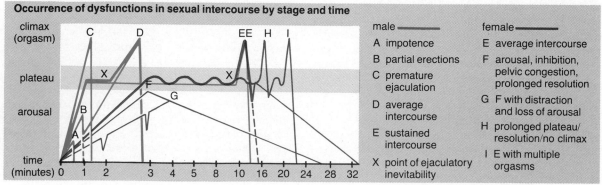

Domeena C. Renshaw, M.D., Loyola University

their own and each other's whole bodies rather than focusing only on genitals and genital arousal, positive, even surprising, sexual responses occur. This is often the kind of affection that couples shared in courtship. Such a therapeutic approach is a modified Masters-Johnson technique, and it may bring about a high rate of symptom reversal in relatively few visits.

In itself, sex therapy may be entirely effective, and further, expensive laboratory tests may be unnecessary. If sex therapy does not solve the problem, further work is indicated to discover nonovert physical or psychological problems. Beyond the general steps in the sexual disorder workup, specific problems are evaluated by means of an increasing array of diagnostic methods. With more precise modes of evaluation, more effective treatment becomes possible.

Impotence

The term impotence refers to the persistent inability to obtain or maintain a penile erection suitable for sexual intercourse. In the U.S. it is estimated that ten million men are chronically impotent. New and more sophisticated diagnostic procedures for the evaluation of impotence have rapidly evolved since 1980 but are still not entirely conclusive.

To exclude endocrine causes of impotence, a medical workup includes blood tests to measure fasting blood sugar, testosterone, luteinizing hormone (LH), prolactin, thyroid-stimulating hormone (TSH), the major thyroid hormone T_4, and the hormone estradiol.

To exclude reduced blood flow as a cause, special noninvasive tests of the penis are undertaken. These include a measurement of nonerect penile blood pressure (normally 80% of pressure in the arm). Penile pulse is measured by a Doppler amplification device. Penile width during sleep erections may be measured in a test called a nocturnal penile tumescence study. Vascular problems may be sought with arteriography studies. Injection of dye into the erect penis, followed by masturbation and X-rays of the penis, can exclude rare but surgically correctable congenital "leakage points." Evaluation of nerves going to and coming from the penis may be done with electrical stimulus methods, known as evoked potential studies.

Recent trials of ultrasound, a technique widely used to check fetal development and test heart function, have suggested that it may be a further method of delineating the cause of an impotence disorder. Better tests for penile rigidity are currently under intense investigation. It is important to develop an objective measure to validate patients' subjective reports of failure to maintain rigidity.

The more extensive, time-consuming, and often costly testing for impotence may be appropriate in cases when (1) the patient reports he has never (or very rarely) been functional in intercourse; (2) he was formerly functional but now has recurrent or frequent

erectile failure with intercourse; (3) he has "soft-tip" erections; i.e., rigidity is insufficient for penetration of the vagina; or (4) a course of brief sex therapy fails despite cooperation of both partners.

Surgical treatment for impotence due to physical causes is available that includes several types of inflatable and permanently rigid, surgically implanted penile prostheses. These devices have made headlines in the past decade, heralding an era of "bionic sex." But such implants alone may not ensure satisfactory intercourse if a couple's relationship is conflictual. Nor are penile devices free of complications—e.g., mechanical failure, tissue infection, or erosion of the device. Both partners must consider such surgery carefully. If a man's partner is receptive, the implant may afford sexual pleasure and closeness. The implant does not, however, give the man a climax or an ejaculation.

Premature ejaculation

In cases of premature ejaculation when no biologic or chemical causes have been found, a major medical workup is not indicated. If a good, explicit sexual history reveals that rapid or "premature" ejaculation is a new or transient symptom and if the physical-genital examination is normal, then the physician can inquire whether the recent cause was high excitement—a new, awkward, or unfamiliar setting; fear of being seen; return to sex after a long abstinence; infrequent coitus; and so forth. Such psychosocial causes of occasional premature ejaculation respond well to reassurance and directives from the physician to make love in a relaxed atmosphere.

On the other hand, if premature ejaculation is lifelong and recurrent, then anxiety, inhibitions, fear of performance, sexual ignorance, or combinations of these are usually causative. Such psychological problems must be addressed.

Contrary to popular belief, masturbation does not cause premature ejaculation. In fact, masturbating before intercourse might assist in correction of the problem because the second erection lasts longer. A frequently prescribed exercise is for the man or his partner to squeeze the penis at the ridge of the tip or at the base for 15 seconds during foreplay. In practice, he then allows an erection to subside, then repeats the squeeze several times before actual intercourse. This is usually done in a position with the man supine and the woman on top. There are many variations of this procedure, which the partners can discover on their own, or they can request instruction about such exercises.

Delayed or absent ejaculation

A medical workup for the problem of delayed or absent ejaculation begins with a physical and genital examination and explicit questions about whether the symptom is "selective" (only with intercourse or after alcohol indulgence or the taking of medications) or "global" (with both intercourse and masturbation and apparently unrelated to chemical ingestion).

If nonselective, or global, then mechanical factors that could obstruct the flow of semen must be sought—*e.g.,* congenital absence of seminal vesicles, an inflammation obstructing the urethra, problems in the neck of the bladder, or problems that arise after prostate surgery (with retrograde ejaculation into the bladder). Neurological and some endocrine lesions may affect ejaculation; therefore, a neurological exam and blood hormone tests (as for impotence) may be indicated. Vasectomy, which causes a barely noticeable reduction in volume of ejaculate, is not the reason for delayed or absent ejaculation.

Female dysfunctions

A medical workup for the female patient can help determine the cause of anorgasmy, pain on intercourse (dyspareunia), or spasm of the vagina (vaginismus). Some women have not ever experienced an orgasm or climax (primary anorgasmy). Others once could achieve orgasm but no longer do so (secondary anorgasmy). A full physical and genital-pelvic examination should include instruction from the physician about the position of the clitoris and its attachments and about the circular muscle of the lower vagina, which a woman can voluntarily contract and relax. She may be given a hand mirror for viewing her genitals and receive accurate education about her genital anatomy so that she may explore and practice on her own or with her partner.

If the vaginal wall is thin or dry, as is common at menopause or after early hysterectomy, then a Pap smear must be done and estrogen treatment possibly given. If there is a vaginal infection, a culture may be done and specific medications prescribed. If there is localized pain, a minor vestibular gland may be infected and require excision under local anesthetic, since this infection rarely responds to antibiotics. If the hymen is still present and tight, a hymenectomy is done so that intercourse can follow.

Sexual apathy

For both male and female complaints of inhibited sexual desire, the medical workup begins with a complete physical and genital exam. Then explicit questions determine whether the symptom is selective (relating to sex with a specific partner or to sex under particular circumstances) or global (at all times). If the latter, then hormonal blood tests may be done, in some cases followed by endocrine treatment. Treatment for an underactive thyroid gland, for example, may be indicated. In some cases neurological problems, which can be diagnosed with various tests and X-ray examinations, are the cause of sexual apathy. Such infrequent physical causes of inhibited desire underscore the need for careful medical evaluation as an integral part of the overall treatment of a sexual problem.

The most common underlying causes of selective inhibited sexual desire have to do with fatigue; career, financial, or time pressures; and conflict between partners. If both partners are motivated to change, then relationship therapy can be highly effective. It can encourage open, honest communication, avoidance of blame, respect for libido differences, and taking turns giving and receiving affection so that each partner may be nurtured and pleasurable sexual exchange may be restored.

Psychological evaluation

Just as no psychological exam can exclude or diagnose a physical problem of the genitals, so too no physical exam will exclude psychological or interpersonal problems. Both evaluations are needed for a comprehensive understanding of a sexual symptom. Even when a physical cause for a sex symptom is determined, there is still an emotional reaction to it. The best psychological evaluation remains an in-depth interview with a skilled therapist regarding the present problem, early and present family life, illness, and both partners' dating, love, and sexual relationships.

The reasons for sometimes administering psychological tests as part of sex therapy are threefold: (1) for each partner to know himself or herself better; (2) for partners to know each other better; and (3) to determine how each regards the relationship. Written tests are helpful in some cases because some people can express themselves better on paper. The therapist selects, facilitates, and interprets such tests. However, there is no standard battery of tests for diagnosing psychological causes of sexual apathy.

Sexual pleasure: a basic human need

The aim of sex therapy today is understanding the needs of each partner and ensuring that these are communicated clearly. The elderly, people with physical disabilities, and many with chronic illnesses continue to have sexual longings and need not be excluded from pleasurable sex. In fact, illness, disability, surgery, body changes, medications, and life stresses may affect intercourse frequency and positions of anyone at any age. But despite temporary or chronic limitations, affectionate kissing, touching, teasing, petting, and innovative sexual play can afford ongoing and highly satisfying intimacy.

In sickness and in health, sexuality is an integral part of each person's personality and humanity and is an important way of relating in and beyond the bedroom. Mutuality of sexual exchange is attained with commitment, caring, sharing, effort, experience, compromise, maturity, trust, and affectionate interpersonal exchange.

Working Out at Home

by Jay S. Stuller

As the running boom reached a peak during the 1970s, many joggers began to find that this form of conditioning had its imperfections. The repetitious pounding on pavement led to pains in the feet, knees, and hips. Upholding the regimen in foul climates proved difficult. Thus, during the 1980s it was not uncommon for devoted exercisers to turn to health clubs.

Such establishments offer a variety of equipment and facilities. A well-stocked club has weights, stationary cycles, a swimming pool, and facilities for handball and racquetball. Some also have indoor running tracks. The sports add competition to the exercise process, breaking the routine of pure conditioning.

However, health clubs can be overcrowded, and managing to fit in a workout during lunch periods, evenings, or weekends is often difficult. Also, membership dues are costly. Consequently, home exercise equipment has become the latest and fastest-growing development in physical conditioning. In 1984 American consumers spent more than $1 billion on stationary cycles, weight-lifting sets, jump ropes, minitrampolines, rowing machines, exercise mats, and related gear. A study commissioned by the National Sporting Goods Association found that roughly ten million people use such equipment more than twice a week. Moreover, as some new and innovative employment arrangements are enabling an increasing number of people to work at home—with, for example, the advent of home computers, more lenient maternity leaves for childbearing working mothers, and more fathers participating in infant raising while mothers work—the trend of home-based exercising is likely to continue. A new trend among the more well-to-do is to have a fitness specialist or exercise instructor pay "house calls."

Exercising in the home does have certain advantages. First is the convenience factor; one can exercise before or after work without fighting packed locker rooms. With personal equipment there is no pressure to rush—either to give the next person in line a chance on the equipment or to get back to the office. Many people who are either embarrassed or self-conscious about their bodies and about exercising in public find the home a congenial setting for getting fit. While riding a stationary cycle indoors is not as pleasant as an outdoor ride on a clear day, a stationary cyclist need not worry about foul weather; collisions with cars, trucks, and pedestrians; potholes; or traffic signals. And though pedaling miles without leaving the family room is indisputably boring, there are numerous diversions the indoor cyclist can turn to; *e.g.,* viewing television, listening to the stereo, or reading. Some exercise bicycles are equipped with handy reading stands. Many people find exercising and accomplishing another task concurrently to be an excellent use of time.

On the other hand, the home often contains many distractions and interruptions, such as family demands, chores to do, and the telephone ringing, that may hinder an exercise regimen. If these cannot be ignored for a 20–30-minute uninterrupted workout, a health club's purposeful setting may provide a better atmosphere for exercising.

Also, home exercise equipment, depending on the type, can consume considerable space. Certain weight devices, for example, can occupy from 60 to 100 or more square feet; few machines are easily stored. Perhaps more important, unused equipment that takes up space is a constant reminder that one might not be devoting the intended effort to fitness.

Herein lie the rubs of home exercise equipment; first, the gear is useless unless employed regularly, and second, the results are not always what is promised in advertisements. The typical sales pitch for a rower or weight machine usually features tautly muscled 19-year-olds and either implies or bluntly states that in a few minutes each day, the equipment will help purchasers to sculpt similar physiques and figures. The process is not that simple, nor will time and genetics allow many individuals to look like models.

Simply put, fitness improvement—at a health club or in the home—is the product of hard work and sweat. So-called passive exercise devices that ostensibly increase fitness with no effort are the stuff of

479

The Buffalo Home Trainer, c. 1886, the first known stationary bicycle, was developed before exercising for fitness was popular or considered important for health. It sold for $30.

quackery. One ad claims, "Ten minutes a day and your potbelly will be gone," and is aimed at busy people "who like to have good meals" but do not want to suffer the consequences. No machine or exercise product, however expensive, itself creates fitness. At best, it is only a tool.

Paths to fitness

For all the attention it receives and the complexity that is therein implied, physical conditioning is actually a simple process. Through various forms of exercise, one can:

● *Improve cardiovascular and respiratory efficiency.* These are achieved essentially through aerobic activity. Aerobic activity is hard and steady exercise, be it running, dancing, cycling, or rowing. The key is working one's heart rate to a "target zone" of 70 to 85% of the maximum rate. (To find the target zone, subtract your age from 220, and multiply by .75.)

Aerobic exercise strengthens the heart muscle and improves lung capacity. A stronger heart pumps more blood with less effort, while an increased "maximal oxygen uptake" more efficiently transfers oxygen through the lungs and into the bloodstream.

Aerobic benefits begin after about 20 minutes of sustained exercise in which one has reached the target zone. For any significant conditioning gain—and

for maintenance—one should participate in aerobic exercise at least three days per week.

● *Strengthen the body's other muscles.* This improvement comes from exercising against some form of resistance. *Isometric* exercise involves pushing against an immovable object, such as a wall; in *isotonic* exercise, one moves a muscle through a range of motion, as in leg lifts and arm presses, against resistance or weight. There are several theories on how best to improve muscle strength. Multiple sets of 10 to 15 repetitions with little resistance or weight is a technique with many adherents; others prefer fewer repetitions of the exercise but with relatively greater weights.

By alternating strenuous lifting sessions with rest days, the muscle tissues undergo a biochemical change. The muscles grow larger and stronger, particularly in men. Women's muscles tighten, gain definition, and, as dedicated women bodybuilders have proved, actually grow.

● *Stretch muscles and gain flexibility.* Stretching is important to any form of physical activity; it carries oxygen-rich blood to those muscles, which helps reduce the possibility of pulls and strains. Increased strength from weight lifting can be a liability unless one also gains and maintains flexibility.

● *Improve balance and eye-hand coordination.* A person's overall kinesthetic sense is often neglected as an element of conditioning. However, certain sports, such as tennis, basketball, volleyball, and racquetball, can enhance physical well-being by tuning up these skills. Except for jumping rope, however, few types of home exercise do much for coordination.

Although burning calories and losing weight may be an exerciser's goal, these are not always as significant or rapidly achieved as some would hope. One notable effect, however, is that workouts tend to lower appetite. An increasingly accepted theory on the mechanisms of weight loss indicates that exercise adjusts the caloric equation—*i.e.*, it raises the rate at which calories are burned, making weight loss and weight control easier. Without the exercise component, last-

Heart-rate threshold range (beats per minute)

age	120	130	140	150	160
25–29				135 to 164	
30–34				132 to 161	
35–39			129 to 157		
40–44			126 to 153		
45–49			124 to 150		
50–54			122 to 148		
55–59		119 to 144			
60–64		117 to 142			
65–69		114 to 138			

Photographs, (left) Karl Schumacher/Time Magazine; (right) Martha Leonard/Time Magazine

Some friends (left) get together to build muscles in a basement home gym in Beltsville, Maryland. The room this woman (right) is proudest of in her suburban Chicago home is her "spa," complete with padded wallpaper, mirrored wall, and nearly $5,000 worth of exercise apparatus.

ing and meaningful weight loss is unlikely to occur.

Calories burned vary with the exercise. A 70-kg (154-lb) person pedaling on a stationary cycle at a brisk rate of 27 km/h (17 mph) will burn 14 cal per minute; in a half-hour ride, that amounts to 420 cal. People at higher weights will burn slightly more calories in the same time, while those at lower weights will burn fewer calories. Thus, at 27 km/h for half an hour a man weighing 82 kg (180 lb) would burn 16 cal per minute (480 cal total); a woman weighing 46 kg (100 lb), only 11 cal (330 cal total). But the average fast-food hamburger contains 400 to 600 cal. To lose weight, limiting food intake is also important.

The basic home gym

With an investment of roughly $50,000 and a big enough space to house the gear, one could duplicate a YMCA or health club gym, furnished with a complete Nautilus system, comprising some 20 pieces of equipment, each of which exercises a specific group of muscles. Add a $3,000 stationary cycle with computer monitoring, an $800 rower, a computerized treadmill, and a cross-country-skiing machine, and an individual could get into fine condition—that is, of course, if the equipment is used.

On the other hand, a set of equipment consisting of a jump rope, an inexpensive barbell set, and a roll-up exercise mat—the other end of the exercise spectrum—if used faithfully, is as good as the most expensive home gym. Cost, of course, is not the only criterion in creating a home gym. Some of the more advanced stationary cycles come with devices that enable the exerciser to measure work load, making these machines true "ergometers." With gauges that display speed, elapsed time, and an estimate of caloric consumption—and a few models allow one to track heart rate—these cycles help the exerciser to measure fitness progress. Some individuals find that being able to chart improvement is an important motivator for adhering to an exercise regimen.

Physical conditions, however, may limit or govern the types of equipment that can or should be purchased. A person with frequent low back pain should not choose rowing machines because most rowers do not provide low back support. For those who suffer pain and frequent injury during jogging, the rower or stationary cycle is an excellent alternative aerobic tool.

Quality in equipment can often be tied directly to price. Gear found in discount or department stores is rarely as good as that sold by dealers specializing in health and fitness equipment. Inexpensive exercise bicycles and rowers will break down sooner and more often than more costly models that are backed by a warranty. And poor equipment may also hinder workouts. For instance, a typical rowing machine creates resistance with cylinders similar to automobile shock absorbers. Cheaply manufactured cylinders can overheat from friction, develop points of wear, and then cause halting and uneven pulling actions. When one begins struggling against the machine as much as the exercise, continued use is unlikely.

On the other hand, higher priced gear is not always necessary. It is unlikely that a slim woman with a small frame who rides a stationary cycle only a few days per week for under half an hour will wear it out; consequently, a less expensive "department store" cycle may be sufficient. But for rugged family use, it is wise to purchase a more durable machine.

Safety is an important facet of quality. While many exercise injuries come from misuse or lack of supervision, slipshod manufacturing occasionally contributes. Several years ago a woman in Texas was seriously injured when a seat post on her stationary cycle sliced through the equipment's plastic seat. Another woman was blinded in one eye when an elastic stretch device on her home exercise equipment snapped, striking her in the face. According to an agency of the U.S. Consumer Products Safety Commission, during 1984 more than 18,000 American home exercisers were injured to a degree that required emergency room

Working out at home

treatment. Strains and sprains were the most frequent injuries, followed by bruises and cuts. Ankles, fingers, and the lower back were the most commonly injured body parts.

When purchasing equipment, one should seek sturdy construction. A good, solid machine will have heavy tubular steel and strong bolts, and movable parts will be protected. One should also consider ease of assembly—does the equipment come fully assembled?—and ease of maintenance. The operative words governing the purchase of home equipment are "buyer beware."

Pedaling to fitness: stationary cycles

Long a standard in YMCAs and health clubs, fixed cycles have become a leading seller in the home exercise market. While a cycle's primary benefit is aerobic, the machines also can be adjusted to provide more resistance against the pedals, which helps strengthen leg muscles. (Some models, such as the Schwinn Air-Dyne, also have "arms," so that the exerciser can row and ride, giving the legs *and* upper body a workout.)

Simple cycles can be purchased for about $100, occasionally less. Most of these, however, are not covered by warranties of any significant length. All stationary cycles have speedometers and some means of making pedaling harder, usually provided by a belt that tightens around a flywheel (an important design feature that smooths the pedaling action). But on inexpensive machines, the resistance settings are rarely consistent; only with a quality cycle can one accurately set work loads day after day. Models with calibration capabilities—allowing one to chart work load, speed, and "distance"—begin at roughly $400. These then are the true ergometers in that they enable the calculation of fitness improvements.

Most cycles have adjustable seat heights and adjustable handlebars. Most also have pedal cuffs, which keep feet from slipping, and also allow an upward pedaling motion that strengthens additional leg muscles.

There are many solid brands of stationary cycles. The Schwinn Air-Dyne, which has a flywheel with windvanes—the air tosses a cooling breeze back onto the rider—retails for about $600. Schwinn also makes a sturdy, smoothly functioning bike that sells for about $250. J. Oglaend, Inc., an American subsidiary of Norway's leading cycle maker, markets five cycles, from its $250 economy model to its Bodyguard 990, a sturdy, welded-frame cycle that retails for about $800. Other leading brands include Monark, Vitamaster, Avita, Panasonic, Tunturi, and Precor.

Computerized cycles, with readings displaying elapsed time, work load, calories burned, and heart rates, are in the $2,000 range. In substance, these do no more for the rider than more basic $400 ergometer cycles do; the difference is in form and "extras." For example, the Heart Mate 200, a Wimbledon Industries product, retails for about $4,000 and comes with a built-in television and AM-FM radio. The owner of the Heart Mate enters his or her age and weight into the machine's computer. The computer automatically combines these data with time and intensity of each workout, along with a 60-second heart rate recovery at the end of the ride. The machine then computes maximum oxygen uptake and provides a numerical fitness readout on a scale of 0 to 100.

Calories used per minute for home exercise activities
weight in pounds*

activity	71 or less	72–82	83–93	94–104	105–115	116–126	127–137	138–148	149–159	160–170	171–181	182–192	193 or more	exercise intensity
ropeskipping														
50–60 skips left foot only (per minute)	4.83	5.25	5.75	6.25	6.66	7.16	7.58	8.08	8.50	9.00	9.41	9.91	10.33	moderate/high
70–80 skips left foot only (per minute)	5.25	5.75	6.25	6.75	7.25	7.75	8.25	8.75	9.25	9.75	10.25	10.75	11.25	moderate/high
90–100 skips left foot only (per minute)	6.16	6.75	7.41	8.00	8.58	9.16	9.75	10.33	10.91	11.50	12.08	12.66	13.25	high
110–120 skips left foot only (per minute)	8.50	9.33	10.16	10.91	11.75	12.58	13.41	14.16	15.00	15.83	16.66	17.41	18.25	very high
130–140 skips left foot only (per minute)	11.33	12.41	13.50	14.58	15.66	16.75	17.83	18.91	20.00	21.08	22.16	23.25	24.33	very high
rowing machine														
easy	2.83	3.08	3.41	3.66	3.91	4.16	4.50	4.75	5.00	5.25	5.58	5.83	6.08	moderate
vigorous	6.16	6.75	7.41	8.00	8.58	9.16	9.75	10.33	10.91	11.50	12.08	12.66	13.25	high
stationary bicycle resistance sufficient to get pulse rate to rate to 130														
10 mph (16 km/h)	4.00	4.33	4.75	5.08	5.50	5.91	6.25	6.66	7.00	7.41	7.75	8.16	8.58	moderate
15 mph (24 km/h)	6.16	6.75	7.41	8.00	8.58	9.16	9.75	10.33	10.91	11.50	12.08	12.66	13.25	high
20 mph (32 km/h)	8.41	9.16	10.00	10.83	11.66	12.41	13.25	14.00	14.75	15.58	16.41	17.16	18.00	very high
weight training	2.83	3.08	3.41	3.66	3.91	4.16	4.50	4.75	5.00	5.25	5.58	5.83	6.08	moderate

*1 lb = 0.454 kg
adapted from Charles T. Kuntzleman, *Diet Free* (Emmaus, Pa.: Rodale Press, 1981)

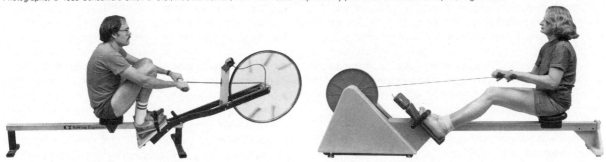

All rowers have sliding seats, but they vary in the way they provide resistance. The flywheel on the rower at left offers smooth stroking and gliding motions. The machine at right has a brake, but many riders find the action is jerky.

The $1,995 Bally Lifecycle 5000 is also computerized. Simple to program, it simulates rides up and down hills by automatically changing pedal resistance. With several different programs, the Lifecycle will take one through a warm-up period, a strong aerobic ride, and a cool-down period; a flashing red light signals the rider to increase or decrease pedal revolutions. The machine's console also indicates the number of calories burned in an hour at any particular work load.

An exercise session on a stationary cycle should begin slowly and deliberately with minimal resistance in order to mobilize joints and increase the body's temperature. This warm-up period should last at least five minutes. After the warm-up one should increase speed gradually until pedaling cadence is not uncomfortable but requires effort and produces light perspiration along with increased breathing and heart rate. Exercise should never end abruptly; one should reduce intensity gradually. Once the cycler can comfortably sustain workout sessions of 10–20 minutes of continuous rigorous pedaling, it is time to increase resistance of work load progessively for higher levels of fitness.

"Row, row, row . . ."

Rowing machines, like cycles, are convenient and relatively compact pieces of home equipment that provide excellent aerobic exercise. Rowers also exercise numerous muscle groups, including the legs, shoulders, arms, lower and upper back, abdomen, and buttocks. Some rowers are advertised as "multigyms" in that the machine's arms can be reconfigured for "presses" and "lifts"; rowing machines can also serve as a platform for sit-ups. However, in a 1985 study by the Consumer's Union, rowers that attempt to double as multigyms were generally judged as failures in both missions. And while rowing against resistance clearly is a strengthening exercise, the primary benefit of the machines, as with cycles, is aerobic.

There are three basic types of rowers. All use sliding seats. The differences between rowers come in the arms or oars and in how they provide resistance. Piston-arm rowers are the largest sellers. The least expensive and most compact of the breed, these provide resistance with modified automotive shock absorbers. Although resistance tension is adjustable, the arm movement is limited to a single plain. Piston rowers are pulled in a foot-to-chest motion rather than the straight-to-the-chest, almost 90-degree pull used in real (outdoor water) rowing.

A second variety uses oarlocks and brackets. Its arms are in a position similar to that of a real scull, pivoting against friction or hydraulic resistance. The arms, however, stick out and take up more floor space than conventional piston-arm machines.

A third rower uses a flywheel. It is long and narrow, and its rowing motion may provide the best simulation of a true stroke. One pulls directly to the chest a single handle attached to a chain, which in turn drives the flywheel. Competitive rowers frequently use flywheel machines for training.

Newer models of rowers with ergometric capabilities, including a few computerized versions, are now

A toy manufacturer sells "play centers" for 1½–5-year-olds, complete with light plastic dumbbells, foot lifts, and other stimulating accessories, designed to make "working out" fun.

Courtesy, Globe United, Inc.

on the market. Price again is a measure of quality. An Avita 950 rower and a Monark 633, both selling for about $300–$350, are good, basic, and reliable piston-type rowers. The Concept II is a popular flywheel rower that, like the Schwinn Air-Dyne cycle, tosses a breeze back on the exerciser. It retails for about $600.

To improve aerobic fitness on a rower, one should begin by setting resistance at a low level over an extended time. Beginners should start with about 12–15 strokes per minute. Others who are in good aerobic shape can usually start at 20 or more strokes per minute. One begins a stroke with legs bent and back straight and uses either an underhand or overhand grip. As one pushes back with the legs, the arm-pull begins. The torso should not be twisted, and the back should remain straight. During the recovery phase— before the next stroke is started—arm tension should loosen. Throughout the workout *all* motions should be smooth. At least 20 minutes of sustained rowing in the "target" heart zone is the goal for achieving good aerobic fitness.

Pumping iron

In the beginning there were basic dumbbells, heavy disks affixed to the ends of a bar. Simply getting into position to do a press on a flat bench became an exercise in daring. Maneuvers such as balancing the bar on the legs, stomach, and then chest were awkward to achieve and caused strain. Today lifting weights is much easier. Replete with pulleys, cables, and levers that enable one to isolate and exercise specific muscle groups, weight-lifting equipment now obviates the dangers of loose weights. Costing from $1,500 to $5,000, such "home gyms" are scaled-down versions of the Universal Gyms system, widely found in schools and health clubs during the 1960s.

While scaled down for home use, most of these weight machines require up to 9.3 sq m (100 sq ft) of space. Their heavy metal construction renders them not easily moved or tucked out of the way. Thus, weight lifters should consider that they are investing in a semipermanent fixture in the home. Recently, however, the Toro Co., known for its lawn mowers, introduced a compact, chairlike weight machine—it takes up only 2.3 sq m (25 sq ft)—that duplicates the function of ten individual Nautilus devices. Called the Power Curve, it is computer controlled; one simply punches in desired weight settings on a console. One can also vary the resistance levels for the upward and downward motions of a lift. The versatile machine carries a suggested retail price of about $5,000.

There are dozens of weight-lifting systems on the market, including the Nautilus machines. Nautilus is noteworthy in that it is one of the few systems that provide even resistance throughout the muscle's entire range of motion. But since individual Nautilus devices are so specific to the muscles they exercise— the characteristic that makes them excellent for health clubs in that exercisers can alternate exercises and rotate from machine to machine—a home exerciser is perhaps better served by one system that exercises many muscle groups.

A basic weight bench that supports conventional barbells is a very serviceable piece of equipment for most home users and can be purchased for less than $100. Many have an attachment for leg extension and "curls." A good weight bench and barbell set should enable one to accomplish the same kind of training possible on expensive, sophisticated machines, although perhaps not as swiftly and sometimes not as safely. Although barbell sets are inexpensive, they must be used with caution; less hazardous models will have a well-designed weight system with smooth levers and pulleys and solid low-back support structures.

Basic setups with levers and bars allow one to perform several lifts and pulls for the upper body. Most also include a chairlike attachment for leg extensions, which doubles as a bench on which to lie flat for leg curls. In this category are the Paramount Fitness Trainer and the Universal Power Pak 400, each of which is designed to allow two people to exercise simultaneously.

For the most convenience and best performance, the weights or resistance levels on a machine should be easily changed. Benches and seating should be stable and well secured. Cylinders and pulleys should glide smoothly.

Sundry gear

Although weights, cycles, and rowers are the mainstays of the home gym, one can also purchase a motorized and computerized treadmill for running in place, a device that simulates the motions used in cross-country skiing, and "stepping" machines for homes that lack real stairs. A toy company has also recently introduced a Kindergym for children, essentially a miniversion of a basic weight bench with leg extension and curl functions. Ostensibly this will keep the child involved with the parent, help develop an exercise ethic, and provide focus for a child's normally high level of activity. Although the Kindergym's weights are of a "play" variety, made of durable plastic and not heavy, sharp, or directly dangerous, the merit of encouraging serious weight training for young children is quite dubious and probably ill advised.

Today's Contact Lenses

by Jay S. Stuller

Imperfect eyesight is one of life's most common banes. At some point in their lives, more than half of all humans require vision correction. The most common vision impairments include myopia, or nearsightedness; hyperopia, known as farsightedness; and astigmatism, which is caused by a misshapen cornea and blurs nearly all fields of vision. And before the age of 50, more than 75% of the world's population develop presbyopia; the muscles that control the eye's lens lose elasticity, creating difficulty in focusing on objects close at hand and making reading glasses or bifocals a necessity.

Eyeglasses are often uncomfortable, to say the least, pinching or slipping down the bridge of the nose and rubbing against tender parts of the ear. The lenses, which can become foggy at the most inopportune time, also acquire mysterious greasy smudges, seemingly without being touched. And except perhaps for sporty, expensive designer frames, spectacles generally do not improve the wearer's appearance.

Hard plastic contact lenses, or contacts, were introduced in 1936 as an alternative to spectacles and were refined and improved throughout the 1940s. These small, clear, vision-correcting disks were designed to lie directly against the cornea of the eye (the transparent outer layer that covers the iris and the pupil), supported by the natural layer of tears that normally moistens the cornea. Made from a plastic material called polymethylmethacrylate (PMMA), hard contacts provide crisp acuity (ability to perceive fine detail) and a peripheral vision that eyeglasses cannot match. But the hard lenses allow neither tears nor oxygen to reach the center of the cornea. This can result in dryness and painful swelling that limit wearing time to about 12 hours.

Soft contact lenses—usually made of water-absorbing plastics called hydrogels—were introduced in 1971 and were a major advance in comfort over hard contacts. But while allowing water and some oxygen to reach the eye, they do not always provide crisp correction, and many types cannot sufficiently correct even moderate astigmatisms. Fragile and hard to handle, soft lenses require daily cleanings in chemical solutions or periodic sterilization in a boiling mixture.

More than 16 million Americans today wear contacts; however, at least as many have invested several hundred dollars in such devices but have given up in utter frustration. Although these people certainly looked better, they found that contacts presented as many problems as they solved. Contacts have often been called "a younger person's product," as it takes a certain amount of youthful vanity to put up with the discomfort and fuss. Lens experts believe that to a large degree they are working as much with a cosmetic product as an optical one. Some people wear contact lenses not because they want to see better than they do with eyeglasses but to *look* better. Women currently are the primary wearers of contact lenses, constituting about 72% of the business.

Materials and designs

The introduction of soft contacts marked a turning point in lens development. Since then, lens makers have rapidly developed soft lenses that can be worn for days and weeks between removals and cleanings. More rigid and durable gas permeable lenses, which allow oxygen to reach the eye surface, are now available for daily wear and may soon be approved by the U.S. Food and Drug Administration (FDA) for extended use. Various types of bifocal contact correction are also, finally, showing promise.

According to a late 1984 report by the U.S. Congressional Office of Technology Assessment, more than 100 different soft contact lenses—among which are 30 to 40 basic types—are available to the public. And while there are numerous hard lenses available, only about a dozen gas permeable lenses have been approved by the FDA. Many of these varied lenses were developed within the past five years, but the advances only hint at what may be on the market five years hence. Literally dozens of new lenses are awaiting approval from the FDA, and even better materials and designs are in the early stages of testing and research.

For example, in anticipation of an "ultimate" lens, technologists are working on a new contact made of fluoropolymers. Fluoropolymers are a special class

485

of plastics that may offer improved gas permeability along with the possibility of extended wear. In preliminary tests, subjects have worn fluoropolymer lenses for more than a year without removal. It will, however, take time to bring such a lens to the public. The FDA's approval process for a new type of soft or gas permeable contact can take from four to seven years. Conventional hard lenses do not carry the potential health problems of the others because PMMA resists bacteria and other deposits. Consequently, they need not undergo FDA review.

Given all the recent technological advances, eye care professionals certainly should be able to fit many more patients with contact lenses than now have them. Twenty-five years ago, U.S. optometrists estimated that there were already ten million contact lens wearers. The 1985 estimate was 23.1 million. With the new generation of lenses, contacts finally may start fulfilling their promise as outright replacements for spectacles.

Ever increasing advances and new products may make disposable contacts a possibility. Already, retailers are selling pairs of replacement lenses for less than $20, although the quality of such products may be suspect. Indeed, ophthalmologists stress that contact lenses are not consumer products on the level of blue jeans, cosmetics, or the latest fashion fad. They are scientific prosthetic devices that must be monitored by a properly qualified medical professional.

Initial considerations

The multitude of lenses available today presents eye care professionals with many choices. Since eyes react individually and differently to various lenses—a patient may experiment with several pairs before finding one that is acceptable—it takes a skilled professional to determine what is best for the patient's vision and health. In the U.S. three categories of eye care professionals serve the public. The ophthalmologist, a medical doctor who specializes in eye diseases and visual disorders, is trained to give the most thorough care. He or she is qualified to prescribe drugs, if necessary, and perform eye surgery. A skilled optometrist, a person licensed to measure and fit corrective lenses, can give almost as detailed an examination as would an ophthalmologist. In the third category is the optician, whose expertise is limited to fitting lenses prescribed by an ophthalmologist or optometrist.

A primary consideration for the eye care professional is whether the patient is strongly motivated to wear contacts. A person must want or need to use them rather than spectacles (be it for cosmetic, professional, or recreational reasons), if only to get past the uncomfortable adjustment period. The patient must also be dedicated to proper hygiene and maintenance of the lenses. Otherwise, the anticipated benefits of the contacts will be lost, other eye problems may develop,

and the patient will have wasted his or her money. The specialist should consider whether the patient has any allergies and take into account the person's work area and life-style in determining whether the patient should choose contacts. Chemicals, cigarette smoke, dust, or other particles in the air can cause eye irritation, especially for a contacts wearer. Eyeglasses may be the preferred method of vision correction if the patient is often exposed to such an atmosphere.

If the specialist and patient agree that contact lenses should be tried, other factors may yet limit the types of lenses that can be used. For example, not all types of contacts can adequately correct astigmatism. If the patient is 40 or older, signs of presbyopia may be apparent, necessitating bifocal correction. Between the ages of 45 and 55, patients often have permanent chemical changes in tear composition. In these cases, even if the patient does not have the condition known as "dry eye," which is another occasional problem, the tears may not sufficiently lubricate the lens and eye. Eyelid structure can also become more flaccid with age, thus providing inadequate support for some types of contact lenses.

Although the "latest" in contacts may be asked for, a competent practitioner will recommend what is best for the patient's condition. The eye care professional may begin with conventional hard lenses, which in many cases provide the best optics. Frequent eye examinations—perhaps as often as once a week for two or three months—are crucial during the adjustment stage. A biomicroscope is used by the examiner to see if the lenses are causing any physical changes in the corneas or any chemical changes in the composition of tears. When the patient's eyes have adjusted to the foreign objects, he or she may later be fitted with other lenses.

A nonharmful film of proteins and lipids will inevitably build up on soft lenses, particularly on the extended-wear ones, which receive infrequent cleanings. How fast the film forms determines how long extended-wear contacts can be left in—from a few days to a month. Bacteria can also build up on soft lenses, and the abuse of extended-wear lenses can lead to serious corneal swelling, allergic responses in the upper eyelid, and even severe infections. Insufficiently cleaned contacts may have contributed to many of the 24 cases of acanthamoeba keratitis reported between April 1985 and January 1986. Until 1984 an average of fewer than three cases per year of this painfully severe, treatment-resistant corneal infection were reported. While extended-wear lenses are FDA approved for "up to 30 days," prudent wearers remove and clean the contacts at least once per week.

Hard, soft, or gas permeable?

Following are the types of lenses now available, as well as some of their applications, benefits, and liabilities:

Conventional hard contacts. With new designs in soft and extended-wear lenses, hard-plastic PMMA lenses soon may be antiquated. Yet they currently hold certain advantages over all soft contacts. For instance, because the lenses are hard they can give clear vision to a patient with a misshapen, astigmatic cornea. Durable and resistant to scratches, these relatively inexpensive lenses can last from five to seven years or longer, are easy to clean, and are available in tints to match or change natural eye color. Moreover, the inert material in a hard contact is free of toxic chemicals and is exceptionally safe for use in the eye.

It takes a month or more, however, for a patient to adapt to hard lenses, because of the lens stiffness and the restriction of oxygen and tear flow to the corneal center. Wearing times must be carefully built up from an hour to several hours and, finally, an entire day. Although attempts have been made to improve hard lens oxygen and tear permeability by drilling small holes in them, a lack of air and lubrication remains a major drawback.

To allow as much oxygen as possible to reach the cornea, hard lenses usually are small in diameter. Consequently, they can be dislodged quite easily; a sudden head or eye movement can cause them to pop loose or to move off of the cornea and into the corner of the eye. A piece of dirt or dust can easily slip under the lens, causing painful irritation.

Soft lenses. Hydrogel lenses are composed primarily of water—from 30 to 70%. As a result they are very flexible and lie softly and comfortably over the cornea. Soft lenses also are highly oxygen permeable. The main difference between extended-wear and daily wear soft lenses is that the former are generally thinner and have a higher water content. The large size of soft lenses is also an advantage. Overlapping a fairly substantial portion of the eye and extending under the lid, these contacts stay in place better than hard lenses. This is particularly important to the individual who has a flaccid eyelid.

Extended-wear soft lenses are an obvious boon, especially for people seeking clear eyesight despite many hours of work at odd times of day or night. They also are useful to persons with physical disabilities— from shaky or arthritic hands to exceptionally poor eyesight—because they need not be handled often.

Soft lenses do have shortcomings. Since they are essentially little "bags of water," they can refract light and thus blur vision. In addition, although the higher water content makes a lens more comfortable, the soft lens is easily torn and is prone to other damage. Maintenance may be another problem. The surface deposits and bacteria that build up on all soft contacts must be removed. Heat disinfectant methods were once the favored technique, but today many cold chemical solutions clean the lenses as well or better with less trouble. However, the cleaning and disinfect-

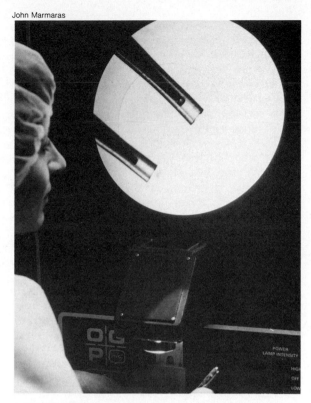

A Bausch & Lomb technician inspects a contact lens for flaws and checks its tensile strength by viewing it through an "optical comparator," which magnifies the lens ten times.

ing solutions are relatively expensive and can cost a soft lens wearer as much as $100 a year or more.

Gas permeables. Gas permeable lenses may offer the greatest promise of all, and contacts manufacturers are conducting intense research into new materials for this type of contact lens. Usually made of a plastic-silicon blend, some of the new gas permeable lenses allow considerably more oxygen to reach the eye than even the best of soft lenses. Yet they are almost as stiff as conventional hard lenses and thus can provide excellent visual acuity. They are durable, too, lasting several years with good care.

The adjustment period with these lenses is about three weeks, slightly longer than for soft lenses. For now, most gas permeables are intended for daily wear only; they must be removed at night and stored in a soaking and cleaning solution. However, some gas permeables are so comfortable that many individuals have been using them as extended-wear lenses, a practice that may be dangerous.

Of the numerous gas permeable materials researchers are investigating, one with promising potential is collagen, a primary component in human tissue. Collagen lenses would consist of up to 90% water but, unlike regular soft lenses, would be durable. Currently being tested in Europe, collagen lenses have not yet been approved by the FDA.

487

Toric lenses. More than a third of all eye patients have an astigmatism. An astigmatic cornea is more oval-shaped than normal and is irregular in its contours. A corrective lens must compensate for the irregularities and must remain in a specific position on the eye. Regular contacts, however, rotate continuously on the eye's surface. While hard contacts simply force the eye's surface into a smooth and spherically correct shape no matter what their rotation, soft lenses cannot easily do so. This is why so many eye care professionals have in the past advised against soft contacts for astigmatics. However, a number of soft toric lenses (from the Latin *torus,* meaning "a protuberance or bulge") are now available. They are specially shaped to accommodate the contours of a patient's cornea.

Somewhat more expensive than regular soft lenses, the toric versions are shaped in such a way that they do not rotate on the eye. This often involves a kind of ballast on the bottom portion of the lens. There are about a dozen different soft toric lenses now on the market. Gas permeable lenses also have good toric potential.

Bifocal contacts. Presbyopes, who require bifocal correction, have long confounded contact lens designers. Although hard contacts with two focal zones, identical to bifocal glasses, have existed for a quarter of a century, they function quite poorly. To counter natural lens rotation and keep the top and bottom zones in place, lens makers thicken and weight the bottom portion of the lens. Patients usually find this uncomfortable. Ballasted soft lenses (by their nature soft lenses do not move as much as hard lenses) provided greater comfort but did not meet acceptable standards of vision correction.

Frequently eye care professionals use what is called the "monovision system," using two completely different lenses to provide contact lens correction of presbyopia. For example, a lens for seeing distant objects is prescribed for the left eye, and a reading lens is used in the right eye. The idea is that the patient will learn to use the eyes separately, and about 75% of those who are fitted with the monovision system adapt within a couple of weeks.

The FDA has recently approved the release of "blended bifocal" or "multifocal" lenses. A "bull's-eye" in the center of these contacts corrects for distance, and the outer ring aids in reading or close vision. An individual adjusts to the concentric fields quite like he or she does with monovision; the brain becomes accustomed to matching the correct focal point with the desired activity.

"Special" lenses. Contact lenses for people with eyes scarred or disfigured by accidents, surgery, or birth defects are now available. A San Francisco-based nonprofit group called the Narcissus Medical Foundation fashions lenses to cover damaged eyes and make them appear normal. Their technicians also have made specially tinted lenses to protect light-sensitive eyes, such as those of albinos.

Cost

Contact lens prices vary greatly, depending on the location of purchase, the practitioner, the type of lens, and other factors. Discount soft lenses, dispensed by fast-service opticians, have recently been advertised for as little as $20 a pair. However, this does not include fees for an eye care professional. Conventional hard lenses, prescribed and fitted by an ophthalmologist or optometrist, are otherwise among the cheapest, costing from $100 to $150. Various types of soft lenses can cost from $150 to $300, including care, with specialty lenses for difficult astigmatisms and other problems reaching $500.

The cost of the lens, however, constitutes a relatively small proportion of these figures. The buyer is actually paying for total eye care, an ophthalmologist's or optometrist's skill in selecting the right lens for the patient's eyes and life-style. The price usually includes follow-up visits and important checks to see that the lens has not caused problems that the patient may not have noticed. Indeed, within a competent eye care professional's fee is allowance for the fact that he or she may fit a patient with two, three, or more different types or brands of lenses before finding one with satisfactory comfort and optics.

The purchase of a cheap or "discounted" pair of lenses is not advised. In fact, the $20 lenses may well cost much more by the time the patient is talked into buying insurance, extra solutions, spare lenses, and so forth. A cheap lens also usually wears out faster, and follow-up care may be limited.

On the horizon

Within the next few years, other technological developments are certain to benefit the contact lens market. For example, lens designers are working on a combination hard and soft contact lens. The center of such a lens is composed of hard or gas permeable material that provides crisp correction; the outer fringe of the lens is made of soft and comfortable hydrogels. Moreover, new drops and solutions that can help clean a lens while it is in the eye are being developed, which would greatly extend wearing periods. Some technologists are even considering the possibility of eyedrops that in themselves will correct vision problems.

More likely, the future of contact lenses rests with some kind of hybrid material. A combination of the best features of soft and gas permeable lenses—providing a durable material that would resist protein and foreign material build-up, could be cleaned with eyedrops, and could be worn for a long time—could overcome many of the current disadvantages and enhance the known advantages of today's lenses.

Surviving the Holidays

by Nancy Seeger

Every year, in the deep mid-winter, there descends upon this world a terrible fortnight. A fortnight, or ten days, or a week, when citizens cannot get about the streets of their cities for the surging pressure of persons who walk therein; when every shop is a choked mass of humanity, and purchases, at the very time when purchases are most numerously ordained to be made, are only possible at the cost of bitter hours of travail; a time when nerves are jangled and frayed, purses emptied to no purpose, all amusements and all occupations suspended in favour of frightful businesses with brown paper, string, letters, cards, stamps, and crammed post offices. This period is doubtless a foretaste of whatever purgatory lies in store for human creatures.

—Rose Macaulay, *Crewe Train*

In contemporary society holidays are given considerable commercial and social emphasis, and large numbers of people anticipate them enthusiastically. Holidays also evoke a wide range of emotional responses and behavior. Because these are trying times for many, people may need help coping.

It goes without saying that the preparation for, and celebration of, holiday festivities can be both positively and negatively stressful. For many a particularly problematic time is the period from Thanksgiving to the New Year. During this extended "Christmas season," society is inundated by a holiday "spirit," which few can escape. Merchants embark on seductive sales promotions; newspapers are filled with advertisements; stores are crammed full of people anxiously making purchases; local public transportation is jammed; public places and homes are bedecked with decorations; many people travel long distances, so that planes, trains, and buses are booked solid; and there are endless social gatherings, parties, and celebratory meals, where vast quantities of food and drink are consumed. Also, many routines are radically changed. Most schoolchildren have extended vacations, and adults' work schedules are altered.

From a religious standpoint, although Hanukka, an important Jewish holiday, occurs around this time, Christmas is given the most all-encompassing societal emphasis. Even if people do not directly participate in the celebration of Christmas, they are affected by others' celebration of it.

Happy times for some, sad times for others

Holidays unquestionably can be times of great joy. At such times a young child may express love for a parent or thanks to a teacher by creating a special present. Aged and debilitated people in nursing homes or young men serving their country overseas may be cheered by letters and gifts from relatives. Patients in hospitals may be entertained by visiting carolers. And consider the thrill of a child sitting on a jolly Santa Claus's lap and hearing he or she will receive a specially desired toy. At Halloween children may delight in the fantasy of changing identities by dressing in imaginative costumes and being welcomed in neighbors' houses, glowing with jack-o-lanterns, where they threaten to play "tricks" so they will receive "treats."

But holiday festivities can be painfully sad for some people, such as the poor, the homeless, the mentally and physically ill, the isolated aged, and those who lack close family or emotional ties. For those who do not have financial resources, these times can be devastating. Christmas can be particularly trying for the economically deprived who want, like everyone else, to give gifts but simply cannot afford to do so. In recent times, owing to widespread unemployment and high inflation, a large segment of the population suffer at holidays for want of resources. Their children in particular are intensely aware that they cannot have what other children have. There are numerous social programs, special funds, food and toy donations, etc., to help the needy and prevent their abandonment at holidays, but a great many people in these categories lack such attention.

Holiday "blues"

Holidays create expectations for new, different, or more fulfilling experiences. There is an illusion or hope that these expectations will be realized. A common one is that families, friends, and co-workers will generate or renew emotional bonds in personal relationships. Children who believe in Santa Claus become excited about the presents that he may bring, while others of all ages hope that sharing, gift giving, social gatherings,

489

and visits with distant relatives will foster affection, warm feelings, and intensified communication.

When they are successful, these occasions fulfill some of the deepest needs people have for reassurance and love. On the other hand, holidays can produce quite the opposite effect; they can cause disorientation, dissatisfactions, letdowns, extreme loneliness, and mild to severe depression.

One example to consider is the man who has an extremely demanding and high-powered job. He may become disoriented by being home from work for many days. Unused to relaxing and directing his energies toward anything but his work, he becomes anxious and depressed and ultimately withdraws from the festivities. Another example is the adolescent girl who is already experiencing a turbulent time in life. If she is then excluded from an important holiday party or has no invitations for New Year's Eve, she then feels so ultimately rejected that she may even attempt suicide. In families of divorce, legal or other arrangements may create a situation in which children spend time with only one parent. This can create a deep sense of loss and sadness for children, parents, grandparents, and other relatives.

If the holidays seem particularly likely to be melancholy times, people can "prepare" by consulting a psychotherapist. Many cities now provide special counseling services and hot lines for people who are overcome with holiday blues.

Holiday overindulgence

One reaction to the stresses of holidays is to overindulge in food and alcohol. And since holidays commonly are celebrated with special meals and drinks, the likelihood of more-than-ordinary consump-

Amid the hustle and bustle and festivities, people who are alone are quite likely to experience holidays as painfully melancholy times.

C. Wolinsky—Stock, Boston

"All right, food people—are you ready?"

tion is great. Many find that they have to have a very strong will to get through holidays without gaining unwanted pounds or suffering indigestion, hangovers, and guilt over broken diets.

Participating in the sharing of food and drink at social gatherings has historically been a way in which people communicate. "Spirits," at least in moderate amounts, help people to relax and release inhibitions, and eating can temporarily quell nervousness and psychological discomfort. Unfortunately, though, with overindulgence people tend to feel a loss of control, particularly during times when stress is already high.

Holiday imbibing. Alcohol has been used for social purposes since ancient times. Apparently, even some of the most primitive cultures incorporated alcoholic drinks into their celebrations. Its capacities for altering moods and releasing tensions and inhibitions have been known for centuries.

But contrary to oft-held notions, alcohol is a depressant drug, not a stimulant. It affects the central nervous system by retarding brain and spinal cord activity. It impairs reaction time and coordination, especially as intoxication increases. A current National Safety Council statistic demonstrates this point. Motor vehicle accidents are the number one cause of death for all Americans between the ages of 5 and 35, and more than 50% of those accidents are alcohol related. Further research has shown that drivers with high blood-alcohol levels have 15 to 25 times more probability of being involved in accidents than nondrinkers who are on the road at the same time and place.

Not surprisingly, rates of alcohol-related accidents are high at holidays. December tradition holds that each holiday season nearly 2,000 unfortunate Americans are likely to die in a motor vehicle accident involving the use of alcohol.

Many authorities recommend that consumption always be limited so that a blood-alcohol level of no higher than 0.055% is reached. This means, for example, that a 59-kg (130-lb) person should consume no more than two drinks in an hour or three drinks in two hours. A smaller person must drink less, while a larger

Nonalcoholic Fourth of July Punch

1 qt cranberry juice	8 oz sugar
6 oz frozen lemon juice	8 oz water
6 oz strong tea	1 liter ginger ale

Boil water and sugar; add tea. Let cool. Add fruit juices. Chill thoroughly. Add ice water to make five quarts of liquid. When ready to serve add one cup fresh or glacé cherries and ginger ale. (Serves 30)

Time required in winter activities to expend calories
(in minutes)

holiday treat	cross-country skiing	downhill skiing	ice skating
fruitcake, 1/3-in slice (57 cal)	4–8	6–10	6–11
candy cane, 1 oz (109 cal)	7–15	11–18	11–22
peanut brittle, 1 oz (119 cal)	8–16	12–20	12–24
sugar cookie, 1 oz (126 cal)	8–17	13–21	13–25
fudge, 1 oz (130 cal)	9–17	13–22	13–26
eggnog, 15% alcohol, 1/2 cup (225 cal)	15–30	23–38	23–45
plum pudding, 2-in slice (270 cal)	18–36	27–45	27–54

person can consume slightly more. It has been established that when this recommended level is exceeded, various reactions occur. Some of the most common are a decrease in positive feelings, deterioration of physical coordination, increase in anxiety, reduction of emotional control, and increase in the possibility of hangover. Other factors affecting an individual's reaction to alcohol are the speed of drinking, metabolic rate, previous experiences with drinking, and foods consumed before, during, and after drinking.

Alcohol enters the bloodstream within minutes of consumption. A typical drink—for example, a can of beer (12 oz of 4½% alcohol), a glass of table wine (5 oz of 12% alcohol), or a shot (1½ oz) of 80-proof whiskey or vodka—generally takes at least an hour to be metabolized by the body. When alcohol is consumed faster than it is metabolized, it accumulates, and progressively higher levels of it are measured in the blood.

Since holiday-inspired imbibing can be such a problem, people should heed the following: (1) Do not drink too fast or too much. (2) Know what you are drinking. Some drinks have a greater amount of alcohol than others. (3) Eat before and while you are drinking, because eating retards absorption of alcohol in the bloodstream. Consume milk about an hour before drinking, as it helps to coat the stomach, as do foods that contain fat, such as cheese and butter. Avoid high-salt foods, like peanuts and chips, because alcohol increases salt retention. Ingestion of excess salt is generally unhealthful; it contributes to high blood pressure, increased thirst, fluid buildup, and discomfort. (4) Know your limits. People respond differently to drinking. A frequent drinker may have a higher tolerance for the effects of alcohol and be better able to anticipate his or her reactions than an infrequent drinker. (5) Never drink to relieve stress or avoid problems. (6) Limit the amount of time spent drinking to one hour or less. It is wise to sip drinks or alternate them with nonalcoholic beverages. (7) When planning or acting as host of a social function, be sure to have fruit juices, soft drinks, and nonalcoholic beverages available, and encourage their consumption. It is also advisable to stop serving alcohol at least an hour before the festivities end. There are numerous alcohol alternatives, including commercial nonalcoholic wines, sparkling wines, and beers sold today. One can

also discover many creative recipes for nonalcoholic holiday punches, ciders, and nogs in most cookbooks and in newspapers around holiday times.

Finally, a most important measure for hosts of holiday festivities to follow is not to allow guests who are intoxicated to drive home. A special program that originated in Sweden, known as the designated driver system, is an excellent way of preventing alcohol-caused driving accidents, which are so high at holidays. With this system one willing and agreed-upon person refrains from drinking alcoholic beverages and is then depended upon by other celebrants to transport them home safely. At the next party a different person volunteers, and the responsibility is rotated. Sometimes designated drivers actually keep their car keys in empty beverage glasses to assure that they are not served.

An all-too-common way of "getting through" the holidays is to overindulge, but the price paid for overdoing it—eating, drinking, and celebrating too much—can be very dear indeed.

"The Cholic" by George Cruikshank, 1819; collection Worcester Art Museum, Worcester, Massachusetts, Samuel B. Woodward Collection

Holiday eating. For most people exercising self-control is extremely difficult, because eating special foods is an inherent part of virtually all holiday festivities. Attempts at self-discipline, although difficult, are worthwhile, especially if indigestion, weight gain, and other consequences are to be prevented. Maintaining or increasing exercise programs is important during times of increased caloric intake and activities that are more sedentary than usual. Even taking short walks can be mentally and physically beneficial.

It is helpful to realize that part of holiday upheaval is caused by changes in routine that involve changes in eating patterns. Although some people try to diet before a holiday so that weight gain can be avoided, these attempts are often unsuccessful. Happily, when routines are reestablished, people generally regain control over their lives, and excessive eating and drinking decline.

Nutrition and health publications offer suggestions and recipes for those who are health and weight conscious. In cooking a holiday meal it is possible to use ingredients that are low in fats, cholesterol, salt, sugar, and calories in quite creative and innovative ways. In fact, with the foods and recipes that are readily available today, the possibilities are endless. For example, a traditional Thanksgiving or Christmas turkey dinner can be healthful as well as festive. A three-ounce serving of white meat without the skin has only 163 calories. Moreover, turkey is relatively low in saturated fats. Gravy should be skipped, but low-fat versions can be substituted. Salad and vegetables can be enjoyed as long as heavy dressings and butter are limited or eliminated. In pumpkin pie, evaporated skim milk can be substituted, and three egg whites used instead of whole eggs. Pie can be topped with low-fat whipped toppings rather than whipped cream.

Food contamination. Platters of delicious foods, frequently served in elaborate fashion, are certainly part of holiday festivities. If improperly stored or prepared, some of these foods can become contaminated and cause discomfort or illness.

The following are good safeguards that will prevent food-borne illness from spoiling your holiday feast: (1) When purchasing frozen foods, be sure that they have been stored below the "frostline" marked on the commercial freezer. (2) Select meat or poultry at the end of the shopping excursion, and put them in the freezer immediately upon returning home. (3) Always thaw meat and poultry in the refrigerator, never at room temperature, because bacteria can grow on unrefrigerated meat and poultry. Allow sufficient time for thawing. (4) Stuff poultry immediately before placing it in the oven, never the night before. (5) Use a meat thermometer to assure that every part of the poultry is heated to at least 74° C (165° F). (6) Refrigerate leftovers immediately after the meal is finished. It is not necessary to cool hot foods before refrigerating them. (7) Refrigerator temperature should be 7° C (45° F) or below, and the refrigerator should be properly defrosted so that cooling coils are in proper working condition.

Indigestion and related disorders. Indigestion is a broad term that is applied to the discomfort caused by overindulgence in food and/or drink. Heartburn is a feeling of burning or warmth that usually develops in the area of the lower half of the breastbone. Heartburn is caused by swallowing something that causes a burning sensation in the esophagus, or by the backup, for various reasons, of stomach acid. The most common cause is overeating, but garlic, onions, and mint have been identified as specific factors in its development. Additional actions that can cause heartburn are lying down within two or three hours after a heavy meal or inhaling too much air, which causes problems when the air reaches the stomach.

Moderated intake of food and drink is the best way to prevent these kinds of stomach and digestive disorders. If symptoms do develop, one should avoid any medications containing aspirin, as well as avoiding smoking, caffeine, alcohol, and all kinds of pepper. These substances increase secretion of stomach acid and thus intensify discomfort. If discomfort is prolonged or severe, it may be necessary to consult a physician.

A last word on surviving

Depending on the circumstances and the individuals involved, people have various ways of dealing with the problematic aspects of holiday times. Sometimes holidays create so much stress that people feel deep relief when they have passed. There are no simple solutions for coping with holiday-triggered upheaval. Essentially, everyone has to determine his or her own method of handling the anxieties and pressures.

Not having overly high expectations, eating and drinking moderately, taking time to get proper rest, and not hesitating to seek help if one feels desperate or unable to cope may be obvious suggestions, but they are nonetheless practical ways of getting through what can be very trying or melancholy times. Some people avoid the impact of "at home" or family activities by taking trips, and others withdraw and limit their social engagements, but most people just "grin and bear" the experiences, hoping that the time will be pleasurable.

Here is how Evelyn Gresham in the novel *Crewe Train* coped: "The seasonable crowds in the streets did indeed get on her nerves and tire her physically and mentally, so she came home after each day's shopping a disintegrated wreck, but she remained a happy wreck."

Gastrointestinal Polyps

by Harvey J. Dworken, M.D.

Gastrointestinal polyps are localized growths, or tumors, on the mucous membranes that line the stomach and intestines. Polyps are quite variable in size and may be either attached by a broad base to the underlying tissue (sessile polyps) or suspended from the intestinal wall by a thin strand, or pedicle, of elongated but otherwise normal mucosa (pedunculated polyps). Polyps may appear in any portion of the gastrointestinal tract, but they are more common in the stomach than in the esophagus or small intestine and most common of all in the large intestine, or colon. Their incidence increases with aging, and it is estimated that among the U.S. population nearly 10% of people over age 40 have at least one polyp in the final 25 cm (10 in) of the large bowel.

Single polyps are usually random in occurrence, while multiple polyps often have an underlying hereditary cause or are associated with a preexisting inflammatory disease, such as ulcerative colitis or Crohn's disease. There are two major kinds of intestinal polyps, neoplastic (*i.e.,* characterized by abnormal growth) and nonneoplastic. This is an important distinction; only neoplastic polyps are believed to have the potential to become cancerous.

Kinds of polyps

Nonneoplastic polyps. Nonneoplastic polyps are divided into three groups: inflammatory, hamartomatous, and metaplastic. Inflammatory polyps rarely exist singly; they occur in areas of acute or chronic inflammation of the mucous membranes (mucosa) and usually result from dilation of mucosal glands and tissue swelling caused by the presence of inflammatory cells. Hamartomatous polyps, or hamartomas, are combinations of tissues that normally appear in the bowel but in other than normal relationships to one another. They are usually caused by the development of smooth muscle cells between glands in the mucosa. Despite the existence of these unusual cell groupings, the lining (epithelial) cells of the mucosa are normal,

and they appear to have no potential to become malignant. Hamartomas may become quite large at times, up to 3–4 cm (1.2–1.6 in) in diameter, and can appear in the stomach, small intestine, or colon.

A hereditary disorder, Peutz-Jeghers syndrome, has been described in which numerous hamartomatous polyps appear, particularly in the small intestine. They may lead to abdominal pain, intestinal obstruction, and bleeding, and their numbers may increase greatly over time. Patients with this disorder also have numerous small deposits of black pigment in their mouths and on their gums and lips. Hamartomas also appear in a rare, nonhereditary, and often fatal syndrome called generalized gastrointestinal polyposis (Cronkhite-Canada syndrome), which generally occurs in persons over age 60. The features include multiple hamartomas of the stomach and colon, areas of brown pigmentation on the face and upper body, anemia, loss of weight, hair loss, changes in fingernails and toenails, and diarrhea and abdominal pain.

Metaplastic polyps are usually quite small, rarely larger than 0.5 cm (0.2 in) in diameter, and appear primarily in the rectum. They are very common in people over age 55, appear to result from delayed degeneration and sloughing of mucosal cells with resulting enlargement of glandular structures, and rarely cause any symptoms.

Neoplastic polyps. Neoplastic polyps are also called adenomatous, or glandular, polyps. Microscopic examination of the tissue reveals the cellular changes clearly indicative of a breakdown in the normal growth-regulation process. Despite these cellular changes, adenomatous polyps do not usually become malignant. In fact, the percentage of adenomatous polyps that do develop into cancer is probably quite small. What is known is that their incidence increases with aging, that they grow slowly, and that the larger ones—more than 3 cm (1.2 in) in diameter—are the most likely to become malignant if they are not removed. In most patients adenomatous polyps occur singly,

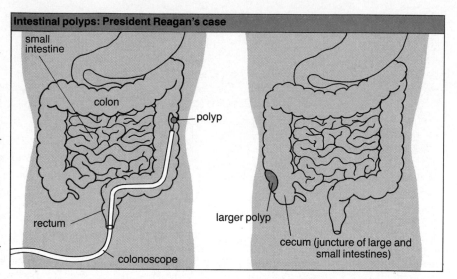

Intestinal polyps: President Reagan's case

small intestine

colon

polyp

rectum

colonoscope

larger polyp

cecum (juncture of large and small intestines)

In July 1985 U.S. Pres. Ronald Reagan underwent colonoscopic surgery for removal of a small polyp from the lower portion of his colon. During the procedure doctors discovered another, larger growth, previously undetected, that required major surgery. The incident heightened public awareness of the potential danger of this relatively common condition and the importance of early detection.

but the likelihood that others will develop at a later date is great.

Adenomatous polyps are further subdivided into three classes, tubular, villous, and tubulovillous, based on their microscopic characteristics. Tubular adenomas are characterized primarily by dilation and enlargement of epithelial glands, while villous adenomas consist of frondlike exaggerations of supporting tissue without prominent glandular enlargement. Tubulovillous adenomas show characteristics of both types. Villous adenomas are more commonly sessile than pedunculated and carry a greater malignant potential than do tubular varieties. They may grow to extremely large sizes, even up to several centimeters in diameter.

While there is no certainty about the causes of cancer of the colon, it is clear that many colon cancers, and probably stomach cancers as well, commence as adenomatous polyps. In fact, many largely benign (*i.e.*, noncancerous) polyps are found on examination to contain localized areas of cancer, while some definitely cancerous polyps contain limited areas that are microscopically benign. Furthermore, surgical specimens of colon cancer often contain one or more satellite benign polyps in their vicinity. There is also a tendency for both random intestinal polyps and colon cancer to occur more often in some families than in others. Removal of polyps, followed by regular follow-up examinations, has been shown to reduce significantly the incidence of colon cancer in large population groups. This evidence supports the view that polyps are likely precursors of colon cancer.

Clear genetic inheritance of the tendency to develop multiple adenomatous polyps (polyposis) of the colon has been described in several uncommon syndromes. One of these is familial polyposis, a dominantly inherited disorder in which, by the time an affected individual reaches the age of 40, the colon has become the site of literally hundreds of adenomatous polyps. The

incidence of cancer is extremely high. Patients with this condition—and their children—must be examined regularly, and all polyps must be removed immediately, usually by surgical removal of involved portions of the colon rather than by simply removing the polyps. Another disorder, known as Gardner's syndrome, also shows dominant inheritance. There are fewer polyps in the colon than in familial polyposis, but growths with a malignant potential may also be found in the small intestine. Patients with Gardner's syndrome also have benign bone and skin tumors and commonly have a tendency to develop cysts in their jaws. In Turcot syndrome, a recessive disorder, patients suffer from both colonic adenomas and malignant tumors of the brain or spinal cord.

Signs and symptoms

Obvious traces of blood in the stool are probably the most common symptom of colonic polyps. If the polyp is located in the stomach or small intestine, however, the blood may be invisible (occult) because it has become mixed with the stool and can be detected only by chemical tests of the feces. Where polyps are large and on lengthy pedicles, they may be pulled by normal intestinal movement, eventually leading to bouts of partial intestinal obstruction manifested by cramps and abdominal distention. Occasionally patients with polyps in the lower colon may notice changes in their bowel habits and a tendency toward less complete evacuations than usual, often with mucus in the stool.

Diagnosis

For the most part, intestinal polyps cause no symptoms at all and are most effectively detected through screening programs for people at greatest risk. Such screening is usually initiated between ages 40 and 50. Healthy people over the age of 40 should probably have annual rectal examinations and at least one test per year for occult fecal blood. Tests for occult blood come in kit form and can be used at home with no inconvenience to the patient. Most tests call for several small stool samples, taken from three or four consecutive bowel movements. The samples are smeared on a card that contains a chemical fixative. The card comes with a special envelope in which it can be returned by mail to the physician or hospital laboratory. The test for occult blood is not always accurate, however, as various factors can cause false-positive results (*i.e.,* indicate the presence of disease in someone who is healthy), and false-negative results also occur in some cases. For these reasons this test is usually used in conjunction with a physical exam.

Examination of the rectum and lower colon with a sigmoidoscope, an instrument that allows the physician to view the colonic mucosa, is also recommended. If two consecutive annual sigmoidoscopic exams are negative, the procedure need not be repeated for four to five years. If polyps are found, however, or if the stool test is positive for occult blood—and remains positive even when the patient eliminates red meat from the diet, one source of false-positive results—a barium X-ray examination of the entire colon should be performed in order to see if other polyps are present or to determine the source of the bleeding. The introduction of a small amount of air (air insufflation) into the barium-filled rectum enhances the contrast and increases the amount of detail the radiologist is able to see.

Some physicians would recommend colonoscopy instead of X-rays. This is an examination of the entire colon by means of a 1.8-m (6-ft)-long fiber-optic instrument that is passed through the rectum into the uppermost portions of the colon. It is true that colonoscopy is more accurate than radiologic studies; in addition, the colonoscope accommodates a wire snare that can be used to remove some kinds of polyps. However, many physicians feel that the expense and trouble of a colonoscopy are not justified unless previous X-ray studies have detected a polyp or other suspicious lesion; this judgment relies upon the fact that significant polyps and tumors are unlikely to be overlooked when a barium enema with air insufflation is performed by an experienced radiologist.

In instances where the barium enema and colonoscopy do not detect the cause of occult bleeding, and the bleeding continues, barium X-ray studies of the esophagus, stomach, and small intestine should be undertaken. Endoscopy (interior visualization) of the upper gastrointestinal tract is indicated if the X-rays do not reveal the probable source of the bleeding.

When a patient has had one or more benign polyps removed, and the remainder of the colon is found to be free of polyps, annual examination of the stools for occult blood should be continued throughout the patient's lifetime. Colonoscopy is repeated a year after the original surgery. If no new polyps are found at this time, the patient is probably safe to revert to the previously described program of two consecutive annual sigmoidoscopic exams, followed by a sigmoidoscopy every four or five years. If this plan is followed carefully and consistently, patients are most unlikely to develop cancer of the colon.

Patients who have had a previous colon cancer should be reexamined annually by colonoscopy for five consecutive years to make certain that the cancer has not recurred and that new polyps have not developed at any other sites. If no new problems have appeared by the end of the five-year period, these patients may revert to the surveillance program recommended for all healthy adults.

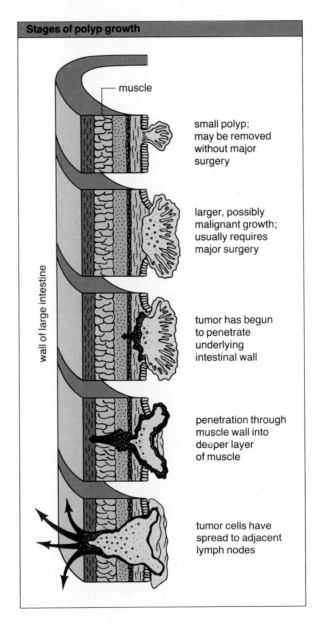

Stages of polyp growth

wall of large intestine

muscle

small polyp; may be removed without major surgery

larger, possibly malignant growth; usually requires major surgery

tumor has begun to penetrate underlying intestinal wall

penetration through muscle wall into deeper layer of muscle

tumor cells have spread to adjacent lymph nodes

Treatment

Once polyps have been diagnosed by X-ray or visual examination, they should be removed, especially if they are larger than 1–2 cm (0.4–0.8 in) in diameter. In most cases removal can be accomplished during colonoscopy or upper gastrointestinal endoscopy, fairly uncomplicated procedures that can be performed with the patient under mild sedation. Neither process requires hospitalization, and both can be completed within 60–90 minutes.

In patients with colonic polyps, the colonoscope is passed upward through the rectum until the site of the polyp is reached. A wire loop snare is then passed around the base of a sessile polyp or around the pedicle of a pedunculated polyp. The loop is tightened, and a low-voltage electrical current is passed through it, separating the polyp from the intestinal wall. The polyp is retrieved and sent to the pathologist for microscopic examination. With this method as many as five or six polyps can be removed during a single procedure. Polyps are removed from the stomach with an upper gastrointestinal endoscope by a similar procedure. Polyps in the small intestine below the duodenum cannot be reached with present-day instruments and can be removed only by means of open abdominal surgery.

Essentially, any patient whose heart and lung functions are stable can undergo the procedure. The risks of endoscopic polypectomy are small. People who are taking anticoagulant medications (blood thinners) should discontinue them several days before the operation, and patients with advanced liver disease should have their blood-clotting functions checked beforehand. If bleeding occurs during the procedure, it usually ceases spontaneously within a few minutes. When bleeding persists, electric cautery with the tip of the wire snare is usually adequate to coagulate the bleeding point. Perforation of the stomach or colon during cauterization, especially in the case of large sessile polyps, is a rare complication and one that is almost never encountered by an experienced endoscopist. Where this complication does occur, however, especially if it is the colon that is perforated, open abdominal surgery is required to close the puncture site because of the danger of bacterial infection of the peritoneal cavity (peritonitis).

Under ideal circumstances pathological examination of excised tissue will reveal that the entire polyp has been removed by endoscopic polypectomy. Where this is not the case, as with some sessile polyps, another endoscopy to relocate the site of the polyp and to remove all remaining abnormal tissue is required. When pathological examination reveals cancer in excised sessile polyps, it is essential that open abdominal surgery be performed to remove the colonic or gastric segment in which the polyp was located, a procedure known as surgical resection. Anything less than resection will not provide complete assurance that all cancer tissue has been eliminated. However, if cancerous changes are found in a pedunculated polyp and the stalk of the polyp contains no malignant cells, it is not necessary to perform a surgical resection; the absence of cancer in the stalk provides assurance that the malignancy is confined entirely to the polyp itself.

Today, with so many questions being asked regarding the costs and effectiveness of medical care, and with prepayment being chosen by increasing numbers of people, it seems relevant to ask what sort of screening programs should be adopted for identifying and removing intestinal polyps at the earliest possible stage. On the one hand, it is known that many cancers of the colon and stomach progress to a surgically incurable state without causing any notable symptoms; on the other hand, it is equally well known that the assiduous search for and routine removal of polyps is costly in terms of time and money and is likely to detect many growths that never will become malignant. Thus, while the neglect of symptoms is certainly unwise, the indiscriminate endoscopic hunt for polyps in the population at large is probably equally misguided.

The general recommendations of the American Cancer Society on prevention of colon cancer probably represent the most prudent course. They call for all healthy people over age 40 to have their stools checked annually or biennially for occult blood, which is the most common manifestation of significant polyps. A rectal examination and a sigmoidoscopic exam every year or two are also recommended, as the largest proportion of colonic polyps and cancers of the colon occur in the lower segment of the bowel (although statistics show that more and more growths are appearing in the upper portions of the intestines, beyond the reach of the sigmoidoscope). Certain people—for example, those with chronic ulcerative colitis or those who have had previous colon cancers—should be examined more often since they are at greater risk.

Shyness

by Jonathan M. Cheek, Ph.D.

Shyness is the tendency to feel tense, worried, or awkward in social situations. Almost everyone has felt somewhat shy at one time or another. Some people experience problems with shyness so frequently and intensely that this characteristic defines an important part of their personality and affects much of their behavior. Shyness is a problem for a surprisingly large number of people in many parts of the world. According to several surveys, for example, almost 40% of the people in the United States consider themselves to be shy.

Not only is shyness a common problem, but it is also an important one. Human beings are social animals; virtually everything done, said, and thought about is either focused directly on social interactions or shaped profoundly by them. Shyness can create barriers to satisfaction in love, work, play, and friendship. Fortunately, understanding the psychology of shyness can help people overcome these difficulties.

There are some people who prefer to spend time alone rather than with others but who also feel comfortable in social settings. These people are "nonanxious introverts." They may be unsociable, but they are not shy. The problem for truly shy people is that their anxiety prevents them from participating in social life when they want or need to.

Even the shyest person does not feel inhibited and anxious all of the time. Certain situations provoke much stronger reactions than others. Shy people have the most difficulty when meeting strangers and entering unfamiliar surroundings. They are painfully self-conscious when they are the focus of attention in a large group or when they are being evaluated in an interview. In these situations the shy person wants to impress others but doubts that he or she will be able to do so. Under these circumstances, the shy person may become so self-preoccupied that he becomes unable to carry on an effective conversation.

Symptoms

Shyness symptoms fall into three categories: feelings, thoughts, and behaviors. Typically, the emotional arousal of shyness is experienced as a general feeling of tension or nervousness. Some shy people also experience specific physiological manifestations of emo-

tional distress; these may include an upset stomach, dry mouth, pounding heart, sweating, blushing, the urge to urinate, or even dizziness. The disturbing impact of these physical symptoms is made worse by the shy person's belief that his or her discomfort is visible to others. Shy people feel afraid, and their strongest fears concern being ridiculed or rejected by others.

Other shyness symptoms are revealed in the thoughts that people have about themselves and others. During social interactions shy people become excessively self-conscious. Rather than participating in the conversation, they talk silently to themselves. Thoughts such as "Why can't I ever think of anything clever to say?" or "She must think I'm really stupid" distract the shy person from paying attention to what others are saying. When they do think about other people, it is in terms of what others are thinking about them; the shy person is preoccupied with worries about being evaluated negatively. Typically, shy people are extremely self-critical, and they expect others to be critical of them as well.

The most easily observed signs of shyness are the behavioral symptoms. Shy people are rarely talkative, and their reticence is most noticeable around strangers and casual acquaintances. When they do speak, shy people avoid arguments and are reluctant to express strong personal opinions. They often show their social discomfort with awkward "body language," gestures such as nervously tugging at their hair or clothing. If they are unable to maintain physical distance by keeping in the background at social gatherings, shy people will try to avoid making eye contact when they do come face to face with others.

Although the feelings, thoughts, and behaviors that are symptomatic of shyness frequently occur together, few shy people experience all of these with equal intensity. Anyone who has persistent problems with at least one category of symptoms can be considered to be a shy person.

Childhood shyness

What causes an individual to become shy? The answers to this question may vary depending on when a particular person first experienced problems with shyness. About half of shy adults report that they have

Actress Carol Burnett, known for her uninhibited comic routines, is one of many performers who claim to be comfortable "in character" but shy in private life.

been shy since early childhood, whereas the other half identify their later childhood and adolescence as the time shyness first appeared. In the case of early-developing shyness, genetic and physiological factors may play a part. Genetically identical twins are significantly more similar to each other in their degree of shyness than are fraternal twins, who, like other siblings, share an average of only 50% of their genes. If one of a pair of identical twins is shy, the other also is likely to be shy—even when they grow up in different environments. This conclusion does not mean that shyness is predetermined by inheritance, or that it cannot be overcome, but simply that some people are born more susceptible to becoming shy than are others.

Studies of infants who are shy and fearful when encountering strangers show that these babies respond physiologically, with unusually high heart rates, to such situations. This observation indicates that the physiological component of early-developing shyness involves having a particularly sensitive nervous system. About 15% of infants exhibit this special sensitivity to stress reactions, and follow-up studies have found that, by the time they start kindergarten, they often are described by their mothers as being shy children. Seventy percent of college students who describe themselves as having been shy in early childhood report that they still have problems with shyness. These findings indicate that when fearful shyness is part of an infant's earliest responses to the environment, it is likely to endure as a characteristic of the adult personality. Early-developing shyness can be overcome, but it usually does not fade away all by itself.

Adolescent shyness

The situation is quite different for the late-developing type of shyness that plagues many adolescents. This form usually first appears between ages 10 and 14 and is caused by the adjustment problems normally involved in the transition from childhood to adolescence. The young adolescent must contend with three major sources of stress: the bodily changes of puberty, the newly acquired ability to think abstractly about the self and the environment, and new demands and opportunities resulting from changing social roles. All of these changes can make adolescents feel intensely self-conscious, as if everyone is watching and judging them, so it is not surprising that more than half of young teenagers describe themselves as shy. For more than 60% of the young people who first experience shyness as adolescents, however, the problem has disappeared by the time they reach age 20. Thus, for many young people adolescent shyness is often no more than a temporarily awkward phase in the process of growing up.

Why are some shy adolescents unable to outgrow the problem? Several factors contribute to the persistence of late-developing shyness. The timing of puberty can intensify the pressures of the adolescent experience; early-maturing girls and late-maturing boys suffer the most severe social adjustment problems with their peers. Moving to a new neighborhood or school can disrupt the development of social skills, which are most easily practiced in safe and familiar surroundings. In addition, shy adolescents need to experience positive social relationships in order to increase their self-esteem. If parents, siblings, teachers, or peers tease and embarrass the shy adolescent, he or she may develop the self-image of being an unworthy and unlikable person. The opposite extreme—neglect rather than unwanted attention—can have equally negative consequences. Shy people suffer when they feel that they are receiving either too much or too little attention from others.

Cultural influences

Cultural factors also contribute to the development and persistence of problems with shyness. In the U.S. and many societies, shyness is generally considered to be a feminine characteristic, and it is more socially acceptable for a girl to be shy than for a boy. During the early childhood years, parents are likely to invest time and effort in helping a son become less inhibited or less timid because these traits are not considered to be masculine; at the same time, they may not regard similar signs of shyness as undesirable in a daughter. Furthermore, the adolescent years put different sets of pressures on girls and boys. In the U.S. and many European countries, television and popular magazines emphasize physical beauty and poise as the image of the ideal woman. Not surprisingly, teenage girls experience more symptoms of self-conscious shyness, such as doubts about their attractiveness and worries about what others think of them, than do boys. On the other hand, because the traditional male role requires initiative and assertiveness in social contacts, the burden of shyness as a behavioral problem appears to be especially severe for adolescent boys. Although the pressures on shy boys are different from the pressures on shy girls, both groups are negatively affected.

Several aspects of contemporary U.S. culture make life more difficult for the shy person. Increased geographic mobility, high divorce rates, and the dissolution of extended family networks are now such pervasive trends that sociologists have called the United States "a nation of strangers." Of course, meeting strangers is the most difficult social situation of all for shy people. In addition, American values also emphasize competition, individual achievement, and material success. It is not surprising, then, that the shy person finds it hard to feel secure and worthwhile in the face of these pressures to excel.

Cross-cultural comparisons

According to surveys conducted in the 1970s, at least three countries have significantly lower rates of shyness than the United States: South Korea, the Philippines, and Israel. South Koreans report the lowest level of shyness of any population that has been surveyed. Korean culture encourages the individual expression of opinions, with the result that Koreans generally enjoy conversation and tend to be more talkative than Americans. In the Philippines children grow up in an extended network of kinship relationships that is maintained and expanded by oral communication. Because their families emphasize communication skills, it is not surprising that Filipinos perceive themselves as outgoing people and report relatively low levels of shyness. In Israel children are praised for being self-confident and often are included in adult conversations, two factors that may account for the low level of shyness reported by Israeli test subjects.

In Japan, on the other hand, the incidence of shyness is much higher than in the United States. Japanese culture values harmony and encourages passive dependence and silent loyalty to one's superiors. Talkative or assertive individuals are considered immature or insincere. The Japanese also tend to be concerned with avoiding the shame of failure. All of these values promote shyness.

These same cultural differences also are reflected within the ethnic subcultures of U.S. society. Among U.S. college students, Japanese-Americans rank as the most shy and students of Jewish background as the least shy. It is clear that, in addition to genetic factors and personal developmental patterns, broad cultural values operate to either promote or diminish the prevalence of shyness.

Consequences

Loneliness is the most obvious undesirable consequence of shyness. Shy children have fewer playmates; shy teenagers date less often; and shy adults report themselves less satisfied with the quality of their social relationships, compared with those who are not shy. Forming and maintaining friendships requires a certain amount of initiative, yet the shy person fears rejection and is reluctant to reach out to others. As a result, shy people may remain painfully isolated, while others are likely to interpret their quietness and withdrawal as unfriendliness or even arrogance. The poet Alfred, Lord Tennyson, expressed this paradoxical dilemma eloquently: "Shy she was, and I thought her cold." By passively keeping in the background, shy people cut themselves off from the very rewards of social life they so desperately desire.

Shyness is also a barrier to fulfilling one's academic and economic potential. In school shy students are likely to avoid contributing to classroom discussions, hesitate to seek help from teachers and advisers, even when they are having trouble, and often develop a negative attitude toward formal education. Ultimately, their passive and conforming approach to fulfilling educational requirements may block the flowering of their creativity.

Upon graduation, shy persons discover that looking for work presents new problems. Job interviews bring them into contact with strangers and appeal to their fears of being negatively evaluated. They tend to avoid high-paying careers that require oral communication skill, such as sales and management. In approaching all aspects of life, including their careers, shy people

For former U.S. president Jimmy Carter, his career in politics and public life depended on overcoming his natural tendency toward shyness.

AP/Wide World

hesitate to take risks; they do not "play to win"—they play not to lose.

The most private consequence of shyness is its effect on the person's self-concept. Shy people come to expect that they will not be successful in social situations, and this expectation may become a self-fulfilling prophecy. If they fail at something, they blame it on their own inadequacy. Yet when they succeed, shy people attribute the results to luck; they are unable to accept personal credit for the positive outcome. Likewise, shy people often doubt that compliments paid to them by others are sincere, yet they have an excellent memory for negative comments or embarrassing events. Unbiased observers of shy people rate them higher on physical attractiveness and social skills than the shy people rate themselves. This negative bias in self-perceptions perpetuates the poor self-image and discourages shy persons from believing that they can overcome their timidity.

Positive consequences

Shyness is not always an entirely negative quality. For example, a study of married couples found that shy people often were described favorably by their spouses as being modest, sincere, and patient.

Shyness has motivated some people to develop the more introspective aspects of their natures; examples are the philosopher Jean-Jacques Rousseau and the novelist Stendhal. Others have learned to cope with their shyness as they rose to prominence in public life; in contemporary U.S. society former president Jimmy Carter, television host Johnny Carson, and actress Carol Burnett are notable examples of this phenomenon. It is clear that shyness does not necessarily ruin a person's life, but becoming less shy can improve the quality of that life.

Therapies

A small minority of shy people suffer so much anxiety in social situations that they habitually avoid almost all contact with other people. These extremely shy persons are diagnosed as having social phobia and, in order to overcome these fears, they usually require professional help. However, most people's experience with shyness falls within the normal range of individual differences in personality characteristics. Nonetheless, the majority of shy people do consider their timidity to be a personal problem and say that they would like to receive help in becoming more socially self-confident. This may explain the popularity of books and magazine articles that promise help in coping with shyness.

Different treatment approaches focus on each of the three categories of shyness symptoms: feelings, thoughts, and behaviors. Relaxation training is used to teach shy people to reduce the intensity of their emotional distress and physical arousal in social situations. In a typical relaxation exercise, the subjects are instructed to breathe slowly and deeply while they vividly imagine being in a situation that makes them mildly anxious; for example, saying hello to a casual acquaintance. When they are able to remain relaxed while thinking about this situation, they gradually move on to imagine increasingly difficult encounters. Eventually each individual arrives at his or her most stressful situation, such as inviting an attractive member of the opposite sex to a party or asking for a raise. By repeatedly practicing this imaging technique, the people learn to feel calm in the presence of others.

Other therapies have been designed to modify the way shy people think about themselves. They are encouraged to change what they say to themselves during social interactions. Negative thoughts, such as "I sound stupid. I don't have anything to say," are replaced with positive statements, such as "So far, so good; continue to speak slowly and ask questions." This strategy helps shy people to become less preoccupied with themselves and to show more interest in others. Shy people also need to learn that their self-perceptions are unrealistically negative, that they are their own worst critics. As they practice taking a positive approach to thinking about themselves, they grow increasingly self-confident.

Once a shy person feels more calm and confident, he or she may still need to learn how to talk and act effectively in social situations. Social skills training focuses on the behavioral symptoms of shyness. The first step is to get shy people to set realistic goals for their own social performance. For example, if a shy man wanted to ask a woman he sees at work out on a date, his first goal might be to have a brief conversation with her about some work-related topic. Before speaking to her, he would practice the conversation with a friend or a counselor. For their second conversation, he would plan to talk about something a little more personal and would again rehearse what he was going to say. After several such conversations, he would be ready to ask her for a date.

Overcoming shyness: one step at a time

The lesson here is that shy people should move forward step by step, gradually taking more risks in social encounters. Persistence and practice are essential for the development of social skills. Shy people also should realize that they need not take all the responsibility for any social failure they might encounter. Sometimes another person is unresponsive for reasons that have nothing to do with the shy person. Sometimes the other person may be shy, too.

Psychological research has demonstrated that these treatment approaches are often successful in changing the feelings, thoughts, and behaviors of shy people. Shyness *can* be overcome, and the formerly shy person *can* enjoy a rewarding social life.

Coping with Spinal Cord Injury

by Thomas O. Brackett, M.D.,
and Kevin M. Kindelan, Ph.D.

The plight of the victim of a spinal cord injury was described in grim but eloquent terms by the English physician Sir William Asher in 1947: "Picture the pathetic patient lying long abed, the urine leaking from his distended bladder, the lime draining from his bones, the blood clotting in his veins, . . . the spirit evaporating from his soul."

Much has changed in the outlook for such patients in the past 40 years, and many lead such active and productive lives that the adjective pathetic is hardly applicable. Nor do victims of spinal cord injury linger long "abed" as did the invalids of old. Many raise families and pursue challenging careers, and many are active in organizations that provide support for others struggling to become similarly independent.

Incidence and outlook

There are about 150,000–170,000 people with traumatic spinal cord injuries in the U.S. today; their number can be expected to increase by about 10,000 each year. The rate of incidence in other industrial countries is about the same as that in the U.S.—40 for every one million people—and other statistical data are also comparable. In simple terms, roughly half of all spinal cord injuries result from road accidents, a quarter from falls and shallow-water diving, and the rest from gunshots, stabbings, and other such wounds. Half of the victims are under the age of 25; 80% are male, and 80% are under the influence of alcohol and/or other drugs at the time of injury. Half are paralyzed from the waist down (paraplegic), half from the neck down (quadriplegic). The typical victim of a spinal cord injury is, therefore, a previously healthy young man, suddenly struck down by a devastating accident.

In the 1940s the average life expectancy of a victim of spinal cord injury was three years, and the initial mortality was more than 50%. The medical treatment of such injuries has improved significantly, however, and, with modern treatment, those who survive the initial injury may expect to live to within 90% of their actuarially predicted life-span.

Adjustment

The adjustment to life after spinal cord injury would be difficult for a person of any age, whether male or female. But the fact that most victims are young and male raises some particularly hard issues. Typically, the victim is someone who, up to the time of the injury, has been physically, socially, and sexually active.

There is no period of gradual restriction of activities, as in progressive degenerative diseases that result in eventual paralysis, but rather a single incident that results in a drastic disruption of all the patient's activities and expectations. Many victims of spinal cord injury are, temporarily or permanently, confined to a wheelchair, which drastically limits their scope of activity. Furthermore, going about in public in a wheelchair inevitably elicits a certain amount of undue attention, inappropriate staring, and other self-conscious behavior on the part of onlookers. Because some friends of the injured person may be unwilling—or simply unable—to accept this situation, a narrowing of social ties may accompany the reduction in physical mobility.

If the injured person's self-esteem has depended principally on the external rewards of social, sexual, and physical achievement, a spinal cord injury will have a devastating impact on the individual's feelings of self-worth. The adjustment process then becomes one of redefining the parameters of self-worth as well as those of the physically accessible world.

Family and friends can be helpful or harmful in the adjustment process. Harmful interventions include both expecting too much from the injured person and expecting too little. Both excessive expectations that the injured person will fulfill the same roles as he did prior to the injury and assumptions that he will perform none of the same roles and have no demands

501

Courtesy, Spinal Injury Awareness, Florida

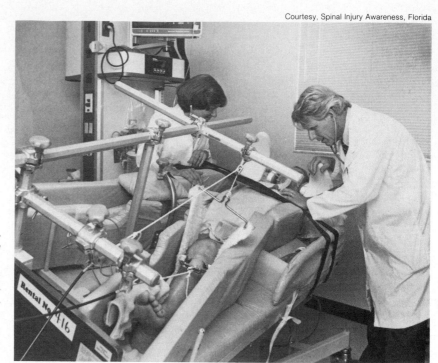

Technological advances have revolutionized the care of the spinal cord injured. This cushioned, rotating bed—designed to prevent the complications that often come with immobilization—like other equipment necessary for acute care, may appear formidable to both patient and family if they do not fully understand its function.

placed on him are equally debilitating. For example, the father who is paralyzed should be expected to continue to function in his parental role; a decision to the contrary could be more crippling than the injury itself. Ideally, helpful interventions on the part of family and friends strike a balance between too much caring and too little.

The initial shock

When they arrive at the hospital emergency room, half of the victims of spinal cord injuries have additional serious injuries to the head, chest, or abdomen, which require immediate treatment. If the spine is broken, it must be stabilized to prevent further injury; in the case of a broken neck, it may be necessary to fasten a metal device to the patient's skull with screws in order that traction can be applied. After all major injuries have been attended to, the patient will be moved to the intensive care unit on a kinetic treatment table—this is a cushioned, motorized bed, which, by maintaining a constant cradlelike rocking motion, helps to prevent pressure sores and other complications that beset the bedridden patient. All necessary intravenous lines and catheters are then set up, along with the equipment needed to monitor the patient's vital functions.

For the victim—and the family, as well—the initial shock of the injury is compounded by the number and complexity of the devices needed for stabilization and support. In terms of emotional care, the first task of the physician and other members of the treatment team is to explain in detail what is being done and why. Both the patient and the family usually have great

difficulty comprehending exactly what has happened. With little or no knowledge of anatomy or physiology, they may ask repeatedly for explanations about damaged nerves, paralysis of muscles, and the need for tubes to drain the bladder or keep the airway clear. The job of the treatment team is to offer lucid explanations as patiently as possible—and as often as may be necessary.

Much has been written in recent years about the

Darryl Stingley, formerly a professional football player, was paralyzed from the neck down in an accident on the playing field. His courage and determination have been an inspiration to other victims of spinal cord injury.

Focus on Sports

The state of Florida has an active program to prevent spinal cord injuries. The "Feet First" emblem, used on T-shirts, buttons, and warning signs, is part of the state's campaign to alert people to the danger of shallow-water diving.

depersonalizing effect of hospitalization and the importance for the patient of retaining essential human dignity. For the patient with a spinal cord injury, who may be dependent upon strangers for the most intimate aspects of personal care, these are crucial issues. Both the family and the treatment team must allow the patient to be involved in decision making about his care insofar as is possible. This is a vital element in maintaining the patient's already shaken sense of self-esteem. To depersonalize the patient by talking about or speaking for him, as if he were mentally as well as physically incapacitated, is further to deprive him of respect. The person who feeds the patient, whether a nurse, aide, or family member, can communicate respect by sitting beside the patient, on his level, and by allowing plenty of time for the meal. Hospital staff, family members, and others visiting the patient can communicate their respect by announcing their presence before entering the room, by conversing with the patient at his own level, rather than looking down, and by making frequent eye contact.

The "normal" reaction

For the victim, the initial shock and emotional numbness will give way to intense feelings of anger, sadness, confusion, fear, denial, and/or hopelessness. Severe depression and a desire to die are common, as are episodes of rage at the injustice of having been struck down. This anger may be expressed in shouting and screaming, refusal to cooperate, or attempts to physically assault those nearby. Even a patient who is paralyzed from the neck down may, out of frustration,

spit at people or attempt to bite them. The patient may feel defeated by helplessness and humiliated by inability to control bowel or bladder function.

Nearly any reaction, no matter how extreme, ought to be considered normal at this time, and the patient should be encouraged to express his or her feelings, no matter how intense or negative. An essential part of the healing process is that the patient be listened to and his feelings accepted. This does not mean agreeing with the feelings but rather listening in a noncritical and nonjudgmental way. If family, friends, or members of the treatment team discourage such expression, they actually postpone the healing process.

A realistic approach

It is crucial for the family to develop some insight into the anatomy and physiology of the injury, so that they have a realistic understanding of the existing problems and are able to provide encouragement on a realistic basis. The physicians, nurses, and therapists working with the patient are responsible for this education process. Simple drawings and anatomic models are useful adjuncts to verbal explanation.

Unrealistic statements and wildly emotional behavior by the family can make life miserable for the patient and for the people caring for him or her. A person lying paralyzed in bed will not be comforted by a weeping, incoherent visitor. Comments such as "You'll be all right" or "Keep your faith, and you'll walk out of here" not only are meaningless but can be harmful. Visitors who act in inappropriate ways must be counseled and, if necessary, excluded.

Simple physical needs assume great importance in a physically dependent person. Help with toothbrushing, shaving, makeup, and other simple grooming needs is greatly appreciated. Tears are a normal part of the emotional healing process, but when they run down the face and into the ears they are a source of discomfort. Wiping the patient's face, drying the ears, and simply holding hands are among the most basic ways of caring and comforting.

For many spinal cord injured people, the fear of loss of sexual prowess and pleasure may be even more devastating than the actual loss of the ability to walk. This is especially true in young people, and most especially in men whose masculinity is threatened by the fear of impotence. Predictions about potency are usually not possible for many weeks following a spinal cord injury. Some men regain the ability to have an erection, and a few are able to ejaculate sperm. Vigorous physical stimulation may be required, and an intelligent and understanding sexual partner is essential. The female spinal cord patient is perfectly capable of conceiving, carrying, and delivering healthy children. With a compassionate partner and much practice, a woman may regain some vaginal and reflex sexual sensations. Orgasm is rare in people with spinal cord injuries. However, since feelings of sexual desire and arousal are largely a psychological function, the combination of psychic and sensory enjoyment can be very satisfying.

The rehabilitation process

Once the patient's condition has been stabilized, typically within a month after the injury, he or she is usually transferred to a spinal injury rehabilitation unit. A sense of loss may be experienced as a result of the separation from the psychologically comfortable atmosphere of the acute care center. This sense of loss can be anticipated and should be openly discussed. Once established in the rehabilitation setting, the patient suddenly becomes only one of many, rather than being unique. An emotional setback is not uncommon at this time. It may take the form of anger at family, friends, or staff, refusal to participate in activities, or withdrawal and symptoms of depression (tearfulness, despondency, sadness, negative expectations of self and of the future). On the other hand, a patient new to the rehabilitation setting will likely observe fellow patients who are even more severely injured. This experience may have a sobering effect on the new patient and may provide some additional motivation for recovery.

For the family the experience of meeting others like themselves and the opportunity to share information, experiences, and feelings are extremely helpful. The goal of rehabilitation—for the patient to return home—may require some changes in the physical environment—doorways may need to be widened, ramps

installed, or bathrooms altered. Classes at the rehabilitation facility acquaint families with the kinds of remodeling that may be needed to accommodate a disabled person.

Acceptance

The patient and his or her family must ultimately learn to function with the reality of the permanence of the injury and the consequent disabilities. The struggle and emotional pain are not to be underestimated, but only through acceptance of the situation can the patient get on with living and engage in self-fulfilling activities. It was the novelist Pearl Buck who wrote, "Endurance of inescapable sorrow is something which has to be learned alone, and only to endure is not enough. There must be acceptance and knowledge that sorrow fully accepted brings its own gifts." As always, an accepting and attentive listener can be a powerful antidote for the patient's feelings of sadness, discouragement, frustration, or anger.

It is true that spinal cord injury may prevent the achievement of some goals; others, however, may be only delayed. Just as modern medicine has extended the lives of paralyzed people, modern technology has expanded their abilities to function in the outside world. Switches activated by voice, air, and even by eye movement allow the operation of telephones, televisions, computers, page turners, and other machines. The physical world, with flattened curbs, access ramps, and widened restrooms, is becoming increasingly accessible to people in wheelchairs. Many paraplegics learn to drive vehicles specially designed to be operated by the hands and arms alone.

Toward better treatment

Active research into the treatment of spinal cord injuries is under way in many centers around the world. Laboratory research focuses on two main areas. First, investigations into the changes in structure, chemistry, and metabolism of injured nerve cells may eventually give researchers an understanding of ways to treat these cells or to reduce the damage. The second major area of research concerns spinal cord regeneration. Unlike all other tissues in the body, cells of the brain and spinal cord do not have the ability to heal—once injured, they never regenerate. Much effort is being directed at finding a drug, an enzyme, or another agent that might stimulate nerve cell regrowth. Finally, there is increasing interest in the use of computerized electrical stimulation of muscles to produce controlled movements. Some remarkable results have been achieved. A few paralyzed patients have been enabled to walk—even to ride bicycles. As computer hardware and software improve, researchers hope to make such advances available outside the experimental laboratory setting.

Systemic Lupus Erythematosus

by Elizabeth S. Raveche, Ph.D.,
and Alfred D. Steinberg, M.D.

Systemic lupus erythematosus (SLE) is a chronic multi-system inflammatory syndrome that afflicts approximately ten million people throughout the world. SLE is an autoimmune disease—that is, one in which the body's immune response is triggered by internal as well as external factors, forming antibodies against its own constituents. The result is inflammation and damage to tissues. Fifty years ago lupus was considered a rare disorder, more often diagnosed at autopsy than during life. Recognition of the diversity of autoantibodies (the "antiself" antibodies) produced by patients with SLE, especially the antinuclear antibodies (*i.e.,* antibodies to DNA and other components of the cell nucleus), has allowed increasing awareness of the disorder and, consequently, an increased rate of diagnosis. Scientists have also come to appreciate the marked variability in signs, symptoms, and laboratory abnormalities from one patient to another. This diversity of clinical findings places SLE within the differential diagnosis of a great many clinical problems and accounts for the fact that it has often been misdiagnosed. In addition, SLE is characterized by periods of exacerbation and remission, which further confound the diagnosis.

Patients with SLE manifest some, but not necessarily all, of the following problems: fatigue, joint pains, anemia, low count of platelets (blood constituents important in clotting), inflammation of the membranes that line and envelop the lungs and heart (causing chest pain), fever, rashes, oral or nasal ulcers, kidney inflammation, and a variety of central nervous system abnormalities, from depression to seizures. Both the types of symptoms and the clinical course of disease vary tremendously from one patient to the next. At one end of the clinical spectrum are patients with rapidly progressive kidney or central nervous system dysfunction. At the other end are patients with a mild illness manifested by fatigue, joint pains, sensitivity to sunlight, and mild skin rashes. The latter individuals might have been viewed in past generations as "frail" or "sickly" without having been given a more specific diagnosis. Most cases fall somewhere between the mildest, requiring little or no treatment, and those with severe major organ involvement, which may require intensive therapy.

Incidence

SLE may occur at any age, but in the majority of patients the onset of illness occurs between ages 13 and 40. In this age range more than 90% of patients are female. The races are not equally susceptible, nor is the extent or course of illness comparable. The chance that a black American woman will develop SLE in her lifetime is approximately one in 200. Polynesians and American Indians of the Sioux family of tribes have a similar incidence. SLE is fairly common in some parts of Asia. The Chinese are probably especially susceptible, but the data on this population are less extensive. Caucasians not only have a lower incidence of the disease (a female Caucasian has only about one chance in 700 of developing SLE) but often have milder cases. Although men are less frequently afflicted, their illness is no milder than that of women.

Genetic and hormonal factors

Both genetic and hormonal factors appear to play important roles in the predisposition to SLE. If one member of a family has SLE, the likelihood of another family member's developing the syndrome increases; the concordance rate is approximately 30% for identical twins and 5–20% for other first-degree relatives (parents, siblings, or offspring of the affected person). Androgens (male hormones) protect against SLE except in certain men who inherit a Y-chromosome (the male sex chromosome) factor from their fathers that predisposes them to SLE. Many patients with SLE demonstrate a tendency to convert disproportionate amounts of sex hormones to highly estrogenic compounds that exacerbate lupus. Overall the data suggest that genetic mechanisms may be different in different families and that, in many cases, more than one gene may be involved in the predisposition to SLE.

Immune function in SLE

SLE is characterized by a multitude of immunologic abnormalities. The hallmark of the disease is excessive activity of the immune system. This immune hyper-activity is usually manifested by increased production of antibodies, proteins formed by the immune system

505

that react with antigens, substances recognized by the body as "foreign" and targeted for destruction. In lupus and other autoimmune diseases, the patient's body produces autoantibodies ("antiself" antibodies) in response to self antigens (those produced by the body's own constituents).

Normally a state of tolerance exists in the body whereby immune responses to particular antigens are held in check. Antibody responses to self antigens are normally suppressed by a class of lymphocytes (white blood cells crucial to normal immunity) called T lymphocytes, or T cells. T lymphocytes regulate the activity of B lymphocytes, or B cells, which ultimately produce the antibodies, including autoantibodies. B cells are only transiently tolerant. Therefore, the body depends on certain T cells—suppressor T cells—to hold self-reactive B cells in check. If any aspect of the production or function of the T cells fails, the B cells are free to produce autoantibodies. Self-tolerance can also be impaired if B cells are directly stimulated by substances that bypass the T cells; for example, B-cell activators such as endotoxins (the toxins created by bacteria). This latter observation may help to explain why a flare-up of SLE is frequently associated with bacterial infection. The cause of abnormal antibody production may be different in different patients. In addition to bacterial—and viral—infections, the following factors are believed to contribute to the disease process: hormonal abnormalities; exposure to ultraviolet light; drugs or foods that increase immune function or depress the suppressor function; and genetic predisposition to hyperimmunity.

Clinical manifestations

In a "typical" case of SLE, a young woman presents her physician with a history of recent sun sensitivity, "butterfly" rash (a reddish rash on the nose and cheeks), arthritis, fever, extreme fatigue, seizures, and kidney dysfunction (nephrotic syndrome, with swelling due to accumulation of fluid in the tissues). There may also be symptoms produced by inflammation of the membrane enveloping the heart and lungs (pleuropericarditis). In fact, only a minority of patients exhibit this so-called typical pattern of complaints. More often, a patient will have only a few signs or symptoms of SLE, such as fatigue and joint pains, and these problems may be transitory. Months or even years after the onset of the first symptoms, additional features of SLE may be manifested. Therefore, the initial complaints may be misleading, preventing the physician from making a definitive diagnosis or accurately predicting the course of the disease.

Based on the clinical features, patients with lupus may be roughly divided into two categories: those who manifest involvement of major organs and whose disease may, therefore, be potentially life-threatening and patients whose disease is more limited, involving

discomfort but no threat of fatality. Approximately half of the patients diagnosed with SLE never develop significant major organ involvement. The majority of lupus patients experience fatigue, fever, joint pain, and weight loss. However, these nonspecific symptoms occur in many disorders. Therefore, before attributing them to SLE, the physician will search for other causes, especially for infections, which may also occur simultaneously with exacerbations of SLE.

The great majority of people with SLE experience some degree of joint pain. Characteristically, the joint problems of lupus are more transitory than those of rheumatoid arthritis; however, with untreated or prolonged disease the pain may become constant, and frank arthritis may develop in SLE, sometimes even including the morning stiffness and joint deformities typical of other arthritic conditions.

The butterfly-shaped rash of lupus, which covers the bridge of the nose and extends onto the cheeks, may in some cases be mistaken for the "rosy" cheeks of robust health. The rash may develop without any exposure to ultraviolet light, but it is commonly exacerbated by such exposure. Patients with SLE also may have rashes that are indistinguishable by both examination and biopsy from an allergic drug reaction.

This patient has the distinctive butterfly-shaped rash that is a classic sign of the autoimmune disorder known as systemic lupus erythematosus, or SLE.

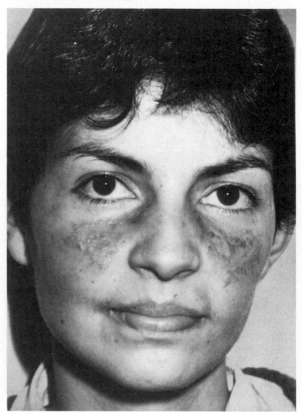

Courtesy, Dr. A. D. Steinberg, NIH

American Rheumatism Association criteria for the diagnosis of systemic lupus erythematosus

criterion	description
malar rash	reddish skin rash, flat or raised, over the bridge of the nose and extending onto the cheekbones ("butterfly" rash)
discoid rash	raised, scaly reddish skin rash; disklike lesions
photosensitivity	skin rash as result of unusual reaction to sunlight
oral ulcers	sores in the mouth, nose, and/or pharynx
arthritis	nonerosive arthritis involving two or more peripheral joints, characterized by swelling, tenderness, or accumulation of fluid
serositis	pleuritis (inflammation of the membrane that envelops the lungs and lines the chest cavity) or pericarditis (inflammation of the membrane that surrounds the heart)
renal disorder	protein or cells in the urine
neurological disorder	seizures or psychosis
hematologic disorder	decrease in number of red cells, white cells, or platelets in the blood
immunologic disorder	abnormal number of LE cells (white blood cells that have ingested the nuclei of other cells) or abnormal amount of anti-DNA antibody (antibody that reacts with the genetic material) or presence of antibody to Sm nuclear antigen or false-positive blood test for syphilis
antinuclear antibody	antibody to constituents of the nuclei within tissue cells

The range of central nervous system involvement observed in different SLE patients is remarkable. Both psychiatric and organic abnormalities are common. Psychological problems include personality disorders and the development of overt psychosis or major affective disorders (*e.g.*, depression, paranoia, mania, or schizophrenia). Seizures, often of the generalized type known as grand mal convulsions, are common in younger patients.

SLE affects the kidneys in most patients. In many the problem is so mild that it escapes detection; in others it is clinically detectable but does not progress to functional impairment. Only in a minority of patients is renal function threatened. It is important to recognize that hypertension (high blood pressure) and lupus nephritis can act together to accelerate destructive changes in the nephrons, the functional units in the kidneys; thus, to be effective, therapy must be directed at both hypertension and nephritis.

Because a majority of SLE patients are women of childbearing age, the question of pregnancy frequently arises. Women with relatively mild disease are usually able to carry a pregnancy to term without complications, especially during periods of remission. The primary difficulties they face are a higher than average incidence of spontaneous abortion and the possibility of an exacerbation of the disease in the postpartum period. Patients with active renal disease due to SLE often experience an exacerbation of symptoms during the pregnancy; they are also at increased risk of preeclampsia, a disorder that is potentially life-threatening to both mother and infant. Most physicians advise against pregnancy for SLE patients with advanced cardiac, central nervous system, or renal involvement.

Diagnosis

Diagnosis of SLE is based upon a combination of characteristic clinical manifestations and compatible laboratory findings. There is no single clinical feature or laboratory test that either establishes or excludes the diagnosis. Thus, making a diagnosis of SLE in a given individual depends upon the combination of symptoms, the nature of immunologic abnormalities indicated by diagnostic tests, and the relative possibility of these abnormalities occurring in a patient with SLE as opposed to a patient with another condition. The American Rheumatism Association (ARA) has developed a list of 11 criteria to be used in the determination of SLE. The ARA criteria include the clinical manifestations discussed above and positive reaction to certain diagnostic tests that indicate immune system dysfunction. According to the ARA, the coexistence of any four of the criteria provides a diagnosis having a specificity and sensitivity greater than 97%. These criteria are not definitive, however. A patient who meets only three of the ARA tests may indeed have SLE; on the other hand, a person with leprosy, not SLE, may have several of the positive indications of lupus. Therefore, clinical judgment must be exercised in each case. Researchers are working to develop more specific diagnostic tests, but none has been discovered thus far.

Main clinical features in systemic lupus erythematosus

feature	approximate percentage
joint pains	90
skin rashes	70
fevers	60
chest pains (especially pleurisy)	45
seizures depression, etc.	45
kidney inflammation	30

Therapy

The value of emotional support, including an optimistic but honest assessment of the condition, cannot be underestimated. Most SLE patients can look forward to a normal life-span, although they may need periodic medical evaluations and a regime of drug therapy. The more active the disease, the more rest and sleep the patient requires. Sunlight (or other sources of ultraviolet light) should be avoided, as should those drugs that augment the effects of ultraviolet light (tetracyclines and psoralens, as well as foods containing large amounts of psoralens, such as celery, parsnips, figs, and parsley). Patients may exercise as much as is possible and comfortable but not to the point of exhaustion. Fatigue and other stresses, including surgery, infection, childbirth, and psychological stress, may exacerbate the disease and require additional treatment.

Since the severity and extent of disease vary greatly from one patient to the next, the drug treatment of SLE also varies. Therapy for patients who have no major organ involvement is symptomatic (*i.e.,* directed at relief of symptoms). Hydroxychloroquine, an antimalarial drug, is especially effective for the skin disease associated with lupus. The nonsteroidal anti-inflammatory drugs, such as aspirin, ibuprofen (Motrin), and naproxen (Naprosyn), are useful for arthritis, inflammation, and fever. Patients who fail to respond to these agents may require treatment with corticosteroids, a group of drugs especially effective in suppressing inflammation. Because of the adverse side effects of long-term corticosteroid therapy, these drugs are administered in the lowest dose capable of eliminating or sufficiently reducing symptoms. Because lupus patients differ widely in their responses to such drugs, establishing an optimum dosage is somewhat of an experiment in each patient. The goal is always to attempt to reduce the dosage and, usually, to establish a schedule of administration on alternating days.

The treatment of major organ disease is directed at preservation of function and prevention of organ failure. Moderate to high daily doses of corticosteroids are usually adequate; however, some patients require very high doses, and in patients with major organ involvement, intravenous administration of cyclophosphamide (Cytoxan, Neosar; a cytotoxic agent also used in cancer chemotherapy) can be lifesaving. Seizures are treated with both corticosteroids and anticonvulsants. Short-acting corticosteroids, such as prednisone or methylprednisolone, are preferred; when administered on an every-other-day basis, these drugs have fewer side effects than when given daily. The long-term management of patients with SLE is often more difficult than the treatment of acute episodes. The inevitable adverse effects of prolonged treatment with high-dose corticosteroids (cataracts, infections, glucose intolerance, hypertension, acne, osteoporosis) must always be balanced against the need for continued vigorous therapy.

Ongoing SLE investigations

The search for specific causes of a variety of immune-mediated diseases, including SLE, continues. Recognition that the genetic factors and immune system abnormalities might be different in different patients may further the scientific understanding of underlying mechanisms and may enable the identification of subgroups of SLE victims. Alternatively, researchers may discover a way to "turn down" the immune thermostat, or "immunostat," lowering the level of activity with genetically engineered antibodies targeted to specific lymphocyte surface antigens, or to modulate the immune system through the administration of soluble factors called cytokines (*e.g.,* interleukins, interferons), which are produced by cells and regulate the function of other cells. These biological products are now becoming widely available through advances in molecular genetics. The approach of direct immunologic manipulation may be much less harmful than the current methods of therapy with high doses of corticosteroids or cytotoxic drugs.

Finally, laboratory experiments have demonstrated that a single gene can prevent SLE in mice. It is possible that appropriate genetic manipulation could someday be applied to human patients. Such treatment offers exciting possibilities, but it must not be prematurely or indiscriminately applied. Under controlled clinical test settings, however, genetic therapy could offer substantial hope for improved treatment of individuals susceptible to SLE.

Oral Contraceptives in the 1980s
by Bruce D. Shephard, M.D.

Oral contraceptives first became available in the United States in 1960. Since then a tremendous amount of information has been gathered about "the Pill," the most effective and popular reversible method of birth control available. To date 150 million women worldwide have used the Pill at some time in their lives. Currently more than 50 million women are using oral contraceptives—among them 10 million in the U.S., 3 million in the U.K., and 1 million in Canada. In industrial countries birth control pills are nearly always purchased from pharmacies or other commercial sources, usually by prescription only. In many less developed countries public and private family-planning programs supply a substantial percentage of women using the Pill. In developed countries purchases of oral contraceptives peaked in the mid-1970s and have since leveled off. By contrast, sales in a number of Latin-American nations have increased about 50% since 1975.

During its more than 25-year history, the Pill has been the subject of intense medical research, becoming one of the most studied drugs in America. Because of their public health importance and impact on millions of women, oral contraceptives (OCs) have received close scrutiny by the press. At times media reports have focused on negative or sensational aspects. When seen in historical perspective, however, the evolution of oral contraceptives has been a steady progression toward increasingly improved products. The greater safety of the Pill and increased public confidence in oral contraception may be attributed to three major factors: the availability of lower-dose formulations, a better identification of risk factors, and increased public awareness of noncontraceptive health benefits associated with OC use.

The evolution of the low-dose Pill
The oral contraceptives of the 1980s differ significantly from those available more than 25 years ago. The combination Pill, used by 99% of women now

taking oral contraceptives, still contains the same two hormones, estrogen and progesterone (in various synthetic forms), but the dosages and formulations have changed, giving the new Pill a wider margin of safety. Present-day birth control pills contain one-fifth the estrogen and one-tenth the progesterone of the first oral contraceptives.

When the Pill was introduced in the U.S. in 1960, there was an initial rush of optimism among consumers and health professionals alike. Oral contraceptives appeared to have all the elements of an ideal method of birth control—effectiveness, safety, and convenience. One of the first hints of trouble came from England in 1967 when the Royal College of General Practitioners reported on the development of blood clots in some otherwise healthy young women taking the Pill. Other large-scale studies in the late 1960s in both the United States and Great Britain confirmed an increased risk of venous thrombosis (blood clots) in OC users. These studies identified a direct relationship between the estrogen dosage and the risk of blood clots. During the early 1970s lowered estrogen dosage became the hallmark of a second generation of birth control pills containing from 50 to 80 micrograms of estrogen; these were half as likely to precipitate blood clots as were the original formulations, which contained 100 to 150 micrograms of estrogen.

Another attempt to prevent adverse side effects—which in the 1970s were attributed almost entirely to the estrogen component—was the introduction of the so-called minipill in 1973. The minipill, which contains only progesterone, has been proved to have a number of disadvantages, compared with the two-hormone combination formulations. The minipill has a higher failure (*i.e.*, pregnancy) rate—3%, compared with less than 1% for the combination Pill—and a rather high incidence of side effects, especially breakthrough bleeding. The minipill is taken by only about 1% of oral contraceptive users in the United States today.

Oral contraceptives in the 1980s

In 1975 a third generation of combination formulations with still lower amounts of estrogen—from 30 to 35 micrograms—was introduced in an attempt to further enhance safety. The "sub-50s," or low-dose pills, as this group became known, soon gained widespread popularity, as they maximized safety without loss of effectiveness. The benefits to be derived from decreased estrogen dosage were clearly indicated by a decline in the rate of venous thrombosis among Pill users from an annual rate of 40 per 100,000 in 1965 to fewer than 10 per 100,000 by 1978. A second advantage to lowered estrogen dosage was that some of the less serious side effects, such as nausea and breast tenderness, were also reduced, although the low-dose formulations did result in slightly higher rates of breakthrough bleeding. By 1980 more than half of all oral contraceptives prescribed contained less than 50 micrograms of estrogen. By 1985 low-dose pills were being used by 65% of all U.S. women taking oral contraceptives.

With the estrogen dosage of the Pill reduced to the lowest therapeutically effective level, medical research has shifted toward a more thorough evaluation of the progesterone component. As early as 1974 a British study by the Royal College of General Practitioners found a correlation between progesterone dosage and the development of high blood pressure. Subsequent studies found that high blood pressure, which was likely to develop in about 5% of Pill users taking higher dose oral contraceptives, reverted to normal when the Pill was stopped. Additional research has also linked birth control pills containing progesterone in high dosages to elevated levels of blood sugar and blood cholesterol. Studies are presently under way to determine whether oral contraceptives containing lower dosages of progesterone will also show these or any other potentially adverse effects. Since progesterone dosage has declined from ten milligrams in the original Pill to one milligram or less in present-day formulations, there appears to be a wide margin of safety for most healthy young women using oral contraceptives.

In the mid-1980s research on the Pill became finely tuned, with greater emphasis on how different types and combinations of hormones influence side effects and safety. The most recent development in this area has been the introduction of a new formulation, the so-called multiphasics, which provide cyclical variation of hormone dosage in an attempt to roughly simulate the changes that occur in a normal menstrual cycle.

Comparison of combination birth control pills by dosage

	brand name	estrogen dose (micrograms)	estrogen component*	progesterone dose (milligrams)	progesterone component*
group I, high dose (more than 50 micrograms of estrogen)	Enovid-E	100	mestranol	2.5	norethynodrel
	Enovid 5	75	mestranol	5	norethynodrel
	Norinyl 1 + 80	80	mestranol	1	norethindrone
	Norinyl 2	100	mestranol	2	norethindrone
	Ortho-Novum 1/80	80	mestranol	1	norethindrone
	Ortho-Novum 2	100	mestranol	2	norethindrone
	Ovulen	100	mestranol	1	ethynodiol diacetate
group II, medium dose (50 micrograms of estrogen)	Demulen	50	ethinyl estradiol	1	ethynodiol diacetate
	Norinyl 1 + 50	50	mestranol	1	norethindrone
	Norlestrin 1/50	50	ethinyl estradiol	1	norethindrone acetate
	Norlestrin 2.5/50	50	ethinyl estradiol	2.5	norethindrone acetate
	Ortho-Novum 1/50	50	mestranol	1	norethindrone
	Ovcon-50	50	ethinyl estradiol	1	norethindrone
	Ovral	50	ethinyl estradiol	0.5	norgestrel
group III, low dose (less than 50 micrograms of estrogen)	Brevicon	35	ethinyl estradiol	0.5	norethindrone
	Demulen 1/35	35	ethinyl estradiol	1	ethynodiol diacetate
	Levlen	30	ethinyl estradiol	0.15	levonorgestrel
	Loestrin 1/20	20	ethinyl estradiol	1	norethindrone acetate
	Loestrin 1.5/30	30	ethinyl estradiol	1.5	norethindrone acetate
	Lo/Ovral	30	ethinyl estradiol	0.3	norgestrel
	Modicon	35	ethinyl estradiol	0.5	norethindrone
	Nordette	30	ethinyl estradiol	0.15	levonorgestrel
	Norinyl 1/35	35	ethinyl estradiol	1	norethindrone
	Ortho-Novum 1/35	35	ethinyl estradiol	1	norethindrone
	Ortho-Novum 10/11†	35	ethinyl estradiol	0.5–1	norethindrone
	Ortho-Novum 7/7/7†	35	ethinyl estradiol	0.5–1	norethindrone
	Ovcon-35	35	ethinyl estradiol	0.4	norethindrone
	Tri-Levlen†	30–40	ethinyl estradiol	0.05–0.125	levonorgestrel
	Tri-Norinyl†	35	ethinyl estradiol	0.5–1	norethindrone
	Triphasil†	30–40	ethinyl estradiol	0.05–0.125	levonorgestrel

*the safety of both hormonal components is a function of *both* dosage and potency
†multiphasic pills

Adapted from Dr. Bruce D. Shephard and Dr. Carroll A. Shephard, *The Complete Guide to Women's Health* (New York: New American Library, 1985)

Some multiphasics vary only the progesterone dosage, while others vary the dosage of both estrogen and progesterone. These formulations also reduce overall dosage somewhat, making multiphasics an attractive alternative among low-dose pills. Further studies are needed to determine how the multiphasics compare, in terms of safety and side effects, with other low-dose oral contraceptives.

Risk factors: who should not take the Pill?

A better understanding of risk factors has dramatically increased the margin of safety for women considering taking birth control pills. "Making Choices," published in 1983 by the Alan Guttmacher Institute (the research branch of Planned Parenthood), represents one of the most comprehensive reviews of oral contraceptive risks and benefits to date. According to this report, 86% of the approximately 500 Pill-related deaths that occur each year could be prevented if women who smoke or who are over age 35 did not take birth control pills. (Smoking, rather than age, is considered the single most important risk factor associated with OC use.) If women who have other cardiovascular risk factors, such as high blood pressure or diabetes, were to avoid the Pill, the risk of cardiovascular complications (blood clots, heart disease) could be reduced even further.

Today, with more accurate methods of identifying women at risk of complications, healthy, nonsmoking women under 35 can take birth control pills with more confidence than ever before. In fact, when the medical risks of pregnancy are considered, the risk of death among nonsmoking women taking the Pill is no more than that of women using less effective methods of birth control. Compared with pregnancy, OC use is at least five times less likely to cause death.

Noncontraceptive health benefits of the Pill

In recent years the identification of a number of health benefits associated with birth control pills has increased public confidence in this type of contraception. The Guttmacher Institute report attempted to quantify health benefits and risks to provide a more nearly accurate overall picture of the Pill's effects. Taking birth control pills prevents about 58,000 hospitalizations per year among Pill users, compared with some 9,000 hospitalizations—mostly for blood clots—that are attributed to Pill use annually, for every ten million women using these drugs. Among hospitalizations prevented, most were for benign breast disease, pelvic inflammatory disease (including sexually transmitted infections), ectopic pregnancy, ovarian cysts, ovarian cancer, and endometrial cancer. It is further estimated that 1,700 cases of ovarian cancer—including 850 deaths from this disease—are prevented each year among Pill users.

Medical benefits associated with OC use can be ex- plained by the Pill's effects on the female reproductive system. The suppression of ovulation, for example, is probably the mechanism responsible for reducing the numbers of ovarian cancers, ovarian cysts, painful menstrual periods, and cases of premenstrual syndrome in Pill users. The presence of progesterone in combination with estrogen is another mechanism that confers health benefits. The antiestrogen effect of progesterone prevents target organs such as the uterus and breast from receiving strong unopposed estrogen stimulation, as they do in a normal menstrual cycle. The protective effect of progesterone is believed to be an important factor in the estimated 50% annual reduction in endometrial cancer among Pill users. Progesterone also plays a part in the prevention of thousands of cases per year of benign breast disease—breast cysts, fibrocystic breast disease, and benign tumors. Because of the antiestrogen effect of progesterone on the uterine lining, Pill users experience shorter, lighter menstrual periods and have a lower incidence of iron deficiency anemia than do nonusers.

Long-term use

There are several special concerns that relate to long-term use of oral contraceptives (*i.e.*, taking the Pill for five or more years). With today's refined knowledge of the Pill's effects, these concerns now specifically involve pregnancy, infertility, cancer, and heart disease.

Pregnancy. Several studies have indicated a slight risk of birth defects in babies born to women who were taking the Pill during the first three months of pregnancy. However, no evidence has linked birth defects or miscarriages to pregnancies conceived immediately after discontinuing OC use. A few years ago women were urged by their physicians to wait six months after stopping the Pill before attempting pregnancy. Today most doctors recommend a waiting time of one to two months, which is all that is necessary to allow for ovulation and a normal menstrual cycle to occur. The primary reason for this precaution is that it enables a more reliable calculation of the due date if pregnancy should occur.

Infertility. The overall fertility of Pill users and nonusers is identical regardless of the length of time of OC use. In the first cycle after use of the Pill is stopped, ovulation is sometimes delayed a few weeks; however, overall capacity for becoming pregnant is unchanged. Women who had irregular periods prior to taking the Pill are more likely than others to experience a prolonged delay (six months or more) in the onset of their first period. In such a case, if the woman desires to become pregnant, ovulation can be restored by means of a drug that stimulates the ovaries. This problem affects fewer than 1% of women using the Pill. And because women who use oral contraceptives have a decreased risk of at least two conditions that are likely to result in infertility—pelvic inflammatory disease and ectopic pregnancy—the use of birth control pills may actually protect women against becoming infertile.

Cancer. There is no firm evidence that oral contraceptives cause any type of cancer. In fact, the Pill has been found to have a protective effect against certain cancers of the female reproductive system—ovarian cancer and uterine cancer. With respect to breast cancer a number of reports, including the largest controlled study to date, the U.S. Centers for Disease Control's Cancer and Steroid Hormone (CASH) study, found no increased risk of breast cancer among Pill users even after ten years of OC use. More research is needed, however, before any link between breast cancer and use of oral contraceptives can be definitely refuted.

The one form of cancer that appears to be associated—at least statistically—with OC use is cancer of the cervix. Although some studies have found an increased risk of abnormal Pap smears, dysplasia (precancerous cellular changes), and cervical cancer in Pill users, most researchers feel that the relationship probably is not causal. The association between cancer of the cervix and use of birth control pills more likely represents the presence of other risk factors for cancer of the cervix—such as increased sexual activity—among Pill users as a group. In most studies of cervical cancer and oral contraceptives, there have not been adequate statistical controls for other important risk factors, such as age at first intercourse and number of sexual partners. Until this issue has been fully resolved, women taking birth control pills are advised to have annual Pap smears.

Cardiovascular disease. Cardiovascular complications—the major adverse effect of taking birth control pills—include blood clot (thromboembolism), heart attack (myocardial infarction), high blood pressure (hypertension), and stroke (cerebral thrombosis or embolus). These complications occur mostly in women over the age of 35 or those who have one or more cardiovascular risk factors. These factors include a personal history of cigarette smoking, high blood pressure, diabetes, or elevated blood lipids (cholesterol or triglycerides). A strong family history of heart disease (especially where heart attacks have occurred before age 50) or insulin-dependent diabetes also increases a woman's risk of cardiovascular disease. In addition, cardiovascular risks are related to total hormone dosage and are thus minimized in low-dose formulations. For most healthy nonsmoking women under 30, the Pill's benefits—both contraceptive and noncontraceptive—outweigh the risks. As a woman approaches age 35, risks increase, especially for women who smoke but very minimally among nonsmokers. After age 35, women who smoke should not take the Pill. Nonsmokers over 35—even those without cardiovascular risk factors—should take birth control pills only

in select circumstances. Many practitioners advise women in this latter group to have a medical checkup every six months, including periodic measurement of blood sugar and cholesterol levels.

To date the Pill has not been found to have long-term effects on the blood vessels or on the development and progression of arteriosclerosis and associated cardiovascular disease. However, more research is needed in this area. In forthcoming studies on possible cardiovascular effects of the Pill, researchers will be evaluating hormone potency as well as dosage. Medical authorities agree that the safest formulations are those with the lowest overall potency and dosage. Combination birth control pills contain one of two types of synthetic estrogen that are roughly similar in potency and one of five types of synthetic progesterone in which the potency varies. Differences in the potency of the progesterones have been difficult to measure precisely. Further research is needed to determine whether formulations with less potent types of progesterone are safer than those with more potent progesterones but with the same dosage.

Educating the public

Although oral contraceptives have evolved toward increasingly more sophisticated and safer products, their popularity has declined in recent years. In 1982 only 20% of married women using contraception selected the Pill, compared with 36% in 1973. The sheer volume of reports in the media, many of them adverse, and some widespread misinformation have shaken public confidence in the Pill. A Gallup Poll in 1985 revealed, for example, that about 75% of U.S. women believe that Pill use carries "substantial health risks." Yet the Guttmacher report found that the Pill is estimated to prevent at least five times as many hospitalizations as it causes.

The general public has not yet begun to take full advantage of new information affecting the decision to choose birth control pills or other contraceptives. For example, some sexually active women with known risk factors still elect to use oral contraceptives when safer methods of birth control are available. Other women who are not at special risk sometimes avoid the Pill because of misconceptions about it; instead, they choose a method less likely to prevent pregnancy. In 1985, despite the recognized greater safety of newer low-dose formulations, more than 3.5 million U.S. women were still taking birth control pills containing 50 micrograms or more of estrogen. Further education is needed to make decision making about contraceptives a more rational process. For women who choose birth control pills over other forms of contraception, such education should emphasize potential risks as well as benefits of oral contraceptives and should explain the importance of low-dose formulations.

Contributors to the World of Medicine

George J. Annas, J.D., M.P.H.
Special Reports Malpractice in Perspective and
The Karen Ann Quinlan Case: A Modern Parable
Edward R. Utley Professor of Health Law and Chief,
Health Law Section, Boston University Schools of
Medicine and Public Health

Kenneth A. Arndt, M.D.
Skin Disorders (coauthor)
Dermatologist-in-Chief, Beth Israel Hospital; Associate
Professor of Dermatology, Harvard Medical School,
Boston

Donna Bergen, M.D.
Neurology
Associate Professor of Neurological Sciences, Rush
Medical College; Associate Attending Neurologist
and Director, Electroencephalography Laboratory,
Rush-Presbyterian-St. Luke's Medical Center, Chicago

Joyce Bermel
Medical Ethics
Managing Editor, *Hastings Center Report,* The Hastings
Center, Hastings-on-Hudson, N.Y.

Michael Bigby, M.D.
Skin Disorders (coauthor)
Associate Dermatologist, Beth Israel Hospital, Boston

Gillian Fansler Brown, Ph.D.
Allergy and Immunology (coauthor)
Section Editor and Project Administrator, Pulmonary
Section, Department of Pediatrics, Tulane University
School of Medicine, New Orleans, La.

Casey Bukro
Environmental Health
Environment Writer, *Chicago Tribune*

Marion C. Chafetz
Alcoholism and Alcohol Abuse (coauthor)
Editor, Health Education Foundation, Washington, D.C.

Morris E. Chafetz, M.D.
Alcoholism and Alcohol Abuse (coauthor)
President, Health Education Foundation; Founding
Director, National Institute on Alcohol Abuse and
Alcoholism; Chairman, Committee on Education and
Prevention, Presidential Commission on Drunk Driving,
Washington, D.C.

Connie S. Chan, Ph.D.
Special Report Addicted to Exercise
Assistant Professor of Human Services, College
of Public and Community Service, University of
Massachusetts at Boston

Miriam Cohen, Ph.D.
Drug Abuse
Assistant Professor, Mount Sinai School of Medicine,
New York City

William J. Cromie
Cancer; Health Care Technology; Transplantation
Executive Director, Council for the Advancement of
Scientific Writing; free-lance medical/science writer,
Oak Park, Ill.

Joy Curtis
Nursing
Associate Professor, College of Nursing, Michigan State
University, East Lansing

Richard D. deShazo, M.D.
Allergy and Immunology (coauthor)
Professor of Medicine and Pediatrics, Department of
Medicine, Tulane University School of Medicine, New
Orleans, La.

Harvey J. Dworken, M.D.
Gastrointestinal Disorders
Professor of Medicine, Case Western Reserve
University, Cleveland, Ohio

Stephen E. Epstein, M.D.
Heart and Blood Vessels (coauthor)
Chief, Cardiology Branch, National Heart, Lung,
and Blood Institute, National Institutes of Health,
Bethesda, Md.

Elizabeth E. Force, Ph.D.
Drugs and Devices
Senior Director, Regulatory Affairs, Merck Sharp and
Dohme Research Laboratories, West Point, Pa.

Arthur L. Frank, M.D., Ph.D.
Occupational Health
Professor and Chairman, Department of Preventive
Medicine and Environmental Health, University of
Kentucky College of Medicine, Lexington

Richard M. Glass, M.D.
Mental Health and Illness
Associate Professor of Psychiatry, University of Chicago

Donald B. Guest, Ph.D.
Health Care Policy
Assistant Professor of Marketing, School of Business,
East Carolina University, Greenville, N.C.

Jan Hudis
Genetics
Science Information Editor, March of Dimes Birth
Defects Foundation, White Plains, N.Y.

Judith L. Jakush
Dentistry
Senior Editor, *American Dental Association News,*
American Dental Association, Chicago

Irving Kushner, M.D.
Arthritis and Rheumatic Diseases
Medical Director, Highland View Rehabilitation Hospital;
Professor of Medicine and Pathology, Case Western
Reserve University, Cleveland, Ohio

Nathan W. Levin, M.D.
Kidney Disease
Head, Division of Nephrology and Hypertension, Henry
Ford Hospital, Detroit; Clinical Professor of Internal
Medicine, University of Michigan, Ann Arbor

Jean D. Lockhart, M.D.
Pediatrics
Director, Maternal, Child, and Adolescent Health,
American Academy of Pediatrics, Elk Grove Village, Ill.

George D. Lundberg, M.D.
Special Report Doctors on the Witness Stand
Editor, *Journal of the American Medical Association;*
Professor of Pathology, Northwestern University,
Chicago, and Georgetown University, Washington, D.C.

Richard M. Nowak, M.D.
Emergency Medicine
Vice-Chairman, Department of Emergency Medicine,
Henry Ford Hospital, Detroit; Assistant Professor,
Section of Emergency Services, University of Michigan,
Ann Arbor

Eugene R. Passamani, M.D.
Heart and Blood Vessels (coauthor)
Associate Director for Cardiology, National Heart,
Lung, and Blood Institute, National Institutes of Health,
Bethesda, Md.

Ralph Pelligra, M.D.
Aerospace Medicine
Medical Services Officer, National Aeronautics and
Space Administration, Ames Research Center, Moffett
Field, Calif.

Richard A. Perritt, M.D.
Eye Diseases and Visual Disorders
Senior Attending Ophthalmologist, Bethany Methodist Hospital, Chicago; Chairman, Eye Section, International College of Surgeons

Thomas L. Petty, M.D.
Lung Diseases
Professor of Medicine and Director, Webb-Waring Lung Institute, University of Colorado Health Sciences Center, Denver

Domeena C. Renshaw, M.D.
Special Report Child Sexual Abuse: When Wrongly Charged
Professor of Psychiatry, Loyola University Stritch School of Medicine, and Director, Loyola Sexual Dysfunction Training Clinic, Maywood, Ill.

David B. Reuben, M.D.
Medical Education
Assistant Professor, Department of Community Health, Brown University Program in Medicine; Associate Physician, Division of General Internal Medicine, Rhode Island Hospital, Providence

Alfred Rockenschaub, M.D.
Special Report Reevaluating Modern Obstetrics: A Study from Vienna
Head, Ludwig-Boltzmann-Institut; Associate Professor of Gynecology and Obstetrics, University of Vienna; formerly Professor of Midwifery and Director, Ignaz Semmelweis-Frauenklinik, Vienna

Allan J. Ryan, M.D.
Sports Medicine
Director, Sports Medicine Enterprise; Editor-in-Chief, *Fitness in Business*, Edina, Minn.

R. Bradley Sack, M.D., Sc.D.
Infectious Diseases
Professor of International Health and Director, Division of Geographic Medicine, Johns Hopkins University School of Hygiene and Public Health, Baltimore, Md.

Serge Schmemann
Special Report The Vice of Vodka: Soviet Attack on Alcoholism
Chief, Moscow Bureau, the *New York Times*

Edward L. Schneider, M.D.
Aging
Deputy Director, National Institute on Aging, National Institutes of Health, Bethesda, Md.

Edith T. Shapiro, M.D.
Special Report Children of Divorce
Psychiatrist in private practice, Englewood, N.J.; Clinical Associate Professor of Psychiatry, College of Medicine and Dentistry, New Jersey Medical School, Newark

Donald R. Shopland
Smoking
Acting Director, Office on Smoking and Health, U.S. Public Health Service, Rockville, Md.

Joanne M. Silberner
AIDS; Awards and Prizes
Biomedicine Editor, *Science News*, Washington, D.C.

Erwin Small, D.V.M.
Veterinary Medicine
Associate Dean and Professor, College of Veterinary Medicine, University of Illinois at Urbana-Champaign

Joseph B. Treaster
Special Report Eruption of Nevado del Ruiz
Chief, Caribbean Bureau, the *New York Times*, Miami, Fla.

Redford B. Williams, Jr., M.D.
Special Report Type A Behavior
Professor of Psychiatry, Associate Professor of Medicine, and Director, Behavioral Medicine Research Center, Duke University Medical Center, Durham, N.C.

Myron Winick, M.D.
Diet and Nutrition
R. R. Williams Professor of Nutrition; Professor of Pediatrics; Director, Institute of Human Nutrition; and Director, Center for Nutrition, Genetics, and Human Development, Columbia University College of Physicians and Surgeons, New York City

Contributors to the Health Information Update

Edward L. Applebaum, M.D.
Hoarseness
Francis L. Lederer Professor and Head, Department of Otolaryngology—Head and Neck Surgery, University of Illinois College of Medicine, Chicago

Thomas O. Brackett, M.D.
Coping with Spinal Cord Injury (coauthor)
Attending Neurosurgeon and Medical Director, Acute Spinal Cord Injury Center, Winter Haven Hospital, Winter Haven, Fla.

Jonathan M. Cheek, Ph.D.
Shyness
Professor of Psychology, Wellesley College, Wellesley, Mass.

Sebastian G. Ciancio, D.D.S.
Dental Plaque
Professor and Chairman, Department of Periodontics, School of Dental Medicine, State University of New York at Buffalo

Harvey J. Dworken, M.D.
Gastrointestinal Polyps
Professor of Medicine, Case Western Reserve University, Cleveland, Ohio

Marc K. Effron, M.D.
Coronary Bypass
Cardiology Faculty, Scripps Memorial Cardiovascular Institute and Specialty Medical Clinic; Clinical Instructor, University of California at San Diego School of Medicine, La Jolla, Calif.

Weylin G. Eng, O.D.
Confronting the Computer: Help for Eyes (coauthor)
Associate Clinical Professor, University of California at Berkeley; Medical Service Corps, United States Navy; consultant to state legislature of California on video display terminals; private practitioner, Oakland, Calif.

Kevin M. Kindelan, Ph.D.
Coping with Spinal Cord Injury (coauthor)
Director, Community Health Center, Winter Haven Hospital, Winter Haven, Fla.

Tom D. Naughton
New Dads and New Babies; The Vulnerable Knee
Managing Editor, *Family Safety and Health Magazine*, National Safety Council, Chicago; free-lance writer

Elizabeth S. Raveché, Ph.D.
Systemic Lupus Erythematosus (coauthor)
Associate Professor, Department of Immunology and Microbiology, Albany Medical College, Albany, N.Y.

Domeena C. Renshaw, M.D.
Sexual Dysfunction: Causes and Cures
Professor of Psychiatry, Loyola University Stritch School of Medicine, and Director, Loyola Sexual Dysfunction Training Clinic, Maywood, Ill.

Nancy Seeger
Surviving the Holidays; Toys: Hazardous to Health?
Public Affairs Specialist, University of Chicago Medical Center; free-lance medical/science writer

Bruce D. Shephard, M.D.
Oral Contraceptives in the 1980s
Clinical Associate Professor, Department of Obstetrics and Gynecology, University of South Florida College of Medicine, Tampa

Alfred D. Steinberg, M.D.
Systemic Lupus Erythematosus (coauthor)
Medical Director, U.S. Public Health Service; Chief, Section on Cellular Immunology, Arthritis and Rheumatism Branch, National Institute of Arthritis and Musculoskeletal and Skin Diseases, National Institutes of Health, Bethesda, Md.

Stephen E. Straus, M.D.
The Epstein-Barr Virus
Head, Medical Virology Section, National Institute of Allergy and Infectious Diseases, National Institutes of Health, Bethesda, Md.

Jay Stuller
Working Out at Home; Today's Contact Lenses
Senior Editor, Public Affairs Department, Chevron Corp., San Francisco; free-lance writer

Robert C. Yeager
Confronting the Computer: Help for Eyes (coauthor)
Senior Publications Editor, Chevron Corp., San Francisco; Consulting Editor, Electric Power Research Institute, Palo Alto, Calif.; free-lance medical writer

Index

This is a three-year cumulative index. Index entries to *World of Medicine* articles in this and previous editions of the *Medical and Health Annual* are set in boldface type, *e.g.* **Alcoholism.** Entries to other subjects are set in lightface type, *e.g.*, amniocentesis. Additional information on any of these subjects is identified with a subheading and indented under the entry heading. The numbers following headings and subheadings indicate the year (boldface) of the edition and the page number (lightface) on which the information appears. The abbreviation "il." indicates an illustration.

Alcoholism 87–280; 86–184; 85–190
    Japanese statistics 85–316
    physicians' treatment 85–195
    polydrug abuse 87–310
    Soviet campaign (special report) 87–277
    unemployment incidence 85–291
  amniocentesis 87–337
    neural tube defects 85–66
    prenatal genetic testing 85–35, 78

All entry headings are alphabetized word by word. Hyphenated words and words separated by dashes or slashes are treated as two words. When one word differs from another only by the presence of additional characters at the end, the shorter precedes the longer. In inverted names, the words following the comma are considered only after the preceding part of the name has been alphabetized. Names beginning with "Mc" and "Mac" are alphabetized as "Mac"; "St." is alphabetized as "Saint." Examples:

    Lake
    Lake, Simon
    Lake Charles
    Lakeland

519

Now there's a way to identify all your fine books with flair and style. As part of our continuing service to you, Britannica Home Library Service, Inc. is proud to be able to offer you the fine quality item shown on the next page.

Booklovers will love the heavy-duty personalized embosser. Now you can personalize all your fine books with the mark of distinction, just the way all the fine libraries of the world do.

To order this item, please type or print your name, address and zip code on a plain sheet of paper. (Note special instructions for ordering the embosser). Please send a check or money order only (your money will be refunded in full if you are not delighted) for the full amount of purchase, including postage and handling, to:

Britannica Home Library Service, Inc.
Attn: Yearbook Department
Post Office Box 6137
Chicago, Illinois 60680

(Please make remittance payable to: Britannica Home Library Service, Inc.)

IN THE BRITANNICA TRADITION OF QUALITY...

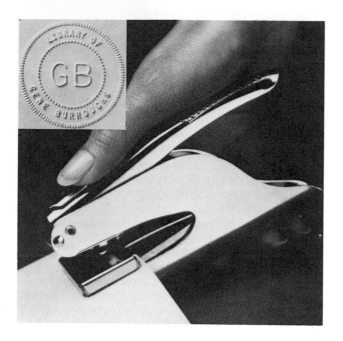

PERSONAL EMBOSSER

A mark of distinction for your fine books. A book embosser just like the ones used in libraries. The 1½″ seal imprints "Library of _____" (with the name of your choice) and up to three centered initials. Please type or print clearly BOTH full name (up to 26 letters including spaces between names) and up to three initials.
Please allow six weeks for delivery.

Just **$20.00**

plus $2.00 shipping and handling

This offer available only in the United States.
Illinois residents please add sales tax

Britannica Home Library Service, Inc.